Lecture Notes in Computer Science 16065

Founding Editors

Gerhard Goos
Juris Hartmanis

Editorial Board Members

Elisa Bertino, *Purdue University, West Lafayette, IN, USA*
Wen Gao, *Peking University, Beijing, China*
Bernhard Steffen, *TU Dortmund University, Dortmund, Germany*
Moti Yung, *Columbia University, New York, NY, USA*

The series Lecture Notes in Computer Science (LNCS), including its subseries Lecture Notes in Artificial Intelligence (LNAI) and Lecture Notes in Bioinformatics (LNBI), has established itself as a medium for the publication of new developments in computer science and information technology research, teaching, and education.

LNCS enjoys close cooperation with the computer science R & D community, the series counts many renowned academics among its volume editors and paper authors, and collaborates with prestigious societies. Its mission is to serve this international community by providing an invaluable service, mainly focused on the publication of conference and workshop proceedings and postproceedings. LNCS commenced publication in 1973.

Claudio Antares Mezzina · Alan Schmitt
Editors

Components Operationally: Reversibility and System Engineering

Essays Dedicated to Jean-Bernard Stefani on the Occasion of His 65th Birthday

Editors
Claudio Antares Mezzina ⓘ
University of Urbino
Urbino, Pesaro-Urbino, Italy

Alan Schmitt ⓘ
Inria
Rennes, France

ISSN 0302-9743　　　　　　ISSN 1611-3349　(electronic)
Lecture Notes in Computer Science
ISBN 978-3-031-99716-7　　　ISBN 978-3-031-99717-4　(eBook)
https://doi.org/10.1007/978-3-031-99717-4

© The Editor(s) (if applicable) and The Author(s), under exclusive license
to Springer Nature Switzerland AG 2026

This work is subject to copyright. All rights are solely and exclusively licensed by the Publisher, whether the whole or part of the material is concerned, specifically the rights of translation, reprinting, reuse of illustrations, recitation, broadcasting, reproduction on microfilms or in any other physical way, and transmission or information storage and retrieval, electronic adaptation, computer software, or by similar or dissimilar methodology now known or hereafter developed.
The use of general descriptive names, registered names, trademarks, service marks, etc. in this publication does not imply, even in the absence of a specific statement, that such names are exempt from the relevant protective laws and regulations and therefore free for general use.
The publisher, the authors and the editors are safe to assume that the advice and information in this book are believed to be true and accurate at the date of publication. Neither the publisher nor the authors or the editors give a warranty, expressed or implied, with respect to the material contained herein or for any errors or omissions that may have been made. The publisher remains neutral with regard to jurisdictional claims in published maps and institutional affiliations.

This Springer imprint is published by the registered company Springer Nature Switzerland AG
The registered company address is: Gewerbestrasse 11, 6330 Cham, Switzerland

If disposing of this product, please recycle the paper.

Preface

This volume is published in honor of Jean-Bernard Stefani's 65th birthday. It is a Festschrift composed of 12 refereed papers authored by close collaborators and friends, and was presented to Jean-Bernard on June 16, 2025, during the one-day workshop CORSE co-located with DisCoTec 2025 – the 20th International Federated Conference on Distributed Computing Techniques, held in Lille.

The contributions gathered in this volume reflect the deep influence of Jean-Bernard's work across a range of foundational and applied topics in computer science. They stand as a testament to his intellectual curiosity, scientific versatility, and tireless research activity, offering both a recognition of his past contributions and a glimpse into future developments inspired by his ideas.

The volume consists of three sections. They comprise scientific papers related to specific research interests of Jean-Bernard:

– concurrency theory and reversibility;
– semantics;
– verification.

We hope this volume serves as both a celebration of Jean-Bernard Stefani's exceptional contributions and an inspiration for future research in the many areas he helped shape.

May 2025
Claudio Antares Mezzina
Alan Schmitt

Organization

Program Committee Chairs

Claudio Antares Mezzina   University of Urbino, Italy
Alan Schmitt   Inria, France

Program Committee

Clément Aubert   Augusta University, USA
Simon Bliudze   Inria, France
Adrian Francalanza   University of Malta, Malta
Gregor Gössler   Inria, France
Ivan Lanese   Università di Bologna, Italy
Sergueï Langlet   Université de Lorraine, France
Michaël Lienhardt   Onera, France
Michele Loreti   Università di Camerino, Italy
G. Michele Pinna   Università di Cagliari, Italy
Irek Ulidowski   University of Leicester, UK
Martin Vassor   Université de Lorraine, France
Nobuko Yoshida   University of Oxford, UK
Gianluigi Zavattaro   Università di Bologna, Italy

Additional Reviewers

Gabriele Cecilia
Kai Pischke

Contents

(Reversible) Concurrency

Encoding Reversible Petri Nets into CCSK 3
    Hernán C. Melgratti, Claudio Antares Mezzina, and G. Michele Pinna

Bounded Reversibility in HOπ 24
    Ivan Lanese, Claudio Antares Mezzina, and Martin Vassor

Bisimulations and Reversibility 46
    Clément Aubert, Iain Phillips, and Irek Ulidowski

Unique-Solution of Equations in Higher-Order Process Calculi
with Passivation 68
    Davide Sangiorgi

Semantics

From Complementary to Zipper Semantics 89
    Serguei̇ Lenglet, Camille Noûs, and Alan Schmitt

CESAn: A Core Erlang Semantics Analyser 103
    Aurélie Kong Win Chang, Jérôme Feret, and Gregor Gössler

Asynchronous Global Protocols, Precisely 116
    Kai Pischke and Nobuko Yoshida

Verification

Applied Formal Methods at ONERA: An Experience Report 137
    Michael Lienhardt

Scalable Verification of Local and Global Properties of Collective Systems ... 154
    Michele Loreti, Michela Quadrini, and Aniqa Rehman

A Hybrid Modelling Approach for Hierarchical Control of Structured CPSs 175
    Simon Bliudze, Sophie Cerf, and Olga Kouchnarenko

Applications

Reversible Computation *vs.* Runtime Adaptation in Industrial IoT Systems 199
 Duncan Paul Attard, Keith Bugeja, Adrian Francalanza,
 Marietta Galea, Gerard Tabone, and Gianluca Zahra

Towards Implementing Distributed Custom Serverless Function
Scheduling in FunLess 218
 Giuseppe De Palma, Saverio Giallorenzo, Jacopo Mauro,
 Matteo Trentin, and Gianluigi Zavattaro

Author Index 237

(Reversible) Concurrency

Encoding Reversible Petri Nets into CCSK

Hernán C. Melgratti[1], Claudio Antares Mezzina[2](✉), and G. Michele Pinna[3]

[1] ICC - Universidad de Buenos Aires, Buenos Aires, Argentina
Melgratthmelgra@dc.uba.ar
[2] Dipartimento di Scienze Pure e Applicate, Università di Urbino, Urbino, Italy
claudio.mezzina@uniurb.it
[3] Dipartimento di Matematica e Informatica, Università di Cagliari, Cagliari, Italy
gmpinna@unica.it

Abstract. Reversibility in computational models is a crucial aspect for applications such as fault-tolerant computing, distributed systems, and quantum computing. Petri nets provide a well-established formalism for modelling concurrent systems, while CCS (Calculus of Communicating Systems) and its reversible extension, CCSK, offer a process algebraic approach to system specification. In this work, we define a method to encode reversible Petri nets into CCSK, ensuring that the structural properties and execution semantics of the original Petri nets are preserved in the translation. We build upon previous research on encoding standard Petri nets into CCS and extend it by incorporating communication keys to track causal dependencies, enabling reversibility.

1 Introduction

In a reversible system, computation can proceed in two directions: forward, executing standard operations, and backward, reversing the effects of the forward computation. Originally, reversible computing was explored for its potential to enable low-energy computation [3]. While energy efficiency remains a relevant concern, reversibility has gained significant attention due to its applications in various domains, such as fault-tolerant computing [9,12,30,42], distributed systems, biochemical systems [14,25,34], and quantum computing. In these contexts, the ability to reverse computations enables error recovery, state exploration, and process rollback, making reversible models crucial for designing robust and resilient systems. Among the formalisms used to describe concurrent systems, Petri nets [36] offer a well-established graphical representation, while process calculi, such as CCS [31] (Calculus of Communicating Systems), provide an algebraic approach to describing interactions and process behaviors.

This work has been supported by the Italian MUR PRIN 2022 project *DeKLA* (F53D23004840006), PRIN 2022 DeLiCE (F53D23009130001), the INdAM-GNCS project CUP_E53C24001950001 *MARQ*, and the European Union - NextGenerationEU program Research and Innovation Program PE00000014 *SEcurity and RIghts in the CyberSpace* (SERICS), projects STRIDE and SWOPS.

In the last decades, many efforts have been made to endow computation models with reversible semantics [2,29]. In particular, two different models have been proposed for CCS: reversible CCS (RCCS) [8,13] and CCS with communication keys (CCSK) [35]. Both of them incorporate a logging mechanism in the operational semantics of CCS that enables the undoing of computation steps. Moreover, it has been shown that they are isomorphic [17] since they only differ on how they log information about past computations: while RCCS relies on some form of memory/monitor, CCSK uses keys. On the Petri nets side there exist several attempts to give a reversible semantics to nets [26–28,32,33], with just [27] providing a suitable class of Petri nets for RCCS.

CCS nets [11] are a subclass of Petri nets aiming at capturing the behavior of CCS. Recently an encoding of CCS nets into CCS processes has been provided [5] showing that a CCS net is strongly bisimilar to the generated CCS process. This paper is motivated by the following question: what is a suitable subclass of Petri nets for CCSK? To answer this question we start from CCS nets and show what the ingredients to first obtain key labelled nets are, that is CCS nets enriched with (i) extra places indicating that a transition has fired and with (ii) particular tokens recording the causal path of a computation. Then we show how it is possible to add reversibility to such kind of nets obtaining CCSK nets. Finally we show how it is possible to generate a CCSK term starting from a CCSK net. This will enable us to obtain a suitable sub-class of (reversible) Petri nets corresponding to CCSK processes.

A Tribute to Jean-Bernard Stefani. This paper is an occasion to celebrate Jean-Bernard Stefani's 65th birthday. Jean-Bernard Stefani has made significant contributions to theoretical computer science, particularly in concurrency theory [21–23], process calculi [37,38,40] and their abstract machines [4,7,24], and component-based software engineering [1,6,39,41]. His research has also advanced the field of reversible computation in concurrent systems with the idea of modelling and verifying fault-handling systems [16,18–20,42], as well as enabling reverse debugging techniques [10,15]. Through his insights, passion, and enthusiasm for computer science–and science more broadly–Stefani has inspired new research directions and fostered generations of computer scientists.

2 CCS and CCSK

A *labelled transition system* (LTS) is the triple $(Q, A, \rightarrow)$ where Q is a set of states, A is a set of labels and $\rightarrow \subseteq Q \times A \times Q$ is a *transition relation*. We write $q \xrightarrow{a} q'$ for $(q, a, q') \in \rightarrow$. When the transition relation $\rightarrow$ can be partitioned into two relations $\rightarrow^f$ and $\rightarrow^b$ (forward and backward) we will write $\rightarrow^f \uplus \rightarrow^b$ instead of $\rightarrow$.

A *strong forward and reverse* bisimulation (FR bisimulation) between two LTSs $(Q_1, A_1, \rightarrow_1^f \uplus \rightarrow_1^b)$ and $(Q_2, A_2, \rightarrow_2^f \uplus \rightarrow_2^b)$ is a relation $\mathcal{R} \subseteq Q_1 \times Q_2$ where if $(q_1, q_2) \in \mathcal{R}$:

1. $\forall q_1' : q_1 \xrightarrow{\mu\ f}_1 q_1'$ implies $\exists q_2' : q_2 \xrightarrow{\mu\ f}_2 q_2'$ and $(q_1', q_2') \in \mathcal{R}$

2. $\forall q_1' : q_1 \xrightarrow{\mu\ b}_1 q_1'$ implies $\exists q_2' : q_2 \xrightarrow{\mu\ b}_2 q_2'$ and $(q_1', q_2') \in \mathcal{R}$
3. $\forall q_2' : q_2 \xrightarrow{\mu\ f}_2 q_2'$ implies $\exists q_1' : q_1 \xrightarrow{\mu\ f}_1 q_2'$ and $(q_1', q_2') \in \mathcal{R}$
4. $\forall q_2' : q_2 \xrightarrow{\mu\ b}_2 q_2'$ implies $\exists q_1' : q_1 \xrightarrow{\mu\ b}_1 q_2'$ and $(q_1', q_2') \in \mathcal{R}$

If we restrict the relation $\mathcal{R}$ to the forward direction, by removing requirements (2) and (4) on the relation $\mathcal{R}$, and $\rightarrow_1^b$, $\rightarrow_2^b$ from the corresponding LTSs, we call $\mathcal{R}$ a strong bisimulation. We denote with $\sim_{fb}$ the largest strong forward and reverse bisimulation, and with $\sim$ the largest strong bisimulation.

2.1 CCS

Let $\mathcal{A} = \{a, b, c, \ldots\}$ be a set of *actions*, and let $\overline{\mathcal{A}} = \{\overline{a} \mid a \in \mathcal{A}\}$ be the set of their corresponding *co-actions*. The set of all possible actions is given by $\text{Act} = \mathcal{A} \cup \overline{\mathcal{A}}$. This set is extended to $\text{Act}_\tau = \text{Act} \cup \{\tau\}$, where $\tau \notin \text{Act}$ is a distinguished *silent* (or internal) action. We use α, β to range over elements of Act_τ. We assume that for each $a \in \text{Act}$, $\overline{\overline{a}} = a$ holds. The syntax of CCS is presented below.

(Actions) $\alpha ::= a \mid \overline{a} \mid \tau$

(Processes) $P ::= \mathbf{0} \mid \alpha.Q \mid P + P'$ (Agents) $Q ::= P \mid Q \parallel Q' \mid (\nu a)Q \mid X$

In CCS, a prefix (or action) can be an input a, an output $\overline{a}$, or the silent action τ. A process can be the inactive process $\mathbf{0}$, a prefixed agent of the form $\alpha.Q$, or a nondeterministic choice among two processes $P + P'$. Agents can be simple processes, a parallel composition of agents $Q \parallel Q'$, the restriction $(\nu a)Q$ that denotes that the name a is *locally bound* to the agent Q and cannot be used for communication outside of Q, or a process name X. Restriction is the only binder in CCS.

Let $\mathcal{P}$ denote the set of all CCS processes that can be obtained by a CCS agent Q and a set of defining equations $\mathcal{D} = \{X_i = Q_i\}$ where each X_i is a process constant and Q_i an agent. For any process $P \in \mathcal{P}$, we write $\text{n}(P)$ for the set of all names occurring in P, and $\text{fn}(P)$ and $\text{bn}(P)$ for the sets of free and bound names of P.

Definition 1 (CCS Semantics). *Given a set of defining equations $\mathcal{D}$ and an agent Q, the operational semantics of CCS is defined as the $LTS(Q, \mathcal{D}) = (\mathcal{P}, \text{Act}_\tau, \rightarrow)$, where the transition relation $\rightarrow$ is the smallest relation closed under the rules in Fig. 1.*

We now comment on the rules in Fig. 1. The ACT rule indicates that an agent of the form $\alpha.Q$ can perform α and evolves to Q. The PAR-L and PAR-R rules specify that either process in a parallel composition can execute an action independently while the other remains inert. The SYN rule regulates synchronization, enabling two parallel processes to interact by simultaneously executing complementary actions (e.g., a and $\overline{a}$). The RES rule enforces name restriction by preventing the bound name from being propagated outside the process Q. The CONS rule handles recursion by replacing a process identifier with its defining expression.

$$\alpha.Q \xrightarrow{\alpha} Q \text{ (ACT)} \qquad \frac{Q_1 \xrightarrow{\alpha} Q_1'}{Q_1 + Q_2 \xrightarrow{\alpha} Q_1'} \text{ (SUM-L)} \qquad \frac{Q_2 \xrightarrow{\alpha} Q_2'}{Q_1 + Q_2 \xrightarrow{\alpha} Q_2'} \text{ (SUM-R)}$$

$$\frac{Q_1 \xrightarrow{\alpha} Q_1'}{Q_1 \parallel Q_2 \xrightarrow{\alpha} Q_1' \parallel Q_2} \text{ (PAR-L)} \qquad \frac{Q_2 \xrightarrow{\alpha} Q_2'}{Q_1 \parallel Q_2 \xrightarrow{\alpha} Q_1 \parallel Q_2'} \text{ (PAR-R)} \qquad \frac{Q_1 \xrightarrow{a} Q_1' \quad Q_2 \xrightarrow{\bar{a}} Q_2'}{Q_1 \parallel Q_2 \xrightarrow{\tau} Q_1' \parallel Q_2'} \text{ (SYN)}$$

$$\frac{Q \xrightarrow{\alpha} Q' \quad \alpha \notin \{a, \bar{a}\}}{(\nu a)Q \xrightarrow{\alpha} (\nu a)Q'} \text{ (R-RES)} \qquad \frac{D(X) = Q \quad Q \xrightarrow{\alpha} Q'}{X \xrightarrow{\alpha} Q'} \text{ (CONS)}$$

Fig. 1. CCS LTS

2.2 CCSK: CCS with Communication Keys

A general framework to obtain a reversible semantics for a calculus given in a particular SOS format is provided in [35]. The main ideas of such approach is to make every operator of a calculus *static*, since dynamic operator are forgetful, and to identify each action with a unique *key*. The result of applying such a framework on CCS is CCSK: that is CCS with communication keys. The syntax of CCSK is then the following one.

(Actions) $\quad \alpha ::= a \mid \bar{a} \mid \tau \qquad$ (Prefixes) $\pi ::= \alpha \mid \alpha[i]$

(Processes) $P ::= \mathbf{0} \mid \pi.Q \mid P + P' \quad$ (Agents) $\quad Q ::= P \mid Q \parallel Q' \mid (\nu a)Q \mid X$

The only difference from CCS is the presence of the past-prefix operator $\alpha[i].Q$, which denotes that the process Q has previously executed the action α, which has been bound to the fresh identifier i.

We write $\mathsf{key}(Q)$ for the set of keys of a process Q, given inductively by:

$\mathsf{key}(X) = \mathsf{key}(\mathbf{0}) = \emptyset \qquad \mathsf{key}((\nu a)Q) = \mathsf{key}(Q) \qquad \mathsf{key}(\alpha[i].Q) = \{i\} \cup \mathsf{key}(Q)$
$\mathsf{key}(\alpha.Q) = \mathsf{key}(Q) \qquad \mathsf{key}(Q_1 + Q_2) = \mathsf{key}(Q_1 \parallel Q_2) = \mathsf{key}(Q_1) \cup \mathsf{key}(Q_2)$

A CCSK process is standard, noted $\mathsf{std}(Q)$, when it does not contain communication keys, that is $\mathsf{std}(Q) \iff \mathsf{key}(Q) = \emptyset$.

Definition 2 (CCSK Semantics). *Given a set of defining equations $\mathcal{D}$ and a CCSK term Q, the operational semantics of CCSK is defined as the labelled transitions system $LTS(\mathcal{D}, Q) = (\mathcal{P}, \{\alpha[i] \mid \alpha \in \mathsf{Act}_\tau \land i \in \mathbb{N}\}, \to \uplus \hookrightarrow)$, where the relations $\to$ and $\hookrightarrow$ are the smallest relations closed under the inference rules in the top and bottom sections, respectively, of Fig. 2.*

We now comment on the inference rules and focus on the most complex forward-transition rules, noting that the backward rules are symmetric.

Rule ACT-1 converts a prefix into a past-action while preserving the prefix's information via a static operator. Rule ACT-2 allows a process under a past-action prefix to progress further. Rule SUM-L allows the execution of the left process of a choice. Unlike CCS, the non-selected branch (Q_2) is preserved rather

$$\alpha.Q \xrightarrow{\alpha[i]} \alpha[i].Q \quad (\text{Act1}) \qquad \frac{Q \xrightarrow{\beta[j]} Q' \quad i \neq j}{\alpha[i].Q \xrightarrow{\beta[j]} \alpha[i].Q'} \quad (\text{Act2}) \qquad \frac{Q_1 \xrightarrow{\beta[j]} Q'_1 \quad \text{std}(Q_2)}{Q_1 + Q_2 \xrightarrow{\beta[j]} Q'_1 + Q_2} \quad (\text{Sum-L})$$

$$\frac{Q_1 \xrightarrow{\beta[j]} Q'_1 \quad j \notin \text{key}(Q_2)}{Q_1 \parallel Q_2 \xrightarrow{\beta[j]} Q'_1 \parallel Q_2} \quad (\text{Par-L}) \qquad \frac{Q_1 \xrightarrow{\alpha[i]} Q'_1 \quad Q_2 \xrightarrow{\bar{\alpha}[i]} Q'_2}{Q_1 \parallel Q_2 \xrightarrow{\tau[i]} Q'_1 \parallel Q'_2} \quad (\text{Syn})$$

$$\frac{Q \xrightarrow{\alpha[i]} Q' \quad \alpha \notin \{a, \bar{a}\}}{(\nu a)Q \xrightarrow{\alpha[i]} (\nu a)Q'} \quad (\text{R-Res}) \qquad \frac{\mathcal{D}(X) = Q \quad Q \xrightarrow{\alpha[i]} Q'}{X \xrightarrow{\alpha[i]} Q'} \quad (\text{Cons})$$

$$\alpha[i].Q \xrightsquigarrow{\alpha[i]} \alpha.Q \quad (\text{Act1}^\bullet) \qquad \frac{Q' \xrightsquigarrow{\beta[j]} Q \quad i \neq j}{\alpha[i].Q' \xrightsquigarrow{\beta[j]} \alpha[i].Q} \quad (\text{Act2}^\bullet) \qquad \frac{Q'_1 \xrightsquigarrow{\beta[j]} Q_1 \quad \text{std}(Q_2)}{Q'_1 + Q_2 \xrightsquigarrow{\beta[j]} Q_1 + Q_2} \quad (\text{Sum-L}^\bullet)$$

$$\frac{Q'_1 \xrightsquigarrow{\beta[j]} Q_1 \quad j \notin \text{key}(Q_2)}{Q'_1 \parallel Q_2 \xrightsquigarrow{\beta[j]} Q_1 \parallel Q_2} \quad (\text{Par-L}^\bullet) \qquad \frac{Q'_1 \xrightsquigarrow{\alpha[i]} Q_1 \quad Q'_2 \xrightsquigarrow{\bar{\alpha}[i]} Q_2}{Q'_1 \parallel Q'_2 \xrightsquigarrow{\tau[i]} Q_1 \parallel Q_2} \quad (\text{Syn}^\bullet)$$

$$\frac{Q \xrightsquigarrow{\alpha[i]} Q' \quad \alpha \notin \{a, \bar{a}\}}{(\nu a)Q \xrightsquigarrow{\alpha[i]} (\nu a)Q'} \quad (\text{R-Res}^\bullet) \qquad \frac{\mathcal{D}(X) = Q \quad Q' \xrightsquigarrow{\alpha[i]} Q}{Q' \xrightsquigarrow{\alpha[i]} X} \quad (\text{Cons}^\bullet)$$

Fig. 2. CCSK LTS: symmetric rules are omitted

than discarded. The requirement on Q_2 of being a standard CCS process ensures that it has not execute any action. Rule Par-L allows the left branch of a parallel composition to execute without synchronizing with the right branch. The side condition ensures that the key created is not used in the right branch. Rule Syn, which accounts for synchronization, requires the two complementary actions to share the same key.

3 Nets

We start by recalling definitions and notions on *multisets*. The symbol $\mathbb{N}$ indicates the set of natural numbers. A *multiset* over a set A is a function $f : A \to \mathbb{N}$. Multisets are assumed to be equipped with the standard operations of union $(+)$ and difference $(-)$. We write $f \subseteq f'$ if $f(a) \leq f'(a)$ for all $a \in A$. The multiset $[\![f]\!]$ is defined such that $[\![f]\!](a) = 1$ if $f(a) > 0$ and $[\![f]\!](a) = 0$ otherwise. We often confuse a multiset f with the set $\{a \in A \mid f(a) \neq 0\}$ when $f = [\![f]\!]$. In such cases, $a \in f$ denotes $f(a) \neq 0$, and $f \subseteq A$ signifies that $f(a) = 1$ implies $a \in A$ for all a. The underlying set of a multiset f, namely the one formed by the elements a with $f(a) > 0$, is precisely $[\![f]\!]$. Additionally, we will employ standard set operations like $\cap$, $\cup$, or $\setminus$. The set of all multisets over A is denoted as μA; the symbol 0 stands for the unique multiset defined such that $[\![0]\!] = \emptyset$. We sometimes denote a multiset f as $\oplus_{a \in [\![f]\!]} f(a) \cdot a$, thus $a \oplus 2b$ would be the multiset f such that $f(a) = 1$ and $f(b) = 2$. Given a multiset f with $\#(f)$ we denote the number of its elements with their multiplicity, hence $\#(f) = \sum_{a \in [\![f]\!]} f(a)$.

A sequence of elements of a given set A is written as usual as $\rho = a_1 a_2 \cdots a_n$, with $a_i \in A$. The length of a sequence $\rho = a_1 a_2 \cdots a_n$, denoted by $len(\rho)$, is n. With ε we denote the empty sequence.

We recall the definition of net which we consider labelled, meaning that we associate to each transition a label from a fixed set.

Definition 3. *A labelled net over* A *is the quintuple* $N = \langle S, T, F, \lambda, \mathsf{A} \rangle$, *where S and T are respectively the set of places and of transitions, and are such that $S \cap T = \emptyset$, $F \subseteq (S \times T) \cup (T \times S)$ is a set of arcs, and $\lambda : T \to \mathsf{A}$ is a labelling mapping.*

Given a labelled net N and $x \in S \cup T$, we define the preset ${}^\bullet x = \{y \mid (y, x) \in F\}$ and the postset $x^\bullet = \{y \mid (x, y) \in F\}$. If x is a place then ${}^\bullet x$ and $x^\bullet$ are sets of transitions; analogously, if $x \in T$ then ${}^\bullet x$ and $x^\bullet$ are sets of places.

Example 1. Consider the labelled net in Fig. 3. The transition t_1 is labelled with a and has s_1 in its preset and s_1, s_2 in the postset. The transition t_4 is labelled with τ and ${}^\bullet t_4 = \{s_2, s_3\}$ whereas $t_4^\bullet$ contains the place s_1 and s_4.

We introduce the notion of *marking* for these nets and describe the token game.

Definition 4. *A marked net is the pair* $\mathsf{N} = (N, m)$ *where* $N = \langle S, T, F, \lambda, \mathsf{A} \rangle$ *is a labelled net and $m : S \to \mathbb{N}$ is a marking.*

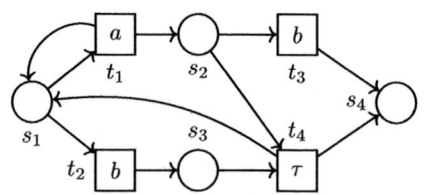

Fig. 3. A labelled net

We will often call *marked nets* simply nets. A transition t is *enabled* at a marking m, written $m\, [t\rangle$, if $\forall s \in {}^\bullet t$. $m(s) > 0$. If a transition t is enabled at a marking m then it may *fire* giving the marking m' defined as follows: $\forall s \in S$. $m(s) - 1$ if $s \in {}^\bullet t \setminus t^\bullet$, $m(s) + 1$ if $s \in t^\bullet \setminus {}^\bullet t$ and $m(s)$ for all others places. The firing of a transition t at m' producing the marking m' is denoted as $m\, [t\rangle\, m'$. A *firing sequence* (shortened as fs) of (N, m) is a sequence σ of markings such that for each $1 \le i < len(\sigma)$ there is a transition t_i enabled at $\sigma(i)$ and $\sigma(i)\, [t_i\rangle\, \sigma(i+1)$ and $\sigma(1)$ is m. A marking m' is *reachable* if there is a firing sequence ending with m'. With $\mathcal{M}_{(N,m)}$ we denote the set of reachable markings of the net (N, m).

Definition 5. *Let* $\mathsf{N} = (N, m)$ *be a net, where* $N = \langle S, T, F, \lambda, \mathsf{A} \rangle$, *then its marking graph is the tuple* $M(N, m) = (\mathcal{M}_{(N,m)}, \mathsf{A}, \longrightarrow, m)$ *where* $\longrightarrow \,\subseteq\, \mathcal{M}_{(N,m)} \times \mathsf{A} \times \mathcal{M}_{(N,m)}$ *is such that* $(m', a, m'') \in \longrightarrow$, *written* $m' \xrightarrow{a} m''$, *if there is a transition t such that $m'\, [t\rangle\, m''$ and $\lambda(t) = a$.*

4 CCS Nets

We start by recalling the notion of CCS net as defined in [5] and inspired by previous works, for instance see [11].

Definition 6. *A CCS net is a labeled net* $N = \langle S, T, F, \lambda, \mathsf{A} \rangle$ *such that for all* $t \in T$ $|{}^\bullet t| \leq 2$ *and if* $|{}^\bullet t| = 2$ *then* $\lambda(t) = \tau$.

A marked CCS net is the pair $\mathsf{H} = (N, m)$ *where* N *is a CCS net and* $m : S \to \mathbb{N}$ *is a marking.*

The unique characteristic of this kind of nets is that transitions have either one incoming arc or two. Thus a place with various outgoing arcs represents the possible choice among various actions. A transition with two incoming arcs is a *synchronization*, and it involves just two places in the preset, to match binary CCS synchronization. We report the algorithm and main result presented in [5] adapted to our notation.

Algorithm 1: Encoding from CCS net to CCS process

Input : CCS net $\langle S, T, F, \lambda, \mathsf{A} \rangle$ and marking $m : S \to \mathbb{N}$
Output: CCS process Q and partial mapping of defining equations $\mathcal{D}$

1 $\mathcal{D} \leftarrow$ Empty mapping of defining equations
2 **for** $s \in S$ **do** $\mathcal{D}(X_s) \leftarrow (Y_{t_1} + Y_{t_2} + \cdots + Y_{t_k})$ where $\{t_1, t_2, \ldots, t_k\} = \{t \mid t \in s^\bullet\}$
3 **for** $t \in \{t \mid t \in T \text{ and } |{}^\bullet t| = 1\}$ **do** substitute Y_t in $\mathcal{D}(X_{s^*})$ with $\lambda(t).(X_{s_1} \mid X_{s_2} \mid \ldots \mid X_{s_k})$ where $(s^*, t) \in F$ and $\{s_1, s_2, \ldots, s_k\} = \{s \mid s \in t^\bullet\}$
4 $A' \leftarrow \emptyset$
5 **for** $t \in \{t \mid t \in T \text{ and } |{}^\bullet t| = 2\}$ **do**
6 $\quad A' \leftarrow A' \cup \{a_t\}$ where a_t is a fresh action
7 $\quad$ substitute Y_t in $\mathcal{D}(X_{s^*})$ with $a_t.(X_{s_1} \mid X_{s_2} \mid \ldots \mid X_{s_k})$
8 $\quad$ substitute Y_t in $\mathcal{D}(X_{s^{**}})$ with $\overline{a_t}.0$ where
    $(s^*, t), (s^{**}, t) \in F$ and $s^* \neq s^{**}$ and $\{s_1, s_2, \ldots, s_k\} = \{s \mid s \in t^\bullet\}$
9 **end**
10 $\{a_1, a_2, \ldots, a_n\} \leftarrow A'$
11 $Q \leftarrow (\nu a_1)(\nu a_2) \ldots (\nu a_n) \left(X_{s_1}^{m(s_1)} \mid X_{s_2}^{m(s_2)} \mid \ldots \mid X_{s_{|S|}}^{m(s_{|S|})} \right)$
12 **return** $(Q, \mathcal{D})$

Theorem 1 (Correctness of Algorithm 1). *Let* (N, m) *be a CCS net system, and let the CCS process* Q *and the set of defining equations* $\mathcal{D}$ *be the result of applying Algorithm 1 to* N *and* m. *Then* $M(N, m)$ *is bisimilar to* $LTS(Q, \mathcal{D})$.

5 Enriching Nets

We want to generalize the notion of CCS net, well suited to encode CCS terms, to obtain a notion of CCSK net, that should be able to encode CCSK terms. We need to add reversing transitions to CCS nets and we must enrich nets to have a way to keep track of the executed transitions. The first step is to establish what the tokens in this kind of nets are, and define the token game accordingly.

We fix an alphabet A of actions containing a special action τ and on that we form what are the *tokens* we will consider in the following. With $\langle\!\langle v_1, \ldots, v_n \rangle\!\rangle$ we denote the tuple with n elements in some set, where the order does not matter, hence $\langle\!\langle v_1, \ldots, v_i, \ldots, v_j, \ldots, v_n \rangle\!\rangle$ is equivalent to $\langle\!\langle v_1, \ldots, v_j, \ldots, v_i, \ldots, v_n \rangle\!\rangle$. $\langle\!\langle v_1, \ldots, v_n \rangle\!\rangle_\sim$ denotes the equivalence class with respect to the equivalence defined above, but we will constantly omit the subscript. The tuple with no elements is $\langle\!\langle \; \rangle\!\rangle$.

Definition 7. *Let* A *be a set of actions containing the special action τ, define a token as follows:* $(\cdot, \langle\!\langle \rangle\!\rangle, \cdot)$ *is a token; if* $w_1, \ldots, w_n$ *are tokens,* $a \in A$ *is an action and* $j \in \mathbb{N}$ *is a number, then* $(a, \langle\!\langle w_1, \ldots, w_n \rangle\!\rangle, j)$ *is a token; and nothing else is a token. With* Tok *we denote the set of tokens.*

Now tokens are not simply anonymous objects but each of them contains a code on how it has been produced. Given a token $w = (a, \langle\!\langle w_1, \ldots, w_n \rangle\!\rangle, j)$, the mappings $\mathsf{kt}(w) = j$, $\mathsf{label}(w) = a$ and $\lfloor w \rfloor = (w_1, \ldots, w_n)$ give respectively the key, the action labelling the transition producing that token and the tuple of tokens used for producing it. The *size* of a token is defined as follows: $\mathsf{size}((\cdot, \langle\!\langle \; \rangle\!\rangle, \cdot)) = 0$ and $\mathsf{size}((a, \langle\!\langle w_1, \ldots, w_n \rangle\!\rangle, j)) = max\{\mathsf{size}(w_i) \mid 1 \leq i \leq n\} + 1$.

Example 2. Take $\mathsf{A} = \{a, b, \tau\}$, tokens are $w_0 = (\cdot, \langle\!\langle \rangle\!\rangle, \cdot)$, $w_1 = (a, \langle\!\langle (\cdot, \langle\!\langle \rangle\!\rangle, \cdot) \rangle\!\rangle, 1)$, $w_2 = (b, \langle\!\langle (\cdot, \langle\!\langle \rangle\!\rangle, \cdot) \rangle\!\rangle, 1)$, $w_3 = (a, \langle\!\langle (\cdot, \langle\!\langle \rangle\!\rangle, \cdot), (b, \langle\!\langle (\cdot, \langle\!\langle \rangle\!\rangle, \cdot) \rangle\!\rangle, 1) \rangle\!\rangle, 2)$ and $w_4 = (\tau, \langle\!\langle (a, \langle\!\langle (\cdot, \langle\!\langle \rangle\!\rangle, \cdot) \rangle\!\rangle, 1), (b, \langle\!\langle (\cdot, \langle\!\langle \rangle\!\rangle, \cdot) \rangle\!\rangle, 2) \rangle\!\rangle, 3)$. Their size is $\mathsf{size}(w_0) = 0$, $\mathsf{size}(w_1) = 1 = \mathsf{size}(w_2)$, $\mathsf{size}(w_3) = 2$ as the size of the tokens $(\cdot, \langle\!\langle \rangle\!\rangle, \cdot)$ and $(b, \langle\!\langle (\cdot, \langle\!\langle \rangle\!\rangle, \cdot) \rangle\!\rangle, 1)$ is 0 and 1 respectively, and finally $\mathsf{size}(w_4)$ is again 2.

The notion of net system changes accordingly: (N, m) with N labelled net and the marking m is now a mapping associating to each place a multiset of tokens, i.e. $m : S \to \mu\mathsf{Tok}$.

To take into account the new notion of tokens, we have to reformulate the notions of enabling of a transition at a given marking, the firing of an enabled transition and accordingly the notion of firing sequence. Let N be a labelled net, and let $m : S \to \mu\mathsf{Tok}$ be a marking. A transition $t \in T$ is *enabled* at m, written $m\,[t\rangle$, if $\forall s \in {}^\bullet t$ it holds that $m(s) \neq 0$, namely the place is marked. Let m be a marking and let t be a transition enabled at m. Then t may fire consuming the tokens w_{s_i} present in the places in ${}^\bullet t = \{s_1, \ldots, s_n\}$ and producing the token $w = (\lambda(t), \langle\!\langle w_{s_1}, \ldots, w_{s_n} \rangle\!\rangle, i)$, where i is just a new index, in the places in the $t^\bullet$, giving the new marking m'. Formally, denoting with w_{s_i} the token used in the place $s_i \in {}^\bullet t$ we obtain the marking m', where for all $s \in S$

$$m'(s) = \begin{cases} m(s) - w_{s_i} + w & \text{if } s = s_i \in {}^\bullet t \cap t^\bullet \\ m(s) - w_{s_i} & \text{if } s = s_i \in {}^\bullet t \setminus t^\bullet \\ m(s) + w & \text{if } s = s_i \in t^\bullet \setminus {}^\bullet t \\ m(s) & \text{otherwise} \end{cases}$$

The firing of a transition t at a marking m is denoted as usual: $m\,[t\rangle\,m'$. The firing sequences are defined in the same way, as well as the notion of reachable marking and of marking graph. A marking $m : S \to \mu\mathsf{Tok}$ is *initial* if $\forall s \in S$. $[\![m(s)]\!] \subseteq \{(\cdot, \langle\!\langle\rangle\!\rangle, \cdot)\}$ and a place s is unmarked if $m(s) = 0$.

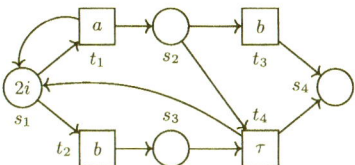 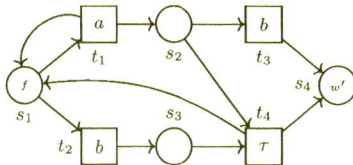

Fig. 4. A labeled net with the initial marking and after the firing of t_1, t_2 and t_4. The tokens are $i = (\cdot, \langle\!\langle\rangle\!\rangle, \cdot)$, $w = (a, \langle\!\langle i\rangle\!\rangle, 1)$, $w' = (\tau, \langle\!\langle (a, \langle\!\langle i\rangle\!\rangle, 1), (b, \langle\!\langle i\rangle\!\rangle, 2)\rangle\!\rangle, 3)$ and $f \in \mu\mathsf{Tok}$ is the multiset $w \oplus w'$.

Example 3. Consider the labelled nets in Fig. 4. On the left only the place s_1 is marked and the marking is $m(s_1) = (\cdot, \langle\!\langle\rangle\!\rangle, \cdot) \oplus (\cdot, \langle\!\langle\rangle\!\rangle, \cdot)$ and all the other places are such that $m(s_j) = 0$ for $j \in \{2, 3, 4\}$. At this marking the enabled transitions are t_1 and t_2. Assume that t_1 is executed. The resulting marking m_1 is $m_1(s_1) = (\cdot, \langle\!\langle\rangle\!\rangle, \cdot) \oplus (a, \langle\!\langle(\cdot, \langle\!\langle\rangle\!\rangle, \cdot)\rangle\!\rangle, 1)$, $m_1(s_2) = (a, \langle\!\langle(\cdot, \langle\!\langle\rangle\!\rangle, \cdot)\rangle\!\rangle, 1)$ and the other places are unmarked. Thus $m\,[t_1\rangle\,m_1$. At m_1 the transitions t_1, t_2 and t_3 are enabled. By executing t_2 using the token $(\cdot, \langle\!\langle\rangle\!\rangle, \cdot)$ we obtain the marking m_2 where $m_2(s_1) = (a, \langle\!\langle(\cdot, \langle\!\langle\rangle\!\rangle, \cdot)\rangle\!\rangle, 1)$, $m_2(s_2) = m_1(s_2)$, and $m_2(s_3) = (b, \langle\!\langle(\cdot, \langle\!\langle\rangle\!\rangle, \cdot)\rangle\!\rangle, 2)$. At this marking all the transitions are enabled and we decide to fire t_4. We get the marking m_3 shown in Fig. 4 in the net on the right. The firing sequence is $m\,[t_1\rangle\,m_1\,[t_2\rangle\,m_2\,[t_4\rangle\,m_3$. If instead of executing t_4 at m_2 we execute t_3 the reached marking would be $m'(s_1) = (a, \langle\!\langle(\cdot, \langle\!\langle\rangle\!\rangle, \cdot)\rangle\!\rangle, 1)$, $m'(s_2) = 0$, $m'(s_3) = (b, \langle\!\langle(\cdot, \langle\!\langle\rangle\!\rangle, \cdot)\rangle\!\rangle, 2)$ and $m'(s_4) = (b, \langle\!\langle(a, \langle\!\langle(\cdot, \langle\!\langle\rangle\!\rangle, \cdot)\rangle\!\rangle, 1)\rangle\!\rangle, 3)$.

The second step is to enrich a labelled net with *key* places whose purpose is to keep a precise record of the fired transitions.

Definition 8. *A* key labelled net *$K = (N, S_k)$ is a pair where $N = \langle S, T, F, \lambda, \mathsf{A}\rangle$ is a labelled net such that there exists a subset $S_k \subseteq S$ of places, called* key places, *such that for all $t \in T$ $|t^\bullet \cap S_k| = 1$ and for all $s \in S_k$. $s^\bullet = \emptyset$ and $|{}^\bullet s| = 1$.*

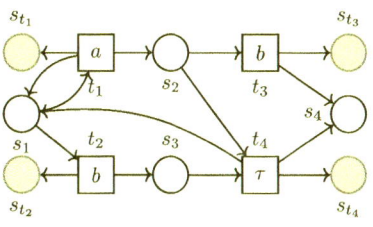

Fig. 5. A key labeled net.

A direct consequence of this definition is that $|T| = |S_k|$. The key place associated to a transition, which is unique, conveys the idea of the key associated to a transition when it gets executed.

Example 4. In Fig. 5 it is shown a key labelled net. Removing the key places we obtain the labelled net depicted in Fig. 4 on the left.

Each labelled net can be transformed into a key labelled net.

Proposition 1. *Let $N = \langle S, T, F, \lambda, \mathsf{A}\rangle$ be a labelled net, and let $S_k = \{s_t \mid t \in T\}$ be a new set of places. Then $\mathcal{K}(N) = (N', S_k)$ where $N' = \langle S \cup S_k, T, F \cup \{(t, s_t) \mid t \in T\}, \lambda, \mathsf{A}\rangle$, is a key labelled net.*

Key places can also be removed from a key labelled net.

Proposition 2. *Let $\mathsf{K} = (N, S_k)$ be a key labelled net with $N = \langle S, T, F, \lambda, \mathsf{A}\rangle$. Then $\mathcal{G}(\mathsf{K}) = \langle S \setminus S_k, T, F \setminus \{(t, s) \mid s \in S_k, t \in T\}, \lambda, \mathsf{A}\rangle$ is a labelled net.*

Observe that, given a labelled net N, $\mathcal{G}(\mathcal{K}(N)) = N$ up to renaming of key places and, given a key labelled net K, $\mathcal{K}(\mathcal{G}(\mathsf{K}))$ is equal to K, again up to renaming of key places. It is straightforward to observe that key places do not influence the token game.

Proposition 3. *Let $\mathsf{K} = (N, S_k)$ be a key labelled net, m a marking and $t \in T$ a transition. Then $m\,[t\rangle$ iff $m_{|S \setminus S_k}\,[t\rangle$ and if $m\,[t\rangle\,m'$ then $m_{|S \setminus S_k}\,[t\rangle\,m'_{|S \setminus S_k}$ where $m_{|S \setminus S_k} : S \setminus S_k \to \mu\mathsf{Tok}$ is the restriction of m to the places in $S \setminus S_k$.*

If $m_{|S \setminus S_k}\,[t\rangle\,m'_{|S \setminus S_k}$ then we have that there is a marking $\widetilde{m} : S \to \mu\mathsf{Tok}$ such that $m_{|S \setminus S_k} = \widetilde{m}$ and $\widetilde{m}\,[t\rangle\,\widetilde{m}'$ with $m'_{|S \setminus S_k} = \widetilde{m}'$.

As each key place is associated to a given transition, we can, using the name of the transition, find the associated key place.

Definition 9. *Let $\mathsf{K} = (N, S_k)$ be a key labelled net and let $t \in T$ be a transition. Then with s^t we denote the key place $s^t \in S_k$ such that $\bullet s^t = \{t\}$. The key place associated to a transition t is denoted with $\mathsf{keypl}(t)$.*

Definition 10. *Let $\mathsf{K} = (N, S_k)$ be a key labelled net where $N = \langle S, T, F, \lambda, \mathsf{A}\rangle$ and let $m : S \to \mu\mathsf{Tok}$ be a marking. We say that m is initial iff (a) $\forall s \in S$. $[\![m(s)]\!] \subseteq \{(\cdot, \langle\!\langle\rangle\!\rangle, \cdot)\}$ and (b) $\forall s \in S_k$. $m(s) = 0$.*

A marking is initial iff all the key places are unmarked and if another place is marked, then it contains the *initial* token $(\cdot, \langle\!\langle\rangle\!\rangle, \cdot)$.

We introduce now *reversing* transitions. The idea is simple: given a transition t we add a transition u that has the effect of *reversing* the execution of t.

Definition 11. *A reversible labelled net with reversing transitions $U \subseteq T$ and key places $S_k \subseteq S$ is the triple $R = (\langle S, T, F, \lambda, \mathsf{A}\rangle, S_k, U)$ where*

1. *$\langle S, T, F, \lambda, \mathsf{A}\rangle$ is a labelled net,*
2. *$(\langle S, T \setminus U, F \setminus (\{(s, u) \mid s \in S, u \in U\} \cup \{(u, s) \mid s \in S, u \in U\}), \lambda, \mathsf{A}\rangle, S_k)$ is a key labelled net, and*
3. *$U \subseteq T$ and $\forall u \in U$. $\exists! \, t \in T \setminus U$ such that (a) $\bullet u = t^\bullet$ and $u^\bullet = \bullet t$, and (b) $\lambda(t) = \lambda(u)$.*

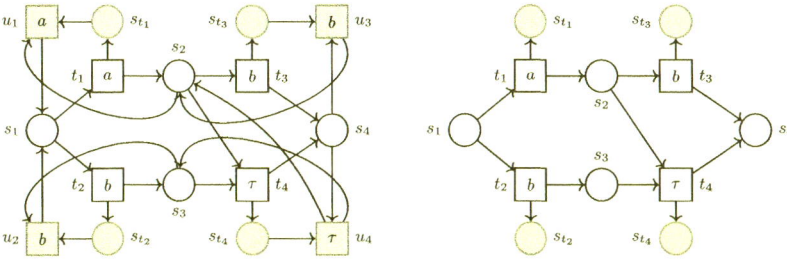

Fig. 6. A reversible labeled net (on the left) and the associated key labelled net.

In a reversible labelled net we have a designated subset U of reversing transitions that are such that, for each reversing transition, there is exactly one *forward* transition (not a reversing one) such that their presets and postsets are exchanged.

Example 5. In Fig. 6 we depict a reversible labeled net and the associated labelled net without the reversing transitions.

Enabling and Firing a Reversing Transition: Executing a reversing transition is different from executing a *normal* one. First of all, it has to undo the effects of firing a transition t, and the token produced in the postset of the transition t depends on the tokens consumed, the labelling of t and a fresh index, thus a reversing transition u has first to check that there is the *same* token in each of the places in its preset.

Definition 12. *Let $R = (\langle S, T, F, \lambda, \mathsf{A}\rangle, S_k, U)$ be a reversible labelled net and let $u \in U$ be a reversing transition, and let $t \in T \setminus U$ the corresponding forward transition. Then u is enabled at the marking m whenever there exist a token $w \in m(s)$ such that $\mathsf{label}(w) = \lambda(t)$ and $w \in m(s)$ for each $s \in {}^\bullet u$ and for each $w' \in \lfloor w \rfloor$ there exists a place $s \in u^\bullet$ such that either there $\exists t \in {}^\bullet s$ and $w' \in m(\mathsf{keypl}(t))$ or $w' = (\cdot, \langle\!\langle\rangle\!\rangle, \cdot)$. The enabling of a reversing transition u at a marking m is denoted with $m \, \llbracket u \rangle$.*

Example 6. Consider the reversible labelled net depicted in Fig. 7 on the left and the marking $m(s_1) = m(s_2) = m(s_3) = m(s_{t_3}) = 0$, $m(s_4) = w_3 = m(s_{t_4})$, $m(s_{t_1}) = (a, \langle\!\langle\!\langle (\cdot, \langle\!\langle\rangle\!\rangle, \cdot)\rangle\!\rangle\!\rangle, 1)$ and $m(s_{t_2}) = (b, \langle\!\langle\!\langle (\cdot, \langle\!\langle\rangle\!\rangle, \cdot)\rangle\!\rangle\!\rangle, 3)$, where $w + 3 = (\tau, \langle\!\langle\!\langle (a, \langle\!\langle\!\langle (\cdot, \langle\!\langle\rangle\!\rangle, \cdot)\rangle\!\rangle\!\rangle, 1), (b, \langle\!\langle\!\langle (\cdot, \langle\!\langle\rangle\!\rangle, \cdot)\rangle\!\rangle\!\rangle, 2)\rangle\!\rangle\!\rangle, 3)$. The reverse transition u_4 is enabled, thus $m \, \llbracket u_4 \rangle$, as in all the places in its preset (namely s_4 and s_{t_4}) the token $w_3 = (\tau, \langle\!\langle\!\langle (a, \langle\!\langle\!\langle (\cdot, \langle\!\langle\rangle\!\rangle, \cdot)\rangle\!\rangle\!\rangle, 1), (b, \langle\!\langle\!\langle (\cdot, \langle\!\langle\rangle\!\rangle, \cdot)\rangle\!\rangle\!\rangle, 2)\rangle\!\rangle\!\rangle, 3)$ is present and the *forward* transitions putting a token in the places in postset of $u_4 = \{s_2, s_3\}$, namely t_1 and t_2, are such that $\mathsf{keypl}(t_1) = s_{t_1}$ contains the token $w_1 = (a, \langle\!\langle\!\langle (\cdot, \langle\!\langle\rangle\!\rangle, \cdot)\rangle\!\rangle\!\rangle, 1)$ and $m(\mathsf{keypl}(t_2)) = m(s_{t_2}) = (b, \langle\!\langle\!\langle (\cdot, \langle\!\langle\rangle\!\rangle, \cdot)\rangle\!\rangle\!\rangle, 2) = w_2$.

The execution of the reversing transition u at the marking m is formalized in the following definition.

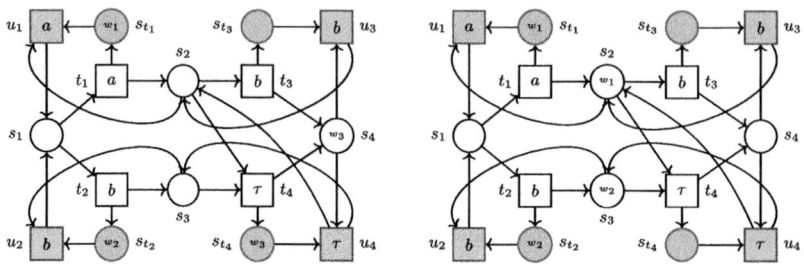

Fig. 7. A reversible labelled net (on the left) after the firing of t_1, t_2 and t_4 starting from an initial marking $m(s_1) = (\cdot, \langle\!\langle\rangle\!\rangle, \cdot) \oplus (\cdot, \langle\!\langle\rangle\!\rangle, \cdot)$. On the right, the marking after undoing the transition t_4.

Definition 13. *Let $R = (\langle S, T, F, \lambda, \mathsf{A}\rangle, S_k, U)$ be a reversible labelled net and let $u \in U$ be a reversing transition. Let m be a marking such that $m [\![u\rangle\!\rangle$ under the token w. Then u may fire at the marking m giving the marking m', written as $m [\![u\rangle\!\rangle m'$ where*

$$m'(s) = \begin{cases} m(s) - w + w' & \text{if } s \in {}^\bullet u \cap u^\bullet \text{ with } w' \in \mathsf{keypl}(t) \text{ for some } t \in {}^\bullet s \\ m(s) + w' & \text{if } s \in u^\bullet \setminus {}^\bullet u \text{ with } w' \in \mathsf{keypl}(t) \text{ for some } t \in {}^\bullet s \\ m(s) - w & \text{if } s \in {}^\bullet u \setminus u^\bullet \\ m(s) & \text{otherwise} \end{cases}$$

Example 7. In the reversible labelled net depicted on the right in Fig. 7 it is shown the marking after the reverse firing of u_4.

Given a reversible labelled net $R = (\langle S, T, F, \lambda, \mathsf{A}\rangle, S_k, U)$, with $\mathcal{B}(R)$ we denote the key labelled net $(\langle S, T \setminus U, F \cap (\{(s, u) \mid s \in S, u \in U\} \cup \{(u, s) \mid s \in S, u \in U\}), \lambda, \mathsf{A}\rangle, S_k)$ as prescribed in Definition 11.

We end this part by defining a marking graph of a reversible labelled net. Consider a reversible labelled net $R = (\langle S, T, F, \lambda, \mathsf{A}\rangle, S_k, U)$, and a marking m. Then the execution of a transition (either forward or reversing) is defined as $m [\![x\rangle\!\rangle m'$ if either $m [x\rangle m'$ if $x \notin U$ or $m [\![x\rangle m'$ if $x \in U$. The firing sequence is defined accordingly and the reachable markings as well. The set of the reachable markings of a reversible labelled net $R = (\langle S, T, F, \lambda, \mathsf{A}\rangle, S_k, U)$ with initial marking m is denoted as usual with $\mathcal{M}_{(R,m)}$.

Definition 14. *Let $R = (\langle S, T, F, \lambda, \mathsf{A}\rangle, S_k, U)$ be a reversible labelled net, then its marking graph is the tuple $M(R, m) = (\mathcal{M}_{(R,m)}, \mathsf{A}, \longrightarrow, m)$ where $\longrightarrow \subseteq \mathcal{M}_{(R,m)} \times \mathsf{A} \times \mathcal{M}_{(R,m)}$ is such that $(m', a, m'') \in \longrightarrow$, written $m' \xrightarrow{a} m''$, if there is a transition $x \in T$ such that $m' [\![x\rangle\!\rangle m''$ and $\lambda(x) = a$.*

Observe that the transition relation $\longrightarrow$ can be partitioned: $\longrightarrow = \longrightarrow_f \uplus \longrightarrow_b$ where $m \xrightarrow{x}_f m'$ when $m [x\rangle m'$ and $m \xrightarrow{x}_b m'$ when $m [\![x\rangle m'$.

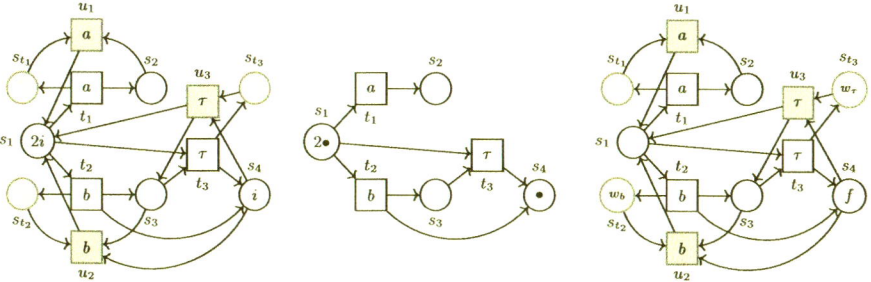

Fig. 8. An initial ccsk-net $\mathsf{G} = (N, S_k, U, m_{in}, m)$, the associated CCS net system $(\mathcal{G}(\mathcal{B}((N, S_k, U))), \widetilde{m})$ where $\widetilde{m}(s) = \#(m(s))$ for all $s \in S \setminus S_k$ and the ccsk-net after the execution of the transitions t_2 and t_3 from the initial marking where s_1 carries the multiset $2i$ and the place s_4 the multiset i, where i is the initial token $(\cdot, \langle\!\langle\rangle\!\rangle, -)$, w_b is the token $(b, \langle\!\langle i \rangle\!\rangle, 1)$, w_τ is $(\tau, \langle\!\langle (b, \langle\!\langle i \rangle\!\rangle, 1), i \rangle\!\rangle, 2)$ and f is the multiset of tokens $i \oplus w_b \oplus w_\tau$.

6 CCSK Nets

We have now all the ingredients to be able to define what a CCSK net is.

Definition 15. *A CCSK net $P = (\langle S, T, F, \lambda, \mathsf{A}\rangle, S_k, U)$ is a reversible labelled net such that $\mathcal{G}(\mathcal{B}(P))$ is a CCS net.*

In fact, a CCSK net is just a reversible labelled net where the labelled net with only the forward transitions and without the key places is precisely a CCS net.

Definition 16. *A CCSK net system (ccsk-net for short) is the tuple $\mathsf{G} = (N, S_k, U, m_{in}, m)$ where (N, S_k, U) is a CCSK net, $m_{in} : S \to \mu\mathsf{Tok}$ is an initial marking of $\mathcal{B}((N, S_k, U))$ and $m : S \to \mu\mathsf{Tok}$ is a marking.*

The requirement that m_{in} should be an initial marking of the key labelled net $\mathcal{B}((N, S_k, U))$ is motivated by the fact that we have to keep track of the starting CCSK process.

Definition 17. *A ccsk-net $\mathsf{G} = (N, S_k, U, m_{in}, m)$ is initial when $m = m_{in}$.*

Example 8. In Fig. 8 we depict, on the left, a ccsk-net and in the middle the associated CCS net system. The initial tokens are of the following form: $i = (\cdot, \langle\!\langle\rangle\!\rangle, \cdot)$. The places s_1 and s_4 are initially marked. The key places are those drawn in red. On the right the same ccsk-net after the executions of t_2 and t_3 (and the only marked key places are indeed s_{t_2} and s_{t_3}). The CCSK term corresponding to the ccsk-net on the left is

$$(\nu s_{t_3})\big((s_{t_3}.\mathbf{0} + a.\mathbf{0} + b.(\overline{s_{t_3}}.\mathbf{0}|\mathbf{0}))|(s_{t_3}.\mathbf{0} + a.\mathbf{0} + b.(\overline{s_{t_3}}.\mathbf{0}|\mathbf{0}))\big)|\mathbf{0})$$

For the ccsk-net on the right in Fig. 8, the CCSK term is

$$(\nu s_{t_3})\big((s_{t_3}.\mathbf{0} + a.\mathbf{0} + b[1].(\overline{s_{t_3}}[2].\mathbf{0}|\mathbf{0}))|(s_{t_3}[2].\mathbf{0} + a.\mathbf{0} + b.(\overline{s_{t_3}}.\mathbf{0}|\mathbf{0}))\big)|\mathbf{0})$$

Proposition 4. Let $\mathsf{G} = (N, S_k, U, m_{in}, m)$ be a ccsk-net, then $(\mathcal{G}(\mathcal{B}((N, S_k, U))), \tilde{m})$, where $\tilde{m} : S \setminus S_k \to \mathbb{N}$ is a marking defined as $\tilde{m}(s) = \#(m(s))$, is a CCS net.

7 From CCSK Net to CCSK Processes

We present now an algorithm that, given a ccsk-net $\mathsf{G} = (N, S_k, U, m_{in}, m)$, gives as output a CCSK process and a partial mapping of defining equations (abbreviated as pmde) $\mathcal{D}$.

An *enhanced* prefix π is a prefix of the form $\pi ::= \alpha \mid \alpha[i] \mid \alpha[s]$ where s belongs to a set S_k of key places, that are sometimes called *key holders*, and $\alpha \in \mathsf{Act}_\tau$. An *enhanced* CCSK term is a CCSK term where the prefixes are enhanced. The mapping ψ transform an enhanced CCSK term into a CCSK one by removing all the key holders. Thus $\psi(a[i].b[s].\mathbf{0} + a[s'].\mathbf{0}) = a[i].b.\mathbf{0} + a.\mathbf{0}$.

Lists of elements are written by listing their elements separated with a ";" in square brackets and $[\,]$ denotes the empty list. Given a list $[e_1; e_2; \ldots; e_n]$ and an element e, with $e :: [e_1; e_2; \ldots; e_n]$ we denote the list $[e; e_1; e_2; \ldots; e_n]$. **hd** and **tl** give respectively the head and the tail of a list, and @ is the usual concatenation operation on lists. The mapping **mklist** receives an element e and a number i and produces a list with i copies of e. Thus $\mathbf{mklist}(e, 3) = [e; e; e]$.

The algorithm receives a ccsk-net and works as follows:

- It runs an adapted version of the Algorithm 1 using $(\mathcal{B}((N, S_k, U)), m_{in})$ as inputs. The algorithm produces a list of enriched CCSK terms and a pmde where each equation is on enriched CCSK terms, together with a list of variables and a set of actions (that are the fresh one to be restricted).
- Using the marking m on the key places it transforms the pmde into another partial mapping of defining equations and a CCSK terms without enhanced prefixes, assigning to CCSK terms the correct index.

Auxiliary functions used in the algorithms are briefly described here.

- **getkeys** takes an enhanced CCSK term of the form $\alpha_1[s_1].(X_1^1 \mid \ldots \mid X_1^{n_1}) + \cdots + \alpha_k[s_k].(X_k^1 \mid \ldots \mid X_k^{n_k})$ and returns the set $\{s_1, \ldots, s_k\}$ of key holders appearing in the enhanced CCSK term,
- **minkeys** takes a set of key holders $\{s_1, \ldots, s_k\}$, a mapping $m : S_k \to \mu\mathsf{Tok}$ and either a token w' or $\bullet$ and gives back a pair (s_i, w) such that $w \in m(s_i)$, $\lfloor w \rfloor$ contains w' if w' is not $\bullet$, and $\text{size}(w)$ is the minimal among those in $m(s_j)$ for each $1 \leq j \leq k$ satisfying the previous conditions,
- **getvar** takes an enhanced CCSK term $\alpha_1[s_1].(X_1^1 \mid \ldots \mid X_1^{n_1}) + \cdots + \alpha_k[s_k].(X_k^1 \mid \ldots \mid X_k^{n_k})$ and a key holder s_i and returns the variables in $(X_i^1 \mid \ldots \mid X_i^{n_i})$,
- **tolist** takes a set of elements and transforms it in a list,
- **toterm** takes a non empty list of variables and gives the parallel compositions of all the variables in the list,
- **var** takes an (enhanced) CCSK term Q and returns the set of variables appearing in it,

Algorithm 2: From CCSK net system to CCSK process and defining equations

Input : CCSK net system $\mathsf{G} = (\langle S, T, F, \lambda, \mathsf{A}\rangle, S_k, U, m_{in}, m)$
Output : CCSK process Q and a pmde $\mathcal{D}$

1 $l_{\mathsf{var}} \leftarrow [\,], A \leftarrow \emptyset, l_{\mathsf{var}}^{\mathsf{res}} \leftarrow [\,], \mathcal{D} \leftarrow \mathcal{D}_\emptyset, l_{\mathsf{tok}} \leftarrow [\,], (\mathcal{D}, l_{\mathsf{var}}, A) \leftarrow Algorithm\ 3(\mathsf{G})$
2 **while** $l_{\mathsf{var}} \neq [\,]$ **do**
3 $\quad (\mathcal{D}, Q) \leftarrow Algorithm\ 4(\mathcal{D}, \mathcal{D}(\mathbf{hd}(l_{\mathsf{var}})))$
4 $\quad \mathcal{D}(X) \leftarrow Q$ **where** X is a new variable
5 $\quad l_{\mathsf{var}}^{\mathsf{res}} \leftarrow X :: l_{\mathsf{var}}^{\mathsf{res}}$
6 $\quad (\mathcal{D}, m, l_{\mathsf{tok}}) \leftarrow Algorithm\ 5(\mathcal{D}, X, m, l_{\mathsf{tok}})$
7 $\quad l_{\mathsf{var}} \leftarrow \mathbf{tl}(l_{\mathsf{var}})$
8 **end**
9 $\{s_{t_1}, \ldots, s_{t_n}\} \leftarrow A, \mathcal{D} \leftarrow \mathbf{clean}(\mathcal{D})$
10 $Q \leftarrow (\nu s_{t_1})(\nu s_{t_2}) \ldots (\nu s_{t_n})\,\mathbf{toterm}(l_{\mathsf{var}}^{\mathsf{res}})$
11 **return** $(Q, \mathcal{D})$

- **findmin** takes a set $\mathcal{S}$ of key holders, a mapping m and a token list l_{tok} and gives a set of pairs (s, w) where s is a key holder and w a token containing the head of the list of tokens, and
- **clean** takes a pmde $\mathcal{D}$ where some terms may be enhanced and gives the pmde $\mathcal{D}$ where the terms are just CCSK ones.

In the following we write the algorithms involved. The empty mapping of defining equations is denoted with $\mathcal{D}_\emptyset$. Algorithm 2 is the main algorithm and after initializing the list of variables, the set of restricted actions, the empty list of tokens, it runs the adaptation of the Algorithm 1, which is the Algorithm 3. The Algorithm 3 returns also a list of variables, and in a **while** loop the Algorithm 2

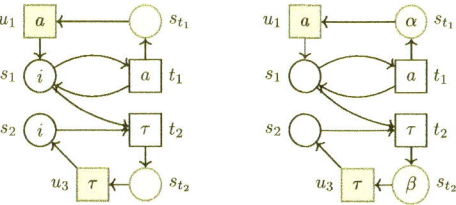

Fig. 9. An initial ccsk-net $\mathsf{G} = (N, S_k, U, m_{in}, m)$ and the same ccsk-net after the execution of transitions a and τ.

first applies the Algorithm 4 to get an enhanced CCSK term Q, with variables renamed, associated to the first element and, because of the renaming of variables, a pmde $\mathcal{D}$. Then it associates Q to a fresh variable which is inserted in a list and it runs the main routine, namely Algorithm 5. The variables in the list of results are transformed in a CCSK term which is given as result together with the defining equations $\mathcal{D}$.

The Algorithm 4 simply adds to the defining equations new variable associated to the equations appearing in an enhanced CCSK term, and the new

Algorithm 3: Encoding from CCSK net systems G to $(\mathcal{D}, l, A')$

Input : CCSK net system $\mathsf{G} = (\langle S, T, F, \lambda, \mathsf{A}\rangle, S_k, U, m_{in}, m)$
Output : pmde $\mathcal{D}$, a list of variables l and a set of fresh actions A'

1 $\mathcal{D} \leftarrow \mathcal{D}_\emptyset,\ A' \leftarrow \emptyset$
2 **for** $s \in S \setminus S_k$ **do** $\mathcal{D}(X_s) \leftarrow (Y_{t_1} + Y_{t_2} + \cdots + Y_{t_k})$ **where**
  $\{t_1, t_2, \ldots, t_k\} = \{t \mid t \in T \setminus U\ \land\ t \in s^\bullet\}$
3 **for** $t \in \{t \mid t \in T \setminus U$ and $|{}^\bullet t| = 1\}$ **do substitute** Y_t **in** $\mathcal{D}(X_{s^*})$ **with**
  $\lambda(t)[\mathsf{keypl}(t)].(X_{s_1} \mid X_{s_2} \mid \ldots \mid X_{s_n})$ **where** $(s^*, t) \in F$ and $s_i \in t^\bullet \setminus S_k$
4 **for** $t \in \{t \mid t \in T \setminus U$ and $|{}^\bullet t| = 2\}$ **do**
5 $\quad A' \leftarrow A' \cup \{a_t\}$ **where** a_t is a fresh action
6 $\quad$ **substitute** Y_t **in** $\mathcal{D}(X_{s^*})$ **with** $a_t[\mathsf{keypl}(t)].(X_{s_1} \mid X_{s_2} \mid \ldots \mid X_{s_n})$
7 $\quad$ **substitute** Y_t **in** $\mathcal{D}(X_{s^{**}})$ **with** $\overline{a_t}[\mathsf{keypl}(t)].0$ **where**
  $\quad (s^*, t), (s^{**}, t) \in F$ and $s^* \neq s^{**}$ and $s_i \in t^\bullet \setminus S_k$
8 **end**
9 $l =$
  $\mathbf{mklist}(X_{s_1}, \widetilde{m_{in}}(s_1))\,@\,\mathbf{mklist}(X_{s_2}, \widetilde{m_{in}}(s_2))\,@\,\ldots\,@\,\mathbf{mklist}(X_{s_{|S|}}, \widetilde{m_{in}}(s_{|S|}))$
10 **return** $(\mathcal{D}, l, A')$

Algorithm 4: Renaming variables and updating $\mathcal{D}$

Input : pmde $\mathcal{D}$ and an enhanced CCSK term Q
Output : pmde $\mathcal{D}$ and an enhanced CCSK term Q
1 **for** $X_i \in \mathbf{var}(Q)$ **do** $\mathcal{D}(X_i') \leftarrow Q\{X_i'/X_i\}$ **where** X_i' is a fresh variable
2 **return** $(\mathcal{D}, Q)$

---

variables are associated to the corresponding definitions. As the new variables are added, nothing is lost.

The main routine is Algorithm 5. This part uses the mapping from key places (key holders) to assign the correct key to the action in an enhanced CCSK term Q identified by its defining equation. It receives also a list of tokens. It runs Algorithm 4 to make copies of the variables in the enhanced CCSK term. If the list of tokens is empty then it checks the key holders in Q. If Q does not have any key holders then it finishes, otherwise it takes one among the shortest keys. The reason for picking one among the shortest keys depends on the need of allocating first the initial keys. The marking is updated and the exploration of the CCSK term continues using the variables *after* the prefix considered. The other parts of the term are made, so to speak, inactive using the mapping ψ which is applied the the term $Q\{\!\{s/\mathsf{kt}(w)\}\!\}$ which is the enhanced CCSK term where the key holder s is replaced with the correct index.

The exploration uses the same Algorithm 5 to the designated variables. If the list of tokens is not empty then the token in the head of the list is used to find another token, if present, which has that token in it, meaning that it is something that is *after* in the CCSK term. Then it does as above, updating the mapping m. Observe that the tokens under inspection are removed and in the case they

Algorithm 5: Assignment of keys to enhanced CCSK terms

Input : A pmde $\mathcal{D}$, a variable X, a mapping $m : S_k \to \mu\mathsf{Tok}$ and a list l_{tok} of tokens

Output : A pmde $\mathcal{D}$, a mapping $m : S_k \to \mu\mathsf{Tok}$ and a list of tokens l_{tok}

1 $Q \leftarrow \mathcal{D}(X)$
2 **if** $l_{\mathsf{tok}} = [\,]$ **then**
3 $\quad S \leftarrow \mathbf{getkeys}(Q)$
4 $\quad$ **if** $\mathcal{S} \neq \emptyset$ **then**
5 $\quad\quad (s,w) \leftarrow \mathbf{findmin}(m,\mathcal{S},\bullet)$
6 $\quad\quad \mathcal{V} \leftarrow \mathbf{getvar}(Q,s)$
7 $\quad\quad \mathcal{D}(X) \leftarrow \psi(Q\{\!\{s/\mathsf{kt}(w)\}\!\})$
8 $\quad\quad$ **if** $\lfloor w \rfloor$ *is* (w_1,w_2) **then** $m(s) = m(s) - w + (\mathsf{label}(w), w_2, \mathsf{kt}(w))$ **else** $m(s) = m(s) - w$
9 $\quad\quad l_{\mathsf{tok}} \leftarrow w :: l_{\mathsf{tok}}$
10 $\quad\quad$ **for** $X \in \mathcal{V}$ **do**
11 $\quad\quad\quad (\mathcal{D}, Q) \leftarrow Algorithm\ 4(\mathcal{D}, \mathcal{D}(X)), \mathcal{D}(X) \leftarrow Q$
12 $\quad\quad\quad (\mathcal{D}, m, l_{\mathsf{tok}}) \leftarrow Algorithm\ 5(\mathcal{D}, X, m, l_{\mathsf{tok}})$
13 $\quad\quad$ **end**
14 $\quad$ **end**
15 **else**
16 $\quad S \leftarrow \mathbf{getkeys}(Q)$
17 $\quad$ **if** $\mathcal{S} \neq \emptyset$ **then**
18 $\quad\quad (s,w) \leftarrow \mathbf{findmin}(m,\mathcal{S},\mathbf{hd}(l_{\mathsf{tok}}))$
19 $\quad\quad \mathcal{V} \leftarrow \mathbf{getvar}(Q,s)$
20 $\quad\quad \mathcal{D}(X) \leftarrow \psi(Q\{\!\{s/\mathsf{kt}(w)\}\!\})$
21 $\quad\quad$ **if** $\lfloor w \rfloor$ *is* (w_1,w_2) **then** $m(s) = m(s) - w + (\mathsf{label}(w), w_2, \mathsf{kt}(w))$ **else** $m(s) = m(s) - w$
22 $\quad\quad l_{\mathsf{tok}} \leftarrow w :: l_{\mathsf{tok}}$
23 $\quad\quad$ **for** $X \in \mathcal{V}$ **do**
24 $\quad\quad\quad (\mathcal{D}, Q) \leftarrow Algorithm\ 4(\mathcal{D}, \mathcal{D}(X)), \mathcal{D}(X) \leftarrow Q$
25 $\quad\quad\quad (\mathcal{D}, m, l_{\mathsf{tok}}) \leftarrow Algorithm\ 5(\mathcal{D}, X, m, l_{\mathsf{tok}})$
26 $\quad\quad$ **end**
27 $\quad$ **end**
28 $\quad l_{\mathsf{tok}} \leftarrow \mathbf{tl}(l_{\mathsf{tok}})$
29 **end**
30 **return** $(\mathcal{D}, m, l_{\mathsf{tok}})$

are tokens representing a synchronization then the token is replaced with one of a smaller size. It is worth to observe that Algorithm 5 converges.

Example 9. Figure 9 depicts an initial CCSK net system (on the left) and the same CCSK net system after the execution of a and τ. The tokens are $\alpha = (a, \langle\!\langle i \rangle\!\rangle, 1)$ and $\beta = (\tau, \langle\!\langle \alpha, i \rangle\!\rangle, 2)$. When we execute the Algorithm 3 we get $\mathcal{D}(X_{s_1}) = a[s_{t_1}].X_{s_1} + c[s_{t_2}].0$ and $\mathcal{D}(X_{s_2}) = \bar{c}[s_{t_2}].0$, the list $[X_{s_1}; X_{s_2}]$ and a set of new actions $A = \{c\}$. The list is not empty and we start with X_{s_1}, and, after applying Algorithm 4, we have that the equations $\mathcal{D}(X''_{s_1}) = a[s_{t_1}].X'_{s_1} + c[s_{t_2}].0$ and $\mathcal{D}(X'_{s_1}) = a[s_{t_1}].X_{s_1} + c[s_{t_2}].0$ are added to $\mathcal{D}$. The new variable X''_{s_1} is added to the list of results and the Algorithm 5 is invoked, with an empty list of tokens and the marking $m(s_{t_1}) = \alpha$ and $m(s_{t_2}) = \beta$. The shortest token among the ones associated to the key holders of $a[s_{t_1}].X'_{s_1} + c[s_{t_2}].0$, namely $\{s_{t_1}, s_{t_2}\}$, is α, and $\lfloor \alpha \rfloor$ is a singleton, therefore $\mathcal{D}(X''_{s_1}) = a[1].X'_{s_1} + c[s_{t_2}].0$, $\mathcal{V} = \{X'_{s_1}\}$, the marking is updated, now being $m(s_{t_1}) = 0$, and the token α is added to the list of tokens. The Algorithm 4 is used to update $a[1].X'_{s_1} + c[s_{t_2}].0$, associated to X''_{s_1}, obtaining $a[s_{t_1}].X'''_{s_1} + c[s_{t_2}].0$ and $\mathcal{D}(X'''_{s_1}) = a[1].X'_{s_1} + c[s_{t_2}].0$. The new invocation of Algorithm 5 is with a list of tokens containing the token α, the variable X'''_{s_1} and the updated marking. The set of key holders contains just s_{t_2}, furthermore the token β is such that $\lfloor \beta \rfloor$ contains α. Furthermore the set of variables is now empty, and the result is that $\mathcal{D}(X'''_{s_1})$ is updated to $a[1].X'_{s_1} + c[2].0$, β is added to the list of tokens and the marking associated to s_{t_2} is updated removing β and adding $(\tau, \langle\!\langle i \rangle\!\rangle, 2)$. At this point β is removed from the list of tokens. Now we end also the first invocation of this algorithm, and we go back to analyze the list $[X_{s_2}]$. We create a new variable X'_{s_2} which is added to the resulting list that now is $[X'_{s_2}; X'_{s_1}]$ and $\mathcal{D}(X'_{s_2}) = \overline{c}[s_{t_2}].0$. The Algorithm 5 will put in the term $\overline{c}[s_{t_2}].0$ the proper key obtaining $\mathcal{D}(X'_{s_2}) = \overline{c}[2].0$ and the token $(\tau, \langle\!\langle i \rangle\!\rangle, 2)$ will be removed from $m(s_{t_2})$. The final result will be $Q = (\nu c)(X'_{s_2} \mid X'_{s_1})$ and the $\mathcal{D}$ constructed so far.

We now state the correspondence between CCSK nets and CCSK.

Theorem 2 (Correctness of Algorithm 2). *Let* $\mathsf{G} = (\langle S, T, F, \lambda, \mathsf{A}\rangle, S_k, U, m_{in}, m)$ *be a ccsk-net, and let the result of applying Algorithm 2 to* G *be the CCSK process* Q *and defining equations* $\mathcal{D}$. *Then* $M(\mathsf{G}, m)$ *is forward-reverse bisimilar to* $LTS(Q, \mathcal{D})$.

8 Conclusions

Inspired by the work in [5] we have provided a class of Petri nets, called CCSK nets, which correspond to CCSK processes. We also have provided an algorithm which, given a CCSK net, constructs the corresponding CCSK term.

There are several directions for future investigations. First we want to improve our results, and to implement the provided algorithm in LEAN[1]. This on one side would allow us to benchmark our results, on the other hand would allow us to mechanise the correctness proof.

Also, a generalisation of CCS nets to multi-synchronization nets should be possible. A direct consequence of this would be to obtain a CCSK with multi-synchronization. Another direction would be to connect CCSK nets with event structures, by finding a suitable notion of (reversible) event structure corresponding to CCSK.

---

[1] https://lean-lang.org/.

References

1. Abdellatif, T., Kornas, J., Stefani, J.-B.: Reengineering J2EE servers for automated management in distributed environments. IEEE Distributed Syst. Online **8**(11) (2007)
2. Aman, B., et al.: Foundations of reversible computation. In: Ulidowski, I., Lanese, I., Schultz, U.P., Ferreira, C. (eds.) RC 2020. LNCS, vol. 12070, pp. 1–40. Springer, Cham (2020). https://doi.org/10.1007/978-3-030-47361-7_1
3. Bennett, C.H.: Notes on the history of reversible computation. IBM J. Res. Dev. **44**(1), 270–278 (2000)
4. Bidinger, P., Schmitt, A., Stefani, J.-B.: An abstract machine for the kell calculus. In: Steffen, M., Zavattaro, G. (eds.) FMOODS 2005. LNCS, vol. 3535, pp. 31–46. Springer, Heidelberg (2005). https://doi.org/10.1007/11494881_3
5. Bogø, B., Burattin, A., Scalas, A.: Encoding petri nets into CCS. In: Castellani, I., Tiezzi, F. (eds.) COORDINATION 2024, LNCS, vol. 14676, pp. 38–55. Springer (2024)
6. Bruneton, E., Coupaye, T., Leclercq, M., Quéma, V., Stefani, J.-B.: The FRACTAL component model and its support in java. Softw. Pract. Exp. **36**(11–12), 1257–1284 (2006)
7. Claudel, B., Sabah, Q., Stefani, J.-B.: Simple isolation for an actor abstract machine. In: Graf, S., Viswanathan, M. (eds.) FORTE 2015. LNCS, vol. 9039, pp. 213–227. Springer, Cham (2015). https://doi.org/10.1007/978-3-319-19195-9_14
8. Danos, V., Krivine, J.: Reversible communicating systems. In: Gardner, P., Yoshida, N. (eds.) CONCUR 2004. LNCS, vol. 3170, pp. 292–307. Springer, Heidelberg (2004). https://doi.org/10.1007/978-3-540-28644-8_19
9. Danos, V., Krivine, J.: Transactions in RCCS. In: Abadi, M., de Alfaro, L. (eds.) CONCUR 2005. LNCS, vol. 3653, pp. 398–412. Springer, Heidelberg (2005). https://doi.org/10.1007/11539452_31
10. Fabbretti, G., Lanese, I., Stefani, J.-B.: Reversibility with holes - (work in progress). In: Æ. Mogensen, T., Mikulski, L. (eds.) Reversible Computation - RC 2024, LNCS, vol. 14680, pp. 69–74. Springer (2024)
11. Gorrieri, R., Versari,C.: A process calculus for expressing finite place/transition petri nets. In: Fröschle, S.B., Valencia, F.D. (eds.) EXPRESS 2010, EPTCS, vol. 41, pp. 76–90 (2010)
12. Koutavas, V., Gazda, M., Hennessy, M.: Distinguishing between communicating transactions. Inf. Comput. **259**(1), 1–30 (2018)
13. Krivine, J.: A verification technique for reversible process algebra. In: Glück, R., Yokoyama, T. (eds.) Reversible Computation RC 2012. Revised Papers, LNCS, vol. 7581, pp. 204–217. Springer (2012)
14. Kuhn, S., Ulidowski, I.: Modelling of DNA mismatch repair with a reversible process calculus. Theor. Comput. Sci. **925**, 68–86 (2022)
15. Lami, P., Lanese, I., Stefani, J.-B., Coen, C.S., Fabbretti, G.: Reversible debugging of concurrent erlang programs: supporting imperative primitives. J. Log. Algebraic Methods Program. **138**, 100944 (2024)
16. Lanese, I., Lienhardt, M., Mezzina, C.A., Schmitt, A., Stefani, J.-B.: Concurrent flexible reversibility. In: Felleisen, M., Gardner, P. (eds.) ESOP 2013. LNCS, vol. 7792, pp. 370–390. Springer, Heidelberg (2013). https://doi.org/10.1007/978-3-642-37036-6_21
17. Lanese, I., Medic, D., Mezzina, C.A.: Static versus dynamic reversibility in CCS. Acta Informatica **58**(1–2), 1–34 (2021)

18. Lanese, I., Mezzina, C.A., Schmitt, A., Stefani, J.-B.: Controlling reversibility in higher-order Pi. In: Katoen, J.-P., König, B. (eds.) CONCUR 2011. LNCS, vol. 6901, pp. 297–311. Springer, Heidelberg (2011). https://doi.org/10.1007/978-3-642-23217-6_20
19. Lanese, I., Mezzina, C.A., Stefani, J.-B.: Reversing higher-order Pi. In: Gastin, P., Laroussinie, F. (eds.) CONCUR 2010. LNCS, vol. 6269, pp. 478–493. Springer, Heidelberg (2010). https://doi.org/10.1007/978-3-642-15375-4_33
20. Lanese, I., Mezzina, C.A., Stefani, J.-B.: Reversibility in the higher-order π-calculus. Theoret. Comput. Sci. **625**, 25–84 (2016)
21. Lenglet, S., Schmitt, A., Stefani, J.-B.: Howe's method for calculi with passivation. In: Bravetti, M., Zavattaro, G. (eds.) CONCUR 2009 - Concurrency Theory, LNVS, vol. 5710 , pp. 448–462. Springer (2009)
22. Lenglet, S., Schmitt, A., Stefani, J.-B.: Normal bisimulations in calculi with passivation. In: de Alfaro, L., (ed.) FOSSACS 2009, LNCS, vol. 5504, pp. 257–271. Springer (2009)
23. Lenglet, S., Schmitt, A., Stefani, J.-B.: Characterizing contextual equivalence in calculi with passivation. Inf. Comput. **209**(11), 1390–1433 (2011)
24. Lienhardt, M., Lanese, I., Mezzina, C.A., Stefani, J.-B.: A reversible abstract machine and its space overhead. In: Giese, H., Rosu, G. (eds.) FMOODS / FORTE 2012, LNCS, vol. 7273, pp. 1–17. Springer (2012)
25. Melgratti, H.C., Mezzina, C.A., Pinna, G.M.: A Petri net view of covalent bonds. Theor. Comput. Sci. **908**, 89–119 (2022)
26. Melgratti, H.C., Mezzina, C.A., Pinna, G.M.: A reversible perspective on petri nets and event structures. ACM Trans. Comput. Log. **25**(4), 1–38 (2024)
27. Melgratti, H.C., Mezzina, C.A., Pinna, G.M.: A truly concurrent semantics for reversible CCS. Log. Methods Comput. Sci. **20**(4) (2024)
28. Melgratti, H.C., Mezzina, C.A., Ulidowski, I.: Reversing place transition nets. Log. Methods Comput. Sci. **16**(4) (2020)
29. Mezzina, C.A., et al.: Software and reversible systems: a survey of recent activities. In: Ulidowski, I., Lanese, I., Schultz, U.P., Ferreira, C. (ed.) Reversible Computation: Extending Horizons of Computing - Selected Results of the COST Action IC1405, LNCS, vol. 12070 , pp. 41–59. Springer (2020)
30. Mezzina, C.A., Tiezzi, F., Yoshida, N.: Checkpoint-based rollback recovery in session programming. Log. Methods Comput. Sci. **21**(1), 2 (2025)
31. Milner, R. (ed.): A Calculus of Communicating Systems. LNCS, vol. 92. Springer, Heidelberg (1980). https://doi.org/10.1007/3-540-10235-3
32. Philippou, A., Psara, K.: A collective interpretation semantics for reversing Petri nets. Theor. Comput. Sci. **924**, 148–170 (2022)
33. Philippou, A., Psara, K.: Reversible computation in nets with bonds. J. Log. Algebraic Methods Program. **124**, 100718 (2022)
34. Phillips, I., Ulidowski, I., Yuen, S.: A reversible process calculus and the modelling of the ERK signalling pathway. In: Glück, R., Yokoyama, T. (eds.) Reversible Computation RC 2012. Revised Papers, LNCS, vol. 7581, pp. 218–232. Springer (2012)
35. Phillips, I.C.C., Ulidowski, I.: Reversing algebraic process calculi. J. Log. Algebraic Methods Program. **73**(1–2), 70–96 (2007)
36. Reisig, W.: Petri Nets: An Introduction, EATCS Monographs on Theoretical Computer Science, vol. 4. Springer (1985)
37. Schmitt, A., Stefani, J.-B.: The m-calculus: a higher-order distributed process calculus. In: Aiken, A., Morrisett, G. (eds.) POPL 2003, pp. 50–61. ACM (2003)

38. Schmitt, A., Stefani, J.-B.: The kell calculus: a family of higher-order distributed process calculi. In: Priami, C, Quaglia, P. (eds.) Global Computing, IST/FET International Workshop, GC 2004, LNCS, vol. 3267 , pp. 146–178. Springer (2004)
39. Seinturier, L., Merle, P., Rouvoy, R., Romero, D., Schiavoni, V., Stefani, J.-B.: A component-based middleware platform for reconfigurable service-oriented architectures. Softw. Pract. Exp. **42**(5), 559–583 (2012)
40. Stefani, J.-B.: A calculus of kells. In: Focardi, R., Zavattaro, G. (eds.) 2nd EATCS Workshop on Foundations of Global Computing, FGC 2003, EPTCS, vol. 85 , pp. 40–60. Elsevier (2003)
41. Stefani, J.-B., Vassor, M.: Encapsulation and sharing in dynamic software architectures: the hypercell framework. In: Pérez, J.A., Yoshida, N. (eds.) FORTE 2019. LNCS, vol. 11535, pp. 242–260. Springer, Cham (2019). https://doi.org/10.1007/978-3-030-21759-4_14
42. Vassor, M., Stefani, J.-B.: Checkpoint/rollback vs causally-consistent reversibility. In: Kari, J., Ulidowski, I. (eds.) Reversible Computation - RC 2018, LNCS, vol. 11106 , pp. 286–303. Springer (2018)

Bounded Reversibility in HOπ

Ivan Lanese[1], Claudio Antares Mezzina[2], and Martin Vassor[3](✉)

[1] Olas Team, University of Bologna & Inria - Université Côte d'Azur, Bologna, Italy
[2] Department of Pure and Applied Sciences, University of Urbino, Urbino, Italy
[3] Université de Lorraine, CNRS, Inria, LORIA, 54000 Nancy, France
martin.vassor@univ-lorraine.fr

Abstract. The higher-order causally-consistent reversible π-calculus, known as **roll**−π, enables the rollback of arbitrary past actions while preserving causal consistency – ensuring that effects are undone before their causes. This prevents the occurrence of actions without justifications, even after a rollback. However, in practical scenarios, not all events can be reversed; for example, once a document is printed, it cannot be *unprinted*.

To better model real-world constraints, we introduce **broll**−π (*bounded* **roll**−π), an extension of **roll**−π that limits reversibility. Our approach imposes two key restrictions: *spatial bounds*, which prevent certain processes from being affected by rollbacks, and *temporal bounds*, which restrict how far back in time a rollback can go. Bounded reversibility allows for more realistic and controlled rollbacks in computational systems. In this paper, we provide an informal introduction to **broll**−π and discuss its implications for modeling reversible processes in practical applications.

1 Introduction

Motivation. Reversibility attracted interest for many relevant application areas, including very fast simulations [3], promising low-energy digital circuits [7], and powerful debugging techniques [6,14]. An application area that attracted the interest of Jean-Bernard was the possibility of using reversibility for reliability [8,9,11,17]. The basic idea here is that in case of errors one could rollback to states before the error occurred, and retry or find an alternative solution. This triggered the introduction of rollback operators in process calculi [9], allowing one to undo an action possibly far in the past, including all and only its consequences. Reversible process calculi often aim at providing *sound* and *complete* rollbacks. Soundness states that rolling back reaches configurations that could be reached using forward-only reductions, while completeness relates to the fact that all events can be reverted (in particular, concurrent rollbacks do not prevent

---

This work has been partially supported by French ANR project SmartCloud ANR-23-CE25-0012, by INdAM – GNCS 2025 project MARQ, code CUP_E53C24001950001, and by the project FREEDA (CUP: I53D23003550006), funded by the frameworks PRIN (MUR, Italy) and Next Generation EU. We thanks reviewers for their comments and suggestions.

each other). While very practical to reason on systems, those requirements do not fit practical applications. For instance:

- in a typical client-server architecture, clients and the server interact, hence their actions are causally related. Reverting a client would also cause to rollback the server, which in turn would rollback other clients.
- in a distributed algorithm, e.g. to implement consensus in a fail-stop model [2, Section 2.7 and Chap. 5], reversibility is very appealing, since it provides fault-tolerance quite transparently. However, in languages such as **roll**−π, processes can always revert to the beginning of the computation, hence there is no eventual termination[1].

The two examples above illustrate the difficulty of using reversible calculi such as **roll**−π in practice: to reason on real world applications, we need notions of abstraction and composition; but reversibility, as it is implemented in **roll**−π, breaks boundaries of subsystems.

This paper introduces **broll**−π, for *bounded* **roll**−π, an extension of **roll**−π with two novelties:

Spatial boundaries: The possibility to restrict rollback to part of the system only. While in **roll**−π communication always establishes a bidirectional causal dependency between sender and receiver, hence rollback of one of them triggers the rollback of the other, this is not always the case in **broll**−π. Indeed, rollback propagates only if both the sender and the receiver agree to do so. This addresses the issue with client-server architectures described above: communications between clients and the server may not establish causality links; hence rollbacks would be contained to individual clients or to the server.

Temporal boundaries: The calculus includes a *commit* primitive. Upon commit, the committed past event cannot be undone any more, thus addressing the second problem we mentioned above. Memories related to committed events become useless, hence this approach allows one to limit the amount of history information that needs to be kept, thus limiting a main issue of reversible computing.

These advantages come at the price of breaking the nice theoretical framework built in [4,13], which assumes every action to be reversible forever. We believe that such a theory needs to be extended to cope with systems which are only partially reversible. This paper only adds a small block in this direction.

Outline. We begin by recalling **roll**−π in Sect. 2. This is instrumental to better understand the rest of the paper, which builds on it. We then give an informal presentation of **broll**−π in Sect. 3, where we also explain the main design choices

---

[1] Even providing an implementation, e.g., a library, that is eventually free of rollback requests, and therefore that is eventually terminating, is not enough. Indeed, there is no way to ensure that the context has no rollback requests targeting states before the call of the library, thus invalidating eventual termination.

$$\begin{aligned}
\mathcal{P}, \mathcal{Q} \ ::=&\ 0 & & \textit{Empty process} \\
&|\ X & & \textit{Variable} \\
&|\ \nu c.\,(\mathcal{P}) & & \textit{Channel restriction} \\
&|\ \mathcal{P} \parallel \mathcal{P} & & \textit{Parallel composition} \\
&|\ c\,\langle \mathcal{P} \rangle & & \textit{Sending message} \\
&|\ c(X) \triangleright_\gamma (\mathcal{P}) & & \textit{Receiving message} \\
&|\ \texttt{roll}\ k\ \ |\ \ \texttt{roll}\ \gamma & & \textit{Rollback primitive} \\
\mathcal{M}, \mathcal{N} ::=&\ 0 & & \textit{Empty configuration} \\
&|\ \nu u.\,(\mathcal{M}) & & \textit{New identifier (name or key)} \\
&|\ \mathcal{M} \parallel \mathcal{N} & & \textit{Parallel configuration} \\
&|\ \kappa : \mathcal{P} & & \textit{Tagged process} \\
&|\ [\mu; k]^\bullet\ \ |\ \ [\mu; k] & & \textit{(Marked) memory} \\
\kappa\ \ ::=&\ k\ \ |\ \ \langle h, \tilde{h} \rangle \cdot k & & \textit{Simple/Complex tag} \\
\mu\ \ ::=&\ \kappa_1 :\ c\langle \mathcal{P} \rangle \parallel \kappa_2 :\ c(X) \triangleright_\gamma (\mathcal{Q}) & & \textit{Memory content}
\end{aligned}$$

Grammar 1.1. Grammar of **roll**−π.

to implement the two new mechanisms. Then, in Sect. 4, we introduce **broll**−π, its syntax and its semantics. We conclude the section with a few examples that illustrate the new features of **broll**−π. The new extensions we introduce allow us to broaden the scope of reversibility. In Sect. 5 we show how our framework can be used to implement a speculative consensus algorithm. In Sect. 6, we discuss the relations between rollback and commit. Section 7 discusses related work and Sect. 8 wraps up with some final considerations.

2 A Recap of roll−π

Reversibility in **roll**−π builds on the mechanisms introduced in ρπ [10,11]. Both calculi extend **HO**π [15] with reversibility. In both **roll**−π and ρπ (as well as in **broll**−π), **HO**π processes do not execute directly, but are embedded in *configurations*: history on the past of the computation is recorded in *memories* and processes are associated with *tags* which uniquely identify processes. Memories also track causal dependencies, namely store which processes interact, and which are the tags of the processes generated by the interaction.

The syntax of **roll**−π is given in Grammar 1.1. Channel names are ranged over by a, b, c, ... We note $[\mu; k]^\circ$ for $[\mu; k]$ or $[\mu; k]^\bullet$.
Processes of **roll**−π are similar to processes of **HO**π: communications happen on channels (e.g. a) between a pending message $a\,\langle P \rangle$ and a receiver, also referred to as *trigger*, $a(X) \triangleright_\gamma (Q)$. The receiver binds the process variable X and the key variable γ in Q. Processes can be composed in parallel ($P \parallel Q$) and channel names can be restricted ($\nu a.\,(P)$ binds a in P). In addition to those primitives, **roll**−π introduces a new rollback primitive roll γ/roll k, used to trigger rollbacks. Contrary to **HO**π, processes of **roll**−π can not be executed directly: instead, they have to be embedded in *configurations*, which add *tags* (to keep track of causal dependencies) as well as *memories* (which record past events).

A tagged process is denoted by $k : P$, where k is the tag of process P. Tags can be restricted at the configuration level with $\nu k.(P)$. When a tagged process is a parallel composition (e.g. $k : P \parallel Q$), k can be split to tag separately P and Q. This leads to complex tags (e.g. $\langle k_1, \tilde{k}\rangle \cdot k : P \parallel \langle k_2, \tilde{k}\rangle \cdot k : P$, where $\tilde{k} = \{k_1, k_2\}$). Complex tags allow one to keep track of independent processes (e.g. P and Q) which depend on (i.e. which were created by) the same event. Finally, when a communication happens, a memory is created to store the state of processes involved in the communication, thus enabling rollbacks. A memory $[\mu; k]$ contains the processes in μ (which are always a pending message and a receiver) and a tag k to keep track of causal chains. For instance, the configuration $k_1 : c\langle\mathcal{P}\rangle \parallel k_2 : c(X) \triangleright_\gamma (Q)$ performs a communication and reduces to $k : Q\{^{\mathcal{P},k}/_{X,\gamma}\} \parallel [k_1 : c\langle\mathcal{P}\rangle \parallel k_2 : c(X) \triangleright_\gamma (Q); k]$. Notice how the created process and the memory share the same tag, thus storing the causal link.

While in $\rho\pi$ there is no policy specifying when to execute forwards and when to execute backwards, in **roll**$-\pi$ normal computation is forward, but processes may trigger a rollback using a dedicated primitive: `roll` k, where k refers to which memory to rollback. Two rollback semantics are provided in [9]: high-level (centralized) and low-level (distributed).

In the high-level semantics (which we focus on in this paper), the rollback happens atomically: in a single step, consequences of the event which created the memory to revert are removed and the configuration μ inside the target memory $[\mu; k]$ is re-instantiated.

Reversible Communication. The reduction rule for **roll**$-\pi$ is as follows[2]:

$$(\text{Com})\ \frac{}{\kappa_1 : a\langle P\rangle \parallel \kappa_2 : a(X) \triangleright_\gamma (Q) \twoheadrightarrow \nu k.\left(k : Q\{^{P,k}/_{X,\gamma}\} \parallel [\kappa_1 : a\langle P\rangle \parallel \kappa_2 : a(X) \triangleright_\gamma (Q); k]\right)}$$

The main idea here is that the original configuration is stored inside the memory, together with a fresh tag k, linking the memory to the continuation of the trigger. The continuation of a memory, if composed by multiple parallel components, is eventually split using the following structural congruence rule:

$$(\text{E.TagP})\quad k : P \parallel Q \equiv \nu h_1, h_2.\left(\langle h_1, \tilde{h}\rangle \cdot k : P \parallel \langle h_2, \tilde{h}\rangle \cdot k : Q\right)$$

where $\tilde{h} = \{h_1, h_2\}$ (this is the binary case, n-ary case follows the same idea).

Rolling Back Using **roll**$-\pi$ *High-Level Semantics.* In the high-level semantics of **roll**$-\pi$, a first rule (H.Start) marks the target memory to revert.

$$(\text{H.Start})\ [\mu; k] \parallel \kappa : \texttt{roll}\ k \twoheadrightarrow [\mu; k]^\bullet \parallel \kappa : \texttt{roll}\ k$$

---

[2] In [9], this rule is used both in the high-level semantics (named (H.Com)) and in the low-level one (named (L.Com)). We name it (Com) in this paper.

Then, rollbacks are atomic (all memories are removed and replaced by the initial process at once). The rollback rule (H.ROLL) is the following:

$$(\text{H.ROLL}) \quad \frac{N \blacktriangleright k \quad \text{complete}(N \parallel [\mu; k])}{N \parallel [\mu; k]^\bullet \twoheadrightarrow \mu \parallel N \wr_k}$$

The two required predicates roughly mean that all processes and memories in N causally depend on k ($N \blacktriangleright k$) and that all successors of k are in N (complete($N \parallel [\mu; k]$)). $N \wr_k$ extracts from memories in N those messages or triggers which do not have k as a causal antecedent, but which participated in communications with causal descendants of k.

All the reductions mentioned above can happen inside evaluation contexts, in particular parallel composition and restriction contexts.

3 Informal Presentation of broll−π

As mentioned in the Introduction, our goal is to set *spatial* and *temporal* boundaries on rollbacks. Those two kinds of boundaries are enforced by two independent mechanisms, and therefore we shall present them independently.

We first present *spatial boundaries*, allowing one to ensure that when two processes communicate, the rollback of one of them does not trigger the rollback of the other. We observe that, in **roll**−π, *memories* are responsible of rolling back both sides of a communication, since they record both the sender and the receiver. Thus restoring the memory restores both the sender and the receiver. Therefore, to decouple both sides of the communication, we modify the *content* of the memory, so that only one side is restored. In the case we present, messages do not have continuations, so they can not be rolled back. Therefore, we choose to only store the receiver process in the memory, dropping the message[3].

To allow the programmer to decide whether rollback should be propagated to the sender or not, we introduce two different usages of names: *bracketed* names (e.g. $\{a\}$) which specify that rollback should not be propagated, or normal (e.g., a). Notice that *usages* of names are normal or bracketed, not names themselves: a name can be used both normally and bracketed, albeit in different places.

Regarding *temporal boundaries*, we introduce a mechanism to make a past action irreversible, allowing one to eventually remove the corresponding memories. Similar to the `roll k` primitive, we introduce `commit k`, which commits memory tagged with k. Two points need attention:

1. if a memory is committed, all the previous memories (i.e. those that are causal ascendants of the target one) also need to be blocked (*commit consistency*);
2. commits need to be compatible with rollbacks, in particular when they are concurrent (*commit/rollback consistency*).

---

[3] In a variant with continuations, we would need to create two independent memories upon communication: one for the receiver, one for the sender.

To deal with commit consistency, **broll**–π adopts a spanning mechanism somewhat similar to that of the low level semantics of rollbacks (cf. [9]), but towards the past. When a memory is to be committed, we iteratively mark all causal ascendant memories as committed as well. Eventually, all marked memories are removed[4].

To deal with commit/rollback consistency, we prevent reverting memories that are marked for commit (by preventing the start of the rollback requests as well as by preventing to revert the memories). To ensure this, to execute a roll k process, we first check that no memory that depends on k is marked. This implies that the presence of a roll k is not enough to guarantee that memory k will actually be reverted. Indeed, a commit k' where k' is a descendant of k may prevent this. This design choice reminds *open-nested transactions* [1], but the behaviour is actually different. In open-nested transactions, children transactions may commit before the father and, if the father cannot commit, then children commits' are compensated. Our case is slightly different: if the children commits then the father cannot rollback any more.

4 The Calculus

We now present the **broll**–π calculus. In Sect. 4.1, we introduce its syntax. In Sect. 4.2, we introduce its semantics. The novelty of the semantics lies in an extra rule for communication on $\{c\}$ (rule (NCOM)), which does not propagate the causal dependency to the sender; and a few new rules for committing memories. The latter is not trivial as it effectively rewrites history via memory removal. Therefore, most of the new rules are intended to properly cleanup leftovers. In Sect. 4.3, we illustrate the new commit semantics using an example, clarifying in particular the interaction between commits and rollbacks.

4.1 Syntax

The syntax of bounded **roll**–π, given in Grammar 1.2, extends the one of **roll**–π [9] (see Grammar 1.1). We note $[\mu; k]^\oplus$ for $[\mu; k]$, $[\mu; k]^\bullet$, or $[\mu; k]^\dagger$. We note α (and decorated variants) for a or $\{a\}$; and define $\text{name}(a) = \text{name}(\{a\}) = a$.

The two main differences between the syntax of **broll**–π and of **roll**–π are as follows. First, there is an additional *commit* primitive, which prevents a memory (identified by its key) to be rolled back. Second, communications can happen in two ways: either causally consistently as in **roll**–π (when both ends of the communication use plain names: c) or in a non causally consistent way (when either end of the communication uses bracketed names: $\{c\}$). This will affect how memories are built.

To accommodate for those two novelties, we have to adapt other elements of the grammar:

---

[4] While garbage collecting memories is not the primary objective of this work, it is a nice side effect to have such a feature.

$$
\begin{array}{rll}
\mathcal{P}, \mathcal{Q} & ::= \ldots & \textit{As in } \text{roll}-\pi \textit{ except Send/Receive} \\
& \mid \alpha \langle \mathcal{P} \rangle & \textit{Sending message} \\
& \mid \alpha(X) \triangleright_\gamma (\mathcal{P}) & \textit{Receiving message} \\
& \mid \texttt{commit } k \quad \mid \quad \texttt{commit } \gamma & \textit{Commit primitive} \\
\mathcal{M}, \mathcal{N} & ::= \ldots & \textit{As in } \text{roll}-\pi \\
& \mid [\mu; k]^\dagger & \textit{Memory marked for removal} \\
& \mid \texttt{init } \kappa & \textit{Tokens: initial tag} \\
\kappa & ::= \ldots & \textit{As in } \text{roll}-\pi \\
\mu & ::= \ldots & \textit{As in } \text{roll}-\pi \\
& \mid \kappa : \alpha(X) \triangleright_\gamma (Q) & \textit{Non-causally consistent memory content} \\
\alpha & ::= \{c\} \mid c & \textit{(Non) reversible channels}
\end{array}
$$

Grammar 1.2. Grammar of bounded roll−π.

- In addition to $\kappa_1 : c\langle \mathcal{P} \rangle \parallel \kappa_2 : c(X) \triangleright_\gamma (Q)$, the content of memory can also be $\kappa : \{c\}(X) \triangleright_\gamma (Q)$ or $\kappa : c(X) \triangleright_\gamma (Q)$ when bracketed names are used (in the second case the bracketed name was on the sender side). In that case, the memory contains only the receiver process, since the sender and the receiver are not causally linked.
- Memories can be marked with †. This mark is used to identify committed memories that will eventually be erased.
- We introduce a token $\texttt{init } k$, which identifies *initial* processes, i.e. processes that are not associated with a memory. This is needed to identify whether a process depends on an existing memory or not.

Initial Configuration. In roll−π, a configuration is initial if it has no memory, tags are unique and simple, and all variables are bound. In addition, initial configurations of broll−π need to have a token $\texttt{init } k$ for each tagged process $k : P$.

4.2 Semantics

As mentioned before, roll−π rollback has been given two semantics. We focus here on the high-level semantics, since it is simpler, while leaving the extension of the low-level one (more easily implementable) for future work. Interestingly, the mechanism used to remove memories upon commit has similarities with the low-level rollback mechanism. We believe this to be a relevant choice, since removing memories is only needed for garbage collection, hence can be done asynchronously.

Structural Congruence. We use the same structural congruence than in [9].

Causally Consistent Communication. When communicating on unbounded channels, communication happens as in roll−π. We use the reduction rule (Com) presented above.

Non Causally Consistent Communication. The first novelty of **broll**–π is *non causally consistent* communication, which decouples the trigger and the message in rollback. In particular, rollbacking the message has no impact on the corresponding trigger. Rolling back the trigger instead does not restore the message (which would be the only possible impact on the message, since messages are asynchronous hence they have no descendants). In order to ensure causal-consistent reversibility as in the previous paragraph, both sender and receiver need to agree by using the channel as normal, e.g. c. If instead any of them wants to communicate in a non-causal consistent way, it can use the channel bracketed, e.g. $\{c\}$. The rule regulating non causally consistent communication is then:

$$(\text{NCom}) \ \frac{\text{name}(\alpha_1) = \text{name}(\alpha_2) \quad \alpha_1 = \{a\} \text{ or } \alpha_2 = \{a\}}{\kappa_1 : \alpha_1 \langle P \rangle \parallel \kappa_2 : \alpha_2(X) \triangleright_\gamma (Q) \twoheadrightarrow \kappa_1 : 0 \parallel \nu k. (k : Q\{^{P,k}/_{X,\gamma}\} \parallel [\kappa_2 : \alpha_2(X) \triangleright_\gamma (Q); k])}$$

Let us note that doing non causal consistent reversibility is a unilateral decision, as it is sufficient that one of the two involved processes is not willing to revert the communication. There are two differences between rule (Com) and rule (NCom). Indeed, in rule (NCom):

1. the created memory only contains the receiver process, and has no link with the message; and
2. the message completely disappears, but for leaving a leftover $\kappa_1 : 0$.

Not storing the message has a limited impact, as it may be restored by rolling back the memory that initially created the message (in case the message was present in the initial configuration, one can add a communication to create a memory creating it).

Since the memory only contains the trigger, then a rollback on the message has no impact on it. However, we need the leftover $\kappa_1 : 0$ to allow for rollback on the sender side. A rollback on the trigger side will leave the sender side unaffected.

Committing Computations. The second novelty of **broll**–π are *commits*. A commit targets a past interaction, by means of the tag of the corresponding memory, and forbids to undo it. In other terms, rollbacks involving the undo of such an interaction, possibly as part of rollbacks of older interactions, are disallowed. Since the committed interaction cannot be rollbacked any more, the corresponding memory and all the memories causing it become useless and can be garbage collected. The garbage collection of memories is similar to the low level semantics of rollbacks (cf. [9]), but it works from the target memory towards the past instead of towards the present.

Commit acts by marking with a dagger the committed memory:

$$(\text{Commit.S}) \ \frac{}{\kappa_1 : \text{commit } k \parallel [\mu; k] \twoheadrightarrow \kappa_1 : \text{commit } k \parallel [\mu; k]^\dagger}$$

In order to understand why this commits the memory, we need to discuss rollbacks.

Definition 1 (Commit-free configuration). *A configuration M is commit-free (noted commit-free(M)) if it does not contain any memory of the form $[\mu; k]^\dagger$.*

Thus, the rollback rule can easily be adapted:

$$(\textsc{B.Roll}) \quad \frac{N \blacktriangleright k \quad \text{complete}(N \parallel [\mu; k]) \quad \text{commit-free}(N)}{N \parallel [\mu; k]^\bullet \twoheadrightarrow \mu \parallel N \downarrow_k}$$

Notice that in this approach a rollback either fully takes place, or it is forbidden, there is no partial rollback.

Garbage Collecting Useless Memories. We now discuss how to garbage collect memories which are no more needed since a commit forbids to rollback them.

First, we need to understand which memories need to be garbage collected. To this end, the mark on a memory is propagated to its ancestors:

$$(\textsc{Commit.M}) \quad \frac{\mu \equiv \kappa_1 : P \parallel M \quad \kappa_1 = \langle \_, \tilde{\_} \rangle \cdot k' \text{ or } \kappa_1 = k'}{[\mu; k]^\dagger \parallel [\mu'; k']^\circ \twoheadrightarrow [\mu; k]^\dagger \parallel [\mu'; k']^\dagger}$$

Notice that a single application of the rule propagates the mark to a single ancestor, multiple applications are needed to cover all the ancestors.

The question then arises of when to stop propagating the mark, and when one can actually start erasing memories. Indeed, we can not distinguish the first memory of a configuration unless we look at the whole system, which is not practicable. To address this issue, we introduce init κ tokens, which mark initial processes. We assume such a token exists for each initial process in an initial configuration[5]. When we mark a memory $[\mu; k]^\dagger$ for erasure and such tokens exist for all processes in μ, we know this memory has no ancestor and can be removed. Upon erasure, we also remove the tokens, and replace them with a new init k token, as the immediate successor of the memory is now the oldest process (or memory) in the configuration.

$$(\textsc{Commit.E}) \quad \frac{}{\left[\prod_{\kappa_i \in \tilde{\kappa}} (\kappa_i : P_i); k\right]^\dagger \parallel \prod_{\kappa_i \in \tilde{\kappa}} (\text{init } \kappa_i) \twoheadrightarrow \text{init } k}$$

To obtain the required init κ_i, we may need to split a token init k into complex keys, if the corresponding processes are split as well.

$$(\textsc{Commit.B}) \quad \frac{\langle h_i, \tilde{h} \rangle \cdot k \text{ occurs in } M}{\text{init } k \parallel M \twoheadrightarrow \prod_{h_i \in \tilde{h}} (\text{init } \langle h_i, \tilde{h} \rangle \cdot k) \parallel M}$$

---

[5] Intuitively, we want to maintain the invariant that, for all processes $k : P$, there exists either a memory $[\mu; k]^\oplus$ or a token init k (and similarly for complex tags).

Finally, introducing commits and memory erasure makes it possible to have dangling roll k or commit k, i.e. where the target tag k does not refer to any memory (if the memory tagged with k is erased or rollbacked). We introduce a rule to clean-up such dangling processes. We identify this case when a key k used for a tag is only used by commit k or roll k processes, or init κ tokens, i.e. when the binder of the key only binds such processes/tokens.

$$(\text{Commit.C1}) \ \frac{\begin{array}{c} M_i = \kappa_i : \text{roll } k \text{ or } M_i = \kappa_i : \text{commit } k \\ I = 0,\ I = \text{init } k \text{ or } I = \prod_{h_i \in h} (\text{init } \langle h_i, \hat{h} \rangle \cdot k) \end{array}}{\nu k. \left(I \parallel \prod_i (M_i) \right) \twoheadrightarrow \nu k. \left(I \parallel \prod_i (\kappa_i : 0) \right)}$$

Notice that we possibly end up with $\kappa_i : 0$ processes (with distinct tags), as in **roll**$-\pi$. In **roll**$-\pi$, those processes need to be kept in order to track causal dependencies (even when a process is 0, it can be reverted and we need the tag to identify which memory lead to this 0). However, in **broll**$-\pi$, thanks to init k tokens, we can sometimes identify that those processes are now *initial* (either because the initial configuration contained them, or because the memory that created those processes were committed). In that case, we can collect them. We also collect the associated init κ to avoid leftovers.

$$(\text{Commit.C2}) \ \frac{}{\text{init } \kappa \parallel \kappa : 0 \twoheadrightarrow 0}$$

As in **roll**$-\pi$, all the reductions mentioned above can happen inside parallel composition and restriction contexts.

4.3 Example

We illustrate **broll**$-\pi$ with an example, which combines both non causally-consistent communications and commits. The initial configuration we consider is:

$$k_P : a(X) \triangleright_\gamma (\text{roll } \gamma \parallel b \langle 0 \rangle) \parallel k_Q : b(Y) \triangleright_\delta (\text{commit } \delta)$$
$$\parallel k_R : \{a\} \langle 0 \rangle \parallel \text{init } k_P \parallel \text{init } k_Q \parallel \text{init } k_R$$

For the sake of conciseness, we do not show all intermediate steps.

Non Causally-Consistent Communications. This configuration first reduces with (NCom):

$$(\text{NCom}) \twoheadrightarrow \nu k'_P . \begin{pmatrix} k'_P : (\text{roll } k'_P \parallel b \langle 0 \rangle) \parallel k_Q : b(Y) \triangleright_\delta (\text{commit } \delta) \\ \parallel [k_P : a(X) \triangleright_\gamma (\text{roll } \gamma \parallel b \langle 0 \rangle); k'_P] \\ \parallel k_R : 0 \parallel \text{init } k_P \parallel \text{init } k_Q \parallel \text{init } k_R \end{pmatrix}$$

Notice that the created memory contains only the receiver part, not the pending message; and an empty process tagged with k_R replaces the message (also in case a rollback occurs). In our case, this leftover is initial (since the message was initial as well), and can be collected with (COMMIT.C2):

$$(\text{COMMIT.C2}) \atop \twoheadrightarrow \quad \nu k'_P. \begin{pmatrix} k'_P : (\text{roll } k'_P \parallel b\langle 0 \rangle) \parallel k_Q : b(Y) \triangleright_\delta (\text{commit } \delta) \\ \parallel [k_P : a(X) \triangleright_\gamma (\text{roll } \gamma \parallel b\langle 0 \rangle); k'_P] \\ \parallel \text{init } k_P \parallel \text{init } k_Q \end{pmatrix}$$

If a rollback occurs, the message would not be reverted:

$$\begin{array}{c}(\text{H.START})^* \\ (\text{B.ROLL}) \\ \leadsto \end{array} \quad \begin{array}{l} k_P : a(X) \triangleright_\gamma (\text{roll } \gamma \parallel b\langle 0 \rangle) \parallel k_Q : b(Y) \triangleright_\delta (\text{commit } \delta) \\ \parallel \text{init } k_P \parallel \text{init } k_Q \end{array}$$

Committing Memories. Instead of rolling back, let's assume forward computation continues with (COM), where $\tilde{k}'_P = \{k'_{P1}, k'_{P2}\}$. For the sake of conciseness, we replace $\nu k'_P, k'_{P1}, k'_{P2}, k'_Q. (\ldots)$ with $\nu \ldots (\ldots)$. We call M the obtained configuration:

$$\twoheadrightarrow^* \nu\ldots \begin{pmatrix} \langle k'_{P1}, \tilde{k}'_P \rangle \cdot k'_P : \text{roll } k'_P \parallel k'_Q : \text{commit } k'_Q \\ \parallel \left[\langle k'_{P2}, \tilde{k}'_P \rangle \cdot k'_P : b\langle 0 \rangle \parallel k_Q : b(Y) \triangleright_\delta (\text{commit } \delta); k'_Q \right] \\ \parallel [k_P : a(X) \triangleright_\gamma (\text{roll } \gamma \parallel b\langle 0 \rangle); k'_P] \\ \parallel \text{init } k_P \parallel \text{init } k_Q \end{pmatrix}$$

At this stage, two reductions can take place: we can initiate a rollback of k'_P; or we can initiate a commit of k'_Q. We focus on the commit, with a short remark on the interplay between rollbacks and commits.

Starting a commit phase happens by triggering (COMMIT.S). This rule requires a commit k process. In our case, we target the tag k'_Q. This rule marks the memory with tag k'_Q with a †.

$$M \xrightarrow{(\text{COMMIT.S})}$$

$$\nu\ldots \begin{pmatrix} \langle k'_{P1}, \tilde{k}'_P \rangle \cdot k'_P : \text{roll } k'_P \parallel k'_Q : \text{commit } k'_Q \\ \parallel \left[\langle k'_{P2}, \tilde{k}'_P \rangle \cdot k'_P : b\langle 0 \rangle \parallel k_Q : b(Y) \triangleright_\delta (\text{commit } \delta); k'_Q \right]^\dagger \\ \parallel [k_P : a(X) \triangleright_\gamma (\text{roll } \gamma \parallel b\langle 0 \rangle); k'_P] \\ \parallel \text{init } k_P \parallel \text{init } k_Q \end{pmatrix}$$

Remark 1 (Concurrent commits and rollback). The roll k'_P process can initiate a rollback with (H.START), thus marking the second memory. To perform the rollback, rule (B.ROLL) needs to apply. However, the memory $[...; k'_Q]^\dagger$ is causally-dependent on k'_P, thus the predicate commit-free(N) does not hold, which forbids (B.ROLL) to apply. On the other hand, rule (COMMIT.M) ignores marks on memories marked for rollback. Thus, memories marked for rollback do not block commits.

Since we now have a †-marked memory, we can trigger the rule (COMMIT.M), which spans the mark to predecessor memories, e.g. the memory with tag k'_P.

$$(\text{COMMIT.M}) \twoheadrightarrow$$

$$\nu .... \begin{pmatrix} \langle k'_{P_1}, \tilde{k}'_P \rangle \cdot k'_P : \text{ roll } k'_P \parallel k'_Q : \text{ commit } k'_Q \\ \parallel \left[\langle k'_{P_2}, \tilde{k}'_P \rangle \cdot k'_P : b\langle 0 \rangle \parallel k_Q : b(Y) \triangleright_\delta (\text{commit } \delta); k'_Q \right]^\dagger \\ \parallel \left[k_P : a(X) \triangleright_\gamma (\text{roll } \gamma \parallel b\langle 0 \rangle); k'_P \right]^\dagger \\ \parallel \text{init } k_P \parallel \text{init } k_Q \end{pmatrix}$$

The memory with tag k'_P has no predecessor. We see that the process it contains (identified with k_P) is an initial process (there is an init k_P token in the configuration). Therefore, we can erase that memory with (COMMIT.E). Notice that in the resulting configuration, the process k'_P, created by the communication recorded in the memory with the same tag, is now initial, and therefore, an init k'_P token is created.

$$(\text{COMMIT.E}) \twoheadrightarrow \nu .... \begin{pmatrix} \langle k'_{P_1}, \tilde{k}'_P \rangle \cdot k'_P : \text{ roll } k'_P \parallel k'_Q : \text{ commit } k'_Q \\ \parallel \left[\langle k'_{P_2}, \tilde{k}'_P \rangle \cdot k'_P : b\langle 0 \rangle \parallel k_Q : b(Y) \triangleright_\delta (\text{commit } \delta); k'_Q \right]^\dagger \\ \parallel \text{init } k_Q \parallel \text{init } k'_P \end{pmatrix}$$

The memory with tag k'_Q is the next one to be erased. However, rule (COMMIT.E) requires a token init $\langle k'_{P_2}, \tilde{k}'_P \rangle \cdot k'_P$, which does not exist. However, $\langle k'_{P_2}, \tilde{k}'_P \rangle \cdot k'_P$ appeared while splitting k'_P, which is initial. Therefore, we can split the token init k'_P to obtain the key needed using (COMMIT.B).

$$(\text{COMMIT.B}) \twoheadrightarrow \nu .... \begin{pmatrix} \langle k'_{P_1}, \tilde{k}'_P \rangle \cdot k'_P : \text{ roll } k'_P \parallel k'_Q : \text{ commit } k'_Q \\ \parallel \left[\langle k'_{P_2}, \tilde{k}'_P \rangle \cdot k'_P : b\langle 0 \rangle \parallel k_Q : b(Y) \triangleright_\delta (\text{commit } \delta); k'_Q \right]^\dagger \\ \parallel \text{init } k_Q \parallel \text{init } \langle k'_{P_1}, \tilde{k}'_P \rangle \cdot k'_P \parallel \text{init } \langle k'_{P_2}, \tilde{k}'_P \rangle \cdot k'_P \end{pmatrix}$$

From this point, we can trigger (COMMIT.E) again, removing the last memory. We are left with commit and roll processes only which refer to nonexistent memories. Those processes can be collected using the cleanup rules

(COMMIT.C1) and (COMMIT.C2), resulting in an empty configuration.

$$(\text{COMMIT.E})$$

$$\nu\ldots\left(\begin{array}{l}\langle k'_{P1}, \tilde{k'_P}\rangle \cdot k'_P : \texttt{roll}\ k'_P \parallel k'_Q : \texttt{commit}\ k'_Q \\ \parallel \texttt{init}\ \langle k'_{P1}, \tilde{k'_P}\rangle \cdot k'_P \parallel \texttt{init}\ k'_Q\end{array}\right) \begin{array}{c}(\text{COMMIT.C1})^3 \\ (\text{COMMIT.C2})^3 \\ \rightarrow\end{array} 0$$

5 Application: a Speculative Consensus Algorithm

We present a practical example which illustrates the use of both non causally-consistent communications and commits: a consensus algorithm with speculative execution. Like a regular consensus protocol [2], we are given n processes (named p_1 to p_n) which aim to agree on a single value. To this end, each process p_i *proposes* a value v_i, and eventually *decides* on the selected value v. To reach this agreement, the distributed system must run a *consensus protocol* such that (i) all p_i eventually decide (termination); (ii) all p_i decide the same value v (agreement); (iii) the value v is one of the proposed v_i (non-triviality); and (iv) every process decides once (integrity). In our case, *decision* occurs on committing the result of the algorithm. Notice that multiple messages may be sent on the decision channels due to rollbacks.

To implement such protocol, we augment **broll**$-\pi$ with high-level language features, such as control flow (if-then-else) and data types (integers and arrays). For the sake of simplicity we do not detail further those features and we assume they integrate seamlessly into **broll**$-\pi$. Our implementation focuses on the consensus protocol, implemented as a (set of) processes C_i, which p_i interact with. In a first step, we describe *how* processes p_i interact with C_i to initiate the consensus protocol and recover the decided value (i.e. we present the user interface of C_i). Then, we delve into C_i, first explaining a few preliminary items before describing the algorithm itself.

Consensus Process Interface. The consensus protocol C_i (which p_i interacts with) is shown in Fig. 1, where the behaviour of a process C_i is presented. To propose a value v_i, p_i sends it on $\texttt{propose}_i$ and C_i then takes over, eventually sending the decided value on $\texttt{decide}_i$, which is to be received by p_i. Our algorithm includes speculative execution: even before all values from peers are received (or even proposed), a value is sent on $\texttt{decide}_i$, which allows p_i to continue. If this value is not consistent with the proposed values from the peers, reversible execution allows to roll back p_i and deciding another value. We assume p_i internally uses only the reversible fragment of **broll**$-\pi$. If p_i use non causally consistent communication during speculative execution, peers would not necessarily be reverted when the speculative execution is aborted[6]. If any p_i initiates

---

[6] Peers that take part in the consensus would be reverted, even though the rollback would not propagate through the communication.

a commit while performing speculative execution, this commit also affects the consensus part, which causally precedes the speculative execution. This permanently spoils the consensus algorithm.

$$s_i \langle \mathtt{A_{init}} \rangle \parallel l_i \langle 0 \rangle \parallel \mathbf{F}(\{s'_i\}(X) \triangleright (X))$$

$$\parallel l_i(X) \triangleright_{\gamma_i} \left(\prod_{1 \leq j \leq n} \left(c_{j \to i}(X_j) \triangleright \left(\{s_i\}(A) \triangleright \left(\begin{array}{l} \text{if } i = j \\ \text{then } \prod_{\substack{1 \leq k \leq n \\ k \neq i}} (c_{i \to k} \langle X_j \rangle) \\ \parallel \{s'_i\} \left\langle \left(\begin{array}{l} s_i \left\langle A\{^{X_j}/_{A[j]}\} \right\rangle \\ \parallel \left(\begin{array}{l} \text{if } \min(A) > X_j \\ \text{then roll } \gamma_i \end{array} \right) \end{array} \right) \right\rangle \\ \parallel \text{if } \bot \notin A \text{ then commit } \gamma_i \end{array} \right) \right) \right) \\ \parallel s_i(A) \triangleright (s_i \langle A \rangle \parallel \text{if } \neg \mathtt{is\_empty}(A) \text{ then } \mathtt{decide}_i \langle \min(A) \rangle) \end{array} \right)$$

$$\parallel \mathtt{propose}_i(v_i) \triangleright (c_{i \to i} \langle v_i \rangle)$$

Fig. 1. The consensus protocol C_i used by process p_i.

Preliminary Items. Before explaining the core content of our algorithm, we shall introduce a few preliminary elements.

First, our algorithm contains a channel l_i, which is initially and exclusively used to set up a rollback point (γ_i) prior to any event. In the following, if an inconsistency happens, the algorithm rolls back to γ_i, thus reverting any consequences of the inconsistency.

Second, our algorithm (for participant i) relies on an array which contains proposed values that are known to participant i. This is an array of n cells, initially empty (we note $\bot$ the absence of value, and we call $\mathtt{A_{init}}$ the initial array). At any time, there is at most one copy of this array in a pending message $\{s_i\} \langle A \rangle$. To access the array, one receives the pending message containing the array. The channels s_i and s'_i are used internally (they are restricted to the algorithm). They allow us to keep known proposed values even during rollback. The channel s_i is used to make the array available. The message is made available using s_i in a causally-consistent way, thus leaving the reader the choice of whether it is read in a causally-consistent way or not. Channel s'_i is used to update the array. Updating the array consists in emitting a message on s_i. To escape the scope of the rollback to γ_i, modifications of the array use $\{s'_i\}$ in a non-causally consistent way. There is a replicating receive-and-execute listener process on $\{s'_i\}$.

To replicate a process, we introduce $\mathbf{F}(P)$ which creates as many copies of P as needed. This replicator is implemented as[7]:

$$\mathbf{F}(P) = \nu c. \begin{pmatrix} c\langle c(X) \rhd_\gamma (P \parallel X \parallel c\langle X\rangle \parallel \mathtt{commit}\ \gamma)\rangle \\ \parallel c(X) \rhd_\gamma (P \parallel X \parallel c\langle X\rangle \parallel \mathtt{commit}\ \gamma) \end{pmatrix}$$

Third, there are channels $c_{j\to i}$ for each pairs of participants. Those channels are used to broadcast proposed values. This includes a channel $c_{i\to i}$, used to forward internally the value proposed by p_i.

Finally, the value that is decided is the lowest proposed value. This is arbitrary, but it ensures the satisfaction of the agreement and non-triviality properties.

The Algorithm. We can now look at the core content of the algorithm, which is the continuation of the trigger on l_i. This continuation is composed of two main parts.

First, let us discuss the actions to take when a new proposed value is received on one of the $c_{j\to i}$ channels (even when $j = i$, which is only marginally different). Upon reception of a proposed value X_j, we read the array (from $\{s_i\}$[8]) and up to three out of the four actions below take place in parallel:

- If the value is from p_i (i.e. if it is the local proposed value), it is sent to all other participants (which eventually trigger the same events on their own channels).
- If the array that has been read is already full, then X_j was already known and all proposed values are known and inconsistencies can no longer happen. In that case, we commit the protocol.
- In any case, we update the content of the array with the value received: we create a new pending message on s_i containing the array updated with X_j in the j-th cell. Notice that this message should persist in case of rollback. To enforce that, we first escape the scope of the rollback to γ_i using $\{s_i'\}$: we send the message $s_i \langle A\{X_j/A[j]\}\rangle$, that contains the updated array on $\{s_i'\}$, thus any future rollback will not revert this message.
- Finally, if X_j is strictly lower than all known values so far, then speculative execution of p_i is inconsistent, and is therefore rolled back: we roll back to γ_i. However, before rolling back, we have to make sure the newly created message on s_i (containing the updated array) has been received by $\{s_i'\}$: if not, an early rollback could rollback the pending message on $\{s_i'\}$, thus erasing the message on s_i contained in it. To prevent this unfortunate scheduling, the rollback decision is sent on $\{s_i'\}$ *together* with the array message itself, therefore the rollback can trigger only after the message on $\{s_i'\}$ is received.

---

[7] The two occurrences of commit γ are not needed strictly speaking, but creating copies also creates memories. We add the commit γ to clean up those memories.

[8] We read the array in a non-causally-consistent way, ensuring the old version of the array is not restored, even in case of rollbacks.

Notice that the two last items are mutually exclusive: if the array is full, then X_j is already in the array and therefore, it can not be strictly smaller than the minimum value of the array.

The first part ensures that the array eventually contains all proposed values, but we still need to return the decided value to p_i, by sending it on decide_i. The second parallel element of the continuation does it. At any time, the array can be read, and (if it is not empty), its minimum value is sent on decide_i, thus made available to p_i. This decision can be speculative, if the array is not full (in which case a rollback may occur in the future). In this process, the array is not modified, which allows us to read it in a causally consistent way. This is needed due to rollbacks: when a rollback occurs, the pending $s_i \langle A \rangle$ is reverted, thanks to the causally-consistent receive, the message consumed by the trigger is restored, and that message is consistent as the array is not modified.

Our reversible approach interferes with the properties of consensus algorithms mentioned above. In particular, it requires a careful definition of what it means *deciding* for a process in our context. In particular, sending on decide_i can not constitute a decide event, since multiple messages can be sent and reverted on that channel, with values inconsistent w.r.t. that of other processes. Such a definition would thus violate agreement and integrity. Instead, the committing commit γ_i constitutes a suitable choice for the *decide* event, for each process executes commit just once (integrity). Agreement and non-triviality should be straightforward, showing that each process ends up with the same array. Termination is less trivial, due to rollbacks and administrative reductions. However, the number of rollback for a process is bounded by n, since the a new element is inserted when rolling back. Administrative reductions (e.g. reducing the $\mathbf{F}(\dots)$) however could be unbounded, and ought to be ignored or limited.

6 Discussion

The two extensions introduced in **broll**–π blur the line between normal (forward-only) calculi and strict causal consistent reversible calculi. In order to illustrate this relaxed boundary, in this section we sketch a few applications of our calculus and highlight some relevant points.

6.1 Reversibility Domains

We call *reversibility domains* a system of multiple processes where subsets of the processes of the system can rollback together in a causally-consistent way, but where such rollbacks are limited to the subset considered. Intuitively, such system could, for instance be a computation distributed across multiple datacenters. Each datacenter could have a local fault-tolerance mechanism based on reversibility, and communications across datacenters would be considered as side-effects, i.e. non-reversible actions.

The **broll**–π calculus is general enough to easily model such behaviour: processes belonging to the same domain would communicate using causally-consistent communications, while processes belonging to different domains would communicate using non causally-consistent communications.

In fact, **broll**–π is strictly more general than a calculus implementing only domains, since channels can be used differently at different steps, while a strict application of reversibility domains would be more static. This allows us to model, for instance, merging or splitting domains.

6.2 Interactions Between Reversible and Recursive Processes.

Following the same idea of reversibility domains, we can also sketch an interesting application of our work: a single system (i.e. a single term of the calculus) can have a part that is programmed using a reversible paradigm, and another part that uses a more conventional forward-only recursive paradigm. Said otherwise, reversibility is seen as any other programming primitive/style/paradigm, not only for fault tolerance or debugging.

For instance, consider the following term:

$$k_p : i\langle 0\rangle \mathbin\Vert i(X) \triangleright_\gamma (\{c\}\langle P\rangle \mathbin\Vert \texttt{roll}\ \gamma) \mathbin\Vert k_q : \mathbf{F}(\{c\}(Y) \triangleright (Q))$$

The first part (with key k_p) is a process that first reduces on an internal (reversible) channel i into $\{c\}\langle P\rangle \mathbin\Vert \texttt{roll}\ \gamma$ (with γ substituted with the key generated during the reduction), i.e. into a process that sends P on $\{c\}$ (i.e. a non causally-consistent communication) and that reverts the first communication, reaching again the initial state. On the second hand, the other part of the term (with key k_q) only uses non causally-consistent communications, as if written in **HO**π (except for commits to cleanup memories). This process uses the $\mathbf{F}(...)$ replicator introduced in Sect. 5, which generates $\{c\}(Y) \triangleright (Q)$ at will.

In summary, the first part is eventually able to send on $\{c\}$, while the second part is eventually able to receive on that channel, and this happens infinitely many times. The second implementation is a classical implementation of recursion in higher-order calculi, while the first one is a novel implementation enabled by the interaction between rollback and non causal-consistent communications.

6.3 On the Duality of Rollbacks and Commits

It is to be noted that commits are, to some extent, dual of rollbacks (similarly to what happens in transactions). This is better seen by representing configurations in a more graphical way, where processes are represented as vertices of a graph, causal dependencies as (directed) edges, and tag references (e.g. in $\texttt{roll}\ k$) as backward edges. Communication rules consist in completing the graph. For instance, consider the configuration

$$k : a\langle P\rangle \mathbin\Vert l : a(\_) \triangleright_\gamma (\texttt{roll}\ \gamma \mathbin\Vert \texttt{commit}\ \gamma)$$

The configuration and its first reduction can be graphically represented as (where dotted arrows represent rollback/commit targets, and plain arrows causal dependencies):

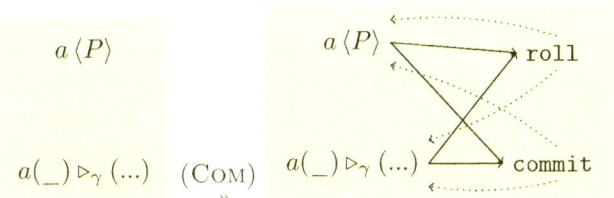

If we abstract away processes (the content of the vertices), and rollback/commit edges, in order to keep the structure of the causal dependencies[9] then any configuration is represented as a directed acyclic graph. In such setting:

- communication reductions consist in adding nodes at the right of the graph;
- executing causally consistent rollbacks consists in removing nodes from the right, i.e. maxima of the underlying poset[10];
- executing commits consists in removing nodes from the left, i.e. minima of the underlying poset.

This seems to show an underlying duality between rollbacks and commits, which are essentially removing one end or the other of the causal dependency poset. This emphasizes that, somehow, only communications are actual computations, while rollbacks/commits are erasing one side or the other of the history.

To further emphasize this duality, instead of having two kinds of reduction (forwards and backwards), we could divide the semantics into three kinds of rules:

1. Computational reductions, i.e. reductions where actual computation occurs; i.e. rules (COM) and (NCOM).
2. Backward reductions, i.e. reductions undoing some computations; i.e. all the rules related to rollbacks.
3. Forward or progress reductions, i.e. reductions that set some computations in stone; i.e. all the rules related to commits.

7 Related Work

Comparison with *Irreversible Actions* in RCCS [5]. When it comes to setting temporal boundaries, we think of *irreversible* actions introduced in RCCS by Danos and Krivine in [5]. Before comparing irreversible actions and commits,

---

[9] This is the graph of the $>$ relation in [9,10], which is a partial order.
[10] This is slightly more subtle though: one can not erase maxima at random, we have to remove atomically all successors of the parents of our target.

we shall first present reversibility in RCCS [4], which is quite different than in **roll**$-\pi/\rho\pi$ (see [12] for an interesting discussion on causal-consistent reversibility in various calculi, including the two aforementioned ones).

In RCCS, each process has a memory stack which grows when the process takes transitions. A synchronisation leads to two memories: one on each side of the communication. Rollbacks occur by popping memories from the stack, and soundness of rollbacks is ensured by the linear structure of the stack of memories. Irreversible actions are implemented by inserting special elements in the memory stack: a token $\langle\circ\rangle$. This token can not be popped, thus ensuring that actions prior to the irreversible ones can no longer be reversed.

There is a fundamental difference between irreversible actions and commits. With irreversible actions, being irreversible is a property of *actions*, while in **broll**$-\pi$, being committed is a property of *memories*. In addition, in **broll**$-\pi$, committing a memory is decided independently of the creation of the memory and, in particular, it is decided after the memory is created. However, in RCCS with irreversible actions, reversible and irreversible actions are two distinct synchronisation primitives, and choosing between the two is decided statically by the programmer.

Implementing Oracles as in $\Omega\rho\pi$ [16]. In [16], a variant of **roll**$-\pi$ called $\Omega\rho\pi$ is introduced. In $\Omega\rho\pi$, configurations of **roll**$-\pi$ are able to communicate with an *oracle*. Sending a message to the *oracle* changes its internal state; and receiving a message from the oracle reads its internal state. Contrary to other processes, the oracle state is not reverted during a rollback. This allows one to perform a computation, store the result, rollback; and then to *guess* the rolled-back result without repeating the computation (hence the name of the *oracle*).

We show that such an oracle can be implemented in **broll**$-\pi$: in fact, this paper is a generalisation of [16]. Following $\Omega\rho\pi$, we use a channel inform to update the state of the oracle. To read its state, we slightly diverge from $\Omega\rho\pi$: we first send a message to request a forecast (channel req_fcast), and then we receive the state on channel forecast as in $\Omega\rho\pi$. This slight modification is required for technical reasons explained below.

The state of the oracle is implemented as a pending message on a channel state. The oracle maintains such pending message, whose content is updated if needed. Then, the oracle consists of two (replicated) processes: one to deal with inform, and the other to deal with forecast. The pending message and the two replicated processes are respectively tagged with s, i and f in the oracle process below. Notice that the oracle is not intended to ever reverse. Thus, it communicates with the environment using only non causally-consistent communications, and memories are periodically committed to avoid leftovers.

$s: \{\texttt{state}\}\langle S\rangle$

$\parallel i: \mathbf{F}(\{\texttt{inform}\}(S') \triangleright (\{\texttt{state}\}(\_) \triangleright_\gamma (\{\texttt{state}\}\langle S'\rangle)))$

$\parallel f: \mathbf{F}(\{\texttt{req\_fcast}\}(\_) \triangleright (\{\texttt{state}\}(X) \triangleright (\{\texttt{forecast}\}\langle X\rangle \parallel \{\texttt{state}\}\langle X\rangle)))$

where $\mathbf{F}(P)$ is the replicator process introduced in Sect. 5.

Both the inform and forecast parts of the oracle are repeating using a process $\mathbf{F}(P)$, which generates as many such processes as needed. Upon receiving an oracle state update on channel inform the pending state$\langle S \rangle$ is consumed and a new one is produced. Upon receiving a forecast request on req_fcast, the pending state$\langle S \rangle$ is read, forwarded on forecast and a new state$\langle S \rangle$ is created. Without this reception on {req_fcast}, pending messages on {forecast} could spawn at will, and there would be no possibility to collect them before updating the oracle state, thus leaving pending messages on {forecast} containing outdated values. Thanks to the introduction of {req_fcast}, we can control the duplication of {forecast}, preventing this issue.

Overall, the process maintains an invariant: there is always at most one pending message on state, which ensures consistency w.r.t. the semantics of $\Omega\rho\pi$. Also, even when there is no such pending message (e.g. during intermediate steps), one is eventually created, thus ensuring the absence of deadlock.

Implementing Compensations as in croll−π [8]. In [8] an enhanced version of **roll**−π, named **croll**−π, featuring compensations is presented. The core idea of **croll**−π is to enhance messages with alternatives, which serve as fallback options. When a memory is hit by a rollback, instead of reactivating the original message, the system uses the attached alternative. This relatively simple change enables the modeling of compensations and supports communicating transactions, where interacting processes may need to jointly recover or backtrack.

While both [8] and the present paper tackles the issue of programming systems which are only partially reversible, the proposed mechanisms are quite different and may not be mutually encodable. We leave however for future work a more detailed comparison, and an integration of the two approaches if none of them would be able to encode the other.

8 Conclusion

In this paper, we introduced **broll**−π, an extension of **roll**−π which allows (i) processes to communicate without recording the causal dependency of the receiver on the sender, and (ii) to commit past actions, making them permanent.

To implement non causally-consistent communications, we changed the content of the memory that is created when receiving a message. Instead of storing both the message and the receiver process, we store the receiver process only. Thus, upon reverting the receiver, the rollback information does not propagate to the sender side (and vice-versa).

To implement commits, **broll**−π introduces a primitive commit k which removes the memory $[\mu; k]$ as well as all memories it causally depends on, effectively making it non-reversible. Concurrent commits and rollbacks are dealt with by preventing memories scheduled for erasure to be rolled back, thus preventing inconsistencies.

There are several promising directions for future work. First, we aim to develop a comprehensive behavioural theory for **broll**−π, providing deeper insights into its fundamental principles. Second, we plan to design a low-level semantics, inspired by distributed algorithms, to demonstrate how coordinated rollback/commit primitives can be implemented effectively. Furthermore, it will be crucial to prove the equivalence between that low-level semantics and the high-level one presented in this paper.

Additionally, we intend to explore whether **broll**$-\pi$ can support the encoding of long-running transactional schemas, which nowadays are used in microservices architectures.

References

1. Buchmann, A.: Open nested transaction models. In: Liu, L., Tamer Özsu, M. (eds.) Encyclopedia of Database Systems, pp. 2597–2601. Springer, New York (2018)
2. Cachin, C., Guerraoui, R., Rodrigues, L.: Introduction to Reliable and Secure Distributed Programming. Springer, Heidelberg (2011)
3. Carothers, C.D., Perumalla, K.S., Fujimoto, R.: Efficient optimistic parallel simulations using reverse computation. ACM Trans. Model. Comput. Simul. **9**(3), 224–253 (1999)
4. Danos, V., Krivine, J.: Reversible communicating systems. In: Gardner, P., Yoshida, N. (eds.) CONCUR 2004. LNCS, vol. 3170, pp. 292–307. Springer, Heidelberg (2004). https://doi.org/10.1007/978-3-540-28644-8_19
5. Danos, V., Krivine, J.: Transactions in RCCS. In: Abadi, M., de Alfaro, L. (eds.) CONCUR 2005. LNCS, vol. 3653, pp. 398–412. Springer, Heidelberg (2005). https://doi.org/10.1007/11539452_31
6. Hoey, J., Lanese, I., Nishida, N., Ulidowski, I., Vidal, G.: A case study for reversible computing: reversible debugging of concurrent programs. In: Ulidowski, I., Lanese, I., Schultz, U.P., Ferreira, C. (eds.) RC 2020. LNCS, vol. 12070, pp. 108–127. Springer, Cham (2020). https://doi.org/10.1007/978-3-030-47361-7_5
7. Landauer, R.: Irreversibility and heat generated in the computing process. IBM J. Res. Dev. **5**, 183–191 (1961)
8. Lanese, I., Lienhardt, M., Mezzina, C.A., Schmitt, A., Stefani, J.-B.: Concurrent flexible reversibility. In: Felleisen, M., Gardner, P. (eds.) ESOP 2013. LNCS, vol. 7792, pp. 370–390. Springer, Heidelberg (2013). https://doi.org/10.1007/978-3-642-37036-6_21
9. Lanese, I., Mezzina, C.A., Schmitt, A., Stefani, J.-B.: Controlling reversibility in higher-order Pi. In: Katoen, J.-P., König, B. (eds.) CONCUR 2011. LNCS, vol. 6901, pp. 297–311. Springer, Heidelberg (2011). https://doi.org/10.1007/978-3-642-23217-6_20
10. Lanese, I., Mezzina, C.A., Stefani, J.-B.: Reversing higher-order Pi. In: Gastin, P., Laroussinie, F. (eds.) CONCUR 2010. LNCS, vol. 6269, pp. 478–493. Springer, Heidelberg (2010). https://doi.org/10.1007/978-3-642-15375-4_33
11. Lanese, I., Mezzina, C.A., Stefani, J.-B.: Reversibility in the higher-order π-calculus. Theor. Comput. Sci. **625**, 25–84 (2016)
12. Lanese, I., Mezzina, C.A., Tiezzi, F.: Causal-consistent reversibility. Bull. EATCS **3**(114) (2014). The concurrency column by Nobuko Yoshida
13. Lanese, I., Phillips, I.C.C., Ulidowski, I.: An axiomatic theory for reversible computation. ACM Trans. Comput. Log. **25**(2), 11:1–11:40 (2024)
14. McNellis, J., Mola, J., Sykes, K.: Time travel debugging: root causing bugs in commercial scale software (2017)

15. Sangiorgi, D.: Bisimulation for higher-order process calculi. Inf. Comput. **131**(2), 141–178 (1996)
16. Vassor, M.: Reversibility and predictions. In: Yamashita, S., Yokoyama, T. (eds.) RC 2021. LNCS, vol. 12805, pp. 163–181. Springer, Cham (2021). https://doi.org/10.1007/978-3-030-79837-6_10
17. Vassor, M., Stefani, J.-B.: Checkpoint/rollback vs causally-consistent reversibility. In: Kari, J., Ulidowski, I. (eds.) RC 2018. LNCS, vol. 11106, pp. 286–303. Springer, Cham (2018). https://doi.org/10.1007/978-3-319-99498-7_20

Bisimulations and Reversibility

Clément Aubert[1], Iain Phillips[2](✉), and Irek Ulidowski[3,4]

[1] Augusta University, Augusta, GA, USA
[2] Imperial College, London, UK
i.phillips@imperial.ac.uk
[3] University of Leicester, Leicester, UK
[4] AGH University of Science and Technology, Kraków, Poland

Abstract. Concurrency and causality can be expressed within a labelled transition system by exploiting reversibility of transitions. It is natural to ask what behavioural equivalences can be captured by bisimulations in the reversible setting. In this paper we work with keyed configuration structures and CCSK, establish an operational correspondence between the two models, and give definitions of hereditary history-preserving bisimulation and history-preserving bisimulation in both models. We then present several characterisation results for the two bisimulations in terms of previously proposed, as well as new, "reverse" bisimulations.

Keywords: Concurrency · Process Algebras · Configuration Structures · Labelled Transition System · Reversibility · Bisimulation

1 Introduction

Bisimulation is the go-to behavioural equivalence in concurrency theory that helps us formally compare the behaviour of two systems—typically processes in a model such as the process algebra Calculus of Communicating Systems (CCS [24]). We say that two processes are bisimilar if they can simulate each other's behaviour in a step-by-step fashion. If one process can perform an action (for example sending a message, or updating a variable), the other process must be able to match the action, and their continuations must also be able to match each other's actions.

Although bisimulation has important properties and enjoys modal logic, proof system and testing characterisations [1,24], thus making it a universally acceptable and widely applicable interleaving equivalence, it does not distinguish processes that have different *causal* or *concurrent* behaviour. One needs to work with non-interleaving semantics, also called *true concurrency* semantics, to be able to fully represent causality, concurrency and conflict—known as true concurrency relations. Consider actions a and b, and processes $a \mid b$, where the actions are executed concurrently, and $a.b + b.a$, where there is a choice between executing a followed by b and b followed by a. These processes are bisimilar: both processes can perform a, b in some matching order. However, they are different under true-concurrency semantics: a, b are concurrent in $a \mid b$ and are not in $a.b + b.a$, where a causes b or b causes a.

There is a wealth of research on adapting bisimulation to capture true-concurrency differences in behaviour. The two main approaches are 1. to generalise what it means to "perform an action", and 2. to require that the elements of behaviour matched by bisimulation are also in a *causal order-preserving* bijection.

In the first approach, one can consider performing "steps", which are sets of concurrent actions, giving *step bisimulation* [7,15,27,30]. We notice that $a \mid b$ and $a.b + b.a$ are not step bisimilar as only $a \mid b$ can perform the step $\{a, b\}$. One can also consider more complex groups of actions such as *pomsets* (partially ordered multisets), thus giving *pomset bisimulation* [27,30]. Consider $a \mid a$ and $(a \mid a) + a.a$. These processes are bisimilar and step bisimilar, but not pomset bisimilar since only the second process can perform the pomset $\{a < a\}$ (two actions a, one causing the other). There are examples of processes [27,30] where even pomset bisimulation is not distinguishing enough. That motives the second approach, which requires that we also keep track of which actions are matched via some bijection. This allows us to record and match causality and concurrency between actions via the bijection. Such bisimulations are called *history preserving* and the two most widely studied are *history-preserving* (HP) bisimulation [29, 30] and *hereditary history-preserving* (HHP) bisimulation [7], both of which we investigate in this paper.

Reversible computation is a model of computing where every computational step can be undone, meaning that a system can evolve backwards as naturally as forwards. When a model represents concurrent as well as sequential execution, we adopt the form of reversibility called *causal-consistent* reversibility [12], which allows one to undo any action provided that its consequences, if any, are undone beforehand. Traditionally, most of the computational paradigms are not reversible; however we now have theories and techniques for automatically converting irreversible models, such as process algebra CCS, to their reversible versions that are causal-consistently correct [16,21,26]. CCSK [26] is such a reversible version of CCS. It employs *communication keys* as a mechanism for undoing previously executed actions and synchronisations. CCSK was shown to be useful in studying true concurrency [25], and its concurrency, causality and conflict relations. Returning to our previous example of $a \mid b$ and $a.b + b.a$, we notice that they can be distinguished in the reversible setting. Both can perform a followed by b, which we mark by "attaching" keys k, l; the first can reverse $a[k]$ but the second cannot since the point of execution is immediately after $b[l]$, which guards $a[k]$. These are written in CCSK as

$$a[k] \mid b[l] \xrightsquigarrow{a[k]} a \mid b[l] \qquad \text{and} \qquad a[k].b[l] + b.a \not\xrightsquigarrow{a[k]} .$$

Similarly, both processes can perform $b[l]$ followed by $a[k]$ (by executing the second branch $b.a$ of $a.b + b.a$), but only the first can initially undo $b[l]$. Since we can reverse $a[k]$ and $b[l]$ in any order in the first process we deduce that a, b are concurrent. Being unable to reverse these actions in the second process shows causal ordering.

We have indicated how reversibility can capture concurrency and causal ordering, and so it is natural to investigate bisimulations where processes not only match actions when computing forwards but also match behaviour when reversing execution. That behaviour can be reversing single actions, steps or pomsets [27], or one can require that order-preserving bijections additionally satisfy the *hereditary* property [7]: when reversing, actions that have been related by the bijection generated when computing forwards must be matched again. Hierarchies of such "reverse" bisimulations have been studied in [3,27]. This paper follows this third approach by adapting bisimulation so that it captures true concurrency relationships between processes via reversibility.

We investigate the existing, and propose new, characterisations of HHP and HP bisimulations. Our new characterisations do away with order-preserving bijections and replace them by properties solely defined in terms of reversing single actions (with keys used in an essential way). Our main contributions are:

1. We answer in the affirmative (Theorem 4.15) the question of whether *forward reverse* (FR) bisimulation (with keys) for CCSK [26] is the same as HHP bisimulation on encodings into configuration structures of *standard* CCSK processes, which are essentially CCS processes.
2. We define FR bisimulation on *configuration structures* with key mappings and show it is equivalent to HHP bisimulation on configuration structures (Theorem 4.8). We note that FR bisimulation (without keys) on configuration structures, called "reverse interleaving-interleaving bisimulation (RI-IB)" in [27], is strictly less discriminating than HHP bisimulation [7,25].
3. We define *back and forth* (BF) bisimulation on configuration structures and show it equivalent to HHP bisimulation (Theorem 4.8). In [3] BF bisimulation was defined for RCCS, and it was shown that BF bisimulation on standard RCCS processes was the same as HHP bisimulation on encodings into configuration structures of CCS processes [3, Cor 31].
4. We define a new bisimulation called *forward-backward* (FB) bisimulation (Definition 4.20). It is the first characterisation of HP bisimulation on the standard processes of a reversible calculus, purely using forward and backward labelled transitions with keys (and no bijections or mention of ordering) (Theorem 4.29).

Figure 1 places our results in the context of the hierarchy of main equivalences obtained by following the three approaches outlined earlier (generalising actions to steps and pomsets, using order-preserving bijections and using reversibility).

Other Related Work. An encoding of CCSK with recursion into *labelled reversible bundle event structures* (LRBES) was given in [14]. The semantics of a process is an LRBES with an initial configuration containing the events corresponding to past actions. However, no connection between this semantics and HHP or HP was investigated. *Reversible* CCS (RCCS) [12] was given an abstract model in [22] in terms of a causally-consistent version of reversible nets [23]. However, no connection between their model and HHP or HP was investigated.

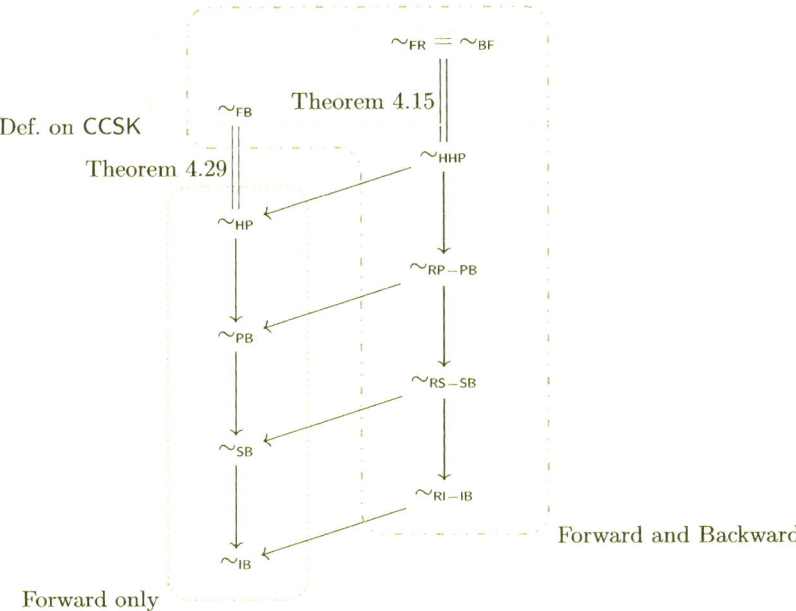

Fig. 1. A hierarchy of equivalences on stable configuration structures, adapted from [27, Fig. 25]. Arrows represent strict inclusion. Here $\sim_{\mathsf{IB}}$ is interleaving bisimilarity (single actions), $\sim_{\mathsf{SB}}$ is step bisimilarity and $\sim_{\mathsf{PB}}$ is pomset bisimilarity, while $\sim_{\mathsf{RI-IB}}$, $\sim_{\mathsf{RS-SB}}$ and $\sim_{\mathsf{RP-PB}}$ are the corresponding equivalences with additional reverse moves. We show the new characterisations $\sim_{\mathsf{FR}}$ and $\sim_{\mathsf{BF}}$ of $\sim_{\mathsf{HHP}}$ (HHP bisimilarity) and $\sim_{\mathsf{FB}}$ of $\sim_{\mathsf{HP}}$ (HP bisimilarity). Note that keys are only used in $\sim_{\mathsf{FR}}$, $\sim_{\mathsf{BF}}$ and $\sim_{\mathsf{FB}}$; these are also the equivalences that are defined for CCSK. One can think of $\sim_{\mathsf{RI-IB}}$ (Definition 4.3) as $\sim_{\mathsf{FR}}$ without using keys; thus adding keys to $\sim_{\mathsf{RI-IB}}$ gives us the extra discriminatory power of $\sim_{\mathsf{HHP}}$.

The idea of giving semantics to a reversible calculus using configuration structures together with a configuration representing past events was used in [9]. The associated reversible calculus uses proof labels on transitions rather than keys to keep track of synchronisation when reversing. Forward bisimilarity and reverse bisimilarity are studied in a reversible setting without synchronisation and keys in [8], where compositionality and axiomatisations of these bisimilarities are proposed.

Many true concurrency bisimulations, including HHP and HP bisimulations, have been given characterisations in terms of modal logics with forward modalities describing causal dependencies between actions [6], or modal logics with reverse modalities (Event Identifier Logic [28]).

Paper Organisation. We recall the definition of CCSK and introduce *keyed* configuration structures in Sect. 2. Operational correspondence between the two models is presented in Sect. 3. We define HHP and HP bisimulations and various "reverse" bisimulations in Sect. 4, where we prove several characterisation results.

Proofs are sketched, or omitted completely, for reasons of space.

2 Preliminary Definitions

We follow the traditional approach [7,30] and define our bisimulations first in a semantic model of configuration structures, and then for a specific reversible calculus CCSK. This section recalls the definitions of these two models.

We write $f\restriction_C$ for the restriction of $f : A \to B$ to $C \subseteq A$, and $f \cup \{a \mapsto b\}$ for the function defined as f on A that additionally maps $a \notin A$ to $b \in B$. We additionally write $\mathrm{dom}(f)$ for the domain of f, namely A, and $\mathrm{img}(f)$ for the subset of B that is the image of f.

Both configuration structures and CCSK processes, defined below, use names, labels and keys:

Definition 2.1 ((Co-)names, labels and keys). *Let* N *be a set of names, ranged over by* a, b *and* c. *A bijection* $\overline{\cdot} :$ N $\to \overline{\mathsf{N}}$, *whose inverse is also written* $\overline{\cdot}$, *gives the complement of a name. The set of labels* L *is* N $\cup \overline{\mathsf{N}} \cup \{\tau\}$, *and we use* α, β *(resp.* λ) *to range over* L *(resp.* L$\setminus\{\tau\}$). *It is convenient to extend the complement mapping to labels by letting* $\overline{\tau} = \tau$.

Let K *be a countably infinite set of keys, ranged over by* k, l, m *and* n. *Keyed labels, denoted* $a[k]$, $a[m]$, $a[n]$, $b[k]$, *etc.,. , are elements of* L $\times$ K.

2.1 CCSK

Definition 2.2 (Operators). *The set* $\mathbb{X}$ *of* CCSK *processes is defined as usual:*

$X, Y \coloneqq$	**0**	(Inactive process)	$\parallel X + Y$	(Sum)
	$\parallel \alpha.X$	(Prefix)	$\parallel X \mid Y$	(Parallel composition)
	$\parallel X\backslash\lambda$	(Restriction)	$\parallel \alpha[k].X$	(Keyed prefix)

The set $\mathbb{P}$ *of* CCS *processes is the set of standard* CCSK *processes, namely those processes that do not use keyed prefixes. We let* P, Q *range over it.*

Definition 2.3 (Keys). *The set of keys in* X, *written* $\mathsf{keys}(X)$, *is defined inductively:*

$$\mathsf{keys}(\mathbf{0}) = \emptyset \qquad \mathsf{keys}(X + Y) = \mathsf{keys}(X) \cup \mathsf{keys}(Y)$$
$$\mathsf{keys}(\alpha.X) = \mathsf{keys}(X) \qquad \mathsf{keys}(X \mid Y) = \mathsf{keys}(X) \cup \mathsf{keys}(Y)$$
$$\mathsf{keys}(\alpha[k].X) = \mathsf{keys}(X) \cup \{k\} \qquad \mathsf{keys}(X\backslash\lambda) = \mathsf{keys}(X)$$

We write $\mathsf{sd}(Y)$ *if* $\mathsf{keys}(Y) = \emptyset$, *i.e.,* Y *is standard. We can convert any* CCSK *process* X *to a standard process* $\mathsf{toStd}(X)$ *by removing all its keys [20].*

Action, Prefix and Restriction

$$\mathsf{sd}(X) \; \dfrac{}{\alpha.X \xrightarrow{\alpha[k]} \alpha[k].X} \; \text{act.} \qquad\qquad k \neq k' \; \dfrac{X \xrightarrow{\beta[k]} X'}{\alpha[k'].X \xrightarrow{\beta[k]} \alpha[k'].X'} \; \text{pre.}$$

$$\alpha \notin \{\lambda, \overline{\lambda}\} \; \dfrac{X \xrightarrow{\alpha[k]} X'}{X \backslash \lambda \xrightarrow{\alpha[k]} X' \backslash \lambda} \; \text{res.}$$

Parallel Group

$$k \notin \mathsf{key}(Y) \; \dfrac{X \xrightarrow{\alpha[k]} X'}{X \mid Y \xrightarrow{\alpha[k]} X' \mid Y} \; |_{\mathrm{L}} \qquad\qquad k \notin \mathsf{key}(X) \; \dfrac{Y \xrightarrow{\alpha[k]} Y'}{X \mid Y \xrightarrow{\alpha[k]} X \mid Y'} \; |_{\mathrm{R}}$$

$$\dfrac{X \xrightarrow{\lambda[k]} X' \quad Y \xrightarrow{\overline{\lambda}[k]} Y'}{X \mid Y \xrightarrow{\tau[k]} X' \mid Y'} \; \text{syn.}$$

Sum Group

$$\mathsf{sd}(Y) \; \dfrac{X \xrightarrow{\alpha[k]} X'}{X + Y \xrightarrow{\alpha[k]} X' + Y} \; +_{\mathrm{L}} \qquad\qquad \mathsf{sd}(X) \; \dfrac{Y \xrightarrow{\alpha[k]} Y'}{X + Y \xrightarrow{\alpha[k]} X + Y'} \; +_{\mathrm{R}}$$

Fig. 2. Forward labelled transition system for CCSK

Definition 2.4 (CCSK LTSes). *The* forward LTS *for CCSK,* $\xrightarrow{\alpha[k]}$*, is given in Fig. 2. The* backward LTS *for CCSK,* $\rightsquigarrow^{\alpha[k]}$*, is defined as the symmetric of* $\xrightarrow{\alpha[k]}$ *[26, Figure 2] [20]. The LTS for CCSK is defined as the union of* $\xrightarrow{\alpha[k]}$ *and* $\rightsquigarrow^{\alpha[k]}$*.*

2.2 Keyed Configuration Structures

We present below *keyed configuration structures*, a variation on *identified configuration structures* [3,4]. Both models are extensions of stable families [11, Definition 12], which are related to stable configuration structures [30, Definition 5.5], completed stable families [34, Section 3.2] and labelled configuration structures [31–33]. How they also relate to e.g., prime event structures and rigid families is discussed in detail in [11, Section 2.2], and they can be proven equivalent to the original definition of event structure [33, Definition 1.1].

While *identified* configuration structures required *every event* to be given an *identifier*, our *keyed* structures simply require *a configuration* to mark its events with *keys*. While keys and identifiers play the exact same role, the important difference is that identified configuration structures could not describe the past and remaining execution at the same time, while keyed configuration structures can. This difference mirrors the difference between RCCS—where memories and actions to be executed are syntactically separate—and CCSK—where past and future actions reside in the same syntax. While it seems trivial that both models are equivalent in terms of expressiveness, we reserve formally proving their correspondence for future work.

Definition 2.5 ((Keyed) Configuration structure). *A* configuration *structure (CS) $\mathcal{C}$ is a tuple (E, C, ℓ) where E is a set of* events *(ranged over by d, e),*

$\ell : E \to L$ is a labelling function and $C \subseteq \mathcal{P}(E)$ is a set of configurations (ranged over by x, y) satisfying:

$$\forall x \in C, \forall e \in x, \exists z \in C \text{ finite}, e \in z, z \subseteq x \qquad \text{(Finiteness)}$$
$$\forall x \in C, \forall d, e \in x, d \neq e \Rightarrow \exists z \in C, z \subseteq x, d \in z \iff e \notin z$$
$$\text{(Coincidence Freeness)}$$
$$\forall X \subseteq C, \exists y \in C \text{ finite}, \forall x \in X, x \subseteq y \Rightarrow \bigcup X \in C \qquad \text{(Finite Completeness)}$$
$$\forall x, y \in C, x \cup y \in C \Rightarrow x \cap y \in C \qquad \text{(Stability)}$$

Given an injective function $\mathsf{x} : x \to \mathsf{K}$ for some $x \in C$, called the key mapping, we write $C \oplus \mathsf{x}$, and say that $\mathcal{K} = (E, C, \ell, \mathsf{x})$ is a keyed configuration structure (KCS) and call C the underlying configuration structure of $\mathcal{K}$.

Other approaches [9,27] use a different model with a similar set of axioms [30]; we conjecture that the differences are mostly stylistic.

Notation. We write $E_\mathcal{C}$, $C_\mathcal{C}$ and $\ell_\mathcal{C}$ for the set of events, of configurations, and for the labelling function of a CS $\mathcal{C}$. We write $\mathbf{0}$ for the empty CS, i.e., with $E = \emptyset$. We write $\mathsf{x}_\emptyset : \emptyset \to \emptyset$ and observe that for all configuration structures $\mathcal{C}$, $\mathcal{C} \oplus \mathsf{x}_\emptyset$ is trivially a KCS, the same way CCSK processes with no keyed prefix are simply CCS processes.

We also write $\mathcal{C}$ for $\mathcal{C} \oplus \mathsf{x}_\emptyset$, and if $\mathsf{x}(e_1) = k_1, \ldots, \mathsf{x}(e_n) = k_n$, we simply write x as $\{e_1 \mapsto k_1, \ldots, e_n \mapsto k_n\}$, assuming that $\{e_1, \ldots, e_n\} \in C_\mathcal{C}$.

3 Operational Correspondence

This section presents operations on KCS, how they are used to give a semantics to CCSK processes, and the operational correspondence between the two models. We start by providing some intuitions on how a CCSK process X is interpreted as a keyed configuration structure $[\![X]\!]$. Consider $\mathcal{C}_1$, $\mathcal{C}_2$ and $\mathcal{C}_3$ in Fig. 3, where directed arrows denote set inclusion. We name the events after their labels, with a subscript if multiple events with the same labels can happen, so that e.g., in $\mathcal{C}_1$, a_1 and a_2 are two events with $\ell(a_1) = \ell(a_2) = a$.

If two events with complementary names as labels can happen at the same time (Fig. 3(c)), then a third event labelled with τ is added. Then we have e.g.,

$$[\![a[k] + a]\!] = \mathcal{C}_1 \oplus \{a_1 \mapsto k\}$$
$$[\![a[k] \mid a[m]]\!] = \mathcal{C}_2 \oplus \{a_1 \mapsto k, a_2 \mapsto m\}$$
$$[\![a[k].b[m] \mid \overline{a}[k]]\!] = \mathcal{C}_3 \oplus \{\tau \mapsto k, b \mapsto m\}$$

with $\{a_1\}$, $\{a_1, a_2\}$ and $\{\tau, b\}$ indeed configurations of respectively $\mathcal{C}_1$, $\mathcal{C}_2$ and $\mathcal{C}_3$.

For simplicity, the keys in the configuration dom (x) will be indicated after the event labels, e.g., as follows for $[\![a[k] \mid a[m]]\!] = \mathcal{C}_2 \oplus \{a_1 \mapsto k, a_2 \mapsto m\}$:

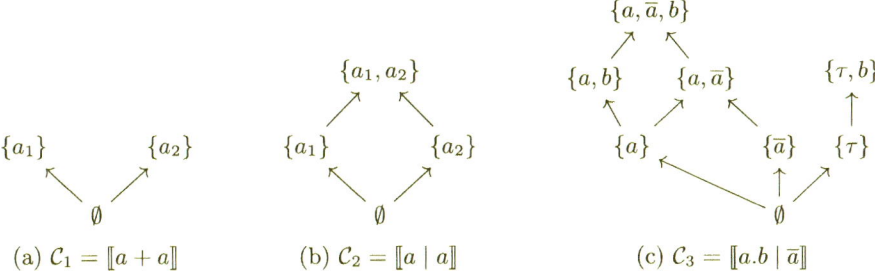

Fig. 3. Examples of configuration structures [3]

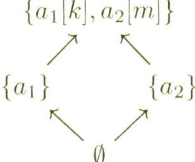

Note that we keep on writing $\{a_1\}$ and $\{a_2\}$, even if the events in those configurations have keys, to indicate that dom (χ) is the configuration containing the events labelled a_1 and a_2. We will also define in Definition 3.4 an operational semantics for KCS, writing e.g., $\{\tau \mapsto k, b \mapsto m\} \overset{b[m]}{\leadsto}_{\mathcal{C}_3} \{\tau \mapsto k\}$ to express that $\mathcal{C}_3$ can backtrack on b and "become" the key mapping $\{\tau \mapsto k\}$ that does not assign any key to b.

3.1 Operations on Keyed Configuration Structures

We define in this section operations on KCS and give intuitions on them. The constructions are standard, except for the keyed part, can be found in previous work [4], and suppose given $\mathcal{K}_i = (E_i, C_i, \ell_i, \chi_i)$, for $i = 1, 2$.

The label prefixing of $\mathcal{K}_1$ by the label a is defined only if $\chi_1 = \chi_\emptyset$, by $a.\mathcal{K}_1 = (E, C, \ell, \chi_\emptyset)$ where, for $e \notin E_1$,

$$E = E_1 \cup \{e\}, \quad C = \{x \mid x = \emptyset \text{ or } \exists x' \in C_1, x = x' \cup e\}, \quad \ell = \ell_1 \cup \{e \mapsto a\}.$$

As an example, we have

$$c. \left(\begin{array}{c} \{a\} \quad \{b\} \\ \nwarrow \quad \nearrow \\ \emptyset \end{array} \right) = \begin{array}{c} \{c,a\} \quad \{c,b\} \\ \nwarrow \quad \nearrow \\ \{c\} \\ \uparrow \\ \emptyset \end{array}$$

The keyed label prefixing of $\mathcal{K}_1$ by the label a and key k is defined by $a[k].\mathcal{K}_1 = a.\mathcal{K}_1 \oplus \chi_1 \cup \{e \mapsto k\}$, provided $\chi_1 \cup \{e \mapsto k\}$ is injective.

As an example, we have

$$c[k] \cdot \left(\begin{array}{ccc} \{a[m]\} & & \{b\} \\ \nwarrow & & \nearrow \\ & \emptyset & \end{array} \right) = \begin{array}{ccc} \{c[k], a[m]\} & & \{c, b\} \\ \nwarrow & & \nearrow \\ & \{c\} & \\ & \uparrow & \\ & \emptyset & \end{array}$$

The restriction by a set of labels L' is denoted $\mathcal{K}_1 \!\upharpoonright_{L'}$ and consists in *removing* events with labels in L' from the set of events and from the configurations of $\mathcal{K}_1$.[1] The labelling and key mappings are then restricted accordingly.

The nondeterministic choice of $\mathcal{K}_1$ and $\mathcal{K}_2$ is defined only if $x_1 = x_\emptyset$ (in which case we let $j = 2$ below) or $x_2 = x_\emptyset$ (in which case we let $j = 1$ below), by $\mathcal{K}_1 + \mathcal{K}_2 = (E, C, \ell, x)$, where, with $\pi_1 : E \to \{1, 2\}$ and $\pi_2 : E \to E_1 \cup E_2$,

$$E = \{\{1\} \times E_1\} \cup \{\{2\} \times E_2\}, \qquad \ell(e) = \ell_i(\pi_2(e)) \text{ for } \pi_1(e) = i,$$

$$C = \{\{i\} \times x \mid x \in C_i\}, \qquad x(e) = \begin{cases} x_j(\pi_2(e)) & \text{if it is defined,} \\ \text{undefined} & \text{otherwise.} \end{cases}$$

We have $C \subseteq \mathcal{P}(E)$ above by seeing $(i, \{e_1, \ldots, e_n\})$ as isomorphic to $\{(i, e_1), \ldots, (i, e_n)\}$.

Although "tagging" the events with 1 or 2 is needed to define the choice properly, we will omit this extra information when discussing this construction, as we can always simplify as follows[2]:

$$\begin{array}{cc} \{b,c\} & \\ \uparrow & \\ \{a[k]\} & \{b\} \\ \uparrow & + \uparrow \\ \emptyset & \emptyset \end{array} = \begin{array}{ccc} & \{(2,b),(2,c)\} & \\ & \uparrow & \\ \{(1,a)[k]\} & & \{(2,b)\} \\ \nwarrow & & \nearrow \\ & \emptyset & \end{array} = \begin{array}{ccc} & \{b,c\} & \\ & \uparrow & \\ \{a[k]\} & & \{b\} \\ \nwarrow & & \nearrow \\ & \emptyset & \end{array}$$

The parallel composition of $\mathcal{K}_1$ and $\mathcal{K}_2$ is $\mathcal{K}_1 \mid \mathcal{K}_2$, and is defined on top of the parallel composition on configuration structures, itself defined in term of categorical product, re-labelling (both omitted here) and restriction. The complete description can be found e.g., in [4, Appendix C.1], we exemplify it below and focus on the construction of the key mapping, which is new.

---

[1] Here we are using restriction as in CCS, in contrast to restriction of functions $f\!\upharpoonright_C$ defined earlier.

[2] Remembering that we additionally use subscripts to differentiate between events with the same label.

Suppose we want to compute
$$\begin{array}{cc} \{a[k], b\} & \{c[m], \bar{a}[k]\} \\ \uparrow & \uparrow \\ \{a[k]\} & | & \{c[m]\} \\ \uparrow & \uparrow \\ \emptyset & \emptyset \end{array}.$$

The first steps are to make the partial product of all pairs of events, using $\star$ to denote "undefined", and then to relabel the pairs of events:

- using the label of the given element if there is only one,
- using τ if the labels of the elements are complementary,
- using a special label $\bot$ otherwise, to mark pairs that need to be discarded.

One then gets:
Event	$(a,\star)$	$(b,\star)$	$(\star,c)$	$(\star,\bar{a})$	(a,c)	$(a,\bar{a})$	(b,c)	$(b,\bar{a})$
Updated label	a	b	c	$\bar{a}$	$\bot$	τ	$\bot$	$\bot$

Computing the new key mapping χ on the non-$\bot$ events then is as follows:

$$\chi(e) = \begin{cases} \chi_1(\pi_1(e)) & \text{if } \chi_1(\pi_1(e)) = \chi_2(\pi_2(e)) \text{ are both defined} \quad (1a) \\ \chi_i(\pi_i(e)) & \text{if } \chi_i(\pi_i(e)) \text{ is defined}, \pi_j(e) = \star, \chi_i(\pi_i(e)) \notin \text{img}(\chi_j), \\ & \text{and } i \neq j \in \{1,2\} \quad (1b) \\ \text{undefined} & \text{otherwise}. \quad (1c) \end{cases}$$

And one obtains that none of the events have a key by (1c), except for

$$\chi(a, \bar{a}) = k \qquad \text{By (1a)} \qquad \chi(\star, c) = m \qquad \text{By (1b)}$$

Importantly, the events labelled a and $\bar{a}$ are not assigned a key, because of the last condition in (1b): the key they were using is now used by the synchronisation event.

Constructing the configurations requires to obey some equations guaranteeing that the universal product is used, and gives the following:

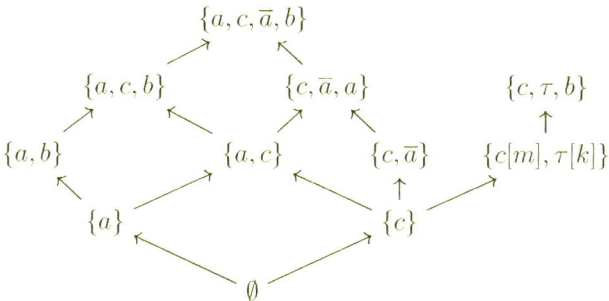

This corresponds to the encoding of $a[k].b \mid c[m].\bar{a}[k]$, where the synchronisation (e.g., the event labelled τ) occurred, but no event labelled a or $\bar{a}$ should be given a key, considering that they did not happen independently.

A possible procedure to compute the new key mapping is as follows:

- First, compute the keys of the events that are actual pairs of events, e.g.,

$$x(a[k], \bar{a}[k]) = k \quad x(a[k], \bar{a}) = \text{undef.} \quad x(a, \bar{a}[k]) = \text{undef.} \quad x(a, \bar{a}) = \text{undef.}$$

- Then, compute the keys of the events where one element is $\star$, e.g.,

$$x(a[k], \star) = \begin{cases} k & \text{if } k \notin \text{dom}(x_2), \\ \text{undef.} & \text{otherwise} \end{cases} \qquad x(a, \star) = \text{undef.}$$

$$x(\star, \bar{a}[k]) = \begin{cases} k & \text{if } k \notin \text{dom}(x_1), \\ \text{undef.} & \text{otherwise} \end{cases} \qquad x(\star, \bar{a}) = \text{undef.}$$

This set of conditions ensures that if $(a[k], \bar{a}[k])$, $(a[k], \star)$ and $(\star, \bar{a}[k])$ are three events in the composition, then only the first gets assigned the key k, as only the event labelled τ "actually occurred".

We now have all the elements to extend the original encoding of CCS processes into CS [35] to represent CCSK processes as KCS:

Definition 3.1 (Encoding a CCSK process). *Given a CCSK process X, its encoding $[\![X]\!]$ as a KCS is built by induction on the process:*

$$[\![X + Y]\!] = [\![X]\!] + [\![Y]\!] \qquad [\![X \mid Y]\!] = [\![X]\!] \mid [\![Y]\!] \qquad [\![X \backslash a]\!] = [\![X]\!] 1_{\{a, \bar{a}\}}$$
$$[\![\alpha.P]\!] = \alpha.[\![P]\!] \qquad [\![\alpha[k].X]\!] = \alpha[k].[\![X]\!] \qquad [\![0]\!] = 0$$

3.2 Operational Semantics

We first define an operational semantics for configuration structures (CS) and keyed configuration structures (KCS).

Definition 3.2 (Forward and backward execution of CS). *Given a configuration structure $\mathcal{C}$ and $x, y \in C_{\mathcal{C}}$ we write $x \xrightarrow{\alpha}_{\mathcal{C}} y$ and $y \rightsquigarrow_{\mathcal{C}} x$ (or simply $x \xrightarrow{\alpha} y$ and $y \rightsquigarrow x$) if there exists $e \in y$ such that $\ell(e) = \alpha$, $e \notin x$ and $y = x \cup \{e\}$.*

Definition 3.3 (Set of key mappings). *Let $\mathcal{C}$ be a configuration structure. We let $K_{\mathcal{C}}$ denote the set of all key mappings of $\mathcal{C}$, i.e., injective functions x such that $\text{dom}(x) = x$ for some $x \in C_{\mathcal{C}}$ and $\text{img}(x) \subset K$.*

Definition 3.4 (Forward and backward execution of KCS). *Given a configuration structure $\mathcal{C}$, and key mappings $x, x' \in K_{\mathcal{C}}$, we write $x \xrightarrow{\alpha[k]}_{\mathcal{C}} x'$ and $x' \xrightsquigarrow{\alpha[k]}_{\mathcal{C}} x$ if*

- *$\text{dom}(x) \xrightarrow{\alpha} \text{dom}(x')$ and,*
- *letting $e = \text{dom}(x') \setminus \text{dom}(x)$, we have $x' = x \cup \{e \mapsto k\}$.*

We shall omit the subscript $\mathcal{C}$ in $x \xrightarrow{\alpha[k]}_{\mathcal{C}} x'$.

This way, when proving the operational correspondence as we do below, we can leave $[\![\mathsf{toStd}(X)]\!]$ as an invariant and simply focus on the key mapping getting extended or restricted per need.

Lemma 3.5 (Operational correspondence). *For all reachable* CCSK *processes X,*

- *if $X \xrightarrow{\alpha[k]} X'$ then $[\![X]\!] \xrightarrow{\alpha[k]} [\![X']\!]$,*
- *if $X \rightsquigarrow^{\alpha[k]} X'$ then $[\![X]\!] \rightsquigarrow^{\alpha[k]} [\![X']\!]$,*
- *if $[\![X]\!] \xrightarrow{\alpha[k]} x'$ then $\exists X'.\ X \xrightarrow{\alpha[k]} X'$ and $[\![X']\!] = x'$,*
- *if $[\![X]\!] \rightsquigarrow^{\alpha[k]} x'$ then $\exists X'.\ X \rightsquigarrow^{\alpha[k]} X'$ and $[\![X']\!] = x'$.*

The operational correspondence between RCCS and identified structures [3, Lemma 19] requires a notion of maximal event and lemmas proving that the maximality is preserved by various operations. For this set-up, the argument is a bit simpler:

- For Lemma 3.5, the key argument is to note that there must exist $e \in E_{[\![\mathsf{toStd}(X)]\!]}$ with $\ell(e) = \alpha$ such that $\mathrm{dom}\left(\mathsf{x}_{[\![X]\!]}\right) \cup e \in C_{[\![\mathsf{toStd}(X)]\!]}$. If multiple such events exist, then tracking down the event matching X's transition is done by induction on the transition derivation. Extending $\mathsf{x}_{[\![X]\!]}$ with $e \mapsto k$ then gives $\mathsf{x}_{[\![X']\!]}$.
- Proving Lemma 3.5 is similar, except that $\mathsf{x}_{[\![X']\!]}$ is obtained by restricting $\mathsf{x}_{[\![X]\!]}$ to a sub-configuration not containing the matching event with label α.
- For Lemma 3.5, one must leverage the fact that $\mathrm{dom}(\mathsf{x}') \setminus \mathrm{dom}\left(\mathsf{x}_{[\![X]\!]}\right)$ must be an event corresponding to a prefix or pair of prefixes, if $\alpha = \tau$, that can be triggered in X. Executing it or them, with the same key as decided in the KCS, gives the required process X'.
- Finally, Lemma 3.5 uses a similar reasoning, as "going down" in the KCS corresponds to undoing a prefix or a pair of prefixes in X.

Definition 3.6 (Causality and maximality [30]). *For all C, $x \in C$ and $d, e \in x$, we let*

$$d \leqslant_x e \iff \forall y \in C \text{ with } y \subseteq x, e \in y \Rightarrow d \in y$$
$$d <_x e \iff d \leqslant_x e \text{ and } d \neq e \qquad \text{(Causality relation on } x\text{)}$$

This last definition is required for Definition 4.1, which in turn is required to define Hereditary History-Preserving Bisimulation.

4 Bisimilarities on Configuration Structures and CCSK

In this section we define hereditary history-preserving (HHP) and history-preserving (HP) bisimulations on both configuration structures and on CCSK. Correspondingly, we present several of their characterisations, including a new forward-backward (FB) bisimulation, all of which purely use forward and backward labelled transitions, and no bijections or mention of ordering.

4.1 Hereditary History-Preserving Bisimulation

We define forward-reverse (FR) and back and forth (BF) bisimulations on configuration structures and show them equivalent to HHP bisimulation (Theorem 4.8). We then show that FR and BF bisimulation on standard CCSK processes are equivalent to HHP on the corresponding KCS (Theorem 4.15).

Notation. *When discussing bisimulations between configuration structures $\mathcal{C}$ and $\mathcal{D}$:*

- *we let x, x' (resp. y, y') range over configurations of $\mathcal{C}$ (resp. $\mathcal{D}$);*
- *we let x, x' (resp. y, y') range over key mappings of $\mathcal{C}$ (resp. $\mathcal{D}$);*

We also write $f\backslash\{e \mapsto e'\}$ for the function defined only if $f(e) = e'$ as f everywhere except on e, where it is undefined.

The following uses the definition of order on events from Definition 3.6.

Definition 4.1 (Label- and order-preserving bijection). *Given configurations $x \in \mathcal{C}$, $y \in \mathcal{D}$, a bijection $f : x \to y$ is label preserving if $\ell_{\mathcal{C}}(e) = \ell_{\mathcal{D}}(f(e))$ for all $e \in x$, and is order preserving if $d \leq_x e \iff f(d) \leq_y f(e)$ for all $d, e \in x$. We say that f is l&o-p if it is label preserving and order preserving.*

Definition 4.2 (HHP on CS [7]). *Let $\mathcal{C}$, $\mathcal{D}$ be configuration structures. A relation $\mathcal{R} \subseteq C_{\mathcal{C}} \times C_{\mathcal{D}} \times (E_{\mathcal{C}} \rightharpoonup E_{\mathcal{D}})$ is a hereditary history-preserving (HHP) bisimulation between $\mathcal{C}$ and $\mathcal{D}$ if $\mathcal{R}(\emptyset_{\mathcal{C}}, \emptyset_{\mathcal{D}}, \emptyset)$ and whenever $\mathcal{R}(x, y, f)$ then f is an l&o-p bijection between x and y and*

- *if $x \xrightarrow{e} x'$ then $\exists y'.\ y \xrightarrow{e'} y'$ and $\mathcal{R}(x', y', f')$, where $f' = f \cup \{e \mapsto e'\}$;*
- *if $y \xrightarrow{e'} y'$ then $\exists x'.\ x \xrightarrow{e} x'$ and $\mathcal{R}(x', y', f')$, where $f' = f \cup \{e \mapsto e'\}$;*
- *if $x \overset{e}{\rightsquigarrow} x'$ then $\exists y'.\ y \overset{e'}{\rightsquigarrow} y'$ and $\mathcal{R}(x', y', f')$, where $f' = f\backslash\{e \mapsto e'\}$;*
- *if $y \overset{e'}{\rightsquigarrow} y'$ then $\exists x'.\ x \overset{e}{\rightsquigarrow} x'$ and $\mathcal{R}(x', y', f')$, where $f' = f\backslash\{e \mapsto e'\}$.*

We say that $\mathcal{R}$ is an HHP bisimulation between x and y if there exists f such that $\mathcal{R}(x, y, f)$ is an HHP bisimulation. We write that x and y are HHP bisimilar ($x \sim_{\mathsf{HHP}} y$) if there is an HHP bisimulation between x and y. We write that $\mathcal{C}$ and $\mathcal{D}$ are HHP bisimilar ($\mathcal{C} \sim_{\mathsf{HHP}} \mathcal{D}$) if there exists an HHP bisimulation between $\emptyset_{\mathcal{C}}$ and $\emptyset_{\mathcal{D}}$.

Definition 4.3 (RI-IB on CS [25,27]). *Let $\mathcal{C}$, $\mathcal{D}$ be configuration structures. A relation $\mathcal{R} \subseteq C_{\mathcal{C}} \times C_{\mathcal{D}}$ is a reverse interleaving-interleaving bisimulation (RI-IB) if whenever $\mathcal{R}(x, y)$ then*

- *if $x \xrightarrow{\alpha} x'$ then $\exists y'.\ y \xrightarrow{\alpha} y'$ and $\mathcal{R}(x', y')$;*
- *if $y \xrightarrow{\alpha} y'$ then $\exists x'.\ x \xrightarrow{\alpha} x'$ and $\mathcal{R}(x', y')$;*
- *if $x \overset{\alpha}{\rightsquigarrow} x'$ then $\exists y'.\ y \overset{\alpha}{\rightsquigarrow} y'$ and $\mathcal{R}(x', y')$;*
- *if $y \overset{\alpha}{\rightsquigarrow} y'$ then $\exists x'.\ x \overset{\alpha}{\rightsquigarrow} x'$ and $\mathcal{R}(x', y')$.*

We say that $\mathcal{R}$ is an RI-IB between x and y if $\mathcal{R}$ is an RI-IB and $\mathcal{R}(x, y)$. We say $x \sim_{\mathsf{RI-IB}} y$ if there is an RI-IB between x and y. We say $\mathcal{C} \sim_{\mathsf{RI-IB}} \mathcal{D}$ if there is an RI-IB between $\emptyset_{\mathcal{C}}$ and $\emptyset_{\mathcal{D}}$.

In fact $\sim_{\text{RI-IB}}$ is strictly coarser than $\sim_{\text{HHP}}$, although the equivalences coincide in the absence of "equidepth auto-concurrency", which is where two events with the same label can occur at the same depth in the same configuration [27, Thm. 9.7]. Note that e.g., $\sim_{\text{HHP}}$ distinguishes configuration structures corresponding to $a.a$ and $a \mid a$, while $\sim_{\text{RI-IB}}$ does not. This was pointed out in [25] in the context of prime event structures ($\sim_{\text{RI-IB}}$ was there called "FR bisimulation"). We therefore adapt $\sim_{\text{RI-IB}}$ to use keys as follows:

Definition 4.4 (FR on CS [25,26]). *Let $\mathcal{C}, \mathcal{D}$ be configuration structures. A relation $\mathcal{R} \subseteq K_\mathcal{C} \times K_\mathcal{D}$ is a* forward-reverse (FR) *bisimulation if whenever $\mathcal{R}(x,y)$ then*

- *if $x \xrightarrow{\alpha[i]} x'$ then $\exists y'$. $y \xrightarrow{\alpha[i]} y'$ and $\mathcal{R}(x',y')$;*
- *if $y \xrightarrow{\alpha[i]} y'$ then $\exists x'$. $x \xrightarrow{\alpha[i]} x'$ and $\mathcal{R}(x',y')$;*
- *if $x \xleftarrow{\alpha[i]} x'$ then $\exists y'$. $y \xleftarrow{\alpha[i]} y'$ and $\mathcal{R}(x',y')$;*
- *if $y \xleftarrow{\alpha[i]} y'$ then $\exists x'$. $x \xleftarrow{\alpha[i]} x'$ and $\mathcal{R}(x',y')$.*

We say that $\mathcal{R}$ is an FR bisimulation between x and y if $\mathcal{R}$ is an FR bisimulation and $\mathcal{R}(x,y)$. We say $x \sim_{\text{FR}} y$ if there is an FR bisimulation between x and y. We say $\mathcal{C} \sim_{\text{FR}} \mathcal{D}$ if there is an FR bisimulation between $\emptyset_\mathcal{C}$ and $\emptyset_\mathcal{D}$.

We can relax the condition in FR bisimulation that keys must match as well as labels to get the following.

Definition 4.5 (BF on CS [3, Definition 24]). *Let $\mathcal{C}, \mathcal{D}$ be configuration structures. A relation $\mathcal{R} \subseteq K_\mathcal{C} \times K_\mathcal{D} \times (K \rightharpoonup K)$ is a* back and forth (BF) *bisimulation if whenever $\mathcal{R}(x,y,f)$ then f is a bijection between $\text{img}(x)$ and $\text{img}(y)$, and*

- *if $x \xrightarrow{\alpha[i]} x'$ then $\exists y',j$. $y \xrightarrow{\alpha[j]} y'$ and $\mathcal{R}(x',y',f')$, where $f' = f \cup \{i \mapsto j\}$;*
- *if $y \xrightarrow{\alpha[j]} y'$ then $\exists x',i$. $x \xrightarrow{\alpha[i]} x'$ and $\mathcal{R}(x',y',f')$, where $f' = f \cup \{i \mapsto j\}$;*
- *if $x \xleftarrow{\alpha[i]} x'$ then $\exists y'$. $y \xleftarrow{\alpha[f(i)]} y'$ and $\mathcal{R}(x',y',f')$, where $f' = f \setminus \{i \mapsto f(i)\}$;*
- *if $y \xleftarrow{\alpha[f(i)]} y'$ then $\exists x'$. $x \xleftarrow{\alpha[i]} x'$ and $\mathcal{R}(x',y',f')$, where $f' = f \setminus \{i \mapsto f(i)\}$.*

We say that $\mathcal{R}$ is a BF bisimulation between x and y if $\mathcal{R}$ is a BF bisimulation and there is a bijection f such that $\mathcal{R}(x,y,f)$. We say $x \sim_{\text{BF}} y$ if there is a BF bisimulation between x and y. We say $\mathcal{C} \sim_{\text{BF}} \mathcal{D}$ if there is a BF bisimulation between $\emptyset_\mathcal{C}$ and $\emptyset_\mathcal{D}$.

Next we show that key mappings related by FR and BF bisimulations naturally give rise to l&o-p bijections, which will help us in showing correspondence with HHP bisimulation.

Lemma 4.6. *Let $\mathcal{C}, \mathcal{D}$ be configuration structures, and $\mathcal{R}$ be an FR bisimulation between them. For any x, y, if $\mathcal{R}(x,y)$ then $y^{-1} \circ x$ is an l&o-p bijection.*

Lemma 4.7. *Let $\mathcal{C}, \mathcal{D}$ be configuration structures, and $\mathcal{R}$ be a BF bisimulation between them. For any x, y, f, if $\mathcal{R}(x,y,f)$ then $y^{-1} \circ f \circ x$ is an l&o-p bijection.*

Theorem 4.8. *Let $\mathcal{C}, \mathcal{D}$ be configuration structures. Then the following are equivalent:*

1. $\mathcal{C} \sim_{\mathsf{HHP}} \mathcal{D}$;   2. $\mathcal{C} \sim_{\mathsf{FR}} \mathcal{D}$;   3. $\mathcal{C} \sim_{\mathsf{BF}} \mathcal{D}$.

Proof (sketch). We show (1) $\Rightarrow$ (2), (2) $\Rightarrow$ (3) and (3) $\Rightarrow$ (1) applying Lemma 4.6 and Lemma 4.7. We define a new bisimulation $\mathcal{R}'$ for each implication as follows:

- (1) $\Rightarrow$ (2) Let $\mathcal{R}$ be an HHP bisimulation between $\mathcal{C}$ and $\mathcal{D}$. Let

$$\mathcal{R}' = \{(\mathsf{x}, \mathsf{y}) : \exists x, y, f.\ \mathcal{R}(x, y, f),\ \mathrm{dom}\,(\mathsf{x}) = x,\ \mathrm{dom}\,(\mathsf{y}) = y,\ f = y^{-1} \circ x\}$$

- (2) $\Rightarrow$ (3) Let $\mathcal{R}$ be an FR bisimulation between $\mathcal{C}$ and $\mathcal{D}$. Let

$$\mathcal{R}' = \{(\mathsf{x}, \mathsf{y}, \mathrm{id}_{\mathrm{img}(\mathsf{x})}) : \mathcal{R}(\mathsf{x}, \mathsf{y})\}$$

- (3) $\Rightarrow$ (1) Let $\mathcal{R}$ be a BF bisimulation between $\mathcal{C}$ and $\mathcal{D}$. Let

$$\mathcal{R}' = \{(\mathrm{dom}\,(\mathsf{x}), \mathrm{dom}\,(\mathsf{y}), y^{-1} \circ f \circ x) : \mathcal{R}(\mathsf{x}, \mathsf{y}, f)\}$$

We show that $\mathcal{R}'$ is an FR, BF and HHP bisimulation respectively. □

We can define FR and BF on (reachable) CCSK processes:

Definition 4.9 (FR on CCSK [25,26]). *Let X, Y etc,. range over CCSK processes. A relation $\mathcal{R}$ is a* forward-reverse (FR) *bisimulation if whenever $\mathcal{R}(X, Y)$ then*

- *if $X \xrightarrow{\alpha[i]} X'$ then $\exists Y'.\ Y \xrightarrow{\alpha[i]} Y'$ and $\mathcal{R}(X', Y')$;*
- *if $Y \xrightarrow{\alpha[i]} Y'$ then $\exists X'.\ X \xrightarrow{\alpha[i]} X'$ and $\mathcal{R}(X', Y')$;*
- *if $X \rightsquigarrow^{\alpha[i]} X'$ then $\exists Y'.\ Y \rightsquigarrow^{\alpha[i]} Y'$ and $\mathcal{R}(X', Y')$;*
- *if $Y \rightsquigarrow^{\alpha[i]} Y'$ then $\exists X'.\ X \rightsquigarrow^{\alpha[i]} X'$ and $\mathcal{R}(X', Y')$.*

We say that $\mathcal{R}$ is an FR bisimulation between X and Y if $\mathcal{R}$ is an FR bisimulation and $\mathcal{R}(X, Y)$. We say $X \sim_{\mathsf{FR}} Y$ if there is an FR bisimulation between X and Y.

Definition 4.10 (BF on CCSK [3, Definition 24]). *Let X, Y etc,. range over CCSK processes. A relation $\mathcal{R}$ is a* back and forth (BF) *bisimulation if whenever $\mathcal{R}(X, Y, f)$ then f is a bijection between $\mathsf{keys}(X)$ and $\mathsf{keys}(Y)$, and*

- *if $X \xrightarrow{\alpha[i]} X'$ then $\exists Y', j.\ Y \xrightarrow{\alpha[j]} Y'$ and $\mathcal{R}(X', Y', f')$, with $f' = f \cup \{i \mapsto j\}$;*
- *if $Y \xrightarrow{\alpha[j]} Y'$ then $\exists X', i.\ X \xrightarrow{\alpha[i]} X'$ and $\mathcal{R}(X', Y', f')$, with $f' = f \cup \{i \mapsto j\}$;*
- *if $X \rightsquigarrow^{\alpha[i]} X'$ then $\exists Y'.\ Y \rightsquigarrow^{\alpha[f(i)]} Y'$ and $\mathcal{R}(X', Y', f')$, with $f' = f \setminus \{i \mapsto f(i)\}$;*
- *if $Y \rightsquigarrow^{\alpha[f(i)]} Y'$ then $\exists X'.\ X \rightsquigarrow^{\alpha[i]} X'$ and $\mathcal{R}(X', Y', f')$, with $f' = f \setminus \{i \mapsto f(i)\}$.*

We say that $\mathcal{R}$ is a BF bisimulation between X and Y if $\mathcal{R}$ is a BF bisimulation and there is a mapping f such that $\mathcal{R}(X, Y, f)$. We say $X \sim_{\mathsf{BF}} Y$ if there is a BF bisimulation between X and Y.

Proposition 4.11. *If $X \sim_{\mathsf{FR}} Y$ then $X \sim_{\mathsf{BF}} Y$.*

Proof. Let $\mathcal{R}$ be an FR bisimulation between X and Y. Then for any X, Y, if $\mathcal{R}(X, Y)$ then $\mathsf{keys}(X) = \mathsf{keys}(Y)$ [20]. Let $\mathcal{R}' = \{(X, Y, \mathsf{id}_{\mathsf{keys}(X)}) : \mathcal{R}(X, Y)\}$. Then $\mathcal{R}'$ is a BF bisimulation between X and Y, by reasoning similar to the proof of Theorem 4.8. □

Example 4.12. The converse of Proposition 4.11 does not hold: if $i \neq j$ then we have $a[i] \sim_{\mathsf{BF}} a[j]$, but not $a[i] \sim_{\mathsf{FR}} a[j]$.

Next we show that encoding of standard CCSK processes into configuration structures preserves FR and BF bisimulations, which is crucial in proving Theorem 4.15. Let P and Q be standard CCSK processes.

Lemma 4.13. $P \sim_{\mathsf{FR}} Q$ *iff* $[\![P]\!] \sim_{\mathsf{FR}} [\![Q]\!]$.

Lemma 4.14. $P \sim_{\mathsf{BF}} Q$ *iff* $[\![P]\!] \sim_{\mathsf{BF}} [\![Q]\!]$.

Theorem 4.15. *The following are equivalent:*

- $P \sim_{\mathsf{FR}} Q$
- $P \sim_{\mathsf{BF}} Q$
- $[\![P]\!] \sim_{\mathsf{FR}} [\![Q]\!]$
- $[\![P]\!] \sim_{\mathsf{BF}} [\![Q]\!]$
- $[\![P]\!] \sim_{\mathsf{HHP}} [\![Q]\!]$

Proof. By Lemma 4.13, Lemma 4.14 and Theorem 4.8. □

We note that a variant of HHP bisimulation was defined on RCCS [3, Definition 28] which used identifiers and transitions of the form $x \xrightarrow{e,i} y$.

4.2 History-Preserving Bisimulation and Forward-Backward Bisimulation

We define FB bisimulation, a coarser form of FR bisimulation, on configuration structures and show it equivalent to HP bisimulation (Theorem 4.22). Then we show that FB bisimulation on standard CCSK processes is equivalent to HP on the corresponding KCS (Theorem 4.29).

Definition 4.16 (HP on CS). *Let $\mathcal{C}, \mathcal{D}$ be configuration structures. A relation $\mathcal{R} \subseteq C_{\mathcal{C}} \times C_{\mathcal{D}} \times (E_{\mathcal{C}} \rightharpoonup E_{\mathcal{D}})$ is a history-preserving (HP) bisimulation between $\mathcal{C}$ and $\mathcal{D}$ if $\mathcal{R}(\emptyset, \emptyset, \emptyset)$ and whenever $\mathcal{R}(x, y, f)$ then f is an l&o-p bijection between x and y and*

- *if $x \xrightarrow{e} x'$ then $\exists y'. \ y \xrightarrow{e'} y'$ and $\mathcal{R}(x', y', f')$, where $f' = f \cup \{e \mapsto e'\}$;*
- *if $y \xrightarrow{e'} y'$ then $\exists x'. \ x \xrightarrow{e} x'$ and $\mathcal{R}(x', y', f')$, where $f' = f \cup \{e \mapsto e'\}$.*

We write that $\mathcal{C}$ and $\mathcal{D}$ are HP bisimilar ($\mathcal{C} \sim_{\mathsf{HP}} \mathcal{D}$) if there exists an HP bisimulation between them.

Clearly, if $\mathcal{C} \sim_{\mathsf{HHP}} \mathcal{D}$ then $\mathcal{C} \sim_{\mathsf{HP}} \mathcal{D}$. However the converse does not hold.

Example 4.17 (Absorption Law [10,30]). Let $\mathcal{C}$ be a configuration structure corresponding to $(b \mid (a+c)) + (a \mid b) + ((b+c) \mid a)$, and let $\mathcal{D}$ be a configuration structure corresponding to $(b \mid (a+c)) + ((b+c) \mid a)$. Then clearly $\mathcal{C} \sim_{\mathsf{HP}} \mathcal{D}$. However, $\mathcal{C} \sim_{\mathsf{HHP}} \mathcal{D}$ fails because after performing a, b in $a \mid b$ of $\mathcal{C}$, which must be matched by a, b in $b \mid (a+c)$ of $\mathcal{D}$, we can reverse a in both configuration structures, but then we can only do c in $\mathcal{D}$ and not in $\mathcal{C}$.

Definition 4.18 (B on CS). *Let $\mathcal{C}, \mathcal{D}$ be configuration structures. A relation $\mathcal{R} \subseteq K_\mathcal{C} \times K_\mathcal{D}$ is a backward (B) bisimulation if whenever $\mathcal{R}(x, y)$ then*

- *if $x \overset{\alpha[i]}{\rightsquigarrow} x'$ then $\exists y'. \ y \overset{\alpha[i]}{\rightsquigarrow} y'$ and $\mathcal{R}(x', y')$;*
- *if $y \overset{\alpha[i]}{\rightsquigarrow} y'$ then $\exists x'. \ x \overset{\alpha[i]}{\rightsquigarrow} x'$ and $\mathcal{R}(x', y')$.*

We say that $\mathcal{R}$ is a B bisimulation between x and y if $\mathcal{R}$ is a B bisimulation and $\mathcal{R}(x, y)$. We say $x \sim_{\mathsf{B}} y$ if there is a B bisimulation between x and y.

Definition 4.19 (F on CS). *Let $\mathcal{C}, \mathcal{D}$ be configuration structures. A relation $\mathcal{R} \subseteq K_\mathcal{C} \times K_\mathcal{D}$ is a forward (F) bisimulation if whenever $\mathcal{R}(x, y)$ then*

- *if $x \xrightarrow{\alpha[i]} x'$ then $\exists y'. \ y \xrightarrow{\alpha[i]} y'$ and $\mathcal{R}(x', y')$;*
- *if $y \xrightarrow{\alpha[i]} y'$ then $\exists x'. \ x \xrightarrow{\alpha[i]} x'$ and $\mathcal{R}(x', y')$.*

We say that $\mathcal{R}$ is an F bisimulation between x and y if $\mathcal{R}$ is an F bisimulation and $\mathcal{R}(x, y)$. We say $x \sim_{\mathsf{F}} y$ if there is an F bisimulation between x and y. We say $\mathcal{C} \sim_{\mathsf{F}} \mathcal{D}$ if there is an F bisimulation between $\emptyset_\mathcal{C}$ and $\emptyset_\mathcal{D}$.

Definition 4.20 (FB on CS). *Let $\mathcal{C}, \mathcal{D}$ be configuration structures. $\mathcal{R} \subseteq K_\mathcal{C} \times K_\mathcal{D}$ is a Forward-Backward (FB) bisimulation if*

- *$\mathcal{R}$ is an F bisimulation;*
- *$\mathcal{R} \subseteq \sim_{\mathsf{B}}$.*

We say that $\mathcal{R}$ is an FB bisimulation between x and y if $\mathcal{R}$ is an FB bisimulation and $\mathcal{R}(x, y)$. We say $x \sim_{\mathsf{FB}} y$ if there is an FB bisimulation between x and y. We say $\mathcal{C} \sim_{\mathsf{FB}} \mathcal{D}$ if there is an FB bisimulation between $\emptyset_\mathcal{C}$ and $\emptyset_\mathcal{D}$.

Note that if in Definition 4.20 we replaced '$\mathcal{R} \subseteq \sim_{\mathsf{B}}$' by '$\mathcal{R}$ is a backward bisimulation' then we would have the (stronger) FR bisimulation. See Example 4.26 for an example of FB bisimulation applied to CCSK.

Proposition 4.21. *Let $\mathcal{C}$, $\mathcal{D}$ be configuration structures. Then*

- *If $x \sim_{FR} y$ then $x \sim_{FB} y$;*
- *If $x \sim_{FB} y$ then $x \sim_F y$ and $x \sim_B y$.*

Proof.
- Any FR bisimulation is both a forward bisimulation and a backward bisimulation. Hence, it is an FB bisimulation.
- Any FB bisimulation is both a forward bisimulation and included in $\sim_B$. □

Theorem 4.22. *Let $\mathcal{C}$, $\mathcal{D}$ be configuration structures. Then $\mathcal{C} \sim_{HP} \mathcal{D}$ iff $\mathcal{C} \sim_{FB} \mathcal{D}$.*

Proof (sketch). ($\Rightarrow$) Suppose $\mathcal{R}$ is an HP bisimulation between $\mathcal{C}$ and $\mathcal{D}$. Let

$$\mathcal{R}' = \{(x,y) : \exists f.\ \mathcal{R}(\mathrm{dom}\,(x), \mathrm{dom}\,(y), f),\ x = y \circ f\}$$

We show that $\mathcal{R}'$ is an FB bisimulation between $\mathcal{C}$ and $\mathcal{D}$.
($\Leftarrow$) Suppose $\mathcal{R}$ is an FB bisimulation between $\mathcal{C}$ and $\mathcal{D}$. Let

$$\mathcal{R}' = \{(\mathrm{dom}\,(x), \mathrm{dom}\,(y), y^{-1} \circ x) : \mathcal{R}(x,y)\}$$

We show that $\mathcal{R}'$ is an HP bisimulation between $\mathcal{C}$ and $\mathcal{D}$. □

We can define backward (B), forward (F) and FB bisimulation on CCSK processes:

Definition 4.23 (B for CCSK). *A relation $\mathcal{R}$ is a backward (B) bisimulation if whenever $\mathcal{R}(X,Y)$ then*

- *if $X \xrightarrow{\alpha[i]} X'$ then $\exists Y'.\ Y \xrightarrow{\alpha[i]} Y'$ and $\mathcal{R}(X',Y')$;*
- *if $Y \xrightarrow{\alpha[i]} Y'$ then $\exists X'.\ X \xrightarrow{\alpha[i]} X'$ and $\mathcal{R}(X',Y')$.*

We say that $\mathcal{R}$ is a B bisimulation between X and Y if $\mathcal{R}$ is a B bisimulation and $\mathcal{R}(X,Y)$. We say $X \sim_B Y$ if there is a B bisimulation between X and Y.

Definition 4.24 (F for CCSK). *A relation $\mathcal{R}$ is a forward (F) bisimulation if whenever $\mathcal{R}(X,Y)$ then*

- *if $X \xrightarrow{\alpha[i]} X'$ then $\exists Y'.\ Y \xrightarrow{\alpha[i]} Y'$ and $\mathcal{R}(X',Y')$;*
- *if $Y \xrightarrow{\alpha[i]} Y'$ then $\exists X'.\ X \xrightarrow{\alpha[i]} X'$ and $\mathcal{R}(X',Y')$.*

We say that $\mathcal{R}$ is an F bisimulation between X and Y if $\mathcal{R}$ is an F bisimulation and $\mathcal{R}(X,Y)$. We say $X \sim_F Y$ if there is an F bisimulation between X and Y.

Definition 4.25 (FB for CCSK). *$\mathcal{R}$ is an FB bisimulation if*

- $\mathcal{R}$ is an F bisimulation;
- $\mathcal{R} \subseteq \sim_B$.

The Absorption Law (Example 4.17) gives us an example of CCSK processes which are FB bisimilar but not FR bisimilar.

Example 4.26. Let $P_1 = b \mid (a+c)$, $P_2 = (b+c) \mid a$, $P = P_1 + P_2$ and $Q = P + (a \mid b)$. We have $P \sim_{FB} Q$ but not $P \sim_{FR} Q$. The latter holds by the same reasoning as already given in Example 4.17. As to the former, the interesting cases for the FB bisimulation $\mathcal{R}$ relating P and Q are the extra states available in Q. We have

$$\mathcal{R}(\,(b \mid (a[m]+c)) + P_2,\ P + (a[m] \mid b)\,) \qquad \text{for all } m \in \mathsf{K} \qquad (2)$$
$$\mathcal{R}(\,P_1 + ((b[n]+c) \mid a),\ P + (a \mid b[n])\,) \qquad \text{for all } n \in \mathsf{K} \qquad (3)$$
$$\mathcal{R}(\,(b[n] \mid (a[m]+c)) + P_2,\ P + (a[m] \mid b[n])\,) \qquad \text{for all } m \neq n \in \mathsf{K} \qquad (4)$$
$$\mathcal{R}(\,P_1 + ((b[n]+c) \mid a[m]),\ P + (a[m] \mid b[n])\,) \qquad \text{for all } m \neq n \in \mathsf{K} \qquad (5)$$

If we undo $a[m]$ in (4) we reach a pair of processes which does not belong to $\mathcal{R}$, and which should not belong to $\mathcal{R}$, since $\mathcal{R}$ needs to be an F bisimulation but forward c is possible on the left but not the right. Similarly if we undo $b[n]$ in (5). Thus $\mathcal{R}$ is not a B bisimulation. However, $\mathcal{R} \subseteq \sim_B$; the pairs of processes in (2–5) are easily seen to be B-bisimilar, noting that the pairs of processes reached by undoing $a[m]$ in (4) and undoing $b[n]$ in (5) are B-bisimilar:

$$(b[n] \mid (a+c)) + P_2 \sim_B P + (a \mid b[n]) \qquad \text{for all } n \in \mathsf{K} \qquad (6)$$
$$P_1 + ((b+c) \mid a[m]) \sim_B P + (a[m] \mid b) \qquad \text{for all } m \in \mathsf{K} \qquad (7)$$

Encoding standard CCSK processes into keyed configuration structures preserves B and FB bisimulations. In the following results let P and Q be standard CCSK processes.

Lemma 4.27. $P \sim_B Q$ iff $[\![P]\!] \sim_B [\![Q]\!]$.

Lemma 4.28. $P \sim_{FB} Q$ iff $[\![P]\!] \sim_{FB} [\![Q]\!]$.

Theorem 4.29. *The following are equivalent:*

- $P \sim_{FB} Q$
- $[\![P]\!] \sim_{FB} [\![Q]\!]$
- $[\![P]\!] \sim_{HP} [\![Q]\!]$

Proof. By Lemma 4.28 and Theorem 4.22. □

5 Conclusion

We have shown that HHP and HP bisimulations can be characterised by several different bisimulations, defined purely in terms of forward and backward transitions, and without using bijections or orderings. This confirms a long-standing view that there are benefits in adopting the reversible setting as one of the standard approaches to research concurrency, particularly "true concurrency" relations. We saw in Fig. 1 how our results fit into the hierarchy of equivalences on stable configuration structures established in [27], and how assigning keys to events in addition to reversibility enables us to capture the full true concurrent discriminatory power of HHP equivalence.

It would be fascinating to explore how the ideas and results of this paper can be applied to other reversible models and calculi. In particular, higher-order pi calculus has been given reversible operational semantics [17–19], and one wonders if it would take much effort to propose true concurrency equivalences for reversible higher-order pi based on our ideas.

Another topic worth a study is *congruence* and a suitable notion of *context* in the reversible setting. Initial ideas and results have been given in [2,5,13,26], paving the way to future research.

Acknowledgements. We thank the referees for their helpful comments and suggestions. C. Aubert thanks John Natale for stimulating discussion on the correspondence between configuration structures and event structures [33, Definition 1.1], and acknowledges the support of the National Science Foundation under grant 2242786.

References

1. Abramsky, S.: Observation equivalence as a testing equivalence. Theor. Comput. Sci. **53**, 225–241 (1987). https://doi.org/10.1016/0304-3975(87)90065-X
2. Aubert, C., Cristescu, I.: Contextual equivalences in configuration structures and reversibility. J. Logical Algebraic Methods Program. **86**(1), 77–106 (2017). https://doi.org/10.1016/j.jlamp.2016.08.004
3. Aubert, C., Cristescu, I.: How reversibility can solve traditional questions: the example of hereditary history-preserving bisimulation. In: Konnov, I., Kovács, L. (eds.) CONCUR. LIPICS, vol. 171, pp. 13:1–13:24. Schloss Dagstuhl - Leibniz-Zentrum für Informatik (2020). https://doi.org/10.4230/LIPIcs.CONCUR.2020.7
4. Aubert, C., Cristescu, I.: How reversibility can solve traditional questions: the example of hereditary history-preserving bisimulation (research report). Technical report version of [3] (2020). arXiv:2005.06814
5. Aubert, C., Varacca, D.: Processes against tests: on defining contextual equivalences. J. Logical Algebraic Methods Program. 100799 (2022). https://doi.org/10.1016/j.jlamp.2022.100799
6. Baldan, P., Crafa, S.: A logic for true concurrency. J. ACM **61**(4), 24:1–24:36 (2014). https://doi.org/10.1145/2629638
7. Bednarczyk, M.A.: Hereditary history preserving bisimulations or what is the power of the future perfect in program logics. Technical report ICS

PAS, Polish Academy of Sciences (1991). https://web.archive.org/web/20240430035238/https://citeseerx.ist.psu.edu/document?repid=rep1&type=pdf&doi=0fb01e8f7466c5d0e4fe4f0e7fd74123485ca56c
8. Bernardo, M., Esposito, A., Mezzina, C.A.: Expansion laws for forward-reverse, forward, and reverse bisimilarities via proved encodings. Electron. Proc. Theor. Comput. Sci. **412**, 51–70 (2024). https://doi.org/10.4204/eptcs.412.5
9. Bernardo, M., Esposito, A., Mezzina, C.A.: Alternative characterizations of hereditary history-preserving bisimilarity via backward ready multisets. In: Abdulla, P.A., Kesner, D. (eds.) FoSSaCS 2025. LNCS, vol. 15691, pp. 67–87. Springer, Cham (2025). https://doi.org/10.1007/978-3-031-90897-2_4
10. Boudol, G., Castellani, I.: On the semantics of concurrency: partial orders and transition systems. In: Ehrig, H., Kowalski, R., Levi, G., Montanari, U. (eds.) CAAP 1987. LNCS, vol. 249, pp. 123–137. Springer, Heidelberg (1987). https://doi.org/10.1007/3-540-17660-8_52
11. Cristescu, I.: Operational and denotational semantics for the reversible π-calculus. Ph.D. thesis, Université Paris Diderot – Paris 7–Sorbonne Paris Cité (2015). http://scholar.harvard.edu/files/cristescu/files/these.pdf
12. Danos, V., Krivine, J.: Reversible communicating systems. In: Gardner, P., Yoshida, N. (eds.) CONCUR 2004. LNCS, vol. 3170, pp. 292–307. Springer, Heidelberg (2004). https://doi.org/10.1007/978-3-540-28644-8_19
13. Fabbretti, G., Lanese, I., Stefani, J.B.: Reversibility with holes. In: Mogensen, T.Æ., Mikulski, L. (eds.) RC 2024. LNCS, vol. 14680, pp. 69–74. Springer, Cham (2024). https://doi.org/10.1007/978-3-031-62076-8_5
14. Graversen, E., Phillips, I.C.C., Yoshida, N.: Event structure semantics of (controlled) reversible CCS. J. Logical Algebraic Methods Program. **121**, 100686 (2021). https://doi.org/10.1016/j.jlamp.2021.100686
15. Lanese, I.: Concurrent and located synchronizations in π-calculus. In: van Leeuwen, J., Italiano, G.F., van der Hoek, W., Meinel, C., Sack, H., Plášil, F. (eds.) SOFSEM 2007. LNCS, vol. 4362, pp. 388–399. Springer, Heidelberg (2007). https://doi.org/10.1007/978-3-540-69507-3_33
16. Lanese, I., Medic, D.: A general approach to derive uncontrolled reversible semantics. In: Konnov, I., Kovács, L. (eds.) CONCUR. LIPICS, vol. 171, pp. 33:1–33:24. Schloss Dagstuhl - Leibniz-Zentrum für Informatik (2020). https://doi.org/10.4230/LIPIcs.CONCUR.2020.33
17. Lanese, I., Mezzina, C.A., Schmitt, A., Stefani, J.-B.: Controlling reversibility in higher-order pi. In: Katoen, J.-P., König, B. (eds.) CONCUR 2011. LNCS, vol. 6901, pp. 297–311. Springer, Heidelberg (2011). https://doi.org/10.1007/978-3-642-23217-6_20
18. Lanese, I., Mezzina, C.A., Stefani, J.-B.: Reversing higher-order pi. In: Gastin, P., Laroussinie, F. (eds.) CONCUR 2010. LNCS, vol. 6269, pp. 478–493. Springer, Heidelberg (2010). https://doi.org/10.1007/978-3-642-15375-4_33
19. Lanese, I., Mezzina, C.A., Stefani, J.-B.: Reversibility in the higher-order π-calculus. Theor. Comput. Sci. **625**, 25–84 (2016). https://doi.org/10.1016/j.tcs.2016.02.019
20. Lanese, I., Phillips, I.C.C.: Forward-reverse observational equivalences in CCSK. In: Yamashita, S., Yokoyama, T. (eds.) RC 2021. LNCS, vol. 12805, pp. 126–143. Springer, Cham (2021). https://doi.org/10.1007/978-3-030-79837-6_8
21. Lanese, I., Phillips, I.C.C., Ulidowski, I.: An axiomatic theory for reversible computation. ACM Trans. Comput. Logic **25**(2), 1–40 (2024). https://doi.org/10.1145/3648474

22. Melgratti, H.C., Mezzina, C.A., Pinna, G.M.: A truly concurrent semantics for reversible CCS. Logical Methods Comput. Sci. **20**(4) (2024). https://doi.org/10.46298/LMCS-20(4:20)2024
23. Melgratti, H.C., Mezzina, C.A., Ulidowski, I.: Reversing place transition nets. Logical Methods Comput. Sci. **16**(4) (2020). https://doi.org/10.23638/LMCS-16(4:5)2020
24. Milner, R. (ed.): A Calculus of Communicating Systems. LNCS, vol. 92. Springer, Heidelberg (1980). https://doi.org/10.1007/3-540-10235-3
25. Phillips, I.C.C., Ulidowski, I.: Reversibility and models for concurrency. In: Hennessy, M.C.B., van Glabbeek, R.J. (eds.) SOS. ENTCS, vol. 192(1), pp. 93–108. Elsevier (2007). https://doi.org/10.1016/j.entcs.2007.08.018
26. Phillips, I.C.C., Ulidowski, I.: Reversing algebraic process calculi. J. Logic Algebraic Program. **73**(1–2), 70–96 (2007). https://doi.org/10.1016/j.jlap.2006.11.002
27. Phillips, I.C.C., Ulidowski, I.: A hierarchy of reverse bisimulations on stable configuration structures. Math. Struct. Comput. Sci. **22**(2), 333–372 (2012). https://doi.org/10.1017/S0960129511000429
28. Phillips, I.C.C., Ulidowski, I.: Event identifier logic. Math. Struct. Comput. Sci. **24**(2) (2014). https://doi.org/10.1017/S0960129513000510
29. Rabinovich, A., Trakhtenbrot, B.A.: Behavior structures and nets. Fund. Inform. **11**(4), 357–404 (1988). https://doi.org/10.3233/FI-1988-11404
30. Glabbeek, R.J., Goltz, U.: Refinement of actions and equivalence notions for concurrent systems. Acta Informatica **37**(4/5), 229–327 (2001). https://doi.org/10.1007/S002360000041
31. Glabbeek, R.J., Plotkin, G.D.: Configuration structures, event structures and Petri nets. Theor. Comput. Sci. **410**(41), 4111–4159 (2009). https://doi.org/10.1016/j.tcs.2009.06.014
32. Winskel, G.: Event structure semantics for CCS and related languages. In: Nielsen, M., Schmidt, E.M. (eds.) ICALP 1982. LNCS, vol. 140, pp. 561–576. Springer, Heidelberg (1982). https://doi.org/10.1007/BFb0012800
33. Winskel, G.: Event structure semantics for CCS and related languages. DAIMI Research Report 159, University of Aarhus, April 1983. Full version of [32], typeset version by Alex Katovsky in April 2011. http://www.cl.cam.ac.uk/~gw104/eventStructures82.pdf. https://tidsskrift.dk/index.php/daimipb/article/%20view/6812/5891
34. Winskel, G.: Event Structures, Stable Families and Concurrent Games. Lecture Notes. University of Cambridge (2017). https://www.cl.cam.ac.uk/~gw104/ecsym-notes.pdf
35. Winskel, G., Nielsen, M.: Models for concurrency. In: Abramsky, S., Gabbay, D.M., Maibaum, T.S.E. (eds.) Semantic Modelling. Handbook of Logic in Computer Science, vol. 4, pp. 1–148. Oxford University Press (1995). https://doi.org/10.1093/oso/9780198537809.003.0001

Unique-Solution of Equations in Higher-Order Process Calculi with Passivation

Davide Sangiorgi[1,2](✉)

[1] Olas Team, Università di Bologna, Bologna, Italy
Davide.Sangiorgi@gmail.com
[2] INRIA, Sophia Antipolis, France

Abstract. Stefani and coauthors, in various papers, have advocated the usefulness of constructs for localities and passivation in higher-order process languages. They have also shown that the constructs may have surprising consequences on the theory of the languages.

In this paper, dedicated to Jean-Bernard Stefani, we show that, in contrast, proof techniques based on unique-solution of equations are robust enough to bear the presence of such constructs.

1 Introduction

Higher-order concurrent calculi (or languages) are process calculi in which terms of the languages may be passed around in communication messages or, similarly, may move from their original syntactic placement to another one. These calculi build on basic process calculi such as CCS and CSP (that have concurrency but are not higher-order), as well on on the λ-calculus (that is higher-order but is inherently sequential).

Jean-Bernard Stefani has conducted pioneering research on the addition of *localities* and *passivation* to higher-order concurrent calculi, e.g., [3,10,12,27–29]. Localities are constructs meant to represent the spatial distribution of the processes. Thus a locality $a[P]$ indicates that process P should run at location a. Localities may be placed in parallel; in certain languages they may also be nested, yielding a forest-like, or tree-like, structure. It may also be possible to move the process running inside a location towards a different location (sometimes indicated as *strong mobility*). Such a possibility may be useful in distributed and network management. *Passivation* refers precisely to the ability of suspending the execution of a running process and then passing it around, typically as a parameter of a message. As argued by Stefani and his coauthors (e.g., [12]):

> Passivation provides basic support for dynamic reconfiguration: with passivation, named parts of a system can be replaced during execution. Dynamic reconfiguration is useful to support patches and system updates while limiting system downtime and increasing availability; to support fault recovery and fault tolerance by providing a basic mechanism for

checkpointing computations and replicating them; and to support adaptive behaviors, whereby a system changes its configuration to adapt to varying operating conditions, with the aim of improving performance and/or dependability.

While expressive and convenient to use, higher-order concurrent languages are often hard to analyse by means of formal methods [9,10,12,16]. In this paper we focus on techniques for establishing behavioural equivalence between higher-order processes. The reference behavioural equivalence for a language is usually contextually defined. An example is *barbed congruence*, which combines the contextual closure with the coinductive method of bisimilarity [15]. Roughly, two processes are barbed congruent if they have the same reductions and the same observables (called *barbs*) in every context.

The universal quantification on all contexts, however, makes it difficult to prove process equalities following the definition of barbed congruence. This is the motivation for studying characterisations without contextual quantifications, typically as forms of labeled bisimilarity. In the bisimulation proof method two terms are deemed bisimilar if there is a bisimulation relation containing them as a pair. An active topic of research investigates proof methods for reducing the work needed in order to establish (labeled) bisimilarity results, notably as enhancements of the bisimulation proof method [17,18]. In such techniques, called *up-to techniques*, the derivatives of two terms in the bisimulation game may be rewritten and manipulated, with the goal of working with candidate relations that need not be bisimulations—it is sufficient that they are *contained* in a bisimulation. Among the most powerful such forms of enhancement is the *up-to context* technique [17,24], which allows one to exploit linguistic algebraic structures so to remove a common context in the derivative terms, and then requires the resulting terms to be related. Up-to context techniques can be particularly effective in higher-order languages. Unfortunately, in such calculi proving the soundness of the techniques can be surprisingly hard. As a consequence, higher-order process calculi are the class of languages in which up-to context techniques are most scarce in the literature. Techniques of this kind have been derived exploiting fully-abstract translations into first-order calculi (CCS-like or π-calculus-like) [13]. However fully abstract translations are sensitive to the grammar of the language chosen: a modification to the grammar may break or prevent a fully abstract translation to be defined, or, at the very least, will require a careful re-examination of the full abstraction proof.

The power of 'up-to contexts' may be recovered with techniques based on *unique solutions of equations*. In these techniques one establishes that two tuples of processes are componentwise bisimilar by establishing that they are solutions of the same system of equations. The method was first proposed by Milner in the setting of CCS [14], and has been used in verification tools based on algebraic reasoning [1,8,21]. Milner's theorem has however syntactic constraints, on the shape of the equations. For instance, the theorem heavily relies on the sum operator – any other operator but sum and prefix is forbidden within the equations. This limits the expressiveness of the method, and prevents its transport onto languages for distributed systems or higher-order languages, which usually do not include the sum operator. Recently, two research directions have been developed to overcome such limitations. The first consists in replacing equations with special inequations called *contractions* [26]. Using contractions, unique-solution theorems may be established under a mild syntactic constraint, namely a guarding condition on the variables of the contractions. The second research direction consists in replacing the syntactic constraints with a semantic condition that has to do with *divergence* [5,7], inspired by results by Roscoe in CSP [19,20]. In this case the theorems assert that a guarded system of equations whose infinite unfolding never produces a divergence has the unique-solution property.

In higher-order concurrent languages, these two directions have been experimented on the Higher-Order π-calculus, HOπ [22,25], a higher-order concurrent language that enriches CCS by allowing communication of messages that may contain processes [6,26]. In HOπ there are no localities and there is no passivation. In this paper we study the extension of such techniques to HOπP, a basic extension of HOπ with localities and passivation, introduced by Lenglet, Schmitt and Stefani [12].

The addition of localities and passivation has often surprising consequences on the theory of the calculi. Examples are proofs of congruence of bisimilarity, characterisations of barbed congruence in term of labeled bisimilarities, more generally proof techniques for reasoning [10,12,27], expressiveness [2]. An instance that is relevant for this paper concerns *normal bisimilarity* as a characterisation of barbed congruence [23]. The distinguishing feature of normal bisimilarity is the lack of universal quantification on the checks that have be made on two matching input actions during the bisimulation game (e.g., quantifications on all possible values that may be received in the input); and similarly for matching output actions. In HOπ, normal bisimilarity has been proved to coincide with barbed congruence, as well as other forms of labeled bisimilarities such as context bisimilarity [4,23]. In HOπP, the problem of whether normal bisimilarity is the same as barbed congruence and context bisimilarity is still open. A partial positive answer has been given by Lenglet, Schmitt and Stefani [11,12] in a subcalculus of HOπP without restrictions. We show in this paper that proof techniques based on unique solutions of contractions and equations do not suffer similar drawbacks, and can indeed be smoothly extended to accommodate localities and passivation (at least in their basic form, as in HOπP).

Throughout the work, behavioural equivalences, hence also bisimilarity, are meant to be *weak* because they abstract from internal moves of terms, as opposed to the *strong* ones, which make no distinctions between the internal moves and the external ones (i.e., the interactions with the environment). Weak equivalences are, practically, the most relevant ones: e.g., two equal programs may produce the same result with different numbers of evaluation steps. The proofs in this paper extend those in [26] and [6]; hence we only provide sketches of the proofs. Similarly, we refer to papers such as [3,27–29] for more discussion and details about uses and theory of passivation.

Paper Outline. We recall the definition of HOπP in Sect. 2: syntax, transition system, and barbed congruence. In Sect. 3 we introduce the format of systems of equations for HOπP. In Sect. 4 we discuss the proof method based on contractions, directly applied to barbed congruence. In Sect. 5 we introduce normal bisimilarity, and recall some of the main differences between its use in HOπ and in HOπP. In Sects. 6 we present unique-solution techniques based on equation and divergence-freedom, for normal bisimilarity, in the subcalculus without restrictions. We conclude in Sect. 7, with a few final remarks.

2 Background: HOπP

We recall here HOπP, the extension of the Higher-Order π-calculus with passivation, from, e.g., [12].

We use abstractions and concretions to represent input and output prefixes; we also use *first-order names*, i.e., names which carry nothing. These are opposed to *higher-order names*, i.e., names which are used to exchange processes. The presence of first-order names is not necessary, but makes the presentation of various results easier. Thus, let $\mathcal{F}$ be the infinite set of first-order names, and $\mathcal{H}$ the infinite set of higher-order names. Then, $\overline{\mathcal{F}} \stackrel{\text{def}}{=} \{\overline{m} \mid m \in \mathcal{F}\}$, $\overline{\mathcal{H}} \stackrel{\text{def}}{=} \{\overline{a} \mid a \in \mathcal{H}\}$, $\mathcal{N} \stackrel{\text{def}}{=} \mathcal{F} \cup \mathcal{H}$ and $\overline{\mathcal{N}} \stackrel{\text{def}}{=} \overline{\mathcal{F}} \cup \overline{\mathcal{H}}$. The special symbol τ, which does not occur in $\mathcal{N}$ or $\overline{\mathcal{N}}$, denotes a silent step. We let μ range over $\mathcal{N} \cup \overline{\mathcal{N}} \cup \{\tau\}$, and ℓ range over $\mathcal{F} \cup \overline{\mathcal{F}} \cup \{\tau\}$ (the set of CCS-like actions). By convention, if $\ell \neq \tau$ then $\overline{\overline{\ell}} = \ell$. We use symbols x, y, z for names in $\mathcal{N}$; symbols m, n for names in $\mathcal{F}$; and symbols a, b, c for names in $\mathcal{H}$. We also assume an infinite set of *process variables*, ranged over by X, Y, Z, and a set *constant identifiers* (or simply *constants*) ranged over by K, H, to write recursively defined processes.

Definition 1. *The syntactic categories of our language and their grammar are:*

$$
\begin{aligned}
\textit{Processes} \quad & P ::= a.F \mid \overline{a}.C \mid \ell.P \mid a[P] \mid P_1 | P_2 \mid \nu x\, P \mid X \mid F \circ P \mid \mathbf{0} \\
\textit{Abstractions} \quad & F ::= (X)\, P \mid K \\
\textit{Concretions} \quad & C ::= \nu x\, C \mid \langle P_1 \rangle P_2 \\
\textit{Agents} \quad & A ::= P \mid F \mid C
\end{aligned}
$$

A prefix $a.(X)\, P$ represents an input, in which the process received at a will replace X in P. Dually, $\overline{a}.\langle P_1 \rangle P_2$ is an output, in which P_1 is emitted at a and P_2 is the continuation. In an application $F \circ P$ process P is supposed to replace the formal parameter of the abstraction F. Localities, $a[P]$, are passivation units; localities may be nested, therefore the structure of localities in a term $a[P]$ is a tree.

The remaining operators are the usual one of CCS and derived calculi. Symbols $P, Q, R, \ldots$ range over processes, F, G over abstractions, C, D over concretions, A, B over agents. Each constant K has a corresponding definition $K \stackrel{\triangle}{=} (X)\, P$ (as P may contain K, the behaviour may be recursive). Recursion can be derived (examples of this will be shown in Sect. 3); however we take constants as primitives because they are useful when reasoning about equations.

The calculus is monadic—abstractions are parametrised over exactly one value. We stick to monadicity for simplicity of presentation.

We sometimes omit trailing occurrences of **0**, therefore abbreviating $\overline{m}.\mathbf{0}$ as $\overline{m}$, and $\overline{a}.\langle Q\rangle\mathbf{0}$ as $\overline{a}.\langle Q\rangle$; we also omit the parameter in constants when it is not needed, therefore simply writing $K \stackrel{\text{def}}{=} P$ and simply using K as a process. We also sometimes use a special form of constants, namely the replication $!P$, that intuitively stands for an infinite number of copies of P in parallel; it can be written as the constant $K_P \stackrel{\text{def}}{=} P|K_P$.

An application redex $((X)P) \circ Q$ can be normalised as $P\{Q/X\}$. An agent is *normalised* if all such application redexes have been contracted. Although the full application $F \circ P$ is often convenient, when it comes to reasoning on behaviours it is useful to assume that all expressions are normalised, in the above sense. Thus in the remainder of the paper *we identify an agent with its normalised expression* (normalisation terminates because the right-hand side of an application is a process, and thus a normalisation step may not create new applications). The application construct $F \circ P$ will play a role in the treatment of equations in the following sections.

An abstraction $(X)P$ binds all free occurrences of X in P; similarly a restriction $\nu x\, P$ binds the free occurrences of x in P. These binders give rise in the expected way to the definitions of alpha conversion, free (process) variables and free names of an agent. An agent is *closed* if it has no free variables (it can have free names). We use a tilde to denote a tuple; all notations are extended to tuples componentwise. $P\{\widetilde{Q}/\widetilde{X}\}$ denotes the componentwise and simultaneous substitution of variables $\widetilde{X}$ with processes $\widetilde{Q}$ (where it is assumed that the members of $\widetilde{X}$ are distinct). We often abbreviate $\nu x_1 \ldots \nu x_n\, A$ as $(\nu x_1, \ldots, x_n)A$. In a statement, we say that a name is *fresh* to mean that it is different from any other name occurring in agents of the statement.

We only admit *standard concretions*, i.e., expressions $\nu\widetilde{x}\,\langle P_1\rangle P_2$ where names in $\widetilde{x}$ are pairwise distinct and $\widetilde{x} \subseteq \mathsf{fn}(P_1)$. Indeed, the remaining concretions have little significance: in $\nu\widetilde{x}\,\langle Q\rangle P$, by alpha conversion, names $\widetilde{x}$ can be assumed to be distinct; and if $x \notin \mathsf{fn}(Q) \cup \{\widetilde{x}\}$ then in $(\nu x, \widetilde{x})\langle Q\rangle P$ the restriction on name x can be pushed inwards, resulting in the standard concretion $\nu\widetilde{x}\,\langle Q\rangle(\nu x\, P)$. In the following, we therefore assume that if $x \notin \mathsf{fn}(Q) \cup \{\widetilde{x}\}$, then $(\nu x, \widetilde{x})\langle Q\rangle P$ denotes $\nu\widetilde{x}\,\langle Q\rangle(\nu x\, P)$.

We wish to extend restriction to operate on abstractions; similarly, localities and (a form of) parallel composition to operate on abstractions and concretions:

- let $F \stackrel{\text{def}}{=} (X)Q$; then we set $a[F] \stackrel{\text{def}}{=} (X)a[P]$; for $X \notin \mathsf{fv}(P)$ we set $F|P \stackrel{\text{def}}{=} (X)(Q|P)$; and we set $\nu x\, F \stackrel{\text{def}}{=} (X)\nu x\, Q$;
- let $C \stackrel{\text{def}}{=} \nu\widetilde{x}\,\langle Q\rangle R$; then we set $a[C] \stackrel{\text{def}}{=} \nu\widetilde{x}\,\langle Q\rangle a[R]$; for $\widetilde{x} \cap \mathsf{fn}(P) = \emptyset$ we set $C|P \stackrel{\text{def}}{=} \nu\widetilde{x}\,\langle Q\rangle(R|P)$, and similarly for $P|C$.

We now present the operational semantics of the calculus. First, we define an operation of pseudo-application between an abstraction $F = (X)P$ and a

Table 1. The transition system of

Prefix	$\mu.A \xrightarrow{\mu} A$
Parallelism	$\dfrac{P_1 \xrightarrow{\mu} A}{P_1\|P_2 \xrightarrow{\mu} A\|P_2}$
First-order communication	$\dfrac{P_1 \xrightarrow{m} P_1' \quad P_2 \xrightarrow{\overline{m}} P_2'}{P_1\|P_2 \xrightarrow{\tau} P_1'\|P_2'}$
Higher-order communication	$\dfrac{P_1 \xrightarrow{a} F \quad P_2 \xrightarrow{\overline{a}} C}{P_1\|P_2 \xrightarrow{\tau} F \bullet C}$
Passivation	$a[P] \xrightarrow{\overline{a}} \langle P \rangle \mathbf{0}$
Locality	$\dfrac{P \xrightarrow{\mu} A}{a[P] \xrightarrow{\mu} a[A]}$
Restriction	$\dfrac{P \xrightarrow{\mu} A}{\nu x\, P \xrightarrow{\mu} \nu x\, A}\quad \mu \notin \{x,\overline{x}\}$
Constants	$\dfrac{F \circ P \xrightarrow{\mu} A}{K \circ P \xrightarrow{\mu} A}\quad K \stackrel{\text{def}}{=} F$

concretion $C = \nu \widetilde{x} \langle Q \rangle R$. By alpha conversion, we can assume that $\widetilde{x} \cap \mathsf{fn}(F) = \emptyset$, and then we set
$C \bullet F \stackrel{\text{def}}{=} \nu \widetilde{x}\,(R|P\{Q/X\})$. Symmetrically, $F \bullet C \stackrel{\text{def}}{=} \nu \widetilde{x}\,(P\{Q/X\}|R)$. While application, indicated by '$\circ$', acts on an abstraction and a process, the pseudo-application, indicated by '$\bullet$', involves a concretion and an abstraction.

The operational semantics of the calculus is reported in Table 1. We have omitted the symmetric forms of the parallelism and communication rules. The following forms of judgements are used:

$P \xrightarrow{a} F$ (higher-order input transition at port a)

$P \xrightarrow{\overline{a}} C$ (higher-order output transition at port a)

$P \xrightarrow{\ell} Q$ (first-order transition)

In turn, a first-order transition can be a first-order input (if $\ell \in \mathcal{F}$), a first-order output (if $\ell \in \overline{\mathcal{F}}$), or an interaction (if $\ell = \tau$, and may also represent the exchange of a process).

The reference behavioural equivalence for a language is normally defined by means of a closure under all contexts. This is indeed the case for *barbed congruence*. A (process) *context* is a process expression that may contain a hole in a process position. (In the paper, unless otherwise stated, a 'context' is meant to be a 'process context', as opposed to an 'abstraction context' or a 'concretion context'.)

We write $P \downarrow_x$ if $P \xrightarrow{x}$ or $P \xrightarrow{\overline{x}}$ (process P 'has a barb at x'). As usual, $\longrightarrow$ abbreviates $\xrightarrow{\tau}$, and $\Longrightarrow$ is the reflexive and transitive closure of $\longrightarrow$; finally $P \Downarrow_x$ holds if there is P' with $P \Longrightarrow P'$ and $P' \downarrow_x$.

Definition 2 (barbed bisimulation and congruence). *A relation $\mathcal{R}$ on (closed) processes is a barbed simulation if whenever $P \mathrel{\mathcal{R}} Q$:*

1. *$P \longrightarrow P'$ implies there is Q' such that $Q \Longrightarrow Q'$ and $P' \mathrel{\mathcal{R}} Q'$;*
2. *if $P \downarrow_x$ then $Q \Downarrow_x$.*

A relation $\mathcal{R}$ is a barbed bisimulation if $\mathcal{R}$ and $\mathcal{R}^{-1}$ are barbed simulations. Barbed bisimilarity, written $\approx_{\mathrm{bar}}$, is the union of all barbed bisimulations. Two processes P and Q are barbed congruent, written $P \approx_{\mathrm{bar}}^{\mathrm{c}} Q$, if for each (closing) context $\mathbb{C}$, it holds that $\mathbb{C}[P] \approx_{\mathrm{bar}} \mathbb{C}[Q]$.

The definition of barbed congruence may be extended to abstractions and concretions by closing under abstraction and concretions contexts (that is, process expressions that may contain a hole in an abstraction or concrete position), in the expected manner.

3 Systems of Equations in HOπP

Intuitively, uniqueness of solutions of equations [14] for a behavioural equivalence $\asymp$ says that if a context $\mathbb{C}$ obeys certain conditions, then all processes P that satisfy the equation $P \asymp \mathbb{C}[P]$ are in the relation $\asymp$.

We use bold letters $\mathbf{X}, \mathbf{Y}, \ldots$ for the variables needed for writing equations, called *equation variables*. An equation variable can represent a process or an abstraction (formally one should thus make a formal distinction between two classes of equation variables, using separate letters or using types; in this paper the distinction will be clear from the context). Correspondingly, the body of an equation is a process or an abstraction possibly containing equation variables.

We call *extended HOπP* the HOπP syntax of Sect. 2 where equation variables may be used as agents. To make the distinction between the ordinary syntax of HOπP and the syntax of extended HOπP, we use bold letters to range over the syntactic categories of the latter. Thus, in extended HOπP, $\mathbf{P}, \mathbf{Q}$ stand for *extended processes*, $\mathbf{F}$ for *extended abstractions*, $\mathbf{C}$ for *extended concretions*, and $\mathbf{A}$ for *extended agents* (the word 'extended' indicates the possible presence of equation variables). The grammars for extended processes and extended abstractions include productions for equation variables.

Definition 3. *Assume that, for each i of a countable indexing set I, we have variables $\mathbf{X}_i$, and agents*

$\mathbf{A}_i$ possibly containing such variables. Then $\{\mathbf{X}_i = \mathbf{A}_i\}_{i \in I}$ is a system of HOπP equations. There is one equation for each variable $\mathbf{X}_i$; moreover each $\mathbf{A}_i$ is a process or an abstraction, depending on whether the corresponding variable $\mathbf{X}_i$ is a process or an abstraction variable.

Example 1. We report some examples of systems of equations, whose solutions are then discussed in Example 2:

1. $\mathbf{X} = (Y)\,(\mathbf{X} \circ Y)$.

2. $\mathbf{X} = (Y)(\mathbf{X} \circ Y | Y)$.
3. $\mathbf{Z} = a.(Y)(\mathbf{Z}|Y)$.
4. $\mathbf{X} = (X) d.(Z)(\mathbf{Y} \circ Z)$
   $\mathbf{Y} = (Z) \ell.(Z|(\mathbf{Y} \circ Z))$
5. $\mathbf{Z} = a.(X)\overline{b}.\langle X \rangle \mathbf{Z}$.

We write $\mathbf{A}[\widetilde{A}]$ for the expression resulting from $\mathbf{A}$ by replacing each variable $\mathbf{X}_i$ in $\mathbf{A}$ with the agent A_i, assuming $\widetilde{A}$ and $\widetilde{\mathbf{X}}$ have the same length.

Remark 1. To avoid issues with restriction, we take the replacement in $\mathbf{A}[\widetilde{A}]$ to be a substitution, not a syntactic replacement.

Definition 4. *Suppose $\{\mathbf{X}_i = \mathbf{A}_i\}_{i \in I}$ is a system of equations, and $\asymp$ a behavioural equivalence:*

- *$\widetilde{A}$ is a solution of the system of equations for $\asymp$ if for each i it holds that $A_i \asymp \mathbf{A}_i[\widetilde{A}]$;*
- *the system has a unique solution for $\asymp$ if whenever $\widetilde{A}$ and $\widetilde{B}$ are both solutions for $\asymp$, then $\widetilde{A} \asymp \widetilde{B}$.*

In the example below the behavioural equivalence $\asymp$ is taken to be barbed congruence.

Example 2. Consider the equations from Example 1 (and $\approx^{\text{c}}_{\text{bar}}$):

1. the equation $\mathbf{X} = (Y)(\mathbf{X} \circ Y)$ is satisfied by any (closed) abstraction.
2. In $\mathbf{X} = (Y)((\mathbf{X} \circ Y)|Y)$, the abstraction $(Y)(!Y)$ is a solution.
3. The solution of $\mathbf{Z} = a.(Y)(\mathbf{Z}|Y)$ is a process that can always receive a process at a and then runs it.
4. The system of equations in Example 1(4) has a unique solution. The abstraction for $\mathbf{X}$ receives a process at d, and then makes it available at ℓ, so that any output at ℓ (from the environment) will start a copy of such process.
5. The solution of the equation $\mathbf{Z} = a.(X)\overline{b}.\langle X \rangle \mathbf{Z}$ is a 'link' process that repeatedly receives a process at a and then emits the process at b.

4 Barbed Contraction

Intuitively, for a behavioural equivalence $\asymp$, its contraction $\succeq_{\asymp}$ is a preorder in which $P \succeq_{\asymp} Q$ holds if $P \asymp Q$ and, in addition, Q has the *possibility* of being at least as efficient as P. That is, if P can do some work (i.e., some interactions with its environment), then Q should be able to do the same work at least as quickly as P (i.e., performing no more τ-steps then those performed by P). Process Q, however, may be nondeterministic and may have other ways of doing the same work, and these could be slow (i.e., involving more τ-steps than those performed by P).

A *system of contractions* is defined as a system of equations, except that the contraction symbol $\succeq$ is used in place of the equality symbol $=$. Thus a system of contractions is a set $\{\mathbf{X}_i \succeq \mathbf{A}_i\}_{i \in I}$ where I is an indexing set and expressions $\mathbf{A}_i$ may contain the contraction variables $\{\mathbf{X}_i\}_{i \in I}$.

Definition 5. *Given a behavioural equivalence $\asymp$ and its contraction $\succeq_\asymp$, and a system of contractions $\{\mathbf{X}_i \succeq \mathbf{A}_i\}_{i \in I}$, we say that:*

- *$\widetilde{A}$ is a solution for $\succeq_\asymp$ of the system of contractions if $\widetilde{A} \succeq_\asymp \mathbf{A}[\widetilde{A}]$;*
- *the system has a unique solution for $\asymp$ if whenever $\widetilde{A}$ and $\widetilde{B}$ are both solutions for $\succeq_\asymp$, then $\widetilde{A} \asymp \widetilde{B}$.*

We adapt the contraction technique to barbed congruence, introducing for this the *barbed congruence contraction*, $\succeq_\mathrm{bar}^\mathrm{c}$. Reasoning about barbed congruence, the contraction symbol $\succeq$ is interpreted as $\succeq_\mathrm{bar}^\mathrm{c}$, and the equivalence $\asymp$ as the barbed congruence relation $\approx_\mathrm{bar}^\mathrm{c}$. Thus $\widetilde{A}$ being a solution for $\succeq_\mathrm{bar}^\mathrm{c}$ of the system of contractions $\{\mathbf{X}_i \succeq \mathbf{A}_i\}_{i \in I}$ means that $\widetilde{A} \succeq_\mathrm{bar}^\mathrm{c} \mathbf{A}[\widetilde{A}]$; and the system having a unique solution for $\approx_\mathrm{bar}^\mathrm{c}$ means that whenever $\widetilde{A}$ and $\widetilde{B}$ are both solutions for $\succeq_\mathrm{bar}^\mathrm{c}$ then $\widetilde{A} \approx_\mathrm{bar}^\mathrm{c} \widetilde{B}$. We consider barbed congruence so to show that it is possible to apply the contraction technique directly to barbed congruence, even though it is contextually defined.

We write $Q \stackrel{\wedge}{\longrightarrow} Q'$ if $Q \longrightarrow Q'$ or $Q = Q'$.

Definition 6 (barbed contraction, barbed congruence contraction). *A relation $\mathcal{R}$ on (closed) processes is a barbed contraction if, whenever $P\,\mathcal{R}\,Q$:*

1. *$P \longrightarrow P'$ implies there is Q' such that $Q \stackrel{\wedge}{\longrightarrow} Q'$ and $P'\,\mathcal{R}\,Q'$;*
2. *$Q \longrightarrow Q'$ implies there is P' such that $P \Longrightarrow P'$ and $P' \approx_\mathrm{bar} Q'$;*
3. *$P \downarrow_x$ implies $Q \downarrow_x$;*
4. *$Q \downarrow_x$ implies $P \Downarrow_x$.*

Barbed contraction, written $\succeq_\mathrm{bar}$, is the union of all barbed contractions. Barbed congruence contraction, written $\succeq_\mathrm{bar}^\mathrm{c}$, relates two processes P and Q if, for each (closing) context $\mathbb{C}$, it holds that $\mathbb{C}[\,]P \succeq_\mathrm{bar} \mathbb{C}[Q]$. □

Barbed congruence contraction is extended to abstractions and concretions in the same way as barbed congruence, by closing under abstraction and concretion contexts.

In the remainder of the paper, for simplicity, we state all results about systems of equations admitting only *process* equations; and the same for contractions. Thus all variables $\mathbf{X}, \mathbf{Y}, \ldots$ will be process variables. The generalisation to equations and contractions involving abstractions is easy, though notationally tedious. We will use abstraction variables and abstraction contractions only in Example 3 below.

Definition 7 (reduction-autonomous contractions). *An extended process $\mathbf{P}$ is reduction-autonomous if for all $\widetilde{P}$ and context $\mathbb{C}$:*

- *if $\mathbb{C}[\mathbf{P}[\widetilde{P}]] \longrightarrow R$, then there is a context $\mathbb{C}'$ such that $R = \mathbb{C}'[\widetilde{P}]$ and, for all $\widetilde{Q}$, also $\mathbb{C}[\mathbf{P}[\widetilde{Q}]] \longrightarrow \mathbb{C}'[\widetilde{Q}]$;*
- *if $\mathbb{C}[\mathbf{P}[\widetilde{P}]] \downarrow_x$ then, for all $\widetilde{Q}$, also $\mathbb{C}[\mathbf{P}[\widetilde{Q}]] \downarrow_x$.*

A system of contractions $\{\mathbf{X}_i \succeq \mathbf{P}_i\}_{i \in I}$ is reduction-autonomous *if each* $\mathbf{P}_i$ *is reduction-autonomous.*

Theorem 1. *Any system of reduction-autonomous contractions has a unique solution for* $\approx^c_{\mathrm{bar}}$.

Proof (Sketch). One first shows that, if $\widetilde{P}$ and $\widetilde{Q}$ are solutions for $\succeq^c_{\mathrm{bar}}$ to a system of reduction-autonomous contractions, then, for any context $\mathbb{C}$, if $\mathbb{C}[\widetilde{P}] \Longrightarrow R$, there is a context $\mathbb{C}'$ such that $R \succeq_{\mathrm{bar}} \mathbb{C}'[\widetilde{P}]$ and $\mathbb{C}[Q] \Longrightarrow \approx_{\mathrm{bar}} \mathbb{C}'[\widetilde{Q}]$.

Using this fact, then one shows that, for $\widetilde{P}$ and $\widetilde{Q}$ solutions, the set of all pairs (P_1, Q_1) such that there is a context $\mathbb{C}$ with $P_1 \approx_{\mathrm{bar}} \mathbb{C}[\widetilde{P}]$ and $Q_1 \approx_{\mathrm{bar}} \mathbb{C}[\widetilde{Q}]$ is a barbed bisimilarity.

Definition 8. *A system of contractions* $\{\mathbf{X}_i \succeq \mathbf{P}_i\}_{i \in I}$ *is* weakly guarded *if, in each* $\mathbf{P}_i$, *each occurrence of any contraction variable is underneath a prefix.*

By inspection of the syntax of a weakly guarded contraction and of the rules of the LTS for HOπP we obtain the following lemma.

Lemma 1. *A system of weakly guarded contractions is reduction-autonomous.*

Corollary 1 (unique solution of contractions for $\approx^c_{\mathrm{bar}}$). *A system of weakly guarded contractions has a unique solution for* $\approx^c_{\mathrm{bar}}$.

Example 3. The example is about two ways of modeling the replication operator. We consider the equality (barbed congruence) between the terms $\overline{c}.\langle R \rangle\, \mathbf{0}$ and $\overline{c}.\langle S \rangle\, \mathbf{0}$, where

$$R \stackrel{\mathrm{def}}{=} b.(Y)\,\nu a\,(M|a[M]) \quad \text{for } M \stackrel{\mathrm{def}}{=} a.(X)\,(Y|X|a[X])$$

and

$$S \stackrel{\mathrm{def}}{=} b.(Y)\,\nu a\,(N|\overline{a}.\langle Y|N \rangle\,\mathbf{0}) \quad \text{for } N \stackrel{\mathrm{def}}{=} a.(X)\,(X|\overline{a}.\langle X \rangle\,\mathbf{0}).$$

Terms $\overline{c}.\langle R \rangle\, \mathbf{0}$ and $\overline{c}.\langle S \rangle\, \mathbf{0}$ send on c processes (R and S) that, in turn, receives a process at b and then replicates this process. Indeed, if P is the process so received, assuming a does not occur free in P, in one case we obtain the term

$$R_P \stackrel{\mathrm{def}}{=} \nu a\,(M\{P/Y\}|a[M\{P/Y\}])$$

and in the other case

$$S_P \stackrel{\mathrm{def}}{=} \nu a\,(N|\overline{a}.\langle P|N \rangle\,\mathbf{0}),$$

and then we have:

$$R_P \longrightarrow P|R_P \longrightarrow P|P|R_P \longrightarrow \cdots$$

$$S_P \longrightarrow P|S_P \longrightarrow P|P|S_P \longrightarrow \cdots$$

The internal structure of R_P and S_P is however different. Moreover, R makes use of passivation, whereas S only uses higher-order communications. A system of contractions that proves $\overline{c}.\langle R\rangle \mathbf{0} \approx^{\mathrm{c}}_{\mathrm{bar}} \overline{c}.\langle S\rangle \mathbf{0}$ is the following:

$$\mathbf{Z}_1 \succeq \overline{c}.\langle \mathbf{Z}_2\rangle \mathbf{0}$$
$$\mathbf{Z}_2 \succeq b.(U)\,(\mathbf{X} \circ U)$$
$$\mathbf{X} \succeq (Y)\,\tau.(Y|\mathbf{X} \circ Y)$$

These contractions are reduction-autonomous, and therefore have a unique solution for barbed congruence. Note that, in the first contraction, a contraction variable occurs within the object of the initial output, and therefore contributes to the synchronisation resulting from such an output. Still, the contraction is weakly guarded, as the variable appears, syntactically, underneath the output prefix. Two solutions for $\succeq^{\mathrm{c}}_{\mathrm{bar}}$ (the barbed congruence contraction) to the above system of three contractions are, respectively:

1. $\overline{c}.\langle R\rangle \mathbf{0}$, R, and $(Y)\,\nu a\,(M|a[M])$;
2. $\overline{c}.\langle S\rangle \mathbf{0}$, S, and $(Y)\,\nu a\,(N|\overline{a}.\langle Y|N\rangle \mathbf{0})$.

To prove that these are solutions, we need a few simple algebraic laws, such as

$$\nu a\,(\overline{a}.\langle Q_1\rangle Q_2 | a.(X)\,Q) \succeq^{\mathrm{c}}_{\mathrm{bar}} \nu a\,(Q_2|Q\{Q_1/X\})\,,$$
$$\nu a\,(a.(X)\,Q | a[a.(X')\,Q']) \succeq^{\mathrm{c}}_{\mathrm{bar}} \nu a\,(Q\{a.(X')\,Q'/X\})\,,$$

(these laws hold because the process on the right is the only possible derivative of the process on the left), and laws that modify the scope of a restriction.

5 Normal Bisimilarity

In the Higher-Order π-calculus (HOπ), barbed congruence can be characterised by means of *normal bisimilarity*, a form of bisimilarity that does not demand universal quantifications in the answers required during the bisimulation game [23]. Lenglet, Schmitt and Stefani [12] have studied normal bisimilarity in HOπP. They have proved 'positive' results, but have also discovered 'negative' results, that is, counterexamples to the transport to HOπP of results true in HOπ. Among the positive result is a characterisation with respect to barbed congruence in the variant of HOπP without the restriction operator; for the proof of completeness, a choice operator is also added to the language. Below, we stick to the HOπP subcalculus without restriction, omitting for simplicity the choice operator (its addition, for the results we present is easy). We call HOπP$^-$ this language. We briefly recall some of the negative results from [12].

The absence of universal quantification in the clauses of normal bisimulation is particularly relevant in the input clause: in HOπ, to evaluate two abstractions $(X)P$ and $(X)Q$, it is not necessary to consider all possible instantiations of the parameter X. It is sufficient to consider the instantiation with a single agent, called *trigger*. A *trigger* is a process of the form $\mathtt{Tr}_m \stackrel{\text{def}}{=} m.\mathbf{0}$, and the input clause of normal bisimulation for two processes P and Q is as follows:

- whenever $P \xrightarrow{a} F$, there exists G s.t. $Q \xRightarrow{a} G$ and $F \circ \mathtt{Tr}_m \, \mathcal{R} \, G \circ \mathtt{Tr}_m$, for m not free in P and Q.

Bisimilarity is preserved by injective substitutions, thus a single trigger, with m fresh, is sufficient. More generally, in HOπ, if P and Q are processes with a free variable X then from the equality between $P\{\mathtt{Tr}_m/X\}$ $Q\{\mathtt{Tr}_m/X\}$ one can infer the equality between $P\{R/X\}$ $Q\{R/X\}$, for any process R.

Surprisingly, the above results break in presence of passivation [12]. As a counterexample, Lenglet, Schmitt and Stefani exhibit the processes

$$P_1 \stackrel{\text{def}}{=} !a[X] | !a[\mathbf{0}] \quad \text{and} \quad Q_1 \stackrel{\text{def}}{=} X | P_1$$

Instantiating the free variable X with the (ordinary) trigger $m.\mathbf{0}$ yields the processes

$$P_m \stackrel{\text{def}}{=} !a[m.\mathbf{0}] | !a[\mathbf{0}] \quad \text{and} \quad Q_m \stackrel{\text{def}}{=} m.\mathbf{0} | !a[m.\mathbf{0}] | !a[\mathbf{0}] \ .$$

These processes are bisimilar. For instance, the move

$$Q_m \xrightarrow{m} \mathbf{0} | !a[m.\mathbf{0}] | !a[\mathbf{0}]$$

is matched by (using the rule for location)

$$P_m \xrightarrow{m} a[\mathbf{0}] | !a[m.\mathbf{0}] | !a[\mathbf{0}]$$

as the derivative process, using the absorption law for replication, can be proved to be the same as $!a[m.\mathbf{0}] | !a[\mathbf{0}]$. It turns out that, however, P_1 and Q_1 may be distinguished by instantiating X with the 'composite' triggers $m.n.\mathbf{0}$, for m, n fresh. Such an instantiation yields the processes

$$P_{m,n} \stackrel{\text{def}}{=} !a[m.n.\mathbf{0}] | !a[\mathbf{0}] \quad \text{and} \quad Q_{m,n} \stackrel{\text{def}}{=} m.n.\mathbf{0} | !a[m.n.\mathbf{0}] | !a[\mathbf{0}] \ .$$

As before, the only possible match for the transition

$$Q_{m,n} \xrightarrow{m} n.\mathbf{0} | !a[m.n.\mathbf{0}] | !a[\mathbf{0}] \stackrel{\text{def}}{=} Q'_{m,n}$$

could be, using location,

$$P_{m,n} \xrightarrow{m} a[n.\mathbf{0}] | !a[m.n.\mathbf{0}] | !a[\mathbf{0}] \stackrel{\text{def}}{=} P'_{m,n}$$

But now we have

$$P'_{m,n} \xrightarrow{\overline{a}} \langle n.\mathbf{0} \rangle !a[m.n.\mathbf{0}] | !a[\mathbf{0}]$$

in which the object of the concretion is a process capable of using n immediately, and this action cannot be matched by $Q'_{m,n}$.

Lenglet, Schmitt and Stefani then elaborate this argument and prove that composite triggers allow one to pinpoint the position of a process variable in the tree structure of localities in a process. That is, if an occurrence of a variable X occurs in a process underneath localities $a_1, \ldots, a_i$ then in a behaviourally equal process there must be an occurrence of X underneath the same localities (and in the same order $a_1, \ldots, a_i$).

We recall the definition of normal bisimilarity in $\mathrm{HO}\pi\mathrm{P}^-$. We write $\mathrm{Tr}_{m,n}$ for the composite trigger $m.n.\mathbf{0}$. As $\mathrm{HO}\pi\mathrm{P}^-$ has no restrictions, all concretions are of the form $\langle P_1 \rangle P_2$.

We write $Q \stackrel{\widehat{\ell}}{\Rightarrow} Q'$ to mean $Q \Longrightarrow Q'$ if $\ell = \tau$, and $Q \stackrel{\ell}{\Rightarrow} Q'$ otherwise.

Definition 9 (normal bisimulation). *A relation $\mathcal{R}$ on the (closed) processes of $HO\pi P^-$ is a normal simulation if $P \mathrel{\mathcal{R}} Q$ implies, for $m, n \notin fn(P, Q)$:*

1. *whenever $P \stackrel{\ell}{\rightarrow} P'$, there exists Q' s.t. $Q \stackrel{\widehat{\ell}}{\Rightarrow} Q'$ and $P' \mathrel{\mathcal{R}} Q'$;*
2. *whenever $P \stackrel{a}{\rightarrow} F$, there exists G s.t. $Q \stackrel{a}{\Rightarrow} G$ and $F \circ \mathrm{Tr}_{m,n} \mathrel{\mathcal{R}} G \circ \mathrm{Tr}_{m,n}$;*
3. *whenever $P \stackrel{\overline{a}}{\rightarrow} \langle P_1 \rangle P_2$, there exist Q_1, Q_2 s.t. $Q \stackrel{\overline{a}}{\Rightarrow} \langle Q_1 \rangle Q_2$ and $P_i \mathrel{\mathcal{R}} Q_i$, for $i = 1, 2$.*

A relation $\mathcal{R}$ is a normal bisimulation if $\mathcal{R}$ and $\mathcal{R}^{-1}$ are normal simulations. Processes P and Q are normal bisimilar, written $P \approx Q$, if $P \mathrel{\mathcal{R}} Q$, for some normal bisimulation $\mathcal{R}$.

Normal bisimilarity is extended to abstraction and concretions along the lines of clauses (2) and (3) above (i.e., for abstractions, providing a fresh composite trigger, and for concretions decomposing the concretion); moreover it is extended to open agents by requiring instantiations of free variables with fresh composite triggers.

In $\mathrm{HO}\pi\mathrm{P}^-$, normal bisimilarity is a congruence, and coincides with barbed congruence on image-finite processes [12].

6 Unique-Solution Theorems for Normal Bisimilarity

We discuss here a unique-solution-of-equation theorem for normal bisimilarity in $\mathrm{HO}\pi\mathrm{P}^-$, appealing to the variant theorem that makes use of a constraint on divergence [5,7] rather than referring to the contraction preorder as done in Sect. 4. The theorem relies on a reasoning about the transitions of unfoldings of the equations. Suppose $\widetilde{P}$ are solutions of a system of equations $\{\mathbf{X}_i = \mathbf{P}_i\}_{i \in I}$, and consider a context $\mathbb{C}$. Then the process obtained from $\mathbb{C}[\widetilde{P}]$ by unfolding the equations once is $\mathbb{C}[\widetilde{\mathbf{P}}[\widetilde{P}]]$; the process obtained by unfolding the equations twice is $\mathbb{C}[\widetilde{\mathbf{P}}[\widetilde{\mathbf{P}}[\widetilde{P}]]]$; and similarly for the n-unfolding. Given $\{\mathbf{X}_i = \mathbf{P}_i\}_{i \in I}$, we write $\mathbf{P}_i^n$ for the extended process obtained from $\mathbf{P}_i$ after n unfoldings.

We introduce the notion of divergence in $\mathrm{HO}\pi\mathrm{P}^-$. A divergence in a process consists of a finite sequence of transitions (of any kind) followed by an infinite sequence of τ transitions. We first introduce the notion of reduct, which then

Unique-Solution of Equations in Higher-Order Process Calculi   81

allows us to define divergence. As usual, *extended* HOπP⁻ is the extension of HOπP⁻ with equation variables. We use the SOS rules of Table 1 also on the syntax of extended HOπP⁻.

Definition 10 (Reducts).

1. We say that $\mathbf{P}$ *reduces to* $\mathbf{P}'$, written $\mathbf{P} \dashrightarrow \mathbf{P}'$, if one of the following holds:
   (a) $\mathbf{P} \xrightarrow{\ell} \mathbf{P}'$;
   (b) $\mathbf{P}' = \mathbf{P}''$ for some $\mathbf{P}''$ and $\mathbf{P}'''$ such that either $\mathbf{P} \xrightarrow{\overline{a}} \langle \mathbf{P}'' \rangle \mathbf{P}'''$ or $\mathbf{P} \xrightarrow{\overline{a}} \langle \mathbf{P}''' \rangle \mathbf{P}''$;
   (c) $\mathbf{P}' = \mathbf{F} \circ \mathrm{Tr}_{m,n}$ for some fresh m, n and some $\mathbf{F}$ such that $\mathbf{P} \xrightarrow{a} \mathbf{F}$.
   Relation $P \dashrightarrow P'$ ("P reduces to P'") is defined in the same way for processes that do not contain equation variables.
2. The *set of reducts* of an extended process $\mathbf{P}$, written $\mathrm{red}(\mathbf{P})$, is given by:

$$\mathrm{red}(\mathbf{P}) \stackrel{def}{=} \bigcup_n \{\mathbf{P}_n \mid \mathbf{P} \dashrightarrow \mathbf{P}_1 \ldots \dashrightarrow \mathbf{P}_n \text{ for some } n \text{ and } \mathbf{P}_i (1 \le i \le n)\}.$$

Again, the set of reducts of a process P, $\mathrm{red}(P)$, is defined in the same way.
3. The *set of reducts of the unfoldings* of a system of equations $\{\mathbf{X}_i = \mathbf{P}_i\}_{i \in I}$, written $\mathrm{red}_\omega(\widetilde{\mathbf{P}})$, is defined as

$$\mathrm{red}_\omega(\widetilde{\mathbf{P}}) \stackrel{def}{=} \bigcup_{n \in \mathbb{N}, i \in I} \mathrm{red}(\mathbf{P}_i^n).$$

Definition 11 (Divergence). A process P *diverges* if there is $P' \in \mathrm{red}(P)$ such that P' can perform an infinite sequence of internal moves; i.e., there are processes P_i, $i \ge 0$ such that $P' = P_0 \xrightarrow{\tau} P_1 \xrightarrow{\tau} P_2 \xrightarrow{\tau} \ldots$.

Intuitively, a system of equations $\widetilde{\mathbf{X}} = \widetilde{\mathbf{P}}$ *protects* its solutions when transitions emanating from $\mathbf{P}[\widetilde{P}]$, where $\mathbf{P} \in \mathrm{red}_\omega(\widetilde{\mathbf{P}})$ and $\widetilde{P}$ is a solution, can be mimicked by transitions of $\mathbf{P}[\widetilde{\mathbf{P}}^n]$ for some n—i.e., by replacing the solutions with unfoldings of the equations.

Definition 12. A system of equations $\widetilde{\mathbf{X}} = \widetilde{\mathbf{P}}$ *protects its solutions* if, for all solution $\widetilde{P}$, and for all $\mathbf{P}' \in \mathrm{red}_\omega(\widetilde{\mathbf{P}})$, the following hold:

1. if $\mathbf{P}'[\widetilde{P}] \Longrightarrow Q$ for some Q, then there exist $\mathbf{P}''$ and n such that $\mathbf{P}'[\widetilde{\mathbf{P}}^n] \Longrightarrow \mathbf{P}''$ and $\mathbf{P}''[\widetilde{P}] \approx Q$.
2. if $\mathbf{P}'[\widetilde{P}] \xrightarrow{\ell} Q$ for some ℓ and some Q, then there exist $\mathbf{P}''$ and n such that $\mathbf{P}'[\widetilde{\mathbf{P}}^n] \xrightarrow{\ell} \mathbf{P}''$ and $\mathbf{P}''[\widetilde{P}] \approx Q$.
3. if $\mathbf{P}'[\widetilde{P}] \xrightarrow{a} F_0$, for some a and some F_0, then there exist $\mathbf{F}_0$ and n such that $\mathbf{P}'[\widetilde{\mathbf{P}}^n] \xrightarrow{a} \mathbf{F}_0$ and $(\mathbf{F}_0 \circ \mathrm{Tr}_{m,n})[\widetilde{P}] \approx F_0 \circ \mathrm{Tr}_{m,n}$, for any m, n fresh.
4. if $\mathbf{P}'[\widetilde{P}] \xrightarrow{\overline{a}} \langle P_1 \rangle P_2$, for some a, P_1, P_2, then there are $\mathbf{P}_1, \mathbf{P}_2$, and n such that $\mathbf{P}'[\widetilde{\mathbf{P}}^n] \xrightarrow{\overline{a}} \langle \mathbf{P}_1 \rangle \mathbf{P}_2$ and $\mathbf{P}_i[\widetilde{P}] \approx P_i$, $i = 1, 2$.

Proposition 1. *A system of equations that protects its solutions has a unique solution for $\approx$.*

Proof (Sketch). We have to show that given two solutions $\widetilde{P}$, $\widetilde{P}'$ of the system of equations $\widetilde{\mathbf{X}} = \widetilde{\mathbf{P}}$, it holds that $\widetilde{P} \approx \widetilde{P}'$. One then proves that the relation

$$\mathcal{R} \stackrel{\text{def}}{=} \{(P_1, P_1') \text{ s.t. there is } \mathbf{P}' \text{ with } P_1 \approx \mathbf{P}'[\widetilde{P}], P_2 \approx \mathbf{P}'[\widetilde{P}'] \text{ and } \mathbf{P}' \in \mathsf{red}_\omega(\widetilde{\mathbf{P}})\}$$

is a bisimulation relation. For this one considers $(P_1, P_1') \in \mathcal{R}$, and makes a case analysis on the possible transitions from P_1.

The syntactic solution of a system of equations can be seen as the result of the infinite unfolding of the equations defining the system.

Definition 13 (Syntactic solution). *Given a system of equations $\{\mathbf{X}_i = \mathbf{P}_i\}_{i \in I}$, its syntactic solution is defined as the tuple of mutually recursive constants $\widetilde{K_\mathbf{P}}$ (there is one $K_{\mathbf{P},i}$ for each $i \in I$), whose defining equations are $K_{\mathbf{P},i} \stackrel{\triangle}{=} \mathbf{P}_i[\widetilde{K_\mathbf{P}}]$.*

For instance, the syntactic solutions of the equation $\mathbf{Z} = a.(X)\overline{b}.\langle X\rangle\mathbf{Z}$ (Example 1(5)) is the constant $K \stackrel{\triangle}{=} a.(X)\overline{b}.\langle X\rangle K$, which repeatedly receives a process at a and emits the process at b.

The syntactic solutions of the system $\widetilde{\mathbf{X}} = \widetilde{\mathbf{P}}$ do not diverge if, for all $i \in I$, $K_{\widetilde{\mathbf{P}},i}$ does not diverge.

Theorem 2 (Unique solution). *A guarded system of equations whose syntactic solutions do not diverge has a unique solution for $\approx$.*

Proof (Sketch). One shows that a guarded system of equations whose syntactic solutions do not diverge protects its solutions, and then appeals to Proposition 1. We explain the schema of the proof, considering, for simplicity, a single equation $\mathbf{X} = \mathbf{P}$. We take a solution P of the equation and a transition $\mathbf{P}'[P] \stackrel{\mu}{\longrightarrow} A$, for $\mathbf{P}' \in \mathsf{red}_\omega(\mathbf{P})$. The goal is to find an n such that, using the n-th unfolding $\mathbf{P}^n$ of $\mathbf{P}$, process $\mathbf{P}'[\mathbf{P}^n]$ can match the transition *without the need of P*; i.e., there is $\mathbf{A}$ with $\mathbf{P}'[\mathbf{P}^n] \stackrel{\hat{\mu}}{\Longrightarrow} \mathbf{A}$ and $\mathbf{A}[P] \approx A$.

One looks for this n incrementally. At each step the length of the transition sequence $\mathbf{P}'[\mathbf{P}^n] \stackrel{\hat{\mu}}{\Longrightarrow} \mathbf{A}$ grows; precisely, the sequence at step n is a strict prefix of the sequence at step $n+1$. This procedure necessarily stops: otherwise, one builds an infinite sequence of transitions involving only the unfoldings of $\mathbf{P}$, and with at most one visible transition: this would yield a divergence in the syntactic solution of $\mathbf{P}$, contradicting the hypothesis.

The theorem may be strengthened by ignoring *innocuous* divergences [5,6], that is, divergences in the conditions of Theorem 2 that show up in a finite unfolding of the equation (i.e., observing such divergences does not require the infinite unfolding).

7 Conclusion

In the paper, we have transplanted proof techniques based on unique-solution of equations onto a higher-order process calculus with localities and passivation. We have shown that the techniques are robust enough to bear the presence of the constructs for localities and passivation. In contrast, other techniques, such as those for congruence of forms of labeled bisimilarity, are strongly affected by the presence of such constructs (e.g., [10,12]). We have considered a technique based on contraction [26], applied to barbed congruence, and a technique based on divergence [5–7], applied to normal bisimilarity; in both cases the proofs closely follow those for HOπ [6,26]. The latter technique can be further strengthened by considering only innocuous divergences [5].

The technique based on divergence could also be applied to barbed congruence. In contrast, we do not know whether the technique based on contractions could be used with normal bisimilarity. One would have first to prove substitutivity properties for the contraction version of normal bisimilarity. As discussed in earlier sections, in presence of localities and passivation, the substitutivity of normal bisimilarity is delicate.

A problem raised by Lenglet, Schmitt and Stefani [12], and still open, is whether normal bisimilarity, in the variant involving composite triggers as in Definition 9, is a characterisation of barbed congruence (and context bisimilarity) on the full calculus HOπP, including the restriction operator.

Acknowledgments. Thanks to the reviewers for their reading of the paper and their suggestions. Above all, big thanks to Jean-Bernard Stefani, for his kindness, his advices, and for countless enlightening discussions, during so many years, on the theory of process calculi, their proof techniques, and their applications. Research partly supported by the MIUR-PRIN project 'Resource Awareness in Programming: Algebra, Rewriting, and Analysis' (RAP, ID P2022HXNSC).

References

1. Baeten, J.C., Basten, T., Reniers, M.A.: Process Algebra: Equational Theories of Communicating Processes. Cambridge University Press (2010)
2. Bernardo, M., Sangiorgi, D., Vignudelli, V.: On the discriminating power of passivation and higher-order interaction. In: Henzinger, T.A., Miller, D. (eds.) Twenty-Third EACSL Annual Conference on Computer Science Logic (CSL) and Twenty-Ninth Annual ACM/IEEE Symposium on Logic in Computer Science (LICS), pp. 14:1–14:10. ACM (2014). https://doi.org/10.1145/2603088.2603113
3. Bidinger, P., Stefani, J.-B.: The kell calculus: operational semantics and type system. In: Najm, E., Nestmann, U., Stevens, P. (eds.) FMOODS 2003. LNCS, vol. 2884, pp. 109–123. Springer, Heidelberg (2003). https://doi.org/10.1007/978-3-540-39958-2_8
4. Cao, Z.: More on bisimulations for higher order π-calculus. Theor. Comput. Sci. **446**, 1–19 (2012). https://doi.org/10.1016/j.tcs.2012.04.014

5. Durier, A., Hirschkoff, D., Sangiorgi, D.: Divergence and unique solution of equations. Log. Methods Comput. Sci. **15**(3) (2019). https://doi.org/10.23638/LMCS-15(3:12)2019
6. Durier, A., Hirschkoff, D., Sangiorgi, D.: Towards 'up to context' reasoning about higher-order processes. Theor. Comput. Sci. **807**, 154–168 (2020)
7. Durier, A., Hirschkoff, D., Sangiorgi, D.: Eager functions as processes. Theor. Comput. Sci. 913, 8–42 (2022). https://doi.org/10.1016/j.tcs.2022.01.043
8. Groote, J.F., Mousavi, M.R.: Modeling and Analysis of Communicating Systems. MIT Press (2014)
9. Jeffrey, A., Rathke, J.: A theory of bisimulation for a fragment of Concurrent ML with local names. In: Proceedings of LICS 2000. IEEE (2000)
10. Lenglet, S., Schmitt, A., Stefani, J.-B.: Howe's method for calculi with passivation. In: Bravetti, M., Zavattaro, G. (eds.) CONCUR 2009. LNCS, vol. 5710, pp. 448–462. Springer, Heidelberg (2009). https://doi.org/10.1007/978-3-642-04081-8_30
11. Lenglet, S., Schmitt, A., Stefani, J.-B.: Normal bisimulations in calculi with passivation. In: de Alfaro, L. (ed.) FoSSaCS 2009. LNCS, vol. 5504, pp. 257–271. Springer, Heidelberg (2009). https://doi.org/10.1007/978-3-642-00596-1_19
12. Lenglet, S., Schmitt, A., Stefani, J.: Characterizing contextual equivalence in calculi with passivation. Inf. Comput. **209**(11), 1390–1433 (2011). https://doi.org/10.1016/j.ic.2011.08.002
13. Madiot, J.-M., Pous, D., Sangiorgi, D.: Bisimulations up-to: beyond first-order transition systems. In: Baldan, P., Gorla, D. (eds.) CONCUR 2014. LNCS, vol. 8704, pp. 93–108. Springer, Heidelberg (2014). https://doi.org/10.1007/978-3-662-44584-6_8
14. Milner, R.: Communication and Concurrency. Prentice Hall (1989)
15. Milner, R., Sangiorgi, D.: Barbed bisimulation. In: Kuich, W. (ed.) ICALP 1992. LNCS, vol. 623, pp. 685–695. Springer, Heidelberg (1992). https://doi.org/10.1007/3-540-55719-9_114
16. Piérard, A., Sumii, E.: Sound bisimulations for higher-order distributed process calculus. In: Hofmann, M. (ed.) FoSSaCS 2011. LNCS, vol. 6604, pp. 123–137. Springer, Heidelberg (2011). https://doi.org/10.1007/978-3-642-19805-2_9
17. Pous, D., Sangiorgi, D.: Advanced Topics in Bisimulation and Coinduction (D. Sangiorgi and J. Rutten editors), chap. Enhancements of the coinductive proof method. Cambridge University Press (2011)
18. Pous, D., Sangiorgi, D.: Bisimulation and coinduction enhancements: a historical perspective. Formal Asp. Comput. **31**(6), 733–749 (2019)
19. Roscoe, A.W.: An alternative order for the failures model. J. Log. Comput. **2**(5), 557–577 (1992)
20. Roscoe, A.W.: The Theory and Practice of Concurrency. Prentice Hall PTR, Upper Saddle River (1997)
21. Roscoe, A.W.: Understanding Concurrent Systems. Springer (2010)
22. Sangiorgi, D.: An investigation into functions as processes. In: Brookes, S., Main, M., Melton, A., Mislove, M., Schmidt, D. (eds.) MFPS 1993. LNCS, vol. 802, pp. 143–159. Springer, Heidelberg (1994). https://doi.org/10.1007/3-540-58027-1_7
23. Sangiorgi, D.: Bisimulation for higher-order process calculi. Inf. Comput. **131**(2), 141–178 (1996)
24. Sangiorgi, D.: On the bisimulation proof method. J. Math. Struct. Comput. Sci. **8**, 447–479 (1998)
25. Sangiorgi, D.: Asynchronous process calculi: the first-order and higher-order paradigms. Theoret. Comput. Sci. **253**, 311–350 (2001)

26. Sangiorgi, D.: Equations, contractions, and unique solutions. ACM Trans. Comput. Log. **18**(1), 4:1–4:30 (2017). https://doi.org/10.1145/2971339
27. Schmitt, A., Stefani, J.: The m-calculus: a higher-order distributed process calculus. In: Aiken, A., Morrisett, G. (eds.) 30th SIGPLAN-SIGACT Symposium on Principles of Programming Languages, pp. 50–61. ACM (2003)
28. Schmitt, A., Stefani, J.-B.: The kell calculus: a family of higher-order distributed process calculi. In: Priami, C., Quaglia, P. (eds.) GC 2004. LNCS, vol. 3267, pp. 146–178. Springer, Heidelberg (2005). https://doi.org/10.1007/978-3-540-31794-4_9
29. Stefani, J.: A calculus of Kells. In: Focardi, R., Zavattaro, G. (eds.) 2nd EATCS Workshop on Foundations of Global Computing. Electronic Notes in Theoretical Computer Science, vol. 85, pp. 40–60. Elsevier (2003)

Semantics

From Complementary to Zipper Semantics

Sergueï Lenglet[1], Camille Noûs[2], and Alan Schmitt[3(✉)]

[1] Université Sorbonne Paris Nord, Villetaneuse, France
[2] Laboratoire Cogitamus, Creteil, France
[3] INRIA, Rennes, France
alan.schmi@inria.fr

Abstract. We present two serialized semantics format for process calculi based on labeled transition systems. *Complementary semantics* are useful to prove the congruence of bisimilarity. *Zipper semantics* are the first step toward the automatic derivation of an abstract machine. Both semantics are based on the same restrictions: inductive rules have at most one premise and some contextual information is kept in the label.

Keywords: Process calculus · Semantics · Labeled transition system · Bisimilarity · Congruence · Abstract machine

1 Introduction

The semantics of process calculi can be defined using a *labeled transition system* (LTS), where a process performs a little bit of computation (it is a *small-step* semantics) while indicating as a label the interaction it is doing. Such a description simplifies semantics with interactions that are not local, such as the sending and receiving of a message between (syntactically) distant processes. Consider for instance the process $(\overline{a} \parallel P) \parallel (Q \parallel a.R)$, where $\overline{a}$ is the sending of (an empty) message on a, and $a.R$ is the receiving of an empty message before continuing as R. The $\parallel$ operator represents the parallel composition. This process may evolve to $P \parallel (Q \parallel R)$ after the communication on a. This can be witnessed by the fact that $\overline{a} \parallel P$ can emit on a to evolve to P, and $Q \parallel a.R$ can receive on a to evolve to $Q \parallel R$. The derivation as an LTS of this computation would typically be shown as follows, where τ denotes an internal step.

$$\dfrac{\dfrac{\cdots}{\overline{a} \parallel P \xrightarrow{\overline{a}} P} \quad \dfrac{\cdots}{Q \parallel a.R \xrightarrow{a} Q \parallel R}}{(\overline{a} \parallel P) \parallel (Q \parallel a.R) \xrightarrow{\tau} P \parallel (Q \parallel R)}$$

This approach has two drawbacks. First, the communication rule has multiple inductive hypotheses, which can raise some transitivity issues when proving some properties of the calculus. This was first described in our work on behavioural equivalences in calculi with passivation [11–13] and is detailed in Sect. 2. Second, the decomposition of a term as a context around a redex is left implicit in the structure of the derivation, while it would be useful to have it as an explicit label, for instance as a first step towards an abstract machine for the calculus as we more recently showed [2,10]. This is described in Sect. 3. Although these questions are quite different, our proposal to address them is very similar: a labeled transition system where each rule has at most one inductive premise, and where contexts or parts of contexts are explicitly given in the labels.

2 Complementary Semantics

To be preserved by context is a desirable property of behavioural equivalences: it means that one can prove that two terms are equivalent by decomposing them into smaller equivalent subterms. Such a property turned out to be difficult to prove for some higher-order process calculi [11,12]. To illustrate this, we use a simple calculus called HOcore [9], for which we define a context bisimilarity. We show what the problem is with its congruence proof, and how it can be solved using complementary semantics.

2.1 HOcore

We recall the syntax and semantics of HOcore, which we use to present complementary and zipper semantics (Sect. 3). HOcore is a minimal higher-order process calculus with no name restriction. We let a, b range over *channel names*, X, Y over *process variables*, and we define the syntax of processes as follows.

$$P, Q, R ::= X \mid \mathbf{0} \mid P \parallel Q \mid a(X).\, P \mid \overline{a}\langle P \rangle$$

The process **0** is the inactive process, $P \parallel Q$ runs P and Q in parallel, and a communication may happen between an input $a(X).P$ and an output $\overline{a}\langle Q \rangle$ that run in parallel. The communication is asynchronous because a message output does not have a continuation [16]. The notions of bound variables (the variable X in $a(X).P$) and free variables are defined as usual. We adopt the *Barendregt convention* that bound variables are always kept distinct from free variable through α-conversion. We write $P\{R/X\}$ for the usual capture-avoiding substitution of X by R in P, and $\widetilde{P}$ for a tuple of processes.

In spite of its minimal number of constructors, HOcore is Turing-complete [9].

We present the semantics of HOcore as a labeled transition system (LTS). A process may evolve towards a process (internal actions $P \xrightarrow{\tau} P'$), an *abstraction* (message input $P \xrightarrow{a} F = (X)Q$), or a *concretion* (message output $P \xrightarrow{\overline{a}} C = \langle R \rangle Q$). The transition $P \xrightarrow{a} (X)Q$ means that P may receive a process R on a to continue as $Q\{R/X\}$. The transition $P \xrightarrow{\overline{a}} \langle R \rangle Q$ means that P may send the process R on a and continue as Q. Note that Q is needed even though our calculus is asynchronous, as it not only contains the direct continuation of the message (which is absent in an asynchronous calculus), but also processes in parallel of the message sending.

Let *agents*, noted A, be the set of processes, abstractions, and concretions. We extend the parallel composition to all agents as follows, relying on the Barendregt convention to avoid capture.

$$(X)Q \parallel P \triangleq (X)(Q \parallel P) \qquad \langle Q \rangle R \parallel P \triangleq \langle Q \rangle (R \parallel P)$$
$$P \parallel (X)Q \triangleq (X)(P \parallel Q) \qquad P \parallel \langle Q \rangle R \triangleq \langle Q \rangle (P \parallel R)$$

A higher-order communication takes place when a concretion interacts with an abstraction. We define a pseudo-application operator $\bullet$ between an abstraction $(X)P$ and a concretion $\langle R \rangle Q$ as follows.

$$(X)P \bullet \langle R \rangle Q \triangleq P\{R/X\} \parallel Q$$

The rules of the LTS are given in Fig. 1, where we omit the symmetric rules for Par and HO.

Abstr
$a(X).P \xrightarrow{a} (X)P$

Concr
$\overline{a}\langle Q \rangle \xrightarrow{\overline{a}} \langle Q \rangle \mathbf{0}$

Par
$$\dfrac{P \xrightarrow{l} A}{P \parallel Q \xrightarrow{l} A \parallel Q}$$

HO
$$\dfrac{P \xrightarrow{a} F \quad Q \xrightarrow{\overline{a}} C}{P \parallel Q \xrightarrow{\tau} F \bullet C}$$

Fig. 1. Labeled Transition System for HOcore

2.2 Context Bisimilarity and Howe's Method

Sangiorgi [15] defines *context* bisimilarity as a behavioural equivalence for higher-order process calculi. When two tested processes P and Q perform a partial action like receiving a message on a, a context may interact with them by sending a message on that channel. Context bisimilarity therefore requires the processes to remain bisimilar after communicating with any such recipient, represented by the abstraction F in the second clause of Definition 1. The principle is symmetric for outputting processes.

Definition 1. *Strong context bisimilarity $\sim$ is the largest symmetric relation on closed processes $\mathcal{R}$ such that $P \mathcal{R} Q$ implies:*

- *for all $P \xrightarrow{\tau} P'$, there exists Q' such that $Q \xrightarrow{\tau} Q'$ and $P' \mathcal{R} Q'$;*
- *for all $P \xrightarrow{a} F$, for all C, there exists F' such that $Q \xrightarrow{a} F'$ and $F \bullet C \mathcal{R} F' \bullet C$;*
- *for all $P \xrightarrow{\overline{a}} C$, for all F, there exists C' such that $Q \xrightarrow{\overline{a}} C'$ and $F \bullet C \mathcal{R} F \bullet C'$.*

Sangiorgi's proof technique to show that context bisimilarity is a congruence unfortunately does not scale to more complex calculi [11]. It explains why we turn to Howe's method [1,6,7], a systematic proof technique to show that a simulation $\mathcal{R}$ is a congruence. The method can be divided in three steps: first, prove some basic properties on the *Howe's closure* $\mathcal{R}^\bullet$ of the relation. By construction, $\mathcal{R}^\bullet$ contains $\mathcal{R}$ and is a congruence. Second, prove a simulation-like property for $\mathcal{R}^\bullet$, and finally prove that $\mathcal{R}$ and $\mathcal{R}^\bullet$ coincide on closed processes. Since $\mathcal{R}^\bullet$ is a congruence, conclude that $\mathcal{R}$ is a congruence.

The definition of the Howe's closure relies on the open extension of $\mathcal{R}$, noted $\mathcal{R}^\circ$: it extends the definition of the relation $\mathcal{R}$ to *open processes*, that are processes with free process variables.

Definition 2. *Let P and Q be two open processes. We have $P \mathcal{R}^\circ Q$ iff $P\sigma \mathcal{R} Q\sigma$ for all process substitutions σ that close P and Q.*

Howe's closure is inductively defined as the smallest congruence which contains $\mathcal{R}^\circ$ and is closed under right composition with $\mathcal{R}^\circ$.

Definition 3. *Howe's closure $\mathcal{R}^\bullet$ of a relation $\mathcal{R}$ is the smallest relation verifying:*

- $\mathcal{R}^\circ \subseteq \mathcal{R}^\bullet$;
- $\mathcal{R}^\bullet \mathcal{R}^\circ \subseteq \mathcal{R}^\bullet$;
- *for all operators op of the language, if $\widetilde{P} \mathcal{R}^\bullet \widetilde{Q}$, then $op(\widetilde{P}) \mathcal{R}^\bullet op(\widetilde{Q})$.*

By definition, $\mathcal{R}^\bullet$ is a congruence. The composition with $\mathcal{R}^\circ$ allows for some transitivity and gives some additional properties to the relation.

In our case, we want to prove that a bisimilarity $\mathcal{B}$ is a congruence. By definition, we have $\mathcal{B} \subseteq \mathcal{B}^\circ \subseteq \mathcal{B}^\bullet$. To have the reverse inclusion, we prove that $\mathcal{B}^\bullet$ is a bisimulation. To this end, we need the following classical properties of the Howe's closure.

Lemma 1. *Let $\mathcal{R}$ be a reflexive relation. If $P \mathcal{R}^\bullet Q$ and $R \mathcal{R}^\bullet S$, then we have $P\{R/X\} \mathcal{R}^\bullet Q\{S/X\}$.*

This lemma is typically used to establish the simulation-like result (second step of the method). We sketch the proof in order to give an idea on why the transitive item $\mathcal{R}^\bullet \mathcal{R}^\circ \subseteq \mathcal{R}^\bullet$ is needed in Definition 3. The proof is by induction on the derivation of $P \mathcal{R}^\bullet Q$. Suppose we have $P \mathcal{R}^\circ Q$. Since $R \mathcal{R}^\bullet S$ and $\mathcal{R}^\bullet$ is a congruence, we have $P\{/X\}R \mathcal{R}^\bullet P\{S/X\}$. Let σ be a substitution that closes P, Q, and S except for X; by open extension definition, we have $P\{S/X\}\sigma \mathcal{R} Q\{S/X\}\sigma$, i.e., we have $P\{S/X\} \mathcal{R}^\circ Q\{S/X\}$. Finally we have $P\{R/X\} \mathcal{R}^\bullet \mathcal{R}^\circ Q\{S/X\}$, hence we have $P\{R/X\} \mathcal{R}^\bullet Q\{S/X\}$. The other cases are easy using the induction hypothesis.

We cannot prove directly that $\mathcal{B}^\bullet$ is symmetric. Instead we use the following lemma.

Lemma 2. *Let $\mathcal{R}$ be an equivalence. Then the reflexive and transitive closure $(\mathcal{R}^\bullet)^*$ of $\mathcal{R}^\bullet$ is symmetric.*

Then one proves that the restriction of $(\mathcal{B}^\bullet)^*$ to closed terms is a bisimulation. Consequently we have $\mathcal{B} \subseteq \mathcal{B}^\bullet \subseteq (\mathcal{B}^\bullet)^* \subseteq \mathcal{B}$ on closed terms, and we conclude that $\mathcal{B}$ is a congruence.

The main difficulty lies in the proof of the simulation-like property for Howe's closure. In the following subsection, we explain why we cannot directly use Howe's method with Definition 1.

2.3 Communication Problem

Proving that a congruence is a simulation raises transitivity issues [11]. In a nutshell, the problem occurs in the communication case, where we have two inductive premises (one for the message sending and one for the message receiving). Applying the induction hypothesis twice results in the final processes being related by $\mathcal{R}\mathcal{R}$ instead of directly $\mathcal{R}$. To avoid the problem, we establish a stronger result. Given a bisimilarity $\mathcal{B}$ based on a LTS $P \xrightarrow{\lambda} A$, the simulation-like result follows the pattern below.

Let $P\ \mathcal{B}^\bullet\ Q$. If $P \xrightarrow{\lambda} A$, then for all $\lambda\ \mathcal{B}^\bullet\ \lambda'$, there exists B such that $Q \xrightarrow{\lambda'} B$ and $A\ \mathcal{B}^\bullet\ B$.

Instantiated with Definition 1, the property would be as follows.

Conjecture 1. If $P\ \mathcal{R}^\bullet\ Q$, then:

- for all $P \xrightarrow{\tau} P'$, there exists Q' such that $Q \xrightarrow{\tau} Q'$ and $P'\ \mathcal{R}^\bullet\ Q'$;
- for all $P \xrightarrow{a} F$, for all $C\ \mathcal{R}^\bullet\ C'$, there exists F' such that $Q \xrightarrow{a} F'$ and $F \bullet C\ \mathcal{R}^\bullet\ F' \bullet C'$;
- for all $P \xrightarrow{\bar{a}} C$, for all $F\ \mathcal{R}^\bullet\ F'$ there exists C' such that $Q \xrightarrow{\bar{a}} C'$ and we have $F \bullet C\ \mathcal{R}^\bullet\ F' \bullet C'$.

The proof of Conjecture 1 fails with higher-order communication. The reasoning is by induction on $P\ \mathcal{R}^\bullet\ Q$. Suppose we are in the parallel case, i.e., we have $P = P_1 \parallel P_2$ and $Q = Q_1 \parallel Q_2$, with $P_1\ \mathcal{R}^\bullet\ Q_1$ and $P_2\ \mathcal{R}^\bullet\ Q_2$. Suppose that we have $P \xrightarrow{\tau} P'$, and the transition comes from rule HO: we have $P_1 \xrightarrow{a} F$, $P_2 \xrightarrow{\bar{a}} C$ and $P' = F \bullet C$. We want to find Q' such that $Q \xrightarrow{\tau} Q'$ and $P'\ \mathcal{R}^\bullet\ Q'$. We also want to use the same rule HO, hence we have to find F', C' such that $Q \xrightarrow{\tau} F' \bullet C'$. However we cannot use the input clause of the induction hypothesis with P_1, Q_1: to have a F' such that $Q_1 \xrightarrow{a} F'$, we have to find first a concretion C' such that $C\ \mathcal{R}^\bullet\ C'$. We cannot use the output clause with P_2, Q_2 either: to have a C' such that $Q_2 \xrightarrow{\bar{a}} C'$, we have to find first an abstraction F' such that $F\ \mathcal{R}^\bullet\ F'$. We cannot bypass this mutual dependency and the inductive proof of Conjecture 1 fails.

To break the circularity, we propose a change in the LTS: instead of requiring the abstraction before providing a matching output, we only require the process that will do the reception (that will reduce to the abstraction). This may seem a very small change, yet it is sufficient to break the symmetry. We return to the communication problem where $P_1 \parallel P_2$ is in relation with $Q_1 \parallel Q_2$. The concretion C' from Q_2 matching the $P_2 \xrightarrow{\overline{a}} C$ step depends only on Q_1, which is known, and not on some unknown abstraction. We can then obtain the abstraction F' from Q_1 that matches the $P_1 \xrightarrow{a} F$ step.

Technically, we do not use concretions and abstractions anymore. In the LTS, when a communication between P and Q occurs, this becomes a transition from P using Q as a label. In other words, we store part of the context of the communication in the label. Higher in the derivation, the actual output from P is discovered, and we switch to dealing with the input knowing exactly the output. The proof of the bisimulation property for the candidate relation relies on this serialization of the LTS and illustrates how symmetry is broken. On the other hand, we can prove that the resulting bisimilarity coincides with context bisimilarity.

2.4 Complementary Semantics and Bisimilarity

$$
\begin{array}{cccc}
\text{In} & \text{Out} & \text{Par} & \text{HO} \\
 & Q \xmapsto{a,R} Q' & P_1 \xmapsto{\lambda} P_1' & P \xmapsto{\overline{a},Q} P' \\
\hline
a(X).P \xmapsto{a,R} P\{R/X\} & \overline{a}\langle R \rangle \xmapsto{\overline{a},Q} Q' & P_1 \parallel P_2 \xmapsto{\lambda} P_1' \parallel P_2 & P \parallel Q \xmapsto{\tau} P'
\end{array}
$$

Fig. 2. Complementary LTS for HOcore.

We define a LTS $P \xmapsto{\lambda} P'$ for HOcore where processes always evolve towards other processes. We have three kinds of transitions: internal actions $P \xmapsto{\tau} P'$, message input $P \xmapsto{a,R} P'$, and message output $P \xmapsto{\overline{a},R} P'$. We called this LTS *complementary* because in a transition $P \xmapsto{\overline{a},R} P'$, we put in the label what is needed to complement P for a communication to happen (here, a receiving process R). Rules of this LTS can be found in Fig. 2, except for the symmetric of rules Par and HO.

Rules for internal actions $P \xmapsto{\tau} P'$ are similar to the one for the contextual LTS $P \xrightarrow{\tau} P'$, except for higher-order communication since we change the message output judgement; we detail the rule HO later. Message input $P \xmapsto{a,R} P'$ means that process P may receive the process R as a message on a and becomes P'. In the contextual style, it means that $P \xrightarrow{a} (X)P''$ and $P' = P''\{R/X\}$ for some P''.

The main difference is in the definition of output actions. The transition $P \xmapsto{\overline{a},R} P'$ means that P may send a message on a, R may receive on a, and the communication on a between P and R results in P'. The transition $P \xmapsto{\overline{a},R} P'$ means that there exists F, C such that $P \xrightarrow{\overline{a}} C$, $R \xrightarrow{a} F$, and $P' = F \bullet C$.

Rules of the LTS (Fig. 2) are classic except rules HO and Out. In rule HO, the premise $P \xmapsto{\overline{a},Q} P'$ means that P and Q can communicate on a name a and the result is P', i.e., $P \| Q \xrightarrow{\tau} P'$ (by communication on a in the classical LTS), which is exactly what the conclusion of the rule states. Rule Out has a premise (unlike its equivalent rule Concr) since in the conclusion we need the result Q' of the input of R on a by Q.

Example 1. We show an example of derivation for a process close to the one given in the introduction.

$$\cfrac{\cfrac{\cfrac{\cfrac{\cfrac{}{a(X).R \xmapsto{a,\mathbf{0}} R\{\mathbf{0}/X\}} \text{In}}{Q \| a(X).R \xmapsto{a,\mathbf{0}} Q \| R\{\mathbf{0}/X\}} \text{Par}}{\overline{a}\langle \mathbf{0}\rangle \xmapsto{\overline{a},Q \| a(X).R} Q \| R\{\mathbf{0}/X\}} \text{Out}}{\overline{a}\langle \mathbf{0}\rangle \| P \xmapsto{\overline{a},Q \| a(X).R} (Q \| R\{\mathbf{0}/X\}) \| P} \text{Par}}{(\overline{a}\langle \mathbf{0}\rangle \| P) \| (Q \| a(X).R) \xmapsto{\tau} (Q \| R\{\mathbf{0}/X\}) \| P} \text{HO}$$

The structure of parallel compositions is not preserved between the source and target processes: the correspondence between the complementary LTS and the LTS of Fig. 1 is up to *structural congruence* [11], an equivalence on processes where parallel composition is commutative, associative, and with $\mathbf{0}$ as neutral. This discrepancy between the semantics is not a problem because our goal is to define a behavioural equivalence, and reordering processes does not change the behaviour of processes in HOcore. In more expressive calculi such as calculi with passivation, we can no longer reason up to structural congruence and the definition of the complementary semantics is more complex as a result [11].

We define complementary bisimilarity as the bisimilarity associated to the complementary LTS.

Definition 4. *Strong complementary bisimilarity $\sim_m$ is the largest symmetric relation on closed processes $\mathcal{R}$ such that $P \mathcal{R} Q$ and $P \xmapsto{\lambda} P'$ implies $Q \xmapsto{\lambda} Q'$ with $P' \mathcal{R} Q'$.*

As in context bisimilarity, in the message output case $P \xmapsto{\overline{a},R} P'$, the matching transition $Q \xmapsto{\overline{a},R} Q'$ still depends on a receiving entity (here R). However, instead of considering a context which directly receives the message (an abstraction F), we consider a process R which evolves toward an abstraction. This nuance allows us to use Howe's method to prove the soundness of $\sim_m$. We extend $\sim_m^\bullet$ to labels λ: we have $\lambda \sim_m^\bullet \lambda'$ iff $\lambda = \lambda' = \tau$, or $\lambda = (\gamma, R)$, $\lambda' = (\gamma, R')$ with $R \sim_m^\bullet R'$. We prove the following simulation-like property for $\sim_m^\bullet$:

Lemma 3. *Let P, Q be closed processes. If $P \sim_m^\bullet Q$ and $P \xmapsto{\lambda} Q$, then for all $\lambda \sim_m^\bullet \lambda'$, there exists Q' such that $Q \xmapsto{\lambda'} Q'$ and $P' \sim_m^\bullet Q'$.*

We do not have the same problem as in Sect. 2.3 with higher-order communication. We remind that in this case, we have $P_1 \| P_2 \sim_m^\bullet Q_1 \| Q_2$ with $P_1 \sim_m^\bullet Q_1$,

$P_2 \sim^\bullet_m Q_2$ and $P_1 \xrightarrow{\overline{a},P_2} P'$. We can apply directly the message output clause of the induction hypothesis: there exists Q' such that $Q_1 \xrightarrow{\overline{a},Q_2} Q'$ and $P' \sim^\bullet_m Q'$. We conclude that $Q_1 \| Q_2 \xmapsto{\tau} Q'$ (by rule HO) with $P' \sim^\bullet_m Q'$ as wished.

Theorem 1. *Relation $\sim_m$ is a congruence.*

We refer to our paper [11] for the proof of the theorem as well as for the proof that complementary and context bisimilarities coincide.

3 Zipper Semantics

Section 2 shows that serializing the LTS makes possible the congruence proof of bisimilarities for higher-order process calculi. The same principle also helps as a first step towards abstract machines for process calculi. We present *zipper semantics*, a small-step semantics inspired by context-based reduction semantics and which can be automatically transformed into an abstract machine [2,10]. Indeed, each rule of a zipper semantics has at most one inductive premise, and the conclusion of the rule is only modified in the case of axioms.

3.1 Context-Based Reduction Semantics

The semantics of process calculi is usually presented either with a structural congruence relation which reorders terms to make redexes appear, bringing input and output processes together, or with a LTS which preserves the structure of the term [16]. Instead, we present it here as a reduction semantics with explicit contexts [3,5], which makes it easier to come up with (or translate into) the corresponding zipper semantics, introduced in the next section.

We represent a context $\mathbb{E}$ as a list of elementary contexts called *frames* $\mathfrak{F}$. The empty list is denoted as $\bullet$ and concatenation of $\mathfrak{F}$ to $\mathbb{E}$ as $\mathfrak{F} :: \mathbb{E}$. Each frame is either of the form $\| P$ or of the form $P \|$. Because it is more convenient for the definition of the zipper semantics, we interpret contexts inside-out [4]: the head of the context is the innermost frame. The definition of plugging a process in a context $\mathbb{E}[P]$ is therefore as follows.

$$\bullet[P] \triangleq P \qquad (\| Q :: \mathbb{E})[P] \triangleq \mathbb{E}[P \| Q] \qquad (Q \| :: \mathbb{E})[P] \triangleq \mathbb{E}[Q \| P]$$

A redex is a parallel composition with an input on one side and an output on the same name on the other side, both surrounded with contexts. The general formulation of such communication sites in a program can be expressed with the following reduction semantics.

$$\mathbb{E}[\mathbb{F}[\overline{a}\langle Q\rangle] \| \mathbb{G}[a(X).P]] \to_{\mathsf{rs}} \mathbb{E}[\mathbb{F}[\mathbf{0}] \| \mathbb{G}[P\{Q/X\}]]$$
$$\mathbb{E}[\mathbb{G}[a(X).P] \| \mathbb{F}[\overline{a}\langle Q\rangle]] \to_{\mathsf{rs}} \mathbb{E}[\mathbb{G}[P\{Q/X\}] \| \mathbb{F}[\mathbf{0}]]$$

Such rules can be read declaratively: if we find a redex in a context $\mathbb{E}$ built according to the given grammar of contexts, where the redex is itself the parallel composition of the sending and receiving of messages inside contexts $\mathbb{F}$ and

$\mathbb{G}$, then we can reduce. Note that the structure of parallel compositions is preserved between the process being reduced and the result of the reduction: the contexts $\mathbb{E}$, $\mathbb{F}$, and $\mathbb{G}$ are left unchanged.

This format of semantics does not make it apparent how to *decompose* a term to find a redex. On the other hand, structural operational semantics (SOS) offers another common semantic format that makes it more explicit how to navigate in a term to find a redex, but it does not store the traversed path. Zipper semantics is a middle ground between these two formats.

3.2 Left-First Zipper Semantics

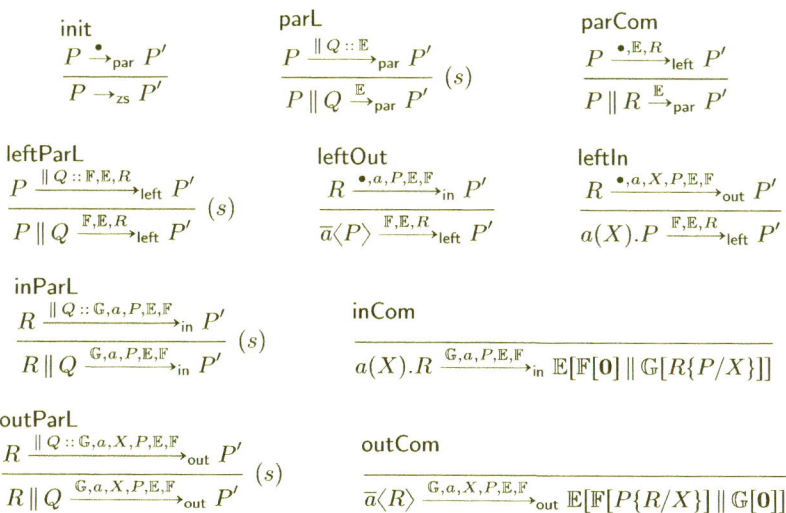

Fig. 3. Left-first Zipper Semantics for HOcore.

A first step towards an abstract machine is to make explicit the step-by-step decomposition of a term into a context and a redex. To this end, we proposed zipper semantics, a combination of SOS and reduction semantics. Like a regular SOS, a zipper semantics goes through a term looking for a redex using structural rules, except the current position in the term is made explicit with a context as in reduction semantics.

Finding an HOcore redex requires us to recognize three constructs (parallel composition along with output and input on a shared name) and build the contexts $\mathbb{E}$, $\mathbb{F}$, and $\mathbb{G}$. Such a search can be conducted in many ways. A possibility is to search first for the parallel composition at the root of the redex $P \| Q$. From there, the communication rules of typical LTSs for process calculi [9,14,16] have two inductive premises looking for the output in P and the input in Q, or the opposite. To be closer to an abstract machine, we sequentialize the search by going left in P to find either an output or an input on some name a, and we then look for a complementary action on the same name in Q. Starting with the left process is an arbitrary choice—going right would produce a symmetric semantics.

Figure 3 presents such a left-first zipper semantics, where we omit the symmetric versions of the rules marked with the symbol (s)–a convention we follow from now on. There exist different kinds of transitions, or *modes*, to reuse a terminology used in abstract machines. We briefly explain the rules by describing them from the conclusion to their promise.

The init rule initializes the search with the par mode, the purpose of which is to decompose the initial process as $\mathbb{E}[P \parallel R]$, where P and R are the communicating processes. The rules parL and (omitted) parR are going through the initial process by focusing on the subprocess on the left or right of the parallel composition. We see why interpreting contexts inside-out is convenient: focusing on a subprocess amounts to pushing the corresponding frame on top of the current context.

Once we find the parallel composition $P \parallel R$ at the root of the redex, the parCom rule switches to the $\xrightarrow{\mathbb{F},\mathbb{E},R}_{\text{left}}$ transition (with $\mathbb{F}$ set to $\bullet$), which looks for an input or an output in P, while building the context $\mathbb{F}$ and remembering $\mathbb{E}$ and R for later. As in the par mode, the rules leftParL and leftParR focus on the left or right subprocess and remembers the other in the context $\mathbb{F}$.

We eventually reach either an output (rule leftOut) or an input (rule leftIn) on some name a. It triggers the search for respectively an input or an output in R on the same name using the transitions $\xrightarrow{\mathbb{G},a,P,\mathbb{E},\mathbb{F}}_{\text{in}}$ or $\xrightarrow{\mathbb{G},a,X,P,\mathbb{E},\mathbb{F}}_{\text{out}}$, constructing the context $\mathbb{G}$ at the same time. The communication on a happens once the decomposition is complete with either rule inCom or outCom.

Example 2. We reuse the same example as before.

$$\cfrac{\cfrac{\cfrac{\cfrac{\cfrac{a(X).R \xrightarrow{Q\parallel::\bullet,a,\mathbf{0},\bullet,\parallel P::\bullet}_{\text{in}} (\mathbf{0}\parallel P)\parallel(Q\parallel R\{\mathbf{0}/X\})}{Q\parallel a(X).R \xrightarrow{\bullet,a,\mathbf{0},\bullet,\parallel P::\bullet}_{\text{in}} (\mathbf{0}\parallel P)\parallel(Q\parallel R\{\mathbf{0}/X\})}\text{ inParR}}{\overline{a}\langle\mathbf{0}\rangle \xrightarrow{\parallel P::\bullet,\bullet,Q\parallel a(X).R}_{\text{left}} (\mathbf{0}\parallel P)\parallel(Q\parallel R\{\mathbf{0}/X\})}\text{ leftOut}}{\overline{a}\langle\mathbf{0}\rangle\parallel P \xrightarrow{\bullet,\bullet,Q\parallel a(X).R}_{\text{left}} (\mathbf{0}\parallel P)\parallel(Q\parallel R\{\mathbf{0}/X\})}\text{ leftParL}}{(\overline{a}\langle\mathbf{0}\rangle\parallel P)\parallel(Q\parallel a(X).R) \xrightarrow{\bullet}_{\text{par}} (\mathbf{0}\parallel P)\parallel(Q\parallel R\{\mathbf{0}/X\})}\text{ parCom}}{(\overline{a}\langle\mathbf{0}\rangle\parallel P)\parallel(Q\parallel a(X).R) \rightarrow_{\text{zs}} (\mathbf{0}\parallel P)\parallel(Q\parallel R\{\mathbf{0}/X\})}\text{ init}}\text{ inCom}$$

Unlike with complementary semantics, the structure of the initial process is preserved. Computation happens only when applying the axiom inCom; the other rules do not change the resulting process in any way.

3.3 Output-First Zipper Semantics

A different strategy to reach the same decomposition is as follows: after finding the parallel decomposition $P \parallel Q$ at the root of the redex, we look for

$$\frac{\text{init}}{P \xrightarrow{\bullet}_{\text{par}} P'} \qquad \frac{\text{parL}}{P \xrightarrow{\| Q :: \mathbb{E}}_{\text{par}} P'}{P \| Q \xrightarrow{\mathbb{E}}_{\text{par}} P'} (s) \qquad \frac{\text{parOutL}}{P \xrightarrow{\bullet, \mathcal{L}, \mathbb{E}, Q}_{\text{out}} P'}{P \| Q \xrightarrow{\mathbb{E}}_{\text{par}} P'} \qquad \frac{\text{parOutR}}{Q \xrightarrow{\bullet, \mathcal{R}, \mathbb{E}, P}_{\text{out}} P'}{P \| Q \xrightarrow{\mathbb{E}}_{\text{par}} P'}$$

$$\frac{\text{outParL}}{P \xrightarrow{\| Q :: \mathbb{F}, \mathcal{S}, \mathbb{E}, R}_{\text{out}} P'}{P \| Q \xrightarrow{\mathbb{F}, \mathcal{S}, \mathbb{E}, R}_{\text{out}} P'} (s) \qquad \frac{\text{outIn}}{R \xrightarrow{\bullet, \mathcal{S}, a, P, \mathbb{E}, \mathbb{F}}_{\text{in}} P'}{\overline{a}\langle P \rangle \xrightarrow{\mathbb{F}, \mathcal{S}, \mathbb{E}, R}_{\text{out}} P'}$$

$$\frac{\text{inParL}}{R \xrightarrow{\| Q :: \mathbb{G}, \mathcal{S}, a, P, \mathbb{E}, \mathbb{F}}_{\text{in}} P'}{R \| Q \xrightarrow{\mathbb{G}, \mathcal{S}, a, P, \mathbb{E}, \mathbb{F}}_{\text{in}} P'} (s) \qquad \frac{\text{inComL}}{b(X).R \xrightarrow{\mathbb{G}, \mathcal{L}, a, P, \mathbb{E}, \mathbb{F}}_{\text{in}} \mathbb{E}[\mathbb{F}[\mathbf{0}] \| \mathbb{G}[R\{P/X\}]]} (s)$$

Fig. 4. Output-first Zipper Semantics for HOcore.

the output in either P or Q, and then for the input in the other process. Again, the choice of looking for the output first is arbitrary, and we could start with the input instead. We give the rule of the output-first strategy in Fig. 4.

The transition $\xrightarrow{\mathbb{E}}_{\text{par}}$ is searching for the parallel composition and proceeds as in Sect. 3.2. Once we find it, we look for the output either on the left or on the right with respectively rules parOutL and parOutR. We record the side we pick with a parameter $\mathcal{S} ::= \mathcal{L} \mid \mathcal{R}$. For example, in rule parOutL, we look for an output in P on the left ($\mathcal{L}$), remembering that we should later search for a corresponding input in Q. We also initialize the context $\mathbb{F}$ surrounding the output with $\bullet$ and remember $\mathbb{E}$ as the context enclosing the whole redex.

The transition $\xrightarrow{\mathbb{F}, \mathcal{S}, \mathbb{E}, R}_{\text{out}}$ decomposes its source process to find an output, building $\mathbb{F}$ at the same time: the other parameters $\mathcal{S}$, $\mathbb{E}$, and R remain unchanged during the search. When we find the output $\overline{a}\langle P \rangle$ (rule outIn), we look for a corresponding input in R using $\xrightarrow{\mathbb{G}, \mathcal{S}, a, P, \mathbb{E}, \mathbb{F}}_{\text{in}}$, which builds the context $\mathbb{G}$ during the search. Once we find an input on a, we compute the result of the communication, which depends whether the output is on the left (rule inComL) or on the right (omitted rule inComR).

Example 3. The output-first derivation for our ongoing example is as follows.

$$\cfrac{\cfrac{\cfrac{\cfrac{\cfrac{\cfrac{}{a(X).R \xrightarrow{Q \| :: \bullet, \mathcal{L}, a, \mathbf{0}, \bullet, \| P :: \bullet}_{\text{in}} (\mathbf{0} \| P) \| (Q \| R\{\mathbf{0}/X\})}}{Q \| a(X).R \xrightarrow{\bullet, \mathcal{L}, a, \mathbf{0}, \bullet, \| P :: \bullet}_{\text{in}} (\mathbf{0} \| P) \| (Q \| R\{\mathbf{0}/X\})}}{\overline{a}\langle \mathbf{0} \rangle \xrightarrow{\| P :: \bullet, \mathcal{L}, \bullet, Q \| a(X).R}_{\text{out}} (\mathbf{0} \| P) \| (Q \| R\{\mathbf{0}/X\})}}{\overline{a}\langle \mathbf{0} \rangle \| P \xrightarrow{\bullet, \mathcal{L}, \bullet, Q \| a(X).R}_{\text{out}} (\mathbf{0} \| P) \| (Q \| R\{\mathbf{0}/X\})}}{(\overline{a}\langle \mathbf{0} \rangle \| P) \| (Q \| a(X).R) \xrightarrow{\bullet}_{\text{par}} (\mathbf{0} \| P) \| (Q \| R\{\mathbf{0}/X\})}}{(\overline{a}\langle \mathbf{0} \rangle \| P) \| (Q \| a(X).R) \rightarrow_{\text{zs}} (\mathbf{0} \| P) \| (Q \| R\{\mathbf{0}/X\})}} \begin{array}{l} \text{inComL} \\ \text{inParR} \\ \text{outIn} \\ \text{outParL} \\ \text{parOutL} \\ \text{init} \end{array}$$

In that particular example, the derivation remains close of the previous one because the output process is on the left of the redex. The difference is in the extra information $\mathcal{L}$ recorded in the label, which tells us where should be the continuation of the output compared to the input.

3.4 Leaf-First Zipper Semantics

The exploration strategies described so far are called *root-first*, because they start the search with the operator at the root of the redex (the parallel composition). In contrast, a *leaf-first* strategy starts with an operator at the leaves of the redex, the input or the output. In the case of HOcore, it does not matter which one we choose. In a process calculus with name restriction [15], the communication is less symmetric because of the scope extrusion of the name restrictions surrounding the message output. In such a calculus, it is more convenient to start with the output [10], so we describe this strategy also in this paper.

The rules are given in Fig. 5, using the same modes out, par, and in as in the output-first strategy, but with a different meaning. The rule init starts the search at the top of the term with the output mode out. The rules outParL and outParR change the current focus to a subterm. When we apply the rule outOut, the initial term is decomposed as $\mathbb{E}[\bar{a}\langle M\rangle]$, and we switch to the par mode.

The par mode searches the parallel composition which separates the output and input processes *from the inside out*, i.e., starting from the leaf (the message sending) and walking the context. The transition $\mathbb{E} \xrightarrow{K,a,M}_{\text{par}} P'$ goes through $\mathbb{E}$ looking for the parallel composition, constructing K (the continuation of the output) while doing so, and remembering that M is sent on a. The rules outOut initializes the continuation of the par mode with $\mathbf{0}$.

If the context is of the shape $\parallel Q :: \mathbb{E}$ or $Q \parallel :: \mathbb{E}$, we consider a process of the form $\mathbb{E}[K \parallel Q]$ or $\mathbb{E}[Q \parallel K]$ and we have two possibilities. If Q is not the process receiving the message, then Q has to be added to the continuation, and we continue searching for the receiver in $\mathbb{E}$ (rules parL and parR). Otherwise, we have found the parallel composition where the communication takes place. We search for the input in Q with a transition $Q \xrightarrow{\mathbb{E},a,M}_{\text{in}} P'$, where $\mathbb{E}$ is the context surrounding Q, initially either $K \parallel :: \mathbb{E}$ (rule parInL) or $\parallel K :: \mathbb{E}$ (rule parInR).

The in mode is then going through the receiving process (from the outside in), pushing the processes in parallel on the context $\mathbb{E}$ (rules inParL and inParR). Once an input $a(X).R$ has been found, the communication happens resulting in $\mathbb{E}[R\{M/X\}]$. The decomposition of the initial process into a redex is not as obvious in rule inCom as in the corresponding rules in Fig. 3 or 4, but one can still prove the correspondence between the leaf-first zipper semantics and the context-based reduction semantics [10].

$$\text{init } \frac{P \stackrel{\bullet}{\to}_{\text{out}} P'}{P \to_{\text{zs}} P'} \qquad \text{outParL } \frac{P \xrightarrow{\|Q::\mathbb{E}}_{\text{out}} P'}{P \| Q \xrightarrow{\mathbb{E}}_{\text{out}} P'} \ (s) \qquad \text{outOut } \frac{\mathbb{E} \xrightarrow{0,a,M}_{\text{par}} P'}{\overline{a}\langle M \rangle \xrightarrow{\mathbb{E}}_{\text{out}} P'}$$

$$\text{parL } \frac{\mathbb{E} \xrightarrow{K \| Q,a,M}_{\text{par}} P'}{\| Q :: \mathbb{E} \xrightarrow{K,a,M}_{\text{par}} P'} \ (s) \qquad \text{parInL } \frac{R \xrightarrow{K \| :: \mathbb{E},a,M}_{\text{in}} P'}{\| R :: \mathbb{E} \xrightarrow{K,a,M}_{\text{par}} P'} \ (s)$$

$$\text{inParL } \frac{R \xrightarrow{\|Q::\mathbb{E},a,M}_{\text{in}} P'}{R \| Q \xrightarrow{\mathbb{E},a,M}_{\text{in}} P'} \ (s) \qquad \text{inCom } \frac{}{a(X).R \xrightarrow{\mathbb{E},a,M}_{\text{in}} \mathbb{E}[R\{M/X\}]}$$

Fig. 5. Leaf-First Zipper Semantics for HOcore.

Example 4. The leaf-first derivation is quite different from the previous ones.

$$\cfrac{\cfrac{\cfrac{\cfrac{\cfrac{\cfrac{\cfrac{a(X).R \xrightarrow{Q \| :: (0 \| P) \| :: \bullet, a, 0}_{\text{in}} (0 \| P) \| (Q \| R\{0/X\})}{Q \| a(X).R \xrightarrow{(0 \| P) \| :: \bullet, a, 0}_{\text{in}} (0 \| P) \| (Q \| R\{0/X\})}}{\| (Q \| a(X).R) :: \bullet \xrightarrow{0 \| P, a, 0}_{\text{par}} (0 \| P) \| (Q \| R\{0/X\})}}{\| P :: \| (Q \| a(X).R) :: \bullet \xrightarrow{0, a, 0}_{\text{par}} (0 \| P) \| (Q \| R\{0/X\})}}{\overline{a}\langle 0 \rangle \xrightarrow{\| P :: \| (Q \| a(X).R) :: \bullet}_{\text{out}} (0 \| P) \| (Q \| R\{0/X\})}}{\overline{a}\langle 0 \rangle \| P \xrightarrow{\| (Q \| a(X).R) :: \bullet}_{\text{out}} (0 \| P) \| (Q \| R\{0/X\})}}{(\overline{a}\langle 0 \rangle \| P) \| (Q \| a(X).R) \xrightarrow{\bullet}_{\text{out}} (0 \| P) \| (Q \| R\{0/X\})}}{(\overline{a}\langle 0 \rangle \| P) \| (Q \| a(X).R) \to_{\text{zs}} (0 \| P) \| (Q \| R\{0/X\})}$$

(annotations on right: inCom, inParR, parInL, parL, outOut, outParL, outParL, init)

This style is where the analogy with the zipper data structure [8] is more obvious: we go up and down in the term by going through the context represented inside-out as a list.

4 Conclusion

We have presented two applications of a serialized semantics format to describe process calculi. First, the *complementary semantics* was introduced to prove congruence properties of higher-order process calculi with passivation. This was done during the PhD of Sergueï Lenglet, supervised by Jean-Bernard Stefani and Alan Schmitt. Many years later, Sergueï and Alan continued working on the semantics of process calculi, and we reused some of these fruitful ideas to define the *zipper semantics* of a calculus, from which an abstract machine (and an implementation) can be automatically derived. We are currently working on the derivation of the zipper semantics itself from a context-based reduction semantics, which would simplify further the experimentation around process calculi.

References

1. Baldamus, M.: Semantics and Logic of Higher-Order Processes: Characterizing Late Context Bisimulation. PhD thesis, Berlin University of Technology (1998)
2. Biernacka, M., Biernacki, D., Lenglet, S., Schmitt, A.: Non-deterministic abstract machines. In: Klin, B., Lasota, S., Muscholl, A. (eds.) 33rd International Conference on Concurrency Theory (CONCUR 2022), Volume 243 of Leibniz International Proceedings in Informatics (LIPIcs), pp. 1–24. Schloss Dagstuhl – Leibniz-Zentrum für Informatik, Dagstuhl, Germany (2022)
3. Danvy, O.: From reduction-based to reduction-free normalization. In: Koopman, P.W.M., Plasmeijer, R., Swierstra, S.D. (eds.) Advanced Functional Programming, 6th International School, AFP 2008, Heijen, The Netherlands, May 2008, Revised Lectures, Volume 5832 of Lecture Notes in Computer Science, pp. 66–164. Springer (2008)
4. Felleisen, M.: Findler, R.B., Flatt, M.: Semantics Engineering with PLT Redex. The MIT Press (2009)
5. Felleisen, M., Hieb, R.: The revised report on the syntactic theories of sequential control and state. Theor. Comput. Sci. **103**(2), 235–271 (1992)
6. Gordon, A.D.: Bisimilarity as a theory of functional programming. Electr. Notes Theoret. Comput. Sci. **1**, 232–252 (1995)
7. Howe, D.J.: Proving congruence of bisimulation in functional programming languages. Inf. Comput. **124**(2), 103–112 (1996)
8. Huet, G.P.: The zipper. J. Funct. Program. **7**(5), 549–554 (1997)
9. Lanese, I., Pérez, J.A., Sangiorgi, D., Schmitt, A.: On the expressiveness and decidability of higher-order process calculi. Inf. Comput. **209**(2), 198–226 (2011). Extended Abstract in Logic in Computer Science (LICS) (2008). Coq formalization available at http://www.irisa.fr/celtique/aschmitt/research/hocore/
10. Lenglet, S., Schmitt, A.: Leaf-first zipper semantics. In: FORTE 2024 - 44th International Conference on Formal Techniques for Distributed Objects, Components, and Systems, Groningen, Netherlands (2024)
11. Lenglet, S., Schmitt, A., Stefani, J.-B.: Characterizing contextual equivalence in calculi with passivation. Inf. Comput. **209**(11), 1390–1433 (2011)
12. Lenglet, S., Schmitt, A., Stefani, J.-B.: Howe's method in calculi with passivation. In: CONCUR '09, Volume 5710 of LNCS, pp. 448–462. Springer (2009)
13. Lenglet, S., Schmitt, A., Stefani, J.-B.: Normal bisimulations in process calculi with passivation. In: FoSSaCS '09, Volume 5504 of LNCS, pp. 257–271. Springer (2009)
14. Sangiorgi, D.: Bisimulation in higher-order process calculi. In: Olderog, E. (ed.) Programming Concepts, Methods and Calculi, Proceedings of the IFIP TC2/WG2.1/WG2.2/WG2.3 Working Conference on Programming Concepts, Methods and Calculi (PROCOMET '94) San Miniato, Italy, 6-10 June, 1994, Volume A-56 of IFIP Transactions, pp. 207–224. North-Holland (1994)
15. Sangiorgi, D.: Bisimulation for higher-order process calculi. Inf. Comput. **131**(2), 141–178 (1996)
16. Sangiorgi, D., Walker, D.: The Pi-Calculus: A Theory of Mobile Processes. Cambridge University Press (2001)

CESAn: A Core Erlang Semantics Analyser

Aurélie Kong Win Chang[1], Jérôme Feret[2], and Gregor Gössler[1(✉)]

[1] Univ. Grenoble Alpes, INRIA, CNRS, Grenoble INP, LIG, 38000 Grenoble, France
gregor.goessler@inria.fr
[2] Département d'Informatique de l'ENS, ENS, CNRS, PSL University,
75005 Paris, France

Abstract. In the concurrent distributed language Erlang, processes interact through message passing and signals. One of the main sources of non-determinism that make Erlang programs difficult to debug, is the order in which messages are handled.

We present a prototype tool called CESAn that implements a small-step semantics that faithfully represents message handling in Core Erlang, enabling the user to investigate the causes of non-determinism in Erlang stemming from message handling. We see CESAn as a building block for debugging and analysis tools for Erlang.

1 Introduction

Understanding and debugging concurrent systems is notoriously difficult, in particular due to the difficulty of reproducing particular, faulty executions of a non-deterministic program. Erlang [1] is a functional language for programming large-scale distributed systems such as telecommunication systems. In Erlang, processes interact through message passing. One of the main sources of non-determinism of Erlang programs is the order in which messages are handled. In [17] we have formalized a small-step semantics of a subset of Core Erlang that faithfully represents how, and in which order, messages are handled.

In this paper we present a tool called CESAn [16] that implements the semantics of [17], and that features a minimalistic implementation of an algorithm based on [15], to explain program errors in terms of non-deterministic choices within the program semantics. After a brief presentation of alternative Erlang semantics and related debugging tools that have proposed in the literature, we present the CESAn tool and discuss some of its underlying design choices. We then discuss its application to a simple example of a Core Erlang program whose outcome depends on a race condition involving signal handling, and sketch how CESAn can help in understanding the causes of the non-deterministic program behavior.

This work has been funded by the ANR grant ANR-18-CE25-0007 DCore.

2 Related Work

Erlang is translated by the Erlang compiler in a language with less syntactic sugar: Core Erlang. We thus chose to base our analysis on a subset of Core Erlang. We are aware that there exists another language in which any Erlang code can be translated, and which is used as compilation language by Elixir, seen as a successor of Erlang: Abstract Erlang. However, as it does not have any formal semantics, and the only relevant document on the matter we found was the official documentation, we considered it wiser to stick with Core Erlang.

Our semantics is by no means the first one for Core Erlang. [5] is the most recent official specification of Core Erlang we found, but whilst useful it is informal and partly obsolete. A small step semantics of a subset of Core Erlang was proposed in [20], making some choices such as the order of evaluation of function arguments based on its implementation rather than the official documentation. In [12] and [13], Huch used a semantics of what he called Core Erlang, but was actually a subset of Erlang. A modular reversible semantics for a fragment of Core Erlang is proposed in [21], focused on causal-consistent reversibility. A semantics dedicated to type inference for a subset of Core Erlang was presented in [11]. More recently, [2] formalized a subset of Core Erlang with a big step semantics, following [20] in some aspects, and validated it with the proof assistant Coq. [4] introduced the concept of medium step semantics, which considers as a step not only assignments, but also some events of interactions between processes. This semantics is used by a declarative debugger [3]. Starting from the code and an expression that returned an incorrect value, it explores the execution with the help of questions asked to the developer whether the current evaluation is correct.

However, all these semantics lack the signal handling and monitoring part. The only semantics we found that finely modeled signals [23] treats them as side effects of operations that are instantaneously dealt with. This implies a strong hypothesis on their order of reception, and prevents the generation of scenarios with a degraded network, which are not uncommon in Erlang [14]. Our work inherited of several aspect of some of these contributions: [5] is our main reference document. Our model of signals sent per process is a slightly more general version of [4]'s messages sent box.

Soter [8] implements an actor model close to a subset of Core Erlang equipped with a parametric abstract interpretation framework, ensuring that several sources of infinite state spaces are reduced to finite representations. In particular, the content of mailboxes is abstracted into a multiset, thus losing the ordering of messages. This abstraction would break our analysis of the causes of non-deterministic program behavior.

With a similar goal as our work but an entirely different approach, the tool Concuerror [10] is dedicated to detecting crash events caused by specific race conditions. Starting with the source code, it searches through, and executes, all possible interleavings of operations with side effects, such as message handling, to identify those in which an error occurs. However, no explanation for the error is provided. CauDEr [19] is a causal-consistent reversible debugger for Erlang:

in order to undo some action, all of its consequences, and only those, need to be undone beforehand. Using a different notion of causality than the construction of explanations in CESAn, both are complementary [18].

3 CESAn

CESAn is open source. It takes as input a Core Erlang program, and outputs its semantic graph G in the form of a labelled transition system, if G is finite. Each state of G is a state of the program execution. Each transition is the application of a rule in the semantic derivation tree of the program. The label of a transition is the name of the rule applied during said transition.

When given, in addition, an execution trace of the program in the form of a path π in the semantic graph, and a subset B of set of states of G that are considered as *failing*, CESAn will construct an explanation identifying the subset of transitions of π that are choices in G that contribute to bringing the execution closer to B, in the sense of [15].

3.1 Design Choices

CESAn is essentially constituted of two parts. One—which we will refer to as the engine—is dedicated to read the inputs and generate the semantic graph, while the other is in charge of the user interface. The engine is written in Maude [7]. The lack of Maude library dedicated to visual representations is why the user interface is written in Python, which comes with libraries for handling graphs and programming user interfaces.

Philosophy. The prototype of [20] has some very good characteristics, such as properly commented code and a functional though slightly outdated Core Erlang parser, and it had been made with modularity on mind. However, the way it was implemented did not allow us to easily implement the graphical user interface we needed. Furthermore, the way some of its modules were intertwined created undesirable dependencies which made it difficult to simply add the semantics we picked to the project. We therefore refactored the code of [20] in order to make it more easily reusable by making it more modular. Some dependencies between modules made it hard to readapt the original code to some specificities of our implementation like the binding with Python instead of just getting a full-text output. Doing so, we also tried to make it easier to read and to change. The adventurous reader wanting to perform such a task will find very useful advice on the matter of refactoring in [9].

We tried to keep the design of CESAn as reusable as possible. As much as possible, we tested our code and automated the test phase with unit tests executable from a makefile command. Right now, everything tested is done so automatically, except for the behavior of the semantics rules, which are visually tested because of a lack of time: the user has to play the role of the oracle. As per the tests themselves, we documented them, saying for each of them what we are testing and, in general, what we are expecting and why if the case is not trivial.

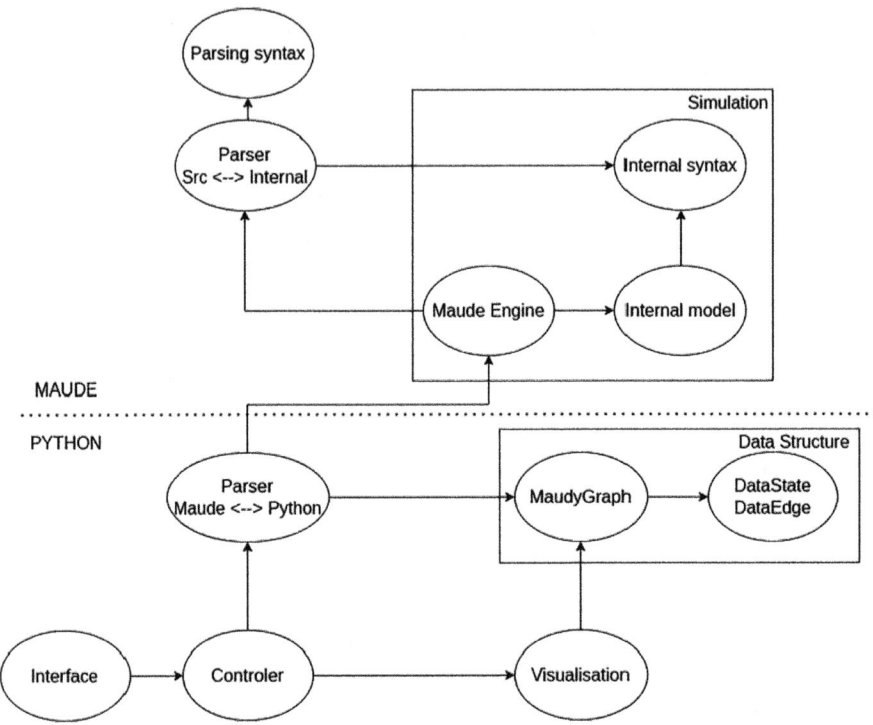

Fig. 1. Dependency graph of the sligthly abstracted structure. Ovals represent groups of modules, and arrows dependencies.

3.2 Structure of the Implementation

Figure 1 shows a simplified representation of the structure of the code. We tried to keep the number of dependencies between modules low. For instance, if one wanted to parse Erlang instead of Core Erlang while keeping our current internal model, only two files have to be changed: the parsed syntax, and the parser translating from the program syntax to the internal one.

Maude Engine. As said earlier, the Maude part is dedicated to generating the semantic graph of the program given as input. The core of the engine is the set of Maude modules which implements the semantics of [17] and its syntax, which is slightly different from Core Erlang. For instance, the receive instruction no longer exists since the OTP 23 update. This modification of Core Erlang has been done in order to fix some behaviors about maps which are out of the scope of this work. It complicates a lot the code representation and, for our model, it has the same behavior as the old receive, which is why we kept a receive in the internal syntax. This transformation is handled by the parsing modules. The curious reader can see how it is done in lines 236 to 271 and 295 to 315 of the parsing.maude file.

$$\text{MONITOR} \quad \frac{fresh\_lid(L) = lid}{\Pi \cup \{(pid_1, (\underline{\text{call}} \ erlang : monitor(\text{process}, pid_2), \theta, \tau, \mathtt{m}, st, \mathtt{r}), sig_{sent}, L)\}}$$
$$\xrightarrow{aux}$$
$$\Pi \cup \{(pid_1, (lid, \theta, \tau, erlang, \mathtt{m}, st, \mathtt{r}), sig_{sent} \cdot (\text{not\_msg}, pid_2, (\text{monitored\_by}, pid_1, lid)),$$
$$L \cup \{(\text{monitoring}, pid_2, lid)\})\}$$

(a) Rule as formalized in [17].

```
crl [monitor] :
    < aux || PID ||
        call atom("erlang") : atom("monitor") (atom("process"), erlPid(ID)) || THETA || TAU ||
        MNAME || STACK || TERMREASON ||
        SIGBOX ||
        LINKSSET ||
        RULENAME >
=>
    < aux || PID ||
    erlLid(NEWID) || THETA || TAU ||
    MNAME || STACK || TERMREASON ||
    #add-sig(SIGBOX, {not-msg, pid(ID), {monitor, PID, lid(NEWID)}}) ||
    LINKSSET ; {monitoring, pid(ID), lid(NEWID)} ||
    monitor >
    if NEWID := #getNewLid(#getLids(LINKSSET))
.
```

(b) Implementation in Maude.

Fig. 2. Implementation of the MONITOR rule in Maude.

The internal syntax, a more explicit variant of the Core Erlang syntax, is used by the Maude engine, where are implemented the rules of our semantics. A simple rule such as MONITOR is implemented in Maude as shown in Fig. 2. For other rules such as SUBEXPR_OK shown in Fig. 3, the translation is somewhat less straight-forward. In order to have Maude rewrite the sub-expressions step by step, we use meta-level rewriting [6].

Python Interface and Graphical Representation. CESAn is started with a command-line interface written in Python. The user is able to describe the initial state—as the one shown in Fig. 4—of the system to be analyzed. This description is then pre-processed with a Perl script based on the one of [20] in order to make it compatible with Maude. The Python side is also in charge of generating a graphical representation of the Maude output. Knowing the kind of framework we ultimately wanted to create, we chose netgraph, a Python library that enables interactive representations. Thanks to it, it is possible to display a wealth of information while still keeping it readable. netgraph offers the possiblity of zooming in the graph, as well as moving nodes and edges, and export the graph. However, netgraph has shown some limits, such as the impossibility to create interactive tables linked to the interactive graph without lengthy code. It would be worthwhile considering the use of more versatile tools, or swap to another language, for the user interface of CESAn.

Figure 5 shows the user interface of CESAn after analyzing the example of Sect. 4. The left-hand side shows the semantic graph generated by the Maude

```
crl [subexpr-do] :
   < aux || PID || do EX1 EX2 || THETA || TAU || MNAME ||
   STACK || TERMREASON || SIGBOX || LINKSSET || RULENAME > =>
   < aux || PID || do EX' EX2 || THETA' || TAU' || MNAME' ||
   STACK || TERMREASON' || SIGBOX' || LINKSSET' || RULENAME' >
   if not(EX1 :: Const)
       /\ < TRTAG' || PID || EX' || THETA' || TAU' || MNAME' ||
          STACK' || TERMREASON' || SIGBOX' || LINKSSET' || RULENAME' > :=
          downTerm( getTerm (metaRewrite(UP-RULE-PYTHON,
   upTerm( < aux || PID || EX1 || THETA || TAU || MNAME ||
   STACK, {do EX1 EX2, THETA, MNAME} || TERMREASON || SIGBOX || LINKSSET || RULENAME > ),
   1)),
       < aux || PID || atom("error: expression not evaluable") || THETA || TAU || MNAME ||
        STACK || TERMREASON || SIGBOX || LINKSSET || subexpr-do > )
      /\ EX' =/= eop
      /\ EX' =/= EX1
```

Fig. 3. Implementing a case of SUBEXPR_OK for do in Maude.

```
< term || pid(0) || call atom("erlang") : atom("spawn") (atom("module"), atom("fonction"), []) ||
#empty-env || #empty-modenv || atom("mname") || #empty-stack || {normal, (#empty-stack)} ||
#empty-box || #no-link || rspawn >
|||
< term || pid(1) || do int(1) int(2) || #empty-env || #empty-modenv || atom("mname") || #empty-stack ||
{normal, (#empty-stack)} || #empty-box || #no-link || rspawn >
||||
#empty-modenv ||||| pid(0), pid(1)
```

Fig. 4. Description of a system.

engine. Each state of the graph represents a state of the program execution, and each arrow represents the semantics rule applied in order to go from one state to another. The label on the arrows indicates the name of the rule that has been applied, and the identifier of the process(es) modified by the rule. Clicking on a state will make a table appear on the right-hand side. This table describes the selected state.

About Testing. Unfortunately, Maude does not seem to have a library dedicated to unit testing. This is why all of the automated tests are written in Python and use the `unittest` Python library. The downside of this situation is that, in order to test Maude code, we are actually comparing strings instead of directly comparing Maude entities. This means, and it happened, that if something changes in the binding Python library about how Maude is translated to Python strings, all of the tests dedicated to Maude parts of the system will fail.

It is possible to run all or part of the automatized tests through commands defined in the Makefile.

3.3 Using CESAn

CESAn is used through command line. As said earlier, from the description of the initial state of the system the user will want to analyze, it will generate its semantic graph. There are two ways to describe such an initial state:

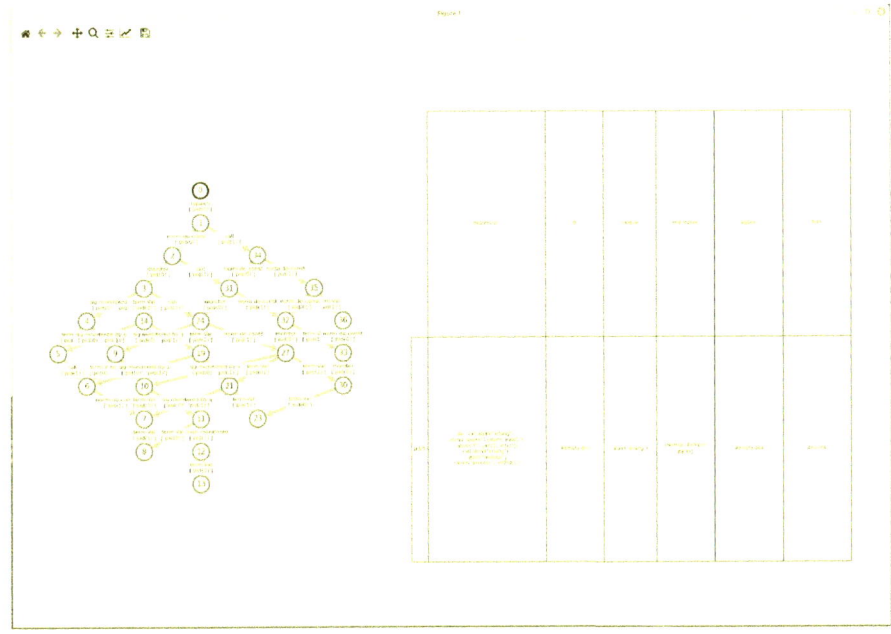

Fig. 5. Interactive user interface showing the semantic graph of a Core Erlang program along with information about the selected state.

- either by giving it directly, in a file, written in the internal language of CESAn,
- or by giving the first expression evaluated by the first process of the system and, if needed, the path to the file in which a Core Erlang module is described.

Directly Describing a State. The first option gives the most freedom to the users, allowing them to describe a system composed of any number of processes, themselves in any valid state. For instance, Fig. 4 shows a system composed of two processes. The one of identifier pid(0) creates a new process by calling the function spawn, and the one of identifier pid(1) evaluates the instruction do 1 2. The two processes are separated with three pipes | | |, and after the description of the processes global information about the system is given, such as the table of the functions loaded by default on any new process of the system, and the list of the identifiers already in use. More information about the way to describe such systems is given in the documentation of CESAn, and more examples can be found in the tests repository. The call to CESAn is then
python CESAn from_file *path*

where *path* is the path of the file containing the description of the system state.

Creating the Initial State from the First Expression Called. It is also possible to ask CESAn to generate itself the initial state of a system, by giving it the first expression evaluated by the first process, and optionally a module in Core Erlang to load. The module can be written by hand or generated by the Erlang compiler.

If no module needs to be loaded, the call to CESAn is

> python CESAn create_state *expr*

where *expr* is the first expression called. If a module needs to be loaded, this call becomes

> python CESAn create_state *expr* --src_module *path*

where *path* is the path of the file of the module, or, in a shorter way:

> python CESAn create_state *expr* --m *path*

Interacting with the Graph. Once the semantic graph is generated, it is possible to interact with it, e.g. by moving nodes and zooming in or out. Clicking on a node gives access to more information about the state it represents, in the table on the right of the graph Fig. 5. For each process of the system at the state represented by the selected node, one can get what is the next expression it will evaluate, the map θ of the affected variable with their value, the module of the last evaluated expression, the value currently stored as the reason of the termination of the process, the list of signals sent by the process, and the links existing between the process and the other ones of the system.

4 Example

Consider a simple program composed of one process, of identifier pid(0), that is about to evaluate the expression

```
do call "erlang": "spawn" ("mod1", "f", [1, 2]) call "erlang"
: "monitor"("process", pid(1))
```

The process spawns a new process, of identifier pid(1), and then creates a monitor link with it. The new process calls function f in module mod1 to evaluate the expression do on its input parameters:

```
1  module 'mod1' ['f' / 2]
2  attributes [ ]
3  ('f' / 2 =
4          fun (X,Y) ->
5              do X Y)
6  end
```

Generating the Semantic Graph. Figure 6 shows the semantic graph of our program as generated by CESAn. The initial state is on the top of the graph, in bold. Each transition is represented with an arrow, and its label tells which rule has been applied and which processes have been modified.

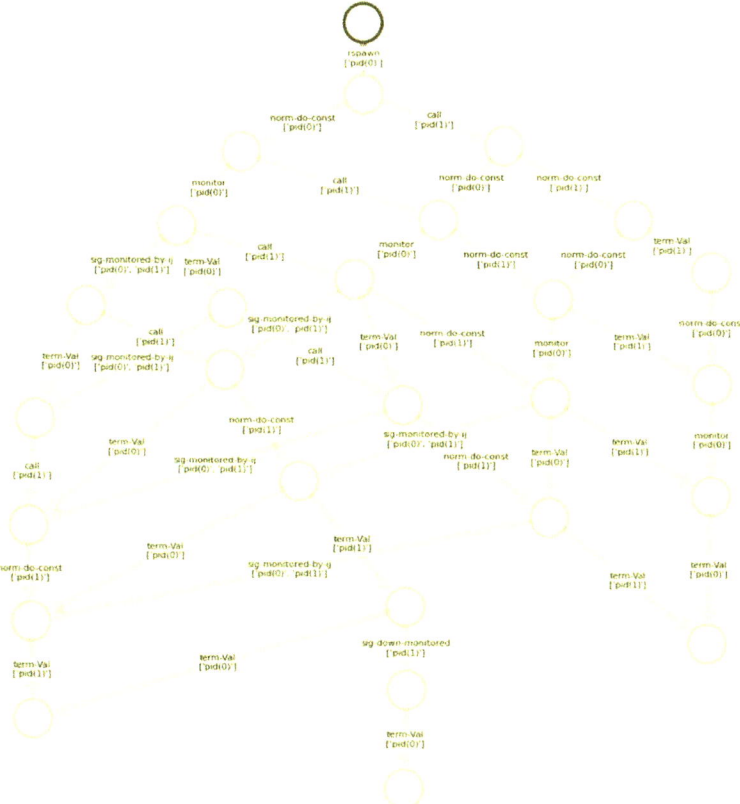

Fig. 6. Semantic graph of the example program.

Explaining a Failure. Consider the program execution shown in bold in the semantic graph of Fig. 7. We assume here that the execution is fully observable. Further suppose that we expect our program to behave in such a way that by the end of the execution of the program, the process in charge of the computation must have sent to its monitoring process the message saying it has ended. This is our expected safety property P. Figure 7 highlights in green the states where the message to the monitoring process has been sent (and hence P is satisfied), and in red the states where the program has ended without the message being sent (and hence P is violated); the colors have been added manually. Obviously, our execution path π violates P.

In order to evaluate how much the order in which messages have been handled causes the observed fault, we use the algorithm of [15]. It describes a game-theoretic approach to explain error traces, which we instantiate for our needs as follows. The state space is partitioned into a set of n layers such that from layer 0 a violation of the safety property is inevitable, and from each layer $1 \leq i \leq n-1$, a single bad choice is sufficient to enter layer $i - 1$. Hence, the layer to which

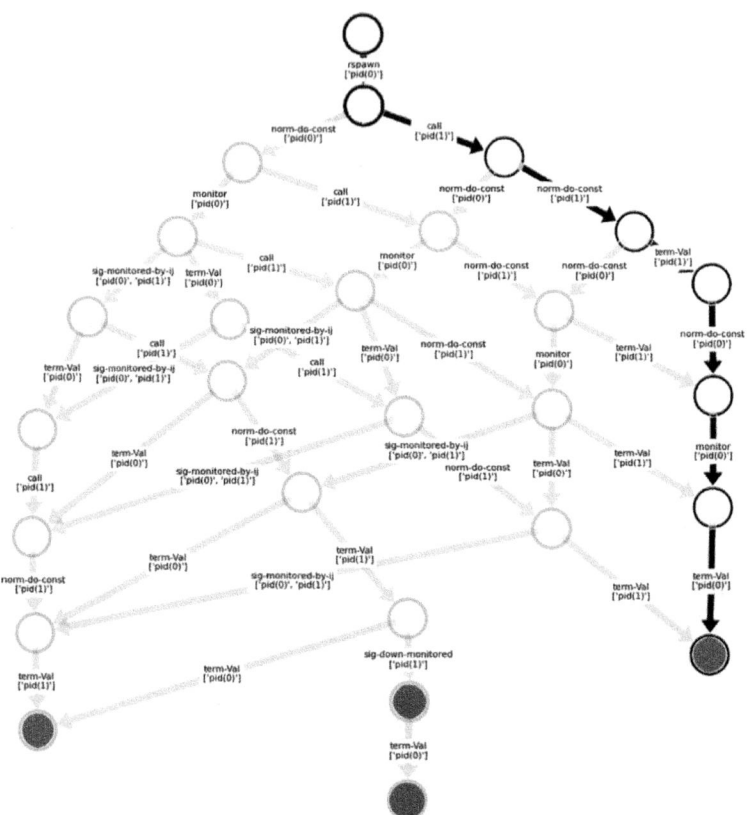

Fig. 7. Semantic graph of the example program. The execution path π is shown in bold. States where the message to the monitoring process has been sent are shown in green. States where the program has ended without the message being sent are shown in red. (Color figure online)

a state belongs indicates how precarious it is, in terms if its distance to the property violation.

Figure 8 shows the result of applying the analysis to the semantic graph of our example. The numbers on the states represent the layer they are part of. The layer from which the property violation is inevitable is shown in orange. A transition crossing layers towards a lower layer contributes to the program execution violating the property, and gives a hint to which order to enforce so as to fix the program. In our example the termination of the process with pid(1) is fatal in the state where it happens. By following, from the last state of the highlighted execution that belongs to layer 1, the *safe alternatives* that remain within layer 1, one can see that satisfaction of P is ensured by the partial order of precedence sig-monitored-by-ij[$"pid(0)", "pid(1)"$] $\prec$ term-Val[$"pid(1)"$] $\prec$ term-Val[$"pid(0)"$].

5 Discussion

CESAn is a proof of concept tool that needs to be improved in many ways, but we hope that it will be useful in exploring new analyses. First an foremost, an abstraction is needed to be able to handle programs with a large or infinite state space, and to focus explanations on an appropriate level of abstraction. Beyond explaining failures, leveraging the mechanisms used for localizing bugs for program *repair* is not a new idea, but doing this in our framework looks like a promising avenue of work.

From the point of view of user experience, our first tests suggest that the—basic—interactive graphical representation of the explanation in CESAn helps the user in grasping the causes of a failure. More specifically, it can be used in order to enrich the programmers' foraging diet [22] and give them some hints

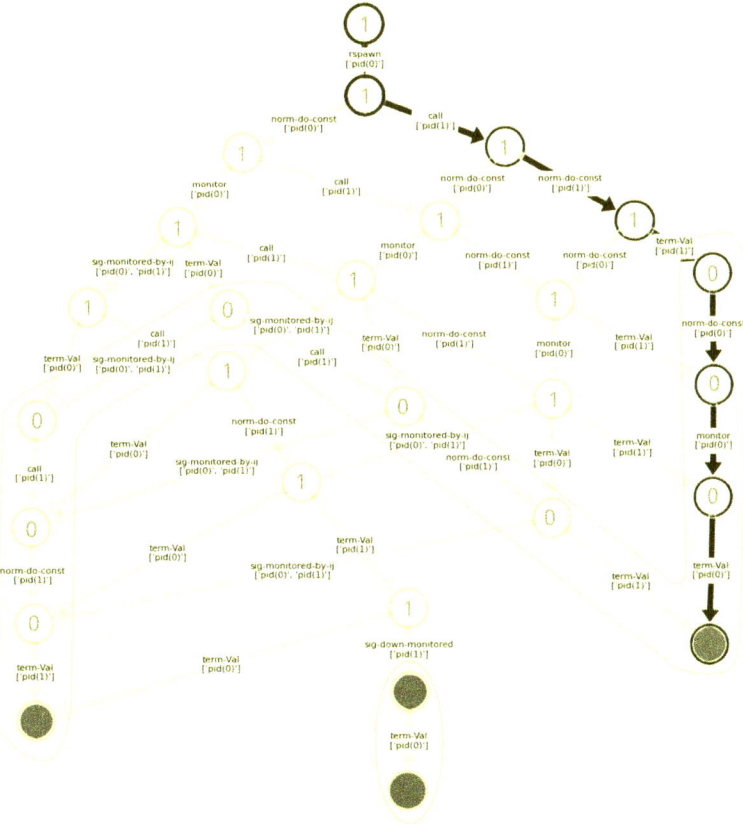

Fig. 8. Semantic graph of the example program, with the premices of our explanation.

during the exploration of the behaviors of the system in order to debug it. For instance, a graphical representation of the layers could provide hints about where to investigate alternatives to transitions bringing the system closer to a failure, enabling the user to explore them interactively. CESAn has, however, not been confronted to the field yet. User feedback would certainly raise many suggestions on how it is actually used, and knowing that the use of a tool can change the way data is explored [24], we would be interested in seeing how developers explore data when using CESAn.

References

1. Armstrong, J.L.: Making reliable distributed systems in the presence of software errors. PhD thesis, The Royal Institute of Technology Stockholm, Sweden, 2003
2. Bereczky, P., Horpácsi, D., Thompson, S.J.: Machine-checked natural semantics for Core Erlang: exceptions and side effects. In: Proceedings of the 19th ACM SIGPLAN International Workshop on Erlang, pp. 1–13, Virtual Event USA, August 2020. ACM
3. Caballero, R., Martin-Martin, E., Riesco, A., Tamarit, S.: Declarative debugging of concurrent erlang programs. J. Log. Algebr. Methods Programm. **101**, 22–41 (2018)
4. Caballero, R., Martin-Martin, E., Riesco, A., Tamarit, S.: A core erlang semantics for declarative debugging. J. Log. Algebr. Methods Programm. **107**, 1–37 (2019)
5. Carlsson, R., et al.: Core Erlang 1.0.3 language specification. Technical report, 2004
6. Clavel, M., et al.: All About Maude - A High-Performance Logical Framework, How to Specify, Program and Verify Systems in Rewriting Logic, LNCS, vol. 4350. Springer, Cham (2007). https://doi.org/10.1007/978-3-540-71999-1
7. Clavel, M., et al.: Maude manual (version 3.1). SRI International University of Illinois at Urbana-Champaign, 2020. http://maude.lcc.uma.es/maude31-manual-html/maude-manual.html
8. D'Osualdo, E., Kochems, J., Ong, C.-H.L.: Automatic verification of erlang-style concurrency. In: Logozzo, F., Fähndrich, M. (eds.) SAS 2013. LNCS, vol. 7935, pp. 454–476. Springer, Heidelberg (2013). https://doi.org/10.1007/978-3-642-38856-9_24
9. Fowler, M.: Refactoring: Improving the Design of Existing Code. Addison-Wesley signature series. Addison-Wesley, Boston, second edition, 2019. OCLC: on1064139838
10. Alkis Gotovos, Maria Christakis, and Konstantinos Sagonas. Test-driven development of concurrent programs using concuerror. In *Proceedings of the 10th ACM SIGPLAN workshop on Erlang - Erlang '11*, page 51, Tokyo, Japan, 2011. ACM Press
11. Harrison, J.: Automatic detection of core Erlang message passing errors. In: Proceedings of the 17th ACM SIGPLAN International Workshop on Erlang, pp. 37–48, St. Louis MO USA, September 2018. ACM
12. Huch, F.: Verification of Erlang programs using abstract interpretation and model checking. In: Proceedings of the fourth ACM SIGPLAN international conference on functional programming, Icfp '99, pp. 261–272, New York, NY, USA, 1999. Association for Computing Machinery. Number of pages: 12 Place: Paris, France

13. Huch, F.: Verification of Erlang Programs using Abstract Interpretation and Model Checking. PhD thesis, RWTH Aachen, 2001
14. Hébert, F.: Stuff goes bad Erlang in anger, 2016. https://www.erlang-in-anger.com
15. Jin, H.S., Ravi, K., Somenzi, F.: Fate and free will in error traces. Int. J. Softw. Tools Technol. Transf. **6**(2), 102–116 (2004)
16. Kong Win Chang, A.: CESAn: a core erlang semantics analyser, 2025. https://gitlab.inria.fr/dcore-pub/erlangsemantics.git
17. Kong Win Chang, A., Feret, J., Gössler, G.: A semantics of core Erlang with handling of signals. In: Proceedings of the 22nd ACM SIGPLAN International Workshop on Erlang, pp. 31–38, Seattle WA USA, August 2023. ACM
18. Lanese, I., Gössler, G.: Causal debugging for concurrent systems. In: Mogensen, T.Æ., Mikulski, L. (eds.), Reversible Computation. RC 2024. LNCS, vol. 14680, pp. 3–9. Springer, Cham (2024). https://doi.org/10.1007/978-3-031-62076-8_1
19. Lanese, I., Nishida, N., Palacios, A., Vidal, G.: Cauder: a causal-consistent reversible debugger for erlang. In: Gallagher, J.P., Sulzmann, M. (eds.) FLOPS 2018. LNCS, vol. 10818, pp. 247–263. Springer, Cham (2018). https://doi.org/10.1007/978-3-319-90686-7_16
20. Neuhäußer, M., Noll, T.: Abstraction and model checking of core erlang programs in maude. Electron. Notes Theor. Comput. Sci. **176**(4), 147–163 (2007)
21. Nishida, N., Palacios, A., Vidal, G.: A reversible semantics for erlang. In: Hermenegildo, M.V., Lopez-Garcia, P. (eds.) LOPSTR 2016. LNCS, vol. 10184, pp. 259–274. Springer, Cham (2017). https://doi.org/10.1007/978-3-319-63139-4_15
22. Piorkowski, D.J., et al.: The whats and hows of programmers' foraging diets. In: Proceedings of the SIGCHI Conference on Human Factors in Computing Systems, pp. 3063–3072, Paris France, April 2013. ACM
23. Svensson, H., Fredlund, L.-Å.: A more accurate semantics for distributed erlang. In: Proceedings of the 2007 SIGPLAN workshop on Erlang Workshop - Erlang '07, p. 43, Freiburg, Germany, 2007. ACM Press
24. Yalçin, M.A., Elmqvist, N., Bederson, B.B.: Cognitive stages in visual data exploration. In: Proceedings of the Sixth Workshop on Beyond Time and Errors on Novel Evaluation Methods for Visualization, pp. 86–95, Baltimore MD USA, October 2016. ACM

Asynchronous Global Protocols, Precisely

Kai Pischke(✉) and Nobuko Yoshida

University of Oxford, Oxford, UK
kai.pischke@cs.ox.ac.uk

Abstract. Asynchronous multiparty session types are a type-based framework that ensures the compatibility of components in a distributed system by specifying a global protocol. Each component can be independently developed and *refined* locally, before being integrated into a larger system, leading to higher quality distributed software. This paper studies the interplay between global protocols and an asynchronous refinement relation, *precise asynchronous multiparty subtyping*. This subtyping relation locally *optimises* asynchronous messaging, enabling a permutation of two actions in a component while still preserving the safety and liveness of the overall composed system. In this paper, we first define the *asynchronous association* between a global protocol and a set of local (optimised) specifications. We then prove the *soundness* and *completeness* of the operational correspondence of this asynchronous association. We demonstrate that the association acts as an *invariant* to provide type soundness, deadlock-freedom and liveness of a collection of components optimised from the end-point projections of a given global protocol.

Keywords: Multiparty session types · Precise asynchronous multiparty session subtyping · Type-safety · Association · Optimisation

1 Introduction

Concurrent and distributed components, often viewed as multiagents, are an effective abstraction for building flexible concurrent and distributed systems. Jean-Bernard Stefani is a pioneer of *component-based software engineering* (CBSE). He has promoted CBSE to both language and system communities, proposing a number of novel frameworks, systems and models. Two of many examples are a software framework for component-based OS kernels, THINK [11], which enables code-reuse and reduction of development times for building embedded systems; and a modular, extensible and language-independent model for configurable software systems, FRACTAL[1], which was first introduced by France Telecom and

---

[1] https://fractal.ow2.io/.

Work supported by: EPSRC EP/T006544/2, EP/K011715/1, EP/K034413/1, EP/L00058X/1, EP/N027833/2, EP/N028201/1, EP/T014709/2, EP/V000462/1, EP/X015955/1, ARIA and Horizon EU TaRDIS 101093006.

© The Author(s), under exclusive license to Springer Nature Switzerland AG 2026
C. A.Mezzina and A. Schmitt(Eds.): Jean-Bernard Stefani Festschrift, LNCS 16065, pp. 116–133, 2026.
https://doi.org/10.1007/978-3-031-99717-4_7

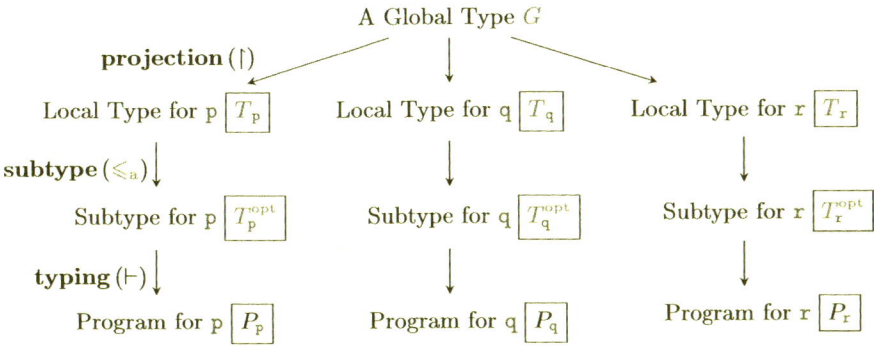

Fig. 1. Top-down methodology of multiparty session types. G denotes a global type, which is projected into the three participants, p, q and r, generating local types T_p, T_q and T_r for each participant. Local types are then refined to T_p^{opt}, T_q^{opt} and T_r^{opt}. Three distributed programs P_p, P_q and P_r follow.

INRIA. THINK has had a significant impact on the embedded systems community, and FRACTAL has been used for developing multiple implementations in different programming languages (such as Java, C, C++, Smalltalk, .Net).

Session types [14,20] are a type discipline for codifying concurrent components. *Multiparty session types* [15,16] (MPST) extend this idea from two-party to multiparty communication, facilitating a programmer in specifying a *global protocol* to coordinate communicating components. Using MPST, we can ensure that typed components interact without type errors or deadlocks *by construction*. Similar to FRACTAL, the MPST framework is *language-agnostic*, and has been adapted into over 20 programming languages [22].

Figure 1 describes the MPST workflow. We assume a set of participants $\mathcal{P}$ in the distributed system. We specify a *global protocol (type)* G, which is projected into a set of *local protocols (types)* $\{T_p\}_{p \in \mathcal{P}}$ from the viewpoint of each participant p. The local type T_p is then *refined* to an optimised local type T_p^{opt} using the *multiparty asynchronous subtyping relation* $\leqslant_a$ [13]. Subtyping $\leqslant_a$ allows for "safe permutations" of actions (explained in § 1), enabling us to type a more optimised program P_p which conforms to T_p^{opt}. Once each program is typed, we can automatically guarantee that a collection of distributed programs $\{P_p\}_{p \in \mathcal{P}}$ satisfy safety, deadlock-freedom and liveness.

This workflow (called *top-down* in [21]) is implemented by the MPST toolchains, SCRIBBLE [25] and νSCR [26], which check whether a given global protocol is well-formed, and if so, generate a corresponding set of local types. Building on this, the Rust toolchain RUMPSTEAK [10] uses νSCR to generate state machines, from which *optimised* APIs are generated using a sound approximation of $\leqslant_a$.

Ring-Choice Example. We explain our workflow by introducing a running example which will be referenced throughout this paper, the ring-choice protocol G_{ring} from [9]:

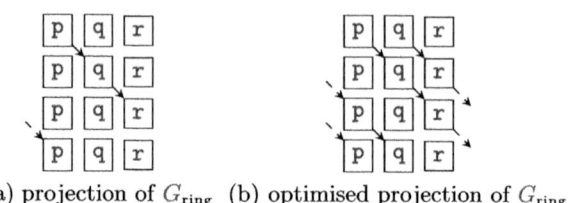

(a) projection of G_{ring} (b) optimised projection of G_{ring}

Fig. 2. Ring protocol: Projected and optimised interactions (from [9])

$$G_{\text{ring}} = \mu t.\text{p}\to\text{q:add(int)}.\text{q}\to\text{r}: \begin{cases} \text{add(int)} . \text{r}\to\text{p}: \{\text{add(int)} . \text{t}\} \\ \text{sub(int)} . \text{r}\to\text{p}: \{\text{sub(int)} . \text{t}\} \end{cases}$$

The global type G_{ring} specifies that:

1. p sends an integer n to q labelled by add;
2. q sends an integer m to r labelled by add or sub;
   (a) if add is selected, it sends the integer $m + k$ labelled by add to p, and the protocol restarts from Step 1; and
   (b) if sub is selected, it sends the integer $m - k$ labelled by sub to p, and the protocol restarts from Step 1.

If we assume *synchronous interactions* as illustrated in Fig. 2(a), no data flow would occur from q to r and from r to p *before* q receives data from p. This synchronisation is captured by the local types which are projected from G:

$$T_{\text{p}} = \mu t.\text{q}\oplus\{\text{add(int)}.\text{r}\&\{\text{add(int)}.\text{t}, \text{sub(int)}.\text{t}\}\}$$
$$T_{\text{q}} = \mu t.\text{p}\&\{\text{add(int)}.\text{r}\oplus\{\text{add(int)}.\text{t}, \text{sub(int)}.\text{t}\}\}$$
$$T_{\text{r}} = \mu t.\text{q}\&\{\text{add(int)}.\text{p}\oplus\{\text{add(int)}.\text{t}\}, \text{sub(int)}.\text{p}\oplus\{\text{sub(int)}.\text{t}\}\}$$

where the notation $\oplus$ is a *selection type* which denotes an internal choice (followed by label and payload), while $\&$ denotes a *branching type*, representing an external choice.

Under *asynchronous interactions* illustrated in Fig. 2(b), assuming that each participant begins with its own initial value, q can concurrently choose one of two labels to send the data to r *before* receiving data from p, letting r and p start the next action. By applying asynchronous subtyping ($\leqslant_a$), we can optimise T_{p} to the following $T_{\text{p}}^{\text{opt}}$, pushing the external choice behind the internal one:

$$T_{\text{q}}^{\text{opt}} = \mu t.\text{r}\oplus\{\text{add(int)}.\text{p}\&\{\text{add(int)}.\text{t}\}, \text{sub(int)}.\text{p}\&\{\text{add(int)}.\text{t}\}\}$$

With process P_{q} typed by $T_{\text{q}}^{\text{opt}}$, we can run the ring protocol more efficiently (see [10]). An overview of the history of asynchronous subtyping is given in [8], encompassing the theory and applications of the relation.

Contributions. This paper proves the *sound* and *complete operational correspondence* between behaviours of global type G and a set of local types $\{T_{\mathsf{p}}^{\mathrm{opt}}\}_{\mathsf{p}\in\mathcal{P}}$, which are refined or optimised by $\leqslant_a$ from G's projection $\{T_{\mathsf{p}}\}_{\mathsf{p}\in\mathcal{P}}$. We say $\{T_{\mathsf{p}}^{\mathrm{opt}}\}_{\mathsf{p}\in\mathcal{P}}$ is *associated* to G.

More formally, given a typing context $\Delta = \{\mathsf{p} : (\sigma_{\mathsf{p}}, T_{\mathsf{p}}^{\mathrm{opt}})\}_{\mathsf{p}\in\mathrm{roles}(G)}, \Delta_{\mathbf{end}}$ where $\mathrm{roles}(G)$ is a set of roles in G, σ_{p} is the type of the queue for participant p, and $\Delta_{\mathbf{end}}$ is a typing context which contains only termination type **end** (which denotes the participant has completed communications), then the *association* between Δ and a global type G is defined as follows:

$$\Delta \sqsubseteq_a G \quad \text{if } G \upharpoonright_{\mathsf{p}} (\sigma_{\mathsf{p}}, T_{\mathsf{p}}) \text{ and } T_{\mathsf{p}}^{\mathrm{opt}} \leqslant_a T_{\mathsf{p}} \text{ for all } \mathsf{p} \in \mathrm{roles}(G) \qquad (1)$$

Once we obtain the soundness and completeness of the association, we can derive the *subject reduction* theorem and *session fidelity* of the top-down approach from the corresponding results of the bottom-up system [13, Theorems 4.11 and 4.13]. The bottom-up system does *not* use global types and their projections, but requires an additional check that the collection of local types (i.e., a typing context) satisfies a *safety* property [19].

More specifically, we divide the steps to derive these results as follows:

Step 1 We define the operational semantics of G (denoted by $G \to G'$) and a typing context Δ (denoted by $\Delta \to \Delta'$).
Step 2 We prove **soundness**: if $\Delta \sqsubseteq_a G$ and $G \to$, then there exist G' and Δ' such that $G \to G'$, $\Delta \to \Delta'$ and $\Delta' \sqsubseteq_a G'$.
Step 3 We prove **completeness**: if $\Delta \sqsubseteq_a G$ and $\Delta \to \Delta'$, then there exists G' such that $G \to G'$ and $\Delta' \sqsubseteq_a G'$.
Step 4 We define the typing rule for multiparty session processes using the association:

$$\frac{\forall \mathsf{p} \in \mathrm{dom}(\Delta) \quad \vdash P_{\mathsf{p}} \triangleright T_{\mathsf{p}} \quad \vdash h_{\mathsf{p}} \triangleright \sigma_{\mathsf{p}} \quad \Delta(\mathsf{p}) = (\sigma_{\mathsf{p}}, T_{\mathsf{p}}) \quad \Delta \sqsubseteq_a G}{\vdash^{\mathrm{top}} \Pi_{\mathsf{p}\in\mathrm{dom}(\Delta)} \, (\mathsf{p} \triangleleft P_{\mathsf{p}} \mid \mathsf{p} \triangleleft h_{\mathsf{p}}) \; \triangleright \Delta} \quad [\textsc{SessTop}]$$

where $\vdash P \triangleright T$ is a typing judgement to assign type T to process P and $\vdash h \triangleright \sigma$ assigns type σ to a FIFO queue h (defined in [13, Figure 5]). $\mathsf{p} \triangleleft P_{\mathsf{p}}$ means process P_{p} is acting as participant p, buffering sent messages in its queue $\mathsf{p} \triangleleft h_{\mathsf{p}}$.

Step 5 We prove **the subject reduction theorem of the top-down system** using the completeness of the association with the subject reduction theorem of the bottom-up system [13, Theorem 4.11]; and **the session fidelity theorem of the top-down system** using the soundness and completeness of the association with the session fidelity theorem of the bottom-up system [13, Theorem 4.13]. We can also derive **safety, deadlock-freedom** and **liveness** from [19] and [13, Theorem 4.12]. We give detailed explanations in Sect. 5.

$$
\begin{array}{rcl}
B & ::= & \text{int} \mid \text{bool} \mid \text{real} \mid \text{unit} \mid \ldots \qquad \text{Basic types} \\
G & ::= & \text{p}{\rightarrow}\text{q}\colon \{\text{m}_i(B_i).G_i\}_{i\in I} \qquad \text{Transmission} \\
& \mid & \text{p}\overset{\text{m}_j}{\rightsquigarrow}\text{q}\colon \{\text{m}_i(B_i).G_i\}_{i\in I} \qquad \text{Transmission en route} \\
& \mid & \mu t.G \quad \mid \quad t \quad \mid \quad \text{end} \qquad \text{Recursion, Type variable, Termination} \\
T & ::= & \text{p}\&\{\text{m}_i(B_i).T_i\}_{i\in I} \qquad \text{External choice} \\
& \mid & \text{p}\oplus\{\text{m}_i(B_i).T_i\}_{i\in I} \qquad \text{Internal choice} \\
& \mid & \mu t.T \quad \mid \quad t \quad \mid \quad \text{end} \qquad \text{Recursion, Type variable, Termination} \\
\sigma & ::= & \varnothing \mid (\text{q},\text{m}(B)) \mid \sigma\cdot\sigma \qquad \text{Empty Queue, Message, Concatenation}
\end{array}
$$

Fig. 3. Syntax of types.

Outline. We provide an extensive exploration of global and local types in Sect. 2.1, including syntax, projection, and subtyping. We define operational semantics for both global types (Sect. 3.1) and typing contexts (Sect. 3.2). We establish the sound and complete operational relationship between these two semantics in Sect. 4. Furthermore, we demonstrate that the top-down typing system ensures subject reduction, session fidelity, and liveness in Sect. 5. Full proofs are found in [18].

2 Multiparty Session Types

This section introduces *global* and *local* types, together with *queue* types. As in [1], our formulation of global types includes special runtime-specific constructs to allow global types to represent en-route messages which have been sent but not yet received, and we give a novel projection relation (Def. 1) which extends the standard coinductive projection [12, Definition 3.6] to asynchronous semantics by simultaneously projecting onto both local and queue types.

2.1 Global and Local Types

Multiparty Session Type (MPST) theory uses *global types* to provide a comprehensive overview of communications between *roles*, such as $\text{p},\text{q},\text{s},\text{t},\ldots$, belonging to a set $\mathcal{R}$. It employs *local types*, which are obtained via *projection* from a global type, to describe how an *individual* role communicates with other roles from a local viewpoint. The syntax of global and local types is presented in Fig. 3, where constructs are mostly standard [19].

Basic types are taken from a set $\mathcal{B}$, and describe types of values, ranging over integers, booleans, real numbers, units, *etc.*

Global types range over $G, G', G_i, \ldots$, and describe the high-level behaviour for all roles. The set of roles in a global type G is denoted by $\text{roles}(G)$. We explain each syntactic construct of global types.

- p→q: $\{\mathtt{m_i}(B_i).G_i\}_{i\in I}$: a *transmission*, denoting a message from role p to role q, with a label $\mathtt{m}_i$, a payload of type B_i, and a continuation G_i, where i is taken from an index set I. We require that the index set be non-empty ($I \neq \emptyset$), labels $\mathtt{m}_i$ be pair-wise distinct, and self receptions be excluded (i.e. p $\neq$ q).
- p$\stackrel{\mathtt{m}_j}{\leadsto}$q: $\{\mathtt{m_i}(B_i).G_i\}_{i\in I}$: a *transmission en route*, representing a *transmission* of the message with index $j \in I$ which has already been sent by role p but has not been received by role q. Note that since q has not yet received the message, all branches are still present even though it is predetermined which will be chosen. This type is only meaningful at runtime.
- $\mu\mathtt{t}.G$: a *recursive* global type, where contractive requirements apply [17, §21.8], i.e. each recursion variable $\mathtt{t}$ is bound within a $\mu\mathtt{t}....$ and is guarded.
- **end**: a *terminated* global type (omitted where unambiguous).

Local types (or *session types*) range over $T, T', T_i, \ldots$, and describe the behaviour of a single role. We elucidate each syntactic construct of local types.

An *internal choice* (*selection*), $\mathtt{p}\oplus\{\mathtt{m_i}(B_i).T_i\}_{i\in I}$, indicates that the *current* role is expected to *send* to role p; an *external choice* (*branching*), $\mathtt{p}\&\{\mathtt{m_i}(B_i).T_i\}_{i\in I}$, indicates that the *current* role is expected to *receive* from role p; a *recursive* local type, $\mu\mathtt{t}.T$, follows a pattern analogous to $\mu\mathtt{t}.G$; finally, we use **end** for *termination* (omitted where unambiguous). Similar to global types, local types also need pairwise distinct, non-empty labels.

Queue types range over $\sigma, \sigma', \sigma_i, \ldots$, and describe the type of queues storing buffered asynchronous messages: $\varnothing$ is the empty queue; $(\mathtt{p}, \mathtt{m}(B))$ is the type of a queued message being sent to participant p with a message label $\mathtt{m}$ and a payload of type B; and $\sigma \cdot \sigma'$ is the concatenation of two queues.

2.2 Projections

Projection. In the top-down approach of MPST, local types are obtained by projecting a global type onto roles. Our definition of *projection*, as given in Def. 1 below, is slightly modified from the traditional presentation of projection as a partial function from global to local types. We define projection coinductively as a relation between global types G and pairs of local types T and queue types σ, allowing the queues to capture buffered messages, projected from en-route transmissions, at the local level.

Definition 1 (Global Type Projection). *The* projection *of a global type G onto a role p is defined coinductively as a relation $G\!\upharpoonright_{\mathtt{p}}(\sigma, T)$ by the rules in Fig. 4.*

where $\sqcap$ is the merge operator for session types *(full merging), defined coinductively as follows:*

- *If* $\mathrm{unf}(T) = \mathbf{end}$ *and* $\mathrm{unf}(T') = \mathbf{end}$ *then* $T \sqcap T' = \mathbf{end}$.
- *If* $\mathrm{unf}(T) = \mathtt{p}\oplus\{\mathtt{m_i}(B_i).T_i\}_{i\in I}$ *and* $\mathrm{unf}(T') = \mathtt{p}\oplus\{\mathtt{m_i}(B_i).T'_i\}_{i\in I}$ *then* $T \sqcap T' = \mathtt{p}\oplus\{\mathtt{m_i}(B_i).T_i \sqcap T'_i\}_{i\in I}$.

$$\frac{\forall i \in I \quad G_i \upharpoonright_{\mathtt{p}} (\sigma, T_i)}{(\mathtt{q} \to \mathtt{r} \colon \{\mathtt{m}_\mathtt{i}(B_i).G_i\}_{i \in I}) \upharpoonright_{\mathtt{p}} (\sigma, \sqcap_{i \in I} T_i)} \; [\text{P-}\sqcap]$$

$$\frac{\forall i \in I \quad G_i \upharpoonright_{\mathtt{p}} (\sigma, T_i)}{\left(\mathtt{q} \overset{\mathtt{m}_j}{\rightsquigarrow} \mathtt{r} \colon \{\mathtt{m}_\mathtt{i}(B_i).G_i\}_{i \in I}\right) \upharpoonright_{\mathtt{p}} (\sigma, \sqcap_{i \in I} T_i)} \; [\text{P-}\sqcap\text{-II}]$$

$$\frac{\forall i \in I \quad G_i \upharpoonright_{\mathtt{p}} (\sigma, T_i)}{(\mathtt{p} \to \mathtt{q} \colon \{\mathtt{m}_\mathtt{i}(B_i).G_i\}_{i \in I}) \upharpoonright_{\mathtt{p}} (\sigma, \mathtt{q} \oplus \{\mathtt{m}_\mathtt{i}(B_i).T_i\}_{i \in I})} \; [\text{P-}\oplus]$$

$$\frac{G_j \upharpoonright_{\mathtt{p}} (\sigma, T)}{\left(\mathtt{p} \overset{\mathtt{m}_j}{\rightsquigarrow} \mathtt{q} \colon \{\mathtt{m}_\mathtt{i}(B_i).G_i\}_{i \in I}\right) \upharpoonright_{\mathtt{p}} (\sigma \cdot (\mathtt{q}, \mathtt{m}_j(B_j)), T)} \; [\text{P-}\oplus\text{-II}]$$

$$\frac{\forall i \in I \quad G_i \upharpoonright_{\mathtt{p}} (\sigma, T_i)}{(\mathtt{q} \to \mathtt{p} \colon \{\mathtt{m}_\mathtt{i}(B_i).G_i\}_{i \in I}) \upharpoonright_{\mathtt{p}} (\sigma, \mathtt{q} \& \{\mathtt{m}_\mathtt{i}(B_i).T_i\}_{i \in I})} \; [\text{P-\&}]$$

$$\frac{\forall i \in I \quad G_i \upharpoonright_{\mathtt{p}} (\sigma, T_i)}{\left(\mathtt{q} \overset{j}{\rightsquigarrow} \mathtt{r} \colon \{\mathtt{m}_\mathtt{i}(B_i).G_i\}_{i \in I}\right) \upharpoonright_{\mathtt{p}} (\sigma, \mathtt{q} \& \{\mathtt{m}_\mathtt{i}(B_i).T_i\}_{i \in I})} \; [\text{P-\&-II}]$$

$$\frac{G\{\mu t.G/t\} \upharpoonright_{\mathtt{p}} (\sigma, T)}{\mu t.G \upharpoonright_{\mathtt{p}} (\sigma, T)} \; [\text{P-L}] \qquad \frac{G \upharpoonright_{\mathtt{p}} (\sigma, T\{\mu t.T/t\})}{G \upharpoonright_{\mathtt{p}} (\sigma, \mu t.T)} \; [\text{P-R}] \qquad \overline{\mathbf{end} \upharpoonright_{\mathtt{p}} (\varnothing, \mathbf{end})} \; [\text{P-End}]$$

Fig. 4. Rules for coinductive projection.

- If $\text{unf}(T) = \mathtt{p}\&\{\mathtt{m}_\mathtt{i}(B_i).T_i\}_{i \in I}$ and $\text{unf}(T') = \mathtt{p}\&\{\mathtt{m}_j(B_j).T'_j\}_{j \in J}$ then $T \sqcap T' = \mathtt{p}\&\{\mathtt{m}_\mathtt{k}(B_k).T''_k\}_{k \in I \cup J}$. Where $T''_k = \begin{cases} T_k \sqcap T'_k & \text{if } k \in I \cap J \\ T_k & \text{if } k \in I \setminus J \\ T'_k & \text{if } k \in J \setminus I \end{cases}$

We make use of an unfolding function, defined by $\text{unf}(\mu t.T) = \text{unf}(T\{\mu t.T/t\})$ when there is a recursion binder at the outermost level otherwise $\text{unf}(T) = T$.

A new rule, [P-⊕-II], allows an en-route message $(\mathtt{q}, \mathtt{m}_j(B_j))$ to be included in the projected queue of outgoing messages. If a global type G starts with a transmission from role p to role q, projecting it onto role p (resp. q) results in an internal (resp. external) choice, provided that the continuation of each branching of G is also projectable. When projecting G onto other participants r (r ≠ p and r ≠ q), a merge operator, as defined in Def. 1, is used to ensure that the projections of all continuations are "compatible". It is noteworthy that there are global types that cannot be projected onto all of their participants as shown in [21, §4.4].

Recall the ring-choice example: projection $G_{\text{ring}} \upharpoonright_{\mathtt{p}} T_{\mathtt{p}}$ can be derived by applying [P-L], [P-R], [P-⊕], [P-⊓], and merging the results of applying [P-&], to the coinductive hypothesis for each branch.

2.3 Asynchronous Multiparty Subtyping

We introduce a *subtyping* relation $\leqslant_a$ on local types, as defined in Def. 2. This subtyping relation is standard [19], and will be used later when defining local type semantics and establishing the relationship between global and local type semantics.

Given a standard subtyping $<:$ for basic types (e.g. including int $<:$ real), we give a summary of *asynchronous subtyping* $\leqslant_a$ introduced in [13]. We first consider the tree representation of local type T (denoted by $\mathfrak{T}(T)$).

We write $\mathbb{T}$ for generic trees and additionally define three specific types of tree. *Single-input* trees (denoted by $\mathbb{V}$) are those which have only a singleton choice in all branchings, while *single-output* trees (denoted by $\mathbb{U}$) are those which have only a singleton choice in all selections. Trees which are both single-input and single-output are called *single-input-single-output (SISO) trees* (denoted by $\mathbb{W}$). These can all be defined coinductively by the following equations.

$$\mathbb{T} = \mathtt{p}\&\{\mathtt{m}_i(B_i).\mathbb{T}_i\}_{i \in I} \mid \mathtt{p}\oplus\{\mathtt{m}_i(B_i).\mathbb{T}_i\}_{i \in I} \mid \mathbf{end}$$
$$\mathbb{U} = \mathtt{p}\&\{\mathtt{m}_i(B_i).\mathbb{U}_i\}_{i \in I} \mid \mathtt{p}!\mathtt{m}(B);\mathbb{U} \mid \mathbf{end}$$
$$\mathbb{V} = \mathtt{p}?\mathtt{m}(B);\mathbb{V} \mid \mathtt{p}\oplus\{\mathtt{m}_i(B_i).\mathbb{V}_i\}_{i \in I} \mid \mathbf{end}$$
$$\mathbb{W} = \mathtt{p}?\mathtt{m}(B);\mathbb{W} \mid \mathtt{p}!\mathtt{m}(B);\mathbb{W} \mid \mathbf{end}$$

We will define reorderings of SISO trees, and to do so, we consider non-empty sequences $\mathcal{A}^{(\mathtt{p})}$ of receives not including p and $\mathcal{B}^{(\mathtt{p})}$ of sends not including p together with receives from any participant. These sequences are inductively defined (where $\mathtt{p} \neq \mathtt{q}$) by:

$$\mathcal{A}^{(\mathtt{p})} = \mathtt{q}?\mathtt{m}(B) \mid \mathtt{q}?\mathtt{m}(B);\mathcal{A}^{(\mathtt{p})} \quad \mathcal{B}^{(\mathtt{p})} = \mathtt{r}?\mathtt{m}(B) \mid \mathtt{q}!\mathtt{m}(B) \mid \mathtt{r}?\mathtt{m}(B);\mathcal{B}^{(\mathtt{p})} \mid \mathtt{q}!\mathtt{m}(B);\mathcal{B}^{(\mathtt{p})}$$

We define the set $\mathtt{act}(\mathbb{W})$ of actions of a SISO tree:

$\mathtt{act}(\mathbf{end}) = \emptyset$; $\mathtt{act}(\mathtt{p}?\mathtt{m}(B);\mathbb{W}) = \{\mathtt{p}?\} \cup \mathtt{act}(\mathbb{W})$; and $\mathtt{act}(\mathtt{p}!\mathtt{m}(B);\mathbb{W}) = \{\mathtt{p}!\} \cup \mathtt{act}(\mathbb{W})$.

Using these definitions, we introduce a *refinement relation* ($\lesssim$) defined coinductively by the following rules:

$$\frac{B' <: B \quad \mathbb{W} \lesssim \mathcal{A}^{(\mathtt{p})};\mathbb{W}' \quad \mathtt{act}(\mathbb{W}) = \mathtt{act}(\mathcal{A}^{(\mathtt{p})};\mathbb{W}')}{\mathtt{p}?\mathtt{m}(B);\mathbb{W} \lesssim \mathcal{A}^{(\mathtt{p})};\mathtt{p}?\mathtt{m}(B');\mathbb{W}'} \text{[Ref-}\mathcal{A}\text{]}$$

$$\frac{B <: B' \quad \mathbb{W} \lesssim \mathcal{B}^{(\mathtt{p})};\mathbb{W}' \quad \mathtt{act}(\mathbb{W}) = \mathtt{act}(\mathcal{B}^{(\mathtt{p})};\mathbb{W}')}{\mathtt{p}!\mathtt{m}(B);\mathbb{W} \lesssim \mathcal{B}^{(\mathtt{p})};\mathtt{p}!\mathtt{m}(B');\mathbb{W}'} \text{[Ref-}\mathcal{B}\text{]}$$

$$\frac{B' <: B \quad \mathbb{W} \lesssim \mathbb{W}'}{\mathtt{p}?\mathtt{m}(B);\mathbb{W} \lesssim \mathtt{p}?\mathtt{m}(B');\mathbb{W}'} \text{[Ref-In]} \qquad \frac{B <: B' \quad \mathbb{W} \lesssim \mathbb{W}'}{\mathtt{p}!\mathtt{m}(B);\mathbb{W} \lesssim \mathtt{p}!\mathtt{m}(B');\mathbb{W}'} \text{[Ref-Out]}$$

$$\frac{}{\mathbf{end} \lesssim \mathbf{end}} \text{[Ref-End]}$$

We can extract sets of single-input and single-output trees from a given tree using the functions $[\![\cdot]\!]_{\mathsf{SI}}$ and $[\![\cdot]\!]_{\mathsf{SO}}$.

$$[\![\mathtt{p}\&\{\mathtt{m_i}(B_i).\mathtt{T}_i\}_{i\in I}]\!]_{\mathrm{SI}} = \bigcup_{i\in I}\{\mathtt{p?m_i}(B_i);\mathbb{V}_i \mid \mathbb{V}_i \in [\![\mathtt{T}_i]\!]_{\mathrm{SI}}\}$$

$$[\![\mathtt{p}\oplus\{\mathtt{m_i}(B_i).\mathtt{T}_i\}_{i\in I}]\!]_{\mathrm{SI}} = \{\mathtt{p}\oplus\{\mathtt{m_i}(B_i).\mathbb{V}_i\}_{i\in I} \mid \forall i \in I : \mathbb{V}_i \in [\![\mathtt{T}_i]\!]_{\mathrm{SI}}\} \quad [\![\mathbf{end}]\!]_{\mathrm{SI}} = \{\mathbf{end}\}$$

$$[\![\mathtt{p}\oplus\{\mathtt{m_i}(B_i).\mathtt{T}_i\}_{i\in I}]\!]_{\mathrm{SO}} = \bigcup_{i\in I}\{\mathtt{p!m_i}(B_i);\mathbb{U}_i \mid \mathbb{U}_i \in [\![\mathtt{T}_i]\!]_{\mathrm{SO}}\}$$

$$[\![\mathtt{p}\&\{\mathtt{m_i}(B_i).\mathtt{T}_i\}_{i\in I}]\!]_{\mathrm{SO}} = \{\mathtt{p}\&\{\mathtt{m_i}(B_i).\mathbb{U}_i\}_{i\in I} \mid \forall i \in I : \mathbb{U}_i \in [\![\mathtt{T}_i]\!]_{\mathrm{SO}}\} \quad [\![\mathbf{end}]\!]_{\mathrm{SO}} = \{\mathbf{end}\}$$

Definition 2 (Subtyping). *We consider trees that have only singleton choices in branchings (called* single-input (SI) *trees), or in selections (*single-output (SO) *trees), and we define the session subtyping $\leqslant_a$ over all session types by considering their decomposition into SI, SO, and SISO trees.*

$$\frac{\forall \mathbb{U} \in [\![\mathfrak{T}(T)]\!]_{SO} \quad \forall \mathbb{V}' \in [\![\mathfrak{T}(T')]\!]_{SI} \quad \exists \mathbb{W} \in [\![\mathbb{U}]\!]_{SI} \quad \exists \mathbb{W}' \in [\![\mathbb{V}']\!]_{SO} \quad \mathbb{W} \lesssim \mathbb{W}'}{T \leqslant_a T'} \quad \text{[Sub]}$$

The refinement $\lesssim$ captures safe permutations of input/output messages, that never cause deadlocks or communication errors under asynchrony; and the subtyping relation $\leqslant_a$ focuses on reconciling refinement $\lesssim$ with the branching structures in session types.

Example 1 (Subtyping the Ring Protocol Projection). To demonstrate that $T_{\mathtt{q}}^{\mathrm{opt}} \leqslant_a T_{\mathtt{q}}$, we must show that for all $\mathbb{U} \in [\![\mathfrak{T}(T_{\mathtt{q}}^{\mathrm{opt}})]\!]_{SO}$ and $\mathbb{V}' \in [\![\mathfrak{T}(T_{\mathtt{q}})]\!]_{SI}$, there exist $\mathbb{W} \in [\![\mathbb{U}]\!]_{SI}$ and $\mathbb{W}' \in [\![\mathbb{V}']\!]_{SO}$ such that $\mathbb{W} \lesssim \mathbb{W}'$. Consider the following sets:

$$[\![\mathfrak{T}(T_{\mathtt{q}}^{\mathrm{opt}})]\!]_{SO} = \left\{\mathtt{r!add(int)};\mathtt{p?add(int)};\ldots,\mathtt{r!sub(int)};\mathtt{p?add(int)};\ldots,\ldots\right\}$$

$$[\![\mathfrak{T}(T_{\mathtt{q}})]\!]_{SI} = \left\{\mathtt{p?add(int)};\mathtt{r} \oplus \left\{\begin{matrix}\mathtt{add(int)}\ldots\\ \mathtt{sub(int)}\ldots\end{matrix}\right\}\right\}$$

Now, we must find for each $\mathbb{U}$ in the first set and $\mathbb{V}'$ in the second, a pair of SISO trees $(\mathbb{W}, \mathbb{W}')$ such that $\mathbb{W} \lesssim \mathbb{W}'$. For instance, if the second $\mathbb{U}$ is chosen, we have $\mathbb{W} = \mathtt{r!sub(int)};\mathtt{p?add(int)};\ldots$ and we can pick $\mathbb{W}' = \mathtt{p?add(int)};\mathtt{p!sub(int)};\ldots$

Then we can apply rule [Ref-$\mathcal{B}$] to validate that it is safe to reorder the send ahead of the receive in the optimised type. We could form a similar argument in the other cases. Thus we conclude that: $T_{\mathtt{q}}^{\mathrm{opt}} \leqslant_a T_{\mathtt{q}}$.

Lemma 1 (Merge preserves subtyping). *Given collections of mergeable types T_i and T_i' ($i \in I$). If for all $i \in I$, $T_i \leqslant_a T_i'$ then $\prod_{i \in I} T_i \leqslant_a \prod_{i \in I} T_i'$.*

3 Operational Semantics

3.1 Semantics of Global Types

We now present the Labelled Transition System (LTS) semantics for global types. To begin, we introduce the transition labels in Def. 3, which are also used in the LTS semantics of typing contexts (discussed later in §3.2).

$$\frac{G[\mu t.G/t] \xrightarrow{\alpha} G'}{\mu t.G \xrightarrow{\alpha} G'} \text{ [GR-}\mu\text{]} \qquad \frac{j \in I}{\text{p}\overset{m_j}{\rightsquigarrow}\text{q}: \{\text{m}_i(B_i).G'_i\}_{i \in I} \xrightarrow{\text{q:p\&m}_j} G'_j} \text{ [GR-\&]}$$

$$\frac{j \in I}{\text{p}\rightarrow\text{q}: \{\text{m}_i(B_i).G'_i\}_{i \in I} \xrightarrow{\text{p:q}\oplus\text{m}_j} \text{p}\overset{m_j}{\rightsquigarrow}\text{q}: \{\text{m}_i(B_i).G'_i\}_{i \in I}} \text{ [GR-}\oplus\text{]}$$

$$\frac{\forall i \in I : G'_i \xrightarrow{\alpha} G''_i \quad \alpha \neq \text{p:q}\oplus\text{m}' \quad \alpha \neq \text{p:r\&m}''}{\text{p}\rightarrow\text{q}: \{\text{m}_i(B_i).G'_i\}_{i \in I} \xrightarrow{\alpha} \text{p}\rightarrow\text{q}: \{\text{m}_i(B_i).G''_i\}_{i \in I}} \text{ [GR-Ctx-I]}$$

$$\frac{j \in J \quad \forall i \in I : G'_i \xrightarrow{\alpha} G''_i \quad \alpha \neq \text{q:p\&m}'}{\text{p}\overset{m_j}{\rightsquigarrow}\text{q}: \{\text{m}_i(B_i).G'_i\}_{i \in I} \xrightarrow{\alpha} \text{p}\overset{m_j}{\rightsquigarrow}\text{q}: \{\text{m}_i(B_i).G''_i\}_{i \in I}} \text{ [GR-Ctx-II]}$$

Fig. 5. Global type reduction rules.

Definition 3 (Transition Labels). *Let α be a transition label of the form:*
$$\alpha ::= \text{p:q\&m} \mid \text{p:q}\oplus\text{m} \quad \text{(receive or send a message)}$$

Definition 4 (Global Type Reductions). *The global type transition $\xrightarrow{\alpha}$ is inductively defined by the rules in Fig. 5. We use $G \rightarrow G'$ if there exists α such that $G \xrightarrow{\alpha} G'$; we write $G \rightarrow$ if there exists G' such that $G \rightarrow G'$, and $G \not\rightarrow$ for its negation (i.e. there is no G' such that $G \rightarrow G'$). Finally, $\rightarrow^*$ denotes the transitive and reflexive closure of $\rightarrow$.*

The semantics of global types reflect the reorderings permitted by asynchronous subtying, allowing transitions according to specific asynchronous behaviours:

- [GR-μ] permits a valid transition to take place under a recursion binder.
- [GR-&] describes the receiving of asynchronous messages, allowing en-route message to be received.
- [GR-$\oplus$] describes the sending of asynchronous messages, resulting in a standard transmission becoming an en-route one.
- [GR-Ctx-I] allows the semantics to anticipate a deeper transition inside a communication type so long as it is not a send between the same participants or receive by the sending participant. The restriction $\alpha \neq \text{p:q}\oplus\text{m}'$ corresponds with the fact that $\mathcal{B}^{(\text{p})}$ does not allow sends preempting sends to the same participant, and the restriction $\alpha \neq \text{p:r\&m}''$ corresponds with the fact that $\mathcal{B}^{(\text{p})}$ does not allow receives preempting sends to the same participant.
- [GR-Ctx-II] is even more flexible. The only restriction, $\alpha \neq \text{q:p\&m}'$ does not place any limits on the sender who has already triggered an en-route message, only requiring the receiver not pre-emptively receive a different message from the same sender, as with $\mathcal{A}^{(\text{p})}$.

In this way, [GR-Ctx-I] and [GR-Ctx-II] enable the semantics to capture the same ideas of safe reorderings which are already present in the existing precise asynchronous subtyping relation. We can safely execute actions pre-emptively exactly when the new behaviour corresponds to a SISO tree which is a refinement of a top level behaviour.

Definition 5 (Balanced$^+$ Global Types). *A global type G is balanced$^+$ iff, for every type G', G'' such that $G \to^* G' \to^* G''$, where $G'' = \mathtt{q} \to \mathtt{r} \colon \{\mathtt{m_i}(B_i).G'''_i\}_{i \in I}$ (or $\mathtt{q} \stackrel{\mathtt{m_k}}{\leadsto} \mathtt{r} \colon \{\mathtt{m_i}(B_i).G'''_i\}_{i \in I}$) and for each of the roles $\mathtt{p} \in \{\mathtt{q}, \mathtt{r}\}$, there exists a $k \geq 0$ such that all fair paths $G' \to G'_1 \to G'_2 \to \ldots$ reach a type $G'' = \mathtt{s} \to \mathtt{t} \colon \{\mathtt{m_j}(B_j).G'''_j\}_{j \in J}$ (or $\mathtt{q} \stackrel{\mathtt{m_k}}{\leadsto} \mathtt{r} \colon \{\mathtt{m_i}(B_i).G'''_i\}_{i \in I}$) in at most k steps with $\mathtt{p} \in \{\mathtt{s}, \mathtt{t}\}$. As is standard when defining projectable types, we assume well-formed global types satisfy this condition. For types without en-route transmisions, this aligns with the normal definition of balanced types (Def 3.3 in [12] and Def 4.17 in [21]). Given en-route types are only runtime behaviour, we also restrict ourselves to global types G' which are the result of running a global type $G \to^* G'$ where G does not contain en-route transmissions.*

Example 2 (Semantics of Global Type for Ring Protocol). Consider the global type for the ring-choice protocol (§1). The asynchronous semantics enable us to apply both [GR-⊕] reductions, corresponding to sends from p to q and from q to r, before any receive reductions (using [GR-&]) are applied. As we will see later, this particular choice of global reduction path corresponds to behaviour which can only be captured by the optimised local type.

We begin by reducing G_{ring} via a send action from p to q:

$$G_{\mathrm{ring}} \xrightarrow{\mathtt{p}:\mathtt{q} \oplus \mathrm{add}} G_{\mathrm{ring}}^{(1)} = \mathtt{p} \stackrel{\mathrm{add}}{\leadsto} \mathtt{q}\colon\mathrm{add}(\mathrm{int}).\mathtt{q} \to \mathtt{r}\colon \begin{cases} \mathrm{add}(\mathrm{int}) \cdot \mathtt{r} \to \mathtt{p}\colon \{\mathrm{add}(\mathrm{int}) \cdot G_{\mathrm{ring}}\} \\ \mathrm{sub}(\mathrm{int}) \cdot \mathtt{r} \to \mathtt{p}\colon \{\mathrm{sub}(\mathrm{int}) \cdot G_{\mathrm{ring}}\} \end{cases}$$

At this point, a message from p to q is in transit. We then perform another [GR-⊕] reduction, using [GR-Ctx-II] to apply the sending from q to r under the existing en-route type:

$$G_{\mathrm{ring}}^{(1)} \xrightarrow{\mathtt{q}:\mathtt{r} \oplus \mathrm{sub}} G_{\mathrm{ring}}^{(2)} = \mathtt{p} \stackrel{\mathrm{add}}{\leadsto} \mathtt{q}\colon\mathrm{add}(\mathrm{int}).\mathtt{q} \stackrel{\mathrm{sub}}{\leadsto} \mathtt{r}\colon \begin{cases} \mathrm{add}(\mathrm{int}) \cdot \mathtt{r} \to \mathtt{p}\colon \{\mathrm{add}(\mathrm{int}) \cdot G_{\mathrm{ring}}\} \\ \mathrm{sub}(\mathrm{int}) \cdot \mathtt{r} \to \mathtt{p}\colon \{\mathrm{sub}(\mathrm{int}) \cdot G_{\mathrm{ring}}\} \end{cases}$$

The state $G_{\mathrm{ring}}^{(2)}$ reflects the two en-route messages: one from p to q and one from q to r. We can the proceed with the corresponding receive actions using the [GR-&] rule. First, q receives the message from p:

$$G_{\mathrm{ring}}^{(2)} \xrightarrow{\mathtt{q}:\mathtt{p} \& \mathrm{add}} G_{\mathrm{ring}}^{(3)} = \mathtt{q} \stackrel{\mathrm{sub}}{\leadsto} \mathtt{r}\colon \begin{cases} \mathrm{add}(\mathrm{int}) \cdot \mathtt{r} \to \mathtt{p}\colon \{\mathrm{add}(\mathrm{int}) \cdot G_{\mathrm{ring}}\} \\ \mathrm{sub}(\mathrm{int}) \cdot \mathtt{r} \to \mathtt{p}\colon \{\mathrm{sub}(\mathrm{int}) \cdot G_{\mathrm{ring}}\} \end{cases}$$

$$\dfrac{k \in I}{\mathtt{p}{:}(\sigma, \mathtt{q}\oplus\{\mathtt{m}_i(B_i).T_i\}_{i\in I}) \xrightarrow{\mathtt{p}:\mathtt{q}\oplus\mathtt{m}_k(B_k)} \mathtt{p}{:}(\sigma\cdot(\mathtt{q},\mathtt{m}_k(B_k)), T_k)} \;[\Delta\text{-}\oplus]$$

$$\dfrac{k \in I}{\mathtt{p}{:}(\sigma, \mathtt{q}\&\{\mathtt{m}_i(B_i).T_i\}_{i\in I}), \mathtt{q}{:}(\sigma'\cdot(\mathtt{p},\mathtt{m}_k(B_k)),T) \xrightarrow{\mathtt{p}:\mathtt{q}\&\mathtt{m}_k(B_k)} \mathtt{p}{:}(\sigma,T_k), \mathtt{q}{:}(\sigma',T)} \;[\Delta\text{-}\&]$$

$$\dfrac{\mathtt{p}{:}T\{^{\mu t.T}/_t\} \xrightarrow{\alpha} \Delta'}{\mathtt{p}{:}\mu t.T \xrightarrow{\alpha} \Delta'}\;[\Delta\text{-}\mu] \qquad \dfrac{\Delta \xrightarrow{\alpha} \Delta'}{\Delta\, x{:}B \xrightarrow{\alpha} \Delta', x{:}B}\;[\Delta\text{-},B] \qquad \dfrac{\Delta \xrightarrow{\alpha} \Delta'}{\Delta\, c{:}T \xrightarrow{\alpha} \Delta', c{:}T}\;[\Delta\text{-},]$$

Fig. 6. Typing context reduction rules.

Then, r receives the message from q:

$$G^{(3)}_{\text{ring}} \xrightarrow{\mathtt{r}:\mathtt{q}\&\mathtt{sub}} G^{(4)}_{\text{ring}} = \mathtt{r}{\to}\mathtt{p}{:}\{\mathsf{sub}(\mathsf{int}) \, . \, G_{\text{ring}}\}$$

Next, r sends to p:

$$G^{(4)}_{\text{ring}} \xrightarrow{\mathtt{r}:\mathtt{p}\oplus\mathtt{sub}} G^{(5)}_{\text{ring}} = \mathtt{r}\overset{\mathsf{sub}}{\leadsto}\mathtt{p}{:}\{\mathsf{sub}(\mathsf{int}) \, . \, G_{\text{ring}}\}$$

Finally, p receives this last message, returning us to the original state of the protocol:

$$G^{(5)}_{\text{ring}} \xrightarrow{\mathtt{r}:\mathtt{p}\&\mathtt{sub}} G_{\text{ring}}$$

In §3.2, we will show that this reduction sequence corresponds to a behaviour of the optimised local implementation for q.

3.2 Semantics of Typing Context

After introducing the semantics of global types, we now present an LTS semantics for *typing contexts*, which are collections of local types. The formal definition of a typing context is provided in Def. 6, followed by its reduction rules in Def. 7.

Definition 6 (Typing Contexts). *Δ denotes a partial mapping from participants to queues and types. Their syntax is defined as:*

$$\Delta ::= \emptyset \mid \Delta, \mathtt{p}{:}(\sigma, T)$$

The context composition Δ_1, Δ_2 is defined iff $\mathrm{dom}(\Delta_1) \cap \mathrm{dom}(\Delta_2) = \emptyset$.

Definition 7 (Typing Context Reduction). *The typing context transition $\xrightarrow{\alpha}$ is inductively defined by the rules in Fig. 6. We write $\Delta \xrightarrow{\alpha}$ if there exists Δ' such that $\Delta \xrightarrow{\alpha} \Delta'$. We write $\Delta \to \Delta'$ iff $\Delta \xrightarrow{\alpha} \Delta'$ for some α and $\Delta \not\to$ for its negation (i.e. there is no Δ' such that $\Delta \to \Delta'$), and we denote $\to^*$ as the reflexive and transitive closure of $\to$.*

Example 3 (Operational Semantics of Optimised Ring Context). As an example, consider the operational semantics of the optimised ring protocol. Each transition captures either a message send or receive, which either enqueues or dequeues a message in the queue of the sending participant.

$$\Delta_0 = \text{p}{:}(\varnothing, T_\text{p}), \text{q}{:}(\varnothing, T_\text{q}^{\text{opt}}), \text{r}{:}(\varnothing, T_\text{r})$$

$$\xrightarrow{\text{p:q}\oplus\text{add(int)}} \Delta_1 = \text{p}{:}(\langle(\text{q}, \text{add(int)})\rangle, \text{r}\&\left\{\begin{array}{l}\text{add(int)}.T_\text{p}\\\text{sub(int)}.T_\text{p}\end{array}\right\}), \text{q}{:}(\varnothing, T_\text{q}^{\text{opt}}), \text{r}{:}(\varnothing, T_\text{r})$$

$$\xrightarrow{\text{q:r}\oplus\text{sub(int)}} \Delta_2 = \text{p}{:}(\langle(\text{q}, \text{add(int)})\rangle, \text{r}\&\left\{\begin{array}{l}\text{add(int)}.T_\text{p}\\\text{sub(int)}.T_\text{p}\end{array}\right\}),$$
$$\text{q}{:}(\langle(\text{r}, \text{sub(int)})\rangle, \text{p}\&\{\text{add(int)}.T_\text{q}^{\text{opt}}\}), \text{r}{:}(\varnothing, T_\text{r}))$$

$$\xrightarrow{\text{q:p}\&\text{add(int)}} \Delta_3 = \text{p}{:}(\varnothing, \text{r}\&\left\{\begin{array}{l}\text{add(int)}.T_\text{p}\\\text{sub(int)}.T_\text{p}\end{array}\right\}), \text{q}{:}(\langle(\text{r}, \text{sub(int)})\rangle, T_\text{q}^{\text{opt}}), \text{r}{:}(\varnothing, T_\text{r})$$

$$\xrightarrow{\text{r:q}\&\text{sub(int)}} \Delta_4 = \text{p}{:}(\varnothing, \text{r}\&\left\{\begin{array}{l}\text{add(int)}.T_\text{p}\\\text{sub(int)}.T_\text{p}\end{array}\right\}), \text{q}{:}(\varnothing, T_\text{q}^{\text{opt}}), \text{r}{:}(\varnothing, \text{p}\oplus\{\text{sub(int)}.T_\text{r}\})$$

$$\xrightarrow{\text{r:p}\oplus\text{sub(int)}} \Delta_5 = \text{p}{:}(\varnothing, \text{r}\&\left\{\begin{array}{l}\text{add(int)}.T_\text{p}\\\text{sub(int)}.T_\text{p}\end{array}\right\}), \text{q}{:}(\varnothing, T_\text{q}^{\text{opt}}), \text{r}{:}(\langle(\text{p}, \text{sub(int)})\rangle, T_\text{r})$$

$$\xrightarrow{\text{p:r}\&\text{sub(int)}} \Delta_0$$

4 Global and Local Type Asynchronous Association

Following the introduction of LTS semantics for global types (Def. 4) and typing contexts (Def. 7), we establish a relationship between these two semantics using the projection relation $\lceil_\text{p}$ (Def. 1) and the subtyping relation $\leqslant_a$ (Def. 2).

Definition 8 (Association of Global Types and Typing Contexts). *A typing context Δ is associated with a global type G written $\Delta \sqsubseteq_a G$, iff Δ can be split into two disjoint (possibly empty) sub-contexts $\Delta = \Delta_G, \Delta_{\text{end}}$ where:*

1. *Δ_G contains projections of G:* $\text{dom}(\Delta_G) = \text{roles}(G)$, *and* $\forall \text{p} \in \text{roles}(G) : \Delta(\text{p}) = (\sigma_\text{p}, T'_\text{p})$ *and* $\exists T_\text{p} : T'_\text{p} \leqslant_a T_\text{p}$ *and* $G\lceil_\text{p}(\sigma_\text{p}, T_\text{p})$;
2. *Δ_{end} contains only end endpoints:* $\forall \text{p} \in \text{dom}(\Delta_{\text{end}}) : \Delta(\text{p}) = (\varnothing, \text{end})$.

The association $\cdot \sqsubseteq_a \cdot$ is a binary relation over typing contexts Δ and global types G. There are two requirements for the association: (1) the typing context Δ must include an entry for each role; and (2) for each role p, its corresponding entry in the typing context ($\Delta(\text{p})$) must be a subtype (Def. 2) of the projection of the global type onto this role.

Looking again at the ring protocol example, we can observe how the reduction of the global type corresponds to updates in the local context. This forms an *operational correspondence* between the global semantics and local process configurations. Each global step is matched by a change in the local context.

$$G_{\text{ring}} \xrightarrow{\text{p:q}\oplus\text{add}} G_{\text{ring}}^{(1)} \xrightarrow{\text{q:r}\oplus\text{sub}} G_{\text{ring}}^{(2)} \xrightarrow{\text{q:p\&add}} G_{\text{ring}}^{(3)} \xrightarrow{\text{r:q\&sub}} G_{\text{ring}}^{(4)} \xrightarrow{\text{r:p}\oplus\text{sub}} G_{\text{ring}}^{(5)}$$

$$\sqsubseteq_a \qquad \sqsubseteq_a \qquad \sqsubseteq_a \qquad \sqsubseteq_a \qquad \sqsubseteq_a \qquad \sqsubseteq_a$$

$$\Delta_0 \xrightarrow{\text{p:q}\oplus\text{add}} \Delta_1 \xrightarrow{\text{q:r}\oplus\text{sub}} \Delta_2 \xrightarrow{\text{q:p\&add}} \Delta_3 \xrightarrow{\text{r:q\&sub}} \Delta_4 \xrightarrow{\text{r:p}\oplus\text{sub}} \Delta_5$$

This idea is illustrated through two main theorems: Thm. 2 shows that the reducibility of a global type aligns with that of its associated typing context; while Thm. 1 illustrates that each possible reduction of a typing context is simulated by an action in the reductions of the associated global type.

Theorem 1 (Completeness of Association). *Given associated global type G and typing context Δ such that $\Delta \sqsubseteq_a G$. If $\Delta \xrightarrow{\alpha} \Delta'$, then there exists G' such that $\Delta' \sqsubseteq_a G'$ and $G \xrightarrow{\alpha} G'$.*

Proof (Sketch). By case analysis on α. For each type of action we consider the possible structure of G permitted by the $\leqslant_a$ relation and find that it must be able to take a corresponding step. See [18] for detailed proofs.

Theorem 2 (Soundness of Association). *Let $\Delta \sqsubseteq_a G$ and assume $G \xrightarrow{\alpha} G'$. Then there exist an action α', a context Δ', and a global type G'' such that*

$$G \xrightarrow{\alpha'} G'', \qquad \Delta \xrightarrow{\alpha'} \Delta', \qquad \Delta' \sqsubseteq_a G''.$$

Proof (Sketch). By induction on the transition $G \xrightarrow{\alpha} G'$. We again consider the possible structure of G permitted by $\leqslant_a$ and conclude that Δ can take a step. We can then use Thm 1 to find a corresponding global type transition which preserves association. See [18] for detailed proofs.

5 Deriving the Main Theorems from Associations

This section demonstrates how to derive the main theorems using soundness and completeness of the associations, together with the corresponding results in [13, Theorems 4.11, 4.12 and 4.13]. Before that, we recall the bottom-up typing system for a multiparty session:

$$\frac{\forall \mathsf{p} \in \text{dom}(\Delta) \quad \vdash P_{\mathsf{p}} \triangleright T_{\mathsf{p}} \quad \vdash h_{\mathsf{p}} \triangleright \sigma_{\mathsf{p}} \quad \Delta(\mathsf{p}) = (\sigma_{\mathsf{p}}, T_{\mathsf{p}}) \quad \varphi(\Delta)}{\vdash^{\text{bot}} \Pi_{\mathsf{p} \in \text{dom}(\Delta)} \, (\mathsf{p} \triangleleft P_{\mathsf{p}} \mid \mathsf{p} \triangleleft h_{\mathsf{p}}) \, \triangleright \Delta} \quad [\textsc{SessBot}]$$

where φ is some desired property, which is usually a *safety* property–a selected label is always available at the branching process [19,23]. In [13], a *liveness* property [13, Definition 4.17] is used instead for proving the preciseness of $\leqslant_a$. See [13, § 7.1].

Deriving Subject Reduction Theorem. We prove the subject reduction theorem of the top-down system using the completeness of the association with the following subject reduction theorem of the bottom-up system. We define asynchronous multiparty session $(M, M_i, \ldots)$ as: $M ::= \text{p} \triangleleft P_\text{p} \mid \text{p} \triangleleft h_\text{p} \mid M \mid M'$.

Theorem 3 (Subject Reduction, Theorem 4.11 [13]). Assume $\vdash^{bot} M \triangleright \Delta$ with Δ live and $M \to^* M'$. Then there exist live Δ', Δ'' such that $\vdash^{bot} M' \triangleright \Delta''$ with $\Delta' \leqslant_a \Delta$ and $\Delta' \to^* \Delta''$.

Theorem 4 (Subject Reduction of the Top-Down System). Assume $\vdash^{top} M \triangleright \Delta$ and $M \to^* M'$. Then there exists Δ such that $\vdash^{bot} M' \triangleright \Delta'$ with $\Delta \to^* \Delta'$.

Proof. Assume $M \equiv \Pi_{\text{p} \in \text{dom}(\Delta)}(\text{p} \triangleleft P_\text{p} \mid \text{p} \triangleleft h_\text{p})$ and $\vdash^{top} M \triangleright \Delta$ is derived with

$$\forall \text{p} \in \text{dom}(\Delta) \quad \vdash P_\text{p} \triangleright T_\text{p} \quad \vdash h_\text{p} \triangleright \sigma_\text{p} \quad \Delta(\text{p}) = (\sigma_\text{p}, T_\text{p}) \quad \Delta \sqsubseteq_a G \qquad (2)$$

by [SessST]. Suppose $M \to M'$. We need to prove that there exist G' and Δ' such that $\Pi_{\text{p} \in \text{role}(G')}(\text{p} \triangleleft P'_\text{p} \mid \text{p} \triangleleft h'_\text{p})$ with $\Delta' \sqsubseteq_a G'$.

Note that Δ is live by [19,23]. Hence by Theorem 3, there exist live Δ', Δ'' such that $\vdash^{bot} \Pi_{\text{p} \in \text{role}(G)} P'_\text{p} \triangleright \Delta''$ with $\Delta' \leqslant_a \Delta$ and $\Delta' \to^* \Delta''$. By Definition 8, $\Delta' \sqsubseteq_a G$. Then by Theorem 1, $\Delta' \to^* \Delta''$ implies $G \to^* G'$ and $\Delta'' \sqsubseteq_a G'$. Hence $\vdash^{top} \Pi_{\text{p} \in \text{dom}(\Delta'')} P'_\text{p} \triangleright \Delta''$ as desired.

Deriving Session Fidelity. We derive session fidelity of the top-down system. We use the soundness and completeness of the association with session fidelity of the bottom-up system

Theorem 5 (Session Fidelity, Theorem 4.13 [13]). Assume $\vdash^{bot} M \triangleright \Delta$ with Δ live. Assume $\Delta \to$. Then there exist M' and Δ' such that $M \to^+ M'$, $\Delta \to \Delta'$ and $\vdash^{bot} M' \triangleright \Delta'$.

Theorem 6 (Session Fidelity of the Top-Down System). Assume $\vdash^{top} M \triangleright \Delta$ is derived by $\Delta \sqsubseteq_a G$ and $G \to$. Then there exist M' and Δ' such that $M \to^+ M'$, $G \to G'$ and $\vdash^{top} M' \triangleright \Delta'$ with $\Delta' \sqsubseteq_a G'$.

Proof. Assume $\Delta \sqsubseteq_a G$. By the soundness of the association, $G \to$ implies $\Delta \to$. Suppose $M \equiv \Pi_{\text{p} \in \text{dom}(\Delta)}(\text{p} \triangleleft P_\text{p} \mid \text{p} \triangleleft h_\text{p})$ and $\vdash^{top} M' \triangleright \Delta$ is derived with (2) above. By Theorem 5, there exist M' and Δ' such that $M \to^+ M'$ and $\Delta \to \Delta'$. Hence by the completeness of the association, and Theorem 4, $G \to G'$ and $\Delta' \sqsubseteq_a G'$ with $\vdash^{top} M' \triangleright \Delta'$, as desired.

Next we show that typed multiparty sessions are live (defined in [13, § 2.3]).

Theorem 7 (Liveness of the Top-Down System). Assume $\vdash^{top} M \triangleright \Delta$. Then for all M' such that $M \to^* M'$, M' is safe, deadlock-free and live.

Proof. We first note that if M is live, then M is safe and deadlock-free. If $\Delta \sqsubseteq_a G$, then Δ is live, hence we have $\vdash^{bot} M \triangleright \Delta$. Then by Theorem 4.12 in [13], M is live.

6 Conclusion

We have proposed an asynchronous association relation and proved its sound and complete operational correspondence. This work is the first to prove these results based on (1) asynchronous precise subtyping and (2) projection with co-inductive full merging. We introduced a new operational semantics for global types, which captures more behaviours allowed by permuting actions than the previous asynchronous global type semantics in [2,16]. We developed a new projection relation which associates global types with a pair of a local type and a queue type for each participant. Using this correspondence, we derived the subject reduction theorem and the session fidelity theorem of the top-down system from the corresponding theorems of the bottom-up system [13, Theorem 4.11 and 4.13]. Since the projection Δ of G is known to be safe, deadlock-free and live [19,24], we can derive that asynchronous multiparty session processes typed by the top-down typing system ([SessTop]) are also safe, deadlock-free and live (Theorem 7). While [13] has proved the subject reduction theorem and session fidelity theorem under the subsumption rule of $\leqslant_a$, it does not use the top-down typing system. On the other hand, [12] has shown that multiparty synchronous subtyping is precise in the synchronous multiparty session calculus using the top-down system. None of the previous work has defined association with respect to asynchronous subtyping or co-inductive projection. An interesting open question is whether the association theorems hold for the sound decidable asynchronous subtyping relations [7,10] (and [4,5] by extending binary to multiparty session types) so that we can derive the subject reduction theorems under those relations.

We have demonstrated the usefulness of association in deriving the main theorems of the top-down system, by *reusing* the theorems in [13]. We have not yet reached a stage to claim that MPST is a theoretical framework for building component-based software systems as Jean-Bernard Stefani has defined. There still needs to be more effort applied to developing practical applications of MPST for testing and maintaining compositionality and reusability of protocols. The most challenging topic is to type individual *components*, each being written in a different programming language or running on a different platform, while ensuring their type-safety and deadlock-freedom, assuming they conform to a shared global protocol. Implementing such a component-based architecture requires significant engineering effort such as defining system requirements, identifying components, splitting the system into components, integrating these components, and designing the interfaces for components. We plan to conduct a serious study along these lines in the near future to make MPST a true *theory of CBSE*.

References

1. Barwell, A.D., Scalas, A., Yoshida, N., Zhou, F.: Generalised Multiparty Session Types with Crash-Stop Failures Technical Report (2022)
2. Barwell, A.D., Scalas, A., Yoshida, N., Zhou, F.: Generalised multiparty session types with crash-stop failures (2022). To appear in LMCS

3. Blair, G., Coupaye, T., Stefani, J.-B.: Component-based architecture: the fractal initiative. Ann. Telecommun. **64**(1–2), 1–4 (2009)
4. Bocchi, L., King, A., Murgia, M.: Asynchronous subtyping by trace relaxation. In: Finkbeiner, B., Kovács, L. (eds.) Tools and Algorithms for the Construction and Analysis of Systems - 30th International Conference, TACAS 2024, Held as Part of the European Joint Conferences on Theory and Practice of Software, ETAPS 2024, Luxembourg City, Luxembourg, 6–11 April 2024, Proceedings, Part I, vol. 14570 of Lecture Notes in Computer Science, pp. 207–226. Springer, Heidelberg (2024)
5. Bravetti, M., Carbone, M., Lange, J., Yoshida, N., Zavattaro, G.: A sound algorithm for asynchronous session subtyping and its implementation. Log. Methods Comput. Sci. **17**(1) (2021)
6. Bruneton, E., Coupaye, T., Leclercq, M., Quéma, V., Stefani, J.B.: The fractal component model and its support in java. Softw. Pract. Exp. **36**(11–12), 1257–1284 (2006)
7. Castro-Perez, D., Yoshida, N.: CAMP: cost-aware multiparty session protocols. Proc. ACM Program. Lang. **4**(OOPSLA), 155:1–155:30 (2020)
8. Chen, T.C., Dezani-Ciancaglini, M., Yoshida, N.: On the preciseness of subtyping in session types: 10 years later. In: Proceedings of the 26th International Symposium on Principles and Practice of Declarative Programming, PPDP '24. Association for Computing Machinery, New York (2024)
9. Cutner, Z., Yoshida, N.: Safe session-based asynchronous coordination in rust. In: Damiani, F., Dardha, O. (eds.) COORDINATION 2021. LNCS, vol. 12717, pp. 80–89. Springer, Cham (2021). https://doi.org/10.1007/978-3-030-78142-2_5
10. Cutner, Z., Yoshida, N., Vassor, M.: Deadlock-free asynchronous message reordering in rust with multiparty session types. In: 27th ACM SIGPLAN Symposium on Principles and Practice of Parallel Programming, PPoPP '22, pp. 261–246. ACM (2022). arxiv:2112.12693
11. Fassino, J.P., Stefani, J.B., Lawall, J.L., Muller, G.: Think: a software framework for component-based operating system kernels. In: Proceedings of the General Track of the Annual Conference on USENIX Annual Technical Conference, ATEC'02, pp. 73–86. USENIX Association (2002)
12. Ghilezan, S., Jakšić, S., Pantović, J., Scalas, A., Yoshida, N.: Precise subtyping for synchronous multiparty sessions. J. Logical Algebr. Methods Program. **104**, 127–173 (2019)
13. Ghilezan, S., Pantović, J., Prokić, I., Scalas, A., Yoshida, N.: Precise subtyping for asynchronous multiparty sessions. ACM Trans. Comput. Logic **24**(2), 1–73 (2023)
14. Honda, K., Vasconcelos, V.T., Kubo, M.: Language primitives and type disciplines for structured communication-based programming. In: Proceedings of ESOP 1998, vol. 1381 of LNCS, pp. 22–138. Springer, Heidelberg (1998)
15. Honda, K., Yoshida, N., Carbone, M.: Multiparty asynchronous session types. In: Proceedings of POPL 2008, pp. 273–284. ACM (2008)
16. Honda, K., Yoshida, N., Carbone, M.: Multiparty asynchronous session types. J. ACM **63**(1), 9:1–9:67 (2016)
17. Pierce, B.: Types and Programming Languages. MIT Press, Cambridge (2002)
18. Pischke, K., Yoshida, N.: Asynchronous global protocols, precisely: Full proofs. https://arxiv.org/abs/2505.17676 (2025)
19. Scalas, A., Yoshida, N.: Less is more: multiparty session types revisited. Proc. ACM Program. Lang. **3**(POPL), 1–29 (2019)

20. Takeuchi, K., Honda, K., Kubo, M.: An interaction-based language and its typing system. In: Halatsis, C., Maritsas, D., Philokyprou, G., Theodoridis, S. (eds.) PARLE 1994. LNCS, vol. 817, pp. 398–413. Springer, Heidelberg (1994). https://doi.org/10.1007/3-540-58184-7_118
21. Udomsrirungruang, T., Yoshida, N.: Top-down or bottom-up? Complexity analyses of synchronous multiparty session types. Proc. ACM Program. Lang. **9**(POPL), 1040–1071 (2025)
22. Yoshida, N.: Programming language implementations with multiparty session types. In: de Boer, F.S., Damiani, F., Hähnle, R., Johnsen, E.B., Kamburjan, E. (eds.) Active Object Languages: Current Research Trends, vol. 14360 of Lecture Notes in Computer Science, pp. 147–165. Springer, Heidelberg (2024)
23. Yoshida, N., Hou, P.: Less is More Revisit (2024)
24. Yoshida, N., Hou, P.: Less is more revisited, 2024. Accepted by Cliff B. Jones Festschrift Proceeding (2004)
25. Yoshida, N., Hu, R., Neykova, R., Ng, N.: The scribble protocol language. In: Abadi, M., Lluch Lafuente, A. (eds.) TGC 2013. LNCS, vol. 8358, pp. 22–41. Springer, Cham (2014). https://doi.org/10.1007/978-3-319-05119-2_3
26. Yoshida, N., Zhou, F., Ferreira, F.: Communicating finite state machines and an extensible toolchain for multiparty session types. In: Bampis, E., Pagourtzis, A. (eds.) FCT 2021. LNCS, vol. 12867, pp. 18–35. Springer, Cham (2021). https://doi.org/10.1007/978-3-030-86593-1_2

Verification

Introduction

Applied Formal Methods at ONERA: An Experience Report

Michael Lienhardt

DTIS, ONERA, Université Paris-Saclay, 91120 Palaiseau, France
michael.lienhardt@onera.fr

Abstract. ONERA is a french national research center developing methods and studies related to the aerospace domain, including physical simulations, event processing, and formal methods. It also produces many software tools at many level of maturity, ranging from prototypes for simple studies, to industrial level software tools in the context of collaborations with industrial partners like Airbus or SAFRAN. While these tools are developed by domain experts, which ensures the quality of their results, their implementation could benefit from expertise in computer-science and formal methods, to help ensure a design consistent with their expected maintainability, evolution and properties.

To illustrate this statement, we present in this paper two recent projects at ONERA where formal methods were actively used in the design of new scientific tools or in the maintenance of existing ones. In particular, we discuss the context of these projects, where formal methods were used, for what purpose and with what results. We also propose a report on some of the dynamics that were used to develop fruitful and long-lasting collaborations between formal methods and experts of very different scientific fields.

1 Introduction

ONERA is an research center dedicated to the aerospace domain. Its subjects of studies cover a large variety of topics, including simulation of physical phenomena [4,15,20,22,25,34,51], aircraft design [26,46] scientific space missions [44], event processing [13], and validation of embedded systems and hardware [7,23,40,49]. The methods and techniques developed at ONERA are often integrated in tools, either in dedicated prototypes to illustrate the validity of the approaches, or in large and long-lived software tools which gather the know-how of experts in various scientific domain and provide a complete set of functionalities for external collaborations, including industrial partnerships.

In this paper, we focus on two kinds of such long-lived software tools. A first category of tools considered here is *scientific data collection and processing* (SDCP): these tools collect data of various nature coming from various sensors and process them to produce information relevant for human operators. The development of such tools is complex because it requires two kinds of expertise: on one hand, specialists must design many specific modules (in form of libraries or small applications) implementing the different steps that must be taken to translate the input data into information of interest; on the other hand, these modules must be integrated into a complete toolchain that must provide the communication means to make them collaborate, and also a dedicated GUI so users can seamlessly configure and pilot these modules in order to actually perform the expected translation.

The second category of tools considered in this paper is *physical simulations*. The development of such a tool is very complex due to two main factors. First, the range of simulations this tool must perform is very large, and so software engineering techniques are necessary to integrate all these different functionalities in a maintainable code base. Second, the simulations performed by such a tool are very computation and memory intensive, and so concurrency and distribution techniques must also be integrated in its development.

Recently, two projects fostered collaborations between experts developing such tools and computer scientists, including in particular techniques taken from formal methods. The goal of these projects was to develop a common understanding between experts of different domains, and use that understanding to develop dedicated frameworks that would capture all the computer-specific implementation details, so that domain-experts could focus on implementing their approaches while enjoying a dedicated framework that would promote code maintainability, evolutivity, and runtime efficiency. The first project was dedicated to SDCP tools and used *Model-Driven Engineering* (MDE) techniques to help automatically generate the code and GUIs necessary to make every modules in the toolchain collaborate and pilotable by end-users. Formal method techniques were used in this project to guide the design of the code generator, define its operational semantics, and propose a deadlock analysis tool. The second project, dedicated to *Computational Fluid Dynamics* (CFD), which is the research field of fluid flow simulations specifically, directly uses various formal methods techniques to propose a new software architecture for such simulation tools. This architecture has successfully been used in the production of a new industrial-level fluid flow simulator called *SoNICS* [27]. This paper gives a brief overview of these two projects and discusses the human aspects of these collaborations: some examples of the difficulties we encountered, and how a fruitful and long-lasting dialogue was established.

The paper is structured as follows: Sect. 2 presents the application of formal methods in the context of scientific data collection and processing (SDCP) tools; Sect. 3 describes how formal methods were central in the development of a CFD-capable software architecture; Sect. 4 discusses the human aspects of these collaborations; and Sect. 5 concludes the paper.

2 Formal Methods in SDCP Tools

This project focused on three scientific data collection and processing tools: *Microscope* [44], *GravTer* and *IPSAT*. Microscope was a mission led by CNES and ONERA to test the Equivalence Principle by measuring with an accuracy of 10^{-15} the difference in free fall of two bodies made of different compositions, improving the best previous experiments by two orders of magnitude. A large part of the project was dedicated to the design and production of a satellite with its onboard tooling to perform the measurements, while another important part was focused on the development of a toolchain to process these measurements. *GravTer* uses multiple sources to compute precise values of the earth's gravity field at every position of the earth (latitude, longitude and altitude). It also stores these values in a database and provides several functionalities to query it. Finally, the *IPSAT* software performs a similar task, but for data related to ionized particles captured in the earth's magnetic field. These data are collected since the 70 s for space weather restitution and forecast.

This project focused on providing a versatile framework capable of: *i*) capturing the functional API of these tools' modules; *ii*) expressing their collaborations; *iii*) generating glue code implementing the specified collaborations; and *iv*) generating GUIs so end-users could pilot and check the computation performed by the generated code. It was structured in three steps. The first step focused on studying the structure of these tools and identifying common design or implementation patterns. The second step was to design a *Domain Specific Language* (DSL) that could capture all the computer-science specific implementation complexities into a user-friendly representation, together with a code generation tool that would translate such representations into executable code. The third step was to iterate with the domain experts, to help them use the DSL in the implementation of their data-processing application, and also update the DSL when design mismatch were encountered or when some functionalities were missing.

2.1 SDCP Tool Structure

While the application domains of these different software tools are very different, their implementations all share the same structure: they consist of multiple domain-specific modules embedded in an ad-hoc toolchain, usually implemented in bash or Python, that take care of assembling the modules in a workflow providing the functionalities and GUIs expected by the end user. Moreover, while maintaining the modules is relatively simple since they implement single tasks, maintaining the toolchain itself is far more difficult as it may require to insert an entirely new pipeline of tasks to implement new functionalities, or rewrite existing communication pathways when the API of a module changes. We illustrate the toolchains of these data-processing tools with an excerpt of the toolchain of *IPSAT*, shown in Fig. 1. This part of the toolchain is dedicated to the correction of the input data. Blue modules are the ones where human inputs are required, while white modules perform an automatic task. First, the user chooses the dataset (called *mission*) from the input database. Then, the *compute characteristics* module collects and combine all information related to this dataset into an understandable format, so the users can choose in the *select representative data* and *select erroneous data* modules which data are clearly correct and which may be erroneous. Moreover, while selecting the correct data, the user chooses

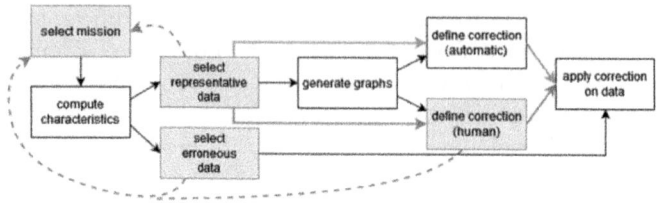

Fig. 1. Excerpt of the *IPSAT* toolchain

how the correction will be computed, either manually or automatically: this is shown with the brown and blue arrows that carry a simple trigger stating which module will perform the computation. Also, if all the data are correct (or if all the data are erroneous), no correction needs to be applied to the dataset, and the user can start a new instance of the workflow, modeled with the dashed purple arrows. The *generate graphs* module analyses the correct data w.r.t. multiple criteria to feed the modules that will define the correction. Depending on which correction method have been chosen by the user, one of these modules will just drop the data it received from the *generate graphs* module, while the other will perform its task and send its result to the *apply correction on data* module that performs the correction and updates the database with the now corrected data. Note that the user has again the possibility to cancel the current workflow and start a new one in the *define correction (human)* module, in case they discover that the supposed erroneous data are actually correct (and so the correction would be the identity). This toolchain is the result of several evolutions, the last one being the integration of the *define correction (automatic)* module, based on AI techniques.

2.2 METAL: a DSL for Toolchains

From the analysis done in the first step of the collaboration, it was clear that the purpose of the DSL was to provide a high-level representation of toolchains orchestrating domain-specific modules. This DSL thus had to provide two kinds of functionalities: *i*) it must concisely capture the workflow of a toolchain by identifying the different modules it contains and the communication patterns necessary for their collaboration; and *ii*) it must concisely capture all aspects related to data management, i.e., how to translate a data between different encodings used by the modules (including unit conversion), and how to present the data in GUIs to efficiently visualize and modify it.

For the data management functionality, a in-house DSL, called Gamme [3], already existed and is still maintained. This DSL is based on the xtext/xtend framework [5], and could produce translation code and GUIs in Java, C++ and Python. On the other hand, to the best of our knowledge, no workflow generation tool was ever used at ONERA. However, many approaches ranging from statecharts [28], component models [1,9,50] or orchestration [10,33,41] are particularly suited to express workflows. Hence, it was decided that while software

```
1   using get_mission(): t_mission;              11  }
2                                                12
3   component type SelectMission {               13  using apply_correction(t_corr, t_data): void;
4     port in reset: void;                       14
5     port out mission: t_mission;               15  component type ApplyCorrection {
6     initial state start:                       16    port in corr: t_corr;
7       [] get_mission() ==> mission;            17    port in err: t_data;
8         next wait;                             18    initial state always:
9     state wait:                                19      [corr, err] apply_correction(corr, err);
10      [reset] get_mission() ==> mission;       20  }
```

Fig. 2. Two Example of Component Types

engineers were focused on extending Gamme with a new DSL layer dedicated to express a workflow and produce C++ and Python code, experts with good knowledge of existing approaches should guide the design of this DSL to ensure that no unexpected problem would arise later in development.

The resulting DSL, called *METAL*, structures a workflow into three parts. First, *component types* inherit a stateful structure from the Aeolus component model [14], and to every state is associated a set of behaviors triggered by a (possibly empty) join pattern [24]. Second, *component assemblies* are described by naming every component instance used in this assembly and connecting their ports using bindings. Finally, a *workflow* is a specific component assembly where references to external modules are bound, and initial values used for the computation are set. We illustrate this DSL by focusing on its first part: let us consider the modules *select mission* and *apply correction on data* of Fig. 1. These two modules can respectively be described with the component types SelectMission and ApplyCorrection of Fig. 2. In this example, types are in blue (we refer to [3] for a description of how these types are declared within the Gamme DSL and how they interact in practice with *IPSAT*'s modules): void has its usual meaning; t_mission is the type of a mission; t_data is the type of mission data, including representatives selected by the *select representative data* module; and t_corr is the types of correction data.

Lines 1 to 11 present the construction of the *select mission* module. It starts with the declaration of the external function get_mission in Line 1. This function presents a GUI to the user with a list of missions to choose from and returns the chosen mission. This function is at the core of the SelectMission component which declares the ports and behaviors that allow this function to collaborate with other component-embedded functions. First, this component declares two ports: an input port reset, typed with void, which models the reception of a trigger cancelling the current computation (the dashed purple arrows in Fig. 1); and an output port mission, typed with t_mission, where the mission chosen by the user will be sent. This component then declares two states. The initial state, called start, has one unique behavior (Lines 7 to 8) triggered by an empty list of ports []. This behavior thus automatically executes: it runs the get_mission() function; sends its result to the mission output port; and changes the current state of the component to wait. This state also has one unique behavior (Line 10) that model the reset of a computation: upon the reception of a trigger on the `reset` input port, it once again runs the `get_mission()` function; send its result to the `mission` output port; and stays in the `wait` state to manage possible future cancelling triggers.

Lines 13 to 20 present the construction of the *apply correction on data* module. Similarly to the previous module, it starts with the declaration of an external function `apply_correction` that takes two parameters, a correction and a data to be fixed, applies the input correction on the input data and stores the result in the mission database, and returns nothing. Lines 15 to 20 wrap this function into the `ApplyCorrection` component. First, this component declares two input ports: `corr` receives the correction parameters of `apply_correction`, and `err` receives the erroneous data to correct. Finally, this component has only one state, called `always` with only one behavior: this behavior triggers upon the reception of a message on both its input ports, and uses these messages (that have the same name as the ports in which they were received) as parameters of the `apply_correction` function.

2.3 The DSL in Practice

We successfully used the DSL to fully describe the toolchains of *GravTer* and *IPSAT*. We did not apply it on *Microscope* simply due to lack of time. This work required several iterations with the developers of these tools, to understand how their workflow worked, and also how the data were structured. The DSL itself did not change much during these iterations: the well-known approaches that were used to design it were robust enough to satisfy the developers of these tools. One concern that was raised several times however was that communication in our DSL is only one way while programmers are used to functions, where parameters are send to a function which then answers with a returning value. This lack of answers in our DSL was slightly confusing when designing the toolchains, and future-based approaches [30,31,52] were considered. However such an extension exposes far more synchronization issues to the user, and so it was decided not to include it.

One extension that was implemented since it did not cause any burden on the user was to provide a concurrent and distributed runtime for the DSL. Since the communication between components is asynchronous in our DSL, this was relatively easy to implement, and seamlessly allowed to run *GravTer* and *IPSAT*, whose toolchains were originally implemented in sequential Python and bash code, in a distributed fashion. In particular, we achieved a 15 times speedup by running *GravTer* on 22 nodes.

3 Formal Methods in Complex Simulations

The usecase of this project was the *elsA* software [11,12,43] which performs precise fluid flow simulations for a large panel of applications, such as planes [51], helicopters [20], turbines [22] and engines [4]. This tool was developed for over more than 25 years, and its structure undertook several evolutions to keep up with the user requests and hardware evolutions. In particular, since fluid dynamics is bound by the unsolved Navier–Stokes equations, Computational Fluid Dynamics (CFD) tools like *elsA* must implement many different approximations of these equations to cover all application cases requested by the users. Moreover, the mesh on which the simulation must be perform also has an important impact on the computation. First, each object within the mesh (e.g., a wing or a rotor) triggers a specific computation to manage that object. Second, the mesh is usually very large, which requires the computation to be performed in a distributed fashion, where every process could need data computed by other processes, leading to possible deadlocks. The last major evolution of *elsA* managed these issues with a modular approach: every single function was encapsulated within an object, called *operator*, and a *factory* [18] created a list of tasks to perform based on the user requests and the mesh specification. Distribution was managed by specific stop points in the task list where communications were allowed. While being modular, this approach suffered from having all the complexity of building the task list centralized into the *factory*. To solve this issue, the development team had the intuition that code generation would help, and tinkered with this idea. Coincidentally, they met the main developer of Gamme, and started discussing code generation techniques and applications. It quickly appeared that other approaches could be helpful for the development of *elsA*, and this first contact started a discussion that completely revisited *elsA*'s factory and split it into three parts: Software Product Lines, Task Graph Generation and Task Graph Transformation.

3.1 Software Product Lines

A *Software Product Line* (SPL) is a set of similar programs, called *variants*, with a common code base and a well documented variability [50]. The field of SPL focuses on solving two problems: i) how to organize the many options of a software to have a clear picture of the configuration space; and ii) how to apply these options in the code to avoid code duplication and facilitate maintenance and evolution. SPLs have been studied for more than two decades, from both a practical and theoretical point of view [19,38,48].

A CFD solver such as *elsA* is a natural usecase for SPL. Indeed, as previously discussed, the computation performed by *elsA* has a lot of variations and, as presented in [37], the configuration space of a CFD solver can be split into three parts. The first part consists of about 2000 options that configure which fluid flow computation to perform, i.e., which approximation of the Navier–Stokes equations to use, together with their configuring constants. The second part is the output information provided to the user: virtually any data could interest them since it depends on which phenomena they are studying. So they must provide the list of these data to *elsA* which in turn must compute them by extending its computation. The last part of the configuration space is the shape of the input mesh itself.

In our refactoring of *elsA*'s factory, we used a well-known standard to organize its options, called *Feature Model* (FM). Such a model organizes options

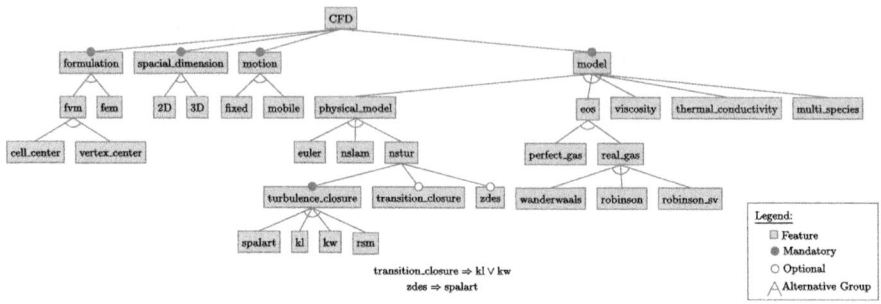

Fig. 3. A Sample of CFD Options Structured into a Feature Model

in a tree hierarchy, with additional constraints on option selection written with boolean formula. A sample of CFD options organized into a FM is presented in Fig. 3. Here, the configuration space is rooted in the CFD option and is split in four categories: formulation states which discretization of the computation to use (e.g., either computes the values in the cells of the mesh, or on its vertices); spacial_dimension states how many dimensions to consider, (2 and 3 dimensions are currently supported); motion states if the computation is stationary or not; and model presents the options to configure the equations used to perform simulation. Below the tree hierarchy, two additional constraints are presented, restricting how the options can be selected: transition_closure $\Rightarrow$ kl $\vee$ kw means that if the user wants a transition closure, then only the turbulent model kl or kw can be selected; and zdes $\Rightarrow$ spalart means that the Zonal Detached Eddy Simulation can only be performed with the spalart turbulence closure.

As discussed in [37], the effect of most of these options is to select which variant of every operator will be used in the computation. This selection is supported by the *Delta-Oriented Programming* (DOP) approach [35,47], which was formalized in various contexts [6,17,39], including [37] which formalizes DOP in the very context discussed in this section.

3.2 Task Graph Generation

This part of the collaboration focused on replacing *elsA*'s factory method to produce its list of tasks into a more robust algorithm. Indeed, while the goal of the list is to ensure that every task has its inputs available before being executed, possibly by executing other tasks beforehand, no such notion of dependency was explicitly used in producing the list, leading to a complex and error-prone implementation of the factory. Instead, with an explicit notion of dependency, this part of the factory becomes a simple dependency analysis, similar to [14,38].

However, while [14,38] use counted names or boolean formula to model their dependencies, none of these approaches can be taken here, due to two factors. First, operators in *elsA* can be generic: e.g., *grad* can compute the gradient of any value. Second, the dependency analysis must be able to capture how the mesh impacts the computation, e.g., how many objects and of what type are in the mesh, and where to insert the corresponding computation. To answer the first factor, we model dependencies as terms, i.e., syntax trees that can contain variables. That way, the *grad* operator can be modeled with $grad : \alpha \to \mathtt{grad}(\alpha)$: the parameter α states that this operator can take any kind of value in input, and $\mathtt{grad}(\alpha)$ states that this operator return the gradient of that input value. In this context, finding which operator can produce a needed dependency can easily be implemented with pattern matching, and the dependency analysis can be implemented as a fixpoint algorithm that solves every dependency by finding a matching operator, until all dependencies have been matched. To answer the second factor, we extended the implementation of our dependency analysis into term rewriting: that way, we can simply translate information contained in the mesh into rewriting rules that will insert the computation triggered by the mesh at the correct spot during the dependency analysis. A complete formalization of this dependency analysis is presented in [37].

Finally, while it was clear that using terms to model dependencies and term rewriting to encode the dependency analysis was a robust approach, it was unclear how expressive the term should be to capture all the dependencies. Indeed, while *elsA* developers had a very deep understanding of *elsA*, its equations and its computation, they never manipulated dependencies and terms before. Consequently, we use unranked trees as terms as formalized in [32] and implemented in [36].

3.3 Task Graph Transformation

Finally, the last element in our refactoring of *elsA*'s factory consists of extending the generate task graph with additional information and computation. For instance, we previously discussed that *elsA*'s computation is distributed with dependencies crossing node boundaries. These external dependencies cannot be managed by the dependency analysis described in the previous section, since it only manages local dependencies. Consequently, a graph transformation pass is needed to ensure that all external dependencies are satisfied on every node. This pass consists of a simple fixpoint algorithm where every node sends its external dependencies to the nodes that can perform the corresponding computation, until every node has all its distant dependencies solved.

Another important transformation to perform on the task graph is to produce its derivative. Indeed, an important aspect of aircraft design is to produce optimal shapes for a specific purpose (like avoiding or minimizing the creation of vortices). And an efficient method to obtain such optimals is to differentiate the function of interest and use iterative approaches like Newton's method or GMRES [45] to compute these optimals. Methods to differentiate imperative codes have been investigated and implemented [29,42], and we adapted these methods to apply them on a task graph [8].

4 Human Aspects of These Collaborations

While the scientific realizations discussed in the previous sections are important achievements, and the expertise of everyone involved was paramount in producing these realizations, the human dynamics was also of great importance to actually create communities where people shared enough mutual understanding to make the collaborations work. In this section, we will discuss several aspects of the dynamics of the collaborations presented in this paper, which we structure in two categories. First, we present some difficulties we encountered in building a common understanding of the different implementation and design techniques that were considered in our projects, in particular with experts not fluent in computer-science idioms. Second, we present few simple principles we used in practice to build fruitful collaborations rooted in mutual respect.

4.1 Difficulties

Most of the difficulties we encountered in our collaborations were caused by a lack of knowledge or vocabulary on specific fields, like component models, product lines, or *boundary condition* (an element of a mesh). This lack of knowledge led, as discussed before, the *elsA* developers to design their own mechanisms and practices to manage the complex configuration space of their tool since they did not have enough knowledge about product lines and the associated vocabulary to assess that some of the techniques developed in this field could help them in this task. It also led to some collaborations failing before even starting, due to computer-scientists misunderstanding the problem to be solved, thinking solutions already existed and dismissing it. More generally, we identified three main difficulties in building collaborations between computer-scientists and domain experts.

The Impossible Specification. An obvious yet challenging difficulty often arises when scientists without knowledge in specific topics want to describe the problems they face and want to solve: they don't have the vocabulary or don't know the concepts to precisely express these problems. Indeed, without knowledge about component architectures and the languages to describe them, developers of SDCP tools could not describe the abstract structure of their implementations nor identify what kind of framework could help them in their development efforts. Similarly, the *elsA* development team struggled for some time with option management without knowing that SPLs existed and could elegantly solve their issues.

On the other hand, some imprecisions in the domain-expert requests might also be caused by the domain itself. This is for instance the case for the notion of dependencies used in Sect. 3.2: since CFD is subject of a very active research and is in constant evolution, it is impossible to predict what kind of term could capture all dependencies that could appear in the next few years.

The Datastructure Monster. Complex and abstract data structures, like components, terms or dependency graphs, can be difficult to understand and manipulate. Moreover, such data structure are useless or even counter-productive in some contexts where arrays and matrices are more suited and give better performances. Consequently, it is not always easy to argue that, e.g., using graphs to structure tasks is more suited than using lists. The acceptance of complex or abstract data structures, like component architectures or terms is gradual, and must follow three main principles: *i*) the data structure must be as simple as possible and its usage as obvious as possible; *ii*) at least one domain expert must understand the data structure and validate its purpose; and *iii*) the data structure and its usage must be explained repeatedly, with simple and applied examples. For instance, the acceptance of terms by the *elsA* development team was gradual, and was actually advocated by the persons who tinkered with code generation: they compared terms to Abstract Syntax Trees. Moreover, while *elsA* developers were slightly apprehensive of using graphs to structure their tasks, many of them had important knowledge about HPC topics and libraries (which was acquired through the development of the distributed features of *elsA*) and knew about dependency graphs through libraries like openMP [16] or runtimes like Legion [2].

The Asynchronous Devil. While there are nowadays many examples where asynchronous communication is more efficient than synchronous ones (like in microkernels), or where synchronous communications cause artificial deadlocks that are avoided using asynchronous ones, building concurrent and distributed software based on asynchronous communications is still avoided by many developers. For instance, the semantics of the component model presented in Sect. 2.2 is naturally expressed using asynchronous communications. However, many end-users of this DSL, upon knowing that communication is asynchronous, start wondering if this won't cause errors in communications or deadlocks. A similar apprehension was present in *elsA* developers, even those experts in HPC: they struggled in making the distributed aspect of their factory works and were very caution toward any deviation from the solution they designed.

In the end, users of the toolchain DSL were reassured by seeing that their toolchain worked even in presence of asynchronous communications, and *elsA* developers were reassured seeing that the refactoring of the factory (that includes an asynchronous implementation of a consensus) did work. However, many explanations and clarification are still required in order for these developers to fully master asynchrony.

4.2 Building Mutual Understanding

To overcome the difficulties previously discussed, we tried few key principles to break the language and expertise barrier. In the following, we present four of these principles which we used with great results.

Listen. Even if some scientists and developers are not labeled as computer-science experts, they can have a lot of experience implementing tools. And so, even if they lack the precise terminology to specify the problem they are tackling, it does not mean that they do not have an idea of how to solve that problem. For instance, even if *elsA*'s factory suffered some design issues, its developers acquired a lot of experience and insights of how to solve these issues during its implementation. Hence it is important to listen and try to understand their description of the problem and ask questions to clarify specific points.

Moreover, developers who did not study computer science may have created their own idioms for the implementation concepts they use, which may not correspond to the "standard" vocabulary. For instance, *elsA* developers use *serialization* in place of *scheduling*. Also, many developers of simulation tools use *object-oriented approach* to refer to the technique of wrapping functions inside objects to easily compose them (possibly via a task graph) into a complete computation. These alternative terms and meanings can be confusing and cause misunderstandings, but it is counter-productive to dismiss them (as it may alienate the people using them): instead, it is better to ask questions to clarify the intended meaning, and then agree on a common vocabulary.

Respect. A property specific of collaborations between computer scientists and experts of other scientific domains is that its actors do not share the same status. Indeed, while experts may struggle to implement their theories and tools and could benefit from computer scientists' insights, the inverse almost never occurs. This situation is analogous to the relationship between a worker and a toolbox, where the worker uses tools from the toolbox, and the toolbox never uses the worker. However, the purpose of the toolbox is to be useful to the worker, and without the worker the toolbox would never exist in the first place.

Moreover, these experts, beyond their knowledge of their own scientific domain of studies, may have a lot of experience implementing their tools. Hence, while some of the code they wrote might look imperfect, or their development practices might look inefficient and error-prone, they are still far more knowledgeable in what they do compared to any external computer-scientists. It is thus important to respect their knowledge and practices: only the implementation related to the problem being specified and for which a common understanding have been reached can be discussed.

Prototypes. Since domain experts may not have a deep expertise in computer science and formal methods, in many cases it is useless to motivate a specific solution to a problem using an intricate discourse. Instead, it is far more efficient to illustrate the solution with a simple prototype that may not implement all the required functionalities right away. Such a prototype shows how the solution could work in practice, and only few in-person arguments presenting how the missing functionalities could be added are usually sufficient to convince collaborators that this solution is worth investigating. Then, when the proposed solution is assessed and agreed upon, the time it could take to implement the complete tool and produce its formal specification becomes less of a problem.

This pattern was used for instance for the task graph generation discussed in Sect. 3.2. Initially, a very simple implementation of terms and pattern matching was done in Python [18], to show that dependency analysis was a promising way to solve many of the issues of *elsA*'s factory. Then, the implementation of a C++ library for unranked term rewriting [36] took more than six month, and its integration into a fully-fledged task graph generation tool, together with its formalization [37], took several additional months.

Power of Theorems. Formal methods are time consuming and it is important to illustrate their interest to collaborators with no expertise in them. In our work, we used the fact that most collaborators are fluent in mathematical concepts: they know about theorems and the importance of proving properties. Consequently, even if many of them manage their code organically, by implementing a first version and patching it until it works for a pre-defined set of tests, they can understand, when explained, the interest of a systemic approach to specify an algorithm, where hypothesis on the inputs and requirements on the outputs are well defined, and a proof shows that the algorithm do perform what it is supposed to do. Moreover, proving an algorithm means studying in detail how it works, and it can happen that while trying to prove an algorithm we discover a more efficient version of it.

5 Conclusion

In this paper, we presented two collaborations between formal methods and experts of various domains. We introduced the problems that motivated these collaborations and how they were solved. We also presented the human aspects of these collaborations, with the difficulties of establishing a common understanding between experts of different fields, and few principles that were used to help create that common understanding.

In future work, we would like to deepen and widen these collaborations. First, we would like to invite more practitioners to use our toolchain DSL, and evaluate if its current expressiveness is enough. Moreover, we would like to continue studying the theoretical foundations of this DSL, for instance by studying its communication patterns and improving their efficiency. Second, while much work was dedicated to the formalization of the new version of *elsA*'s factory, some of its aspects still need to be formalized, like the transformation to produce the derivative of a computation. Finally, an important aspect of simulation that was not discussed in this paper is *coupling* [21], i.e., making two simulators collaborate. For instance, having a CFD simulator and a chemical simulator collaborate to simulate together an engine with its fuel combustion. *Coupling* involves interesting synchronization issues such as exchanging specific values at specific times of the simulation, which may unexpectedly change during the simulation itself. Studying such synchronization patterns from a formal method point of view could help implementing efficient and safe coupling methods.

Acknowledgements. The author would like to thank all the persons involved in the collaborations presented in this paper, the *Microscope* design and development team, the *GravTer* team, the *IPSAT* team, the *elsA* and *SoNICS* team: without all these persons, their work, time and understanding, nothing presented here would have been possible. Moreover, the author would like to thank the reviewers for their useful and constructive comments.

References

1. Alliance, T.O.: OSGi Service Platform. IOS Press Inc., Amsterdam (2003)
2. Bauer, M., Treichler, S., Slaughter, E., Aiken, A.: Legion: expressing locality and independence with logical regions. In: Hollingsworth, J.K. (ed.) SC Conference on High Performance Computing Networking, Storage and Analysis, SC 2012, Salt Lake City, UT, USA, 11–15 November 2012, p. 66. IEEE/ACM (2012). https://doi.org/10.1109/SC.2012.71
3. Bedouet, J., Huynh, N., Kervarc, R.: Gamme, a meta-model to unify data needs in simulation modeling (WIP). In: Wainer, G.A., Mosterman, P.J., Barros, F.J., Zacharewicz, G. (eds.) 2013 Spring Simulation Multiconference, SpringSim 2013, San Diego, CA, USA, 7–10 April 2013, Proceedings of the Symposium on Theory of Modeling and Simulation - DEVS Integrative M&S Symposium, p. 14. ACM (2013). http://dl.acm.org/citation.cfm?id=2499648
4. Berthelon, T., Dugeai, A., Langridge, J., Thouverez, F.: Ground effect on fan forced response. In: Proceedings of the 15th International Symposium on Unsteady Aerodynamics, Aeroacoustics and Aeroelasticity of Turbomachines, vol. ISUAAAT15-094. American Society of Mechanical Engineers (2018)
5. Bettini, L.: Implementing Domain Specific Languages with Xtext and Xtend. Packt Publishing, Birmingham (2016)
6. Bettini, L., Damiani, F., Schaefer, I.: Compositional type checking of delta-oriented software product lines. Acta Inform. **50**(2), 77–122 (2013). https://doi.org/10.1007/S00236-012-0173-Z
7. Boniol, F., Pagetti, C., Sensfelder, N.: Identification of multi-core interference. In: Yu, D., Nguyen, V., Jiang, C. (eds.) 19th IEEE International Symposium on High Assurance Systems Engineering, HASE 2019, Hangzhou, China, 3–5 January 2019, pp. 98–106. IEEE (2019). https://doi.org/10.1109/HASE.2019.00024
8. Bourasseau, S., Michel, B., Lienhardt, M., Nunez Ramirez, J., Maugars, B., Content, C.: Algorithmic differentiation on operator graphs and applications. In: 2025 SIAM Conference on Computational Science and Engineering, Fort Worth, United States (2025). https://hal.science/hal-05002641
9. Bruneton, E., Coupaye, T., Leclercq, M., Quéma, V., Stefani, J.: The FRACTAL component model and its support in java. Softw. Pract. Exp. **36**(11–12), 1257–1284 (2006). https://doi.org/10.1002/SPE.767
10. Busi, N., Gorrieri, R., Guidi, C., Lucchi, R., Zavattaro, G.: Towards a formal framework for choreography. In: 14th IEEE International Workshops on Enabling Technologies (WETICE 2005), 13–15 June 2005, Linköping, Sweden, pp. 107–112. IEEE Computer Society (2005). https://doi.org/10.1109/WETICE.2005.57
11. Cambier, L., et al.: An overview of the multi-purpose elsA flow solver. Aerosp. Lab (2), 1–15 (2011). https://hal.science/hal-01182452
12. Cambier, L., Heib, S., Plot, S.: The Onera elsA CFD software: input from research and feedback from industry. Mech. Ind. **14**(3), 159–174 (2013)

13. Carle, P., Choppy, C., Kervarc, R., Piel, A.: Safety of unmanned aircraft systems facing multiple breakdowns. In: Choppy, C., Sun, J. (eds.) 1st French Singaporean Workshop on Formal Methods and Applications (FSFMA 2013). Open Access Series in Informatics (OASIcs), vol. 31, pp. 86–91. Schloss Dagstuhl – Leibniz-Zentrum für Informatik, Dagstuhl (2013). https://doi.org/10.4230/OASIcs.FSFMA.2013.86
14. Catan, M., et al.: Aeolus: mastering the complexity of cloud application deployment. In: Lau, K.-K., Lamersdorf, W., Pimentel, E. (eds.) ESOCC 2013. LNCS, vol. 8135, pp. 1–3. Springer, Heidelberg (2013). https://doi.org/10.1007/978-3-642-40651-5_1
15. Coiro, E., Lefebvre, S., Ceolato, R.: Infrared signature prediction for low observable air vehicles. In: AVT-324 Specialists' Meeting on Multi-disciplinary design approaches and performance assessment of future combat aircraft, pp. MP–AVT–324–08. NATO, Online (2020). https://doi.org/10.14339/STO-MP-AVT-324-08
16. Dagum, L., Menon, R.: OpenMP: an industry-standard API for shared-memory programming. IEEE Comput. Sci. Eng. **5**(1), 46–55 (1998). https://doi.org/10.1109/99.660313
17. Damiani, F., Hähnle, R., Kamburjan, E., Lienhardt, M.: A unified and formal programming model for deltas and traits. In: Huisman, M., Rubin, J. (eds.) FASE 2017. LNCS, vol. 10202, pp. 424–441. Springer, Heidelberg (2017). https://doi.org/10.1007/978-3-662-54494-5_25
18. Damiani, F., Lienhardt, M., Maugars, B., Michel, B.: Towards a Modular and Variability-Aware Aerodynamic Simulator. In: Ahrendt, W., Beckert, B., Bubel, R., Johnsen, E.B. (eds.) The Logic of Software. A Tasting Menu of Formal Methods. LNCS, vol. 13360, pp. 147–172. Springer, Cham (2022). https://doi.org/10.1007/978-3-031-08166-8_8
19. Damiani, F., Lienhardt, M., Paolini, L.: On logical and extensional characterizations of attributed feature models. Theor. Comput. Sci. **912**, 56–80 (2022). https://doi.org/10.1016/J.TCS.2022.01.016
20. Wall, B.G., et al.: From aeroacoustics basic research to a modern low-noise rotor blade. J. Am. Helicopter Soc. **62**(4), 1–16 (2017)
21. Errera, M., et al.: Multi-physics coupling approaches for aerospace numerical simulations. Aerosp. Lab (2), 1–16 (2011). https://hal.science/hal-01182439
22. F Blonde, M.S., F Lebœuf, M.L.: Modelling unsteadinesses and polydispersion in wet steam flows using the quadrature method of moments and a two-equation model. In: 10th European Conference on Turbomachinery Fluid dynamics & Thermodynamics. European Turbomachinery Society (2013)
23. Finzi, A., Craciunas, S.S., Boyer, M.: Integrating sporadic events in time-triggered systems via affine envelope approximations. In: 30th IEEE Real-Time and Embedded Technology and Applications Symposium, RTAS 2024, Hong Kong, 13–16 May 2024, pp. 15–28. IEEE (2024). https://doi.org/10.1109/RTAS61025.2024.00010
24. Fournet, C., Gonthier, G.: The reflexive CHAM and the join-calculus. In: Boehm, H., Jr., G.L.S. (eds.) Conference Record of POPL 1996: The 23rd ACM SIGPLAN-SIGACT Symposium on Principles of Programming Languages, Papers Presented at the Symposium, St. Petersburg Beach, Florida, USA, 21–24 January 1996, pp. 372–385. ACM Press (1996). https://doi.org/10.1145/237721.237805
25. Garaud, J.D., et al.: Z-set -suite logicielle pour la simulation des matériaux et structures. In: 14ème Colloque National en Calcul des Structures. Presqu'île de Giens, France (2019). https://hal.science/hal-02115875

26. Gray, J.S., Hwang, J.T., Martins, J.R.R.A., Moore, K.T., Naylor, B.A.: OpenMDAO: an open-source framework for multidisciplinary design, analysis, and optimization. Struct. Multidiscip. Optim. **59**(4), 1075–1104 (2019). https://doi.org/10.1007/s00158-019-02211-z
27. Gueyffier, D., Plot, S., Soismier, M.: SoNICS: a new generation CFD software for satisfying industrial users needs. In: OTAN/STO/Workshop AVT-366. Online, France (2022). https://hal.science/hal-04045165
28. Harel, D.: StateCharts: a visual formalism for complex systems. Sci. Comput. Program. **8**(3), 231–274 (1987). https://doi.org/10.1016/0167-6423(87)90035-9
29. Hascoët, L., Pascual, V.: The tapenade automatic differentiation tool: principles, model, and specification. ACM Trans. Math. Softw. **39**(3), 20:1–20:43 (2013). https://doi.org/10.1145/2450153.2450158
30. Johnsen, E.B., Hähnle, R., Schäfer, J., Schlatte, R., Steffen, M.: ABS: a core language for abstract behavioral specification. In: Aichernig, B.K., de Boer, F.S., Bonsangue, M.M. (eds.) FMCO 2010. LNCS, vol. 6957, pp. 142–164. Springer, Heidelberg (2011). https://doi.org/10.1007/978-3-642-25271-6_8
31. Johnsen, E.B., Owe, O., Yu, I.C.: Creol: a type-safe object-oriented model for distributed concurrent systems. Theor. Comput. Sci. **365**(1-2), 23–66 (2006). https://doi.org/10.1016/J.TCS.2006.07.031
32. Kutsia, T., Marin, M.: Regular expression order-sorted unification and matching. J. Symb. Comput. **67**, 42–67 (2015). https://doi.org/10.1016/J.JSC.2014.08.002
33. Lanese, I., Montesi, F., Zavattaro, G.: The evolution of Jolie. In: De Nicola, R., Hennicker, R. (eds.) Software, Services, and Systems. LNCS, vol. 8950, pp. 506–521. Springer, Cham (2015). https://doi.org/10.1007/978-3-319-15545-6_29
34. Langenais, A., Vuillot, F., Peyret, C., Chaineray, G., Bailly, C.: Assessment of a two-way coupling methodology between a flow and a high-order nonlinear acoustic unstructured solvers. Flow Turbul. Combust. **101**(3), 681–703 (2018). https://doi.org/10.1007/s10494-018-9928-0
35. Lienhardt, M.: PYDOP: a generic python library for delta-oriented programming. In: Arcaini, P., et al. (eds.) Proceedings of the 27th ACM International Systems and Software Product Line Conference - Volume B, SPLC 2023, Tokyo, Japan, 28 August–1 September 2023, pp. 30–33. ACM (2023). https://doi.org/10.1145/3579028.3609011
36. Lienhardt, M.: The hrewrite library: a term rewriting engine for automatic code assembly. In: Ogata, K., Martí-Oliet, N. (eds.) WRLA 2024. LNCS, vol. 14953, pp. 165–178. Springer, Cham (2024). https://doi.org/10.1007/978-3-031-65941-6_9
37. Lienhardt, M., Beek, M.H., Damiani, F.: Product lines of dataflows. J. Syst. Softw. **210**, 111928 (2024). https://doi.org/10.1016/J.JSS.2023.111928
38. Lienhardt, M., Damiani, F., Johnsen, E.B., Mauro, J.: Lazy product discovery in huge configuration spaces. In: Rothermel, G., Bae, D. (eds.) ICSE 2020: 42nd International Conference on Software Engineering, Seoul, South Korea, 27 June–19 July 2020, pp. 1509–1521. ACM (2020). https://doi.org/10.1145/3377811.3380372
39. Lienhardt, M., Damiani, F., Testa, L., Turin, G.: On checking delta-oriented product lines of statecharts. Sci. Comput. Program. **166**, 3–34 (2018). https://doi.org/10.1016/J.SCICO.2018.05.007
40. Macedo, N., Brunel, J., Chemouil, D., Cunha, A.: Pardinus: a temporal relational model finder. J. Autom. Reason. **66**(4), 861–904 (2022). https://doi.org/10.1007/S10817-022-09642-2
41. Montesi, F., Guidi, C., Lucchi, R., Zavattaro, G.: JOLIE: a java orchestration language interpreter engine. In: Boella, G., Dastani, M., Omicini, A., van der

Torre, L., Cerná, I., Linden, I. (eds.) Combined Proceedings of the Second International Workshop on Coordination and Organization (CoOrg 2006) and the Second International Workshop on Methods and Tools for Coordinating Concurrent, Distributed and Mobile Systems (MTCoord 2006), Bologna, Italy, 13 June 2006. Electronic Notes in Theoretical Computer Science, vol. 181, pp. 19–33. Elsevier (2006). https://doi.org/10.1016/J.ENTCS.2007.01.051
42. Moses, W.S., et al.: Scalable automatic differentiation of multiple parallel paradigms through compiler augmentation. In: Proceedings of the International Conference on High Performance Computing, Networking, Storage and Analysis, SC 2022. IEEE Press (2022)
43. Plot, S.: The high level of maturity of the elsA CFD software for aerodynamics applications. In: EUCASS 2019, Madrid, Spain (2019). https://hal.science/hal-02502351
44. Rodrigues, M., et al.: Microscope mission scenario, ground segment and data processing. Classical Quantum Gravity **39**(20), 204004 (2022). https://doi.org/10.1088/1361-6382/ac4b9a
45. Saad, Y., Schultz, M.H.: GMRES: a generalized minimal residual algorithm for solving nonsymmetric linear systems. SIAM J. Sci. Stat. Comput. **7**(3), 856–869 (1986). https://doi.org/10.1137/0907058
46. Saves, P., et al.: SMT 2.0: a surrogate modeling toolbox with a focus on hierarchical and mixed variables gaussian processes. Adv. Eng. Softw. **188**, 103571 (2024). https://doi.org/10.1016/J.ADVENGSOFT.2023.103571
47. Schaefer, I., Bettini, L., Bono, V., Damiani, F., Tanzarella, N.: Delta-oriented programming of software product lines. In: Bosch, J., Lee, J. (eds.) SPLC 2010. LNCS, vol. 6287, pp. 77–91. Springer, Heidelberg (2010). https://doi.org/10.1007/978-3-642-15579-6_6
48. Schröter, R., Krieter, S., Thüm, T., Benduhn, F., Saake, G.: Feature-model interfaces: the highway to compositional analyses of highly-configurable systems. In: Dillon, L.K., Visser, W., Williams, L.A. (eds.) Proceedings of the 38th International Conference on Software Engineering, ICSE 2016, Austin, TX, USA, 14–22 May 2016, pp. 667–678. ACM (2016). https://doi.org/10.1145/2884781.2884823
49. Sensfelder, N., Brunel, J., Pagetti, C.: On how to identify cache coherence: case of the NXP QorIQ T4240. In: Völp, M. (ed.) 32nd Euromicro Conference on Real-Time Systems, ECRTS 2020, 7–10 July 2020, Virtual Conference. LIPIcs, vol. 165, pp. 13:1–13:22. Schloss Dagstuhl - Leibniz-Zentrum für Informatik (2020). https://doi.org/10.4230/LIPICS.ECRTS.2020.13
50. Szyperski, C.A., Gruntz, D., Murer, S.: Component Software - Beyond Object-Oriented Programming, 2nd edn. Addison-Wesley component software series, Addison-Wesley (2002). https://www.worldcat.org/oclc/248041840
51. Thollet, W., Dufour, G., Carbonneau, X., Blanc, F.: Body-force modeling for aerodynamic analysis of air intake-fan interactions. Int. J. Numer. Methods Heat Fluid Flow **26**(7), 2048–2065 (2016)
52. Yonezawa, A.: ABCL: An Object-Oriented Concurrent System. MIT Press, Cambridge (1990)

Scalable Verification of Local and Global Properties of Collective Systems

Michele Loreti[✉][iD], Michela Quadrini[iD], and Aniqa Rehman[iD]

University of Camerino, Via Madonna delle Carceri, 7, 62032 Camerino, Italy
{michele.loreti,michela.quadrini,aniqa.rehman}@unicam.it

Abstract. Collective adaptive systems (CAS) are composed of many entities that interact with each other to reach local or global goals. In CAS, two kinds of behaviour can be considered: *local behaviour* and *global behaviour*. The former is the behaviour of each entity operating in the system. The latter is the system's behaviour as a whole and *emerges* from the local computations. Many languages have been proposed to model CAS to forecast the effect of local computations at the global level. Moreover, logics and tools have also been proposed to specify the properties of collectives and verify their satisfaction. Unfortunately, due to the problem of state-space explosion, standard exact model-checking techniques cannot be used. This paper presents a methodology that supports scalable analysis of CAS. Based on mean-field approximation, the proposed technique can be used to verify the behaviour of the single agents in a context approximated in terms of a deterministic process. A simple example shows how the proposed approach can be used to support the analysis of CAS.

Keywords: Collective Systems · Formal Languages · Local and Global Properties · Mean-Field Model Checking

1 Introduction

In the last three decades, much research has been done to study languages and tools that can capture the intricacies of distributed computations. The diffusion of the Internet stimulated this research line. The execution of programs moved from the *single computer* to the *Wide Area Network* (WAN). A new application class was developed based on a distributed software architecture of many heterogeneous computational entities, named *sites*. Different authorities generally manage network sites with different administrative policies and security requirements. In 2002, a research project named Mikado, coordinated by Jean-Bernard Stefani, was founded with the goal of studying new formal programming models based upon the notion of domain as a computing concept. These models support reliable, distributed mobile computation and provide the mathematical basis for a secure standard for distributed computing in open systems. One of the key Mikado results involved the Kernel Language for Agents Interaction and Mobility (KLAIM) [7,8], an experimental language for global computing.

Thanks to the constantly increasing pervasiveness of software and the availability of *smart-devices* that can interact with the environment where they are deployed, a new class of systems has attracted attention: Collective Systems. These systems are composed of heterogeneous entities that interact with each other and emerge into complex and dynamic behaviour. They range from biological ecosystems to social networks, and distributed systems exhibit complex behaviour that evolves over time. The research work done in projects like Mikado laid the basis on which formal languages and techniques have been developed to model CS [21,25].

Together with the languages and models to represent behaviour of CS, formal tools are needed to describe their properties and to verify their satisfaction. Indeed, for this class of systems, it is crucial to use tools that can forecast the emerging behaviour. In [23] the logic GLoTL has been proposed. This logic permits describing properties of CS from two different point of view: local and global. *Local properties* capture the behaviour of individual agents and describe how the individual agent behaviour influences the behaviour of the system at a global level while *global properties* permit us to describe the system's overall behaviour and a way to describe the emergent properties of multi-agent that arises through individual agents interactions.

In this paper, we introduce GLoTL+, a variant of GLoTL to specify *branching time properties* at the global level and *linear time logic* at the local one. In GLoTL+, a new operator is introduced that permits amounting the average fraction of agents satisfying a given local property. Moreover, we will also discuss how scalable analysis is crucial to understanding complex and dynamic behaviour and allows us to deal with such large-scale systems by approximating the behaviour of individuals. Scalable analysis techniques like *mean-field* permit us to abstract the identity of the individuals as well as focus on the aggregate behaviour of the system as a whole. As a result, computational complexity is reduced.

The paper is structured as follows. Section 2 introduces different approaches to model Collective Systems in terms of Stochastic Processes that represent behaviour at different levels of abstractions. Section 3 presents the syntax and semantics of GLoTL+, while in Sect. 4 an algorithm is proposed to perform exact model-checking. Moreover, to support scalable analysis, an algorithm based on mean-field approximation is proposed in Sect. 5. Finally, Sect. 6 concludes the paper.

2 Modelling Collective Systems

This section presents a family of Markovian Processes that can describe CAS at different levels of abstraction, from individuals to collectives. Following an approach similar to the one presented in [20], we assume that a *system* consists of a population of N identical interacting objects. At any step of the computation, each object can be in any of its finitely many states. Objects evolve following a *clock-synchronous* computation. Each member of the population must either execute one of the transitions that are enabled in its current state (by executing an *action*), or remain in such a state. This choice is based on a probability distribution that depends on the system state.

From Individuals to Fraction of Population. A CAS consists of many entities, the agents, that interact with each other to reach local or global goals. To reason about the behaviour of CAS, models are needed to specify possible computations formally and, in the case of quantitative analysis, to provide tools that permit measuring the *probability* of the set of computations of our interest. These models should represent the behaviour of a system at two different levels. A *global level*, where the whole state is considered, and a *local level*, where one can focus on the behaviour of every single agent.

Let $\mathcal{S}$ be a (countable) set of *agent states*, the behaviour of a collection of agents can be rendered in terms of a set of random variables $\{X(t), t \in T\}$ describing the state of the N agents operating in the system at a given time T.

Example 1 (Red/Blue Scenario 1/2). Let us consider a simple *running scenario* that will be used throughout the paper to help the reader understand the different concepts. We consider a system composed of N agents that can be either *blue* or *red* coloured. The goal is to guarantee that, without any centralised control, agents evolve to a *balanced configuration* where the number of *blue agents* is *similar* to the number of *red agents*. Each agent can autonomously change colour in the system according to their perceptions of the other agents' states.

We can assume that each agent in the system can be either in the state B, indicating that the agent is *blue coloured*, or in the state R, when the agent is *red*. At each computational step, an agent changes its state according to the colour of the agents that it has *observed*. In particular, an agent changes its state whenever an agent with the same colour is observed.

The global state of a system can be described at three different levels of abstraction: *individuals*, *counting vectors* and *fraction of population*.

At the level of *individuals*, the global state is rendered as a tuple in $\mathcal{S}^N$. Each agent's *identity* is preserved along the different states via the index when this approach is used. We let $\mathbf{s}^{(N)}$ denote an element in $\mathcal{S}^N$, we will use $\mathbf{s}$ when the value of N is clear from the context. Let $\mathbf{s} \in \mathcal{S}^N$, we let $\mathbf{s}(i)$ and s_i denote the i-th value in $\mathbf{s}$. Finally, for any $\mathbf{s} \in \mathcal{S}^N$ and $i < N$, we let $\mathbf{s}[i..]$ denote the state of individuals $\mathbf{s}' \in \mathcal{S}^{N-i}$ such that $\mathbf{s}'(j) = \mathbf{s}(i+j)$.

When the global state is rendered as a *counting vector*, the identity of the single agent is lost, and only the number of agents in the different state in $\mathcal{S}$ is considered. Following this approach, a global state with $N \in \mathbb{N}$ agents is represented in $N^{\mathcal{S}} \subseteq \mathbb{N}^{\mathcal{S}}$ consisting of the vector $\mathbf{m}$ associating to each element in $\mathcal{S}$ an integer value such that

$$\sum_{s \in \mathcal{S}} \mathbf{m}(s) = N$$

where $\mathbf{m}(s)$ denotes the element s in the vector $\mathbf{m}$.

Definition 1. *Given an element* $\mathbf{s} \in \mathcal{S}^N$ *we let* $\mathbf{m_s}$ *denote the counting vector in* $N^{\mathcal{S}}$ *such that for any* $s \in \mathcal{S}$

$$\mathbf{m_s}(s) = \sum_i \chi_s(\mathbf{s}(i)) \tag{1}$$

For any $s \in \mathcal{S}$, $\chi_s : \mathcal{S} \to \{0,1\}$ *is the function associating to each* $s' \in \mathcal{S}$ 1 *if* $s = s'$, 0 *otherwise. Finally, for any* $\mathbf{m} \in N^{\mathcal{S}}$, *we let* $[\mathbf{m}] = \{\mathbf{s} \mid \mathbf{m_s} = \mathbf{m}\}$. □

Let $s \in \mathcal{S}$, we let $\mathbf{1}_s$ denote the counting vector in $1^{\mathcal{S}}$ associating 1 to s and 0 to all the other states. Moreover, given $\mathbf{m}_1 \in N^{\mathcal{S}}$ and $\mathbf{m}_2 \in M^{\mathcal{S}}$, we let $\mathbf{m}_1 + \mathbf{m}_2$ denote the counting vector $\mathbf{m} \in (N+M)^{\mathcal{S}}$ such that $\mathbf{m}(s) = \mathbf{m}_1(s) + \mathbf{m}_2(s)$ for any $s \in \mathcal{S}$. We will also write $\mathbf{m}_1 = \mathbf{m}_2 - \mathbf{m}_3$ whenever $\mathbf{m}_1 + \mathbf{m}_3 = \mathbf{m}_2$. Finally, given $\mathbf{m} \in N^{\mathcal{S}}$ and $k \in \mathbb{N}$, we let $k \cdot \mathbf{m}$ denote the counting vector $\mathbf{m}' \in (kN)^{\mathcal{S}}$ such that $\mathbf{m}'(s) = k \cdot \mathbf{m}(s)$, for any $s \in \mathcal{S}$.

If one is not interested in the actual size N of the population, a representation based on *fraction of population* can be considered. In this case, global states are represented via elements in $\mathcal{U}^{\mathcal{S}}$, that is the *unit simplex* on $\mathcal{S}$, consisting of the set of vectors $\boldsymbol{\mu}$ associating to each state $s \in \mathcal{S}$ a value in $[0,1]$ where for any $\boldsymbol{\mu} \in \mathcal{U}^{\mathcal{S}}$

$$\sum_{s \in \mathcal{S}} \mu(s) = 1$$

For each $s \in \mathcal{S}$ and $\boldsymbol{\mu} \in \mathcal{U}^{\mathcal{S}}$, $\mu(s)$ denotes the fraction of agents in the system in the state s. Moreover, given a counting vector $\mathbf{m} \in N^{\mathcal{S}}$, we let $\boldsymbol{\mu}_{\mathbf{m}}$ be vector in $\mathcal{U}^{\mathcal{S}}$ such that for any $s \in \mathcal{S}$, $\boldsymbol{\mu}_{\mathbf{m}}(s) = \frac{\mathbf{m}(s)}{N}$. Moreover, for any $\mathbf{s} \in \mathcal{S}^N$ we use $\boldsymbol{\mu}_{\mathbf{s}}$ to denote $\boldsymbol{\mu}_{\mathbf{m_s}}$.

Multi-agent Discrete Time Model. The behaviour of the agents can be described in terms of a *Multi-Agent Discrete Time Model* (MADTM) $\mathcal{M}$ that consists of a pair $(\mathcal{S}, \mathcal{P})$ where $\mathcal{S}$ is a finite set of *agent states* while $\mathcal{P} : \mathcal{U}^{\mathcal{S}} \to \mathcal{S} \times \mathcal{S} \to [0,1]$, represents the agent transition probability. Given a $\boldsymbol{\mu} \in \mathcal{U}^{\mathcal{S}}$, $\mathcal{P}^{\mu}[s_1, s_2]$ is the probabiility that agent s_1 evolves in one step in s_2, giving that s_1 operates in an environment where the fraction of agents in each state is described by $\boldsymbol{\mu}$.

Example 2 (Red/Blue Scenario 2/3). In the case of our running scenario, we can consider the MADTM $(\mathcal{S}_{rb}, \mathcal{P}_{rb})$, where $\mathcal{S}_{rb} = \{\mathsf{B}, \mathsf{R}\}$ is the set of states introduced in Example 1, while $\mathcal{P}_{rb}$ is the agent transition probability defined as follows:

$$\mathcal{P}^{\mu}[\mathsf{R}, \mathsf{B}] = \alpha_m \cdot \mu(R) \qquad \mathcal{P}^{\mu}[\mathsf{R}, \mathsf{R}] = 1 - \alpha_m \cdot \mu(R)$$

$$\mathcal{P}^{\mu}[\mathsf{B}, \mathsf{R}] = \alpha_m \cdot \mu(B) \qquad \mathcal{P}^{\mu}[\mathsf{B}, \mathsf{B}] = 1 - \alpha_m \cdot \mu(B)$$

where α_m is the probability that an agent meets another agent in a computational step. We can observe that the higher the number of agents of a given colour, the higher the probability that one of them will change it.

DTMC of Individuals. Given a MADTM $\mathcal{M} = (\mathcal{S}, \mathcal{P})$, we let $\mathcal{I}_{\mathcal{M}}^{(N)}$ denote the DTMC $(\mathcal{S}^N, \mathbf{P}_{\mathcal{I}}^{\mathcal{P}})$ of *individuals* with size N. Each state in $\mathcal{I}_{\mathcal{M}}^{(N)}$ is a vector in $\mathcal{S}^N$ and represents the state of each of the N agents operating in the system. Probability matrix $\mathbf{P}_{\mathcal{I}}^{\mathcal{P}}$ is defined as follows:

$$\mathbf{P}_{\mathcal{I}}^{\mathcal{P}}[\mathbf{s}, \mathbf{s}'] = \mathcal{P}_I^{\mu_\mathbf{s}}[\mathbf{s}, \mathbf{s}'] \tag{2}$$

where

$$\mathcal{P}_I^{\mu}[\mathbf{s}, \mathbf{s}'] = \Pi_{i=1}^{N} \mathcal{P}^{\mu}[s_i, s_i'] \tag{3}$$

Here, probability matrix of $\mathbf{P}_{\mathcal{I}}^{\mathcal{P}}$ of individuals is expressed in terms of a $\mathcal{P}_I$ where, $\mathcal{P}_I$ describes the transition probabilities product of individual agents under μ in a configuration $\mathbf{s}$ to $\mathbf{s}'$.

The DTMC $\mathcal{I}_{\mathcal{M}}^{(N)}$ can be used to describe the behaviour of N agents operating in the same context. Any path $\pi \in Path(\mathcal{I}_{\mathcal{M}}^{(N)})$ represents a computation that can be experienced in the system described by $\mathcal{I}_{\mathcal{M}}^{(N)}$. If we focus on the specific agent i in the sequence of states occurring in π, we have a *local* perspective of the computation executed by agent i. Indeed, each agent is identified by an index (its position in the vector) preserved throughout the computation.

Given a *global* path π, we let $\pi \downarrow i$ denote the *local path* obtained from π by considering infinite sequence of agent states $s_0 s_1 \ldots$ ($s_i \in \mathcal{S}$) such that for any j, $s_j = \pi[j][i]$. We say that $\pi_\ell = s_0 s_1 \ldots$ is a *local path* for agent i from the state $\mathbf{s} \in \mathcal{S}^N$ if and only if there exists $\pi \in Paths_{\mathcal{I}_{\mathcal{M}}^{(N)}}(\mathbf{s})$ such that $\pi_\ell = \pi \downarrow i$. We let $Paths_{\mathcal{M}^N}^i(\mathbf{s})$ denote the set of local paths of agent i from $\mathbf{s}$, while $Paths_{\mathcal{M}^N}^i = \cup_{\mathbf{s} \in \mathcal{S}^N} Paths_{\mathcal{M}^N}^i(\mathbf{s})$.

DTMC of Counting Vectors. When we consider the system at the individual level, via $\mathcal{I}_{\mathcal{M}}^{(N)}$, we have a detailed view of the behaviour of a population of N agents described in terms of a MADTM $\mathcal{M}$. Unfortunately, when this approach is used, the number of configurations that must be considered increases exponentially with the population size. Indeed, given a set of agent states $\mathcal{S}$, a system composed by N agents can reach $\mathcal{O}(|\mathcal{S}|^N)$ different configurations. However, we can observe that the behaviour of a single agent does not depend on its index. Indeed, it is easy to see that For any $\mathbf{s}_1, \mathbf{s}_2 \in N^{\mathcal{S}}$, and for any pair of indexes $i, j \in \mathbb{N}$ such that $1 \leq i, j \leq N$:

$$\mathbf{P}_{\mathcal{I}}^{\mathcal{P}}[\mathbf{s}_1, \mathbf{s}_2] = \mathbf{P}_{\mathcal{I}}^{\mathcal{P}}[\mathbf{s}_1[i \leftrightarrow j], \mathbf{s}_2[i \leftrightarrow j]]$$

When an agent's specific identity is irrelevant, the system state can be defined in terms of a *counting vector*. Indeed, each $\mathbf{m} \in N^{\mathcal{S}}$ can be used to represent all the *individual states* in $[\mathbf{m}]$ (see Definition 1). We can also observe that given $\mathbf{m}, \mathbf{m}' \in N^{\mathcal{S}}$, for any pair of vectors of individuals $\mathbf{s}, \mathbf{s}' \in [\mathbf{m}]$ the probability that they can jump to a state in $[\mathbf{m}']$ is the same:

$$\mathbf{P}_{\mathcal{I}}^{\mathcal{P}}[\mathbf{s}, [\mathbf{m}']] = \mathbf{P}_{\mathcal{I}}^{\mathcal{P}}[\mathbf{s}', [\mathbf{m}']]$$

Given a MADTM $\mathcal{M} = (\mathcal{S}, \mathcal{P})$, we can abstract the identities of the single agent to consider the DTMC $\mathcal{C}_{\mathcal{M}}^{(N)}$ be the DTMC $(N^{\mathcal{S}}, \mathbf{P}_{\mathcal{C}}^{\mathcal{P}})$ that describe the behaviour of a *population* with size N. Each state in $\mathcal{C}_{\mathcal{M}}^{(N)}$ is a vector in $N^{\mathcal{S}}$ and is used to count the number of agents in the different states.

Probability matrix $\mathbf{P}_{\mathcal{C}}^{\mathcal{P}}$ is defined as follows:

$$\mathbf{P}_{\mathcal{C}}^{\mathcal{P}}[\mathbf{m}, \mathbf{m}'] = \mathcal{P}_{\mathcal{C}}^{\mu_\mathbf{m}}[\mathbf{m}, \mathbf{m}'] \tag{4}$$

where:

$$\mathcal{P}_{\mathcal{C}}^{\mu}[\mathbf{m}_1, \mathbf{m}_2] = \mathcal{P}_{\mathcal{I}}^{\mu}[\mathbf{s}_{\mathbf{m}_1}, [\mathbf{m}_2]] \tag{5}$$

The probability matrix of a counting vector is expressed in terms of an individual transition probability matrix where an element $\mathbf{s_m}$ from a vector $\mathbf{m}$ is mapped to any state in vector $\mathbf{m}'$.

It is easy to see that $\mathcal{C}_{\mathcal{M}}^{(N)}$ preserves the probabilistic behaviour of $\mathcal{I}_{\mathcal{M}}^{(N)}$ if one ignores agents identity. However, the number of states is reduced to $\mathcal{O}(N^{|\mathcal{S}|})$.

DTMC of Population Fractions. One could be interested in comparing the system behaviour when considering different population sizes in the various system design steps. For instance, one can compare the probability of reaching a given configuration when the population size increases by a given factor. For this reason, states of the system can be described in terms of fractions of population and formalised via elements in the *unit simplex* on $\mathcal{S}$, $\mathcal{U}^{\mathcal{S}}$.

Let $\mathcal{U}_N^{\mathcal{S}} \subseteq \mathcal{U}^{\mathcal{S}}$ be the subset of vectors $\boldsymbol{\mu}$ such that for any $s \in \mathcal{S}$, $N \cdot \boldsymbol{\mu}(s) \in \mathbb{N}$. We denote these with $\boldsymbol{\mu}^{(N)}$. We observe that $N \cdot \boldsymbol{\mu}^{(N)}$ denotes a the counting vector in $\mathbf{m} \in N^{\mathcal{S}}$ such that $\mathbf{m}(s) = N \cdot \boldsymbol{\mu}(s)$, for any $s \in \mathcal{S}$. Finally, we can observe that for any $k > 0$ and $N \in \mathbb{N}$, $\mathcal{U}_{k \cdot N}^{\mathcal{S}} \subseteq \mathcal{U}_N^{\mathcal{S}} \subseteq \mathcal{U}^{\mathcal{S}}$. Moreover, for any $\boldsymbol{\mu}^{(N)} \in \mathcal{U}_N^{\mathcal{S}}$ and $k \in \mathbb{N}$, we let $k \circ \boldsymbol{\mu}^{(N)}$ denote the element in $\mathcal{U}_{k \cdot N}^{\mathcal{S}}$ representing the population fractions scaled by a factor k.

Given a MADTM $\mathcal{M} = (\mathcal{S}, \mathcal{P})$, we let $\mathfrak{F}_{\mathcal{M}}^{(N)}$ be the DTMC $(\mathcal{U}_N^{\mathcal{S}}, \mathbf{P}_{\mathfrak{F}}^{\mathcal{P}})$ of *population fractions* with size N. Each state in $\mathfrak{F}_{\mathcal{M}}^{(N)}$ is a vector in $\mathcal{U}_N^{\mathcal{S}}$ counts the fraction of agents in the different states. Probability matrix $\mathbf{P}_{\mathfrak{F}}^{\mathcal{P}}$ is defined as follows:

$$\mathbf{P}_{\mathfrak{F}}^{\mathcal{P}}[\boldsymbol{\mu}_1, \boldsymbol{\mu}_2] = \mathcal{P}_{\mathfrak{F}}^{\mu_1}(\boldsymbol{\mu}_1, \boldsymbol{\mu}_2) \tag{6}$$

where:

$$\mathcal{P}_{\mathfrak{F}}^{\mu}[\boldsymbol{\mu}_1, \boldsymbol{\mu}_2] = \mathcal{P}_{\mathcal{C}}^{\mu}[N \cdot \boldsymbol{\mu}_1, N \cdot \boldsymbol{\mu}_2] \tag{7}$$

Here, the probability matrix of a population fraction is expressed in terms of the global transition probability matrix $\mathbf{P}_{\mathcal{C}}^{\mathcal{P}}$ (Eq. 4).

Given a *population fraction* DTMC $\mathfrak{F}_{\mathcal{M}}^{(N)} = (\mathcal{U}_N^{\mathcal{S}}, \mathbf{P}_{\mathfrak{F}}^{\mathcal{P}})$ and $k \in \mathbb{N}_{>0}$, let $k \circ \mathfrak{F}_{\mathcal{M}}^{(N)}$ be the *scaling* of $\mathfrak{F}_{\mathcal{M}}^{(N)}$ denoted as $\mathfrak{F}_{\mathcal{M}}^{(k \cdot N)} = (\mathcal{U}_{k \cdot N}^{\mathcal{S}}, \mathbf{P}_{\mathfrak{F}}^{\mathcal{P}})$. For any $\boldsymbol{\mu}^{(N)} \in \mathcal{U}_N^{\mathcal{S}}$ and $\mathfrak{F}_{\mathcal{M}}^{(N)} = (\mathcal{U}_N^{\mathcal{S}}, \mathbf{P}_{\mathfrak{F}}^{\mathcal{P}})$ we can consider the family of random processes $\left\{ X_{k \circ \boldsymbol{\mu}^{(N)}}^{k \circ \mathfrak{F}_{\mathcal{M}}^{(N)}} \right\}_{k \in \mathbb{N}_{>0}}$.

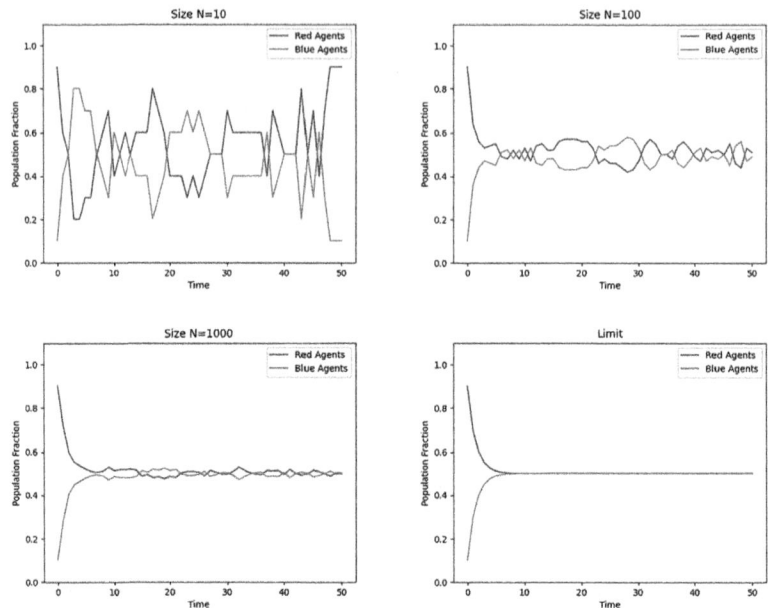

Fig. 1. Red/Blue Scenario: Simulation Results (Color figure online)

The study of this set of random processes permits checking if the expected behaviour of our system is preserved when we scale up the number of agents without changing the fraction of them in the different states. This scaling will help to analyze the agent's behaviour under various conditions because when the population increases, the system's behaviour might exhibit different dynamics and patterns. The following theorem guarantees that if $\mathcal{P}$ is continuous in $\mathcal{U}^\mathcal{S}$ then $\left\{X_{k\circ\mu^{(N)}}^{k\circ\widetilde{\mathfrak{F}}_\mathcal{M}^{(N)}}\right\}_{k\in\mathbb{N}_{>0}}$ converges to a deterministic process.

Theorem 1. *For any $\mathcal{M} = (\mathcal{S}, \mathcal{P})$, such that for any $s, s' \in \mathcal{S}$, $\mathcal{P}(\mu)[s, s']$ is continuous in μ for any $\mu_0 \in \mathcal{U}_N^\mathcal{S}$ and for any fixed t, almost surely:*

$$\lim_{k\to\infty} X_{k\circ\mu_0}^{k\circ\widetilde{\mathfrak{F}}_\mathcal{M}^{(N)}}(t) = \hat{\mu}(t)$$

where $\hat{\mu}(0) = \mu_0$ and $\hat{\mu}(t+1) = \hat{\mu}(t) \cdot \mathcal{P}(\hat{\mu}(t))$.

Proof. The proof follows directly like in [19].

In Fig. 1, simulations of the *Red/Blue Scenario* introduced in Example 1 and Example 2 are presented. The first three figures report the result of a single run when we let the number of agents vary from $N = 10$ to $N = 1000$. The last one reports the behaviour of the limit process of Theorem 1. We can observe

Global State Formulas

$$\Phi ::= \text{true} \mid \neg\Phi \mid \Phi_1 \wedge \Phi_2 \mid \mathcal{P}_{\bowtie p}[\Psi] \mid \mathcal{E}[\phi] \bowtie p \mid \mathcal{P}_{\bowtie p}[\phi@s]$$

Global Path Formulas

$$\Psi ::= \mathcal{X}\,\Phi \mid \Phi_1\,\mathcal{U}^{[k_1,k_2]}\,\Phi_2$$

Local Path Formulas

$$\phi ::= \text{true} \mid \alpha \mid \neg\phi \mid \phi_1 \wedge \phi_2 \mid \mathcal{X}\,\phi \mid \phi_1\,\mathcal{U}^{[k_1,k_2]}\,\phi_2$$

Fig. 2. Syntax of GLoTL+ formulas.

that when the number of agents increases, the experienced behaviour gets closer to the deterministic one. Moreover, if we start from an unbalanced state, an unbalanced configuration can eventually be reached and preserved.

3 Specifying Global and Local Properties in GLoTL+

GLoTL+ extends GLoTL [23] with branching time constructs like PCTL to describe the system properties from a global perspective. Moreover, a new operator is introduced to compute the average fraction of agents that, at a local level, will present a given behaviour.

The syntax of GLoTL+ formulas is reported in Fig. 2. We can see that this is a branching time logic, à la PCTL [2,17]. Three categories of formulas are considered: *global state formulas*, *global path formulas* and *local path formulas*. These formulas are used to specify properties of system states and computations from a *global perspective*, and, in a *local perspective*, to specify properties of single agents.

A *global formula* Φ is built from standard *Boolean operators* (true, $\neg$ and $\wedge$) and *probabilistic operator* ($\mathcal{P}_{\bowtie p}[(\Psi)]$) borrowed from PCTL is used to specify that the probability of the computations satisfying Ψ is $\bowtie p$, where $\bowtie \in \{\leq, <, >, \geq\}$. Finally, novel operators $\mathcal{E}[\phi] \bowtie p$ and $\mathcal{P}_{\bowtie p}[\phi@s]$ are introduced to specify that the *average fraction of agents* satisfying *local formula* ϕ is $\bowtie p$, and that a single agent s in a global context satisfying a *local formula* ϕ is $\bowtie p$. Global path formulas are standard and are built from well-known temporal operators ($\mathcal{X}\,\Phi$ and $\Phi_1\,\mathcal{U}^{[k_1,k_2]}\,\Phi_2$).

A *local formula* ϕ, that has the same syntax of GLoTL, is used to specify properties of the single agents and is built from *atomic proposition* $\alpha \in \mathcal{AP}$ via standard *Boolean operators* (true, $\neg$ and $\wedge$), and *temporal operators* ($\mathcal{X}\,\phi$ and $\phi_1\,\mathcal{U}^{[k_1,k_2]}\,\phi_2$).

Other logical operators can be derived as macros of the above-defined ones. Figure 3 reports a list of derivable operators.

GLOBAL STATE FORMULAS   LOCAL PATH FORMULAS

false $= \neg$true   false $= \neg$true

$\Phi_1 \vee \Phi_2 = \neg(\neg\Phi_1 \wedge \neg\Phi_2)$ $\phi_1 \vee \phi_2 = \neg(\neg\phi_1 \wedge \neg\phi_2)$

$\Phi_1 \rightarrow \Phi_2 = \neg\Phi_1 \vee \Phi_2$ $\phi_1 \rightarrow \phi_2 = \neg\phi_1 \vee \phi_2$

$\mathcal{E}[\,\phi\,] \in [a,b] = \mathcal{E}[\,\phi\,] \geq a \wedge \mathcal{E}[\,\phi\,] \leq b$ $\Diamond^{\leq k}\phi = \text{true}\,\mathcal{U}^{\leq k}\,\phi$

$\mathcal{E}[\,\phi\,] \notin [a,b] = \neg \mathcal{E}[\,\phi\,] \in [a,b]$ $\Box^{\leq k}\phi = \neg\Diamond^{\leq k}\neg\phi$

GLOBAL PATH FORMULAS

$\Diamond^{[k_1,k_2]}\Phi = \text{true}\,\mathcal{U}^{[k_1,k_2]}\,\Phi$

$\mathcal{P}_{\bowtie p}\left[\,\Box^{[k_1,k_2]}\Phi\,\right] = \mathcal{P}_{\bowtie(1-p)}\left[\,\Diamond^{[k_1,k_2]}\neg\Phi\,\right]$

Fig. 3. Derivable Logical Operators

3.1 GLoTL+ Semantic

In this section, we will show how GLoTL+ formulas can be interpreted. Given a MADTM $\mathcal{M} = (\mathcal{S}, \mathcal{P})$, *global state formulas* can be interpreted over states of the models $\mathcal{I}_{\mathcal{M}}^{(N)}$, $\mathcal{C}_{\mathcal{M}}^{(N)}$ and $\mathfrak{F}_{\mathcal{M}}^{(N)}$ while the paths generated from these models are used to define the semantics *global path formulas*. The interpretation of *local path formulas* is defined over a *hybrid* model $\mathcal{H}_{\mathcal{M}}^{(N)}$, that will be defined below, and that describes the behaviour of a single agent operating in a system composed by other N agents.

Semantic of Local Path Formulas. To compute the probability that a given agent $s \in \mathcal{S}$ satisfies a specific *local path* formula, we have to consider the behaviour of the single agent s with respect to the context where it is operating. Following the same approach considered in [17], we consider our system as composed of two parts: one agent and its context.

Given a MADTM $\mathcal{M} = (\mathcal{S}, \mathcal{P})$, we let $\mathcal{H}_{\mathcal{M}}^{(N)}$ be the DTMC $(\mathcal{S} \times \mathcal{U}_N^{\mathcal{S}}, \mathbf{P}_{\mathcal{H}}^{\mathcal{P}})$ of population of size N. Each state in $\mathcal{H}_{\mathcal{M}}^{(N)}$ is a vector in $\mathcal{S} \times \mathcal{U}_N^{\mathcal{S}}$ and the probability matrix $\mathbf{P}_{\mathcal{H}}^{\mathcal{P}}$ is defined as follows:

$$\mathbf{P}_{\mathcal{H}}^{\mathcal{P}}[(s_1,\boldsymbol{\mu}_1),(s_2,\boldsymbol{\mu}_2)] = \mathcal{P}^{(\mu_1+\mathbf{1}_{s_1})}[s_1,s_2] \cdot \mathcal{P}_{\mathfrak{F}}^{(\mu_1+\mathbf{1}_{s_1})}[\boldsymbol{\mu}_1,\boldsymbol{\mu}_2]$$

where $\mathbf{1}_{s_1}$ denotes the counting vector in $\mathbf{1}^{\mathcal{S}}$ associating 1 to s and 0 to all the other states, while $\boldsymbol{\mu}_1^{(N)}+\mathbf{1}_{s_1}$ denotes the population fraction in $\boldsymbol{\mu}^{(N+1)} \in \mathcal{U}_{N+1}^{\mathcal{S}}$ such that $\boldsymbol{\mu}^{(N+1)} = \frac{N \cdot \boldsymbol{\mu}_1^{(N)}+\mathbf{1}_{s_1}}{N+1}$.

Any pair in $(s_1, \boldsymbol{\mu}_1) \in \mathcal{S} \times \mathcal{U}_N^{\mathcal{S}}$ represents an agent s_1 operating in an environment composed of N distributed in the different state according to $\boldsymbol{\mu}_1$. In the rest of this paper, we will refer to the states of $\mathcal{H}_{\mathcal{M}}^{(N)}$ as *hybrid states*. Probability matrix $\mathbf{P}_{\mathcal{H}}^{\mathcal{P}}$ gives the probability that $(s_1, \boldsymbol{\mu}_1)$ evolves in one step in $(s_2, \boldsymbol{\mu}_2)$. This probability is computed as the probability that s_1 evolves in one step in s_2 multiplied by the probability that $\boldsymbol{\mu}_1$ evolves in one step in $\boldsymbol{\mu}_2$. These probabilities are computed by using functions $\mathcal{P}$ of the MADTM $\mathcal{M}$ and function $\mathcal{P}_{\mathfrak{F}}$ of Eq. 7.

$$\pi_\ell \models_\ell^{\mathcal{H}_\mathcal{M}^{(N)}, \mathcal{L}} \text{true}$$

$$\pi_\ell \models_\ell^{\mathcal{H}_\mathcal{M}^{(N)}, \mathcal{L}} \alpha \iff \pi_\ell[0] = (s, \mu) \text{ and } \alpha \in \mathcal{L}(s)$$

$$\pi_\ell \models_\ell^{\mathcal{H}_\mathcal{M}^{(N)}, \mathcal{L}} \neg\phi \iff \pi_\ell \not\models_\ell^{\mathcal{H}_\mathcal{M}^{(N)}, \mathcal{L}} \phi$$

$$\pi_\ell \models_\ell^{\mathcal{H}_\mathcal{M}^{(N)}, \mathcal{L}} \phi_1 \wedge \phi_2 \iff \pi_\ell \models_\ell^{\mathcal{H}_\mathcal{M}^{(N)}, \mathcal{L}} \phi_1 \wedge \pi_\ell \models_\ell^{\mathcal{H}_\mathcal{M}^{(N)}, \mathcal{L}} \phi_2$$

$$\pi_\ell \models_\ell^{\mathcal{H}_\mathcal{M}^{(N)}, \mathcal{L}} \mathcal{X} \phi \iff \pi_\ell[1..] \models_\ell^{\mathcal{H}_\mathcal{M}^{(N)}, \mathcal{L}} \phi$$

$$\pi_\ell \models_\ell^{\mathcal{H}_\mathcal{M}^{(N)}, \mathcal{L}} \phi_1 \mathcal{U}^{[k_1, k_2]} \phi_2 \iff \exists h \in [k_1, k_2] : \pi_\ell[h..] \models_\ell^{\mathcal{H}_\mathcal{M}^{(N)}, \mathcal{L}} \phi_2$$
$$\wedge \forall i \in [0, h) : \pi_\ell[i..] \models_\ell^{\mathcal{H}_\mathcal{M}^{(N)}, \mathcal{L}} \phi_1$$

Fig. 4. Local Formulas: Satisfaction relation

Let $\mathcal{M}$ be the MADTM $(\mathcal{S}, \mathcal{P})$ and $\mathcal{L} : \mathcal{S} \to 2^{\mathcal{AP}}$ be a labelling function associating each *state* s in $\mathcal{S}$ with the set of atomic proposition $\mathcal{A} \in \mathcal{AP}$ satisfied by s, *local path formulas* are interpreted over the paths of the DTMC $\mathcal{H}_\mathcal{M}^{(N)} = (\mathcal{S} \times \mathcal{U}_N^\mathcal{S}, \mathbf{P}_\mathcal{H}^{\mathcal{P}^{(N)}})$. The satisfaction relation is defined in Fig. 4. Any $\pi_\ell \in Paths_{\mathcal{H}_\mathcal{M}^{(N)}}$ satisfies true, π_ℓ satisfies α if and only if the first element in π_ℓ has the form (s, μ) and α occurs in $\mathcal{L}(s)$, $\phi_1 \wedge \phi_2$ is satisfied by π_ℓ if and only if both ϕ_1 and ϕ_2 are satisfied, while $\neg\phi$ is satisfied if and only if π_ℓ does not satisfy ϕ. Temporal formula $\mathcal{X} \phi$ is satisfied by π_ℓ if the computation starting from step 1 satisfies ϕ. Finally, π_ℓ satisfies $\phi_1 \mathcal{U}^{[k_1, k_2]} \phi_2$ if and only if there exists an index $h \in [k_1, k_2]$ such that $\pi_\ell[h..]$ satisfies ϕ_2 and for any index i less then h, $\pi_\ell[i..]$ satisfies ϕ_1.

Given a set $s \in \mathcal{S}$ and a $\boldsymbol{\mu} \in \mathcal{U}_\mathcal{M}^{(N)}$, we let $\mathbb{P}\left\{ (s, \boldsymbol{\mu}^{(N)}) \models_\ell^{\mathcal{H}_\mathcal{M}^{(N)}, \mathcal{L}} \phi \right\}$ denote the probability of all the paths in $\mathcal{H}_\mathcal{M}^{(N)}$ starting from (s, μ) that satisfy ϕ:

$$\mathbb{P}\left\{ (s, \mu^{(N)}) \models_\ell^{\mathcal{H}_\mathcal{M}^{(N)}, \mathcal{L}} \phi \right\} = \mathbb{P}\left\{ \pi_\ell \in Paths_{\mathcal{H}_\mathcal{M}^{(N)}}(s, \mu^{(N)}) \,\middle|\, \pi_\ell \models_\ell^{\mathcal{H}_\mathcal{M}^{(N)}, \mathcal{L}} \phi \right\} \quad (8)$$

Global State and Path Formulas. Given a MADTM $\mathcal{M} = (\mathcal{S}, \mathcal{P})$, *global state formulas* are interpreted over states of the DTMC $\mathfrak{F}_\mathcal{M}^{(N)}$. Note that, the other variants $\mathcal{I}_\mathcal{M}^{(N)}$ and $\mathcal{C}_\mathcal{M}^{(N)}$, where *individuals* and *counting vectors* are considered, could be used. However, for the scope of this paper, it is more convenient to use a state representation based on the fraction of individuals that are in the different states.

Formula $\mathcal{E}[\phi] \bowtie p$ is satisfied by a state $\boldsymbol{\mu}$ if the *average fraction* of agents satisfying ϕ in μ meets the bound $\bowtie p$. Finally, $\mathcal{P}_{\bowtie p}[\Psi]$ is satisfied by μ if the probability of the set of paths starting from $\mu^{(N)}$ satisfying Ψ meets the bound

STATE FORMULAS

$$\mu^{(N)} \models^{\mathfrak{F}_{\mathcal{M}}^{(N)},\mathcal{L}} \text{true}$$

$$\mu^{(N)} \models^{\mathfrak{F}_{\mathcal{M}}^{(N)},\mathcal{L}} \neg \Phi \iff \mu^{(N)} \not\models^{\mathfrak{F}_{\mathcal{M}}^{(N)},\mathcal{L}} \Phi$$

$$\mu^{(N)} \models^{\mathfrak{F}_{\mathcal{M}}^{(N)},\mathcal{L}} \Phi_1 \wedge \Phi_2 \iff \mu^{(N)} \models^{\mathfrak{F}_{\mathcal{M}}^{(N)},\mathcal{L}} \Phi_1 \text{ and } \mu^{(N)} \models^{\mathfrak{F}_{\mathcal{M}}^{(N)},\mathcal{L}} \Phi_2$$

$$\mu^{(N)} \models^{\mathfrak{F}_{\mathcal{M}}^{(N)},\mathcal{L}} \mathcal{E}[\,\phi\,] \bowtie p \iff \sum_{s \in \mu} \mu(s) \cdot \mathbb{P}\left\{ (s, \mu - \mathbf{1}_s) \models_{\ell}^{\mathcal{H}_{\mathcal{M}}^{(N-1)},\mathcal{L}} \phi \right\}$$

$$\mu^{(N)} \models^{\mathfrak{F}_{\mathcal{M}}^{(N)},\mathcal{L}} \mathcal{P}_{\bowtie p}[\,\phi@s\,] \iff \mathbb{P}\left\{ (s, \mu) \models_{\ell}^{\mathcal{H}_{\mathcal{M}}^{(N)},\mathcal{L}} \phi \right\}$$

$$\mu^{(N)} \models^{\mathfrak{F}_{\mathcal{M}}^{(N)},\mathcal{L}} \mathcal{P}_{\bowtie p}[\,\Psi\,] \iff \mathbb{P}\left\{ \pi \models_{\ell}^{\mathcal{H}_{\mathcal{M}}^{(N)},\mathcal{L}} \Psi \,\middle|\, \pi \in Paths_{\mathfrak{F}_{\mathcal{M}}^{(N)}}(\mu^{(N)}) \right\}$$

PATH FORMULAS

$$\pi \models^{\mathfrak{F}_{\mathcal{M}}^{(N)},\mathcal{L}} \mathcal{X}\,\Phi \iff \pi[1] \models^{\mathfrak{F}_{\mathcal{M}}^{(N)},\mathcal{L}} \Phi$$

$$\pi \models^{\mathfrak{F}_{\mathcal{M}}^{(N)},\mathcal{L}} \Phi_1\,\mathcal{U}^{[k_1,k_2]}\,\Phi_2 \iff \exists i \in [k_1, k_2] : \pi[i] \models^{\mathfrak{F}_{\mathcal{M}}^{(N)},\mathcal{L}} \Phi_2$$
$$\forall j \in [0, i) : \pi[j] \models^{\mathfrak{F}_{\mathcal{M}}^{(N)},\mathcal{L}} \Phi_1$$

Fig. 5. Global Formulas: Satisfaction relation

$\bowtie p$. The satisfaction relation of *global path formulas* is standard and reported in Fig. 5.

Example 3 (Properties for Red/Blue Scenario). We can continue the red/blue model to specify the properties of the model through GLoTL+. First, we can specify that the system is balanced:

$$\Phi_{bal} = \mathcal{E}[\,red\,] \in [0.5 - \varepsilon, 0.5 + \varepsilon]$$

Another typical requirement is that the system can eventually reach a balanced state within k_1 steps with a probability greater than a threshold p_1:

$$\Phi_{eb} = \mathcal{P}_{\geq p}[\,\lozenge^{\leq k_1} \Phi_{bal}\,]$$

All the properties above consider the systems from a global perspective. Sometime, we are interested in considering properties from a local point of view. In this For instance, we could check if an agent is *locally stable*. We say that an agent is *stable* if it preserves its state for at least 5 time units. This property can be specified as follows:

$$\phi_{ls} = (\square^{\leq 5} red) \vee (\square^{\leq 5} blue)$$

Local stability can be used to specify that "*with a probability greater than p_2 the average fraction of stable agents is greater than 0.9.*"

$$\Phi_{ls} = \mathcal{P}_{>p_2}[\,\mathcal{E}[\,\phi_{ls}\,] > 0.9)\,]$$

Algorithm 1. Checking Satisfaction of Global State Formulas

```
 1: function SAT(M = (S,P), L, μ^(N), Φ)
 2:     switch Φ do
 3:         case true:
 4:             return ⊤
 5:         case ¬Φ_1:
 6:             return ¬SAT(M, L, μ^(N), Φ_1)
 7:         case Φ_1 ∧ Φ_2:
 8:             return SAT(M, L, μ^(N), Φ_1) ∧ SAT(M, L, μ^(N), Φ_2)
 9:         case E[ φ ] ⋈ p:
10:             e ← 0
11:             for s ∈ dom(μ^(N)) do
12:                 e ← e + μ^(N)(s) · COMPUTELP(M, L, s, μ^(N) − 1_s, φ)
13:             end for
14:             return e ⋈ p
15:         case P_⋈p[ φ@s ]:
16:             return COMPUTELP(M, L, s, μ^(N), φ) ⋈ p
17:         case P_⋈p[ Ψ ]:
18:             return COMPUTEGP(M, L, μ^(N), Ψ) ⋈ p
19: end function
```

4 Model Checking GLoTL+

In this section, an algorithm is presented to check if a given state $\boldsymbol{\mu}^{(N)}$ satisfies a global formula Φ. The proposed algorithm follows an approach similar to the one proposed in [19]. Only the part of the model that is needed to check a formula Φ is visited.

The model-checking algorithm is defined by the function SAT in Algorithm 1. This function takes as arguments a MADTM $\mathcal{M}$ a labelling function $\mathcal{L}$, a local state $\boldsymbol{\mu}^{(N)}$ and a global state formula Φ and returns ⊤ if $\boldsymbol{\mu}^{(N)}$ satisfies Φ, ⊥ otherwise. This function is defined inductively on the structure of Φ. The first three cases are trivial. If Φ is true, ⊥ is returned. The negation of SAT($\mathcal{M}, \mathcal{L}, \mu^{(N)}, \Phi_1$) is returned when $\Phi = \neg \Phi_1$. Finally, if $\Phi = \Phi_1 \wedge \Phi_2$ then the function yields the conjunction of SAT($\mathcal{M}, \mathcal{L}, \mu^{(N)}, \Phi_1$) and SAT($\mathcal{M}, \mathcal{L}, \mu^{(N)}, \Phi_2$).

When the given formula Φ involves a local path formula, the auxiliary function PRBLP, which is defined in Algorithm 2, is used. This function, which will be described below, given a MADTM $\mathcal{M}$, labelling function $\mathcal{L}$, a local state s, a global state $\boldsymbol{\mu}^{(N)}$ and a local formula ϕ, yields the probability that the hybrid state $(s, \boldsymbol{\mu}^{(N)})$ satisfies ϕ. When $\Phi = \mathcal{E}[\, \phi \,] \bowtie p$ function COMPUTELP is used to compute, for any $s \in \boldsymbol{\mu}^{(N)}$, i.e. $\boldsymbol{\mu}^{(N)}(s) > 0$, the probability that s satisfies ϕ. This probability is computed by considering a context composed of $\boldsymbol{\mu}^{(N)} - \mathbf{1}_s$ agents. This probability value is accumulated in the variable e that, at the end, will contain the average fraction of agents satisfying ϕ. Value ⊤ is returned if $e \bowtie p$, ⊥ otherwise. Similarly, if $\Phi = \mathcal{P}_{\phi@s}[\, \bowtie p \,]$ COMPUTELP is used to com-

Algorithm 2. Compute Satisfaction Probability of Local Formulas

1: **function** COMPUTELP($\mathcal{M} = (\mathcal{S}, \mathcal{P}), \mathcal{L}, s_1, \mu_1^{(N)}, \phi$)
2:    **if** $\phi \uparrow$ **then**
3:       **return** 1.0
4:    **end if**
5:    **if** $\phi \downarrow$ **then**
6:       **return** 0.0
7:    **end if**
8:    after$(\phi, \mathcal{L}(s_1)) = \phi'$
9:    $p \leftarrow 0$
10:   **for** $(s_2, \mu_2^{(N)}) \in (\mathcal{S} \times \mathcal{U}_N^{\mathcal{S}})$ **do**
11:      $p \leftarrow p + \mathbf{P}_{\mathcal{H}}^{\mathcal{P}^{(N)}}\left[\left(s_1, \mu_1^{(N)}\right), \left(s_2, \mu_2^{(N)}\right)\right] \cdot \text{COMPUTELP}(\mathcal{M}, \mathcal{L}, s_2, \mu_2^{(N)}, \phi')$
12:   **end for**
13:   **return** p
14: **end function**

$$\frac{}{\text{true} \uparrow} \qquad \frac{}{\text{false} \downarrow} \qquad \frac{\phi_i \uparrow}{(\phi_1 \vee \phi_2) \uparrow} \qquad \frac{\phi_1 \downarrow \quad \phi_2 \downarrow}{(\phi_1 \vee \phi_2) \downarrow}$$

$$\frac{\phi_i \downarrow}{(\phi_1 \wedge \phi_2) \downarrow} \qquad \frac{\phi_1 \uparrow \quad \phi_2 \uparrow}{(\phi_1 \vee \phi_2) \uparrow} \qquad \frac{\phi \downarrow}{(\neg \phi) \uparrow} \qquad \frac{\phi \uparrow}{(\neg \phi) \downarrow}$$

Fig. 6. Accepting and Rejecting Relations

pute the probability that $(s, \boldsymbol{\mu}^{(N)})$ satisfies ϕ and the obtained result is compared with the given threshold p.

In case of $\mathcal{P}_{\bowtie p}[\Psi]$, the result of $\text{SAT}(\mathcal{M}, \mathcal{L}, \mu^{(N)}, \Phi)$ is obtained by calling a function COMPUTEGP$(\mathcal{M}, \mathcal{L}, \mu^{(N)}, \Psi)$ defined in Algorithm 3.

Computing Satisfaction Probability of Local Formulas. Given a MADTM $\mathcal{M}$, a labelling function $\mathcal{L}$, a state s_1 in $\mathcal{S}$, $\mu_1^{(N)} \in \mathcal{U}_N^{\mathcal{S}}$ and a local formula ϕ, function COMPUTELP$(\mathcal{M}, \mathcal{L}, s_1, \mu_1^{(N)}, \phi)$ defined in Algorithm 2 can be used to recursively compute $\mathbb{P}\left\{(s, \boldsymbol{\mu}^{(N)}) \models_\ell^{\mathcal{H}_\mathcal{M}^{(N)}, \mathcal{L}} \phi\right\}$ of Eq. 8. Function COMPUTELP relies on the accepting/rejecting relations ($\phi \uparrow$ and $\phi \downarrow$) defined in Fig. 6, and on the function after defined in Fig. 7. If the formula ϕ is accepting ($\phi \uparrow$) function COMPUTELP just returns 1.0, while 0.0 is returned when ϕ is rejecting (($\phi \downarrow$). If ϕ is neither accepting nor rejecting, first the formula ϕ' obtained from ϕ *after* the labelling $\mathcal{L}(s_1)$ of s_1 is computed, then the resulting probability is obtained by recursively invoke the COMPUTELP for the hybrid states reachable in one step from state s_1 and summing results from each iteration $\mathbf{P}_{\mathcal{H}}^{\mathcal{P}^{(N)}}\left[\left(s_1, \mu_1^{(N)}\right), \left(s_2, \mu_2^{(N)}\right)\right] \cdot \text{PRBLP}(\mathcal{M}, \mathcal{L}, s_2, \mu_2^{(N)}, \phi')$, for any $(s_2, \boldsymbol{\mu}_2^{(N)})$ reachable from $(s_1, \boldsymbol{\mu}_1^{(N)})$.

$$\text{after}(\text{true}, \mathcal{A}) = \text{true} \qquad \text{after}(\text{false}, \mathcal{A}) = \text{false}$$

$$\frac{\alpha \in \mathcal{A}}{\text{after}(\alpha, \mathcal{A}) = \text{true}} \qquad \frac{\alpha \notin \mathcal{A}}{\text{after}(\alpha, \mathcal{A}) = \text{false}}$$

$$\text{after}(\phi_1 \wedge \phi_2) = \text{after}(\phi_1) \wedge \text{after}(\phi_2) \qquad \text{after}(\phi_1 \vee \phi_2) = \text{after}(\phi_1) \vee \text{after}(\phi_2)$$

$$\text{after}(\neg \phi, \mathcal{A}) = \neg \text{after}(\phi, \mathcal{A}) \qquad \text{after}(\mathcal{X}\, \phi, \mathcal{A}) = \phi \qquad \text{after}(\phi_1\, \mathcal{U}^{[0,0]}\, \phi_2, \mathcal{A}) = \text{after}(\phi_2)$$

$$\text{after}(\phi_1\, \mathcal{U}^{[k_1+1, k_2]}\, \phi_2, \mathcal{A}) = \text{after}(\phi_1) \wedge \text{after}(\phi_1\, \mathcal{U}^{[k_1, k_2-1]}\, \phi_2, \mathcal{A})$$

$$\text{after}(\phi_1\, \mathcal{U}^{[0, k_2+1]}\, \phi_2, \mathcal{A}) = (\text{after}(\phi_1) \wedge \text{after}(\phi_1\, \mathcal{U}^{[0, k_2]}\, \phi_2, \mathcal{A})) \vee \text{after}(\phi_2)$$

Fig. 7. Preservation function after.

We can observe that in COMPUTELP, the exploration of the state space reachable from $(s_1, \mu_1^{(N)})$ is made *on-the-fly*. This means that we do not need an explicit generation of the entire state space.

Lemma 1. *For any $\mathcal{M} = (\mathcal{S}, \mathcal{P})$, a labelling function $\mathcal{L}$, a state s_1 in $\mathcal{S}$, $\mu_1^{(N)} \in \mathcal{U}_N^{\mathcal{S}}$ and a local formula ϕ:*

$$\text{COMPUTELP}(\mathcal{M}, \mathcal{L}, s_1, \mu_1^{(N)}, \phi) = \mathbb{P}\left\{ (s, \mu^{(N)}) \models_{\ell}^{\mathcal{H}_{\mathcal{M}}^{(N)}, \mathcal{L}} \phi \right\}$$

Proof. The proof follows directly from the semantics of local formulas.

Computing Satisfaction Probability of Global Path Formulas. The function starts to check with temporal $\mathcal{X}\, \Phi$ operator and compute the probabilities for every $\mu_2 \in \mathcal{U}_N^{\mathcal{S}}$ and the result is the sum of the probabilities of the transitions from $\mu_1^{(N)}$ to those next states $\mu_2^{(N)}$ that satisfy Φ_2. After that it checks the temporal $\Phi_1\, \mathcal{U}^{[k_1, k_2]}\, \Phi_2$ that is obtained by calling another function COMPUTEBU($\mathcal{M} = (\mathcal{S}, \mathcal{P}), \mathcal{L}, \mu_1^{(N)}, \Phi_1, k_1, k_2, \Phi_2$) defined in an Algorithm 4. This function starts to check with a bound k_1 if it is equal to 0 and Φ_2 is satisfied then it returns 1. If the bound k_2 is 0 and Φ_1 is not satisfied it returns 0. Other than this function COMPUTEBU compute the probabilities by updating the bounds and for every $\mu_2 \in \mathcal{U}_N^{\mathcal{S}}$ it invokes recursively COMPUTEBU($\mathcal{M} = (\mathcal{S}, \mathcal{P}), \mathcal{L}, \mu_1^{(N)}, \Phi_1, k_1, k_2, \Phi_2$) for the states reachable in one step from $\mu_1^{(N)}$ and summing the result for each iteration $\mathbf{P}_{\mathfrak{F}}^{\mathcal{P}^{(N)}}[\mu_1^{(N)}, \mu_2^{(N)}] \cdot \text{COMPUTEBU}(\mathcal{M}, \mathcal{L}, \mu_2^{(N)}, \Phi_1, k_1', k_2', \Phi_2)$ for any $\mu_2^{(N)}$ reachable from $\mu_1^{(N)}$.

Correctness. The following theorem guarantees the correctness of the proposed model-checking algorithm.

Algorithm 3. Computing Satisfaction Probability of Global Path Formulas

1: **function** COMPUTEGP($\mathcal{M} = (\mathcal{S}, \mathcal{P}), \mathcal{L}, \mu_1^{(N)}, \Psi$)
2:    **switch** Ψ **do**
3:       **case** $\mathcal{X}\ \Phi$:
4:          $p \leftarrow 0$
5:          **for** $\mu_2^{(N)} \in \mathcal{U}_N^{\mathcal{S}} : \mathbf{P}_{\mathfrak{F}}^{\mathcal{P}^{(N)}}[\mu_1^{(N)}, \mu_2^{(N)}] > 0$ **do**
6:             **if** SAT($\mathcal{M}, \mathcal{L}, \mu_2^{(N)}, \Phi$) **then**
7:                $p \leftarrow p + \mathbf{P}_{\mathfrak{F}}^{\mathcal{P}^{(N)}}[\mu_1^{(N)}, \mu_2^{(N)}]$
8:             **end if**
9:          **end for**
10:         **return** p
11:       **case** $\Phi_1\ \mathcal{U}^{[k_1, k_2]}\ \Phi_2$:
12:          **return** COMPUTEBU($\mathcal{M}, \mathcal{L}, \mu_1^{(N)}, \Phi_1, k_1, k_2, \Phi_2$)
13: **end function**

Algorithm 4. Until-Based Global Path Computation

1: **function** COMPUTEBU($\mathcal{M} = (\mathcal{S}, \mathcal{P}), \mathcal{L}, \mu_1^{(N)}, \Phi_1, k_1, k_2, \Phi_2$)
2:    **if** $(k_1 == 0) \land$ SAT($\mathcal{M}, \mathcal{L}, \mu_1^{(N)}, \Phi_2$) **then**
3:       **return** 1
4:    **end if**
5:    **if** $(k_2 == 0) \lor \neg$SAT($\mathcal{M}, \mathcal{L}, \mu_1^{(N)}, \Phi_1$) **then**
6:       **return** 0
7:    **end if**
8:    $p \leftarrow 0$
9:    $k_1' = \max(0, k_1 - 1)$
10:   $k_2' = \max(0, k_2 - 1)$
11:   **for** $\mu_2 \in \mathcal{U}_N^{\mathcal{S}} : \mathbf{P}_{\mathfrak{F}}^{\mathcal{P}^{(N)}}[\mu_1^{(N)}, \mu_2^{(N)}] > 0$ **do**
12:      $p \leftarrow p + \mathbf{P}_{\mathfrak{F}}^{\mathcal{P}^{(N)}}[\mu_1^{(N)}, \mu_2^{(N)}] \cdot$ COMPUTEBU($\mathcal{M}, \mathcal{L}, \mu_2^{(N)}, \Phi_1, k_1', k_2', \Phi_2$)
13:   **end for**
14:   **return** p
15: **end function**

Theorem 2. *Let $\mathcal{M} = (\mathcal{S}, \mathbf{P})$ be a MADTM and $\mathcal{L} : \mathcal{S} \to 2^{\mathcal{AP}}$ be a labelling function. For any state $\mu^{(N)}$ of $\mathfrak{F}_\mathcal{M}^{(N)}$, $\mu^{(N)} \models^{\mathfrak{F}_\mathcal{M}^{(N)}, \mathcal{L}} \Phi$ if and only if* SAT($\mathcal{M}, \mathcal{L}, \mu^{(N)}, \Phi) = \top$.

Example 4 (Model-checking in action). Figure 8 contains the result of model-cheking of formulas Φ_{bal}, Φ_{eb} of Example 3[1]. In the plots of Fig. 8, we show the probability that these formulas are satisfied after k steps. We can observe that Φ_{bal} is satisfied with probability 1.0 after a few steps, while Φ_{ev} is always satisfied. This means the system is working as expected: it can reach a stable configuration and preserve this property.

---

[1] These analysis have been performed with Sibilla [13].

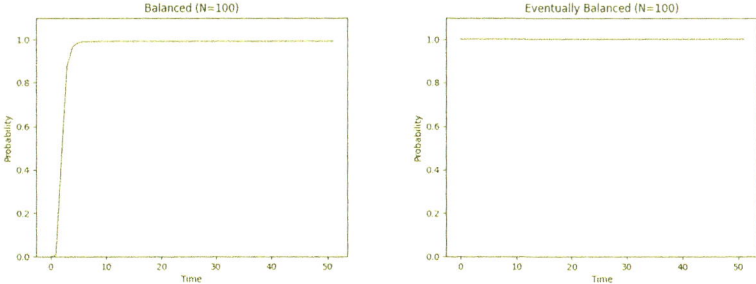

Fig. 8. Red/Blue Scenario: Verification of Formulas of Example 3. (Color figure online)

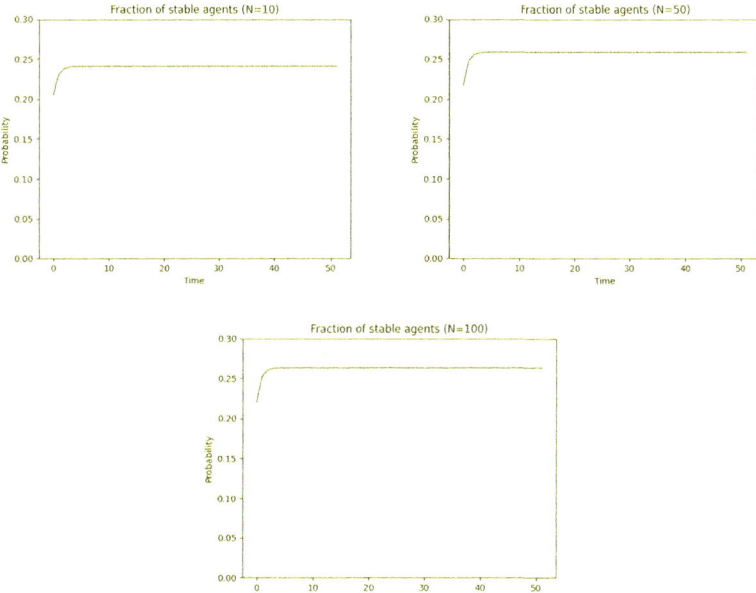

Fig. 9. Red/Blue Scenario: Fraction of Stable Agents. (Color figure online)

However, if we consider the fraction of agents that satisfy formula ϕ_{ls}, we realise that things are not doing as expected at a local level. If we observe Fig. 9, which depicts the fraction of *stable-agents* when we let the number of agents N vary from 10 to 100, we can soon realise that only 25% of agents preserve their state for 10 time units, even when the system reaches a balanced configuration. However, this fraction depends on the number of agents in the system.

5 Mean-Field Model-Checking of GLoTL+

Given $\mathcal{M} = (\mathcal{S}, \mathcal{P})$ and a labelling function $\mathcal{L}$, the algorithm introduced in the previous section can be used to check if a given global state $\boldsymbol{\mu}^{(N)}$ satisfies or not a formula Φ. The proposed algorithm is polynomial in the size of the model (that is $N^{|S|}$) and linear with the size of the formula. It is clear that when the number of agents N involved in the system increases, this computation becomes hard or even impossible. For this reason, tools are needed to guarantee that an approximated result can be obtained even if the number of involved agents is increasing.

For this reason, in this section, a *mean-field* model-checking algorithm is proposed for GLoTL+. The proposed approach follows the same approach as in [18].

In the proposed approach, given $\mathcal{M} = (\mathcal{S}, \mathcal{P})$, what we can do is approximate the behaviour of a system starting from state $\boldsymbol{\mu}_0 \in \mathcal{U}_N^{\mathcal{S}}$ in terms of the deterministic process $\hat{\boldsymbol{\mu}}(t)$ defined as follows:

- $\hat{\boldsymbol{\mu}}(0) = \boldsymbol{\mu}_0$;
- $\hat{\boldsymbol{\mu}}(t+1) = \hat{\boldsymbol{\mu}}(t) \cdot \mathcal{P}(\hat{\boldsymbol{\mu}}(t))$

We have already seen in Theorem 1 that when we let N go to infinit, the chain of random variables $\{X_{k \cdot \boldsymbol{\mu}(N)}^{k \cdot \hat{\mathfrak{s}}_{\mathcal{M}}^{(N)}}(t)\}_{k \in \mathbb{N}}$ converges *almost surely* to $\hat{\boldsymbol{\mu}}$.

A similar approach can be used to consider the behaviour of a single agent s operating in a context that is approximated by $\hat{\boldsymbol{\mu}}(t)$. Given a state $s_0 \in \mathcal{S}$ and $\boldsymbol{\mu}_0 \in \mathcal{U}^{\mathcal{S}}$ we can consider the *time inhomogeneous* stochastic process $\hat{\mathcal{H}}_{\mathcal{M}}^{(s_0, \boldsymbol{\mu}_0)}$ that assumes values in $\mathcal{S} \times \mathcal{U}^{\mathcal{S}}$ that is defined as follows:

- $\mathbb{P}\{\hat{\mathcal{H}}_{\mathcal{M}}^{(s_0, \boldsymbol{\mu}_0)}(0) = (s, \boldsymbol{\mu})\} = \delta_{(s_0, \boldsymbol{\mu}_0)}(s, \boldsymbol{\mu})$
- $\mathbb{P}\left\{\hat{\mathcal{H}}_{\mathcal{M}}^{(s_0, \boldsymbol{\mu}_0)}(t+1) = (s', \boldsymbol{\mu}') | \hat{\mathcal{H}}_{\mathcal{M}}^{(s_0, \boldsymbol{\mu}_0)}(t) = (s, \boldsymbol{\mu})\right\} = \begin{cases} \mathcal{P}^{\boldsymbol{\mu}}[s, s'] & \text{if } \boldsymbol{\mu}' = \boldsymbol{\mu} \cdot \mathcal{P}(\boldsymbol{\mu}) \\ 0 & \text{otherwise} \end{cases}$

where $\delta_{(s_0, \boldsymbol{\mu}_0)}$ is the probability distribution associating 1 to $(s_0, \boldsymbol{\mu}_0)$ and 0 to all the other values.

Both $\hat{\boldsymbol{\mu}}$ and $\hat{\mathcal{H}}_{\mathcal{M}}$ can be used to evaluate satisfaction of global and local GLoTL+ formulas. In Fig. 10, the mean-field satisfaction of global state formulas is reported. We can observe that since $\hat{\boldsymbol{\mu}}$ is deterministic, this evaluation has lost any probability evaluation. This is evident if we look at the satisfaction of global path formulas. Indeed, $\hat{\boldsymbol{\mu}}(t)$ represents at the same time both the state observed at step t and the (deterministic) path starting from the same point.

The following theorem guarantees that when we let N goes to infinite, the result of the evaluation of a formula on $\boldsymbol{\mu}^{(N)}$ converges *almost surely* to the same result as $\hat{\boldsymbol{\mu}}$.

Theorem 3. *For any $\mathcal{M} = (\mathcal{S}, \mathcal{P})$, labelling function $\mathcal{L}$ and formula Φ, if we let k goes to infinite, almost surely $\boldsymbol{\mu}^{k \cdot N} \models^{\hat{\mathfrak{s}}_{\mathcal{M}}^{(N)}, \mathcal{L}} \Phi$ if and only if $\hat{\boldsymbol{\mu}} \models_{\mathcal{M}, \mathcal{L}} \Phi$.*

Proof. The proof follows directly from Theorem 1.

STATE FORMULAS

$\hat{\mu}(t) \models_{\mathcal{M},\mathcal{L}} \text{true}$

$\hat{\mu}(t) \models_{\mathcal{M},\mathcal{L}} \neg \Phi \iff \hat{\mu}(t) \not\models_{\mathcal{M},\mathcal{L}} \Phi$

$\hat{\mu}(t) \models_{\mathcal{M},\mathcal{L}} \Phi_1 \wedge \Phi_2 \iff \hat{\mu}(t) \models_{\mathcal{M},\mathcal{L}} \Phi_1 \text{ and } \hat{\mu}(t) \models_{\mathcal{M},\mathcal{L}} \Phi_2$

$\hat{\mu}(t) \models_{\mathcal{M},\mathcal{L}} \mathcal{E}[\phi] \bowtie p \iff \sum_{s \in S} \hat{\mu}(t)(s) \cdot \mathbb{P}\left\{(s, \hat{\mu}(t)) \models_{\ell}^{\hat{\mu}_{\mathcal{M},\mathcal{L}}} \phi\right\}$

$\hat{\mu}(t) \models_{\mathcal{M},\mathcal{L}} \mathcal{P}_{\bowtie p}[\Psi] \iff \hat{\mu}(t) \models_{\mathcal{M},\mathcal{L}} \Psi \wedge (1 \bowtie p)$

PATH FORMULAS

$\hat{\mu}(t) \models_{\mathcal{M},\mathcal{L}} \mathcal{X} \Phi \iff \hat{\mu}(t+1) \models_{\mathcal{M},\mathcal{L}} \Phi$

$\hat{\mu}(t) \models_{\mathcal{M},\mathcal{L}} \Phi_1 \mathcal{U}^{[k_1,k_2]} \Phi_2 \iff \exists i \in [k_1, k_2] : \hat{\mu}(t+i) \models_{\mathcal{M},\mathcal{L}} \Phi_2$
$\forall j \in [0, i) : \hat{\mu}(t+j) \models_{\mathcal{M},\mathcal{L}} \Phi_1$

Fig. 10. Global Formulas: mean-field satisfaction relation

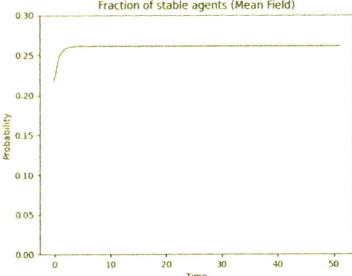

Fig. 11. Red/Blue Scenario: Fraction of Stable Agents (Mean Field). (Color figure online)

Figure 11 reports results of mean-field model-checking of the local stability of agents. We can observe that, also in this case, the fraction of agents that remain stable for 10 time units is around 25%. However, while the analyses of Example 4 needed the order of one minute, the one reported in Fig. 11 has been obtained in few milliseconds on a standard Laptop.

6 Concluding Remarks

Mean-field analysis has been applied to numerous case studies in the area of *collective adaptive systems* i.e., clustered networks, epidemic models, gossip protocols, and bike-sharing scenarios. All these systems are composed of a large number of entities. When this number of entities is large, then the system behaviour can be approximated to one or more entities by another random or stochastic process depending on the mean of the rest of the system. The behaviour of CAS can be approximated either in *continuous* time and *discrete* time. We are focusing on discrete time, and in this time, the mean-field can be approximated by the deterministic solution of a set of difference equations. Analytical analysis of Gossip protocols via mean-field approximation is presented in [3,4]. They analyze the properties of large-scale communication networks and apply the mean-field approximation in discrete time. They use the convergence results similar to the approach discussed in [20], but their approach does not cover the analysis of individual behaviour in terms of a large population. In [16,17], a combination of exact model checking with the mean-field analysis is presented to verify some PCTL properties of selected individuals. In [6], generic results of a model of interacting objects to the solution of an ordinary differential equation are presented. They also highlight the relation between the original stochastic process of N objects and the stationary regime of ODE.

In [24], semantic to Weighted Synchronous Calculus of Communicating Systems (WSCCS) in terms of mean-field is presented. These semantics capture the average behaviour over time without considering the system's whole state space. However, their approach only covers the mean-field equations for some possible WSCCS models. Mean-field analysis is applied to the Continuous Time Markov Chain (CTMC) to analyze the performance problems in large-scale systems in [10]. Still, they also needed to cover the model-checking algorithms. Differently from the approach presented in [3,10], the one shown in this paper focuses on scalable aspects and, due to the use of a simpler formalism, it is equipped with efficient model checking algorithms. We proposed on-the-fly mean-field approximation algorithms from both global and local perspectives. In literature, we found some global symbolic model checking algorithms that are not only computationally efficient but also found in many model checkers both in stochastic [1,15] and qualitative settings [11]. In stochastic model checking, these algorithms can be reduced to optimized and well-known algorithms such as transient analysis. In the case of qualitative settings, these algorithms follow a *bottom up fashion* where a set of states satisfies a formula is constructed recursively and, as a result, before applying an algorithm, the underlying model can be reduced to fewer states. Due to the state space exploration issues, these algorithms always require attention despite their success. Local model checking algorithms [9,12,14] also proposed in literature that based on on-the-fly approach and follows *top down fashion*. These algorithms does not requires the complete knowledge of state space. The state space is generated in a stepwise manner until the desired state satisfies the required formula. Local model checking can be useful in a case when we have large or infinite state space and their global model checking would impossible to use. Therefore, in this paper we focused on both local and global mean-field model checking algorithms that permit us to deal with scalability issues and provide comprehensive analysis from both perspectives.

As a future direction we plan to integrate GLoTL+ and its analysis techniques with exiting formalisms specifically thought for spatial properties [22]. Indeed, for Collective Systems the spatial dimension plays a crucial role. Moreover, to improve the performance, we plan to study the use of parallel architectures like in [5].

References

1. Baier, C., Haverkort, B., Hermanns, H., Katoen, J.P.: Model-checking algorithms for continuous-time Markov chains. IEEE Trans. Softw. Eng. **29**(6), 524–541 (2003)
2. Baier, C., Katoen, J.P.: Principles of Model Checking. MIT Press (2008)
3. Bakhshi, R., Cloth, L., Fokkink, W., Haverkort, B.: Mean-field analysis for the evaluation of gossip protocols. In: 2009 Sixth International Conference on the Quantitative Evaluation of Systems, pp. 247–256. IEEE (2009)
4. Bakhshi, R., Endrullis, J., Endrullis, S., Fokkink, W., Haverkort, B.: Automating the mean-field method for large dynamic gossip networks. In: 2010 Seventh International Conference on the Quantitative Evaluation of Systems, pp. 241–250. IEEE (2010)
5. Belenchia, M., Corradini, F., Quadrini, M., Loreti, M.: libmg: a python library for programming graph neural networks in μg. Sci. Comput. Program. **238**, 103165 (2024). https://doi.org/10.1016/J.SCICO.2024.103165
6. Benaim, M., Le Boudec, J.Y.: A class of mean field interaction models for computer and communication systems. Perform. Eval. **65**(11–12), 823–838 (2008)
7. Bettini, L., et al.: The Klaim project: theory and practice. In: Priami, C. (ed.) GC 2003. LNCS, vol. 2874, pp. 88–150. Springer, Heidelberg (2003). https://doi.org/10.1007/978-3-540-40042-4_4
8. Bettini, L., Ferrari, G., Loreti, M., Pugliese, R., Tiezzi, F., Tuosto, E.: Klaim in the making. In: Margaria, T., Steffen, B. (eds.) ISoLA 2024, Part I. LNCS, vol. 15219, pp. 27–49. Springer, Cham (2024). https://doi.org/10.1007/978-3-031-73709-1_3
9. Bhat, G., Cleaveland, R., Grumberg, O.: Efficient on-the-fly model checking for CTL. In: Proceedings of Tenth Annual IEEE Symposium on Logic in Computer Science, pp. 388–397. IEEE (1995)
10. Bobbio, A., Gribaudo, M., Telek, M.: Analysis of large scale interacting systems by mean field method. In: 2008 Fifth International Conference on Quantitative Evaluation of Systems, pp. 215–224. IEEE (2008)
11. Clarke, E.M., Emerson, E.A., Sistla, A.P.: Automatic verification of finite-state concurrent systems using temporal logic specifications. ACM Trans. Program. Lang. Syst. (TOPLAS) **8**(2), 244–263 (1986)
12. Courcoubetis, C., Vardi, M., Wolper, P., Yannakakis, M.: Memory-efficient algorithms for the verification of temporal properties. Formal Methods Syst. Design **1**, 275–288 (1992)
13. Giudice, N.D., Matteucci, L., Quadrini, M., Rehman, A., Loreti, M.: Sibilla: a tool for reasoning about collective systems. Sci. Comput. Program. **235**, 103095 (2024). https://doi.org/10.1016/J.SCICO.2024.103095
14. Gnesi, S., Mazzanti, F.: An abstract, on the fly framework for the verification of service-oriented systems. In: Wirsing, M., Hölzl, M. (eds.) Rigorous Software Engineering for Service-Oriented Systems. LNCS, vol. 6582, pp. 390–407. Springer, Heidelberg (2011). https://doi.org/10.1007/978-3-642-20401-2_18
15. Kwiatkowska, M., Norman, G., Parker, D.: Probabilistic symbolic model checking with prism: a hybrid approach. Int. J. Softw. Tools Technol. Transf. **6**, 128–142 (2004)
16. Latella, D., Loreti, M., Massink, M.: On-the-fly fast mean-field model-checking. In: Abadi, M., Lluch Lafuente, A. (eds.) TGC 2013. LNCS, vol. 8358, pp. 297–314. Springer, Cham (2014). https://doi.org/10.1007/978-3-319-05119-2_17
17. Latella, D., Loreti, M., Massink, M.: On-the-fly PCTL fast mean-field approximated model-checking for self-organising coordination. Sci. Comput. Program. **110**, 23–50 (2015)

18. Latella, D., Loreti, M., Massink, M.: On-the-fly PCTL fast mean-field approximated model-checking for self-organising coordination. Sci. Comput. Program. **110**, 23–50 (2015). https://doi.org/10.1016/j.scico.2015.06.009
19. Latella, D., Loreti, M., Massink, M.: FlyFast: a mean field model checker. In: Legay, A., Margaria, T. (eds.) TACAS 2017. LNCS, vol. 10206, pp. 303–309. Springer, Heidelberg (2017). https://doi.org/10.1007/978-3-662-54580-5_18
20. Le Boudec, J.Y., McDonald, D., Mundinger, J.: A generic mean field convergence result for systems of interacting objects. In: Fourth international conference on the quantitative evaluation of systems (QEST 2007), pp. 3–18. IEEE (2007)
21. Loreti, M., Hillston, J.: Modelling and analysis of collective adaptive systems with CARMA and its tools. In: Bernardo, M., De Nicola, R., Hillston, J. (eds.) SFM 2016. LNCS, vol. 9700, pp. 83–119. Springer, Cham (2016). https://doi.org/10.1007/978-3-319-34096-8_4
22. Loreti, M., Quadrini, M.: A spatial logic for simplicial models. Log. Methods Comput. Sci. **19**(3) (2023).https://doi.org/10.46298/LMCS-19(3:8)2023
23. Loreti, M., Rehman, A.: A logical framework for reasoning about local and global properties of collective systems. In: Ábrahám, E., Paolieri, M. (eds.) QEST 2022. LNCS, vol. 13479, pp. 133–149. Springer, Cham (2022). https://doi.org/10.1007/978-3-031-16336-4_7
24. McCaig, C., Norman, R., Shankland, C.: From individuals to populations: a mean field semantics for process algebra. Theoret. Comput. Sci. **412**(17), 1557–1580 (2011)
25. Nicola, R.D., Ferrari, G., Pugliese, R., Tiezzi, F.: A formal approach to the engineering of domain-specific distributed systems. J. Log. Algebraic Methods Program. **111**, 100511 (2020). https://doi.org/10.1016/J.JLAMP.2019.100511

A Hybrid Modelling Approach for Hierarchical Control of Structured CPSs

Simon Bliudze[1](✉), Sophie Cerf[1], and Olga Kouchnarenko[2]

[1] Univ. Lille, Inria, CNRS, Centrale Lille, UMR 9189 CRIStAL, 59000 Lille, France
{Simon.Bliudze,Sophie.Cerf}@inria.fr
[2] Université Marie et Louis Pasteur, CNRS UMR6174, Institut FEMTO-ST,
25000 Besançon, France
Olga.Kouchnarenko@femto-st.fr

Abstract. Cyber-physical systems (CPSs) include engineered interacting networks of physical and computational components. As they are widely used in many application domains, guaranteeing their correct and proper behaviour is an essential and a challenging issue. This paper aims to contribute to a flexible design and development of *structured* CPSs, composed of similar elements, and capable of (self-)adaptation to satisfy evolving internal and external constraints, e.g., using control theory. To this end, we make use of their structure and of their behavioural characteristics for modelling by hierarchical motifs both systems' elements and controllers. The motivations and contributions are illustrated on a smart building example.

1 Introduction

Cyber-physical systems (CPSs) are widely used in many application domains. Guaranteeing their correct and proper behaviour is an essential and a challenging issue [11]. CPSs are smart systems that include engineered interacting networks of physical and computational components [30]. More and more devices are now organised as networked communicating systems with additional constraints on the whole system architecture, e.g., some robots put together and playing sounds more or less loudly depending on their respective positions. In this paper, we consider *structured* CPSs, composed of similar elements organized in motifs, responsible for carrying out some common functionalities. For example, a smart building composed of (modular) rooms and hallways is an example of CPSs with flexible and hierarchical structure, where a temperature regulation must be assured as a common functionality.

Managing (self-)adaptation is a topic of increasing attention and importance in software engineering [38], as it is crucial for functional as well as non-functional requirements, e.g., performance, power consumption or reliability. Component-based models allow dealing with both types of requirements while assuring correct-by-construction system development [15]. In addition, component-based models are well-suited to perform dynamic reconfigurations modifying system's architecture, as e.g., in BIP [5] and

---

This work was partially supported by the ANR grant ANR-23-CE25-0004 (ADAPT).
O. Kouchnarenko was supported by the EIPHI Graduate School (grant number ANR-17-EURE-0002). This work was partially carried out during her research leave at Inria Lille.

DR-BIP [4]. However, a recent survey [13] emphasizes the need of a suitable methodology to ensure the correctness of reconfigurations in component-based systems (CBSs).

Self-adaptation of software elements has been extensively studied, notably using the formalism of the well-known MAPE loop [25], extended to MAPE-K with the knowledge management. Feedback control theory has recently emerged as a suitable adaptation methodology in line with the MAPE-K formulation [33]. The MAPE-K approach has however shown to favor monolithic controllers rather than structured controllers [14], that are more appropriate for (self-)adaptive software systems. Moreover, structured CPSs may have their implicit software regulators and explicit controllers interwoven, whereas in general, controller design is too strongly decoupled from the system under control. This is why designing and implementing more flexible controllers is challenging.

This paper aims to contribute to a flexible design and development of structured CPSs capable of (self-)adaptation to satisfy evolving internal and external constraints. This raises the following research questions:

RQ1 How to define a model accounting for the structural, behavioural and data aspects of CPSs that would be naturally amenable to hierarchical control?

RQ2 How to formulate the control problem of such structured CPSs with distributed elements?

To answer these questions, this paper's contribution consists in defining a notion of hierarchical motifs allowing the modelling of both the functional and the control components of CPSs.

The rest of the paper is organized as follows. Section 2 presents the control theory background, and Sect. 3 introduces the motivating example of a smart building temperature control. Section 4 introduces hierarchical motifs and illustrates this notion on the smart building example. Their composition semantics is presented in Sect. 5 (addressing RQ1). In Sect. 6, based on control motifs, the hierarchical control is expressed (tackling RQ2). Related work is presented in Sect. 7, and Sect. 8 concludes the paper.

2 On Control Theory

Control theory (CT) aims to stabilize and configure systems that evolve through time. CT is also a promising methodology for systems' (self-)adaptation [18,23]. In particular, feedback controllers are algorithms that compute the adequate values for systems *knobs*, so that the *measures* meet their desired *reference* values. This decision making is repeated in a loop, allowing dealing with dynamic systems behaviour. In the control theory literature, knobs are also refereed to as control signals, actions or inputs, while measures can also been called outputs or sensors signals.

To control a system, the general methodology consists in (1) identifying a plant Ψ, e.g., the model of the system to be controlled, and (2) designing its associated controller C, the component that makes adaptation decisions to be applied to the plant [18]. Note that even if the systems considered are CPSs or software, *continuous* control is an adequate technique for self-adaptation [35]. Also, a *linear* control formulation has provided significant results even when used on complex and potentially non-linear software systems.

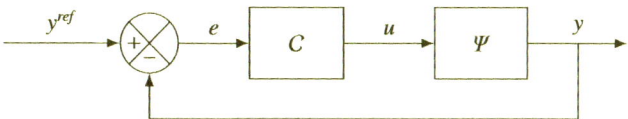

Fig. 1. Schema of a control feedback loop with notations.

A block-schema representation of a feedback loop is given in Fig. 1: The plant Ψ captures the impact of changes of the values of knobs u on the measurements y, while the controller C sets the value of the knobs u based on the measurements y and their reference (e.g. objective value) y^{ref}, though the error e. Knobs and measures are signals that evolve with time, taking continuous (possibly quantified) values. Note that there can also be disturbances, modelled by external and uncontrolled signals that impact the system's behaviour.

Transfer Functions. Both the plant Ψ and the controller C are represented using transfer functions. A transfer function is a mathematical model representing the transformation of signals, e.g., how the knobs signal u affects the measurements signal y. One can thus write

$$y = \Psi u, \qquad (1)$$

where a simple linear relation describes the system behaviour.

3 Motivating Example: Temperature Control in a Smart Building

To illustrate controlled CPSs with flexible and hierarchical structure, let us consider the temperature regulation of a smart building composed of rooms and hallways (see Fig. 2a). Some rooms are modular, meaning they can merge thanks to folding walls to form larger spaces. The rooms are interconnected due to temperature exchanges through walls, ceilings, and floors. Rooms are equipped with controllable heating systems. The target temperature for a room can vary depending on its type (e.g., office, corridor, server room) and occupation status (vacant or with people inside). Time or weather constraints (e.g., open/closed building, winter/summer) can also modify the temperature objectives.

The heat control is hierarchically structured, with (1) the lower level regulating the temperature in a single room, with one radiator each, (2) the middle level consisting of sets of modular rooms that can merge or split, (3) and the higher level setting temperature targets for the different rooms.

As the configuration of a room evolves, it changes room structure inside its set. The temperature regulation of such a smart building illustrates the control of flexible, hierarchically structured systems. For the following of the example, we build on the existing control formulations for building temperature regulation, using optimal control techniques for multi-room apartments [21,22] and distributed control [29] for a multi-zone system, for which we add flexibility and hierarchical considerations.

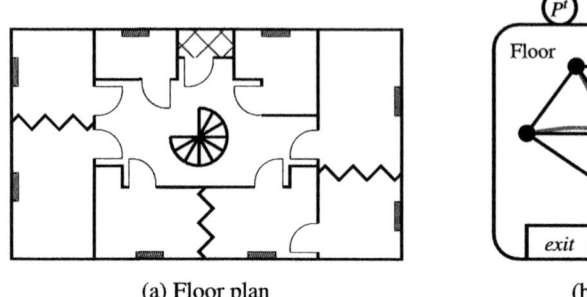 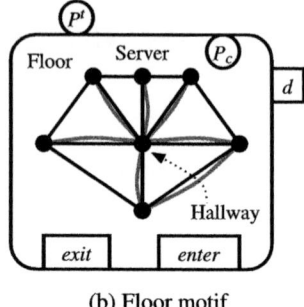

(a) Floor plan   (b) Floor motif

Fig. 2. One floor of the building (In (*a*), zigzag lines indicate foldable partition walls, the server room is shaded. In (*b*), double edges are for visual clarity only, they represent predicates on the underlying graph.) (Color figure online)

4 Hierarchical Motifs

To address RQ1, the key element of our approach is the notion of motifs inspired by Dynamic Reconfigurable BIP (DR-BIP) [4]. In DR-BIP, the main role of motifs is to specify the interconnections among components throughout the lifetime of a system by relying on *maps*. In [4], maps are defined as "abstract concepts that denote arbitrary collections of inter-connected nodes (positions)".

In this paper, we adapt and extend the notion of motifs to allow a flexible design, hierarchical composition and control of *structured* CPSs. Moreover, as this paper focuses on hierarchical control, we rely on maps of the motifs to specify how measurements and control commands are propagated through the system hierarchy. For the purposes of this paper, a *map* is a directed graph with predicates on nodes and edges.

Definition 1 (Map). *A map is a tuple* $\mu = (N, E, \mathcal{P})$, *where N is a set of nodes, $E \subseteq N \times N$ is a set of edges, and $\mathcal{P}$ is a set of predicates on N and E.*

For the sake of conciseness, we will write $n \in \mu$ and $(n_1, n_2) \in \mu$, meaning, respectively, $n \in N$ and $(n_1, n_2) \in E$, for $\mu = (N, E, \mathcal{P})$. We include a set of system-specific predicates to specify the nature of some nodes (e.g., centre of a star) or particularities of their arrangement (e.g., one node is located to the north of another).

Example 1. *Figure 2b shows a motif modelling the smart building floor shown in Fig. 2a. In particular, the motif comprises the corresponding map. The central node in the map represents the hallway. Other nodes represent the rooms (a modular room is also represented by a single node). We use two predicates (edge colours) to specify the possibility of heat transfer (black) and the presence of doors (blue) between nodes. Additionally, we use two node predicates:* Server *to identify the node representing the server room, and* Hallway *to identify the node representing the hallway.*

To be assembled hierarchically, motifs expose *interfaces*, which can be *external* (towards higher levels of the hierarchy) or *internal* (towards the sub-systems located in the nodes of the motif's map). An external interface provides an abstract view of the state space of the sub-tree of the hierarchical assembly rooted in the motif w.r.t. both coordination (i.e.the set of *possible* discrete actions) and control (i.e.the set of *possible* measured values and the set of possible knob positions). Dually, an internal interface specifies the sets of *acceptable* actions, measurements and knob positions for the sub-tree rooted in a given node of the motif.

Let us assume given a universe of actions *Act*. Furthermore, let *Act* be a bounded lattice with the usual lattice operations ∨ (join) and ∧ (meet), and bounds ⊥ (bottom) and ⊤ (top).

Definition 2 (Interface). *An interface is a tuple* $I = (A, S_Y, S_U, S_D, Y, U, D)$, *where* S_Y, S_U, *and* S_U *are vector spaces,* $A \subseteq Act$ *(with* $\bot \in A$ *and* $\top \notin A$*),* $Y \subseteq S_Y$, $U \subseteq S_U$, *and* $U \subseteq S_U$ *are, resp., the set of actions A and the domains of the measurements, knobs and the disturbances exposed by the interface.*

The product of two interfaces is defined component-wise: $I^1 \times I^2 \stackrel{def}{=} (A^1 \cup A^2, S_Y^1 \times S_Y^2, S_U^1 \times S_U^2, S_D^1 \times S_D^2, Y^1 \times Y^2, U^1 \times U^2, D^1 \times D^2)$.

Clearly the product operation on interfaces is associative. Therefore, we will use the standard ∏-notation for products involving more than two interfaces. Although this operator is only commutative up to isomorphism due to the ordering of coordinates in the vector spaces, in this paper, we will only occasionally need an order of operands to be fixed. For the sake of clarity, we do not fix such an order explicitly but assume that *an* order is implicitly given and used consistently.

Example 2. *The external interface of the Floor motif is* $I_{Floor} = (\{enter, exit\}, \mathbb{R}, [0, MAX_{hs}], \mathbb{R}, [0, MAX_{hs}], \mathbb{R}^6, -)$, *with the actions enter and exit representing people arriving at and leaving the floor. The measure and knob* $P_c, P^t \in [0, MAX_{hs}] \subseteq \mathbb{R}$ *represent the power consumed since the previous measure and the target power consumed by the entire heating system of the floor (with* MAX_{hs}—*the maximal total power achievable—a parameter of the motif defined at instantiation). Finally, the disturbance* $d \in \mathbb{R}^6$ *(we omit the range for conciseness) represents the temperature of the room floor* T_f, *the walls* T_w, *the outdoor air* T_o *and the ground* T_g, *the solar radiation on the walls and windows* $\mathcal{R}_s$.

The internal interface of the Floor motif is the product of the external interfaces of its nodes, corresponding, resp., to the control of the 3 Modular Rooms, 3 Rooms, and one Hallway. The map of the Room Control motif (see Fig. 3c) only has one node corresponding to the controlled room.[1]

Example 3. *The external interfaces of the motives Modular Room (see Fig. 3a), Room (see Fig. 3b), and Hallway (not shown) coincide. That interface* $I_{Room} = (\{enter, exit\}, \mathbb{R} \times \mathbb{R} \times \mathbb{N}, [0, MAX_{hmr}] \times [-MAX_{tmr}, MAX_{tmr}] \times [0, MAX_{pmr}], \mathbb{R} \times \mathbb{N}, [0, MAX_{hmr}] \times [0, MAX_{pmr}], \mathbb{R}^6, -)$, *has two actions, enter and exit, as in the Floor motif. The measure* $P_c \in [0, MAX_{hmr}] \subseteq \mathbb{R}$ *is the same as for the Floor interface (with* $MAX_{hmr} \leq MAX_{hs}$). *The knob* $P \in [0, MAX_{hmr}] \subseteq \mathbb{R}$ *represents the power to be applied by the room radiator(s). The measure and the knob cnt, max* $\in [0, MAX_{pmr}] \subseteq \mathbb{N}$

---

[1] We use the same (control) motif for all the nodes of the Floor motif.

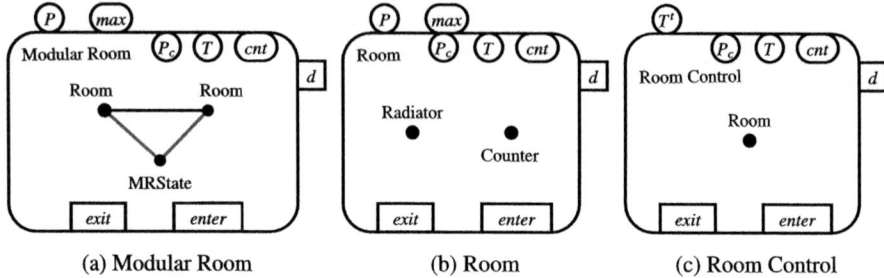

Fig. 3. Modular Room, Room and Room Control motifs (Square boxes on the inside represent actions, on the outside—disturbances, rounded boxes on the inside represent measures, on the outside—knobs.)

represent the current and the maximum admissible numbers of people. The measure $T \in [-MAX_{tmr}, MAX_{tmr}] \subseteq \mathbb{R}$ represents the temperature of the room. The disturbance is the same as for the Floor motif.

The internal interface of the Modular Room motif is the product of the interfaces corresponding to the nodes of its map. For the Room nodes, these coincide with the external interface of the Room motif. For the singleton MRState node, the interface is $I_{MRState} = (\{merge, split, isMerged, isSplit\}, \{\cdot\}, \{\cdot\}, \{\cdot\}, \emptyset, \emptyset, \emptyset)$, i.e. it has four actions and no measures, knobs, or disturbances. The actions correspond, resp., to merging/splitting the room and signalling its current state, i.e. whether it is merged or split.

Finally, the external interface of the Room Control motif (see Fig. 3c) is the same as that of the Room motif, except for the knobs. Instead of $P \in [0, MAX_{hmr}] \subseteq \mathbb{R}$, it has the knob $T \in [-MAX_{tmr}, MAX_{tmr}] \subseteq \mathbb{R}$, which sets the desired temperature within the controlled room.

Observe Example 1 and Example 3 to notice that the role of the Floor motif is to derive target temperatures for each room based on the power consumption budget allocated to the floor. The controllers of each node are then responsible for achieving these temperatures by setting the power and the maximal capacity in their corresponding rooms.

Let us assume given two interfaces $I^{int} = (A^{int}, S_Y^{int}, S_U^{int}, S_D^{int}, Y^{int}, U^{int}, D^{int})$ and $I^{ext} = (A^{ext}, S_Y^{ext}, S_U^{ext}, S_D^{ext}, Y^{ext}, U^{ext}, D^{ext})$.

Definition 3 (Aggregation). *An aggregation over (I^{int}, I^{ext}) is a mapping $\mathcal{A} : 2^{A^{int}} \times S_Y^{int} \to S_Y^{ext}$, such that $\mathcal{A}(2^{A^{int}} \times Y^{int}) \subseteq Y^{ext}$.*

An aggregation combines the measurements from the nodes of a motif and propagates the result to the next level of the hierarchy. Notice that the aggregation depends on the state of the motif represented by the set of enabled internal actions.

Example 4. *The external measure P_c of the Floor motif is the sum of the corresponding internal measures in the nodes: $P_c = \sum_{n \in \mu} n.P_c$.[2] This aggregation does not depend on the enabledness of the enter and exit actions.*

Example 5. *For the Modular Room motif, only the nodes corresponding to sub-rooms have to be taken into account for the power consumption aggregation (cf. Example 1): $P_c = \sum_{n \in \mu \wedge \text{Room}(n)} n.P_c$.*

Temperature measures provided by the sub-rooms can be aggregated to get the global temperature of a Modular Room. We define the aggregation as the simple averaging: $T = \frac{1}{\#\text{Room}} \sum_{n \in \mu \wedge \text{Room}(n)} n.T$, where #Room denotes the number of nodes satisfying Room. More advanced processing based on room topology and the positions of the radiators can be used if necessary.

Finally, the aggregation of the occupancy counters depends on the state of the modular room:[3] $cnt = \mathcal{A}(A_{en}^{MRState}, \ldots)$, with

$$\mathcal{A}(A_{en}^{MRState}, \ldots) = \begin{cases} \frac{1}{\#\text{Room}} \sum_{n \in \mu \wedge \text{Room}(n)} n.cnt & \text{if isMerged} \in A_{en}^{MRState}, \\ \sum_{n \in \mu \wedge \text{Room}(n)} n.cnt & \text{if isSplit} \in A_{en}^{MRState}. \end{cases}$$

Indeed, when a modular room is merged, it is impossible to know whether a person is located in one sub-room or another. Therefore, we make the counters in all sub-rooms mirror each other counting the total number of people in the modular room.

Definition 4 (Control profile). *A control profile over (I^{int}, I^{ext}) is a mapping $\Phi : 2^{A^{int}} \times S_Y^{int} \times S_U^{int} \times S_U^{ext} \times S_D^{ext} \to S_U^{int}$, such that $\Phi(2^{A^{int}} \times Y^{int} \times U^{int} \times U^{ext} \times D^{ext}) \subseteq U^{int}$.*

A control profile specifies how the control command from the hierarchy (i.e.the external knob position) is propagated to the sub-nodes. Based on the control command and the current internal measurements and knob positions, it computes the updated knob positions at the nodes. Similarly to aggregations, profiles depend on the state of the corresponding motifs.

Example 6. *The control profile of the Floor motif sets the temperature target for each room depending on the total power consumption budget (external node) as follows:*

$$n.T' = \begin{cases} 15, & \text{if Server}(n), \\ 18 + T_{cor}, & \text{if Hallway}(n), \\ 19 + T_{cor}, & \text{otherwise}, \end{cases} \quad \text{with} \quad T_{cor} = \begin{cases} 0, & \text{if } \sum_{n \in \mu} n.P_c < P^t, \\ 2 \cdot \frac{P^t - P_c}{P^t \cdot 10\%}, & \text{otherwise}. \end{cases}$$

If the total consumed power is below the budget, the temperatures are assigned according to the room profile. If power consumption exceeds budget, a correction is applied to reduce the target temperatures in the rooms and the hallway.

---

[2] The control interposed between the Floor and the Modular Room motifs propagates the measures from the plant up.

[3] See Example 10 in Sect. 5 for further detail.

Example 7. *The control profile of the Modular Room depends on its state: when the room is merged, the same power is applied to the radiators in both sub-rooms, when it is split, the radiator power is set proportionally to the room capacity:*

$$\Phi_P(A_{en}^{MRState}, \dots) = \begin{cases} (P/2)^{n \in \mu \wedge \text{Room}(n)} & \text{if isMerged} \in A_{en}^{MRState}, \\ \left(\dots, \dfrac{n_i.MAX_{pmr}}{\sum_{n \in \mu \wedge \text{Room}(n)} n.MAX_{pmr}} \cdot P, \dots\right), & \text{if isSplit} \in A_{en}^{MRState}. \end{cases}$$

Similarly, for the capacity control:

$$\Phi_{max}(A_{en}^{MRState}, \dots) = \begin{cases} (max)^{n \in \mu \wedge \text{Room}(n)} & \text{if isMerged} \in A_{en}^{MRState}, \\ \left(\dots, \dfrac{n_i.MAX_{pmr}}{\sum_{n \in \mu \wedge \text{Room}(n)} n.MAX_{pmr}} \cdot max, \dots\right), & \text{if isSplit} \in A_{en}^{MRState}. \end{cases}$$

(As in Example 5, the counters are mirrored when the room is merged.)

A disturbance profile specifies the disturbances at the nodes of the map based on the external disturbances and the internal measures.

Definition 5 (Disturbance profile). *A disturbance profile over (I^{int}, I^{ext}) is a mapping $\Delta : 2^{A^{int}} \times S_Y^{int} \times S_D^{ext} \to S_D^{int}$, such that $\Delta(2^{A^{int}} \times Y^{int} \times D^{ext}) \subseteq D^{int}$.*

Example 8. *We omit precise description of the disturbance propagation for the sake of conciseness. Differentiating the temperature of the outdoor air on the four sides of each room, the disturbance profile of the Modular Room motif consists in assigning the temperature measure of each sub-room in the place of the outdoor air disturbance on the corresponding side of its adjacent sub-room(s). Similarly, the ambient temperature disturbance of the Radiator component is defined by the Room temperature measure.*[4]

Given a map $\mu = (N, E, \mathcal{P})$, and associated node and external interfaces $(I^n)_{n \in \mu}$ and I^{ext}, resp., coordination of the sub-system actions is specified using a First Order Logics (FOL).

Definition 6 (Interaction constraints). *An interaction logic $\mathcal{L}(\Sigma)$ over (μ, I^{int}, I^{ext}), where $I^{int} = (I^n)_{n \in \mu}$, is FOL with the signature Σ, such that*

$$\{\mathbf{E}\} \cup \{\mathbf{P}^p \mid p \in \mathcal{P}\} \cup \{\mathbf{a}^{ext}, \mathbf{a}^{int}, \mathbf{y}^{int}, \mathbf{u}^{ext}, \mathbf{d}^{ext}\} \subseteq \Sigma \quad (2)$$

with the usual FOL satisfaction relation $\models$.

The interpretation domain of $\mathcal{L}(\Sigma)$ is as follows (we use $\mathcal{I}$ and v to denote an interpretation of non-logical symbols and a valuation of variables, resp.):

- *the variables range over the nodes of the map μ, i.e. $\text{codom}(v) = N$,*
- *the predicate $\mathcal{I}(\mathbf{E})(n_1, n_2) = ((n_1, n_2) \in E)$ encodes graph connectivity in the map,*
- *symbols $\mathbf{P}^p$ are interpreted as the corresponding map predicates: $\mathcal{I}(\mathbf{P}^p) = p$,*
- *the constant $\mathcal{I}(\mathbf{a}^{ext}) : \{\cdot\} \to A^{ext}$ determines which external action is to be fired under the interpretation $\mathcal{I}$,*

---

[4] The Room temperature measure depends on the Radiator casing temperature measure, thereby creating a feedback loop affecting the radiator control.

- the function $\mathcal{I}(\mathbf{a}^{int}) : N \to \bigcup_{n \in N} A^n$, such that $\mathcal{I}(\mathbf{a}^{int})(n) \in A^n$, for any $n \in N$, determines which internal actions are to be fired under the interpretation $\mathcal{I}$,
- the function $\mathcal{I}(\mathbf{y}^{int}) : N \to \bigcup_{n \in N} Y^n$, such that $\mathcal{I}(\mathbf{y}^{int})(n) \in Y^n$, for any $n \in N$, determines the internal measures,
- the constant $\mathcal{I}(\mathbf{u}^{ext}) : \{\cdot\} \to U^{ext}$ determines the external knob position,
- finally, the constant $\mathcal{I}(\mathbf{d}^{ext}) : \{\cdot\} \to D^{ext}$ determines the external disturbance value.

An *interaction constraint* over (μ, I^{int}, I^{ext}) is a formula $\varphi \in \mathcal{L}(\Sigma)$, such that $(\bot, (\bot)_{n \in \mu}, y^{int}, u^{ext}, d^{ext}) \models \varphi$, for any $y^{int} \in Y^{int}$, $u^{ext} \in U^{ext}$, and $d^{ext} \in D^{ext}$.

Intuitively, the interaction constraint specifies what actions can be taken by each of the motif's sub-systems in view of the received measurements and control command and how these actions are combined to be exposed through the external interface.

Notice that we do not limit the signature of $\mathcal{L}(\Sigma)$ to the symbols explicitly stated in Definition 6. In particular, symbols can be included to represent internal knob positions or external measurements, or, alternatively, aggregation and profile mappings. Other symbols may represent additional non-persistent information, i.e. carrying values that are discarded from one interaction to another.

Example 9. *The interaction constraint defines the syncrhonisations of the internal and external actions of the Modular Room motif:*

$$\forall n(\text{Room}(n)), \left((\mathbf{a}^{int}(n) = enter \implies \mathbf{a}^{ext} = enter) \land \right. \tag{3}$$

$$\left. \land (\mathbf{a}^{int}(n) = exit \implies \mathbf{a}^{ext} = exit)\right) \land \tag{4}$$

$$\exists! n_{MRState} : \text{MRState}(n_{MRState}) \land \tag{5}$$

$$\mathbf{a}^{ext} \in \{enter, exit\} \implies \mathbf{a}^{int}(n_{MRState}) \in \{isMerged, isSplit\} \land \tag{6}$$

$$\mathbf{a}^{int}(n_{MRState}) = isMerged \implies$$

$$\left(\mathbf{a}^{ext} = exit \implies \forall n(\text{Room}(n)), \mathbf{a}^{int}(n) = exit \right. \tag{7}$$

$$\left. \land \mathbf{a}^{ext} = enter \implies \forall n(\text{Room}(n)), \mathbf{a}^{int}(n) = enter\right) \land$$

$$\mathbf{a}^{int}(n_{MRState}) = isSplit \implies$$

$$\left(\mathbf{a}^{ext} = exit \implies \exists! n(\text{Room}(n)) : \mathbf{a}^{int}(n) = exit \right. \tag{8}$$

$$\left. \land \mathbf{a}^{ext} = enter \implies \exists! n(\text{Room}(n)) : \mathbf{a}^{int}(n) = enter\right) \land$$

$$\left(\mathbf{a}^{int}(n_{MRState}) \in \{merge, split\} \implies \forall n(\text{Room}(n)), \mathbf{y}^{int}(n).cnt = 0\right). \tag{9}$$

Lines (3) and (4) above specify that a person can only enter or exit a sub-room if they, resp., enter or exit the modular room. Line (5) states that there is a node, denoted $n_{MRState}$, that keeps track of the modular room's state. Line (6) states that when executing enter or exit of the room, the state signal must necessarily be consulted. If the room is merged (lines (7)), exiting or entering the modular room means doing so for all sub-rooms (cf. Examples 5 and 7). If the room is split (lines (8)), there must be exactly one sub-room on which the same action is performed. Finally, line (9) requires that the room be empty whenever its state is changed.

Notice that the "signalling" actions isMerged and isSplit are not exported directly. They are only fired as part of interactions with enter and exit actions of the nodes. These interactions are exported as the corresponding external actions of the motif.

To summarise, a motif comprises all the elements introduced in Definitions 1 to 6.

Definition 7 (Motif). *A* motif *is a tuple* $M \stackrel{def}{=} (\mu, (I^n)_{n \in \mu}, I^{ext}, \mathcal{A}, \Phi, \Delta, \varphi)$, *where μ is a map, I^n (for each $n \in \mu$) and I^{ext} are, resp., node and external* interfaces, *such that $A^{ext} \subseteq Act$, $A^n \subseteq Act$, for each $n \in \mu$, and every external action $a \in A^{ext}$ is a join of internal ones, i.e. there exists $N \subseteq \mu$ and $a_n \in A^n$, for each $n \in N$, such that $a = \bigvee_{n \in N} a_n$.*

Denote $I^{int} \stackrel{def}{=} \prod_{n \in \mu} I^n$ the internal interface *of the motif. The remaining four components, $\mathcal{A}$, Φ, Δ, and φ, are then, resp., an aggregation, a control profile, a disturbance profile, and an interaction constraint over (μ, I^{int}, I^{ext}).*

Internal measures Y^{int}, external knobs U^{ext}, and external disturbances D^{ext} can be construed as inputs of a motif. Dually, external measures Y^{ext}, internal knobs U^{int}, and internal disturbances D^{int} can be construed as its outputs.

5 Composition Semantics

In the context of structured CPSs, their model is a tree with motifs at all internal nodes and components defining the systems' behaviour at the leaves. Figure 4 shows a fragment of such a tree modelling the Smart Building example. The children of each internal node correspond to the nodes of the map of the motif. The flexibility of our approach lies with the fact that we do not restrict the nature of components, which may be instantiated motifs (see Definition 9 below), simple, timed or hybrid automata,[5] or any other kind of objects that have an operational semantics expressible as a Labelled Transition System (LTS) of the following kind.

Definition 8 (Object). *An* object *implementing the interface $(A, S_Y, S_U, S_D, Y, U, D)$ is an entity that can be given an operational semantics in the form of an LTS defined by the transition relation $\rightarrow \subseteq (2^A \times Y \times U) \times (A \times U \times D) \times (2^A \times Y \times U)$, such that,*

- *for any transition $((A^{en}, y, u), (a, \widetilde{u}, d), (A^{en'}, y', u')) \in \rightarrow$, we have $a \in A^{en}$ and $u' = \widetilde{u}$,*
- *for any state (A^{en}, y, u) and any $u' \in U$, $d \in D$, there exist $A^{en'}$, y', such that $((A^{en}, y, u), (\bot, u', d), (A^{en'}, y', u')) \in \rightarrow$.*

We write $(A^{en}, y, u) \xrightarrow{a, u', d} (A^{en'}, y', u')$ to denote $((A^{en}, y, u), (a, u', d), (A^{en'}, y', u')) \in \rightarrow$.

The state of an object is thus defined by the set of *enabled actions* and the current measurements and knob positions. The conditions imposed on the transition relation mean that (1) only enabled actions can be fired, (2) the knob positions can only be set externally and are not affected by the behaviour of the object, and (3) the bottom action is always enabled.

---

[5] Our approach to modelling timed and hybrid aspects is based on [7,8]. We do not present it here for the sake of conciseness.

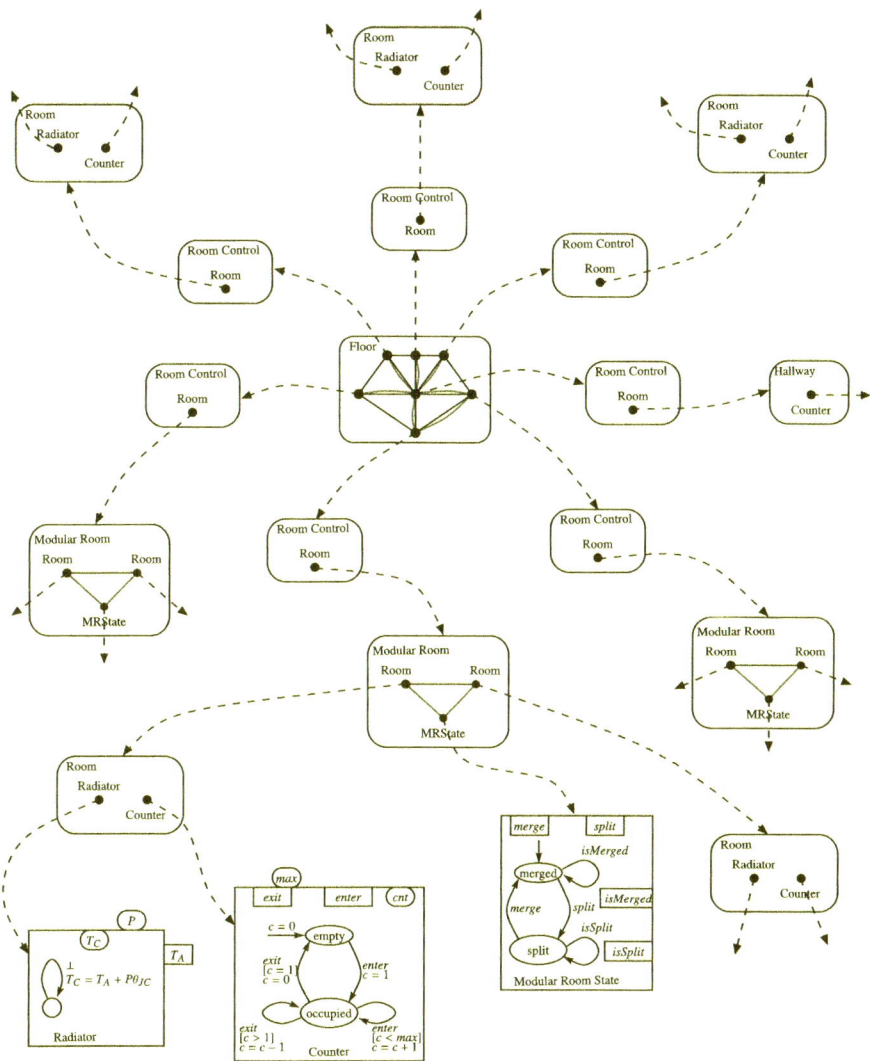

Fig. 4. Fragment of the Smart Building assembly (omitting explicit modelling of time).

Example 10. *Radiator, Counter, and Modular Room State components shown at the leaves of the assembly tree in Fig. 4 are objects in the sense of Definition 8. The Modular Room State component type[6] implements the interface of the MRState node in the Modular Room motif (cf. Example 3). It has been extensively used in the examples of the previous section. It is worth noting the self-loop transitions labelled by the actions isMerged and isSplit. Their purpose is to signal that the component is, resp., in one of the states* `merged` *and* `split`.

---

[6] The full assembly comprises three instances—one for each Modular Room.

To allow hierarchical composition of motifs, we need to define what it means to instantiate a node of a motif with another one.

Definition 9 (Instantiation). *A motif instantiation is a triple* $(M, N, \{O_n \mid n \in N\})$ *with M a motif, $N \subseteq \mu_M$ a set of nodes, and, for each node $n \in N$, O_n an object implementing the corresponding interface I^n of M. An instantiation is* closed *if N is the set of all nodes of μ_M. Otherwise, it is* open.

To allow the use of instantiated motifs as objects to, in turn, instantiate motifs at higher hierarchical levels, we must define their operational semantics. The semantics of a closed motif instantiation $(M, \mu_M, \{O_n \mid n \in \mu_M\})$ is given by the following Structural Operational Semantics (SOS) [32] rule.

$$\frac{\begin{array}{c} a \in A^{en} \quad a = \bigvee_{n \in \mu} a_n \quad u' \in U^{ext} \quad (a, (a_n)_{n \in \mu}, (y_n)_{n \in \mu}, u) \models \varphi \\[4pt] (u'_n)_{n \in \mu} = \Phi\big(\bigcup_{n \in \mu} A_n^{en}, (y_n)_{n \in \mu}, (u_n)_{n \in \mu}, u'\big) \quad (d_n)_{n \in \mu} = \Delta\big(\bigcup_{n \in \mu} A_n^{en}, (y_n)_{n \in \mu}, d\big) \\[4pt] \forall n \in \mu, \; (A_n^{en}, y_n, u_n) \xrightarrow{a_n, u'_n, d_n} (A_n^{en'}, y'_n, u'_n) \\[4pt] A^{en'} = \left\{ a' = \bigvee_{n \in \mu} a'_n \in A^{ext} \;\middle|\; a'_n \in A_n^{en'} \wedge (a', (a'_n)_{n \in \mu}, (y'_n)_{n \in \mu}, u') \models \varphi \right\} \\[4pt] y = \mathcal{A}\big(\bigcup_{n \in \mu} A_n^{en}, (y_n)_{n \in \mu}\big) \quad y' = \mathcal{A}\big(\bigcup_{n \in \mu} A_n^{en'}, (y'_n)_{n \in \mu}\big) \end{array}}{(A^{en}, y, u) \xrightarrow{a, u', d} (A^{en'}, y', u')} \quad (10)$$

Informally, given an enabled joint action $a \in A^{en}$ (premises 1, 2) and a proposed position of the external knob u' (premise 3), such that a, the current internal measurements $(y_n)_{n \in \mu}$, and the current external knob position u satisfy the interaction constraint φ (premise 4), and the actuation of the internal knobs $(u'_n)_{n \in \mu}$ defined by the profile (premise 5) confronted with their disturbances $(d_n)_{n \in \mu}$ (premise 6) allow transitions within the objects at the nodes of the motif map (premises 7, 9), the motif instantiation can change its state accordingly (rule conclusion) with the set of enabled actions and the aggregation of the measurements in the target state being determined by the enabled actions, the proposed position of the external knob and the measurements exposed at the nodes of the motif (premises 8, 10).

Notice that, this semantics is an abstraction of the true behaviour of the object since it hides the internal measures. Therefore, subject to model checking, it can produce false positives. However, its execution in the context of simulation or control is driven in the bottom-up fashion using only the true values of the internal measures.

Proposition 1. *The semantics (10) defines an object in the sense of Definition 8.*

Proof (Proof sketch). We have to show that, in the composed LTS, (1) only enabled actions can be fired, (2) the knob positions can only be set externally and are not affected by the behaviour of the object, and (3) the bottom action is always enabled.

The first two items follow trivially from premise 1 and the conclusion of the rule, resp. To show the third item, consider $a = \bot$. Rule (10) reduces to

$$\frac{\begin{array}{c} u' \in U^{ext} \\ (u'_n)_{n \in \mu} = \Phi\left(\bigcup_{n \in \mu} A_n^{en}, (y_n)_{n \in \mu}, (u_n)_{n \in \mu}, u'\right) \quad (d_n)_{n \in \mu} = \Delta\left(\bigcup_{n \in \mu} A_n^{en}, (y_n)_{n \in \mu}, d\right) \\ \forall n \in \mu, \; (A_n^{en}, y_n, u_n) \xrightarrow{\bot, u'_n, d_n} (A_n^{en'}, y'_n, u'_n) \\ A^{en'} = \left\{ a' = \bigvee_{n \in \mu} a'_n \in A^{ext} \;\middle|\; a'_n \in A_n^{en'} \wedge (a', (a'_n)_{n \in \mu}, (y'_n)_{n \in \mu}, u') \vDash \varphi \right\} \\ y = \mathcal{A}\left(\bigcup_{n \in \mu} A_n^{en}, (y_n)_{n \in \mu}\right) \quad y' = \mathcal{A}\left(\bigcup_{n \in \mu} A_n^{en}, y'_n\right)_{n \in \mu} \end{array}}{(A^{en}, y, u) \xrightarrow{\bot, u', d'} (A^{en}, y', u')} \quad (11)$$

Indeed, from premise 2 of rule (10), we have $a_n = \bot$, for all $n \in \mu$. Since Definition 6 requires that the interaction constraint does not block $\bot$, the premise 4 is trivially satisfied. The premise 7 (premise 4 in rule (11)) is satisfied because the motif is instantiated with objects. All the remaining premises are non-blocking. □

This semantics is synchronous in the sense that transitions of both the motif and all the objects in its instantiation are taken atomically in one step. This is reflected by the last premises in (10) and (11), since the updated measurements y'_n are necessary to compute y'.

6 Control Protocols

This section focuses on linking the proposed modelling approach with the classical Control Theory. That link is necessary for defining control functions for the control motifs of the assembly. First we define control motifs—a special case of motifs defined in Sect. 4. Second, in order to address RQ2, we establish a link between the control formulation presented in Sect. 2 and the definition of motifs. Finally, we focus on hierarchical systems, establishing the plant formulation for instantiated motifs (i.e. sub-trees of the assembly tree).

6.1 Control Motifs

Based on preliminaries from Sect. 2, we consider the basic control signals: measures y, reference values for these measures y^{ref}, and knobs u, a tunable signal that allows leveraging the measures signal. Some authors explicitly consider the error between reference and measure values. In our approach, it can be computed from these signals. In addition, we include the (external) disturbances in the control motif.

Consider an object implementing the interface $(A, S_Y, S_U, S_D, Y, U, D)$. Its control is realized by a *control function* $c : 2^A \times S_Y \times S_U \times S_Y \times S_D \to S_U$. The first parameter of the control function is the *control mode* determined by the set of enabled actions in the current state of the object. Given the control mode $A^{en} \subseteq A$, the current aggregated measurement $y \in Y$, the knob position $u \in U$, a reference value $y^{ref} \in Y$, and disturbance $d \in D$, the control function defines the corresponding new value of the knob $u' = c(A^{en}, y, u, y^{ref}, d) \in U$ of the object.

We define *control motifs*, which are a special case of motifs in Definition 7 characterised by such control functions. We put $M_c = (\{\cdot\}, I^{int}, I^{ext}, id, c, id, true)$, where $\{\cdot\}$ is a singleton map (one node, no edges), $I_c^{int} = (A, S_Y, S_U, S_D, Y, U, D)$ (same as the interface implemented by the object), $I_c^{ext} = (A, S_Y, S_Y, S_D, Y, Y, D)$, $id : S_Y \to S_Y$ is the identity aggregation, the control function c plays the role of the control profile, and $id : S_D \to S_D$ is the identity disturbance profile. The use of the constant predicate *true* means that no interaction constraints are imposed by the motif. In the external interface of a control motif, the knob is replaced by the reference values of the measures. An control profile arising in the context of our running example is shown in Fig. 3c.

We do not impose any constraints on the nature of the control function. However, in the remainder of the paper, we consider linear controllers.

6.2 Linking Control Formulation and Motifs

The notions of plant, controller and their transfer function can be linked with the motifs as defined in Definition 7 and specified in Sect. 6.1.

Let us first consider a motif M in the most general case. The *plant* transfer function Ψ, as defined in Eq. (1), captures the impact of changes of knobs u on measurements y. It is a mathematical model linking elements in the motif's external interface I^{ext}, with $u \in U^{ext}$ and $y \in Y^{ext}$. The impact of disturbances d on measurements is also taken into account in the model, e.g., by artificially augmenting the measurement vector y with the disturbances.

Example 11. *The room plant Ψ_{room} is the model that represents the impact of the heating power on the temperature. It can be expressed as a multi-input multi-output model: Following Examples 2 and 3, the evolution of the Room motif temperature y_{room} (denoted T in Fig. 3b) can be computed based on the temperature of the floor T_f, of the walls T_w, of the outdoor air T_o and of the ground T_g, as well as the solar radiation on the walls and windows R_s, and the radiation coming from the people in the room $cnt \cdot R_o$, where R_o is the average radiation per person and cnt is the counter (see the Counter component in Fig. 4). The heat power control knob u_{room} (denoted P in Fig. 3b) is the internal heat flux in the room coming from the radiators.*

We define x as the set of all relevant disturbances (temperatures and radiations):

$$x \stackrel{def}{=} \begin{bmatrix} y_{room} & T_f & T_w & T_o & T_g & R_s & cnt \cdot R_o \end{bmatrix}^T = \begin{bmatrix} y_{room} & d_{room} \end{bmatrix}^T. \quad (12)$$

Note that for a room connected to several others, T_w can be a vector. The evolution of indoor temperatures can be modelled as:

$$\begin{cases} x' = Ax + Bu_{room}, \\ y_{room} = Cx \end{cases} \quad (13)$$

where x' denotes either the derivative of x in the continuous-time case, or its value at the next time-step in the discrete-time case.[7] *A and B are matrices taking into account*

---
[7] Note that the conventional notation in control formulation is rather x^+.

the convection, thermal resistances, and capacity of the various elements around the room[8]. The matrix C selects the room temperature among all the indoor ones: $C = \begin{bmatrix} 1 & 0 & 0 & 0 & 0 & 0 & 0 \end{bmatrix}$.

The transfer function Ψ_{room} is then classically computed based on the matrices of the model as:

$$\Psi_{room}(s) = C(sI - A)^{-1}B, \tag{14}$$

with I the identity matrix of adequate size and s the complex variable. Note that the model takes into account the count of occupants in the room, to compute the induced radiation, and is thus a hybrid system, with both discrete- and continuous-state interfaces. However, in the following, we focus on linear continuous control, e.g., by considering all the elements of the state x as continuous in the control formulation, and let the hybrid control formulation as future work.

The plant Ψ is thus a partial view of a motif, only concerned with the external interface signals evolution. Its dependence with internal elements can be explored in the case where the map is specified, as presented in the next section.

We now consider a *control motif* M_c. The *controller C* captures the impact of the reference and the measures (often through their difference, i.e. the reference tracking error), and the disturbances d on the knobs signal:

$$u = C(y^{ref}, y, d). \tag{15}$$

Thus, the controller C models the link between the elements of the internal and external interfaces of the control motif M_c.

Example 12. *For our running example, the **controller** C_{room} computes the heat power knob value u_{room} based on the target temperature y_{room}^{ref}, the room measured temperature y_{room} and all the disturbances, that is the x vector. For the linear time-invariant system that we consider, the optimal controller can be computed as a state feedback, with precompensation for the reference tracking:*

$$u_{room} = -Kx + Gy_{room}^{ref}, \tag{16}$$

where K is the state feedback gain; and G is the precompensation gain, both being vectors of appropriate sizes. K is computed based on the plant Ψ_{room}, more particularly on A and B, by pole placement. It allows specifying the desired closed-loop behavior, for instance the speed of reactivity of the control. The precompensation is computed based on A, B, C, and K, ensuring that the measure follows the reference. In this example, the controller C_{room} is thus composed of two transfer functions: K and G.

Note that this controller is a state feedback (i.e. the control is computed based on x, meaning a measure of all its elements is needed), output feedback could rather be used (i.e. using only y_{room} in the control formulation: $u_{room} = -Ky_{room} + Gy_{room}^{ref}$) if the plant extended with the disturbances d_{room} is observable. In this case, a Luenberger observer or a Kalman filter could be used to estimate the full state x.

---

[8] Computing the exact values of the A and B matrices is out of the scope for this work, the interested reader can refer to [21] for an example of those matrices.

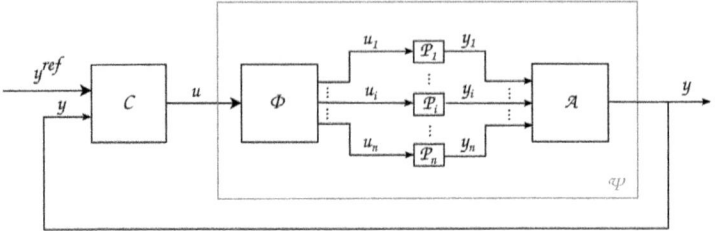

Fig. 5. Hierarchical control schema.

6.3 Hierarchical Control

We consider CPSs with a hierarchical structure, in which there is at least one controller. At a given level, the motif map and interfaces are instantiated, and we fix an order on the nodes of the map. A schematic representation of the control schema is given in Fig. 5. Note that here the disturbances are not explicitly written in the following formulations for the sake of simplicity, as it can be considered as part of the measurement vector y (model extension with disturbance model).

The plant Ψ modeling the knobs-to-measures behaviour of the motif M, can be expressed using the control profile Φ, the aggregation $\mathcal{A}$, and recursion over the lower level motifs. At a given level, the measure $y \in Y^{ext}$ (external interface) is the aggregation of the measures of the lower levels y_i:

$$y = \mathcal{A}\mathbf{y}, \qquad (17)$$

with $\mathbf{y} = [y_1, \cdots, y_i, \cdots, y_n]^T \in Y^{int}$ (internal interfaces). The controller C computes the knob $u \in U^{ext}$ (external interface), that is distributed among the lower levels as u_i by the profile function Φ:

$$\mathbf{u} = \Phi u, \qquad (18)$$

with $\mathbf{u} = [u_1, \cdots, u_i, \cdots, u_n]^T \in U^{int}$ (internal interfaces).

The measure at a lower level can be derived from the value of the knob that was enforced, and is modelled by the subsystem transfer function P_i:

$$y_i = P_i u_i. \qquad (19)$$

Note that if the lower level is not controlled, then $P_i = \Psi_i$. Otherwise, it is the transfer function of the controlled closed loop.

The hierarchical control consists then in designing C to regulate the plant Ψ, recursively formulated as:

$$\Psi = \mathcal{A}\mathbf{P}\Phi, \qquad (20)$$

with $\mathbf{P} \stackrel{def}{=} [P_1, \cdots, P_i, \cdots, P_n] \times \mathbf{I}_n$.

Example 13. *Following Examples 11 and 12, let us now consider the hierarchical level of a modular room, composed of n rooms. The hierarchical control formulation allows deriving the model of the modular room Ψ_{mr} based on the room models $\Psi_{room,i}$, and on* the aggregation and profile. At the lower levels, each room is controlled by a feedback controller, their equivalent closed-loop transfer function is thus:[9]

$$P_i = \frac{C_{room,i} \Psi_{room,i}}{1 + C_{room,i} \Psi_{room,i}}.$$

The modular room relevant temperature is the average temperatures in all rooms when it is merged, and the individual temperature measures otherwise. The aggregation $\mathcal{A}_{mr}$ can be written as:

$$\mathcal{A}_{mr} = \begin{cases} \left[\frac{1}{n} \cdots \frac{1}{n}\right] & \text{if state = merged,} \\ \boldsymbol{I}_n & \text{if state = split.} \end{cases} \quad (21)$$

The profile Φ_{mr} distributes equally the temperature references, if we consider that all rooms are of similar use, and can be expressed as:

$$\Phi_{mr} = \begin{bmatrix} 1 \cdots 1 \end{bmatrix}^T. \quad (22)$$

Overall, the modular room plant is then:

$$\Psi_{mr} = \mathcal{A}_{mr} \mathbf{P}_{room} \Phi_{mr}, \quad (23)$$

with $\mathbf{P}_{room} = [P_{room,1} \cdots P_{room,n}] \times \boldsymbol{I}_n$.

7 Related Work

On Component-Based Models with Layered Architectures. In this paper, only generic concepts of component-based systems are considered to allow applying the paper's proposals on hierarchical motifs to various component-based models, see e.g., a recent survey [13] for a list of component-based models. There are many approaches to model CBSs in general, and those supporting hierarchical style in particular [6,10,12,16]. In [37], C2SADEL, a software architecture description and evolution language, defines C2-style architectures that can be seen as a network of concurrent components linked together by connectors, which are message routing devices. On its side π-ADL [31], which is formally derived from π-calculus, also allows defining architectural styles using it.

BIP [5] and DR-BIP [4] are suitable frameworks for developing CBSs with a layered structure. Some of these frameworks support monitoring and run-time property verification. However the hierarchical motifs integrating control that may usefully impact systems' architecture design and development and bring new verification and validation results, are original contributions of the present paper. Our use of motifs was inspired by DR-BIP. The results of this paper serve as a proof of concept aiming to implement a (DR-)BIP extension integrating hierarchical control motifs. Similarly, we use automata-based models of components and their underlying parallel and hierarchical compositions to represent the behavioural aspects of motifs and composed systems. It

---

[9] Note that, for simplicity, this formulation assumes that the controller is based on output feedback, i.e.not state feedback and without precompensation.

should be noted that, in a sense, our notion of instantiation is dual to the notion of *deployment* used in DR-BIP. Instead of specifying the nodes where each component is deployed, we specify objects, which may be components or motifs, that are located in nodes. Instantiation allows us to assemble motifs hierarchically. Hence, there is no need to have multiple components deployed on the same node. Instead, they can be arranged in an intermediate motif instantiating the node in question.

Fractal [10] allows defining a component assembly by linking their interfaces. Components' interfaces can be of two types dedicated either to the component content or to its membrane (control interfaces). Control interfaces allow building controllers, namely LifeCycleController, BindingController and AttributeController for primitive components, or ContentController for composite components. Standard control interfaces provided by Fractal components make it possible to create new components, modify the content of composites by adding or removing subcomponents, and to create or remove connections between interfaces. Differently from previous works, our approach provides the model of hierarchical motifs for both system's entities and their control. Dealing with attributes becomes possible at the composite level too thanks to motif's profile and aggregation functions. It greatly contributes to a flexible controllers design for systems with layered architectures.

Even more relevant is a less known work by Jean-Bernard Stefani [36], which introduced the G-Kells framework to describe dynamic structures with sharing. According to [36], G-Kells can be understood as an outgrowth of prior work by Stefani and Di Giusto [20], where they proposed a process calculus interpretation of the BIP model. As such G-Kells, DR-BIP and the hierarchical motif framework proposed in this paper share significant strands of genetic material. One common characteristic shared by G-Kells and our current proposal is the focus on the structuring elements of the system. Indeed, both approaches avoid specifying exactly the nature of the primitive behaviours, assuming only that their semantics can be defined in terms of a certain type of LTSs. Beyond that, one of the two principal characteristics of the G-Kells framework, arguably, is sharing: a given component (location) can be simultaneously attached to several other locations (e.g., a process can be a *functional component* of a larger system all while being *hosted* by a virtual machine). Moreover, no constraints are imposed on the attachment graph, which need not even be a Directed Acyclic Graph (DAG). In contrast, our current approach relies on a tree structure. In the future, we plan to generalise the approach to DAGs, which will require addressing the issue of conflict resolution, notably w.r.t. the control theoretic aspects of our work. The other principal characteristic of G-Kells is the structure dynamicity. While already addressed in DR-BIP, we leave the dynamicity in hierarchical motifs for future work.

On Feedback Control for Software Systems. An overview on discrete-time control approaches for self-adaptive systems can be found in [15]. Control theory is a promising methodology for computing systems' (self-)adaptation [18,23]. In [33], a feedback control for both continuous-time and discrete-time cases has been related to the well-known MAPE-K loop in the framework of autonomic computing [25]. Control is then defined as a problem of restricting the uncontrolled system's behaviour, in order to enforce the desired behaviour, and avoid the undesirable one.

In [39], it is considered that MAPE addresses adaptation of software rather than physical properties or resources, whereas control theory (CT) loops are powerful at keeping some variables either at prescribed set points or within ranges, in the face of disturbances. [2] focuses on CPSs, trying to avoid that the issues in the software part affect the physical part. A safety controller is generated that a decision module can substitute to the complex controller to avoid violations of formal safety properties, in a sandboxing approach. Such a system augmentation is automatically generated thanks to reachability methods for hybrid systems. Hardware failure is not however considered. Controller synthesis for multi-agent control has recently been considered in [27], where signal temporal logic is used to express temporal behaviors of system, deriving continuous-time assume-guarantee contracts. Hierarchical organisation of systems is however not considered in this work.

In the model predictive control (MPC), the upper layer commands are fed to the lower levels adapting its behaviour when the conditions require such an action. Our work contributes to a conjecture in [39] by illustrating that in adaptive software the CT and MPC control scheme can be re-used, where the upper layer may be realized using MAPE. Finally, with relation to [26] focusing on brownout as opposed to blackout, the novelty of our approach consists in considering distributed or hierarchical control, and in handling different functionalities, i.e., in enabling a multi-variable control.

Formal Methods for Validating Control Systems. Using formal methods for designing and validating systems' controllers with the aim to guarantee their desired properties, e.g., safety properties, is not new. However, as emphasized in [17], it is hard to formally verify properties of such feedback control systems.

In this context, used formal models are often focused on discrete time control part while abstracting continuous-time dynamics, at least partially. For example, static analysis techniques used in [3] for analysing automata modeling the control structure of synchronous embedded controllers, do not address continuous-time system control. In [1], theorem provers usefully provide static sufficient conditions for ensuring desirable safety properties for the closed-loop control designs. Differently from these approaches, we integrate the dynamics of the plants together with disturbances into the motif notion, in order to control and adapt hierarchical systems.

Verification of data-driven systems' representations controlled with feedback techniques is described in [17], where neural networks (NN) are used for their modeling with the aim to enforce properties such as reachability, safety, and stability of the feedback laws. This data-driven approach is promising, however in [17], systems with a layered control structure are not dealt with.

In [28] the authors aim to establish a common language to unify the study of architecture at different spatio-temporal scales. The proposed language for layered control architectures (LCAs) allows for a form of a hierarchy of control loops. Feedback control is however only considered at the lowest level, while other layers use other decision making techniques. Unlike this work, our approach allows modeling of structured systems with controllers potentially available at each level. For LCA systems, [24] introduces a new multiclock logic (MCL) to express assume-guarantee contracts, in order to prove global stability properties of a system using the stability properties of its components. Differently from [24], we use automata-based models of components and their compositions. Our logic is used to express FOL interaction constraints among hierarchical motifs including control motifs, whereas MCL uses variables and clocks for assume-guarantee contracts at system-level and component-level verification.

In [34], the authors aim to verify properties of a broad class of continuous-time systems composed of interconnected components. The approach defines weak and strong semantics of assume-guarantee contracts for a compositional reasoning, where the week semantics is sufficient to deal with acyclic interconnections, and the strong one is required to reason on cyclic interconnections. In our framework, we aim to extend the class of the systems beyond those described by differential inclusions and invariance assume-guarantee contracts, where this strong-week semantics relationship applies.

8 Conclusion

This paper provided theoretical underpinnings to modeling both the system and its control by using hierarchical motifs with the aim to allow structured CPSs to be adaptive. More precisely, hierarchical motifs have been introduced in a control-compatible manner. We expect our paper to pave the way for the larger challenge of preserving control properties (convergence speed, transient response etc.), in addition to stability of feedback laws studied, e.g., in [17,24].

As a future work direction, we intend to consider systems with discrete state changes, so that theory of control for hybrid systems would be necessary to study the behaviour of such systems, and the preservation of properties such as stability.

Behavioural refinement is another future work direction. We intend to exploit the notions of approximate simulation relations introduced in [19] that are suitable for safety critical systems' control and its refinement. In addition, we intend to integrate the interaction logic for parameterized systems in [9], which is decidable as it can be embedded in WSkS.

Finally, the key limitation of our approach is the tree structure of the considered hierarchical models. In future work, we intend to generalise to directed acyclic graphs by adding a conflict resolution layer in front of the motif's profile. Such a generalisation would allow the modelling of dynamically reconfigurable systems, where an object has to be redeployed from one node to another in a non-atomic manner.

References

1. Aréchiga, N., Loos, S.M., Platzer, A., Krogh, B.H.: Using theorem provers to guarantee closed-loop system properties. In: 2012 American Control Conference (ACC), pp. 3573–3580 (2012). ISSN 2378-5861
2. Bak, S., Manamcheri, K., Mitra, S., Caccamo, M.: Sandboxing controllers for cyber-physical systems. In: IEEE/ACM International Conference on Cyber-Physical Systems, pp. 3–12 (2011)
3. Balakrishnan, G., Sankaranarayanan, S., Ivančić, F., Gupta, A.: Refining the control structure of loops using static analysis. In: Proceedings of the 7th ACM International Conference on Embedded software, EMSOFT 2009, pp. 49–58. ACM (2009)

4. El Ballouli, R., Bensalem, S., Bozga, M., Sifakis, J.: Programming dynamic reconfigurable systems. In: Bae, K., Csaba Olveczky, P. (eds.) Proceedings of International Conference on FACS 2018. LNCS, vol. 11222, pp. 118–136. Springer (2018)
5. Basu, A., et al.: Rigorous component-based system design using the BIP framework. IEEE Softw. **28**(3), 41–48 (2011)
6. Baude, F., et al.: GCM: a grid extension to fractal for autonomous distributed components. Ann. des Télécommunications **64**(1–2), 5–24 (2009)
7. Bliudze, S., Furic, S.: An operational semantics for hybrid systems involving behavioral abstraction. In: Proceedings of the 10th International Modelica Conference, Linköping Electronic Conference Proceedings, pp. 693–706, Linköping. Linköping University Electronic Press, Linköpings universitet (2014)
8. Bliudze, S., Furic, S., Sifakis, J., Viel, A.: Rigorous design of cyber-physical systems: Linking physicality and computation. Int. J. Softw. Syst. Model. **18**(3), 1613–1636 (2019)
9. Bozga, M., Esparza, J., Iosif, R., Sifakis, J., Welzel, C.: Structural invariants for the verification of systems with parameterized architectures. In: Biere, A., Parker, D. (eds.) Proceedings of International Conference on TACAS 2020, Part I. LNCS, vol. 12078, pp. 228–246. Springer (2020)
10. Bruneton, E., Coupaye, T., Leclercq, M., Quéma, V., Stefani, J.-B.: The fractal component model and its support in java: experiences with auto-adaptive and reconfigurable systems. Softw. Pract. Exper. **36**(11–12), 1257–1284 (2006)
11. Bures, T., Calinescu, R., Weyns, D.: Special issue on software engineering for trustworthy cyber-physical systems. J. Syst. Softw. **178**, 110972 (2021)
12. Bures, T., Hnetynka, P., Plásil, F.: SOFA 2.0: balancing advanced features in a hierarchical component model. In: Proceedings of International Conference on SERA 2006, pp. 40–48. IEEE Computer Society (2006)
13. Coullon, H., Henrio, L., Loulergue, F., Robillard, S.: Component-based distributed software reconfiguration: a verification-oriented survey. ACM Comput. Surv. **56**(1), 2:1–2:37 (2024)
14. de Lemos, R.: Software self-adaptation and industry: blame MAPE-K. In: Proceedings of International Symposium on SEAMS 2023, pp. 88–89. IEEE (2023)
15. Lemos, R., et al.: Software engineering for self-adaptive systems: research challenges in the provision of assurances. In: de Lemos, R., Garlan, D., Ghezzi, C., Giese, H. (eds.) Software Engineering for Self-Adaptive Systems III. Assurances. LNCS, vol. 9640, pp. 3–30. Springer, Cham (2017). https://doi.org/10.1007/978-3-319-74183-3_1
16. Ding, Z., Chen, Z., Liu, J.: A rigorous model of service component architecture. In: Pu, G., Stolz, V. (eds.) Proceedings of International Workshop TTSS 2007. ENTCS, vol. 207, pp. 33–48. Elsevier (2007)
17. Dutta, S., Jha, S., Sankaranarayanan, S., Tiwari, A.: Learning and verification of feedback control systems using feedforward neural networks. IFAC-PapersOnLine **51**(16), 151–156 (2018)
18. Filieri, A., et al.: Software engineering meets control theory. In: Proceedings of IEEE/ACM International Symposium on Software Engineering for Adaptive and Self-Managing Systems, pp. 71–82. IEEE (2015)
19. Girard, A., Pappas, G.J.: Hierarchical control using approximate simulation relations. In: Proceedings of the 45th IEEE Conference on Decision and Control, pp. 264–269 (2006)
20. Giusto, C., Stefani, J.-B.: Revisiting glue expressiveness in component-based systems. In: De Meuter, W., Roman, G.-C. (eds.) COORDINATION 2011. LNCS, vol. 6721, pp. 16–30. Springer, Heidelberg (2011). https://doi.org/10.1007/978-3-642-21464-6_2
21. Hazyuk, I., Ghiaus, C., Penhouet, D.: Optimal temperature control of intermittently heated buildings using model predictive control: Part I - Building modeling. Build. Environ. **51**, 379–387 (2012)

22. Hazyuk, I., Ghiaus, C., Penhouet, D.: Optimal temperature control of intermittently heated buildings using model predictive control: Part II – Control algorithm. Build. Environ. **51**, 388–394 (2012)
23. Hellerstein, J.L., Diao, Y., Parekh, S., Tilbury, D.M.: Feedback Control of Computing Systems. Wiley (2004)
24. Incer, I., Csomay-Shanklin, N., Ames, A.D., Murray, R.M.: Layered control systems operating on multiple clocks. IEEE Control Syst. Lett. **8**, 1211–1216 (2024)
25. Kephart, J.O., Chess, D.M.: The vision of autonomic computing. Computer **36**(1), 41–50 (2003)
26. Klein, C., Maggio, M., Årzén, K.-E., Hernández-Rodriguez, F.: Brownout: building more robust cloud applications. In: Jalote, P., Briand, L.C., van der Hoek, A. (eds.) Proceedings of International Conference on ICSE 2014, pp. 700–711. ACM (2014)
27. Liu, S., Saoud, A., Dimarogonas, D.V.: Controller synthesis of collaborative signal temporal logic tasks for multi-agent systems via assume-guarantee contracts. IEEE Trans. Autom. Control 1–16 (2025)
28. Matni, N., Ames, A.D., Doyle, J.C.: A quantitative framework for layered multirate control: toward a theory of control architecture. IEEE Control Syst. Mag. **44**(3), 52–94 (2024)
29. Moroşan, P.-D., Bourdais, R., Dumur, D., Buisson, J.: Building temperature regulation using a distributed model predictive control. Energy Build. **42**(9), 1445–1452 (2010)
30. National Institute of Standards and Technology (NIST, USA). Framework for cyber-physical systems (special publication 1500-201) (2017)
31. Oquendo, F.: pi-ADL: an architecture description language based on the higher-order typed pi-calculus for specifying dynamic and mobile software architectures. ACM SIGSOFT Softw. Eng. Notes **29**(3), 1–14 (2004)
32. Plotkin, G.D.: A structural approach to operational semantics. Technical Report DAIMI FN-19, University of Aarhus (1981)
33. Rutten, E., Marchand, N., Simon, D.: Feedback control as MAPE-K loop in autonomic computing. In: de Lemos, R., Garlan, D., Ghezzi, C., Giese, H. (eds.) Software Engineering for Self-Adaptive Systems III. Assurances. LNCS, vol. 9640, pp. 349–373. Springer, Cham (2017). https://doi.org/10.1007/978-3-319-74183-3_12
34. Saoud, A., Girard, A., Fribourg, L.: Assume-guarantee contracts for continuous-time systems. Automatica **134**, 1–13, Article 109910 (2021)
35. Shevtsov, S., Berekmeri, M., Weyns, D., Maggio, M.: Control-theoretical software adaptation: a systematic literature review. IEEE Trans. Software Eng. **44**(8), 784–810 (2018)
36. Stefani, J.-B.: Components as location graphs. In: Revised Selected Papers of the 11th International Symposium on Formal Aspects of Component Software (FACS 2014). LNCS, vol. 8997, pp. 3–23. Springer (2014)
37. Taylor, R.N., et al.: A component- and message-based architectural style for GUI software. IEEE Trans. Software Eng. **22**(6), 390–406 (1996)
38. Weyns, D.: Software Engineering of Self-adaptive Systems. In: Cha, S., Taylor, R., Kang, K. (eds.) Handbook of Software Engineering, pp. 399–443. Springer, Cham (2019). https://doi.org/10.1007/978-3-030-00262-6_11
39. Weyns, D., et al.: Towards better adaptive systems by combining MAPE, control theory, and machine learning. In: Proceedings of International Symposium SEAMS@ICSE 2021, pp. 217–223. IEEE (2021)

Applications

Reversible Computation *vs.* Runtime Adaptation in Industrial IoT Systems

Duncan Paul Attard, Keith Bugeja, Adrian Francalanza(✉), Marietta Galea, Gerard Tabone, and Gianluca Zahra

University of Malta, Msida, Malta
{duncan.attard,keith.bugeja,adrian.francalanza,marietta.galea,
gerard.tabone,gianluca.zahra.16}@um.edu.mt

Abstract. This paper presents a comparative study between two software engineering techniques, reversible computation and runtime adaptation, in the context of industrial IoT. We frame our comparison around a representative Industry 5.0 shop floor case study that focuses on the high-precision manufacturing of integrated circuits. The case study identifies four error scenarios that can arise in typical shop floor operations and evaluates how reversible computation and runtime adaptation address them, highlighting the strengths and limitations of each approach.

Keywords: reversible computation · runtime adaptation · industrial IoT · industry automation

1 Introduction

Industrial automation has seen significant recent advancements, driven by the robotisation developments of Industry 4.0 [48], and further extended to collaborative robots (or *cobots*) under Industry 5.0 [29]. These advancements have made production automation increasingly accessible to small and medium-sized enterprises (SMEs). This uptake has enabled production automation in low-volume and small-batch manufacturing, sectors that were previously considered beyond the reach of such technologies [28,78]. Indeed, achieving lean small-batch manufacturing through automated production is now considered central to the future of industrial development and competitiveness, particularly in high-precision and safety-critical domains [8], *e.g.*, microelectronics, automotive, and aerospace.

Industrial IoT (IIoT) plays a central role in enabling the *sensor-driven* infrastructure underpinning Industry 4.0 and 5.0 [9,63]. It facilitates real-time monitoring and control in robotised environments, where safety-critical feedback mechanisms govern human-robot interaction [11]. *Robotisation* fundamentally relies on the digitisation of the physical factory shop floor and assembly line. This process is typically governed by two requirements [11,64]:

Funded by the IPCEI-UM (No: E24LO17-01) project under Malta Enterprise.

Automation robustness requires robotised manufacturing to anticipate, detect and avert uncertainties, errors, and abnormalities. Not meeting these conditions could lead to equipment damage, production defects, and in the case of cobots, human injuries and fatalities.

Automation flexibility requires manufacturing robots to be resilient to errors and unexpected situations. As much as possible, production should remain uninterrupted in order to reap the benefits of automation and maximise production gains.

There are various approaches that are used to attain high levels of automation robustness and flexibility [62]. At one end of the spectrum, *static* solutions augment the digital models of shop floors and assembly lines. Static solutions incorporate uncertainty and error occurrences via techniques such as Monte Carlo simulations [18] and machine learning [41]. The latter offline error prediction techniques then permit the design of robust production processes that tolerate uncertainty [23,52]. However, static approaches are still susceptible to break down whenever unexpected errors fall outside predicted scenarios [64]. In addition, static solutions often require vast amounts of resources to model all eventualities and work adequately (*e.g.* data gathered for machine learning purposes and computational power required to analyse the data). These prohibitive upfront costs can render them beyond the reach of SMEs [59]. At the other end of the spectrum are the sensor-based *dynamic* approaches, where set-ups such as vision-based control systems [71,87], often fused with other sensory inputs *e.g.* LiDARs, provide greater automation flexibility in handling uncertainty through dynamic intervention [27]. Yet, this enhanced flexibility comes at a higher cost, such as, installing additional (expensive) high-precision sensors [73,85], which can be prohibitive to many SMEs. Additionally, the runtime computational overhead required may exceed the capabilities of the robot hardware, where determining the right course of action on-the-fly under tight latency constraints may be intractable [59]. Due to these constraints, full-blown dynamic techniques might ultimately resort to more standard graceful degradation approaches [33] for a number of situations.

There are other techniques that strike a balance between static and dynamic approaches to maintain cost-efficiency, thereby extending production automation to a wider range of enterprises. At the same time, these techniques incorporate static information about the shop floor digital model to alleviate the need for high-precision hardware and minimise the runtime computation needed to effect interventions in a timely and precise manner [59]. Runtime Monitoring [17,37] and Reversible Computing [54,75] are two prominent techniques with these characteristics. This paper compares these two approaches in order to understand their commonalities, relative advantages, and limitations. We also investigate how the two techniques can be used to benefit one another. This comparison is given in the context of a representative Industry 5.0 high-precision shop floor case study that manufactures integrated circuits (ICs).

The paper is structured as follows. Section 2 outlines the main characteristics of our shop floor case study, and Sect. 3 summarises the key elements of the runtime monitoring and reversibility techniques. Section 4 considers a selection of error situations that may arise in our shop floor case study and argues how these can be handled by the respective techniques. It also discusses how the two approaches can be combined to leverage their complementary strengths. Section 5 concludes. Our survey does not assume prior knowledge of the aforementioned software engineering techniques. Familiarity with industrial IoT and the challenges in Industry 4.0 and 5.0 is beneficial.

2 Industry 5.0 Factory Shop Floors

Industry 4.0 and 5.0 smart factories comprise fast-paced shop floors where self-driving vehicles and other machinery need to adapt to dynamic changes in real-time. Autonomous mobile robots (AMRs) meet this need by using various sensing devices, *e.g.* cameras, LiDARs, and inertial measurement units [77], to perceive their surroundings, plan optimal navigation routes, and execute real-time obstacle avoidance.

The fleet management system (FMS), or *fleet manager*, coordinates the interaction between different machines on a shop floor, *e.g.* AMRs, high-precision machines, and conveyor systems [43]. It acts as a central coordinator for route planning, movement synchronisation, task assignment, *etc.*, by issuing high-level commands to machines. For instance, the command *'move from A to B via waypoints $1, 2, 3$'* plans the route of an AMR between two stations; *'wait at waypoint 3 until the docking station at A becomes unoccupied'* synchronises its movement w.r.t. other machines; and *'pick up object at A'* tasks the AMR with moving objects around the shop floor. A machine interprets fleet manager commands via its onboard planning module that decomposes them into a detailed motion plan. The plan is subsequently converted into fine-grained control instructions, *e.g.* joint trajectories and velocity profiles, and fed to the motion controller, which manages machine actuators in real-time via continuous feedback loops. Modern FMSs function as coordinating hubs that expose APIs to enable integration with external systems, *e.g.* manufacturing execution systems (MESs), quality control, and digital twin platforms. These APIs offer capabilities such as robot coordination, task assignment, and real-time monitoring of mobile robots.

The diagnostics exposed by the FMS APIs may not always offer sufficient capabilities to external supervision systems wanting to provide added robustness, automation flexibility, quality control, and human safety on top of existing functionality. IIoT systems can be deployed as an *overlay network* [81] of bespoke devices attached to the FMS and factory shop floor equipment to collect specific or high-precision data about machinery and its operating environment. For instance, LiDAR sensors affixed to an AMR base can establish equipment safety perimeters; vibration sensors mounted on a robotic arm can detect excessive force during pick-and-place operations; and particulate sensors can reveal increased risks of contamination in sensitive industrial processes. Integrating sensor data through fusion algorithms enhances operational awareness by providing a multi-faceted view of system behaviour. This can enable faster anomaly detection and more informed, context-aware decision-making [80]. Section 4 describes an external MES that manages the operation of a factory shop floor model (see Sect. 2.1) via a conceptual FMS API and IIoT sensor network overlay.

Factory shop floor designs follow one of three approaches [43]. The *fully-autonomous* approach relegates the fleet manager to a monitoring capacity. Each machine has a *local* planner that plans its routes between stations and resolves conflicts (*e.g.* movement synchronisation, collision avoidance) with other machines [30]. In the *semi-autonomous* approach, machines offload the route planning onto the fleet manager to optimise the overall movement across the shop floor but retain their conflict resolution capability [36]. The *centralised* approach utilises the FMS fully [20]. It computes a *global* route plan for every machine, inherently avoiding conflicts and streamlining navigation on the shop floor. This centralised approach relieves individual machines from autonomous decision-making but comes at the cost of additional computational and communication overhead when dynamic changes in the environment (*e.g.* unforeseen obstacles) oblige the FMS to recompute all routes.

2.1 Integrated Circuit Manufacturing Model

We focus on a subclass of Industry 5.0 manufacturing plants that specialise in automotive-grade ICs, MEMS, and microcontrollers, *e.g.* [72,79,82]. A plant receives wafers containing thousands of ICs for assembly, testing, and packaging. The process begins with wafer dicing, where each chip (or *die*) is separated from the wafer. After dicing, dies are individually mounted onto a package substrate using a die attach material, such as epoxy or solder. This is followed by wire or flip-chip *bonding*, which establishes electrical connections between the die and package substrate wiring. The chip is then *encased* in protective housing, *e.g.* epoxy moulding compound (EMC), to shield it from mechanical damage, moisture, and other contaminants, while also permitting efficient heat dissipation. Lastly, the encapsulated ICs undergo *deflashing* to remove the thin layer of excess epoxy that can bleed between connections during the die encasing process.

Figure 1 depicts a fragment of the manufacturing process described above for a particular shop floor [69]. It consists of *high-precision* machines that perform the final steps of the process, namely wire bonding, EMC die encasing, and deflashing. Stockers are specialised clean storage units that accommodate *die trays* containing batches of dies in various stages of completion. High-precision machines and Stockers have docking stations, which are designated interfaces where die trays are deposited for processing and retrieved after completion. Mobile manipulators (MMs), which are hybrid machines comprising a robotic arm for picking die trays mounted on an AMR base, transport die trays between the high-precision machines and stockers. The FMS orchestrates the operation of the entire shop floor, adopting the centralised approach as described in Sect. 2. Human intervention on the shop floor is limited to specific tasks, such as material handling and replenishment, quality control and inspection, and machine servicing and fault repair. Figure 1 shows machines outfitted with IoT sensors. This use case employs (i) *LiDAR* sensors affixed to MM bases to establish safety

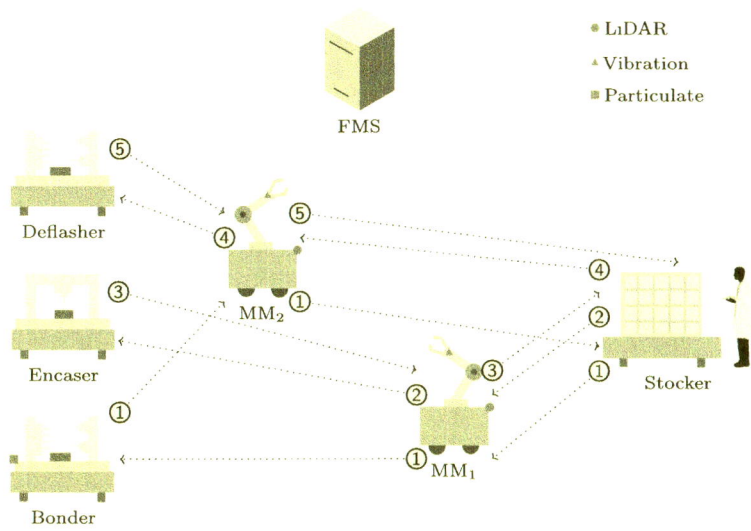

Fig. 1. A typical factory shop floor at an IC manufacturing plant

perimeters around human operators; (ii) *vibration* sensors mounted on robotic arm grippers to detect excessive force during pick-and-place manoeuvres; and (iii) *particulate* sensors to monitor airborne contamination on the shop floor.

Example 1. Figure 1 captures one hypothetical workflow computed by the FMS:

① (a) MM_1 picks a tray of diced dies from the Stocker and delivers it to the Bonder.
① (b) *Simultaneously*, MM_2 retrieves a tray of bonded dies from the Bonder and deposits it into the Stocker.
② MM_1 picks the die tray handled by MM_2 in step ① from the Stocker and delivers it to the Encaser.
③ MM_1 retrieves the processed tray of encased dies from the Encaser and deposits it into the Stocker.
④ MM_2 picks the die tray handled by MM_1 in step ③ from the Stocker and delivers it to the Deflasher.
⑤ MM_2 picks the processed tray of deflashed dies and deposits it into the Stocker. ∎

3 Techniques for Modifying System Behaviour at Runtime

In a non-automated factory shop floor, it is routine for human operators to either report issues or intervene as they arise. Simply replacing humans with their corresponding automated production equivalent robs the shop floor of this implicit but essential supervision. Thus, to attain an automated shop floor with functionality comparable to the non-automated one, one also needs *automated issue detection and remediation*. Section 1 argues that IIoT systems, such as those described in Sect. 2, are often hard to model fully (*e.g.* due to partial knowledge about the environment or phenomena, such as dust particles, that are too complex to model) or maintain continually (*e.g.* prototype refinement over iterations). More critically, certain system attributes cannot be *analysed* (*e.g.* profiling [42]) or *modified* (*e.g.* restarting failed components [53]) unless the system is running. Runtime monitoring and reversible computation are two techniques that enable the runtime analysis and modification of IIoT systems such as the one presented in Fig. 1.

3.1 Runtime Monitoring and Adaptation

Runtime monitoring (RM) is a family of dynamic analysis techniques [17,40]. It uses *monitors*: machines that incrementally analyse a *finite* prefix of the *execution* (or *trace*) exhibited by the system under scrutiny (SuS) to check whether its behaviour meets prescribed criteria. In RM, these criteria take the form of correctness *properties* [3,4], often expressed in high-level formalisms such as temporal logics [13,17]. Properties encode *prior* knowledge about the SuS as correct behaviour that the system is expected to exhibit. Monitors are synthesised from correctness properties (*e.g.* see [2,12,14,70]) and *instrumented* with the SuS to gather trace events (*e.g.* sensor data) during execution. The resulting set-up captures an *unfolding* model of the SuS [5] compared to full (or complete) models used in techniques such as Model Checking [47].

RM is well-suited to IIoT scenarios where human supervision is *impractical*, *e.g.* cognitive fatigue [84] or continuous manual oversight and intervention [51], or *infeasible*, *e.g.* autonomous warehouses [16] or lights-out manufacturing [74]. It can analyse black-box (proprietary) components (*e.g.* AMRs) without needing access to their internals. Moreover, IIoT systems encompass aspects, such as mechanical wear and tear or human negligence, that are complex to predict and model statically. More importantly, control software often needs to intervene in the execution of the cyber-physical processes (in case of safety violations).

There are two main RM intervention methods [25,35]. Runtime enforcement (RE) ensures the execution of the SuS meets correctness properties [6,7]. Enforcement monitors take *preventive* action, steering the operation of the system within the bounds of properties' specifications. RE assumes the SuS to be highly instrumentable, as monitors must enforce its execution continually. This prerequisite is often too stringent for IIoT systems comprising black-box or proprietary components. Runtime adaptation (RA) is a less stringent alternative to RE. RA takes remedial actions (also called adaptations) *after* monitors detect violations to a correctness property [24,49]. This RM variant is less invasive than RE since it does not need to instrument the SuS to the same degree. Adaptation monitors aim to *restore* the SuS to a *good state* from where the intended execution can potentially continue. This fits the black-box nature of industrial machines (such as the ones of Fig. 1) since monitors reason about and react to the *observable behaviour* of components rather than their internal states. Moreover, since monitor and system components can run in *isolation* [5,15,40], RA can offer better safeguards against inadvertently affecting the SuS execution.

RA relies on two forms of prior knowledge on the SuS. The first is an abstract notion of states the SuS can be in, together with a set of observable *events* that capture the transitions between these states. The second kind of SuS knowledge assumed is the correctness behaviour defined over these states, defined in terms of either execution graphs or traces labelled by events. The latter identify a range of states that should *not* be reached during execution, and trigger adaptation monitors to administer *predetermined* remedial actions to steer the SuS back to a non-violating state. Note that the state reached following a series of remedial actions need not be a state visited prior to the violation. For instance, an AMR that ends up off-track on the shop floor can be directed back to its starting point by a RA, but an AMR that develops a mechanical fault may need to be powered off, which constitutes an *unvisited* state that permits graceful degradation without compromising safety.

3.2 Reversible Computation

Reversible computation (RC) is a software engineering paradigm where computations are partitioned as either executing *forwards* or *backwards* [10,75]. This technique allows program executions to be undone whenever a number of backward computation steps are the reverse of forward steps, providing an *efficient* mechanism for error recovery and fault-tolerance. RC was originally motivated by the need for low-energy computing and heat dissipation reduction [56]. It has since been applied to other areas, including programming languages [46,86] and debugging [34,45,55], modelling and algorithm design [19,31,32,54,65,66], as well as to robotics [61,62]. In IIoT settings such as the one outlined in Fig. 1, RC is useful because many physical operations have a natural (or *direct*) reverse counterpart that undoes the effect of the original operation, *e.g.* a MM moving to the left by one unit can be reversed by moving to the right by the same unit. This provides an opportunity to create a layer of abstraction that facilitates programming and enables code reuse. The relationship between forward operations and their reversible counterpart is not always direct, particularly in cases where operations have external dependencies or side effects. In such cases, reversibility may be achieved by traversing reversible computational paths that differ from the original computation. One way to achieve this *indirect* reversibility makes use of checkpoints [38,57,68,83] that allow systems to rollback to a known reversible state, or else, by explicitly creating separate functions that perform the reverse operations. In some cases, auxiliary mechanisms (*e.g.*, memory for execution histories) are employed to reconstruct past states and enable reversibility [21,60,67]. Operations that cannot be directly or indirectly reversed are considered *irreversible* [62].

The above concepts extend naturally to industrial automation settings, such as the factory shop floor discussed in Sect. 2, where computation corresponds to sequences of physical actions [62]. Every operation has its own reversibility characteristics defined by its intrinsic nature and its effect on the shop floor workflow. Some operations are directly reversible due to their confined side effect on other entities on the shop floor, such as a MM retracing its path or recharging the MM batteries. Others require indirect reversal. For example, a MM pushing a batch into a Stocker must instead grasp the batch before pulling it back. Picking the last die from the Stocker in Fig. 1 is also indirectly reversible when the resulting empty Stocker affects the operation of the other MMs. This is the case since in addition to returning the die to the Stocker, reversing the operation needs to inform the other MMs that the Stocker is no longer empty. There are also operations like soldering or gluing, which are inherently irreversible because there are no obvious recovery operations that apply. A RC framework may also lift the terms directly reversible, indirectly reversible, and irreversible to *strategies*. Strategies are defined as sequences of operations. A strategy is a *forward* strategy when it consists exclusively of forward operations; backward strategies are defined analogously. Forward strategies are reversible whenever there exists a backward strategy that restores the computation to the original state. A forward strategy is *directly reversible* when its backward strategy is composed of the inverse of its forward operations in reverse order. Conversely, an *indirectly* reversible strategy is one where its backward strategy does not satisfy the above condition [61,62].

3.3 RA and RC Side-by-Side

There are a few key distinguishing aspects of RA, discussed in Sect. 3.1, and RC, discussed in Sect. 3.2. The first one lies in how error states are defined and handled. In RC, there is a fixed delineation between good and error states, where backward computation is triggered only when the program transitions to an error state [58]. By contrast, error states in RA are captured implicitly by the correctness property being considered: an erroneous state for one property may be a good state for a different property. In certain cases, RA and RC may converge when a particular state is inherently erroneous for any correctness property (*e.g.* a damaged robotic arm). A second, but related, differentiating aspect is that correct behaviour is more explicit in RA, formally stated in terms of a (declarative) specification logic [37]. These specifications then permit the automated synthesis of the (algorithmic) runtime adaptation procedure in terms of monitors. The expected correct behaviour is typically left implicit in the case of RC. Leaving this expected behaviour implicit rules out the possibility of applying automated program synthesis techniques, where the reversible program generally needs to be hand-coded by the software engineer. The third distinguishing feature is that in RC, reversible operations *guarantee* a return to a specific previous state in the (forward) computation or an equivalent state for some notion of state equivalence [10,32,60], *e.g.* causal-consistent reversibility where two states are equivalent modulo the order of concurrent actions [59]. RA offers no such guarantees. This permits the formulation of trial-and-error repetition strategies to deal with unpredictable (minor) variations or extraneous conditions on the shop floor that are not captured via high-precision sensors. For

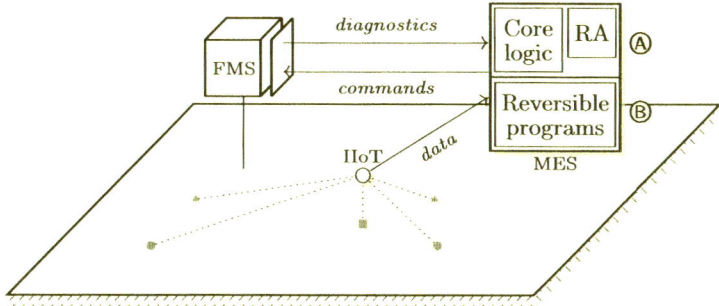

Fig. 2. MES monitoring and controlling shop floor via FMS and IIoT sensor network.

example, a MM that misses the docking station when moving forward (possibly due to tiny obstructing objects), can be reattempted after moving backwards. This reduces reliance on manual tuning and calibration to handle special cases, thereby improving the efficiency and adaptability of automated production lines. In practice, repetition strategies are limited. For example, a MM retracing the same route consumes battery power and contributes to mechanical wear, making unbounded repeated attempts costly and unsustainable. Such operations are considered *partially repeatable*, as they can only be performed a limited number of times. Schultz et al. [76] address this by introducing upper bounds on repetitions, for instance by associating retries with a finite number of tokens, enabling more predictable and resource-aware reversible strategies.

4 Recovering from Issues on the Factory Shop Floor

Human safety, error recovery, and graceful degradation are critical concerns in Industry 4.0 and 5.0 systems. We study how RA and RC from Sect. 3 can be used to address these challenges via a selection of scenarios describing potential issues that could arise in the factory shop floor model presented in Sect. 2.1.

4.1 Target Architecture

Our shop floor is managed by one MES that orchestrates the movement of MMs and coordinates the high-precision machines and Stocker operations through the FMS. Figure 2 depicts this centralised set-up. The MES receives diagnostic information from the FMS API, e.g. $\mathsf{blok}(\mathsf{dev} = \mathsf{MM}_1, \mathsf{at} = \mathsf{Stocker})$, and issues commands in response, e.g. $\mathsf{move}(\mathsf{dev} = \mathsf{MM}_1, \mathsf{from} = \mathsf{Stocker}, \mathsf{to} = \mathsf{Bonder}, \mathsf{waypts} = [1,2,3])$, which the FMS relays to machines on the shop floor. Our MES supplements FMS diagnostics by LiDAR, vibration, and particulate sensor data collected through the IIoT network deployed on the shop floor, e.g. $\mathsf{vibr}(\mathsf{dev} = \mathsf{MM}_1, \mathsf{amt} = 5)$.

Figure 2 illustrates two alternative methods of implementing the MES. Method Ⓐ implements the MES using *conventional* programs instrumented with

RA monitors, whereas method Ⓑ implements the MES as *reversible* programs. RA induces a *separation-of-concerns*, delineating the core program logic that handles normal-case operation and the RA monitor control flow, which intervenes when unexpected conditions arise [26]. By comparison, RC integrates the core logic and the error-handling mechanisms within a *single* program. Props. P_1 to P_4 in Sect. 4.2 showcase how remedial interventions can be implemented in terms of the RA and RC paradigms.

4.2 RA and RC for Handling Runtime Errors

Blocked Docking Station. Recall that in Fig. 1, each high-precision machine and Stocker own a designated docking station where MMs can deposit or pick up ICs. MMs are equipped with LiDAR modules to perceive and map the environment in real-time. Machine docking stations must be unobstructed for a MM to dock successfully. One property we want to hold is:

$$\text{`MMs never block when entering a docking station.'} \qquad (P_1)$$

Suppose the shop floor executes step ① from Sect. 2.1. The MES starts by issuing a pick command to the FMS, instructing MM_2 to lift the tray of bonded dies from the Bonder, *i.e.*, pick(dev = MM_2, from = Bonder, obj = Bonded_Dies). Subsequently, the FMS relays a second MES command to MM_2 to move the machine from the Bonder to the Stocker via specific waypoints, move(dev = MM_2, from = Bonder, to = Stocker, waypts = [1,2,3]). If the LiDAR on MM_2 detects obstructions at the Stocker docking station, it transmits the data lidr(dev = MM_2, dst = 0.1) to the MES. Since MM_2 is unable to dock, the FMS also sends the blok(dev = MM_2, at = Stocker) signal to the MES. Both lidr and blok enable the MES to detect a violation of prop. P_1.

Runtime Adaptation. To remedy the violation of prop. P_1, the MES RA monitor would instruct MM_2 to return to the Bonder via the command:

$$\text{move(dev} = MM_2, \text{from} = \text{Stocker}, \text{to} = \text{Bonder}, \text{waypts} = [3,2,1]). \qquad (1)$$

To promote *automation flexibility* (see Sect. 1) and minimise blockage on the factory shop floor, the RA monitor could also redirect MM_2 to deposit the bonded ICs at a second Stocker, if available. This manoeuvre is expressed as the command move(dev = MM_2, from = Stocker, to = Stocker′, waypts = [3,4,5]).

Reversible Computation. Forward computation comprises the operation sequence:

$$\text{pick(dev} = MM_2, \text{from} = \text{Bonder}, \text{obj} = \text{Bonded\_Dies}); \qquad (2)$$
$$\text{move(dev} = MM_2, \text{from} = \text{Bonder}, \text{to} = \text{Stocker}, \text{waypts} = [1,2,3]) \qquad (3)$$

When the MES receives the signal blok(dev = MM_2, at = Stocker) from the FMS, the system transitions to an error state. This triggers the RC program on the MES to perform the backward computation for op. (3) and reverse the system to a good state. Op. (1) is the *direct inverse* of the forward computation 3, which takes MM_2 back to the Bonder along the reverse waypoints 3, 2, 1.

Note that RC *reverses* the system to a previous good state, while RA reverts to a good state that need not be the previous one. In this instance, RA offers more flexibility since it permits the MM to deposit ICs at a different Stocker.

Damaged Dies. Recall steps ①, ③ and ⑤ from Sect. 2.1 where MMs are tasked with fetching batches of dies from and depositing them to Stockers. Dies are highly sensitive and slight mishandling, *e.g.*, sudden jolts during transport, can render them defective. Although in such cases testing can be performed to assess whether dies are damaged, it is often cheaper and easier to discard suspect dies in practice. To detect potential damage, vibration sensors are mounted on MM chassis and arm grippers. The following property safeguards the integrity of dies:

$$\text{'High-precision machines never receive trays with damaged dies.'} \quad (\text{P}_2)$$

Suppose a gripper vibration sensor reports values above a predefined threshold (say, 3 units) to the MES:

$$\text{vibr}(\text{dev} = MM_1, \text{amt} = 5) \quad (4)$$

At this point, we assume that the batch of dies in transit is likely damaged, in which case an error state is reached.

Runtime Adaptation. A RA-driven MES can discard the potentially damaged batch of dies at a designated disposal unit, *e.g.* by issuing the operation sequence

$$\text{move}(\text{dev} = MM_1, \text{from} = \text{Current}, \text{to} = \text{Disposal\_Unit}, \text{waypts} = [5,6]); \quad (5)$$
$$\text{plce}(\text{dev} = MM_1, \text{to} = \text{Disposal\_Unit}, \text{obj} = \text{Dies}) \quad (6)$$

and instruct the MM to fetch a fresh batch from the Stocker.

Reversible Computation. The sequence of ops. (4) to (6) can be viewed as a RC. The forward computation consists of MM_1 transporting a batch of dies to the high-precision machine. Upon detecting a problem, signalled by op. (4), the MES instructs MM_1 to discard the potentially faulty batch, ops. (5) and (6). Discarding the batch reverses the effect of the error. This strategy is *indirectly reversible*, since a good state (*i.e.*, a high-precision machine receiving functional dies) is reached via a series of operations rather than via one inverse operation. We remark that since the batch of remaining functional dies in the Stocker is necessarily limited, this reverse strategy is also *partially repeatable*.

Damaged Robotic Arm. Robotic arm damage, *e.g.* human or other equipment colliding with the arm, can be indirectly detected through the MM vibration sensors mentioned earlier. The next property captures this requirement:

$$\text{`Robot arm vibration levels never exceed 50.'} \qquad (\text{P}_3)$$

Suppose MM_2 in Fig. 1 experiences a collision in step ④ whilst executing the FMS command move(dev = MM_2, from = Stocker, to = Deflasher, waypts = [1,4,7]). The vibration sensor signals the MES, vibr(dev = MM_2, amt = 100), which triggers a violation of the prop. 3.

Runtime Adaptation. A RA monitor that flags this violation can decommission the affected MM by instructing it to return to the repair bay, *e.g.*, move(dev = MM_2, from = Current, to = Repair_Bay, waypts = [2,3]). The MES can then reassign the pending tasks of MM_2 to other MMs in the fleet, and optionally, notify a technician on the shop floor to assess the damage. The following operation sequence is a hypothetical adaptation the MES initiates via the FMS to reassign the affected task to MM_1.

pick(dev = MM_1, from = Stocker, obj = Encased_Dies);
move(dev = MM_1, from = Stocker, to = Deflasher, waypts = [6,3,1])

Reversible Computation. Damage to the robotic arm is irreversible since the MES cannot restore MM_2 to an operational state using a backward computation.

Degraded Air Quality. Industrial environments can generate particulate matter from physical processes, *e.g.*, wafer dicing and IC deflashing (see Sect. 2.1), foot traffic, *etc.* This can damage the assembly of ICs, and in higher amounts, degrades sensor accuracy and endangers human health [44]. For instance, an ISO Class 5 cleanroom according to ISO 14644-1 allows a maximum of 3,520 particles/m^3 that are $0.5\,\mu m$ in size or larger [1]. Our shop floor of Fig. 1 is equipped with particulate sensors that monitor air quality and report readings to the MES via the IIoT network. The shop floor is also outfitted with high efficiency particulate air (HEPA) filters to purify the air when required. A property that ensures cleanroom air quality levels is:

$$\text{`Particulate matter levels never exceed 3,520.'} \qquad (\text{P}_4)$$

Particulate sensors sample the air quality at the end of every workflow round, *i.e.*, after all MMs have completed their tasks and return to their respective docking stations. Suppose that at the termination of one such round, *e.g.* step ⑤ of ex. 1, the particulate sensor detects degraded air quality and transmits the reading part(amt = 5001) to the MES, which violates prop. P_4.

Runtime Adaptation. The RA monitor for prop. P_4 can trigger a recovery procedure that activates the HEPA filtration system to purify the air

$$\text{hepa(spdlvl = 5, duration = 10)}; \qquad (7)$$

and instructs MMs to execute wheel-cleaning routines at designated adhesive cleaning zones

move(dev = MM_1, from = Stocker, to = Adhesive_Zone, waypts = [2,4,6]); (8)

move(dev = MM_2, from = Deflasher, to = Adhesive_Zone, waypts = [1,6]) (9)

Reversible Computation. The handling of a violation of prop. P_4 is not a directly reversible RC operation. In fact, reversing the MMs to their original position on the shop floor (*e.g.*, reroute MM_1 back to the Stocker in step ①) does not restore the air quality, since this is a by-product of the physical production process. Activating the HEPA filtration system, however, *indirectly reverses* the system to a state of optimal air quality. More generally, restoring the air quality may require repeated activations of the filtration system, *e.g.* performing op. (7) twice, until a safe air quality level is reached. Lastly, if our notion of reversing the system to a previous good state includes the MM wheel-cleaning procedure, the indirect reversal strategy can be extended to include the ops. (8) and (9). Notably, the reversal ops. (8) and (9), together with op. (7) can be executed concurrently. This appears to contrast with previous assumptions about reversibility strategies necessarily being structured as sequences of operations, and suggests the application of more elaborate reversibility theories [32,59,65] to IIoT, *e.g.* approaches such as [22] that allow for concurrent compensation actions.

4.3 RA and RC Complementarity

RA and RC can be viewed as *complementary* software design principles. It is possible to implement RA properties using *only* the reversible operations in a reversible programming language: props. P_1 and P_2 in Sect. 4.2 are instances of this approach. Conversely, RC can be engineered in terms of RA, where adaptation actions encapsulate the *ad hoc* implementation logic that corresponds to high-level reversible operations, *e.g.* see discussion on prop. P_4. Other examples of the latter view include recent work [26,38,39], which proposes reversibility for reliable and fault-tolerant message-passing concurrency via choreographed RA monitors. We discuss other aspects of RA and RC next.

Reversible Programs via RA. Categorising operations and strategies as (i) *directly reversible*, *i.e.*, invertible and can be reversed automatically, (ii) *indirectly reversible*, *i.e.*, requires a manually-defined reverse possibly consisting of multiple operations, or (iii) *irreversible*, enables compilers to provide *static* guarantees about reversible programs [62]. Writing reversible programs requires explicit reasoning about *forward* and *backward* computations layered over implicit notions of good and error states. Reasoning about such programs may be challenging, as the logic for correct behaviour and error mitigation is embedded directly in the code. RA can alleviate this burden by *decoupling* the monolithic program logic that intertwines forward and backward system computation. Much like aspect-oriented programming in mainstream languages [50], this approach treats reversibility as a *cross-cutting* concern. It structures reversible programs into two parts: forward-computation (executable) code and declarative high-level RA properties whose adaptation actions capture the backward-computation logic of the program *exclusively* through reversible operations. Once RA synthesises properties into executable monitor code, it *weaves* it with the forward-computation program code to generate the complete reversible program. This two-stage approach to generating reversible programs through RA has three benefits. First, it simplifies program reasoning by separating the forward- and backward-computation logic, and automating the generation of the completed reversible program. Second, backward-computation code can be further decomposed into fine-grained RA actions that are layered around the core forward-computation logic, improving modularity and enabling incremental development. The last crucial benefit is that by limiting RA actions to reversible operations inherits the static guarantees enjoyed by the RC programming language.

Combining RA with Reversibility. Irreversible RC strategies cannot revert a system to a previous good state. RA is not bound by these all-or-nothing reversibility constraints. This makes RA applicable to cases where *partial recovery* is sufficient to achieve graceful degradation and uphold automation flexibility outlined, *e.g.* prop. 3 in Sect. 4.2. RA can still benefit from reversible operations and the static guarantees they bring about. This can be obtained at two different levels. The first method organises RA properties where *each* property expresses its remedial procedure using either *ad hoc* logic *or* reversible operations. The second method mixes both *ad hoc* logic and reversible operations within the same RA property. For instance, the remedial RA actions that uphold prop. 3 in Sect. 4.2 instruct MM_2 to return to its base. The 'returning to base' operation may need to be reversed if the base of MM_2 is blocked, and this part of the property can easily be expressed using reversible operations (see prop. P_1). However, reassigning pending tasks via the fleet manager in prop. 3 is not a backward computation, and this latter segment of the remedial action can be easily expressed using *ad hoc* logic.

5 Conclusion

This paper compares the strengths and limitations of runtime adaptation (RA) and reversible computation (RC) as software paradigms for detecting and recovering from errors in industrial IoT (IIoT) environments. We use a representative IC manufacturing shop floor use case to showcase how both approaches can be used to address common issues, *e.g.* equipment damage and environmental hazards, emphasising different design trade-offs.

We observe that RA can support *ad hoc* recovery and graceful degradation in the presence of irreversible operations. It delineates the reasoning about forward computations, analysed as runtime events, and remedial actions, executed as adaptation actions. RA is ideal for integrating cross-cutting behaviour as monitors, modularising and supporting incremental IIoT systems development.

By contrast, RC guarantees fine-grained reversibility and supports repetition strategies for trial-and-error recovery. The static guarantees given by RC are counterbalanced by the (i) upfront effort required to encode high-level correctness criteria directly into program logic, (ii) cognitive overhead of reasoning about interleaved forward and backward computations, and (iii) limited applicability of the approach in scenarios involving irreversible actions. We also explore the complementary nature of RA and RC. RA can benefit from incorporating reversible operations to gain predictability and verification guarantees, while RC development processes may be enriched by declarative RA specifications to facilitate development and enhance modularity. Future work will explore automated synthesis of hybrid RA-RC monitors and their use in real-world smart manufacturing settings.

References

1. ISO/TC 209. ISO 14644-1: Cleanrooms and Associated Controlled Environments. Technical report, Iinternational Organization for Standardization (2025)
2. Aceto, L., Achilleos, A., Attard, D.P., Exibard, L., Francalanza, A., Ingólfsdóttir, A.: A monitoring tool for linear-time μhml. SCP, **232**, 103031 (2024)
3. Aceto, L., Achilleos, A., Francalanza, A., Ingólfsdóttir, A., Lehtinen, K.: Adventures in monitorability: from branching to linear time and back again. PACMPL, **3**, 52:1–52:29 (2019)
4. Aceto, L., Achilleos, A., Francalanza, A., Ingólfsdóttir, A., Lehtinen, K.: An operational guide to monitorability with applications to regular properties. SSM **20**, 335–361 (2021)
5. Aceto, L., Attard, D.P., Francalanza, A., Ingólfsdóttir, A.: Runtime instrumentation for reactive components. In: ECOOP, LIPIcs, vol. 313, pp. 2:1–2:33. Schloss Dagstuhl - Leibniz-Zentrum für Informatik (2024)
6. Aceto, L., Cassar, I., Francalanza, A., Ingólfsdóttir, A.: On runtime enforcement via suppressions. In: CONCUR. LIPIcs, vol. 118, pp. 34:1–34:17 (2018)
7. Aceto, L., Cassar, I., Francalanza, A., Ingólfsdóttir, A.: On first-order runtime enforcement of branching-time properties. Acta Informatica **60**(4), 385–451 (2023)
8. Adlin, N., Nylund, H., Lanz, M., Lehtonen, T., Juuti, T.: Lean Indicators for small batch size manufacturers in high cost countries. Procedia Manuf. **51**, 1371–1378 (2020). 30th International Conference on Flexible Automation and Intelligent Manufacturing (FAIM2021)
9. Ahmed, S.F., et al.: Industrial internet of things enabled technologies, challenges, and future directions. CEE **110**, 108847 (2023)
10. Aman, B., et al.: Foundations of reversible computation. In: Reversible Computation: Extending Horizons of Computing: Selected Results of the COST Action IC1405, pp. 1–40 (2020)
11. Anandan, R., Gopalakrishnan, S., Pal, S., Zaman, N.: Intelligent Analytics for Predictive Maintenance. Wiley, Industrial Internet of Things (IIoT) (2022)
12. Attard, D.P., Aceto, L., Achilleos, A., Francalanza, A., Ingólfsdóttir, A., Lehtinen, K.: Better late than never or: verifying asynchronous components at runtime. In: Peters, K., Willemse, T.A.C. (eds.) FORTE 2021. LNCS, vol. 12719, pp. 207–225. Springer, Cham (2021). https://doi.org/10.1007/978-3-030-78089-0_14

13. Attard, D.P., Cassar, I., Francalanza, A., Aceto, L., Ingólfsdóttir, A.: Introduction to runtime verification. In: Behavioural Types: from Theory to Tools, Automation, Control and Robotics, pp. 49–76. River (2017)
14. Attard, D.P., Francalanza, A.: A monitoring tool for a branching-time logic. In: Falcone, Y., Sánchez, C. (eds.) RV 2016. LNCS, vol. 10012, pp. 473–481. Springer, Cham (2016). https://doi.org/10.1007/978-3-319-46982-9_31
15. Attard, D.P., Francalanza, A.: Trace partitioning and local monitoring for asynchronous components. In: Cimatti, A., Sirjani, M. (eds.) SEFM 2017. LNCS, vol. 10469, pp. 219–235. Springer, Cham (2017). https://doi.org/10.1007/978-3-319-66197-1_14
16. Balakrishnan, A., et al.: Safety assurance for autonomous systems with multiple sensor modalities. In: MEMOCODE, pp. 106–111 (2024)
17. Bartocci, E., Falcone, Y., Francalanza, A., Reger, G.: Introduction to runtime verification. In: Bartocci, E., Falcone, Y. (eds.) Lectures on Runtime Verification. LNCS, vol. 10457, pp. 1–33. Springer, Cham (2018). https://doi.org/10.1007/978-3-319-75632-5_1
18. Baydar, C.M., Saitou, K.: Off-line error prediction, diagnosis and recovery using virtual assembly systems. JIM **15**(5), 679–692 (2004)
19. Bennett, C.H.: Logical reversibility of computation. IBM J. Res. Dev. **17**(6), 525–532 (1973)
20. Berndt, M., Krummacker, D., Fischer, C., Schotten, H.D.: Centralized robotic fleet coordination and control. In: Mobile Communication - Technologies and Applications; 25th ITG-Symposium, pp. 1–8 (2021)
21. Bocchi, L., Lanese, I., Mezzina, C.A., Yuen, S.: revTPL: the reversible temporal process language. LMCS, **20**(1) (2024)
22. Bruni, R., Melgratti, H., Montanari, U.: Theoretical foundations for compensations in flow composition languages. In: POPL, pp. 209–220. ACM (2005)
23. Buch, J.P., et al.: Applying simulation and a domain-specific language for an adaptive action library. In: Brugali, D., Broenink, J.F., Kroeger, T., MacDonald, B.A. (eds.) SIMPAR 2014. LNCS (LNAI), vol. 8810, pp. 86–97. Springer, Cham (2014). https://doi.org/10.1007/978-3-319-11900-7_8
24. Cassar, I., Francalanza, A.: Runtime adaptation for actor systems. In: Bartocci, E., Majumdar, R. (eds.) RV 2015. LNCS, vol. 9333, pp. 38–54. Springer, Cham (2015). https://doi.org/10.1007/978-3-319-23820-3_3
25. Cassar, I., Francalanza, A., Aceto, L., Ingólfsdóttir, A.: A survey of runtime monitoring instrumentation techniques. In: PrePostiFM, EPTCS, vol. 254, pp. 15–28 (2017)
26. Cassar, I., Francalanza, A., Mezzina, C.A., Tuosto, E.: Reliability and fault-tolerance by choreographic design. In: PrePostiFM, EPTCS, vol. 254, pp. 69–80 (2017)
27. Chen, H., Zhang, G., Zhang, H., Fuhlbrigge, T.A.: Integrated robotic system for high precision assembly in a semi-structured environment. Assembly Autom. **27**(3) (2007)
28. Christensen, H., et al.: A Roadmap for US Robotics - From Internet to Robotics, vol. 2020. Now Publishers Inc, Edition (2021)
29. European Commission, Directorate-General for Research, Innovation, M. Breque, L. De Nul, and A. Petridis. Industry 5.0 – Towards a sustainable, human-centric and resilient European industry. Publications Office of the European Union (2021)
30. Conesa-Muñoz, J., Gonzalez-de-Soto, M., González de Santos, P., Ribeiro, R.: Distributed multi-level supervision to effectively monitor the operations of a fleet of autonomous vehicles in agricultural tasks. Sensors, **15**(3), 5402–5428 (2015)

31. Danos, V., Krivine, J.: Formal molecular biology done in CCS-R. In: BioConcur@CONCUR, Electronic Notes in Theoretical Computer Science, vol. 180, pp 31–49. Elsevier (2003)
32. Danos, V., Krivine, J.: Reversible communicating systems. In: Gardner, P., Yoshida, N. (eds.) CONCUR 2004. LNCS, vol. 3170, pp. 292–307. Springer, Heidelberg (2004). https://doi.org/10.1007/978-3-540-28644-8_19
33. Donald, B.R.: Error Detection and Recovery in Robotics. LNCS, vol. 336. Springer, New York (1989). https://doi.org/10.1007/BFb0039640
34. Fabbretti, G., Lanese, I., Stefani, J.-B.: Causal-consistent debugging of distributed erlang programs. In: Yamashita, S., Yokoyama, T. (eds.) RC 2021. LNCS, vol. 12805, pp. 79–95. Springer, Cham (2021). https://doi.org/10.1007/978-3-030-79837-6_5
35. Falcone, Y., Krstic, S., Reger, G., Traytel, D.: A taxonomy for classifying runtime verification tools. STTT **23**, 255–284 (2021)
36. Forte, P., Mannucci, A., Andreasson, H., Pecora, F.: Online task assignment and coordination in multi-robot fleets. IEEE Robot. Autom. Lett. **6**(3), 4584–4591 (2021)
37. Francalanza, A., et al.: A foundation for runtime monitoring. In: Lahiri, S., Reger, G. (eds.) RV 2017. LNCS, vol. 10548, pp. 8–29. Springer, Cham (2017). https://doi.org/10.1007/978-3-319-67531-2_2
38. Francalanza, A., Mezzina, C.A., Tuosto, E.: Reversible choreographies via monitoring in erlang. In: Bonomi, S., Rivière, E. (eds.) DAIS 2018. LNCS, vol. 10853, pp. 75–92. Springer, Cham (2018). https://doi.org/10.1007/978-3-319-93767-0_6
39. Francalanza, A., Mezzina, C.A., Tuosto, E.: Towards choreographic-based monitoring. In: Ulidowski, I., Lanese, I., Schultz, U.P., Ferreira, C. (eds.) RC 2020. LNCS, vol. 12070, pp. 128–150. Springer, Cham (2020). https://doi.org/10.1007/978-3-030-47361-7_6
40. Francalanza, A., Pérez, J.A., Sánchez, C.: Runtime verification for decentralised and distributed systems. In: Bartocci, E., Falcone, Y. (eds.) Lectures on Runtime Verification. LNCS, vol. 10457, pp. 176–210. Springer, Cham (2018). https://doi.org/10.1007/978-3-319-75632-5_6
41. Garrett, C.R., Lozano-Pérez, T., Kaelbling, L.P.: Backward-forward search for manipulation planning. In: IROS, pp. 6366–6373. IEEE (2015)
42. Graham, S.L., Kessler, P.B., McKusick, M.K.: Gprof: a call graph execution profiler. In: SIGPLAN Symposium on Compiler Construction, pp. 120–126. ACM (1982)
43. Hažík, J., Dekan, M., Beňo, P., Duchoň, F.: Fleet management system for an industry environment. JRC **3**(6), 779–789 (2022)
44. Hayes, D.: Making chips with dust-free poison. Sci. Cult. **1**(1), 89–104 (1987)
45. Hoey, J., Lanese, I., Nishida, N., Ulidowski, I., Vidal, G.: A case study for reversible computing: reversible debugging of concurrent programs. In: Reversible Computation: Extending Horizons of Computing: Selected Results of the COST Action IC1405, pp. 108–127 (2020)
46. Hoey, J., Ulidowski, I.: Reversing an imperative concurrent programming language. SCP **223**, 102873 (2022)
47. Clarke, E.M., Grumberg, O., Peled, D.A.: Model Checking. MIT Press, Cambridge (1999)
48. Kagermann, H., Wolfgang, W., Helbig, J.: Recommendations for implementing the strategic initiative INDUSTRIE 4.0. Technical report, Work. Group. Acatech, Frankfurt am Main, Ger., (2013)

49. Kalareh, M.A.; Evolving Software Systems for Self-Adaptation. PhD thesis, University of Waterloo, Ontario, Canada (2012)
50. Kiczales, G., et al.: Aspect-oriented programming. In: Akşit, M., Matsuoka, S. (eds.) ECOOP 1997. LNCS, vol. 1241, pp. 220–242. Springer, Heidelberg (1997). https://doi.org/10.1007/BFb0053381
51. Knežević, N., Savić, A., Gordić, Z., Ajoudani, A., Jovanović, K.: Toward Industry 5.0: a neuroergonomic workstation for a human-centered, collaborative robot-supported manual assembly process. IEEE Robot. Autom. Mag. 2–13 (2024)
52. Koval, M.C., King, J.E., Pollard, N.S., Srinivasa, S.S.: Robust trajectory selection for rearrangement planning as a multi-armed bandit problem. In: IROS, pp. 2678–2685. IEEE (2015)
53. Kuhn, R., Hanafee, B., Allen, J.: Reactive Design Patterns. Manning (2016)
54. Kutrib, M.: Reversible and irreversible computations of deterministic finite-state devices. In: Italiano, G.F., Pighizzini, G., Sannella, D.T. (eds.) MFCS 2015. LNCS, vol. 9234, pp. 38–52. Springer, Heidelberg (2015). https://doi.org/10.1007/978-3-662-48057-1_3
55. Lami, P., Lanese, I., Stefani, J.-B., Coen, C.S., Fabbretti, G.: Reversible debugging of concurrent erlang programs: supporting imperative primitives. JLAMP **138**, 100944 (2024)
56. Landauer, R.: Irreversibility and heat generated in the computing process. IBM J. Res. Dev. **5**, 183–191 (1961)
57. Lanese, I., Mezzina, C.A., Schmitt, A., Stefani, J.-B.: Controlling reversibility in higher-order Pi. In: Katoen, J.-P., König, B. (eds.) CONCUR 2011. LNCS, vol. 6901, pp. 297–311. Springer, Heidelberg (2011). https://doi.org/10.1007/978-3-642-23217-6_20
58. Lanese, I., Mezzina, C.A., Stefani, J.-B.: Controlled reversibility and compensations. In: Glück, R., Yokoyama, T. (eds.) RC 2012. LNCS, vol. 7581, pp. 233–240. Springer, Heidelberg (2013). https://doi.org/10.1007/978-3-642-36315-3_19
59. Lanese, I., Mezzina, C.A., Stefani, J.-B.: Reversibility in the higher-order π-calculus. TCS **625**, 25–84 (2016)
60. Lanese, I., Nishida, N., Palacios, A., Vidal, G.: A theory of reversibility for erlang. JLAMP **100**, 71–97 (2018)
61. Lanese, I., Schultz, U.P., Ulidowski, I.: Reversible execution for robustness in embodied AI and industrial robots. IT Prof. **23**(3), 12–17 (2021)
62. Laursen, J.S., Ellekilde, L.-P., Schultz, U.P.: Modelling reversible execution of robotic assembly. Robotica **36**(5), 625–654 (2018)
63. Liao, Y., Freitas, E., Loures, R., Deschamps, F.: Industrial internet of things: a systematic literature review and insights. IEEE Internet Things J. **5**(6), 4515–4525 (2018)
64. Loborg, P.: Error Recovery in Manufacturing Control Systems. PhD thesis, School of Engineering, Linköping University, Sweden (1994)
65. Melgratti, H., Mezzina, C.A., Michele Pinna, G.: A truly concurrent semantics for reversible CCS. LMCS, **20**(4) (2024)
66. Melgratti, H., Mezzina, C.A., Ulidowski, I.: Reversing Place transition nets. LMCS, **16** (2020)
67. Mezzina, C.A., Pérez, J.A.: Causally consistent reversible choreographies: a monitors-as-memories approach. In: PPDP, pp. 127–138. ACM (2017)
68. Mezzina, C.A., Tiezzi, F., Yoshida, N.: Checkpoint-based rollback recovery in session programming. LMCS, **21**(1), 2 (2025)
69. ST Microcontroller Division Applications. Application Note: Introduction to Semiconductor Technology (2000)

70. Mostafa, M., Bonakdarpour, B.: Decentralized runtime verification of LTL specifications in distributed systems. In: IPDPS, pp. 494–503 (2015)
71. Neto, P., Mendes, N., Araujo, R., Norberto Pires, J., Paulo Moreira, A.: High-level robot programming based on CAD: dealing with unpredictable environments. Ind. Robot, **39**(3) (2012)
72. NXP Semiconductors. Official Website (2024). https://www.nxp.com
73. Okumura, S., Take, N., Okino, N.: Error prevention in robotic assembly tasks by a machine vision and statistical pattern recognition method. Int. J. Prod. Res. **43**(7), 1397–1410 (2005)
74. Pasha, A.: Lights-Out Manufacturing: Revolutionizing the Factory Floor with Automation. Technical report, Bosch (2025)
75. Kalyan, S.: Perumalla. Introduction to Reversible Computing, CRC Press (2014)
76. Schultz, U.P., Bordignon, M., Støy, K.: Robust and reversible execution of self-reconfiguration sequences. Robotica, **29**(1), 35–57 (2011)
77. Sehrawat, D., Gill, N.S.: Smart sensors: analysis of different types of IoT sensors. In: 2019 3rd International Conference on Trends in Electronics and Informatics (ICOEI), pp. 523–528 (2019)
78. Sparc: The partnership for Robotics in Europe. Robotics 2020:Multi-Annual Roadmap for Robotics in Europe. Technical report, EU Robotics AISBL, Brussels (2017)
79. STMicroelectronics. Official Website (2024). https://www.st.com
80. Tan, M., Wang, P., Luo, W.: Optimized real-time monitoring and fault diagnosis system for industrial robots with integrated sensor data. In: ICIPCN, pp. 764–768 (2024)
81. Tarkoma, S.: Overlay Networks: Toward Information Networking. Auerbach (2010)
82. Texas Instruments. Official Website (2024). https://www.ti.com
83. Vassor, M., Stefani, J.-B.: Checkpoint/rollback vs causally-consistent reversibility. In: Kari, J., Ulidowski, I. (eds.) RC 2018. LNCS, vol. 11106, pp. 286–303. Springer, Cham (2018). https://doi.org/10.1007/978-3-319-99498-7_20
84. Villani, V., Gabbi, M., Sabattini, L.: Promoting operator's wellbeing in Industry 5.0: detecting mental and physical fatigue. In: 2022 IEEE International Conference on Systems, Man, and Cybernetics (SMC), pp. 2030–2036 (2022)
85. Wang, Y., et al.: Probabilistic graph based spatial assembly relation inference for programming of assembly task by demonstration. In: IROS, pp. 4402–4407. IEEE (2015)
86. Yokoyama, T., Axelsen, H.B., Glück, R.: Principles of a reversible programming language. In: Conference Computing Frontiers, pp. 43–54. ACM (2008)
87. Zhang, B., Wang, J., Rossano, G., Martinez, C.: Vision-guided robotic assembly using uncalibrated vision. In: 2011 IEEE International Conference on Mechatronics and Automation, pp. 1384–1389 (2011)

Towards Implementing Distributed Custom Serverless Function Scheduling in FunLess

Giuseppe De Palma[1,2], Saverio Giallorenzo[1,2], Jacopo Mauro[3], Matteo Trentin[1,2,3], and Gianluigi Zavattaro[1,2(✉)]

[1] Università di Bologna, Bologna, Italy
{giuseppe.depalma2,saverio.giallorenzo2,matteo.trentin2, gianluigi.zavattaro}@unibo.it
[2] OLAS research team, INRIA, Lille, France
[3] University of Southern Denmark, Odense, Denmark
mauro@imada.sdu.dk

Abstract. APP is a declarative language for the definition of custom function scheduling on the worker nodes available in serverless Function as a Service (FaaS) platforms. Current APP implementations assume a central control point that users can access to issue the execution of functions. We propose an extension of APP's implementation to allow for multiple control points, tackling both scaling and resilience issues of existing implementations. To substantiate our proposal, we present an implementation of our extension using the FunLess FaaS platform, tailored for private edge-cloud and multi-cloud environments. We show initial experiments that indicate performance improvements in setups where both the platform and function invocations are spread across multiple locations.

Keywords: Serverless · Function Scheduling · Decentralisation

1 Introduction

This paper has been devised for the Jean-Bernard Stefani's festschrift, as it presents research conducted within our group that aligns closely with his interests. Jean-Bernard has long been an advocate for innovative approaches to the development of distributed software systems, particularly those grounded in modular and compositional principles. Recent trends in modular and compositional distributed software developments tend to minimise the complexity

---

This work has been partially supported by the research project FREEDA (CUP: I53D23003550006) funded by the framework PRIN 2022 (MUR, Italy), RTM&R (CUP: J33C22001170001) funded by the MUR National Recovery and Resilience Plan (European Union - NextGenerationEU) and the French ANR project SmartCloud ANR-23-CE25-0012.

of the components and limit (and possibly avoid) component's interdependencies. This property allows components in the system to autonomously scale in order to make the entire system more resilient. However, as these components scale, the complexity in the management of the overall system, including its computing infrastructure, also increases, creating the need for efficient—ideally automatic—management systems. Serverless computing emerged to address these challenges by offering a model that abstracts away the underlying infrastructure, allowing developers to build applications as compositions of stateless (hence, less complex), event-driven functions, determining the paradigm of Function-as-a-Service (FaaS), that a platform can automatically scale up and down based on demand.

The language of Allocation Priority Policies (APP) (and its variants) emerged as a declarative solution allowing developers to define custom function scheduling policies and placement constraints across worker nodes in serverless platforms [7–11,13,15,16]. Thanks to APP, developers can express fine-grained placement preferences, enabling improved execution performance on diverse criteria, including resource requirements and locality principles. This declarative approach abstracts away the complexities of infrastructure management while giving users control over critical aspects of function placement. For instance, developers can ensure compute-intensive functions run on nodes with specific hardware accelerators, co-locate functions that frequently communicate to reduce latency, or implement compliance requirements by restricting certain functions to specific geographical regions.

Being a platform-agnostic solution, APP-based scheduling can be implemented on multiple serverless platforms, like it has been done for Apache OpenWhisk [16,23] and FunLess [7,12]. Similarly to other open-source alternatives, like OpenFaaS [22], and KNative [1], these platforms typically assume a centralised controller that handles the scheduling of functions. Indeed, serverless platform architectures typically consist of two main components: *controllers* and *workers*. Workers constitute the majority of FaaS platform deployment, as these nodes are responsible for executing the functions. The prevalent deployment model features a single central controller that manages the scheduling and execution of functions across the available workers. This controller acts as the brain of the system: it receives invocation requests, keeps track of system state, and assigns work (i.e., the execution of functions) to the available worker nodes.

Problem. The centrality of the controller in APP-based implementations is paramount: it is the component that realises the semantics of APP-governed scheduling, working as the single entry point of a serverless architecture and having complete control over the functions executing on the workers—it maintains their status and constantly knows which functions run on which workers at any time. While this design simplifies coordination and is efficient at small and moderate scales, it poses limitations as deployments grow. The central controller can become a performance bottleneck and a single point of failure, especially under heavy load or in geographically distributed environments.

The need for multiple controllers arises primarily from scalability, locality, and fault-tolerance concerns. As serverless deployments increase in size—both in terms of number of functions and the geographic spread of infrastructure—a single controller can hardly satisfy the number and quality of service of user requests. The controller must handle a growing volume of requests, maintaining a global view of a large and dynamic system and managing communication with all nodes. This scalability issue can lead to degraded performance and increased latency, particularly when the controller becomes overwhelmed or is physically distant from parts of the system it manages. Moreover, the larger the geographical distribution of users that access the system, the more relevant the problem of having a controller at a single location becomes—e.g., the farther the users are from the controller, the higher is their experienced interaction latency with the system. Regarding faults, having a single coordinator for a given deployment means that all user interactions can fail due to a controller's failure.

Distributing the control logic across multiple controllers addresses these challenges, enhancing scalability, reducing latency, and increasing the overall robustness of the platform. Decentralisation enhances scalability by providing multiple access points to the platform and improves fault-tolerance by eliminating a single point of failure—if one controller fails, only the function requests managed by that controller fail, while users of other, healthy controllers remain unaffected and can continue their operations. In geographically-distributed scenarios, users have the option of interacting with the controller closest to them, reducing latency and improving responsiveness. These aspects are especially critical in IoT and edge computing environments, where constraints such as geographic locality, limited resources, and intermittent connectivity are common.

Contribution. In this paper, we propose an extension of APP's architectural implementation to allow for multiple control points, thereby addressing both scaling, locality, and resilience issues of existing implementations. By enabling decentralised, APP-based scheduling, each controller shall operate autonomously while still respecting the application-level constraints expressed via APP. Indeed, although having multiple controllers solves the mentioned issues, introducing decentralised control in APP-based platforms brings in a new set of challenges, particularly in maintaining distributed state consistency. When scheduling, each controller must maintain an accurate and coherent view of the system's state while respecting APP policies. We explore the architectural and protocol-level modifications needed to make decentralised control possible, and we discuss the key trade-offs between maintaining consistency and achieving responsiveness.

To substantiate our proposal, we present an implementation based on FunLess—a serverless platform tailored for private edge-cloud and multi-cloud environments. Through our implementation and experiments, we demonstrate performance improvements in setups where both the platform and function invocations are spread across multiple locations. Our results indicate that decentralising APP control points improves overall system performance, particularly in geographically distributed deployments.

2 Background

Before presenting our proposal, we briefly overview the FaaS paradigm, the typical architecture of FaaS platforms, APP, and the design of FunLess.

2.1 Serverless and Functions-as-a-Service

A serverless application emerges from the combination of software units called functions, which run in short-lived environments, triggered by events—such as HTTP requests, database updates, file uploads, and scheduled intervals. When an event triggers a function execution, the FaaS platform runs the code after initialising an execution environment—a secure, isolated context that provides the resources for the function lifecycle. FaaS platforms mainly use virtual machines and containers to implement portable, isolated function execution environments.

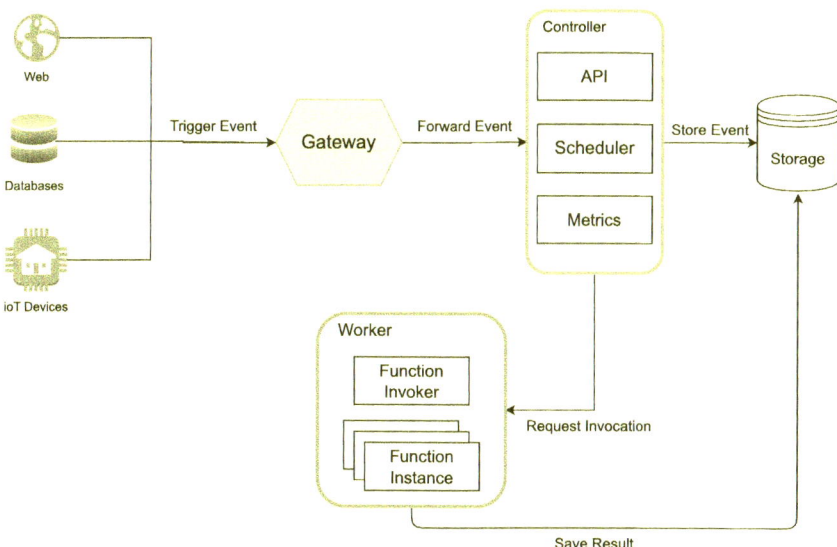

Fig. 1. A typical serverless platform architecture.

Serverless platforms generally follow the (simplified) architecture design reported in Fig. 1. As visible in the figure, the main components of a FaaS platform's architecture are the controllers and the workers. The controller receives requests from external sources, such as users or other systems, and it orchestrates the allocation of functions on the available worker nodes. In particular, the scheduler controller's component determines which worker should execute a function, based on factors such as the worker's current load, the function requirements, and resource availability. Upon receiving a function-execution request, the targeted worker executes the function, handling the function's execution environment lifecycle, including provisioning, scaling, and teardown.

Serverless platforms usually adopt a communication layer that facilitates communication between the controller node and worker nodes, handling messages and data transfer between components—omitted, in Fig. 1, for clarity. In particular, message queues or event brokers (e.g., RabbitMQ [5], Kafka [2]) support asynchronous communication between components, allowing decoupling and scalability. Internal APIs support synchronous communication for tasks such as function deployment, status updates, and resource allocation. Monitoring tools also appear in these architectures to collect metrics on resource usage, function execution times, and error rates. Metrics provide visibility into system performance, function execution, and overall health and enable debugging, troubleshooting, and performance optimisation.

Among the leading providers of serverless computing platforms, Amazon Web Services (AWS) Lambda [24] stands out as a pioneer in the field. AWS Lambda was the first publicly available serverless platform, allowing developers to pay only for the compute time consumed by their functions. Briefly thereafter, other platforms followed suit, such as Microsoft Azure Cloud Functions [3] and Google Cloud Platform (GCP) Cloud Functions [6]. A number of open-source serverless platforms have also emerged, such as OpenWhisk [23], Knative [1], and OpenFaaS [22]. One can deploy these platforms on-premises or on the cloud, as a more flexible and customisable solution compared to the proprietary ones.

2.2 Allocation Priority Policies (APP)

The scheduling of functions, i.e., which worker, among the available ones, executes a given function, can substantially influence their performance. Indeed, effects like *code locality* [18]—due to latencies in loading function code and runtimes—or *session locality* [18]—due to the need to authenticate and open new sessions to interact with other services—can substantially increase the run time of functions. Usually, serverless platforms implement opinionated policies that favour some performance principle tailored for one or more of these locality principles. This shortcoming motivated De Palma et al. [17] to introduce a YAML-like declarative language used to specify scheduling policies to govern the allocation of serverless functions on the nodes that make up a cluster, called APP. Thanks to APP, the same platform can support different scheduling policies, each tailored to meet the specific needs of a set of related functions.

To define function-specific policies, APP assumes the association of each function with a tag. In our examples, we directly use the function's reference name as the tag, but the relation can be one-to-many, to specify a policy shared among a set of functions. Then, APP associates a tag to a policy, so that, at runtime, the scheduler of the platform can pair each function with its APP policy and follow the latter's scheduling logic.

```
1 f:
2   - workers: [ w1, w2, w3 ]
```

```
3         strategy: best_first
4         invalidate: max_concurrent_invocations: 10
5       - workers: *
6         strategy: random
7         invalidate: capacity_used: 80
```
Listing 1.1. APP script used for the tests.

We show an example APP script, illustrating one policy in Listing 1.1. In an APP script, users can specify a sequence of blocks—each identified by YAML's list unit -—associated with a tag. In the example, the policy tag is f, at line 1. Each block indicates on which workers the scheduler can allocate the function. At function invocation, the scheduler tries to allocate the function following the logic in the first block, passing to the next only if none of the workers specified in that block can host the function, and so on. Exhausting all blocks causes the invocation's failure. In APP, workers is the keyword used in the scripts to specify the label of the worker nodes available to that block; in Listing 1.1, the workers labelled w1, w2, and w3 are the ones specified in the first block, at line 2; the universal * at line 5 indicates the selection of all available workers in a given deployment. Besides workers, APP lets users specify the strategy the scheduler shall follow to select among the indicated workers and when to invalidate a worker, which would not be able to execute the function under scheduling. Examples of strategies are random, to chose uniformly at random among the workers in a block, e.g., for load-balancing (line 6) and best_first , to follow a top-to-bottom ordering (line 3), e.g., to indicate the workers from the most to the least powerful. The invalidation constraints can, for example, set a maximal threshold of concurrent functions running on a worker (line 4) or define a maximum number of resources (cpu, memory) occupied by other functions on the worker (line 7).

2.3 The FunLess Serverless Platform

FunLess [12,14] is a serverless platform for private edge-cloud and multi-cloud environments that consists of mainly two components: the Core and the Worker. The Core corresponds to the controller and acts as a user-facing API to *i*) create, fetch, update, and delete functions and *ii*) schedule functions on workers. The Worker is the component deployed on every node tasked to run the functions. Besides Core and Workers, FunLess includes a Postgres database, to store functions and metadata, and Prometheus, to manage the metrics of the platform.[1] Both main components are written in Elixir [19], and take advantage of the BEAM [25] message passing model to communicate with each other.

The Core controls the platform, exposing an HTTP REST API for user interaction, handling authentication and authorisation, and managing functions' lifecycle and invocations. The Core can automatically discover Workers within

---

[1] Resp. at https://www.postgresql.org/ and https://prometheus.io.

the same network employing the Multicast UDP Gossip algorithm for baremetal deployments and Kubernetes' service discovery for containerised environments. Functionality-wise, users create functions by compiling source code to WebAssembly and uploading the binary to the Core, which stores it in the database with a name. Users can group functions in modules and specify memory requirements for function execution. When an invocation request is received, the Core selects a suitable Worker to run the function, to which it then sends the request parameters. In case the Worker does not have a function's binary, it returns an error to the Core, which send said binary alongside the request.

The Worker runs functions via Wasmtime, a security-oriented runtime for WebAssembly. Workers have a local cache with a configurable size limit, where they store recently run binaries, to minimise network traffic during function invocations. Upon reception of an invocation request, the Worker checks its cache for the function's binary, returning an error as mentioned above. After an invocation, the Worker returns its result (successful or not) to the Core.

3 From Centralised to Decentralised APP Scheduling

Usually, open-source serverless platforms employ centralised function scheduling, where a single controller manages the scheduling of functions across worker nodes. In this model, the controller maintains comprehensive knowledge of all workers' states—the only divergence between the status of a worker and the knowledge the controller has is that the worker can become unreachable—and workers are primarily passive components that execute assigned functions and report results or timeouts. APP-based platform implementations particularly rely on the centrality of the controller to ensure the satisfaction of the specified function scheduling constraints found in APP scripts.

While effective at smaller scales, this centralised approach faces significant challenges when scaling to larger, geographically distributed deployments. This section explores the transition from centralised to decentralised function scheduling, examining different decentralisation strategies, their underlying challenges, and their respective trade-offs.

3.1 Challenges in Decentralised Scheduling

Moving from a centralised to a decentralised scheduling architecture introduces several fundamental challenges. First, maintaining state consistency becomes complex as multiple controllers must hold a coherent view of the system state, including worker availability, resource utilisation, and function execution status. Second, coordination overhead emerges when controllers must synchronise scheduling decisions to avoid conflicts, introducing additional communication and potential latency. Third, network limitations, particularly in edge computing scenarios, mean the bandwidth and latency costs of coordination messages can significantly impact performance.

We identify two primary approaches to decentralising serverless scheduling architectures: transaction-based decentralisation and optimistic decentralisation. Each approach offers distinct advantages and limitations.

Transaction-Based Decentralisation. In transaction-based centralisation, each controller maintains a local view of the global system state, and distributed transactions are used to ensure consistency across controllers. Every scheduling decision involves a coordinated update to these local views, guaranteeing that all controllers operate on a consistent snapshot of the system. While this method provides strong consistency guarantees, it is also communication-intensive, as each scheduling operation incurs the overhead of a distributed coordination protocol.

Within this context, two main coordination strategies emerge: distributed transactions and leader election. In both cases, the systems in place ensure that controllers maintain a consistent view of worker states and avoid race conditions between controllers during function scheduling, which could generate a misalignment between the knowledge of the controllers and the state of the workers. Thus, before proceeding with the actual scheduling, controllers must reach consensus on the scheduling decisions. In this case, workers maintain their passive role as in centralised architectures, as transactions entail global state management.

Distributed transactions provide a mechanism to ensure consistent state across controllers. When applied to function scheduling, these transactions enable multiple controllers to coordinate their view of worker availability and resource allocation. One foundational protocol in this domain is two-phase commit [4], which operates in phases: first, a controller sends a "proposal" request to the other controllers; each controller validates the proposed scheduling action against its local state and votes to commit or abort; finally, the initial controller collects all votes and issues either a global commit or abort instruction. This approach guarantees that all controllers either collectively apply or collectively reject a scheduling decision.

As an alternative, leader-election protocols, such as PAXOS [20] and RAFT [21], can reduce the number of messages needed to issue a scheduling instruction by having an elected leader among the controllers govern the global state and regulate scheduling requests from the other controllers, usually called "followers". In practice, followers inform the leader when they receive a request from a user (since the leader maintains the state of the system, requests to the leader can proceed directly, informing the followers of the scheduling decision it takes) to schedule a function, and the leader directs the follower on how to proceed (where to schedule the function or whether the scheduling fails, e.g., because no worker has enough capacity to run that function).

Both approaches become problematic with large-distance topologies, where transaction-based scheduling, leader election and coordination may incur high latency—imagine that a controller with high communication latency becomes the leader, with which all other controllers have to coordinate to schedule their functions. This aspect is particularly relevant in constrained network environments, such as edge computing, where the costs of these messages can be significant—in terms of energy (edge devices may rely on batteries to power them), bandwidth, latency and, ultimately, scheduling time.

Another limitation of this approach arises when a controller is already a bottleneck for incoming scheduling requests. In such cases, enforcing coordination through distributed transactions or relying on a single leader to govern scheduling decisions may exacerbate the problem. The overhead introduced by coordination protocols can further delay responses, compounding the controller's inability to handle requests in a timely manner. This aspect is especially critical in high-load scenarios, where even minor delays can lead to significant degradation in system responsiveness or throughput. Practically, the additional communication and synchronisation steps required by this approach can undermine scalability and reactivity.

Optimistic Decentralisation. To avoid the overhead of distributed transactions, one can pursue an "optimistic" approach, where controllers attempt to schedule functions on workers and delegate to the workers themselves the task of verifying whether they can effectively execute the scheduled functions.

Thus, controllers can maintain partial knowledge of worker states because the workers themselves perform the verification whether their current status is compatible with the constraints to run a function. This approach is safe from a scheduling point of view, because despite the fact that controllers have an under-approximated view of the load on the workers (the one they issued and not the one issued by the other controllers), workers deny the execution functions targeted at them if their state does not satisfy the function's scheduling constraints (e.g., minimal amount of resources, too many concurrent invocations).

Hence, under the optimistic decentralisation approach, workers become active components. To ensure the satisfaction of the scheduling constraints (the invalidation properties) of a policy, controllers must send in their scheduling request both the (reference to the) function to execute (as done in the centralised case) and the invalidation constraints.

Generally, at scheduling time, this modality saves messages compared to the transaction-based version. In the best case, we have at most two messages: one between the controller and worker for function scheduling and, depending on the architecture, possibly a response message to the controller (alternatively, the worker could store the response in a database). In the worst case, for each block of the policy and for each worker in the block, two messages are exchanged: one for scheduling and one to signal the failure of scheduling from the worker.

Since controllers ignore the current status of the worker, it can happen that multiple requests to execute a family of functions related to the same scheduling policy could target the same workers in a small timeframe, leading to many failures and the relative messages. In these contexts, one can introduce an exponential back-off system whereby, after the failure of scheduling with respect to a certain policy, the controller waits for an exponentially increasing time before forwarding scheduling requests, allowing the interested workers to regain some capacity to run new functions by waiting for the termination of the ones they are running.

We conclude our discussion about the optimistic decentralisation approach by observing that, given that controllers have no need to store the current status of the workers, we can consider controllers almost as stateless services—the only stateful element is the management of the response back to the user, which one can delegate to a dedicated, lightweight service that users can receive their responses from. Having stateless controllers allows one to implement standard scale-in and scale-out techniques to dynamically increase/decrease the number of instances of controllers. In this way, the system can elastically adapt to possible modifications of the traffic of incoming function execution requests.

4 Implementation

We proceed to present an APP-based FunLess implementation that uses decentralised function scheduling and supports the execution of multiple controllers.

We remark that since FunLess' main focus is the edge-cloud continuum and multi-cloud scenarios, we have a context in which the communication delays between system's nodes is not negligible. Using a transaction- or leader-based coordination policy among several cores possibly deployed on edge and cloud nodes in different geographical zones can significantly slow down the system due to coordination messages—even in the "lighter" case of leader-based coordination, the leader and followers can experience latencies that would slow down scheduling. For instance, imagine a configuration where the leader is in the cloud and requests for the edge must coordinate with the cloud for scheduling on the edge itself. This configuration represents a clear antipattern, because executing the functions at the edge entails bringing computation closer to the consumer/producer of the response/computation and going through the cloud for coordinating the execution of these functions would diminish the benefits of the cloud-edge approach. The opposite configuration is even more inconvenient: the leader is on the edge and the traffic from the cloud has to reach out to the edge, leaving the Cloud data centre, making the communication substantially slower. For these reasons, we chose to implement the distributed version of FunLess following the optimistic approach.

4.1 A Decentralised Variant of FunLess's Architecture

We draw our proposal for a FunLess' decentralised architecture variant in Fig. 2, including the flow of function creation and execution therein. The architecture includes several Workers and, differently from previous Funless architectures [12, 14], several Cores and a distributed database, which allows for multi-instance deployments. First, we discuss the workflow followed by Cores and Workers in the FunLess standard implementation. Then, we comment on the modifications to these workflows necessary to implement the optimistic decentralisation approach.

Core. Upon receiving a function creation request (as shown in Fig. 2, step 1. Upload), a Core stores the binary in the database by accessing the closest instance (2. Store) and notifies the Workers (3. Broadcast) to cache a local copy (4. Cache), to reduce cold-start overheads. The components communicate via BEAM's distributed inter-process messaging system. When a function invocation reaches a Core (5. Invoke), it retrieves it (if any) from the database (6. Retrieve). Using the latest collected metrics, the Core selects a Worker with enough memory to execute the function (7. Request) if no APP policy is specified, otherwise it follows the policy instruction. Once it selects the Worker, the Core issues the execution of the function therein, waiting to receive the result back, which it relays to the user (10a/13b. reply).

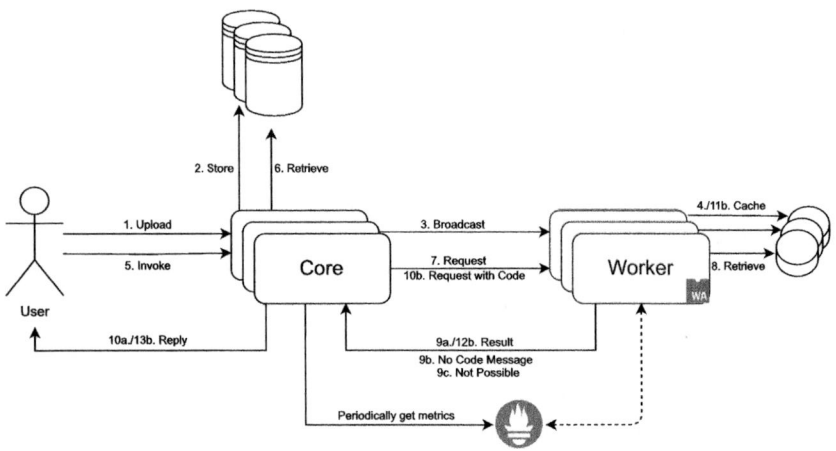

Fig. 2. FunLess decentralised architecture variant, with multiple controllers.

Worker. The Worker runs functions via Wasmtime, a runtime for WebAssembly. When a Worker receives the request to run a function (7. Request), it checks its cache for the function's binary (8. Retrieve). If it finds the binary, it runs the function and returns the result to the Core (9a. Result) that contacted it. Otherwise, the Worker informs the Core (9b. No Code Message), which re-sends the request with the code (10b. Request with Code) for caching (11b. Cache) and execution (12b. Result). Alternatively, if the Worker is unable to execute the function, it notifies the Core (9c. Not Possible). The above logic supports efficient function fetching and execution w.r.t. containers, thanks to the small size of Wasm binaries compared to the larger/heavier container images. For caching and eviction, Workers have a configurable cache memory threshold.

Modifications. From a practical standpoint, extending the implementation to support the optimistic approach involved modifying the Worker's control flow to recognise the violation of APP invalidation constraints. In particular, when a Worker receives a function allocation request, it checks its current state, namely the number of functions currently scheduled and its actually used capacity (unknown to the Core that sent the request). In case, the current state invalidates the constraints contained in the APP script, the Worker sends a dedicated notification back to the Core, as a new response type from the Worker. On the Core side, the new implementation adds logic to interpret this message. In case such failure message is received, the Core proceeds with the scheduling of the function by selecting an alternative Worker (if any) following the APP policy of that function, starting a new message exchange with the selected Worker.

5 Experiments

In this section, we show how our FunLess decentralised architectural variant can improve system performance in multi-controllers deployments. We conduct our evaluation with a series of tests involving function invocations from different locations, specifically from EU and US regions, considering two scenarios where the platform has: i) one Core in the US region and two Workers, one in the EU and one in the US region, and ii) two Cores, one in the EU and one in the US, each with one Worker (as in scenario i). In both scenarios, we send 1000 consecutive invocations from the EU and US regions to the (nearest) Core, first without applying any APP script, in order to have "vanilla" invocations, then, repeating the same tests with an APP script that specifies an ad-hoc policy for Worker assignment.

We designed these experiments to evaluate the impact of geographical distribution and scheduling policies on serverless function execution performance. To this aim, we consider a cross-regional deployment with nodes in both the US and EU regions so that we can draw observations from a realistic multi-region deployment scenario, common in production environments to support global user bases and implement resilient service strategies. By placing nodes in geographically distant regions (US and EU), we can clearly measure the effects of network latency on function execution times, particularly the effect of round-trips that occur when requests cross regional boundaries multiple times. The scenarios are particularly suited to measure the impact of scheduling decisions, supporting the direct comparison between local scheduling, remote scheduling, and default (vanilla) scheduling behaviours and quantify the benefits of decentralised vs centralised scheduling decisions in geographically distributed serverless applications.

5.1 Setup

The platform is deployed over 4 nodes in Google Cloud Platform (GCP) in 2 different regions. Each node being a type e2-medium virtual machine with 2 vCPUs and 2 GB of RAM. Two nodes are located in the EU region (europe-west1) and two in the US region (us-central1). In each zone, 1 node is used as a FunLess Worker and the other as a FunLess Core. Both nodes acting as Cores also deploy a PostgreSQL database with a bidirectional replication in order to provide the Cores a consistent view of the system state. In addition, the EU Core hosts the Prometheus instance. Finally, two Locust[2] instances are also hosted in the Core nodes to generate the localized traffic.

The function invoked is a simple Rust function that returns a sample string compiled to WebAssembly. Listing 1.2 shows the APP script used for the tests.

```
 1  - default:
 2      - workers: '*'
 3
 4  - eu:
 5      - workers:
 6          - 'euworker'
 7      followup: default
 8
 9  - us:
10      - workers:
11          - 'usworker'
12      followup: default
```

Listing 1.2. APP script used for the tests.

5.2 Results

Single Core Test. For the single Core scenario, where the Core was deployed in the US region, three different test runs were performed:

- **APP for both Workers (Local Scheduling)**: the requests from the EU node were tagged with eu and assigned to the EU Worker, while the requests from the US node were tagged with us and therefore assigned to the US Worker.
- **APP for US Worker (Only US Scheduling)**: all requests were tagged with us and assigned to the US Worker, regardless of their origin.
- **Vanilla**: no function was tagged, corresponding of the situation in which no APP script is used.

Table 1 shows the measurements of the three test runs, including the average, median, and standard deviation of the response times for each requests' origin. There is a notable difference in the response times between the usage for a near-Core Worker and a far-Core Worker. With APP using both Workers, the latencies for requests from the EU region is significantly higher than the requests from the US region, while it is halved when using just the US Worker. It shows the significant impact of the double round-trip effect when the requests are assigned to the EU Worker. First the request is sent from the EU Locust instance to the US Core, then the Core sends the request back to the EU region for the Worker

---

[2] https://locust.io.

Table 1. Statistics of function invocation requests for 1 Core US Only (in milliseconds).

Scenario	Avg	Median	Std
APP Local Scheduling - requests from EU	230.68	230.57	14.35
APP Local Scheduling - requests from US	15.46	15.17	1.49
APP Only US Scheduling - requests from EU	120.58	119.62	5.01
APP Only US Scheduling - requests from US	15.62	15.07	2.22
Vanilla - requests from EU	201.15	231.22	64.00
Vanilla - requests from US	80.64	127.77	61.82

to execute the function. The result is then sent back to the US region for the Core to process it and send the final response back to the EU Locust instance.

With vanilla invocations, both Cores can use any Worker, and the scheduling is done based on CPU load and memory usage via the scraped metrics from Prometheus updated on a 5-second interval. In our run we observed that both Cores sent the invocation requests mainly to the EU Worker, performing similarly to the APP script with both Workers with requests from the EU region. The requests from the US region also generally performed worse due to the round-trip to the EU Worker. Figure 3 shows a distribution of the response times for the vanilla invocations. It clearly shows the bimodal distribution when the Cores switch from one Worker to the other.

The most stable conditions are observed when the requests reach the nearest Core and the functions are allocated to the nearest Worker.

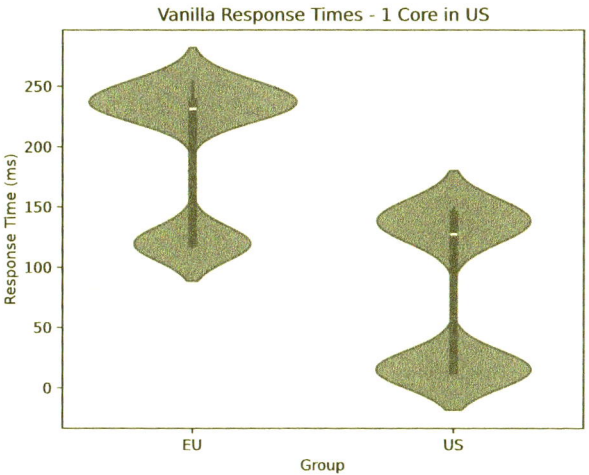

Fig. 3. Distribution of function response time without the APP script. The bimodal distribution is due to the Cores switching from one Worker to the other.

Multi-core Test. For the multi-core scenario, where each region has its own Core, two test runs were performed by sending 1000 requests from the EU and US regions to their respective Cores, at the same time. First using the APP script from Listing 1.2 to assign the requests to the nearest Worker, and once without tagging any function and therefore simulating the vanilla scenario in which an APP script is not available.

The results of the test runs are shown in Table 2. The optimal performance is achieved when the invocations are requested from Workers co-located with the Core, which is the case for all requests when using APP. With vanilla invocations, as seen in the experiment with only one Core, both Cores primarily used the EU Worker due to the low impact of the function execution and the delay of the scraping interval, leading to the response times from the US region being significantly higher.

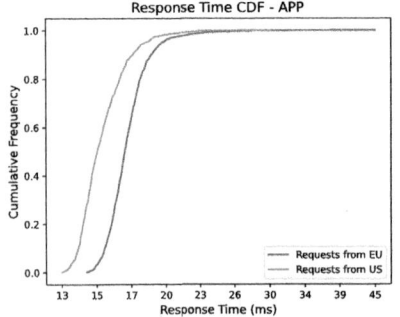

Fig. 4. Distribution of response time for invocations with the APP script.

Fig. 5. Distribution of response time for invocations without the APP script.

Table 2. Statistics of function invocation requests with 2 Cores (in milliseconds).

Scenario	Avg	Median	Std
APP Local Scheduling - requests from EU	17.31	17.03	1.80
APP Local Scheduling - requests from US	15.67	15.30	1.57
Vanilla - requests from EU	32.45	16.38	60.73
Vanilla - requests from US	62.52	15.51	87.36

It is interesting to note that the APP script used for these multi-core experiments is the same as the one used in the experiments with the single Core experiments named "APP Local Scheduling" in Table 1. Hence, a comparison between these two scenarios is a fair way to evaluate the advantages of a decentralised architecture for APP-based function scheduling. We have that in the decentralised architecture both the groups of function invocations from EU have a fast average response time (US: 17.31 ms, EU: 15.67 ms) while in the centralised case one of the two groups—the functions requests from the region without the Core—shows the worst performance (US: 15.46 ms, EU: 230.68 ms). This experimental evidence confirms that the decentralised approach can positively impact the performance of serverless applications, especially when they are geographically distributed and use locality-based scheduling policies.

Figures 4 and 5 present the cumulative distribution functions (CDFs) of response times in log scale for the two test scenarios—with and without the APP script, respectively. When using APP, the response times are stable and distributed between 13 and 24 milliseconds. When using vanilla invocations, more than 80% of the requests from the EU region used the EU Worker, therefore, keeping response times similar to those with the APP script. With the remaining 20% of the requests, the EU Core switched to the US Worker, significantly increasing latency up to more than 140 milliseconds. This behaviour is also visible from the US region, where, in this case, half of the requests were assigned to the US Worker, and the other half to the EU Worker.

6 Related Work and Conclusion

In this work, we introduce and evaluate a decentralised variant of the APP scheduling architecture, implemented in the FunLess serverless platform. The extension enables multiple controllers to cooperate in scheduling functions, improving scalability, responsiveness, and fault tolerance, especially in edge and multi-cloud deployments. Our implementation follows an optimistic decentralisation strategy where workers locally validate scheduling constraints. This approach removes the need for global coordination and enables controllers to be almost stateless, improving elasticity and system adaptability controller-wise, meaning that controllers can dynamically (dis)appear depending on, e.g., load conditions.

The problem of supporting multiple controllers in APP has also been tackled in previous work [9], through the introduction of a variant of the language, called TAPP (Topology-Aware APP) that enables targeted function scheduling within specific topological zones, implemented on Apache OpenWhisk [23]. Compared to our work, in TAPP, each controller has privileged access to local workers and limited access to remote ones. In our approach, all controllers have full access to all workers. Furthermore, TAPP maintains a single platform entry point, while our implementation enables direct access to individual controllers, significantly reducing latency in geographically distributed scenarios.

We note that OpenWhisk itself supports multiple controllers. However, it does not inherently offer coordination or consistency guarantees for scheduling decisions across them. This aspect limits its usage in scenarios requiring policy-aware scheduling across distributed control points, as controllers may race or generate conflicting decisions due to lack of coordination. Our approach addresses these aspects by embedding constraint checks within the workers themselves.

Similarly, other serverless platforms such as Knative and OpenFaaS support multiple ingress points or decentralized deployments (e.g., via Kubernetes autoscaling, multiple gateways, etc.). However, these systems primarily rely on platform-level load balancing and do not offer declarative, fine-grained scheduling guarantees like those expressible in APP. In both cases, scheduling is either opaque or relies on infrastructure-specific heuristics (e.g., pod autoscaling, metric-based routing), with no mechanism to express or enforce function-level policies, such as prioritisation, locality, or resource constraints.

We see different open directions to pursue in the future. Notably, while the decentralised variant of FunLess ensures that a function can be executed on a worker only if it satisfies the scheduling constraints in APP—because the constraints are checked by the worker before execution—it can introduce behaviours that are not allowed by the centralised scheduling architecture—globally, the behaviours of the centralised and decentralised variants of the platform can differ. This divorce can happen because in the centralised version each scheduling instance happens atomically, while in the decentralised variant multiple scheduling instances can interleave, reaching configurations that the centralised case would not. We plan to study the consequences of this discrepancy, and, in case they determine significant limitations, we foresee the investigation of modifications to the scheduling protocols or consistency models that can reconcile these anomalies, while retaining scalability and decentralisation. We also envision applying techniques similar to the ones presented in this paper to other serverless platforms and evaluating whether one can extend the latter to offer policy-aware scheduling guarantees in the likes of APP-based FunLess.

References

1. Knative (2023). https://knative.dev/
2. Apache Software Foundation : Apache Kafka (2025). https://kafka.apache.org/
3. Azure, M.: Microsoft azure functions (2022). https://azure.microsoft.com/
4. Bernstein, P.A., Newcomer, E.: Principles of Transaction Processing. Morgan Kaufmann, 2nd edn. (2009)
5. Broadcom: Rabbitmq (2025). https://www.rabbitmq.com/
6. Cloud, G.: Google cloud functions (2022). https://cloud.google.com/functions/
7. De Palma, G., Giallorenzo, S., Laneve, C., Mauro, J., Trentin, M., Zavattaro, G.: Leveraging static analysis for cost-aware serverless scheduling policies. Int. J. Softw. Tools Technol. Transf. **26**(6), 781–796 (2024). https://doi.org/10.1007/S10009-024-00776-9
8. De Palma, G., Giallorenzo, S., Mauro, J., Trentin, M., Zavattaro, G.: Custom serverless function scheduling policies: An APP tutorial. In: Dorai, G., Gabbrielli, M., Manzonetto, G., Osmani, A., Prandini, M., Zavattaro, G., Zimmermann, O. (eds.) Joint Post-proceedings of the Third and Fourth International Conference on Microservices, Microservices 2020/2022, May 10-12, 2022, Paris, France. OASIcs, vol. 111, pp. 5:1–5:16. Schloss Dagstuhl - Leibniz-Zentrum für Informatik (2022). https://doi.org/10.4230/OASICS.MICROSERVICES.2020-2022.5
9. De Palma, G., Giallorenzo, S., Mauro, J., Trentin, M., Zavattaro, G.: A declarative approach to topology-aware serverless function-execution scheduling. In: IEEE

International Conference on Web Services, ICWS 2022, Barcelona, Spain, July 10–16, 2022, pp. 337–342. IEEE (2022). https://doi.org/10.1109/ICWS55610.2022.00056
10. De Palma, G., Giallorenzo, S., Mauro, J., Trentin, M., Zavattaro, G.: Formally verifying function scheduling properties in serverless applications. IT Prof. **25**(6), 94–99 (2023). https://doi.org/10.1109/MITP.2023.3333071
11. De Palma, G., Giallorenzo, S., Mauro, J., Trentin, M., Zavattaro, G.: Function-as-a-service allocation policies made formal. In: Margaria, T., Steffen, B. (eds.) Leveraging Applications of Formal Methods, Verification and Validation. REoCAS Colloquium in Honor of Rocco De Nicola - 12th International Symposium, ISoLA 2024, Crete, Greece, October 27–31, 2024, Proceedings, Part I. Lecture Notes in Computer Science, vol. 15219, pp. 306–321. Springer (2024). https://doi.org/10.1007/978-3-031-73709-1_19
12. De Palma, G., Giallorenzo, S., Mauro, J., Trentin, M., Zavattaro, G.: Funless: functions-as-a-service for private edge cloud systems. In: IEEE International Conference on Web Services, ICWS 2024, Shenzhen, China, July 7–13, 2024. pp. 961–967. IEEE (2024). https://doi.org/10.1109/ICWS62655.2024.00114
13. De Palma, G., Giallorenzo, S., Mauro, J., Trentin, M., Zavattaro, G.: An openwhisk extension for topology-aware allocation priority policies. In: Castellani, I., Tiezzi, F. (eds.) Coordination Models and Languages - 26th IFIP WG 6.1 International Conference, COORDINATION 2024, Held as Part of the 19th International Federated Conference on Distributed Computing Techniques, DisCoTec 2024, Groningen, The Netherlands, June 17–21, 2024, Proceedings. Lecture Notes in Computer Science, vol. 14676, pp. 201–218. Springer (2024). https://doi.org/10.1007/978-3-031-62697-5_11
14. De Palma, G., Giallorenzo, S., Mauro, J., Trentin, M., Zavattaro, G.: Webassembly at the edge: Benchmarking a serverless platform for private edge cloud systems. IEEE Internet Comput. **1**, 1–8 (2024). https://doi.org/10.1109/MIC.2024.3513035
15. De Palma, G., Giallorenzo, S., Mauro, J., Trentin, M., Zavattaro, G.: Affinity-aware serverless function scheduling. In: 22nd IEEE International Conference on Software Architecture, ICSA 2025, Odense, Denmark, March 31–April 4, 2025. IEEE (2025)
16. Palma, G., Giallorenzo, S., Mauro, J., Zavattaro, G.: Allocation priority policies for serverless function-execution scheduling optimisation. In: Kafeza, E., Benatallah, B., Martinelli, F., Hacid, H., Bouguettaya, A., Motahari, H. (eds.) ICSOC 2020. LNCS, vol. 12571, pp. 416–430. Springer, Cham (2020). https://doi.org/10.1007/978-3-030-65310-1_29
17. De Palma, G., Giallorenzo, S., Mauro, J., Zavattaro, G.: Allocation priority policies for serverless function-execution scheduling optimisation. In: Service-Oriented Computing - 18th International Conference, ICSOC 2020, Dubai, United Arab Emirates, December 14–17, 2020, Proceedings. Lecture Notes in Computer Science, vol. 12571, pp. 416–430. Springer (2020). https://doi.org/10.1007/978-3-030-65310-1_29
18. Hendrickson, S., Sturdevant, S., Harter, T., Venkataramani, V., Arpaci-Dusseau, A.C., Arpaci-Dusseau, R.H.: Serverless computation with openlambda. In: 8th {USENIX} Workshop on Hot Topics in Cloud Computing (HotCloud 16) (2016)
19. Juric, S.: Elixir in action. Manning (2024)
20. Lamport, L.: The part-time parliament. ACM Trans. Comput. Syst. **16**(2), 133–169 (1998)
21. Ongaro, D., Ousterhout, J.K.: In search of an understandable consensus algorithm. In: Gibson, G., Zeldovich, N. (eds.) Proceedings of the 2014 USENIX Annual Technical Conference, USENIX ATC 2014, Philadelphia, PA, USA, June 19–20, 2014,

pp. 305–319. USENIX Association (2014). https://www.usenix.org/conference/atc14/technical-sessions/presentation/ongaro
22. OpenFaaS: Openfaas (2022). https://www.openfaas.com/
23. OpenWhisk, A.: Apache openwhisk (2022). https://openwhisk.apache.org/
24. Services, A.W.: Introducing AWS lambda (2022). https://aws.amazon.com/about-aws/whats-new/2014/11/13/introducing-aws-lambda/
25. Stenman, E.: Beam: a virtual machine for handling millions of messages per second (invited talk). In: Proceedings of the 10th ACM SIGPLAN International Workshop on Virtual Machines and Intermediate Languages, p. 4. VMIL 2018, Association for Computing Machinery, New York (2018). https://doi.org/10.1145/3281287.3281289

Author Index

A
Attard, Duncan Paul 199
Aubert, Clément 46

B
Bliudze, Simon 175
Bugeja, Keith 199

C
Cerf, Sophie 175

D
De Palma, Giuseppe 218

F
Feret, Jérôme 103
Francalanza, Adrian 199

G
Galea, Marietta 199
Giallorenzo, Saverio 218
Gössler, Gregor 103

K
Kong Win Chang, Aurélie 103
Kouchnarenko, Olga 175

L
Lanese, Ivan 24
Lenglet, Serguëi 89
Lienhardt, Michael 137
Loreti, Michele 154

M
Mauro, Jacopo 218
Melgratti, Hernán C. 3

Mezzina, Claudio Antares 3, 24

N
Noûs, Camille 89

P
Phillips, Iain 46
Pinna, G. Michele 3
Pischke, Kai 116

Q
Quadrini, Michela 154

R
Rehman, Aniqa 154

S
Sangiorgi, Davide 68
Schmitt, Alan 89

T
Tabone, Gerard 199
Trentin, Matteo 218

U
Ulidowski, Irek 46

V
Vassor, Martin 24

Y
Yoshida, Nobuko 116

Z
Zahra, Gianluca 199
Zavattaro, Gianluigi 218

GPSR Compliance

The European Union's (EU) General Product Safety Regulation (GPSR) is a set of rules that requires consumer products to be safe and our obligations to ensure this.

If you have any concerns about our products, you can contact us on ProductSafety@springernature.com

In case Publisher is established outside the EU, the EU authorized representative is:

Springer Nature Customer Service Center GmbH
Europaplatz 3
69115 Heidelberg, Germany

Batch number: 09118841

Printed by Printforce, the Netherlands

PSYCHOLOGIE ET SCIENCES HUMAINES

Michel Legrand

Léopold Szondi
son test, sa doctrine

Préface de Jean Oury

PIERRE MARDAGA, EDITEUR
2, GALERIE DES PRINCES, BRUXELLES

© by Pierre Mardaga, Bruxelles 1979
37, rue de la Province, 4020 Liège
2, Galerie des Princes, 1000 Bruxelles

Préface

Ce livre est un événement. Nous étions beaucoup à attendre quelque chose de cet ordre, quelque chose qui nous fasse accéder rigoureusement à la pensée de Léopold Szondi et à une technique nuancée de ce qu'on nomme encore le «Test». Ce travail est réalisé. Il suffit maintenant de le lire, de l'expérimenter, de l'apprécier. Une des plus grandes vertus de cet ouvrage c'est qu'il donne à penser, qu'il ne se referme pas sur un dogme. Je ne suis qu'un lecteur parmi d'autres, survivant comme je peux dans les sillons pas encore effacés d'une psychiatrie exsangue.

La première fois que j'ai entendu parler de L. Szondi, c'était il y a déjà trente ans, en 1948. J'étais à l'Hôpital Psychiatrique de Saint-Alban, en Lozère. Qui dit Saint-Alban, dit François Tosquelles. J'ai eu cette chance insigne de le rencontrer et d'articuler, dans une austérité éblouissante, la clinique psychiatrique avec le travail des groupes, les recherches biologiques, le champ analytique, la phénoménologie et les explorations de Szondi et de Rorschach. Rencontre, destin, profil d'une existence. Les circonstances, comme on dit pudiquement, ont fait que pendant une dizaine d'années je me suis trouvé éloigné, presque marginalisé. Puis nous avons fondé ce qu'on a appelé le G T Psy. Creuset difficile, densité des échanges. C'est dans ce cadre que j'ai appris à mieux connaître Jacques Schotte. «Szondi» revenait, articulé dans un système de pensée d'une richesse et d'une rigueur sans précédent. Il y a eu la notice de 1963 («Notice pour introduire le problème structural de la Schicksalsanalyse» — Szondiana V, 1963)... Les années ont passé, avec leur poids, l'inertie des groupes, les défaillances des collectifs, les niaiseries d'idéologies majoritaires, la destructuration d'un travail profondément révolutionnaire. Des failles se sont creusées, définitives, dans les différents groupes de recherche. Il y a des plages mortes, à jamais stériles.

C'est en décembre 1971 que J. Schotte est venu une semaine à La Borde. Il a exposé l'essentiel de sa réflexion sur Szondi. C'est depuis que j'ai eu l'idée d'une « greffe » : greffe de transfert, comme le dit Gisela Pankow, greffe d'une recherche ouverte sur une sémiologie pratique, réanimation de champs dévastés. Ça continue d'agir; sans éclat, péniblement. Claude Van Reeth est venu, avec une patience digne d'un berger attentif, recommençant, mois après mois, à épeler, pour qui voulait l'entendre, l'alphabet szondien. Long travail, aride; jachère souvent inaccessible, préjugés tenaces. Quelques prairies semblent cependant se dessiner, timidement. Simple émergence d'une couleur vivante. Aube déjà vieille des nouveaux temps. Il faut continuer de ne pas savoir qu'on a de l'espoir, ne pas le proclamer; sinon tout redeviendra terne, monotone, dans une errance infinie.

Nous avions déjà beaucoup de textes excellents: de J. Schotte, de J. Melon, de M. Legrand, de Cl. Van Reeth, etc. Mais il me semblait nécessaire, pratique, utile, qu'un rassemblement didactique soit à nouveau tenté dans une forme aussi rigoureuse qu'accessible. C'est alors que Michel Legrand me proposa le texte de cet ouvrage afin que j'en rédige la préface. J'en fus surpris. Ai-je l'aptitude suffisante pour présenter un tel travail ? J'en ai, malgré tout, accepté l'hommage.

Donc, voici enfin ce livre. Chaque page est un « ouvert ». Il n'y a pas repliement défensif, ostentation réductrice. C'est un essai d'énonciation de catégories qui permettent de déchiffrer et de délimiter : découpe qui s'appuie sur le « réel », enchaînement polyphonique qui tisse les différentes places d'une tablature complexe, phénoménalité du corps dans ses différentes manifestations. Le Réel passe par là, sans échappatoire. Le tableau ne doit être qu'écran, comme tout tableau, afin que se manifeste, dans la marge, ce qui ne peut être dit. L'Œuvre de Szondi c'est un peu ça aussi : surgissement d'un tableau, non pas d'une totalisation, mais d'un tableau total qui ne peut fonctionner que dans sa délimitation.

Ça reste toujours à faire. Mais ce « programme » ne peut pas être sans mise en équations. On assiste à des enchaînements qui ne sont pas linéaires : comme si un « caisson noir » s'entrouvrait pour articuler causes et effets dans le domaine du « continu-discontinu » ou, plus précisément, dans la relation « variables de contrôle » et « variables d'état ». Dans cette lecture matricielle du tableau de Szondi, on assiste à un enchevêtrement d'états stables et d'états instables, et la « dominante » peut apparaître quelquefois comme indicatrice de points de rebroussement du système ou, même, comme « zone de catastrophe ».

Michel Legrand reprend ici ce qu'il a déjà élaboré dans sa thèse (« Psychanalyse, Schicksalsanalyse et épistémologie » — Louvain, juillet 1972) mais l'articule d'une façon plus concrète, dans une visée plus didactique. Il s'appuie, bien sûr, sur l'extraordinaire richesse de l'enseignement de Jacques Schotte et adopte d'emblée la lecture triadique que celui-ci a instaurée. C'est plus qu'une lecture, c'est l'application concrète d'une « phénoménologie triadique », nommément celle de Deese qui, comme le souligne J. Schotte, a orienté sa propre réflexion.

Dans la pratique répétitive de chaque jour, on risque toujours de perdre le sens de ce qu'on fait. Dans ce champ de la psychiatrie, tout devient vite indiscernable, confus, uniformisé. Une fois les grandes déclarations proclamées, on se retrouve devant la tâche quotidienne, lourde, écrasé par les préjugés sordides ou nobles. La ségrégation est devenue le « ça va de soi » de tout citoyen, spécialisé ou analphabète. Il a été de bon ton de parler du « fou »; c'est vite devenu une valeur commerciale dont les éditeurs connaissent bien les arcanes pour améliorer le « tirage ». Les impératifs sociaux, les statuts professionnels, les intérêts « philosophiques » n'ont guère dépassé l'efficience des bonnes œuvres de l'entre-deux guerre. Il faut beaucoup de courage pour parler encore de l'ascèse nécessaire à l'abord concret de l'existence psychotique. On risque la lapidation si l'on parle d'une « covivance » avec la psychose, surtout si l'on précise que c'est affaire d'Ethique et que la première démarche est celle de l'« exposition » (au sens d'E. Levinas).

La réflexion que nous apporte M. Legrand peut nous servir à rester techniquement à ce niveau de «l'exposition», passivité de la passivité, attention extrême à cette sorte de déclosion du Dire. Elle nous tient à proximité de ce dont il s'agit. Chaque cas prend relief, couleur, ouvre des lointains. La nosologie s'estompe tandis qu'une nosographie complètement renouvelée et polydimensionnelle vient se poser, non comme grille de lecture, mais comme tableau de réinterprétation.

La grande novation semble être la généralisation de l'intuition freudienne de la Spaltung, du clivage. La dialectique, ou plus précisément les dialectiques, interfactorielles, intervectorielles, entre l'avant-plan et les arrière-plans, entre les « conjonctures pulsionnelles » (M. Legrand), sont bien plus qu'une syntaxe; de même que l'ensemble des tendances est bien plus qu'un lexique. C'est au niveau des catégories que le jeu apparaît, et, qui dit catégorie, pose la polysémie orientée de chacune des cases, mais également l'ouverture des concepts dans une délimitation de plus en plus affirmée. Le tableau n'est pas un fourre-tout d'un système classificatoire, mais une proposition d'un jeu où la pensée prend corps.

C'est ce « jeu » qu'il me semblait urgent de greffer dans la pratique décadente de la psychiatrie sérielle. Cette greffe a du mal à prendre. Le terrain est encore très altéré, quasi mort par endroits, trop fibreux à d'autres. Mais ce serait être complice de cette destruction que de déclarer faillite. Le livre de M. Legrand, vous verrez que ça peut donner de l'espoir, de la passion, même quand tout semble affadi. Mais, bien sûr, ce n'est pas une « technique » qui peut être « appliquée » sans conditions minutieuses. L'usage qu'on peut en faire ne dépend pas tellement d'une intentionnalité, mais d'un travail au niveau de la « base ». L'acculturation est difficile, surtout au niveau d'un Collectif: le bon usage d'un tel livre peut le poser comme instrument de « soins » pour ceux qui ont à faire avec le monde de la psychose, mais également pour tout « honnête homme »: soins, je veux dire entreprise thérapeutique personnelle, ajointement des concepts, redistribution des valeurs.

Je voudrais reprendre le problème du tableau des catégories. Ce tableau se présente comme un ensemble délimité dont chaque élément est lui-même tableau. Catégories dont chacune est un opérateur, productrice d'interprétations et d'interpénétrations, l'ensemble des parties de chaque case produisant une matrice de systèmes transfinis. Ceci se complexifie encore lorsque l'on suit l'indication de J. Schotte d'une « application », sur chacune des quatre cases d'un vecteur, de chacun des vecteurs: par exemple, à la succession p-k +k- p+ correspond, dans l'élaboration de J. Schotte, la suite: C S P SCH. Nous évoquons là le problème des circuits intravectoriels dont la configuration ne semble pas encore avoir trouvé sa forme définitive. Sans vouloir entrer ici dans une argumentation détaillée, je préfère l'option de Schotte à celles de Szondi, ou de M. Legrand, ou de Jacques Servais et d'autres. La richesse du texte de M. Legrand se révèle ici : tout en prenant position pour telle ou telle configuration, il nous donne des arguments pour que nous puissions élaborer nous-mêmes la succession logique qui nous semble la plus adéquate.

Ce livre permet non seulement de pratiquer le test de Szondi avec toutes les nuances désirables, mais il incite également à la réflexion, à l'élaboration théorique, aux recherches personnelles, lectures complémentaires, etc. Michel Legrand n'hésite pas, par exemple, à renvoyer le lecteur, pour l'approfondissement de certaines notions, aux ouvrages de Jean Melon (en particulier : « Théorie et pratique du Szondi » - Liège, 1975).

Nous suivons, tout au long de la lecture, une démarche de critique épistémologique de l'œuvre de Szondi, démarche dans laquelle s'articulent psychanalyse, phénoménologie et émergence d'un « champ autologique » (Schotte) de la psychiatrie. Sous cette critique, quelquefois extrêmement sévère, du travail de Szondi, s'affirme cependant la dimension géniale de cet inventeur infatigable.

Ce que j'écris là n'échappe pas à la faiblesse inhérente à toute préface. Il y a risque de redondance, de substitution d'une « présentation » (Darstellung), le livre, par une autre présentation, la préface. En effet, ce livre est lui-même une présentation de l'œuvre de Szondi. On risque donc de se trouver dans une succession de mises en abymes plus ou moins déjointées. On ne peut échapper partiellement à ce piège du « dit », à cette « coupure fermée » de la « Darstellung », qu'en essayant de saisir ce qui se manifeste au niveau de « l'exposition », au niveau du Dire. Le dit s'établit en surplomb, et son ombre portée, sur le Dire, fait apparaître mille nuances, une texture fine, un treillis de systèmes « inouïs », où il n'est question que d'Autrui déjà là, dans sa proximité inatteignable. Les « photos » du test ne sont que « visages » proposés, et non figures spatiales. Ces visages, traces d'un impossible lekton, sont ce qui s'expose fugitivement à notre regard. Piège à regard, sa surface et ses inflexions dessinent dans une topologie nouvelle ce qu'il en est non seulement de mon rapport au monde mais de l'émergence silencieuse du dire de « lalangue ». Dimension — ou « dit-mension » comme le dit J. Lacan — qui me « montre », au niveau du Dire, dans une diagrammatique dont le protocole du test n'est qu'un reflet. Je ne peux écrire que dans le tableau, participant par chaque sillon que je trace à son surgissement. Il est, lui-même, surgissement : c'est-à-dire, découpe qui se distingue du réel, articulation qui porte jugement sur ce qu'il piège dans cette distanciation. « Partition » primordiale, Urteilung ; clivage primordial, Urspaltung. Il est le corps qui dispose l'inscription du Réel, accumulant des signifiants qui me singularisent. Notre travail d'interprétation n'est pas simple déchiffrage d'un protocole, mais défrichage nécessaire pour rendre le Dire à sa jachère.

Il me semble bien que le texte de M. Legrand, tout en nous livrant avec minutie et précision le mode technique d'exploitation du test, a la sagesse de laisser jouer le tableau dans sa relative contingence. Il ne le fige pas dans une « nécessité » dogmatique mais laisse le travail se faire sans en extirper le levain. Cette distance est prise par une hypothèse qui me semble être à la base de toute une élaboration : le profil général d'un protocole ne peut être que ce qui apparaît d'un clivage primordial, entre l'avant-plan et l'arrière-plan théorique, ce clivage n'étant que ce qui résulte d'une «instance déterminante invisible» (pour reprendre une expression dérivée d'Alain Badiou commentant Althusser). Cette détermination «ouvre une porte» dans le mur imaginaire des théorisations réductrices du champ psychiatrique. C'est en même temps la schize originaire et la détermination décisive. C'est aussi ce à partir de quoi je peux «dire», en prenant la parole. A partir de cette schize qui me détermine dans ce que ça veut bien dire d'écrire une «préface», je «m'expose». Et cette exposition indique, non pas un chemin, ni un itinéraire, mais une trace à suivre: trace d'un discours ouvert qui ne prend sens que de son dire.

Puis-je espérer que mon «dit» ne soit qu'écran dont le jeu expérimenté fasse apparaître ce qui reste en deçà du texte, dans sa «texture», dans ses interlignes, dans ses marges, en deçà de toute intentionnalité, dans ce qui garde un contact avec son originarité.

Jean Oury
Décembre 1978

Avant-propos

Par cet ouvrage, nous espérons offrir au lecteur d'expression française un instrument qui permette de pénétrer dans l'univers du psychiatre Léopold Szondi, qui ouvre l'accès à la doctrine de Szondi et à son entreprise scientifique en général, interrogée jusque dans ses fondements épistémologiques, aussi bien qu'à son célèbre outil diagnostique, ledit test de Szondi, présenté jusque dans les détails les plus fins de son application. Car nous nous sommes efforcé de répondre à deux ambitions distinctes, apparemment éloignées, mais en réalité enchâssées et même fondues l'une dans l'autre : introduire à l'œuvre szondienne dans ses articulations les plus fondamentales d'une part, proposer les éléments les plus fouillés d'une initiation à la pratique du test d'autre part.

Tout d'abord, nous avons voulu donner une présentation d'ensemble de l'œuvre szondienne. Cette présentation, nous l'avons articulée autour des rapports complexes mais exemplaires qu'entretiennent dans la démarche de Szondi la théorie et la pratique, la doctrine et l'instrumentation testologique. La succession même de nos quatre grandes parties, qui s'organise selon la logique du déroulement historique de l'œuvre, rend visible à elle seule l'incessant va-et-vient dialectique qui conduit de la théorie vers la pratique instrumentale, de la pratique instrumentale vers la théorie. S'originant dans une théorie biogénétique du destin humain et des pulsions (Première partie), la démarche szondienne trouve aussitôt un prolongement dans un instrument diagnostique, conçu à l'origine comme simple matérialisation d'une doctrine constituée (Deuxième partie). Mais l'outil testologique s'avère plus riche que soupçonné au départ et redynamise la théorie pour l'ouvrir à de nouvelles dimensions plus congéniales à la psychanalyse : ainsi se constitue et se précise peu à peu une doctrine psychopulsionnelle profondément originale, cœur même de l'entreprise szondienne (Troisième partie). Toutefois, le test, redevenu instrument d'une théorie renouvelée qu'il présuppose, continue d'appeler une interrogation : ses principes de fonctionnement, sa validité, restent problématiques (Quatrième partie).

Mais nous avons voulu aussi introduire de manière aussi concrète et précise que possible à la pratique du test de Szondi. L'étudiant et le praticien trouveront ici l'essentiel des informations qui leur donneront accès à l'administration et à l'interprétation du test. A la limite, le lecteur qui souhaiterait en un premier temps se limiter à cet aspect pourra effectuer une lecture délibérément sélective de l'ouvrage : il se concentrera d'abord sur le paragraphe A de la deuxième partie, qui l'initiera à l'administration du test et à l'inscription de ses résultats, et passera ensuite au chapitre I de la troisième partie, qui l'introduira à la doctrine des pulsions, guide nécessaire de toute lecture du test, aussi bien qu'aux diverses méthodes d'interprétation.

Nous tenons à exprimer notre gratitude à toutes les personnes qui d'une façon ou d'une autre ont permis de mener à bien la rédaction et la publication de cet ouvrage. Nous remercions en particulier : Jacques Schotte, dont la rencontre cruciale a infléchi un itinéraire intellectuel qui a pu dès lors croiser un long moment l'œuvre szondienne ; Jean Oury et Antoine Vergote, pour leur encouragement bienveillant ; Jean-Paul Abraham, Paul Pellemans et les Presses Universitaires de Namur, pour l'appui décisif qu'ils ont apporté à la publication du travail ; Nicole Renkin, pour la qualité de son aide dactylographique.

Introduction
Léopold Szondi et l'analyse du destin

1. Vie et Œuvre de Szondi

D'origine juive, Szondi est né le 11 mars 1893 à Nyitra en Slovaquie[1].

En 1898, sa famille s'installe à Budapest: c'est dans cette ville que Szondi vivra et poursuivra ses activités jusqu'aux événements dramatiques de la guerre 1940-45.

Dès les toutes premières années de ses études de médecine, qu'il commence en 1911, Szondi manifeste un intérêt spécifique pour la neuropsychiatrie. A la même époque, il a l'occasion de travailler aux côtés de Ranschburg, disciple de Wundt et introducteur de la psychologie expérimentale en Hongrie.

Après l'intermède de la guerre 14-18, qui voit Szondi mobilisé dans les services sanitaires de l'armée de son pays, Szondi obtient rapidement son diplôme de médecin spécialiste en neuropsychiatrie. Il commence par travailler comme assistant dans une polyclinique de Budapest, tout en continuant à collaborer aux activités du laboratoire de psychologie dirigé par Ranschburg. Bientôt, il est lui-même nommé directeur du laboratoire de psychopathologie et de psychothérapie de l'Institut supérieur d'orthopédagogie de Budapest, dont il devient également professeur, fonction qu'il occupera jusqu'en 1941.

Dans le courant de cette période, entre 1921 et 1940, Szondi publie plusieurs ouvrages et une multiplicité de petits articles, écrits pour la plupart en langue hongroise. Nous n'en établirons pas ici la liste, établie par D. Larese (1976, pp. 33-36), mais nous nous bornerons à remarquer que les publications

---

[1] Les données les plus complètes concernant la vie et l'œuvre de Szondi sont contenues dans: Dino Larese, *Leopold Szondi*, 1976.

de l'époque témoignent d'une préoccupation dirigée vers les troubles psychiatriques au sens large, en particulier la neurasthénie et la débilité, et attestent une recherche guidée d'après les orientations de la biologie : endocrinologie, neurologie, génétique. Dès 1930, on observe en effet un mouvement de polarisation progressive autour de la génétique et de ses méthodes d'investigation (la recherche généalogique et la méthode des jumeaux). Soucieux de mettre au jour les facteurs héréditaires des affections mentales, Szondi établit de vastes arbres généalogiques. Il est ainsi conduit à formuler son hypothèse du génotropisme, dont il divulgue le contenu dans : *Analysis of marriages* (La Haye, 1937). Par ailleurs, toujours au cours de la même période, il met au point son épreuve testologique, destinée à l'origine à servir la recherche généalogique.

Mais la guerre 1940-45 bouleverse l'existence de Szondi, amené, comme bien d'autres Juifs, à subir la persécution nazie. En 1941, son poste de professeur lui est enlevé. En 1944, il est déporté à Bergen-Belsen. Il ne devra sa liberté qu'à un échange négocié avec les nazis à l'initiative d'un groupe d'intellectuels juifs américains. Toujours est-il que, six mois après sa déportation, il peut gagner la Suisse, devenue depuis lors sa nouvelle patrie. En 1946, il s'installera à Zurich pour y vivre jusqu'à aujourd'hui et y développera une activité de psychiatre praticien. C'est donc également en Suisse qu'il publiera, en langue allemande, ses cinq grandes œuvres :

1. La *Schicksalsanalyse* (l'Analyse du destin), 1944, jette les bases de la doctrine génétique des pulsions.
2. Le *Lehrbuch der experimentellen Triebdiagnostik* (le Traité du diagnostic expérimental des pulsions), 1947 (réédité en 1960 dans une version entièrement remaniée), introduit au test et à ses méthodes d'interprétation.
3. La *Triebpathologie* (la Pathologie pulsionnelle), 1952, recentre la doctrine des pulsions autour du thème de la dialectique pulsionnelle et développe une approche systématique des maladies mentales.
4. La *Ich-Analyse* (l'Analyse du moi), 1956, expose la théorie szondienne du moi.
5. La *Schicksalsanalytische Therapie* (la Thérapie de l'Analyse du destin), 1963, dégage les implications thérapeutiques de l'Analyse du destin et propose une méthode originale de traitement des affections psychiatriques lourdes.

Nous citerons désormais ces cinq grandes œuvres selon le système d'abréviations suivant : 1. *Scha*, 2. *TrD* (édition de 1960), 3. *TrP*, 4. *IchA*, 5. *SchaTh*.

Signalons pour terminer que Szondi est l'auteur de deux essais, qui parachèvent son œuvre, consacrés à deux figures bibliques : Caïn (*Kain*, Gestalten des Bösen, 1969) et Moïse (*Moses*, Antwort auf Kain, 1973).

2. Le mouvement de l'Analyse du destin

Szondi n'est pas seulement l'auteur d'une œuvre individuelle, il est aussi le fondateur d'une Ecole dite de l'Analyse du destin, l'initiateur d'un mouvement collectif, qui s'est structuré depuis 1947 en « Association internationale de recherche en psychologie du destin », diffuse périodiquement une revue (« Szondiana ») et organise tous les trois ans un colloque international.

Toutefois, cette Ecole n'a connu et ne connaît encore qu'un retentissement limité. Dès l'origine, la doctrine et le test de Szondi ont rencontré des résistances, qui ont freiné leur diffusion dans le monde de la psychologie universitaire et par là même dans le monde des praticiens formés par l'université. Nous connaissons encore mal les causes précises qui ont suscité ces résistances : leur mise au jour exigerait le concours de l'anthropologue, de l'épistémologue et du sociologue de la connaissance. On doit néanmoins faire allusion ici à un phénomène caractéristique des années 50, observable aussi bien aux U.S.A. qu'en France. A cette époque, le test de Szondi est l'objet d'une divulgation : en 1949, Susan Deri, une élève de la première heure émigrée aux U.S.A., publie son *Introduction to the Szondi test* (citée *IS*), restée jusqu'à aujourd'hui l'une des meilleures introductions au test de Szondi ; en 1952, les P.U.F. publient sous la signature de Madame Pruschy-Bejarano, la traduction française du *Diagnostic expérimental des pulsions* (cité *DP*). Aussitôt le test de Szondi suscite la curiosité. De nombreux chercheurs des universités, aux U.S.A. en particulier, s'efforcent de vérifier sa « validité », sans succès, du moins aux yeux de la majorité d'entre eux. L'intérêt retombe, voire même se dissipe. Sans vouloir prendre parti dès à présent — nous examinerons en temps opportun les travaux consacrés à la validité du test —, nous croyons pouvoir dire que ce mouvement de critique négative des années 50 a été pour beaucoup dans l'échec du test de Szondi à pénétrer dans le monde universitaire. Aussi la communauté szondienne, malgré la richesse de sa vie interne, est-elle restée une communauté relativement isolée.

Mais les évolutions récentes permettent d'espérer un changement. La fondation en 1972 d'un Institut Szondi d'enseignement et de recherche, dont le siège est à Zurich, offre désormais de nouveaux moyens pour la diffusion de l'Analyse du destin. Mais surtout, depuis quelques années, la pensée de Szondi connaît un rayonnement nouveau à partir de l'Université de Louvain et de ce qu'y anime Jacques Schotte. Par son enseignement et par les multiples liens scientifiques qu'il noue infatigablement, Schotte a su sensibiliser un public croissant aux ressources trop négligées qu'offre l'œuvre de Szondi pour la fécondation d'une psychiatrie fondamentale, à l'intersection de l'anthropologie philosophique et des sciences humaines, de la psychanalyse freudienne et de la psychiatrie classique. C'est dans ce contexte qu'à sa façon notre ouvrage s'inscrit, comme s'y était inscrit déjà avant le nôtre le travail de Jean Melon, « *Théorie et pratique du Szondi* » (cité *TP*)[1].

---

[1] Précisons que l'ouvrage de J. Melon, publié en 1975 et première bonne introduction à Szondi écrite en langue française, ne fait pas double emploi avec le nôtre : loin d'être rivaux, les deux ouvrages sont largement complémentaires, même s'ils se rejoignent sur certains points, comme il était fatal. Ainsi, notre ouvrage est plus riche à propos des fondements théoriques et épistémologiques de l'œuvre szondienne, de même qu'il traite plus en détail les méthodes d'interprétation du test, et constitue par là une introduction plus précise à ce dernier. Par contre, l'ouvrage de J. Melon consacre de longs développements à la psychopathologie szondienne, qui sont absents de notre propre travail.

Première partie
Analyse du destin et Doctrine génétique des pulsions

A. Destin et figures du destin

D'entrée de jeu, Szondi découpe dans le tissu du réel un domaine qu'un mot unique servira à désigner de bout en bout : son objet propre sera le « destin » et sa discipline « Analyse du destin ». Mais qu'entendre en première approximation par ce terme ?

En élisant ce terme, Szondi se propose de dénommer la vie individuelle de l'homme, qui ne peut être réduite d'après lui à une succession d'événements aléatoires, mais apparaît grosse d'un sens : une cohérence se fait jour à travers l'existence individuelle envisagée dans son déroulement total, de la naissance à la mort, comme si une nécessité y advenait. Bien plus, dans le cours de cette existence, quelques événements font sens plus que d'autres, orientent de manière décisive le destin, lui ouvrent des perspectives qui désormais le marquent, comme si, en certains points de sa trajectoire, l'existence était à un tournant et prenait alors une orientation nouvelle et déterminante : la liaison amoureuse, l'engagement professionnel, le devenir-malade, la mort elle-même, sortes de figures exemplaires du destin, sont autant d'événements marquants de la trajectoire destinale de l'individu.

Mais là n'est encore qu'un point de départ intuitif. Szondi en convient : il est temps que le domaine du destin soit enfin élevé à l'état de domaine d'études scientifiques. L'orientation majeure de Szondi sera dès lors de construire une théorie du destin et de ses diverses modalités.

Cette théorie, dont Szondi jette les bases dans sa première grande œuvre, la *Schicksalsanalyse*, incorpore une composante biogénétique et une composante psychanalytique qui viennent s'y articuler dans une synthèse tout aussi originale que problématique. Tentons de la recomposer analytiquement, morceau par morceau, pour nous élever petit à petit jusqu'à une présentation d'ensemble.

B. La détermination génético-biologique des figures du destin ou choix destinaux

Le destin, précisera toujours Szondi, est choix, et les grandes figures du destin sont autant de formes de choix : choix en amour et amitié, choix de la maladie, choix de la profession, choix de la forme de mort.

Terminologie paradoxale quand on sait que Szondi postule un fondement génétique des « choix » destinaux. Mais à vrai dire, l'association quasi spontanée que l'homme moderne établit, depuis Descartes, entre choix et liberté est dénouée. Un seul constat de départ : à l'intérieur d'une existence individuelle, des orientations sont prises, des choix s'accomplissent, qu'il s'agisse du choix d'une maladie à l'intérieur d'un éventail de possibilités morbides, ou encore du choix d'une profession à l'intérieur d'un éventail de professions potentielles.

Mais à l'intérieur même des figures du destin redéfinies comme choix, Szondi distinguera de bout en bout les figures dites « morbides » et les figures dites « socialisées ». Chacun de ces deux groupes appelle un développement spécifique.

1. La détermination génético-biologique des figures morbides du destin (maladies mentales et morts suicidaires)

Figures morbides ou maladives : choix de la maladie, choix de la forme de mort. Mais non pas choix de la maladie tout court, non pas choix de la forme de mort tout court. Certes un cancer ou un infarctus qui s'achèvent dans la mort sont des événements marquants et dramatiques d'une vie individuelle. Pourtant, la doctrine szondienne, malgré quelques flottements, ne prétend pas couvrir les maladies organiques et leurs conséquences mortelles possibles : elle s'adresse aux maladies « mentales » et aux formes de mort suicidaires.

Mais formulons la thèse szondienne. Il existerait, dans le bagage héréditaire de l'être humain, huit groupes de gènes dont les variétés alléliques récessives seraient productrices de maladies mentales spécifiques*. Ou encore : le champ de la maladie mentale s'articulerait en huit formes majeures, produites génétiquement par des combinaisons homozygotes récessives. Groupées deux par deux de manière à former quatre cycles, ces huit maladies mentales de base régies par l'hérédité seraient les suivantes : 1. les maladies sexuelles (l'homosexualité et le sadisme), 2. les maladies paroxysmales (l'épilepsie et l'hystérie), 3. les maladies schizoformes (les schizophrénies catatonique et paranoïde), 4. les maladies circulaires (la mélancolie et la manie).

Quant aux formes de mort suicidaires, elles se différencieraient d'après le choix du « moyen ». Les mêmes facteurs héréditaires qui donnent lieu à une maladie mentale déterminée peuvent conduire aussi à une mort suicidaire à modalité spécifique. Ainsi, l'homosexualité et la paranoïdie entretiendraient

---

* Dans une annexe à notre première partie (p. 28), nous définissons quelques termes de la génétique. Le lecteur est donc prié de s'y référer chaque fois qu'il buterait sur un terme technique.

une relation spécifique avec un suicide utilisant le poison ou le révolver. Le suicide sadique recourerait à la corde ou au couteau. L'épileptique se donnerait la mort par le feu ou par saut dans le vide. Le catatonique s'abandonnerait à une mort passive (se laisser mourir de faim ou de froid, se jeter sur une voie de chemin de fer, ...). Enfin, des formes suicidaires « orales » (par absorption d'alcool ou de drogue p. ex.) pourraient accompagner les maladies circulaires (Scha, pp. 359-360).

Mais, dès lors que nous avons pris connaissance de la thèse énoncée dans toute sa généralité, nous ne pouvons manquer de nous interroger sur les formes de preuve empirique que Szondi avance à son appui.

Tout d'abord Szondi en appelle le plus souvent à la recherche psychiatrique en matière d'hérédité. Dans un texte classique, Szondi affirme que la doctrine psychiatrique de l'hérédité aurait déjà reconnu trois cycles héréditaires autonomes de maladies mentales (le cycle schizoforme Sch, le cycle circulaire ou maniaco-dépressif C, le cycle épileptique ou paroxysmal P), auxquels on devrait ajouter à présent le cycle héréditaire S des maladies sexuelles (Scha, p. 72).

De plus, en l'un ou l'autre endroit de son œuvre, Szondi nous donnera quelques précisions quant aux recherches effectuées, soit par la méthode des jumeaux, soit par la méthode familiale, qui attesteraient la détermination héréditaire des huit maladies mentales de base.

Enfin, Szondi lui-même effectuera une recherche originale, présentée sous forme d'une communication en 1939 et insérée dans la troisième édition de la Scha (1965). Cette recherche, s'appuyant sur 2.449 sujets, tend à accréditer l'hypothèse selon laquelle l'épilepsie, la migraine et le bégayement sont liés à des facteurs héréditaires communs: le cours héréditaire de ces affections serait dimère, polyallélique et récessif.

Telles sont, grossièrement résumées, les données empiriques sur lesquelles Szondi prétend fonder sa thèse d'une détermination héréditaire des figures morbides du destin, et en particulier des maladies mentales. L'examen de ces données appelle d'emblée une remarque. Car saisissant est l'écart qui sépare les recherches empiriques citées, y compris la propre recherche de Szondi, et les thèses que ces dernières ont l'ambition de soutenir.

Ainsi, pour ne dégager que deux aspects de cet écart:

a) Au vu des recherches citées, le cours héréditaire des huit maladies mentales de base semble devoir être plus complexe (dimère, voire polymère) que ne le postule théoriquement Szondi (cours monomère).
b) Les recherches citées font le plus souvent appel à une allélie multiple ou polyallélie, alors que Szondi retient la seule hypothèse de deux variations alléliques, l'une dominante, l'autre récessive.

En bref, nous devons dire que si l'hypothèse d'une hérédité au moins partielle des troubles mentaux n'est pas à exclure, en tout cas le processus de détermination héréditaire paraît être beaucoup plus complexe que ne le laissent supposer les thèses théoriques de Szondi.

2. *La détermination génético-biologique des figures socialisées du destin (choix amoureux, choix professionnel): le génotropisme*

Si un individu tombe malade, d'une maladie mentale particulière, si éventuellement il se suicide selon la modalité propre à sa maladie, c'est donc qu'il porterait dans son bagage héréditaire, en combinaison homozygote, le gène récessif responsable de cette maladie.

Mais comment expliquer génétiquement d'autres figures du destin, d'autres choix destinaux: le choix en amour, le choix de la profession? C'est sur ce terrain que Szondi innove, et dans son innovation même, suscite le scepticisme, voire l'opposition.

Certes Szondi prétend s'appuyer sur ce qu'il présente comme des acquis de la recherche génétique. Si la génétique a commencé par nier l'efficacité phénotypique du gène récessif «latent», elle a dû progressivement battre en retraite, du moins dans une certaine mesure. Le gène latent peut lui aussi influencer le phénotype. Il arrive que le caractère porté par le gène latent se manifeste au plan visible, mais sous une forme affaiblie. Ainsi l'individu porteur à l'état hétérozygote du gène récessif de la surdité: il ne sera pas sourd certes, mais son ouïe ne sera pas d'aussi bonne qualité que l'ouïe de l'homozygote dominant. Bien plus, la génétique, formulant en cela la thèse dite de l'hétérosis, aurait réussi à montrer que la présence latente d'un gène maladif peut être à l'origine d'un renforcement de la puissance vitale.

Szondi n'est donc pas le premier à affirmer l'efficacité propre des gènes récessifs latents. Mais, dans un mouvement d'audace, il va dépasser l'hétérosis pour poser la thèse du génotropisme. Selon lui, les gènes latents pourraient être à l'origine de certains actes de choix de l'individu, ou encore de certaines figures du destin individuel qui s'expriment sous forme de choix. Plus précisément, les gènes latents guideraient le choix en amour (libidotropisme) ou amitié (sociotropisme), le choix de la profession (opérotropisme).

Pour développer cette thèse, nous nous arrêterons au seul phénomène du libidotropisme.

En quel sens les gènes latents peuvent-ils donc guider le choix en amour d'un individu? A cette question, Szondi répond que l'individu porteur d'un gène latent récessif sera attiré par un individu porteur du même gène et aura tendance à s'unir à lui dans un lien amoureux.

Que penser de cette thèse? Examinons l'appui empirique dont elle peut se réclamer. En réalité, une partie importante de la Scha est consacrée à un essai de fondation empirique de la thèse du génotropisme appliquée au choix en amour, ou plus précisément encore au choix du conjoint. Szondi y procède à l'examen de cas particuliers de conjoints à propos desquels il s'interroge chaque fois: «les deux conjoints sont-ils porteurs du même gène récessif latent?». Ainsi que l'écrit Szondi: «notre théorie ne sera démontrée scientifiquement que lorsque nous aurons établi sans équivoque que les partenaires sont effectivement des individus hétérozygotes, donc des conducteurs possibles» (Scha, p. 91). Mais comment établir la nature de conducteur des conjoints? Par la méthode généalogique. Nous examinerons la parenté proche et éloignée de chacun des conjoints, nous y relèverons les caractères portés par les gènes récessifs (en particulier les maladies) et nous en inférerons le bagage héréditaire latent des deux conjoints.

Illustrons la procédure par l'évocation d'un cas très simple proposé par Szondi lui-même (cfr Tableau I). En l'occurence, les deux conjoints (1 et 2) sont sains et psychiquement normaux (s): chez aucun d'entre eux nous ne relevons trace de maladies ou tares héréditaires. En d'autres termes, ni l'un ni l'autre n'est porteur homozygote d'un gène récessif morbide. Par contre, le frère de l'époux (3), l'un des deux enfants du couple (4), ainsi que le neveu de l'épouse (5), sont débiles (d).

Tableau I

Un exemple de vérification du génotropisme
(d'après Scha, p. 86)

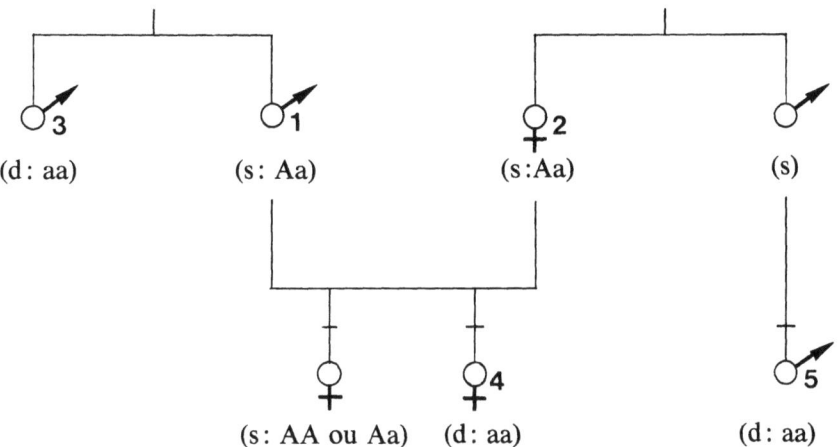

Szondi en conclut : les époux sont donc, du point de vue du caractère « débilité », conducteurs (Scha, p. 85). En effet, à supposer que : 1. la débilité soit un trouble héréditaire, 2. le cours héréditaire de la débilité soit réglé par un seul couple de gènes, dont les variantes alléliques seraient respectivement A et a, 3. la débilité soit liée au gène récessif a, dès ce moment nous pouvons conclure en toute certitude que nos deux conjoints sont porteurs latents (conducteurs) du gène récessif responsable de la débilité.

Or, ce seul cas est riche d'enseignements : il révèle clairement les présupposés dont dépend la juste démonstration de la thèse du génotropisme. Tout d'abord, la démonstration présuppose que soit établie l'hérédité du caractère observé, ici en l'occurence l'hérédité de la débilité. Car, à supposer que nous mettions en question la nature héréditaire de la débilité (qui, il faut bien le dire, est loin d'être établie), la démonstration szondienne devient sans objet. De plus, la démonstration présuppose que soit connu le cours héréditaire précis du caractère (cours héréditaire monomère, dimère, polymère ; récessif, dominant, ...). Or, dans bien des cas, le cours héréditaire n'est pas établi avec précision et de toute manière ne peut être que très complexe, beaucoup plus complexe en tout cas que la simple monomérie récessive. En conséquence, la démonstration ne pourra qu'être entachée d'imprécision et d'incertitude : elle sera bien éloignée de la netteté, sans doute elle-même factice, que laisse présumer le cas abusivement simple que nous venons d'évoquer.

Pour terminer ce premier examen critique de la thèse du génotropisme, une dernière question mérite d'être posée. Szondi, nous l'avons dit, fonde sa thèse sur un certain nombre de cas qui paraissent la confirmer. Mais ce nombre, forcément limité, est-il suffisant pour doter la proposition d'un degré significatif de corroboration ? De plus, cette limitation nécessaire ne laisse-telle pas place, dès lors, à une opération de sélection ? Szondi n'aurait-il pas arbitrairement retenu les seuls cas confirmatoires ? Et quand bien même nous ferions crédit à son honnêteté scientifique, ne pourrions-nous pas trouver, parmi les cas qu'il n'a pu examiner, l'un ou l'autre cas qui infirme sa thèse ? Ces questions, nous devons l'avouer, n'ont jamais été soulevées et affrontées par Szondi et lui ont valu de nombreuses critiques.

Mais il est temps à présent de prendre quelque recul pour relancer notre démarche et lui ouvrir de nouvelles perspectives. Nous l'avons vu, Szondi prétend ouvrir à l'enquête scientifique le domaine du destin individuel et des choix cruciaux qui marquent ce destin individuel, pour chercher aussitôt dans la génétique l'explication des grandes formes du choix destinal. Ainsi le choix d'une maladie mentale relèverait de gènes récessifs donnés en combinaison homozygote, alors que le choix d'un partenaire amoureux serait l'effet d'un gène récessif présent en combinaison hétérozygote. Nous avons ainsi énoncé, comme des thèses distinctes et non articulées, deux thèses génétiques : la thèse de l'hérédité des maladies mentales, la thèse du génotropisme. Or ces deux thèses ne sont pas étrangères l'une à l'autre, mais s'intègrent dans une doctrine génétique globale, dont l'unité ne peut apparaître qu'à la seule condition d'introduire un nouveau thème jusqu'ici abstraitement disjoint : le thème de la pulsion.

C. La doctrine génétique des pulsions

Répétons-le, nous n'avons dissocié le thème de la pulsion du thème du destin qu'à des fins analytiques. D'entrée de jeu, chez Szondi, destin et pulsion sont intimement entrelacés, comme le sont de même destin et gènes, comme vont l'être enfin, en dernière instance, destin, pulsion et gènes, dans une forme complexe d'intrication dont nous avons à démêler les fils.

Donc : en même temps qu'il soumet le destin à un déterminisme héréditaire, Szondi a l'intuition originaire du lien intime qui unit le destin à des forces dynamiques, relativement indéterminées, poussant de l'intérieur, d'un lieu situé à la limite du somatique et du psychique, excitant le psychisme, l'incitant à un travail incessant, bref à ce que Freud et la psychanalyse freudienne ont désigné comme pulsions.

Ayant introduit le thème du destin comme choix, et bien plus comme choix régi par des tendances qui nous sont transmises de nos ancêtres, Szondi précise tout aussitôt : « Nous devrions toujours ajouter le terme "pulsionnel" comme complément au mot "destin" » (Scha, p. 34). Le destin, la vie individuelle et ses vicissitudes, est, dans ce que l'Analyse du destin en rencontre, un destin pulsionnel, commandé par les pulsions ; et ses diverses figures sont autant de destins possibles des pulsions : les choix qui viennent comme cristalliser le destin sont des formes d'apparition, des modalités phénoménales (Erscheinungsformen) des pulsions. Ainsi, dira toujours à nouveau Szondi, les maladies mentales sont avant tout des maladies pulsionnelles.

Mais si le destin est tout à la fois régi par les gènes et commandé par les pulsions, alors un lien étroit doit être noué entre gènes et pulsions, tous deux conducteurs du destin humain. L'articulation, on le devine, sera très simple. Les pulsions, ces forces internes incitatrices des actes de choix qui scandent le destin individuel, auront elles-mêmes une source génétique. Par là, Szondi ne prendrait-il pas Freud au sérieux, qui avait attribué aux pulsions une source organique, sans jamais avoir osé, il est vrai, définir la nature précise de cette source ? Au flou prudent de Freud, Szondi substitue une affirmation crue : « les sources des pulsions sont : les gènes pulsionnels » (Scha, p. 65). Dans le bagage héréditaire total de l'être humain, à côté des gènes qui « déterminent des réactions partiellement corporelles, partiellement psychiques non pulsionnelles, par ex. des réactions intellectuelles, mentales, des possibilités de conception ou de représentation » (TrD, p. 29), existeraient des gènes qui régissent un domaine spécifique des activités psychiques de l'homme : le domaine de ses activités pulsionnelles, identiques aux grands actes de choix destinal.

Szondi se trouve donc engagé ainsi dans une tentative de fondation génétique du registre pulsionnel entendu dans son concept psychanalytique, et de ce qui, des pulsions non directement visibles, se manifeste, à savoir les événements marquants du destin individuel définis comme actes de choix. Une tentative qui, nous le verrons, n'ira pas sans engendrer des effets précis sur la génétique pulsionnelle elle-même.

Repartons de ce que nous appellerions volontiers la logique de la démarche génétique. Qu'effectue dans sa démarche la génétique ? Tout d'abord, elle découpe, dans la réalité visible des organismes, des domaines de variation et en détache des caractères distincts : par ex. la « couleur des yeux » (domaine de variation, dimension spécifique de l'organisme vivant), elle-même « bleue » ou « brune » (deux caractères distincts du domaine ou registre « couleur des yeux »). En plus, elle cherche à mettre en évidence la récurrence héréditaire, de génération en génération, des caractères : à cette fin elle procède à des observations empiriques orientées, soit sous forme d'un croisement actif et programmé des organismes, soit encore sous forme de relevés généalogiques rétrospectifs; et selon les modalités propres de la récurrence héréditaire observée, elle conclut au cours héréditaire des caractères (cours dominant, récessif; cours monomère, polymère, ...). Dès ce moment, les caractères macroscopiques visibles peuvent être attribués à la présence, dans le matériel chromosomique, de ces particules « microscopiques, invisibles, immortelles » que sont, selon les termes de Szondi, les gènes.

Or, dans son essai de fondation génétique de l'ordre pulsionnel, Szondi ne fait rien d'autre que mettre conséquemment en pratique la démarche dont nous venons d'énoncer les moments constitutifs.

Tout d'abord, Szondi distingue des domaines de variation. Plus précisément, il distingue, au sein du registre pulsionnel, huit domaines de variation : huit dimensions irréductibles, huit dispositions pulsionnelles autonomes, ce qu'il appelle huit besoins pulsionnels fondamentaux. Bien plus, à l'intérieur de chacun des huit domaines de variation, il repère des caractères distincts. « Tout besoin pulsionnel », écrit Szondi, « peut se manifester sous trois modalités phénoménales, et plus précisément : 1. sous forme extrême-négative, c'est-à-dire sous une forme morbide; 2. sous une forme physiologique, normale; 3. sous une forme extrême-positive, c'est-à-dire sous une forme socialisée ou sublimée » (Scha, p. 77). En bref, tout besoin pulsionnel autonome s'articule en trois caractères : « morbide », « sain », « socialisé » ou « sublimé ».

Mais d'où émane ce dernier découpage ? Dans l'énumération des trois formes fondamentales d'apparition des pulsions, Szondi est indubitablement tributaire de la psychanalyse freudienne. Les pulsions qui travaillent l'homme sont des forces dont les effets se déploient « du ciel, à travers le monde, jusqu'à l'enfer » (Freud), ou encore, selon une formulation szondienne, de l'humain à l'inhumain, du plus élevé au plus bas. Les pulsions sont à l'œuvre dans les plus hautes vocations humaines (religion, art, science, ...) aussi bien que dans les figures de la maladie mentale. C'est bien cette spécificité du concept psychanalytique de pulsion qui, croyons-nous, conduit Szondi à poser deux modalités extrêmes du besoin pulsionnel, non seulement une modalité dite « morbide » ou « maladive », mais encore une modalité « socialisée » ou encore « sublimée ». Mais c'est aussi la même prise en compte qui produit, dans la doctrine de l'hérédité pulsionnelle, des effets singuliers, que nous aidera à détecter la mise au jour d'un problème inévitablement soulevé par la lecture de Szondi encore que jamais thématisé par Szondi lui-même. Mais pour faire apparaître ce problème, nous devons nous engager dans le second moment constitutif de la démarche génétique : le moment de la mise en évidence des récurrences héréditaires des caractères.

On le soupçonne, la première pièce que Szondi verse au dossier d'une récurrence héréditaire des caractères pulsionnels est donnée par la thèse de l'hérédité des huit maladies mentales de base, dont la recherche psychiatrique aurait vérifié le cours héréditaire. Cette thèse, retranscrite dans les termes de la doctrine génétique des pulsions, s'exprimera comme suit : les gènes qui régissent les besoins pulsionnels sont responsables, en combinaison homozygote récessive (aa), d'une maladie mentale, elle-même identifiée à la modalité pathologique extrême du besoin. En bref, le caractère « morbide » du besoin pulsionnel est porté par un gène (« pulsionnel ») récessif.

Mais pour accréditer la doctrine génétique des pulsions, il ne peut suffire d'avoir établi la récurrence héréditaire du caractère « maladif » du besoin. Il reste à montrer comment les mêmes gènes pulsionnels qui donnent lieu à une forme d'expression pathologique peuvent aussi se manifester sous forme « socialisée » ou « sublimée ». C'est précisément en ce point que nous rencontrons, sur un mode problématique, la seconde thèse génétique de Szondi : la thèse du génotropisme.

Car, on doit le souligner, la liaison n'est en aucune manière immédiate et évidente entre une thèse qui affirme l'hérédité des maladies mentales (redéfinies comme « pulsionnelles ») et attribue ces dernières à l'efficacité de gènes récessifs (« pulsionnels ») et une thèse qui pose l'effet « génotropique » des gènes latents. Dans sa formulation générale, la thèse du génotropisme concerne toute espèce de gène récessif latent possible : gène récessif responsable de dons spécifiques, comme gène récessif porteur de caractères morbides, organiques aussi bien que psychiques (y compris « pulsionnels »). Nous avons vu d'ailleurs comment Szondi, dans sa pratique génotropique concrète, s'intéressait à des individus porteurs du gène récessif de la débilité; d'autres exemples illustratifs concernent des conducteurs de la cécité, de la surdité, du diabète (Scha, pp. 86 et ss.).

Cependant, une nouvelle observation doit aussitôt nuancer ce premier constat. Si nous examinons avec soin la pratique génotropique de Szondi, nous devons conclure que les gènes récessifs pulsionnels (c'est-à-dire responsables de maladies mentales) jouissent d'un privilège indéniable dans la production de l'effet génotropique : ce qui préoccupe Szondi au premier chef, c'est de montrer que les conducteurs de maladies mentales (schizophrénie paranoïde, épilepsie,...), bref les conducteurs de gènes pulsionnels morbides, effectuent des choix socialisés significatifs, qu'il s'agisse de choix en amour ou de choix professionnels.

La thèse du génotropisme concerne donc moins les conducteurs en général que les porteurs de gènes pulsionnels latents. La raison nous en paraît simple. Dès le moment où Szondi avait choisi de rendre compte en termes génétiques du registre pulsionnel dans ses connotations psychanalytiques, il se trouvait dans l'obligation de dériver, non seulement un effet morbide des gènes pulsionnels (auquel se serait opposé sans plus un effet « sain »), mais encore un effet extrême inverse, à savoir un effet positif dit de « socialisation » ou « sublimation », dont l'une des trois combinaisons génétiques possibles de deux allèles pulsionnels (AA, Aa, aa) devait être productrice. La thèse inédite et proprement inouïe du génotropisme, qui attribue la production d'actes de choix socialisés à la combinaison hérérozygote Aa, était comme imposée par les exigences d'une explication génétique de l'ordre pulsionnel : par elle, le choix du partenaire amoureux, le choix de la profession (le caractère « socialisé » du besoin pulsionnel), et le choix de la maladie mentale et de la forme de mort suicidaire (le caractère « morbide » du besoin) étaient enracinés dans un terrain héréditaire commun. Ainsi était construite une doctrine génétique unitaire des pulsions et des figures du destin pulsionnel.

Il nous importe, pour terminer notre première partie, de mettre un moment l'accent sur le choix professionnel, que Szondi désigne sous le terme d'opérotropisme.

Certes, au regard d'exigences logiques, ces quelques considérations auraient eu davantage leur place là où nous avons introduit la thèse du génotropisme. Car l'opérotropisme est bien une forme fondamentale du génotropisme. Au vu des nombreux arbres généalogiques reconstitués par Szondi, des choix professionnels précis et significatifs sont accomplis par les membres des familles où circule une maladie mentale (la paranoïa ou l'épilepsie par ex.) : les mêmes gènes récessifs y circuleraient et se manifesteraient tantôt, pour les uns, homozygotes, sous forme maladive (choix de l'épilepsie, par ex.), tantôt pour les autres, hétérozygotes, sous forme socialisée (choix d'une existence « sainte », par ex.).

Mais l'intérêt d'une pareille articulation maladie-profession nous paraît ressortir bien plus encore, dès lors qu'a été mentionnée la composante psychanalytique (pulsionnelle) de la doctrine génétique de Szondi. Qu'une énergie pulsionnelle puisse être investie dans l'activité professionnelle, ou encore, qu'une activité professionnelle puisse offrir un débouché, une voie d'expression, une forme de satisfaction, à des pulsions qui sans celui-ci auraient peut-être donné lieu à maladie, c'est là une proposition dont la congénialité au projet psychanalytique est hors de doute. Jean Laplanche n'écrivait-il pas il y a quelques années : « la théorie et l'expérience psychanalytique fournissent suffisamment de données pour développer une psychologie du travail — ou plus des différentes sortes de travail — et pour montrer la diversité des sources pulsionnelles auxquelles il peut emprunter de l'énergie » ?[1] Mais

---

[1] Laplanche J., Notes sur Marcuse et la psychanalyse, dans *Marcuse cet inconnu*, *La Nef*, n° 36, 1969, p. 134.

Laplanche se doutait-il que les bases de cette psychopulsionnelle des « différentes sortes de travail » avaient été jetées par Szondi dès 1944, dans la Scha, bien au-delà d'ailleurs de ce que la théorie et l'expérience psychanalytiques ont pu élaborer depuis lors ? Quel que soit l'arrière-fond doctrinal qui a présidé à sa constitution — et on ne peut ignorer que les hypothèses d'une génétique pulsionnelle ont guidé Szondi —, la catégorisation pulsionnelle des professions établie par Szondi reste comme une mine encore trop peu exploitée par la psychologie actuelle. Elle constitue l'un des apports les plus intéressants de l'Analyse du destin (on consultera à cet égard les tableaux de la Scha, pp. 338-341, du DP, p. 18, ou de l'Introduction à l'Analyse du destin, I, 1972, pp. 148-149).

CONCLUSIONS

Il se dégage ainsi de la première œuvre de Szondi, la *Schicksalsanalyse*, les grandes lignes d'une doctrine, tout à la fois pulsionnelle et génétique, du destin : pulsionnelle puisque le concept freudien de pulsion est à l'œuvre dans la reconnaissance et la délimitation des figures du destin, en particulier à travers la polarité du morbide et du sublimé; génétique puisqu'en dernier ressort, les formes du destin pulsionnel individuel sont rapportées à des combinaisons postulées de gènes « pulsionnels ».

Mais comment apprécier cette doctrine ?

Soulignons d'abord une difficulté inévitable à laquelle se heurte la froide appréciation de la doctrine génétique de Szondi. Celle-ci a suscité et se trouve toujours apte à susciter des émois idéologiques, d'où qu'ils viennent. Rejetée d'emblée et sans examen par les uns au nom d'options spiritualistes ou humanistes — comment les choix d'une existence humaine instauratrice de sens pourraient-ils être le produit mécanique de combinaisons génétiques ? —, elle pourrait tout autant mobiliser aujourd'hui l'opposition farouche et spontanée des tenants d'une sociologie marxiste : ne sert-elle pas à occulter l'incidence sur le destin humain d'un milieu social travaillé par la lutte des classes ? L'immanquable entrelacement des options idéologiques et des arguments scientifiques rend toujours hasardeuse une discussion étroitement épistémologique, articulée sur des critères de scientificité.

Si toutefois nous nous risquons à celle-ci, nous interrogerons la doctrine de Szondi quant à sa cohérence logique et sa validation empirique. Est-elle clairement formulée ? Est-elle confirmée empiriquement ?

Sur ces points, nous avons déjà émis quelques réserves. Ainsi nous avons noté l'écart persistant entre les thèses génétiques de Szondi et les travaux empiriques appelés à les appuyer : le fossé est pour ainsi dire béant entre la simplicité excessive de la théorie (deux allèles pulsionnels, un cours monomère) et la complexité du domaine empirique à dériver; et si cette théorie prise dans sa littéralité ne tient pas le coup alors même qu'il s'agit de dériver la seule modalité morbide du besoin pulsionnel (une maladie mentale comme l'épilepsie par ex.), comment pourrait-elle tenir le coup dès lors qu'elle est mobilisée pour expliquer aussi une modalité socialisée du besoin ?

Szondi a d'ailleurs reconnu pratiquement cette difficulté. Dans la suite de son œuvre, il a été amené à raffiner sa doctrine génétique, ne serait-ce que pour rendre compte de certains phénomènes empiriques qui ressortissent au registre du destin pulsionnel. Ainsi la mobilité des choix destinaux est remarquable : ceux-ci « ne sont pas des manifestations héréditaires stables, comme par ex. un naevus sur la peau » (IchA, p. 79). Un individu jusqu'alors sain peut tout à coup tomber malade. Comment expliquer ce brusque virage destinal ? Sans doute, répondra Szondi, doit-on supposer qu'une disposition héréditaire récessive, dominée jusqu'alors par un gène sain dominant, a réussi brutalement, à la faveur d'événements internes ou externes au milieu génétique, à renverser la dominance : « nous réévaluons dans ce nouveau sens fonctionnel le vieux concept génétique de "changement de dominance" » (IchA, p. 79).

Que penser dès lors en dernière instance de cette doctrine génétique ? Même si nous nous situons à l'intérieur de l'unité plus ou moins problématique que constitue la pratique théorique et empirique de Szondi à l'époque de la Scha, la réponse ne saurait être claire. Certes, si nous raisonnons en épistémologue puriste et intransigeant, attaché à une cohérence sans faille de la théorie ou à une articulation nette et non ambiguë de la théorie sur un matériel de faits empiriques, nous devons récuser cette doctrine. Mais on le sait de plus en plus, le purisme épistémologique est souvent éloigné de la réalité concrète d'une pratique scientifique toujours tâtonnante et tissée de contradictions. Si à coup sûr, les thèses génétiques de Szondi sont trop simples dans leur formulation théorique littérale — personne ne pourra croire aujourd'hui qu'un seul gène récessif soit responsable de la schizophrénie —, et nonobstant des options sociologistes — que nous partageons mais qui ne sont pas incompatibles avec une efficacité partielle de déterminations héréditaires, dont l'idéologisation doit toutefois être combattue —, ne doit-on pas à tout le moins laisser la question ouverte, et donc admettre la légitimité d'un travail scientifique qui continue de projeter l'hypothèse non seulement d'un terrain héréditaire des maladies mentales, mais surtout — car c'est là que Szondi ouvre de toutes nouvelles perspectives — d'un terrain héréditaire commun à des choix aussi divers que le choix d'une maladie et le choix d'une profession, bref l'hypothèse d'un terrain pulsionnel héréditaire ?

Mais nous ne pouvons ignorer non plus que nous avons comme figé ou arrêté la pratique szondienne à un moment précis de son développement. Il nous importe dès maintenant de la mettre en mouvement. Or, ce mouvement même, loin d'aplanir les difficultés, loin de résorber les incohérences ou les contradictions internes, les exacerbe tout au contraire. Szondi va se trouver conduit à développer plus avant sa doctrine des pulsions et des besoins pulsionnels, qui demeuraient, dans la Scha, comme un intermédiaire évanescent entre les gènes pulsionnels et les modalités visibles d'apparition des pulsions. Prenant de plus en plus de consistance et de poids, les pulsions elles-mêmes s'avèrent progressivement et toujours davantage irréductibles à ce qui est pourtant censé les fonder encore : les gènes pulsionnels. C'est donc moins une contradiction externe, de la doctrine génétique avec des faits falsificateurs, qu'une contradiction interne, de cette même doctrine avec de nouveaux développements doctrinaux, qui va être dès à présent au premier plan de notre propos. Et puisqu'il nous apparaît que dans l'envol de cette évolution doctrinale le « test de Szondi » ou « Diagnostic expérimental des pulsions » a joué le rôle d'un catalyseur crucial, c'est donc à ce dernier que nous devons immédiatement consacrer un chapitre propre.

ANNEXE

Quelques notions de génétique

Les *gènes*, entités organiques élémentaires porteuses des caractères héréditaires, se combinent deux à deux sous forme de *couple* ou de paire.

Lorsqu'une dimension de l'individu vivant, ou ce que nous avons appelé un *domaine de variation* (par exemple la couleur des yeux, ou, selon la théorie de Szondi, un besoin pulsionnel), est régi par un seul couple de gènes, le cours héréditaire de cette dimension est dit *monomère*. Lorsqu'une dimension est régie par deux couples de gènes, ou par plusieurs couples de gènes, son cours héréditaire est appelé *dimère* ou *polymère*.

Les gènes qui régissent une dimension vitale présentent des variétés distinctes, chacune de ces variétés déterminant un caractère ou une propriété spécifique de la dimension (par exemple, pour ce qui concerne la dimension « couleur des yeux », un gène de variété A déterminera le caractère « brun », un gène de variété a régira le caractère « bleu »). Ces gènes de variété ou de qualité distincte sont appelés gènes *allèles*. Lorsque le nombre des allèles est supérieur à deux, on parle d'une *allélie multiple* ou *polyallélie* (ainsi, pour Szondi, le domaine des manifestations épileptiformes est régi par des gènes spécifiques qui connaissent trois variations alléliques: A, a', a).

Certains allèles sont appelés dominants, d'autres sont appelés récessifs. Un allèle *dominant* (généralement inscrit en majuscule: A, B,...) peut manifester le caractère qu'il détermine, même s'il est accompagné par un allèle récessif porteur d'un autre caractère. A l'inverse, l'allèle *récessif* (inscrit en minuscule: a, b, ...) ne peut manifester son caractère s'il est accompagné d'un allèle dominant. On dit qu'un caractère a un cours héréditaire dominant, lorsqu'il est déterminé par un allèle dominant. On dit qu'un caractère a un cours héréditaire récessif lorsqu'il est porté par un allèle récessif. On parle de *combinaison homozygote* pour désigner un couple ou une paire de gènes dont les allèles sont tous deux soit dominants (AA), soit récessifs (aa), et de *combinaison hétérozygote* pour désigner un couple de gènes dont les allèles sont l'un dominant, l'autre récessif (Aa). L'individu hétérozygote est appelé *conducteur* (conducteur ou porteur d'un caractère qu'il ne manifeste pas au plan visible). Szondi parle de gène *latent* pour désigner le gène récessif présent en combinaison hétérozygote.

Deuxième partie
Le diagnostic expérimental des pulsions
et le mouvement de la pratique szondienne

INTRODUCTION

Science et instrumentation

L'épistémologie reste étrangement discrète à propos de l'instrumentation scientifique. Qu'elle soit théoriciste, attachée au travail du concept et à ce que celui-ci rend possible comme dépassement d'une appréhension première et idéologiquement marquée de la réalité, ou qu'elle soit empiriciste, préoccupée d'une articulation étroite, non équivoque, de la théorie sur le réel (immédiatement) observable, elle procède à une neutralisation de l'instrument scientifique. Bien sûr, elle n'en nie pas l'existence, mais elle en méconnaît l'originalité en l'absorbant, soit dans la théorie, soit dans l'empirie : l'instrument scientifique sera, pour les uns matérialisation de théorie, pour les autres extension de nos moyens d'observation empirique.

Or, une vue plus juste de l'instrumentation scientifique ne nous oblige-t-elle pas à formuler une théorie médiane ? Certes, nous accordons à l'épistémologie théoriciste que l'instrument est bien davantage que l'opérateur d'un branchement sur des faits réels, plus fins et plus précis que ne le seraient les faits donnés par nos moyens d'observation naturels. Ainsi que nous l'a appris Bachelard, l'instrument scientifique est constructeur de faits. Mais les faits construits par l'instrument sont-ils toujours et par avance maîtrisés par une théorie explicite ? L'instrument est-il sans plus cet outil passif et malléable par lequel une théorie constituerait des faits contrôlés de part en part ? Nous ne le croyons pas. L'instrument a aussi une autonomie relative et par conséquent une productivité propre : un pouvoir de mobilisation créatrice de la science. Dans le mouvement par lequel il engendre des faits, selon une dynamique propre non entièrement gouvernée par la théorie qui pourtant le guide, il appelle la théorie à un retour constant sur elle-même, à un questionnement critique perpétuel; parfois même il en ébranle les assises, en précipite l'éclatement.

Quelle que soit la validité générale de cette proposition, il n'est pas douteux que le diagnostic expérimental des pulsions ait joué, dans le mouvement de la pratique szondienne, le rôle que nous venons de dire: construit sous la dictée consciente d'une théorie, élaboré pour mettre au jour des faits qu'une doctrine constituée était en état d'interpréter — précisons: des faits ininterprétables si ce n'est en termes théoriques, en quoi dès l'origine il était plus qu'un simple instrument empirique d'observation —, le diagnostic expérimental des pulsions devait bientôt se révéler plus riche que ne pouvait en expliquer la doctrine qui pourtant l'avait initialement inspiré: il suscitait dès lors les développements théoriques inédits dont il était implicitement gros, il interrogeait et mettait en question la théorie initiale de référence — en quoi il était davantage que la pure matérialisation d'une théorie.

Mais avant d'observer le détail de ce procès, qui emporte théorie, technique et observables dans une dialectique subtile, il est nécessaire de procéder à une présentation du diagnostic expérimental des pulsions, appelé plus communément test de Szondi.

A. Première présentation du test de Szondi

Dans ce pragraphe, nous présenterons successivement le matériel du test, les modalités de son administration et les modalités de l'enregistrement de ses résultats: transcription des résultats bruts, transformation des résultats bruts dans le langage des réactions pulsionnelles et constitution des profils pulsionnels.

Précisons-le, cette présentation, qui a aussi une visée d'information pratique, est extemporanée. Si elle est conforme à la pratique courante actuelle, elle ne fait pas état de la constitution historique de cette pratique, que nous aurons à examiner dans un second temps.

1. Le matériel du test

Le matériel du test est constitué de six séries de photographies en noir et blanc, représentant des êtres humains, de sexe masculin ou féminin, au visage entièrement visible de face[1].

Les êtres humains représentés sur les photos sont des malades mentaux. Plus précisément, chacune des six séries comporte huit photos, parmi lesquelles: la photo d'un homosexuel (h), d'un sadique (s), d'un épileptique (e), d'un hystérique (hy), d'un schizophrène catatonique (k), d'un schizophrène paranoïde (p), d'un dépressif mélancolique (d) et d'un maniaque (m).

Le matériel total est donc composé de 6 × 8 photos: soit 48 photos, parmi lesquelles 6h, 6s,... 6m.

Au dos de chacune des photos, figurent à gauche, en chiffres romains, le numéro de la série à laquelle la photo appartient (I, II, ..., VI), à droite l'initiale de la maladie dont souffre la personne représentée (h, s, ..., m).

---

[1] Le matériel du test est édité par Hans Huber, Berne.

2. L'administration du test

L'administration du test procède en deux phases.

On commence par donner au sujet les instructions suivantes : « je vais vous présenter huit photographies. Regardez-les bien toutes et donnez-moi la photo que vous trouvez relativement la plus sympathique, et ensuite la photo qui vous paraît la plus sympathique en second ». On étale alors, devant le sujet, de manière aussi simultanée que possible, les huit photos de la première série, en deux rangées de quatre photos, et suivant un ordre prescrit (au dos de chaque photo, figure au centre un chiffre arabe, qui indique le numéro d'ordre de chaque photo dans sa série : 1., 2., ..., 8.). Lorsque le sujet a choisi les deux photos qui étaient pour lui les plus sympathiques, on range ces deux photos à droite et on lui demande alors : « choisissez maintenant la photo la plus antipathique et la photo la plus antipathique en second ». On range les deux photos choisies sur la gauche et les quatre photos qui n'ont été choisies ni comme sympathiques ni comme antipathiques sont replacées dans la boîte du test. On procède ensuite de la même manière pour les cinq autres séries. De sorte qu'au terme de la présentation des six séries nous disposons à notre droite de douze photos (2 × 6 photos) choisies comme sympathiques et à notre gauche de douze photos choisies comme antipathiques. Dans la boîte du test demeurent six séries de quatre photos.

Dès ce moment, commence la seconde phase de l'administration, qui utilise les photos non choisies. Nous disons au sujet : « maintenant, je vais vous présenter les quatre photographies qui restent. Choisissez la plus antipathique et ensuite la plus antipathique en second ». Nous étalons devant le sujet, en une rangée, les quatre photos restantes de la première série, et le sujet ayant effectué son choix, nous plaçons les deux photos sur notre gauche, de manière à constituer un nouveau tas. Nous plaçons ensuite les deux photos non choisies sur notre droite et les considérons comme relativement plus sympathiques. Nous procédons de même pour les photos restantes de chacune des cinq autres séries, de sorte qu'au terme nous disposons de deux nouveaux petits tas de douze photos chacun : à notre gauche douze photos antipathiques, à notre droite douze photos sympathiques.

L'administration du test est ainsi terminée. Commence alors :

3. L'inscription des résultats bruts

L'inscription des résultats bruts s'effectue sur une double grille qui, remplie, pourrait se présenter comme suit :

	S		P		Sch		C	
	h	s	e	hy	k	p	d	m
	6	4						
	5	2			5			3
	3	1		2	6	4		1
	2	5	4	1	1	2	4	
		6		3	3		6	
				5				

1

	S		P		Sch		C	
	h	s	e	hy	k	p	d	m
							3	6
				6			2	5
	4	3	5	4		1	1	2
	1		1		2	3	5	4
			2		4	5		
			3			6		
			6					

Mais explicitons la manière de parvenir à ce résultat.

Nous commençons par inscrire les résultats du premier choix, et cela dans le plus grand des deux rectangles (le rectangle supérieur). Les douze photos sympathiques sont inscrites dans les cases qui se situent au-dessus de la ligne médiane. Chacune des douze photos est inscrite dans une case sous la forme du numéro de la série à laquelle elle appartient (1, 2, ..., 6), et cela dans la colonne correspondant à sa catégorie psychiatrique (h, s, ..., m). Nous inscrivons de la même manière les douze photos antipathiques dans les cases qui se situent au-dessous de la ligne médiane. Enfin, nous inscrivons, d'après les mêmes principes, dans le rectangle inférieur, les vingt-quatre photos qui résultent du second choix (douze photos sympathiques au-dessus de la ligne médiane, douze photos antipathiques au-dessous de la ligne médiane).

On le voit, par cette procédure, toutes les informations issues de l'administration du test sont intégralement transcrites : une fois notre double grille remplie, nous savons avec exactitude quelles photos précises le sujet a choisies, comme sympathiques, comme antipathiques, dans chacune des six séries, au cours des deux phases de l'administration.

Ajoutons immédiatement qu'il est recommandé de répéter dix fois l'administration du test sur le même sujet, et cela en répétant chaque fois la même procédure. Deux administrations successives doivent être séparées au minimum d'un intervalle de temps de 24 heures : il est donc déconseillé de procéder, avec le même sujet, à deux administrations sur une même journée.

Au terme des dix administrations, dix doubles grilles identiques à celle que nous avons présentée et contenues sur une feuille unique de notation seront donc complétées.

4. La transformation des résultats bruts en réactions pulsionnelles et la constitution des profils pulsionnels

Une fois les résultats bruts transcrits, il importe de les traduire dans le langage des réactions pulsionnelles et de constituer ainsi les profils pulsionnels.

Énonçons d'abord quelques remarques au sujet des réactions pulsionnelles.

L'expression « réaction pulsionnelle » désigne la réaction momentanée qu'un sujet adopte au cours d'une phase de l'administration du test par rapport aux photos d'une catégorie psychiatrique déterminée (h, s, ..., m).

Les réactions pulsionnelles possibles sont au nombre de quatre :

La réaction nulle (symbolisée par le signe : o) signifie que le sujet n'a pas choisi ou n'a quasiment pas choisi de photo d'une même catégorie psychiatrique ;

La réaction positive (+) signifie que le sujet a choisi comme sympathiques plusieurs photos d'une catégorie et par ailleurs n'en a quasiment pas choisis comme antipathiques ;

La réaction négative (−) signifie à l'inverse que le sujet a choisi comme antipathiques plusieurs des photos d'une catégorie et n'en a quasiment pas choisis comme sympathiques ;

La réaction ambivalente (±) signifie que le sujet a choisi de nombreuses photos d'une même catégorie, mais tout à la fois comme sympathiques et comme antipathiques.

Mais ces premières définitions demeurent vagues. En réalité, des critères tout à fait précis et non équivoques nous permettent d'assigner l'une des quatre réactions à tout ensemble momentané de choix relatifs aux photos de l'une ou l'autre des huit catégories psychiatriques. Le tableau II nous révèle le contenu de ces critères.

On voit ainsi qu'à toute combinaison de choix positifs et négatifs correspond une seule réaction pulsionnelle.

Ajoutons encore qu'au cas où un minimum de quatre photos d'un groupe psychiatrique auraient été choisies comme sympathiques ou comme antipathiques, la réaction sera dite accentuée. Une réaction sera gratifiée d'une accentuation (inscrite sous forme d'un point d'exclamation) lorsque quatre photos auront été choisies comme sympathiques ou comme antipathiques, de deux accentuations (!!) lorsque cinq photos auront été choisies comme sympathiques ou comme antipathiques, enfin de trois accentuations (!!!) lorsque six photos auront été choisies dans une même direction.

Au cas où l'accentuation concerne une réaction ambivalente, le point d'exclamation figure à côté du + ou du -, selon que les quatre photos choisies dans une même direction l'auront été comme sympathiques ou comme antipathiques. Le tableau III résume cet état de choses.

Tableau II: Critères d'attribution des réactions pulsionnelles.

Ensembles des choix de photos d'une catégorie psychiatrique *	Réactions
$\frac{0}{0}$; $\frac{1}{0}$; $\frac{0}{1}$; $\frac{1}{1}$;	o
$\frac{2}{0}$; $\frac{2}{1}$; $\frac{3}{0}$; $\frac{3}{1}$; $\frac{4}{0}$; $\frac{4}{1}$; $\frac{5}{0}$; $\frac{5}{1}$; $\frac{6}{0}$;	+
$\frac{0}{2}$; $\frac{1}{2}$; $\frac{0}{3}$; $\frac{1}{3}$; $\frac{0}{4}$; $\frac{1}{4}$; $\frac{0}{5}$; $\frac{1}{5}$; $\frac{0}{6}$;	-
$\frac{2}{2}$; $\frac{3}{2}$; $\frac{2}{3}$; $\frac{3}{3}$; $\frac{4}{2}$; $\frac{2}{4}$;	±

* *Les choix positifs figurent au numérateur, les choix négatifs au dénominateur.*

Tableau III: Réactions pulsionnelles accentuées.

	Combinaisons de choix donnant lieu à accentuation(s)	Formes d'inscription de la réaction pulsionnelle
une accentuation	$\frac{4}{0}$; $\frac{4}{1}$;	+!
	$\frac{0}{4}$; $\frac{1}{4}$;	-!
	$\frac{4}{2}$;	±!
	$\frac{2}{4}$;	±!
deux accentuations	$\frac{5}{0}$; $\frac{5}{1}$;	+!!
	$\frac{0}{5}$; $\frac{1}{5}$;	-!!
trois accentuations	$\frac{6}{0}$;	+!!!
	$\frac{0}{6}$;	-!!!

Les indications qui précèdent rendent à présent aisée la compréhension du processus de transformation des résultats bruts en réactions pulsionnelles.

Nous partons des résultats bruts inscrits sur la première feuille de notation et considérons séparément les résultats de chacune des administrations du test.

Soit par exemple les choix bruts enregistrés sur la double grille de la p. 32. Examinant d'abord les résultats du premier choix, nous passons en revue successivement les combinaisons de choix qui correspondent à chaque catégorie psychiatrique (les choix de photos h, puis de photos s, et ainsi de suite, jusqu'aux choix de photos m) et nous remplaçons chacune des huit combinaisons observées par une réaction pulsionnelle, que nous inscrivons alors dans le tableau figurant en haut d'une seconde feuille de notation (Tableau IV). Et puisque nous sommes en train de considérer les résultats de la première administration, nous inscrivons les réactions pulsionnelles dans la rangée n° 1. Au-dessous des initiales des diverses catégories psychiatriques figurera donc l'une des quatre réactions pulsionnelles, éventuellement accentuée, en l'occurrence :

	S		P		Sch		C	
	h	s	e	hy	k	p	d	m
1.	+	±	o	-	±	o	-	+

Nous transformons ensuite de la même manière les données brutes issues du second choix. Néanmoins une particularité apparaît. Lorsque le sujet, au cours du premier choix, a choisi cinq ou six photos d'une catégorie psychiatrique, il ne pourra pas choisir plus d'une photo de cette catégorie au moment du second choix : quelle que soit la forme brute de son choix ($\frac{1}{0}$; $\frac{0}{1}$; $\frac{0}{0}$), ce choix sera crédité d'une réaction nulle. On parle dans ce cas d'une réaction nulle contrainte ou forcée et on l'inscrit sous forme d'un zéro barré (ø). Quoi qu'il en soit, les réactions pulsionnelles du second choix sont donc inscrites à leur tour, et cela dans la grille qui figure en bas de la seconde feuille de notation. En l'occurence nous obtenons pour ce qui concerne la première administration :

	S		P		Sch		C	
	h	s	e	hy	k	p	d	m
1.	o	ø	-!	+	-	-	+	+

Nous procédons de même pour les résultats des neuf autres administrations du test, si bien qu'au terme de l'opération de transcription les deux grilles extrêmes (du haut et du bas) de la feuille de notation sont entièrement couvertes de signes. La première grille, sur laquelle sont enregistrées les réactions pulsionnelles révélées par le premier choix, constitue le profil d'avant-plan (Vordergrundprofil ou VGP). Quant à la seconde grille, résultant du second choix, elle constitue le profil complémentaire empirique (Empirische Komplementärprofil ou EKP).

Mais, comme il est loisible de l'observer, une troisième grille, coincée entre les deux premières, reste vide et doit à son tour être occupée. Cette grille, qui constituera le profil complémentaire théorique (Theoretische Komplementärprofil ou ThKP), sera remplie en inversant purement et simplement les

Vordergrundprofile (VGP)

Nr.	Soz.-Wert	S		P		Sch		C	
		h	s	e	hy	k	p	d	m
1		+	±	0	−	±	0	−	+
2		+!	+	±	−	−	−	0	±
3		+	+	±	0	−	−	0	+
4		+	+	±	−	−	−	+	+
5		+	+	+	0	−	−	±	−
6		+!!	+	+	−	−	−!	0	0
7		+	+	0	±	−	−!	0	+
8		+!	+!	0	−	−	−	−	+
9		+!!	+	0	−	−	−	0	±
10		+	+	+	−	−	−!	0	±

Theoretische Komplementärprofile (ThKP)

Nr.	Soz.-Wert	S		P		Sch		C	
		h	s	e	hy	k	p	d	m
1		−	0	±	+	0	±	+	−
2		−!	−	0	+	+	+	±	0
3		−	−	0	±	+	+	±	−
4		−	−	0	+	+	+	−	−
5		−	−	−	±	+	+	0	+
6		−!!	−	−	+	+	+!	±	±
7		−	−	±	0	+	+!	±	−
8		−!	−!	±	+	+	+	+	−
9		−!!	−	±	+	+	+	±	0
10		−	−	−	+	+	+!	±	0

Empirische Komplementärprofile (EKP)

Nr.	Soz.-Wert	S		P		Sch		C	
		h	s	e	hy	k	p	d	m
1		0	ø	−!	+	−	−	+	+
2		ø	+	−	±	+	−!	±	ø
3		+	−	ø	−!	+	0	±	+
4		+	+	0	+	−	−	+	−
5		+	−	−	±	0	−	0	+
6		ø	±	−	+	+	−	±	+
7		+	+	−	ø	−	−	+!	0
8		+	0	±	+	±	−	+	0
9		ø	+	±	±	−	−	+	ø
10		+	+	−	−!	+	0	±	+

Tableau IV : Les trois profils pulsionnels d'un sujet concret signes du profil d'avant-plan. Par exemple, à une réaction + du VGP correspondra une réaction - du ThKP. Le tableau suivant indique les diverses possibilités :

VGP	+(!,	!!,	!!!)	- (!,	!!,	!!!)	± (±!, ±!)	o
ThKP	-(!,	!!,	!!!)	+ (!,	!!,	!!!)	o	±

Ainsi se trouvent constitués les profils pulsionnels à partir desquels les diverses méthodes d'interprétation du test vont alors se mettre en route.

B. Le test et le mouvement de la pratique szondienne

Nous venons à l'instant de livrer quelques informations pratiques, précieuses en ce qu'elles donnent une première connaissance du matériel du test et permettent déjà de l'administrer et d'en inscrire les résultats. Mais en même temps, ces informations, tout utiles et précises qu'elles soient, demeurent inintelligibles. Quel pourrait donc être le sens de toutes ces manipulations pratiques ? Nous devons commencer de nous interroger à ce propos, et d'abord, renouant en cela le fil de notre exposé, situer la procédure du test par rapport à l'état doctrinal que notre première partie avait pour portée de situer.

1. Le test dans la doctrine génétique

On ne peut ignorer que le diagnostic expérimental des pulsions, construit à la fin des années 1930, à l'époque même où Szondi est engagé dans le vif de son travail génétique, a été élaboré comme instrument au service de la recherche familiale génotropique et appelé — conformément à ce but — un génotest. Mais comment donc le test se trouve-t-il approprié, dans son matériel, ses instructions et ses résultats, à servir les buts de la recherche génotropique ?

La recherche génotropique cherche à établir la nature de conducteur des individus, et cela qu'elle se propose de vérifier la thèse du génotropisme ou qu'elle veuille s'en servir à des fins de connaissance individuelle.

Une méthode paraît d'emblée indiquée : la méthode généalogique, dont nous avons défini les principes. Mais cette méthode présente un gros inconvénient qui incite justement à lui trouver un substitut : son application demande de longues et minutieuses recherches. Ce substitut, ce sera précisément le diagnostic expérimental des pulsions.

Nous désirons connaître les gènes pulsionnels latents qui font partie du bagage héréditaire d'un individu. Or que déterminent au niveau macroscopique ces entités microscopiques ? Selon la théorie du génotropisme, des choix et notamment des choix en amour et amitié, et bien plus des choix dirigés sur les porteurs des mêmes gènes latents. Le principe du test devient clair. Trois moments scandent la démarche : 1° nous créons une situation expérimentale qui reproduit adéquatement les conditions de choix à l'œuvre dans la vie réelle; 2° nous demandons au sujet de choisir selon son attrait; 3° enfin, nous concluons de la nature de ses choix à son bagage héréditaire latent.

Examinons plus attentivement ces trois éléments :

1. Le matériel du test est constitué de visages humains, mais non de visages humains quelconques, choisis au hasard, mais bien des représentants des huit

dimensions pulsionnelles fondamentales. Pourquoi cette sélection délibérée ? La théorie génétique des pulsions, ici présupposée, pose huit besoins pulsionnels élémentaires portés chacun par un couple de gènes. De plus, parmi les gènes qui composent l'espace de variation allélique du besoin pulsionnel, nous avons un gène récessif morbide, qui, présent à double dose, donnera lieu à un trouble mental. Dès lors, selon les termes mêmes de la théorie génétique, huit gènes récessifs, un gène pour chaque besoin pulsionnel, peuvent faire partie du bagage héréditaire latent des individus, et ils seront révélés, selon la thèse du génotropisme, par l'attrait que leur porteur ressentirait à l'endroit de porteurs de ces mêmes gènes. D'où le choix nécessaire, pour constituer le matériel testologique, de porteurs des huit gènes morbides considérés par la théorie.

2. Quant aux instructions, elles prescrivent de choisir parmi les visages présentés selon un critère de sympathie ou d'attrait. Le sujet est somme toute prié d'effectuer, dans la situation de test, ces choix qu'il effectue dans la vie réelle lorsqu'il opte pour un partenaire en amour ou en amitié.

3. Quels sont enfin les résultats pertinents ? A l'époque de la Scha, Szondi distingue deux grandes réactions de choix : *a*) la réaction nulle : des six images appartenant à une même catégorie psychiatrique, le sujet n'en a choisi aucune, ou en tout cas n'en a pas choisi plus d'une ; *b*) la réaction pleine : le sujet a choisi les six images, ou en tout cas quatre ou cinq images, d'une même catégorie psychiatrique. Quelles conclusions tirer de ces résultats, concernant la constitution génétique du sujet soumis au test ? S'il est vrai, comme le postule la théorie, que le déterminant du choix selon l'attrait est bien la présence dans le bagage héréditaire de gènes pulsionnels latents, nous pouvons conclure que les réactions pleines révèlent la nature spécifique de conducteur de la personne. Nous pouvons dès lors attribuer à cette personne toutes les propriétés que la théorie assigne au porteur du gène pulsionnel récessif latent. Ainsi, si un individu choisit à six reprises l'image de l'épileptique, nous conclurons qu'il possède dans son bagage héréditaire latent un gène pulsionnel épileptique morbide. Nous saurons du même coup que ses partenaires amoureux sont ou seront aussi des conducteurs de l'épilepsie (selon la thèse du libidotropisme), ou encore qu'il a choisi ou choisira comme profession l'une de celles qui socialisent le besoin épileptoïde (selon la thèse de l'opérotropisme). Quant à la réaction nulle, elle correspond, soit aux manifestations franchement pathologiques du besoin (elle renvoie dans ce cas à une formule génétique homozygote récessive aa), soit aux manifestations saines de celui-ci (dans ce cas, la formule, homozygote dominante, sera AA).

2. *L'excès du test sur la doctrine génétique*

Nous venons donc de montrer, suivant en cela les indications fournies par Szondi lui-même, comment le test dans ses divers aspects peut prétendre s'articuler sur la doctrine génétique des pulsions. Or le lecteur, déjà averti de la procédure testologique, ne peut manquer d'avoir été frappé de ce que les résultats pris en compte par la recherche génotropique (réactions pleines et nulles) n'épuisent nullement les données produites dès l'origine par le test. Car non seulement les réactions de choix mobilisées à l'appel du test peuvent être différenciées en réactions nulles et réactions pleines, mais encore les réactions pleines elles-mêmes peuvent être différenciées plus avant, et le sont dès l'origine, en réactions positives, négatives et ambivalentes, ce qui découle en droite ligne des instructions originaires du test, qui prescrivent au sujet de choisir les photos selon sa sympathie *et* selon son antipathie.

Mais que les réactions positives et négatives n'aient pas été prises en compte dans leur différence par la recherche génotropique (elle-même soustendue par la doctrine génétique) n'a rien d'étonnant. Car si la doctrine génétique élabore bien une doctrine du choix, et en particulier une doctrine du choix en amour et amitié, elle ne discerne pas le choix d'antipathie et le choix de sympathie. Elle ne considère que le seul choix d'attirance positive. La thèse du génotropisme est muette quant à la constitution génétique des personnes qui se repoussent ou s'abhorrent.

Nous sommes donc autorisé à affirmer que dès l'origine le test produisait plus que ce que permettait d'en dériver une doctrine constituée.

Or ces données qu'une théorie génétique laissait en friche appelaient inévitablement une interprétation, demandaient une traduction conceptuelle, bref devaient susciter tôt ou tard des développements théoriques inédits. Que ceux-ci se soient révélés de plus en plus irréductibles à la doctrine initialement fondatrice du fonctionnement du test, c'est ce que nous devons maintenant analyser dans le détail.

3. Le test dans la doctrine des pulsions

a) Premier moment : l'Analyse du destin (1944)

En réalité, les développements théoriques nouveaux, dont il vient d'être question, étaient déjà contenus, du moins dans quelques-unes de leurs composantes embryonnaires, au sein de l'unité plus ou moins problématique que constitue la doctrine szondienne à l'époque de la Scha : appelés par le test et les aspects de son fonctionnement que la doctrine génétique était impuissante à interpréter, ils allaient prendre un appui direct, en partie tout au moins, sur des éléments présents dès l'origine dans la Scha, et bien plus sur des éléments qui déjà alors affolaient la doctrine génétique. En ce sens, le test aurait moins été un créateur qu'une espèce de catalyseur. C'est là ce qu'il nous faudrait montrer.

La doctrine génétique, nous l'avons vu, rapporte diverses formes d'apparition des pulsions à des combinaisons de gènes pulsionnels. Mais entre ces deux termes vient d'emblée s'insinuer un registre intermédiaire : le registre des besoins pulsionnels, non identiques ni aux gènes qui les fondent, ni aux formes de leur manifestation visible (la maladie, la profession, ...). Que d'emblée les besoins pulsionnels jouissent d'une spécificité, nous en voyons l'indice dans ce que Szondi s'efforce dès la Scha d'en donner une première définition générale, qui les situe en deçà de leur mode d'apparition empirique. Au nombre de huit, désignés à l'aide de l'initiale des maladies mentales auxquelles ils peuvent donner lieu, ils se trouvent néanmoins définis en des termes psychopathologiquement neutres :

1. Le besoin pulsionnel h : besoin de tendresse.
2. Le besoin pulsionnel s : besoin d'agression.
3. Le besoin pulsionnel e : besoin d'accumulation des affects grossiers.
4. Le besoin pulsionnel hy : besoin de se porter au regard.

5. Le besoin pulsionnel k : besoin de rétrécissement du moi.
6. Le besoin pulsionnel p : besoin d'élargissement du moi.
7. Le besoin pulsionnel d : besoin d'acquisition d'objets.
8. Le besoin pulsionnel m : besoin d'accrochage aux objets acquis.

(Scha, pp. 74-75)

 Jusqu'ici aucun problème : une paire de gènes régit l'état d'un besoin pulsionnel qui, selon la nature des allèles qui le déterminent, se manifestera sous forme normale, pathologique ou socialisée. Ainsi si nous considérons les gènes pulsionnels qui régissent le besoin s, la combinaison AA produit une forme d'apparition normale du besoin d'agression, la combinaison aa une modalité pathologique du même besoin (un sadisme criminel, par exemple), la combinaison Aa une manifestation socialisée (par exemple l'exercice du besoin d'agression dans une activité professionnelle : la boucherie, la chirurgie,...).

 Mais les problèmes surgissent dès le moment où Szondi, décidant de raffiner sa conception d'un registre pulsionnel propre, précise que tout besoin pulsionnel est originairement ambitendant, ou partagé entre deux tendances polairement opposées (Scha, p. 75). Et Szondi de compléter aussitôt son esquisse de l'ordre pulsionnel, à quel instant précis, croyons-nous, la doctrine génétique est affolée :

I.	Féminité, besoin h	1.	Tendance à la tendresse sensuelle personnelle ;
		2.	Tendance à la tendresse collective, humanisée.
II.	Masculinité, besoin s	3.	Tendance à l'agression ;
		4.	Tendance au dévouement collectif.
III.	Besoin éthique, besoin e	5.	Tendance au mal, à l'accumulation d'affects brutaux ;
		6.	Tendance au bien, à la justice collective.
IV.	Besoin moral, besoin hy	7.	Tendance à « se porter au regard » ;
		8.	Tendance à la pudeur collective.
V.	Rétrécissement du moi, besoin k	9.	Tendance à l'autisme, l'égoïsme ;
		10.	Tendance à l'adaptation à la collectivité.
VI.	Expansion du moi, besoin p	11.	Tendance à l'expansion du moi (inflation) ;
		12.	Tendance à l'élargissement spirituel des besoins humains à la collectivité.
VII.	Besoin d'acquisition, besoin d	13.	Tendance à l'acquisition de valeurs aux dépens des autres ;
		14.	Tendance au refus au bénéfice d'autres êtres humains.
VIII.	Besoin d'accrochage, besoin m	15.	Tendance à l'accrochage à l'objet ;
		16.	Tendance à la séparation.

(d'après Scha, pp. 76-77)

 Il est clair que les tendances pulsionnelles ainsi énumérées et définies exigent une fondation génétique, tout aussitôt trouvée. Car les deux tendances constitutives d'un besoin ont un répondant génétique tout désigné : le gène ou l'allèle pulsionnel A ou a, B ou b, C ou c, ... Mais une conséquence inévitable découle d'un tel enracinement génétique : les deux tendances doivent être, l'une, portée par l'allèle A, physiologique ou normale, l'autre portée par l'allèle a, maladive ou pathologique; ou encore, les deux tendances doivent être identiques aux deux formes d'apparition normale et maladive des pulsions. Or cette identification parfaitement conséquente est impraticable.

Une preuve s'en dégage à l'examen du tableau qui, dans la Scha (pp. 78-81), succède immédiatement aux propositions d'une articulation en besoins et tendances du registre pulsionnel. Ce tableau, dont le but est d'énumérer les manifestations possibles des huit besoins pulsionnels, inclut les seize tendances pulsionnelles comme formes d'apparition des pulsions, et cela dans les termes mêmes qui ont servi à les définir tout juste auparavant, comme composantes élémentaires de l'ordre pulsionnel, mais d'une manière qui est incohérente avec la doctrine génétique des pulsions. Alors même que, conformément à la doctrine génétique, les deux tendances devraient correspondre, la première à une forme d'apparition pathologique, la seconde à une forme d'apparition normale du besoin, nous y remarquons pour chaque besoin que l'une de ces tendances (pour le besoin h par exemple, la tendresse individuelle) figure comme sa forme d'apparition normale et que l'autre (la tendresse collective) y intervient comme sa forme d'apparition socialisée.

Dès la Scha, un décalage s'est comme institué entre une doctrine des pulsions qui fait place en son sein aux tendances pulsionnelles et une doctrine génétique des formes d'apparition des pulsions. Mais ce décalage va se creuser encore davantage, et se muer en rupture, dès lors que Szondi se trouve conduit à interpréter les faits produits par son test.

b) Deuxième moment : le Diagnostic des pulsions (1947)

Nous l'avons vu, Szondi dispose d'un corps d'hypothèses qui autorise une interprétation légitime des données testologiques (les réactions de choix) en termes de gènes. Or rapidement un virage s'accomplit au sein du langage interprétatif : l'interprétation s'effectue non plus dans le langage des gènes, mais dans le langage des pulsions.

Szondi est d'ailleurs lui-même à l'initiative de ce mouvement, puisque, lorsqu'il publie en 1947 son premier traité du « Diagnostic expérimental des pulsions », il présente son test comme une « épreuve qui sert à l'exploration des constitutions et des mécanismes pulsionnels individuels » (DP, p. 23). Les réactions de choix, écrit-il, sont des « réactions déterminées par les pulsions » (DP, p. 23) : elles sont indices de processus pulsionnels et non traces d'une constitution génétique (latente).

Mais comment les réactions de choix sont-elles interprétées en langage pulsionnel? C'est dans le chapitre 7 de la première partie du « Diagnostic des pulsions » que Szondi nous livre les règles fondamentales de l'interprétation des choix; et c'est aussi à même ce texte que nous allons repérer le mouvement par lequel Szondi dépasse la doctrine génétique.

Szondi y distingue un double point de vue dans l'analyse des réactions de choix : le point de vue de la quantité des choix et le point de vue de leur direction de tendance.

Au plan de la quantité des choix, deux grandes formes de réaction peuvent être différenciées : les réactions nulles (ou réactions o) et les réactions pleines. Nous rencontrons donc ces deux modalités du choix qui intéressaient l'interprétation génotropique, et nous devons constater que leur interprétation psychopulsionnelle est en quelque sorte homologue à leur interprétation génétique. La réaction nulle, propose Szondi, indique qu'un besoin est déchargé, ou se décharge, se manifeste, s'extériorise (DP, p. 45). Par contre, la réaction pleine révèle qu'un besoin est chargé et dès lors exerce une action dynamique (DP, p. 47). Au gène latent (dominé) qui n'arrivait pas à manifester son caractère par voie directe, mais était néanmoins producteur d'effets (génotropiques) indirects, se substitue un besoin qui sur un mode analogue ne parvient pas à décharger la tension accumulée en lui et devient dès lors source de dynamisme (réaction pleine); et encore: le gène récessif extériorise son caractère, le besoin est déchargé (réaction nulle).

Mais ce n'est pas tant au plan de l'interprétation des réactions d'après la quantité qu'apparaît la nouveauté conductrice d'un éclatement de la doctrine génétique des pulsions. C'est davantage là où il s'agit d'interpréter les réactions de choix selon qu'elles sont des réactions d'attirance ou de répulsion. Nous n'en sommes d'ailleurs pas surpris puisque nous savons déjà que la doctrine génétique ne différencie pas choix de sympathie et choix d'antipathie. A ce niveau, nous observerons d'abord la conjonction qui s'accomplit entre choix positifs et négatifs d'une part et tendances pulsionnelles d'autre part. Jusqu'alors en effet la polarité des tendances pulsionnelles, déjà introduite au plan théorique dans la Scha, et la polarité choix de sympathie - choix d'antipathie, dès l'origine inhérente à la pratique du test, étaient restées dans un état d'indifférence réciproque. C'est avec le « Diagnostic des pulsions » que s'opère en premier la liaison explicite, et cela dans les deux sens, depuis les tendances et depuis les réactions de choix.

Depuis les tendances: les deux tendances constitutives du besoin sont présentées désormais comme tendance positive et tendance négative, bien plus, en référence au symbolisme de la pratique du test qui traduit les choix de sympathie et d'antipathie, comme tendance + et tendance -. Ainsi les deux tendances constitutives du besoin h seront désignées comme tendance h+ et tendance h- (cfr les tableaux du DP, pp. 16-17).

Depuis les réactions de choix: car différenciées en réactions positives (+) et réactions négatives (-), selon le critère de la direction de tendance, les réactions de choix révèlent l'une ou l'autre des deux tendances pulsionnelles qui articulent polairement le besoin. Mais comment effectuer le saut qui mène de la direction de tendance (+ ou -) des choix aux tendances pulsionnelles ?

Interrogeons à présent le second point de vue interprétatif que nous annoncions: le point de vue de la direction de tendance.

Conduit à rendre compte de la différenciation des choix d'attirance et de répulsion que produit sa pratique mais n'explique pas sa doctrine instituée, Szondi est contraint à enrichir celle-ci. Or, plutôt que de compléter sa doctrine génétique en déterminant le fondement génétique des choix guidés par l'antipathie, Szondi formule une proposition qui déborde sans recours le contexte d'une doctrine héréditaire.

Pour expliquer la différence entre choix de sympathie et choix d'antipathie, Szondi introduit l'idée d'un pouvoir actif du « sujet » ou du « moi ». Dans le choix de sympathie, le sujet ou le moi approuve le besoin, dans le choix d'antipathie il refuse le besoin, le refoule, l'entrave. Une réaction positive (+) indique donc l'affirmation du besoin par le moi, une réaction négative (-) sa négation par le moi; quant à la réaction ambivalente (±), elle révèle un moi qui hésite entre l'affirmation et la négation du besoin.

Le saut de la direction de tendance des choix vers les tendances pulsionnelles s'éclaire en conséquence. Car les deux tendances d'un besoin se forment à l'intervention de la prise de position du moi, également active dans la situation du test. La tendance positive du besoin naît de l'approbation du besoin lui-même et de la direction qui lui est comme naturellement inhérente : elle se situera donc dans le prolongement direct du besoin. Alors que la tendance négative résulte du refus que le moi oppose au besoin : elle travaillera donc dans une direction inverse au besoin et à son orientation spontanée. Ainsi, pour ne prendre qu'un seul exemple, le besoin hy, défini dans son essence générale comme besoin de « se porter au regard », se divise en une tendance positive, la tendance à « se porter au regard » elle-même, et une tendance négative, la tendance inverse à se cacher.

Szondi est ainsi amené, à l'appel du test, à invoquer un choix — ou une composante du choix — régi, non par l'hérédité et les gènes latents, mais par une instance extragénétique, psychologique : le moi de l'individu capable de prendre position par rapport au besoin. Une question en découle : si le moi exerce un pouvoir déterminant dans l'effectuation des choix testologiques, qu'en advient-il du génotropisme ?

Au lieu d'affronter la question, Szondi adopte une attitude curieuse. Incapable de renoncer au génotropisme et à son efficace dans la situation de test, mais tout aussi impuissant désormais à l'articuler de manière rigoureuse sur le test et son fonctionnement, il en postule arbitrairement l'action là où est en jeu son « analogon » psychodynamique intrinsèque.

On peut se demander si la thèse du génotropisme n'est pas la résultante d'une inscription dans les gènes de principes psychodynamiques congéniaux au registre pulsionnel. Ce serait un peu comme si, au moment de leur appariement, les deux gènes allèles étaient engagés dans un rapport de forces, dont le plus fort, l'allèle dominant, finirait par sortir vainqueur ayant repoussé son partenaire récessif, sans que toutefois ce dernier se reconnaisse tout à fait battu : dans l'impossibilité d'une expression directe, il réussirait néanmoins à produire des effets indirects de choix. Ne reconnaissons-nous pas là, transposés dans les gènes, les principes d'une psychodynamique des pulsions (le conflit, le refoulement, le retour et l'expression indirecte du refoulé) ?

Or, qu'affirme Szondi dès le moment où l'interprétation psychopulsionnelle des réactions de choix commence à se développer sur un mode autonome ? Que les réactions d'antipathie (et non pas les réactions pleines tout court) sont révélatrices des exigences pulsionnelles qui guident les choix génotropiques (d'attirance) du sujet (DP, p. 51). On saisit d'emblée ce qu'un pareil énoncé a de conceptuellement illégitime : il ne s'appuie pas sur une doctrine générale du choix d'antipathie ou de répulsion (inexistante, nous le savons), qui aurait été ensuite adéquatement rapportée à la situation de test. Mais il n'est pas non plus quelconque, fruit d'un pur hasard. Il a sa nécessité textuelle propre : par lui, le mécanisme génotropique se trouve référé aux réactions de choix (en l'occurrence : les réactions négatives) qui, à ce stade de la doctrine pulsionnelle, en révèlent l'« analogon » psychodynamique intrinsèque (le refoulement et le retour indirect du refoulé).

c) *Troisième moment : la pathologie pulsionnelle (1952)*

Entre 1947 et 1952, une innovation modifie la pratique du test, la seule d'ailleurs qui soit jamais intervenue. Le second choix est introduit, et la pratique du test amène désormais à la formation de trois profils pulsionnels : le profil établi sur base du premier choix, lui-même redéfini comme profil d'avant-plan (VGP), et les deux profils complémentaires, empirique et théorique (EKP et ThKP).

Mais d'où procède cette innovation? Il ne semble pas qu'au départ un concept théorique clairement formulé ait engendré la modification. Si l'on se fie à une confidence de Szondi, l'idée lui en serait venue à la suite d'une suggestion d'un patient, qui aurait attiré son attention sur les photos non choisies [1]. Effectivement, la procédure en usage jusqu'alors n'épuisait pas les possibilités matérielles offertes par le test: au terme du choix, vingt-quatre photos demeuraient sans emploi. Pourquoi ne pas les utiliser à leur tour ? Mais aussi: pourquoi les utiliser ? Pourquoi cette suggestion anodine d'un patient n'est-elle pas tombée dans l'oreille d'un sourd ?

Szondi ne s'en est jamais expliqué, mais on peut penser qu'une idée très générale, présente de bout en bout à son esprit et accrochée aux matériaux les plus divers, a dû implicitement jouer: nous visons le principe psychodynamique déjà contenu, à l'état voilé, dans la thèse du génotropisme. Est-ce que derrière les tendances les plus manifestes révélées par les réactions du premier choix ne se cacheraient pas d'autres tendances dissimulées, voire même barrées par les premières, mais néanmoins actives et dynamiques à leur façon ? Que cette idée soit intervenue au moment même où a été arrêtée la modification de la pratique, c'est tout au plus une hypothèse. Ce qui est sûr en tout cas, c'est qu'après coup, une fois décidée l'introduction du second choix et conséquemment la construction de deux nouveaux profils pulsionnels, cette idée a été mise explicitement en œuvre dans l'interprétation des nouvelles données produites par le test. A l'arrière des tendances pulsionnelles visibles de l'avant-plan s'agitent des tendances latentes (dites précisément d'arrière-plan) qui, toutes latentes qu'elles soient, n'en sont pas moins aussi réelles que les premières. Telle est bien l'interprétation théorique majeure à la lumière de laquelle Szondi rend compte des résultats de ses nouvelles manipulations pratiques. Que par ailleurs ce soit le profil complémentaire théorique, et non tellement le profil complémentaire empirique, qui d'après Szondi révèle les tendances latentes d'arrière-plan (le profil complémentaire théorique est le seul arrière-plan réel, dira toujours à nouveau Szondi), nous touchons là un problème considérable, mais que nous ne pouvons aborder en ce moment.

Or l'interprétation théorique dont il vient d'être question engendre à son tour des énoncés théoriques complémentaires et interconnectés, que Szondi a formulés dans la TrP (même s'il n'en a jamais pensé l'interconnection nécessaire), et dont il a tiré les conséquences au plan de la signification des choix testologiques, dans la seconde édition du TrD (1960). Nous tenterons d'en dégager deux: un premier qui concerne les tendances pulsionnelles, un second qui intéresse le rôle du moi.

1. La réalité « aprioristique » des tendances pulsionnelles

Si les nouvelles manipulations pratiques et l'interprétation qui leur est associée sont légitimes, alors il résulte que les seize tendances pulsionnelles existent a priori. En effet, tant qu'un profil pulsionnel unique était établi, il s'imposait que seule une partie des tendances pulsionnelles était active chez un sujet. Mais dès le moment où un profil complémentaire théorique est construit, selon la procédure que nous avons apprise (il contiendra toujours

---

[1] Pour plus de détails sur ce point, cfr M. Legrand, 1978.

les tendances qui ne sont pas inscrites dans l'avant-plan) et doté de la signification que nous connaissons (il contient des tendances réelles), nous devons conclure que les seize tendances pulsionnelles fonctionnent dans leur entièreté, les unes à l'avant-plan, les autres à l'arrière-plan.

Cet énoncé, Szondi l'a surtout formulé lorsqu'il envisage à nouveaux frais, dans la TrP, la signification des tendances négatives. Il est temps à présent, y écrit Szondi, de proposer une interprétation dynamique plus profonde des réactions négatives : « toute tendance négative est en soi une tendance élémentaire de la pulsion totale, aussi autonome, aprioristique ... que la tendance positive opposée » (TrP, p. 148). Et Szondi d'appliquer aussitôt sa proposition générale à toutes les variétés de tendance négative (h-, s-, e-, hy-,...). Ainsi il écrit : h- est la disposition aprioristique à l'amour de l'humanité et elle ne naît pas simplement par répression de l'amour personnel (h+).

Mais en réalité ce texte pointe déjà vers le second énoncé essentiel qu'engage la construction d'un arrière-plan théorique.

2. *La transformation du rôle du moi*

Dans la doctrine pulsionnelle qu'esquisse le DP de 1947, les huit besoins pulsionnels sont les constituants de base de la vie pulsionnelle : les uns se déchargeant dans le comportement sous forme d'une manifestation directe (réaction nulle), les autres se chargeant et produisant dès lors des effets dynamiques (réaction pleine). Mais en quelle mesure le moi intervient-il dans ces processus ? Le moi est comme absent des réactions nulles : en tel cas, le besoin se décharge par voie directe, sans médiation du moi. Le moi n'est en vérité présent qu'aux réactions pleines, via l'effectuation d'une prise de position par rapport aux besoins qui s'accumulent en lui, soit que cette prise de position abonde dans le sens du besoin (+), soit qu'elle lui oppose un refus (-). Au fond, à ce stade, le moi constitue les tendances par sa prise de position. Ou peut-être plus justement, il constitue la tendance négative. Car l'interprétation promue en 1947 présuppose une orientation originaire du besoin, que le moi ne constitue pas, à laquelle il peut tout au plus opposer un refus, induisant par là une mutation au sein du besoin — mutation éventuellement transformatrice jusqu'à la sublimation : ainsi la direction originaire du besoin h orientée vers l'amour sensuel se transmue, par le refus du moi (h-), en une tendance à l'amour humain collectif.

Or ce système d'interprétation devient intenable dès le moment où est construit un arrière-plan théorique. La réaction o n'est plus une pure réaction de décharge, puisque le besoin est chargé à l'arrière (±) à l'instant même où la réaction nulle (o) s'inscrit à l'avant. De plus, la réalité aprioristique des tendances conduit à récuser l'idée d'une orientation positive originaire du besoin (à laquelle une tendance négative inverse s'opposerait secondairement), comme la possibilité d'une transmutation sublimatrice du besoin qui arriverait à en effacer l'orientation asociale primitive. En quoi Szondi s'opposera dès 1952 à ce qu'il présente comme une doctrine freudienne de la sublimation. La sublimation ne peut être définie comme la réorientation créatrice et transformatrice du besoin dans une direction sociale. La tendance asociale du besoin est à tout jamais constitutive du bagage pulsionnel humain et peut être tout au plus évacuée à l'arrière-plan. Ainsi, la sublimation du besoin h, signée par la tendance h-, ne suspend pas son orientation asociale, présente à l'arrière-plan (h+).

Mais du même coup, le rôle du moi demande à être réévalué. Si la tendance négative est tout aussi aprioristique que la tendance positive, elle n'est plus comme telle formée par le moi. Le moi ne constitue plus les tendances pulsionnelles. Comment intervient-il donc?

C'est dans les analyses qu'il consacre en 1960 aux réactions positives et négatives que Szondi explicite le nouveau mode d'intervention du moi. Il écrit : « La direction du choix est un signe manifeste de la prise de position du moi vis-à-vis de la tendance concernée. Le profil pulsionnel ne diagnostique donc pas seulement les motions pulsionnelles d'un être humain, mais aussi la prise de position de son moi par rapport à ces tendances pulsionnelles »; et un peu plus bas, il précise significativement : « 1. Réaction positive : le moi choisit actuellement la tendance pulsionnelle positive ... 2. Réaction négative : le moi choisit actuellement la tendance pulsionnelle négative » (TrP, p. 59). De 1947 à 1960, un seul mot a changé : « tendance » s'est substitué à « besoin ». A travers les choix, positifs ou négatifs, qu'il effectue, le moi ne prend plus position vis-à-vis du besoin, mais bien vis-à-vis des tendances qui lui sont données a priori et avec lesquelles il a à s'expliquer. Mais comment prend-il position? Ici encore, comme auparavant, en approuvant et désapprouvant, à cette différence près que l'approbation et la désapprobation du moi ne s'exercent plus tout à fait de la façon dont elles s'exerçaient jusqu'alors. A présent, le moi approuve chaque fois qu'il pose un choix, lorsqu'il choisit positivement certes, mais aussi lorsqu'il choisit négativement, sur le mode de l'antipathie : à ce moment, il approuve la tendance négative du besoin. Mais quand donc le moi désapprouve-t-il? Non plus lorsqu'il choisit négativement, mais tout simplement lorsqu'il ne choisit pas. L'absence de choix est encore choix si l'on peut dire, elle est refus de tendances qui sont dès lors inscrites à l'arrière-plan. L'engagement du moi est ainsi généralisé à toutes les réactions, y compris aux réactions nulles.

En termes synthétiques, le moi n'est plus l'instance qui constitue, par sa prise de position positive ou négative, les tendances pulsionnelles, mais bien l'instance responsable de leur clivage : assumant une part des tendances aprioristiques (positives ou négatives), en refusant l'autre part, le moi clive les seize tendances pulsionnelles en tendances d'avant-plan et en tendances d'arrière-plan.

Telle est la restructuration de la doctrine pulsionnelle qui accompagne la transformation de la pratique testologique, mais du même coup, selon le principe que nous avons déjà énoncé, engendre un nouveau déplacement du mécanisme du génotropisme.

Quelles seront donc désormais les véritables tendances latentes, tendant « à se manifester par des voies indirectes, dans des actes de choix tropiques », sinon les tendances désapprouvées de l'arrière-plan? Implication ultime : si nous effectuons un retour sur la situation testologique de choix, nous devons conclure que la réaction nulle de l'avant-plan, corrélative d'une charge maximale du besoin à l'arrière-plan (±), révèle les besoins génotropiquement actifs (TrP, p. 147). Conséquence inattendue, en totale contradiction avec l'application conceptuelle légitime de la thèse du génotropisme, mais dotée d'une cohérence dès le moment où le génotropisme s'accroche là où son « analogon » psychodynamique est postulé.

CONCLUSIONS

Tout au long de notre paragraphe B, nous nous sommes efforcé de ressaisir le mouvement de la pratique szondienne et ce qui dans ce mouvement atteste l'entremêlement complexe de la pratique technicienne, instrumentale et de la pratique théorique.

Evoluant selon sa dynamique instrumentale propre, le diagnostic expérimental des pulsions nous est apparu comme incessant producteur de faits qui venaient inquiéter une doctrine instituée : choix négatifs et choix positifs différenciés et inscrits sous forme de réactions pulsionnelles + et − tout d'abord ; second choix instigateur de la constitution de deux nouveaux profils pulsionnels ensuite. Mis en demeure de rattraper le retard pris par sa théorie sur sa pratique, Szondi étoffe sa doctrine, tantôt en puisant à des éléments déjà contenus en germes dans son œuvre antérieure (ainsi en 1947, l'appel à une notion de tendance pulsionnelle déjà incluse dans la Scha), tantôt en osant une hypothèse franchement inédite (ainsi l'intervention du moi dans le choix). Sont progressivement mis en place les éléments d'une doctrine psychopulsionnelle, dont deux aspects ont été au centre de notre propos : l'articulation de l'ordre pulsionnel en besoins et tendances, le rôle exercé par le moi vis-à-vis de ces mêmes besoins et tendances. Mais loin de compléter harmonieusement la doctrine génétique qui avait au départ guidé une pratique instrumentale, loin d'en combler les lacunes et de la mettre en état de maîtriser ce qui lui aurait — un moment seulement — échappé, les développements théoriques nouveaux s'avèrent de plus en plus incompatibles avec cette doctrine. Certes Szondi déploie des efforts en vue de les récupérer au profit d'une doctrine génétique maintenue en état, mais des efforts qui cachent mal leur échec. Ainsi Szondi cherche à fonder les tendances dans les allèles pulsionnels, mais du même coup il est conduit à des conclusions qui contredisent sa doctrine génétique elle-même, voire la génétique scientifique tout court.

Car si les tendances pulsionnelles aprioristiques sont fondées dans des gènes allèles, il en découle que tout individu est hétérozygote quant à chacun des huit besoins pulsionnels. Ce qui est scientifiquement insoutenable. Génétiquement, on ne peut exclure l'existence de combinaisons homozygotes AA ou aa, bref le « manque héréditaire » de certaines tendances, possibilité que Szondi rejette explicitement pour des raisons inhérentes à sa doctrine psychopulsionnelle (cfr TrD, p. 99).

Quant au rôle du moi, Szondi lui-même avouera que sa reconnaissance marque les limites d'une doctrine génétique, le point où une doctrine génétique demande, non à être abandonnée — ce à quoi il se refusera jusqu'au bout —, mais à être complétée. Le choix n'est pas entièrement déterminé par l'hérédité, il peut être aussi déterminé par le moi. Le moi a une capacité de prise de position par rapport aux tendances offertes par l'hérédité. Comme si l'hérédité donnait à l'être humain les tendances aprioristiques inscrites génétiquement sous les espèces d'une combinaison hétérozygote (Aa) et engagées dans un rapport incertain de dominance relative, et comme si le moi intervenait pour infléchir le rapport de forces. Mais peut-on sérieusement adhérer à pareille problématique ? Comment donc le moi pourrait-il « contrôler » l'hérédité (Scha Th, p. 87) ?

Au vu des difficultés qui compromettent la doctrine génétique, la seule attitude raisonnable et opportune ne consisterait-elle pas à développer pour elle-même, selon son génie propre, la doctrine psychopulsionnelle qui sert d'ailleurs de base fondamentale à l'interprète du test et dont nous n'entrevoyons encore qu'une esquisse embryonnaire, et cela sans plus aucun souci d'une hypothétique et même invraisemblable fondation génétique ?

Cependant, une difficulté considérable ne peut être voilée. Szondi, il est vrai, complexifie sa doctrine psychopulsionnelle à l'instigation des faits produits par son test. Ainsi il distingue plus finement des tendances pulsionnelles positives et négatives, révélées par les choix de sympathie et d'antipathie. Mais on doit savoir que cette complexification même s'effectue au prix d'une méconnaissance de ce qui autorise le passage ou le saut des choix bruts de photos aux tendances pulsionnelles.

Dans le premier état de la doctrine szondienne, le saut qui s'accomplit des choix testologiques aux gènes pulsionnels latents est légitimé par une hypothèse explicite (le génotropisme). Par contre, dans un état de doctrine qui désormais abandonne toute référence héréditaire, se formule en termes strictement psychopulsionnels et engendre une pratique autonome du test (en vue de «détecter des processus pulsionnels»), le saut des réactions brutes de choix aux processus pulsionnels n'est plus légitimé. Ainsi, la pratique psychopulsionnelle du test supposera que cinq choix positifs de photos d'homosexuels (inscrits : h+!!) au cours d'une administration du test révèle, non plus un gène pulsionnel latent, mais bien une forte tendance à la tendresse personnelle. Mais pourquoi une vive attirance pour les homosexuels révélerait-elle une tendance à la tendresse personnelle ? En termes plus généraux : quels sont les processus psychopulsionnels qui se produisent au moment où s'effectuent les choix et nous autorisent à passer de ces choix au dynamisme pulsionnel diagnostiqué par le test ? Non seulement Szondi n'a jamais répondu à la question, mais encore il n'a jamais formulé la question elle-même.

Une tâche nous incomberait donc : ayant déblayé le terrain par l'écartement du génotropisme, soulever en termes explicites la problématique du fonctionnement du test et jeter les bases d'une doctrine du choix testologique qui légitimerait la pratique psychopulsionnelle du test.

Mais cette tâche, qui sans doute ne pourra être menée jusqu'à son aboutissement, nous ne l'attaquerons pas dans l'immédiat, n'y venant qu'en fin de notre itinéraire. Il nous suffisait de prévenir dès maintenant le lecteur : l'exposé de la doctrine psychopulsionnelle, qui nous occupera à présent et constitue le cœur même de cet ouvrage, s'effectuera dans la mise entre parenthèses d'un problème crucial, qui hypothèque, et hypothèquera peut-être encore longtemps, l'entreprise szondienne.

Troisième partie
La doctrine psychopulsionnelle

Dans cette troisième partie, nous nous donnons comme objectif d'exposer la doctrine psychopulsionnelle de Szondi, et cela indépendamment de toute référence à un arrière-fond génétique héréditaire. Qu'il y soit peu question du diagnostic expérimental des pulsions ne doit point abuser: les développements théoriques dans lesquels nous allons nous engager donnent aussi les éléments de base d'une interprétation du test de Szondi.

Nous parcourrons trois étapes.

Dans un premier temps, nous aurons à exposer la théorie des pulsions elles-mêmes, irréductibles aux effets empiriques qu'elles produisent, introduisant par là comme une coupure au sein de l'ordre pulsionnel, dissociant les pulsions formatrices de système de leurs formes d'apparition empirique (pathologie mentale, socialisation professionnelle,...).

Un second temps nous amènera à poser pour elle-même la problématique de la liaison entre le système pulsionnel et ses manifestations empiriques. Comment le fonctionnement autonome des pulsions engendre-t-il des formes d'apparition visibles? Cette question, nous l'aborderons à propos du domaine empirique qui a retenu l'attention privilégiée de Szondi: le domaine des maladies mentales.

Enfin, dans un troisième temps, nous réfléchirons quelque peu sur la position remarquable occupée par le moi à l'intérieur de l'ordre pulsionnel.

Chapitre I
La théorie des pulsions

L'exposé de la théorie szondienne des pulsions procédera en deux phases. Tout d'abord, dans un premier paragraphe, nous étudierons le système pulsionnel de Szondi et ses constituants de base, ce qu'on pourrait appeler en terme métaphorique l'anatomie des pulsions. Ensuite, dans un second paragraphe, nous examinerons le fonctionnement, que Szondi a appelé dialectique, de ce même système pulsionnel: sorte de physiologie des pulsions.

A. LE SYSTEME PULSIONNEL ET SES CONSTITUANTS ELEMENTAIRES

Le système pulsionnel est composé de quatre pulsions, elles-mêmes constituées chacune de deux besoins, articulés l'un et l'autre en deux tendances. Donc: quatre pulsions, huit besoins, seize tendances, tels sont les constituants élémentaires du système pulsionnel dont nous avons à définir la nature ou l'essence.

Mais quelques remarques préalables nous paraissent nécessaires.

Le point de départ de Szondi paraît être largement intuitif. Szondi aurait eu comme une illumination soudaine qui l'aurait amené à poser son système pulsionnel dans la constitution que nous lui connaissons — on raconte même que le tableau des pulsions lui serait d'abord apparu en rêve. Mais le coup de force initial accompli, s'ouvre un champ considérable d'investigations théoriques. Les constituants du système posés, il reste à en élaborer conceptuellement le contenu. Certes dès l'origine, le système est plus qu'un pur squelette formel: non seulement les composantes élémentaires sont introduites dans leur nombre et dans leur organisation formelle (ordre quaternaire des pulsions, articulation bipolaire des pulsions et des besoins), mais un contenu leur est déjà attribué. Nous savons déjà que d'emblée Szondi nous proposait de premières définitions des besoins et des tendances pulsionnels. Cependant, ses premières définitions, toutes précieuses qu'elles aient pu être, restaient encore très imparfaites. La théorie du système pulsionnel ne se présentait donc pas à l'origine comme une théorie achevée, mais comme l'institution d'un cadre formel, au contenu encore pauvre : elle appelait un enrichissement conceptuel, obtenu à la faveur de démarches tâtonnantes et progressives de recherche.

Les conséquences de cette situation sont considérables. Mais avant même d'en énoncer quelques-unes, posons-nous la question : comment Szondi et les chercheurs qui se réclament de lui procèdent-ils dans cette pratique d'élaboration conceptuelle ? Le processus est assurément très complexe, mais en première approximation nous pourrions dire que cette démarche d'enrichissement théorique se développe en perpétuelle référence à un double champ : le champ du théorique existant et le champ de la clinique. Précisons ces deux points.

1. Relation au champ théorique existant

Szondi tentera d'élaborer la signification des composantes du système pulsionnel en référence à des concepts déjà construits dans le champ de ce qu'il appelle «la psychologie des profondeurs».

Notons à cet égard que les références szondiennes sont très variées et ne se limitent pas à la psychanalyse freudienne au sens strict : si Freud est bien le plus sollicité, des psychologues aussi différents que Jung, Kretschmer ou I. Hermann seront aussi mis à contribution.

Mais cet emprunt au champ théorique existant ne peut être laissé au hasard. Que dire de la logique qui l'anime ? Nous pouvons au moins souligner un élément. Généralement le noyau des significations présomptivement acquises guidera et contrôlera la démarche. Ainsi, si l'on s'efforce aujourd'hui d'éclairer les processus pulsionnels à la lumière de concepts linguistiques ou de concepts lacaniens [1], on prendra soin de se rapporter aux significations déjà construites et de prendre un premier appui sur elles, quitte à devoir parfois les critiquer et les rectifier pour des raisons fondées au plan théorique.

Nous ajouterons cependant que l'interaction n'est pas à sens unique. Le système pulsionnel szondien peut être aussi le stimulant d'une production théorique originale. Car il n'est pas dit que les concepts nécessaires à l'élaboration de ses composantes soient déjà tous contenus dans quelque doctrine existante, auquel cas il suffirait de les exporter dans la théorie pulsionnelle. Le système pulsionnel lui-même pourrait appeler la construction de concepts inédits qui du même coup aideraient à la juste formulation de problèmes toujours en suspens et au déblocage de leur solution.

2. La relation au champ clinique

Nous devrions préciser : relation au champ clinique via le diagnostic expérimental des pulsions. Nous voulons dire par là que le travail conceptuel de Szondi se nourrit d'un appel constant à la clinique psychopathologique qui

---

[1] Nous visons ici le travail remarquable d'Alfred Zenoni (1974).

emprunte le détour du test. Mais ce détour lui-même présente deux aspects qu'il importe de bien distinguer.

Tout d'abord, l'élaboration conceptuelle des processus pulsionnels peut se revendiquer des maladies mentales par le truchement desquelles ils sont diagnostiqués. Ainsi, nous savons que le besoin p est appréhendé par l'intermédiaire de choix de photos de paranoïaques. N'est-ce pas là supposer que le besoin p entretient une liaison intime avec la paranoïa et ce qui s'y joue de déterminant ? La paranoïa pourra donc servir de point d'appui constant dans l'élaboration conceptuelle du besoin p[1]. C'est d'ailleurs bien la référence aux maladies pulsionnelles de base, inscrite dans le matériel du test, qui a guidé Szondi dans la formulation de ses premières définitions conceptuelles : les concepts introduits, empruntés le plus souvent au champ théorique existant, mais déjà producteurs d'effets de connaissance inédits (ne serait-ce que d'être rapportés à un syndrome psychopathologique pour la compréhension duquel ils n'avaient jamais été invoqués jusque là), devaient en tout cas être aptes à ressaisir la problématique en jeu dans les huit grandes maladies pulsionnelles.

Mais c'est d'une autre manière encore que le test ouvre un champ de références cliniques susceptible de stimuler la recherche conceptuelle. Nous n'avons parlé jusqu'ici que de la clinique engagée dans la constitution même de l'appareil méthodologique. C'est moins la clinique des sujets « testants » que la clinique des sujets « testés » qui doit être à présent invoquée. Que signifie un h- ? Que signifie un p+ ? Le problème n'avancerait-il pas si nous confrontions les signes produits par la pratique testologique (un h- ou un p+, par exemple) avec les particularités cliniques, observables par ailleurs, des sujets qui donnent ces signes ? Supposons que les sujets en phase mélancolique aiguë donnent régulièrement la réaction k+ : la recherche conceptuelle sera appelée à élaborer une signification du processus k+ qui dégage la voie d'une compréhension de la mélancolie, soit qu'elle privilégie la référence à une théorie déjà construite de la mélancolie (le dynamisme k+ ne serait-il pas identique au processus d'introjection que Freud a tenu pour générateur de la mélancolie ?), soit qu'elle forge un nouveau concept.

Un procès de travail conceptuel est ainsi mis en route, stimulé par le champ théorique existant et par le champ clinique, et plus encore par le perpétuel chassé-croisé dialectique qu'il institue entre eux. Mais la manière même dont est conduite la recherche n'est pas sans engendrer plusieurs conséquences qui se marquent dans l'état actuel de la doctrine du système pulsionnel. Si Szondi est parti moins d'une théorie achevée que d'un schéma formel au contenu initial pauvre, progressivement enrichi à la faveur d'observations cliniques et d'emprunts théoriques effectués ici ou là dans un relatif désordre, rien d'étonnant à ce que nous devions constater :

1. du fait de la variété des emprunts théoriques, une grande hétérogénéité des significations, les unes s'inspirant du dualisme pulsionnel freudien « Eros et Thanatos », d'autres des notions d'accrochage et de recherche issus de I. Hermann, d'autres encore des mécanismes de défense du moi (refoulement, projection,...),... ;

---

[1] S. Deri (1949) nous donne peut-être le plus bel exemple de cette démarche : chaque fois qu'elle engage la discussion d'un besoin pulsionnel, elle a le souci prioritaire d'en rapporter la définition aux malades mentaux qui le mobilisent à la faveur de l'épreuve testologique.

2. du fait de l'inévitable progressivité de la démarche, une inégalité des formulations, les unes avancées, les autres retardées (ainsi, dès la première édition du DP, la doctrine de la pulsion du moi s'avérait la plus élaborée, ce que la suite de l'œuvre ne fera que confirmer, alors même que la théorie de la pulsion sexuelle est restée jusqu'à aujourd'hui largement en friche);

3. du fait du recours toujours possible à la clinique, l'impureté théorique de certaines formulations (car, en l'absence d'une élaboration conceptuelle adéquate, il sera toujours tentant d'y substituer une particularité empirique observée sur le terrain de la clinique).

C'est dans ce contexte que l'effort exemplaire de Jacques Schotte prend toute sa signification.

D'emblée, dans son premier grand article inaugural (1963), Schotte élevait à l'état de question ce qui, pour Szondi, demeurait impensé. Il attirait l'attention sur une des propriétés les plus remarquables du système pulsionnel de Szondi: sa fermeture. Contrairement à toutes les classifications empiriques, toujours ouvertes, toujours prêtes à s'élargir au gré de découvertes empiriques aléatoires, le système de Szondi, l'octave pulsionnel, s'affirmait clos, rappelant ainsi, par ses caractéristiques épistémologiques, quelques précédents célèbres, tel le tableau des substances de Mendeleïev, dont Bachelard avait déjà célébré la complétude et l'éloignement « de toutes les tentatives de classification empirique »[1]. Mais, remarquait Schotte, tout en fermant son schéma pulsionnel et en excluant ainsi que l'une ou l'autre dimension puisse en être retranchée ou lui être ajoutée, Szondi donnait prise, par ses formulations insuffisantes, à l'opérationisme positiviste. L'exigence était dès lors énoncée par Schotte de substituer à ce qui pouvait encore apparaître comme une collection ou une addition de dimensions hétérogènes, définies en référence à des contenus empiriques trop particuliers, un système beaucoup plus unifié et articulé de catégories abstraites, déconnectées de toute particularité empirique étroite. Car seule l'unification et la cohérence conceptuelle pouvaient avoir quelque chance de légitimer la complétude postulée du système. Et Schotte d'en appeler aussitôt dans cet esprit à des registres humains eux-mêmes diversifiés en un nombre limité de dimensions, tels le registre des sens ou le système des beaux arts, pour en faire apparaître l'homologie avec le système des huit catégories pulsionnelles de Szondi.

Mais, par la suite, au-delà de son article initial, Schotte devait reprendre à nouveaux frais la même problématique[2]. Il promouvait une articulation ternaire du système pulsionnel, à portée tout à la fois structurale et génétique. Selon lui, trois dimensions fondamentales, de complexité structurale croissante et tour à tour éveillées par le déroulement temporel de l'existence humaine, seraient constitutives du schéma szondien: elles correspondraient aux vecteurs: 1.C, 2.S et P et 3.Sch. Homologues par ailleurs à quelques grandes triades anthropologiques, ressaisies à la faveur d'une fine réflexion phénoménologique — ne citons, parmi d'autres, que les triades: base-fondement-origine; enfance-adolescence-âge adulte; ... —, elles seraient électivement perturbées dans les figures majeures de la maladie mentale et y deviendraient, dès lors, selon le principe freudien du cristal, clairement reconnaissables[3]. Du même coup, un éclairage nouveau était projeté sur le champ de la pathologie mentale: dans cette perspective, une attention particulière était accordée aux perturbations basales de

---

[1] G. Bachelard, *Le matérialisme rationnel*, P.U.F., 2ᵉ éd., 1963, p. 100.

[2] Depuis 1971 jusqu'à aujourd'hui, le parcours de Schotte est jalonné par quelques grands cours professés à l'Université de Louvain. Sur ce point, nous renvoyons à la bibliographie.

[3] Les dernières formulations de Schotte, les plus achevées, sont contenues dans: *La nosographie psychiatrique comme patho-analyse de notre condition* (1977-1978), en particulier dans le chapitre IV (pp. 113-142).

l'humeur [1], ainsi qu'à la schisophrénie, définie non comme un raté des toutes premières étapes de l'humanisation, mais comme un trouble de l'origine, se jouant et se décidant non dans les débuts primitifs de l'existence humaine, mais au moment où celle-ci entre dans sa phase finale de constitution créatrice [2]. Notons aussi que sur le terrain d'une approche renouvelée des vecteurs pulsionnels, Schotte devait être suivi à Louvain même par Alphonse de Waelhens (1971), ressaisissant les quatre grands vecteurs en termes de rapport-à: rapport à autrui (C), rapport au corps (S), rapport à la loi (P), rapport à soi (Sch). Enfin, Schotte s'engageait dans une analyse interne des grands vecteurs pulsionnels, en particulier: dans une analyse fouillée du vecteur du contact, qu'il prolongeait déjà sous forme de notes prometteuses, en direction des vecteurs S et P [3], et dans l'analyse du vecteur du moi [4].

Enfin, le tout dernier parcours de Schotte devait être marqué par une réflexion renouvelée sur le système pulsionnel szondien à partir d'une confrontation avec les vues du linguiste rennois J. Gagnepain (1976-77), mais plus encore par la promotion de l'idée de circuit pulsionnel. Cette dernière idée, reprise à Szondi, qui la limitait toutefois au vecteur Sch, était élargie à tous les vecteurs: à l'intérieur de chaque vecteur pulsionnel s'effectuerait une circulation mobilisant les quatre tendances selon un ordre de complexité croissante et reproduisant le mouvement qui traverse le système pulsionnel dans son ensemble (de C à Sch, par S et P) (1975-76, pp. 89 et ss.). La théorie du système pulsionnel et de son fonctionnement, inter et intra-vectoriel, trouvait par là un regain de cohérence. De plus, la problématique interne à chaque vecteur pouvait être reprise sur de nouvelles bases [5]. Enfin, plusieurs questions toujours en suspens (en particulier les questions des clivages vectoriels et des profils complémentaires) étaient relancées.

Nous venons ainsi de dresser le cadre à l'intérieur duquel s'inscrivent aujourd'hui les recherches conceptuelles sur le système des pulsions et ses composantes élémentaires. Mais que dire de notre propre contribution? Nous l'avouons franchement: notre intervention se situe nettement en-deçà des exigences auxquelles devrait idéalement obéir tout développement de la théorie du système pulsionnel. Et cela non pas d'abord en raison d'une insuffisance personnelle, mais surtout en raison même de l'état d'inachèvement de la théorie. Que la doctrine du système pulsionnel doive se présenter dans l'avenir sous la forme d'un système unifié et cohérent de concepts théoriques abstraits déliés des formes empiriques qu'ils fondent par ailleurs, c'est bien là l'exigence dont elle est elle-même porteuse. Mais c'est là aussi, nous l'avons vu, un but que personne n'a encore atteint, malgré les avancées décisives d'un Schotte. D'où le fait que notre exposé n'atteigne pas une pureté théorique pourtant souhaitable et se réfère déjà, dans le but d'une saisie de fonctions pulsionnelles abstraites, à des contenus ou à des formes

---

[1] Cfr en particulier: 1977-1978, chapitre III (pp. 79-112).

[2] A ce titre les élaborations de Schotte pourraient contenir à l'état potentiel une doctrine de la schizophrénie qui permettrait de dépasser l'impasse dans laquelle celle-ci semble être actuellement enfermée. Cfr par exemple, *L'analyse du moi* (1973-1974) et ses considérations finales: Perspective, rétrospective et prospective, pp. 134-151, et *La nosographie psychiatrique comme photo-analyse de notre condition*, (1977-1978), pp. 119-123.

[3] Cfr *L'œuvre de Szondi* (1971-1972), Deuxième partie: Etude phénoménologique des vecteurs pulsionnels, chapitre I: le vecteur C, pp. 63-167, et chapitre 2: le vecteur S et le passage au vecteur P, pp. 1-33.

[4] Cfr *L'analyse dy moi* (1973-1974).

[5] Sur ce point, on consultera J. Melon (1977).

empiriques particulières, surtout psychopathologiques. D'où la nécessaire modestie de nos ambitions : présenter les significations les plus courantes des fonctions pulsionnelles, point de départ obligé de toute recherche comme de toute initiation à l'interprétation du test, mais parfois les soumettre à critique et à rectification, ouvrir enfin, au-delà de Szondi, des pistes que les limitations de notre exposé nous empêcheront de poursuivre, mais que des indications bibliographiques permettront au lecteur de prolonger s'il le désire.

1. La pulsion ou vecteur du contact

a) Le vecteur du rapport à l'objet

En promouvant une pulsion du contact, Szondi entend se démarquer de Freud, encore qu'il s'appuie sur un élément de la doctrine freudienne des pulsions[1].

On sait que Freud avait distingué quatre dimensions constitutives de toute pulsion : la source, la poussée, le but et l'objet. Or, Szondi prétend élever à l'état de pulsion autonome ce qui restait, chez Freud, une composante interne de la pulsion, et particulièrement de la pulsion sexuelle : le rapport à l'objet, affirme Szondi, est le domaine d'une pulsion propre, dite du contact, distincte de la pulsion sexuelle.

Entendons bien, pour prévenir une objection, que la pulsion du contact n'est pas seule à instituer un rapport à l'objet. La pulsion sexuelle est engagée elle aussi dans toute liaison objectale. En d'autres termes, tout investissement pulsionnel d'objet est toujours en même temps investissement sexuel d'objet. Mais — et en cela réside l'originalité déclarée de Szondi — les mouvements sexuels n'épuiseraient pas le lien pulsionnel à l'objet : des mouvements non sexuels y seraient toujours impliqués, que Freud n'aurait pas suffisamment discernés.

Seule l'analyse interne de la pulsion du contact éclairera le contenu de l'objection et sa possible pertinence. Mais avant de nous y engager, une dernière précision : qu'entend-on par « objet » dans l'expression « rapport à l'objet » ? Sans doute le terme « objet » ne doit-il pas être entendu dans un sens qui le rendrait opposable au terme de « sujet » : la constitution corrélative d'un sujet et d'un objet posés dans leur différence ne relève pas de la pulsion du contact. Le terme doit davantage être pris dans le sens le plus général d'« objet de la pulsion » : il désigne tout « x » que puisse investir une pulsion, c'est-à-dire à la limite n'importe quoi. Et à cet égard, Szondi fait de la notion un usage beaucoup plus extensif que Freud : l'objet en jeu dans la pulsion du contact peut être un objet partiel comme le sein ou les fèces, il peut être l'alcool ou l'argent, mais encore un objet « total », une personne (le père, la mère, le conjoint,...), un objet « collectif » (la famille, le peuple, la nation, la race,...) voire un objet « culturel » (la religion, l'idéologie,...).

---

[1] Dans les pages qui suivent, consacrées à l'analyse des vecteurs, nos références à Szondi visent pour l'essentiel le TrD et sa deuxième partie (Psychologie des facteurs et vecteurs pulsionnels, pp. 63-202).

b) Les mouvements objectaux du contact

Il importe à présent de préciser la nature des mouvements élémentaires, non sexuels (mais sexualisés à l'intervention de la pulsion S), qui composent la pulsion du contact.

1. Les deux facteurs du contact

Comme tout vecteur, le vecteur du contact est composé de deux facteurs, en l'occurence des facteurs m et d. Quel contenu leur attribuer en première approximation ?

Plutôt que de suivre Szondi et nombre de ses disciples, qui rapportent les besoins m et d respectivement aux phases orale et anale du développement de la libido, nous préférons nous guider d'après une suggestion de De Waelhens (1971). « Au point où chacun de nous se trouve placé », écrit De Waelhens, « deux groupes d'option se présentent, de toute nécessité. L'un de ces groupes concerne principalement les objets déjà possédés ou acquis et que, par conséquent, nous avons aussi déjà perdus ou sommes en voie de perdre, conformément à la loi de toute vie, qui marche vers la dépossession et la mort. » Ainsi est visé le groupe des mouvements objectaux du facteur m. « Mais, d'autre part », poursuit-il, « puisqu'il est vrai tout autant qu'une vie, si usée soit-elle, n'arrête pas d'esquisser un certain avenir, fut-il médiocre et précaire, il est vrai encore que cette vie engendre sans arrêt la possibilité de se tourner vers des objets nouveaux ... L'autre groupe d'attitudes se rapporte à la quête d'objets nouveaux » (pp. 308-309). Le groupe des mouvements du facteur d a été à son tour pointé.

Mais tentons de repérer à même une situation concrète, les différents mouvements qui s'esquissent, pour y détailler ce qui relève respectivement des facteurs m et d.

2. Le rapport oral au sein

Le rapport oral au sein, bien que non privilégié, est sans doute propice à la mise en évidence des quatre tendances élémentaires du contact. Encore que la saisie pulsionnelle que nous en effectuons ne soit pas à l'abri d'un reproche sérieux : la concrétude chatoyante d'un modèle fait souvent obstacle à une juste appréhension conceptuelle. Mais nous ne nous expliquerons sur ce point qu'au terme du développement naïf d'un exemple surtout invoqué pour sa valeur « pédagogique ».

Partons de l'enfant au sein et interrogeons-nous sur l'attitude de l'enfant par rapport au sein acquis ou possédé (facteur m). Le langage courant nous fait dire que l'enfant prend le sein, sans d'ailleurs que le terme « prend » ait ici la moindre connotation d'une prise active, voire agressive (peut-être l'enfant prendra-t-il un jour le sein de cette manière, mais un autre registre que le contact sera alors entré en scène). La tendance m+ désigne précisément cette sorte de prise élémentaire sur un objet ou sur le monde (au sens où l'on demande : « avez-vous prise ? »), ou encore une tenue élémentaire (« vous y tenez ? », « vous tenez », très différent d'un « vous le tenez ? » connotant la maîtrise). Elle désigne, selon l'expression la plus couramment utilisée par Szondi, l'accrochage (« vous accrochez ? »).

Mais qu'en est-il de l'attitude de l'enfant au sein par rapport aux objets nouveaux, toujours potentiellement ouverts à une quête (facteur d) ? Au moment où il prend le sein, l'enfant ne cherche pas d'objet nouveau: non seulement il tient le sein, mais le maintient, le retient, le conserve. Les expressions de « maintien », « rétention », « conservation », servent à désigner la tendance d-, qu'il n'est pas toujours simple de différencier de m+. Disons que le d- procède du refus d'un mouvement possible de quête ou de recherche de nouveaux objets, qui, associé à m+, a le sens d'un « maintenir la situation objectale de tenue d'un objet », d'une persévération dans la tenue ou l'accrochage, ou encore d'une fidélité à l'objet actuel. Le d- ajoute à l'attitude momentanée du m+ une dimension temporelle d'ouverture sur l'avenir.

Mais supposons que l'enfant parvienne à satiété. Dès ce moment, il se déprend, se détache, se décroche de l'objet qu'il avait acquis (m): il lâche le sein. La tendance m- est mise en jeu. Et cette déprise effectuée, l'enfant repu ne se situe pas par rapport à de nouveaux objets éventuels (d), il ne part pas à la recherche, mais ne refuse pas non plus de partir à la recherche (do), pas plus qu'il ne s'accroche ni ne lâche (mo). Sa vie de contact est comme adynamique (Coo). Jusqu'à ce que, tenaillé par la faim, il pleure et crie, appelle un nouvel objet. La tendance d+ entre alors en action: l'enfant est à la recherche d'un objet, non au sens d'une recherche active, comme s'il partait activement à la quête d'un objet dans le monde, mais au sens d'une disponibilité ou d'une ouverture vis-à-vis de nouveaux objets.

Le sein obtenu ou conquis, l'enfant cessera d'être en recherche, il s'accrochera au sein et le maintiendra. Un nouveau cycle du contact sera mis en route.

3. Pulsion et mouvements du contact

Nous venons ainsi de cerner les tendances élémentaires du contact, dont nous pouvons résumer les significations majeures:
m+ : prendre, tenir, accrocher;
m- : lâcher, se déprendre, se décrocher, se détacher;
d+ : être à la recherche de;
d- : ne pas être à la recherche; maintenir, retenir, conserver, persévérer; ou, selon une terminologie courante, coller.

Avant d'observer le fonctionnement des mêmes tendances dans d'autres situations que la situation d'un rapport primitif au sein, il nous importe de dénoncer ce que notre modèle oral et sa lecture pulsionnelle avaient d'erroné.

Nous le savons, Szondi prétend se dissocier de Freud, et peut-être commençons-nous de percevoir en quel sens. Ce qui se joue dans le rapport oral au sein n'est pas ordonné à la seule recherche d'un plaisir érogène: des mouvements non sexuels s'y accomplissent. Mais, soulignons-le, les mouvements du contact partagent avec les mouvements de la sexualité une caractéristique qui en signe la spécificité pulsionnelle: ils sont irréductibles à une fonction biologique d'auto-conservation. Comme la pulsion sexuelle, la pulsion de contact s'étaye sur la fonction d'auto-conservation, au sens où elle s'y adosse, à savoir: s'appuie sur elle et lui tourne le dos. Ainsi, l'enfant exerce la prise au moment où il boit et se conserve en vie; mais cela même qu'il tient et prend dans le mouvement pulsionnel m+ n'est pas comme tel l'objet de l'auto-conservation ou de l'instinct alimentaire (le lait), mais un objet dévié par rapport à l'objet instinctif: le sein [1], pas plus que la satisfaction qu'il retire de cette prise n'est subordonnée à la qualité du lait, mais à la qualité d'une relation interhumaine que Spitz, parmi d'autres psychologues, a cernée dans ses étapes précoces, pour en mesurer les enjeux.

C'est pourquoi aussi notre modèle oral était trompeur. Les mouvements du contact y étaient présentés comme indissociables, ou en tout cas comme toujours étroitement corrélatifs, des mouvements de l'auto-conservation alimentaire: ainsi, l'accrochage épousait la prise de lait et la satisfaction de la faim. Mais en réalité, dès le moment où la pulsion de contact s'est déconnectée du besoin alimentaire, rien n'empêche l'enfant de s'accrocher au sein alors même qu'il a cessé de boire et se trouve en état de totale réplétion.

Signalons à ce propos qu'une genèse des relations objectales a été construite, où s'observe en clair la dissociation des mouvements du contact et des mouvements de l'auto-conservation (TrP, pp. 421-422). Si l'on en croit cette reconstruction hypothétique, les relations objectales du nouveau-né commenceraient en Coo: bien que l'enfant soit en proie au besoin et le satisfasse via l'allaitement, sa vie pulsionnelle de contact serait vide. Aucun mouvement de contact ne participerait encore à sa relation au sein, marquée du seul sceau du besoin et de sa satisfaction. Mais une expérience réitérée de séparation viendrait comme introduire une rupture dans la relation primitive, qui mobiliserait de premières fonctions du contact: ayant perdu le sein, l'enfant le rechercherait désormais pour s'y accrocher (C++). Plus tard, à l'époque du sevrage oral, il s'en détacherait (C+±), pour entrer bientôt dans une phase anale centrée sur l'exploration éperdue de l'environnement et la recherche perpétuelle d'objets chaque fois nouveaux (C+-).

4. Une relation interhumaine passagère

Mais les mouvements pulsionnels du contact ne s'observent pas uniquement dans le rapport oral à l'objet. Ils s'observent dans toute rencontre interhumaine, à quelque époque de l'existence qu'elle se situe. Ainsi, si nous avons à participer à une soirée, nous pouvons n'y aller que par convenance et nous y maintenir de bout en bout dans une position de réserve ou de retenue: nous sommes indisponible pour de nouveaux contacts (d-), peut-être parce que nous sommes accroché à un autre objet auprès duquel nous restons. Mais nous pouvons aussi être ouvert à une rencontre, en appel ou en attente d'un contact qui peut-être n'arrivera jamais à s'amorcer (d+). A moins que tout à coup, l'ambiance créée (et l'alcool aidant?), l'étincelle jaillisse et le feu prenne: le sentiment d'être en prise sur les choses et les êtres (m+) nous étreindra désormais, que nous passions la soirée avec une seule personne ou avec plusieurs, que des motions sexuelles prennent ou non leur part à notre exaltation. Mais viendra bientôt la séparation d'avec cette ambiance et les personnes que nous avons rencontrées. Si nous avons accroché, le réveil sera pénible: nous flotterons quelque temps dans une atmosphère de tristesse vague, partagé entre une situation ancienne à laquelle le souvenir nous rattache encore et le déroulement d'une vie qui continue et se renouvelle. Très vite, un processus de détachement (m-) nous arrachera à un passé révolu.

---

[1] Sur la pulsion et ce qu'elle comporte de déviation par rapport à l'instinct, cfr J. Laplanche, *Vie et mort en psychanalyse*, Flammarion, 1970.

5. La relation interhumaine durable et le processus du deuil

L'ensemble des mouvements du contact s'observe aussi dans la relation interhumaine durable dès lors qu'elle se trouve interrompue par le deuil.

Un être vient à disparaître, brutalement enlevé au commerce interhumain par la mort. Dès ce moment, la personne qui l'avait investi de longue date et continuait de se maintenir à son contact (d-m+) engage un processus de deuil. L'endeuillé commence par rester attaché à l'être aimé, davantage encore que de son vivant, refusant sa disparition, s'accrochant à lui et à ce qu'il laisse dans le souvenir (m+ !). Mais une exigence de réalité appelle à la séparation : il n'est plus là et ne reviendra pas. La tendance m- est enclenchée, d'abord dans l'ambivalence (m±), puis à l'état pur. Bientôt, au terme d'un processus douloureux, le détachement est effectué, et l'endeuillé s'installe en C-o : il n'est plus attaché (mo), mais il n'est pas non plus en recherche d'un nouvel objet ; il persévère dans son état (d-), peut-être par fidélité à un être mort auquel pourtant il n'est plus vraiment accroché. Mais un jour peut-être renoncera-t-il à une fidélité asséchante et dépassée : il aspirera à un contact frais (d+), investira de nouveaux objets (m+), et enfin choisira de se maintenir au contact de l'un d'entre eux (d-m+). Un attachement durable aura été recréé ; un cycle complet du contact aura été parcouru.

Mais ce dernier exemple, outre qu'il illustre à nouveau les significations attribuées aux tendances du contact, nous ouvre aussi à une nouvelle problématique. Car, on l'aura remarqué, le cycle que nous venons de parcourir a privilégié une configuration du contact : s'il a mobilisé tour à tour toutes les tendances, il a néanmoins pris son point de départ comme trouvé son point d'arrivée dans une constellation précise, élevée ainsi à l'état de station normative, comme s'il était « normal » à l'être humain d'y être installé et d'y retourner si par malchance elle devait un moment être compromise.

c) Normalité et maladivité du contact

Le problème que nous abordons à présent n'est pas propre au vecteur du contact, encore qu'il s'y pose sans doute de façon exemplaire. Bien plus, il est comme l'écho d'une question plus générale à laquelle toute démarche de sciences humaines doit s'affronter.

A première vue, les tendances du contact sont égales en dignité et ne font l'objet d'aucun jugement de valeur. Pourtant, un examen plus attentif révèle qu'elles échappent difficilement à toute forme d'appréciation qualitative. Il est fréquent en effet que les tendances du contact soient qualifiées, les unes de « bonnes » ou « favorables », les autres de « mauvaises » ou « défavorables ». Mais au nom de quels critères sinon au nom d'options idéologiques implicites et non déclarées ?

Ainsi, la tendance m+ sera considérée comme la tendance du contact la plus mûre et la plus heureuse. L'individu qui s'y installe en permanence disposerait d'une solide base existentielle à laquelle il devrait sa confiance inébranlable dans la vie et son optimisme foncier. Inversement la tendance m- sera volontiers tenue pour négative, voire dangereuse : l'individu n'aurait plus rien à quoi (se) tenir, plus rien sur quoi s'appuyer ; tout sentiment de bonheur l'aurait déserté ; seul, abandonné, sans axe de référence, il deviendrait la proie facile des plus inquiétantes tentations, disposé aux solutions extrêmes, prêt à commettre les actes antisociaux les plus graves (le meurtre, le suicide). Or ne pouvons-nous voir dans cette discrimination qualitative l'effet d'une idéologie conservatrice qui privilégie les valeurs de stabilité et de fidélité aux dépens des valeurs de changement et de rupture ? Ne pourrions-nous soutenir à l'inverse que la capacité d'arrachement au familier et au déjà donné constitue, de toutes les orientations du contact, la plus éminemment humaine ?

On le voit, toute direction du contact, comme toute orientation pulsionnelle en général, est susceptible d'une valorisation ou d'une dévalorisation selon qu'est assumée telle ou telle option idéologique. Sans doute un idéal peut-être illusoire — car peut-on échapper à la prise de position ? — commanderait-il d'éviter une appréciation parfois à la limite de la moralisation et de se tenir toujours au plus près d'une signification neutre, qui n'aurait pas encore franchi le seuil de la qualification. Pour le moins toute tendance devrait-elle être épargnée d'une qualification univoque et préservée dans son potentiel de diversification polymorphe.

Au demeurant, le cas du processus de deuil nous invitait déjà à une vue un peu plus nuancée. Que l'être humain puisse trouver son bonheur dans l'investissement durable, dans la tenue et la retenue d'un objet, soit. Mais n'est-ce pas le lot de tout être humain que son objet de tenue puisse lui être enlevé ? L'homme vit toujours suspendu à la menace d'une perte d'objet, et, on le sait, toute la vie humaine de contact est marquée, depuis la naissance jusqu'à la mort, par une succession de pertes qui appellent chaque fois élaboration. Car, la perte intervenue, un travail long et pénible devint nécessaire. La « normalité » ne commande plus alors de tenir et de s'accrocher, mais de faire son deuil.

Mais ne tenons-nous pas à présent une définition plus adéquate de la normalité et de la maladivité du contact ? Désormais nulle fonction du contact ne peut être dite normale ou maladive en soi, mais chacune est en état de devenir l'une ou l'autre. Ainsi la tendance m+, et plus encore la configuration d-m+, cesse d'être normative si elle nourrit un accrochage forcené à une relation objectale révolue qui en viendrait à bloquer tout processus de deuil, alors que la tendance m- le devient dès le moment où elle s'inscrit comme un moment temporaire dans le mouvement d'élaboration d'une perte. Plus généralement, la normalité du contact pourrait être définie comme la capacité de mettre en jeu, lorsque les circonstances l'exigent, l'ensemble des mouvements du contact, la maladivité du contact comme l'immobilisation du travail de deuil dans une position figée et immuable.

Et il est vrai que les grandes figures maladives du contact reconnues par l'Analyse du destin peuvent être ressaisies comme autant de fixations consécutives à une perte. En d'autres termes, toute tendance du contact se pathologise dès le moment où elle se fige et s'exacerbe (une exacerbation qui s'exprimera, dans le langage pulsionnel, sous forme d'une ou plusieurs accentuations). Reprenons à cet égard les grandes significations pathologiques qui résulteraient de l'arrêt à chacune de ces stations.

Les stations du travail de deuil :
(C-+) → C-+! → C--! → C-!o → C+!o → C++! → (C-+)
Les formes de maladivité du contact
m+! (!!, !!!) : le sujet, abandonné par un objet ou se sentant abandonné par

lui, s'y accroche désespérément. Forme de contact dominante chez les individus souffrant de névrose d'acceptation, qui exigent d'un objet une acceptation totale, intransigeante, inconditionnelle, mais toujours insatisfaite.

m-! (!!, !!!) : le sujet, déçu par un objet, s'en détache et se maintient dans une situation de refus de tout contact, car tout objet sera nécessairement décevant, aucun ne méritant plus le moindre investissement. Figure prévalente dans la phase maniaque de la psychose maniaco-dépressive.

d-! (!!, !!!) : le sujet refuse toute recherche par fidélité à l'objet perdu et à une situation objectale dépassée, qui n'a plus d'actualité, mais dont il nourrit une nostalgie compromettant toute forme de changement objectal.

d+! (!!, !!!) : le sujet s'engage dans une recherche éperdue d'objets, mais une recherche toujours déçue et toujours relancée, parce qu'aucun objet n'arrive à restituer la présence de l'objet ancien. Forme prévalente dans la phase mélancolique de la psychose maniaco-dépressive.

m+! (!!, !!!) : le sujet arrive à s'accrocher à un objet-ersatz, substitutif de l'objet perdu, et il vit désormais avec lui dans une union ininterrompue. Figure dominante dans l'alcoolisme et les toxicomanies.

Mais, malgré le progrès que nos dernières propositions permettent de réaliser, elles emportent encore un présupposé qu'il nous reste à déconstruire. Nous l'avons déjà dit, une configuration du contact (C-+) continue d'être promue au rang de configuration privilégiée. Comme si l'être humain occupait naturellement une position qui assure à sa pulsion de contact une pleine satisfaction, une gratification adéquate, et que seuls les accidents ou les aléas d'une existence viendraient régulièrement mais temporairement compromettre. N'est-ce pas là aller à l'encontre de ce que la pulsion, dans son concept freudien, contient d'original et d'irréductible à l'instinct, en ce qu'elle ne connaît pas de forme prédéterminée de satisfaction? Mais comment dissiper cette dernière illusion?

Nous reprendrons à notre compte, tout en la nuançant sur un point, une idée développée, après d'autres, par De Waelhens. La vie humaine de contact, affirme De Waelhens, serait marquée par la perte originaire et irrémédiable d'un objet primordial, et les diverses figures du contact seraient autant de réponses incertaines et périlleuses au manque fondamental qui depuis les origines s'inscrit au creux du destin humain. Citons De Waelhens (1971) :

A l'arrière de tous nos rapports à l'objet « se profile la relation originelle au tout premier objet » (p. 309). Tous nos contacts « portent le sceau de la déception originelle toujours ... recommencée. A chaque fois ressuscitent les plus anciennes options. Refuser l'objet et s'en détourner puisque de toute manière, il nous trahira. Feindre de le tenir pour ce qui va, enfin me combler absolument. N'accepter et ne voir en lui que le représentant et le substitut d'un certain autre auquel nous lie l'espoir aussi bien que le ressentiment, et le ressentiment aussi bien que l'espoir. Transformer toute rencontre en une quête sans trêve ni repos où le désir ne se donne jamais que pour l'amorce d'un autre désir, qui sera, enfin heureux » (p. 307).

Dans le texte qu'on vient de citer, on reconnaîtra aisément les quatre tendances du contact, dont plus aucune n'est privilégiée, pas même la tendance m+, mode tout aussi risqué, tout aussi peu adéquatement satisfaisant, de l'explication de l'être humain avec sa béance originelle, avec sa maladie constitutive.

Doit-on le préciser, l'idée est séduisante, et elle seule permet sans doute de dépasser ce qu'il restait d'un dernier clivage classificateur du normal et du pathologique. Mais en même temps elle nous tend une ultime embûche, qu'il nous importe, pour achever, de surmonter.

Il est courant d'identifier objet primordial perdu et sein maternel, en sorte que l'homme serait tout au long de sa vie la proie malheureuse d'une nostalgie du sein maternel. Szondi lui-même ne manque pas de procéder à l'identification lorsqu'il écrit :

« Le sein maternel reste pour toute la vie l'objet originaire de tous les mouvements pulsionnels d'aller-à-la-recherche et de tous les mouvements d'accrochage. Car : dans l'essence de toutes les formes du « venir-en-contact », nous trouvons toujours le besoin de chercher un objet-ersatz pour le sein maternel et de s'accrocher à cet objet. » (TrD, p. 175)

Or la perte originaire, instauratrice d'une béance qui dynamise les besoins du contact, leur interdisant d'être jamais tout à fait comblés et les élevant ainsi à l'état pulsionnel, a le statut d'un mythe fondateur : elle n'est pas identique à la perte d'un objet réel, pas plus qu'elle n'est situable dans la temporalité concrète de l'existence humaine, même pas dans son tout début. S'il est vrai, certes, que le sein maternel (ou plus généralement un objet oral) est le premier objet d'accrochage, de détachement, de recherche et de maintien, il est tout aussi vrai que le dynamisme pulsionnel qui se joue dans le rapport de l'enfant au sein n'est lui-même concevable que sur le fond d'une perte toujours déjà effectuée[1] ; et c'est à notre sens un tout autre poblème, que nous ne pouvons débattre ici, que de savoir si, d'être la première relation objectale, la relation primitive (mais non originaire) au sein maternel laisse des traces indélébiles et se répercutent définitivement sur le destin des relations objectales que l'existence ultérieure sera amenée à forger. Disons-le tout net : non, l'homme ne cherche pas au fil des contacts qu'il établit à trouver ou retrouver le sein maternel, mais tout au long de son existence il noue et dénoue des relations qui ont leur densité et leur consistance propre, sans rien devoir à un rapport primitif au sein, mais n'en sont pas moins toujours travaillées de l'intérieur par le malaise ou l'insécurité qui est au cœur de sa condition.

2. La pulsion ou vecteur sexuel

a) *Le vecteur du rapport au corps*

Apparemment, nous voici en terre connue. Car s'il est une pulsion qui a été, depuis Freud, reconnue et étudiée, c'est bien la pulsion sexuelle. Mais précisément y a-t-il total recouvrement entre ce que Freud a désigné comme pulsion sexuelle et ce que Szondi vise sous la même expression ?

C'est de manière bien curieuse, il faut le dire, que Szondi a prétendu fonder la nature sexuelle du vecteur S et de ses composants internes. Si l'on doit en

---

[1] On doit remarquer que la genèse des relations objectales à laquelle nous avons fait allusion distinguait clairement une perte originaire mobilisatrice des premiers mouvements de contact et la perte réelle du sein maternel corrélative d'une première crise objectale, nous voulons parler de la crise du sevrage.

croire les déclarations explicites de Szondi, les tendances constitutives du vecteur S seraient sexuelles parce qu'elles poursuivraient un but physiologique commun, à savoir le but de l'accouplement et de la reproduction. Or, pareille proposition ne peut manquer de choquer un esprit formé à la psychanalyse freudienne. Car si nous ne devions retenir qu'un seul des enseignements que Freud nous a transmis, sans doute retiendrions-nous que la sexualité ne s'épuise pas dans un acte sexuel à visée reproductrice et n'a pas de but physiologique prédéterminé, tel l'accouplement reproducteur. Nous pouvons certes accorder à Szondi que les fonctions du vecteur S sont directement mises en jeu dans l'acte sexuel, y compris dans un acte hétérosexuel à effet reproducteur potentiel, mais nous ne pouvons pas définir ce vecteur dans son essence par l'acte génital et moins encore par la visée reproductrice. Nous devons en quelque sorte procéder en sens inverse: d'abord définir les tendances du vecteur S dans toute leur extension, et ensuite seulement indiquer au passage en quel sens ces mêmes tendances pourraient intervenir dans un acte sexuel aboutissant à l'accouplement génital.

A cette fin, nous nous tournerons à nouveau, au titre d'un point de départ, vers une formulation de De Waelhens: le vecteur S est le vecteur du rapport au corps. Non pas que le vecteur S soit seul à mobiliser le corps, qui traverse sans doute le système pulsionnel en son entier. Mais tout au moins met-il en branle des investissements corporels spécifiques, qui font défaut au vecteur C et se diffractent en deux dimensions distinctes. Ecoutons à ce propos De Waelhens (1971).

«La première composante ... qualifie ... la tendance du sujet à se replier sur son corps, à s'enfoncer en lui pour en tirer une jouissance. On pourrait la résumer assez exactement par le terme français de sensualité...»

Quant à la complémentarité de cette attitude, elle se trouvera «dans la corporéité vécue comme prise, comme dépassement des limites propres. Le corps y est adonné non à lui-même mais à la domination de ce qui n'est pas lui» (pp. 309-310).

Donc, repli du corps sur soi dans une sorte d'immanence sensuelle, facteur h; transcendance du corps, dépassement de ses limites, dans l'exercice d'une prise active sur le monde et sur l'environnement, facteur s. Deux pôles du vecteur S, deux investissements corporels divergents, qui se laissent reconnaître comme en une figuration saisissante dans les professions de coiffeur et de terrassier. Car si le corps est intéressé à titre essentiel dans l'une comme dans l'autre, il l'est aussi sur deux modes antithétiques: un attachement doux et tendre, une attaque agressive du monde.

Mais engageons-nous d'emblée dans l'analyse détaillée des composants internes de la sexualité.

b) Le facteur h

1. Essence générale

Le premier des concepts qui sert traditionnellement à définir le facteur h appelle à notre sens une opposition résolue. Que nous enseigne Szondi en effet, sinon que le facteur h est un facteur d'Eros. Le terme serait judicieux s'il se bornait à évoquer l'érotisme, mais, pris dans le sens conceptuel dont l'a doté la seconde doctrine freudienne des pulsions, il devient tout à fait inadéquat. Car Szondi précise aussitôt: le facteur h est un facteur d'Eros parce qu'il régit toute liaison ou formation de lien. Que le facteur h participe à la formation des liens objectaux, marquant cette dernière de son empreinte propre, assurément. Mais qu'il soit le responsable exclusif et privilégié d'une formation de liens qui en définirait dès lors l'essence spécifique, comment pourrions-nous le croire après avoir pris connaissance de la nature des tendances du contact ? Au demeurant, Szondi a été le premier à reconnaître la multidimensionnalité pulsionnelle de toute formation de liens, qui puise toujours, selon ses propres termes, à plusieurs sources (il précise même : aux sources énergétiques des besoins m, h et p).

Mais quelle définition adopter dès lors ? Celle-là même, pensons-nous, qui découle en ligne directe de nos formulations initiales. Nous l'avons vu, le facteur h est un facteur de sensualité, nous aimerions ajouter à présent : d'érotisation ou d'érogénéisation du corps. Car le facteur h ne révèle-t-il pas l'investissement d'un corps qui se complaît en lui-même et tire jouissance de cette complaisance intime ? Et ne dirions-nous pas tout aussi bien qu'il obtient une prime de plaisir de son auto-stimulation ? Le corps dont il s'agit n'est-il pas au bout du compte ce corps érogène que Freud et la psychanalyse ont placé au centre de leur théorie de la sexualité ? Le facteur h n'est-il pas, de tous les facteurs du système pulsionnel, le plus proche de la sexualité entendue dans son concept freudien ? Auquel cas aussi, de tous les termes invoqués par Szondi pour le ressaisir, le terme de libido serait le plus pertinent.

Nullement forcée, bien que jamais formulée en des termes aussi nets, la définition à laquelle nous avons abouti commande la critique d'une autre conceptualisation du facteur h, encore davantage usitée, mais elle aussi insuffisante. Le facteur h sera fréquemment défini comme facteur de tendresse. Or n'a-t-on pas pris l'habitude depuis Freud de différencier à l'intérieur même de la sexualité un investissement à prédominance sensuelle, qui vise un corps à corps érogénéisant, et un investissement à base de tendresse, d'affection, qui résulterait d'une inhibition, voire même d'une sublimation de la sensualité ? La sensualité, sous sa forme sublimée, se transforme en tendresse, reconnaît De Waelhens lui-même (1971, p. 310). En d'autres termes, si elle appartient bien au facteur h au titre d'un de ses avatars, elle n'en constitue pas moins que l'une de ses composantes, impuissante dès lors à en exprimer dans toute son extension l'essence générale. Mais l'examen approfondi des deux tendances du facteur h nous éclairera davantage sur ce point.

2. La tendance h+

La tendance h+ abonde dans le sens du besoin, elle participe de son mouvement qu'elle prolonge et accomplit : elle sera donc définie comme tendance à une jouissance ou à un plaisir érotique obtenu par stimulation du corps érogène.

Pour sa part, Szondi l'a définie comme une tendance à la tendresse personnelle ou individuelle, dirigée sur une personne particulière. Mais n'évacue-t-on pas de la sorte la dimension de perversité polymorphe qui est inhérente à la sexualité dans son concept freudien ? Certes, lorsque Szondi parle de personne particulière, il ne vise pas une personne toujours identique à elle-même, mais bien une personne quelconque : l'essentiel serait l'obtention du plaisir plutôt que la rencontre avec un être humain différencié. Mais, malgré cette nuance, la référence à la personne ne restreint-elle pas indûment le champ de la tendance h+ ? Ne connaît-on pas d'activité sexuelle qui se déploie en dehors de tout contact concret avec une personne humaine ? Sans doute, et c'est pourquoi la référence exclusive à la personne comme pôle de cette tendance doit être critiquée.

Lorsqu'elle s'exacerbe (!,!!, ...), la tendance h+ est le lieu d'une accumulation de tension ouverte à deux vicissitudes majeures. Parfois, la tension n'est que provisoire et évolue rapidement vers la décharge (ho): la libido est momentanément satisfaite. Mais il lui arrive aussi de se maintenir sans jamais parvenir à résolution: elle est responsable dès lors d'une frustration, dont l'origine est soit externe — liée aux circonstances actuelles d'une existence —, soit interne — due aux défenses qui de l'intérieur du sujet s'opposent à l'exercice de l'érotisme. Dans ce dernier cas, la tendance h+ (!, ...), incapable de se décharger selon des voies directes, pourra trouver des formes indirectes de dérivation : elle nourrira par exemple, des symptômes somatiques, selon le mécanisme reconnu au fondement des névroses actuelles (Freud). Mais ses modes d'apparition psychopathologiques ne sont pas épuisés pour autant. Fréquente dans les troubles psychosomatiques, la tendance h+ (!,...) est aussi observée dans les formes les plus diverses de la pathologie mentale: névroses, psychoses, psychopathies, perversions. Car ces syndromes maladifs réinvestissent tous de quelque façon les pulsions partielles autoérotiques, bref l'énergie de la tendance h+.

3. La tendance h-

Comme toute tendance négative, la tendance h- pourrait marquer un refus, en l'occurence ici le refus d'une érogénéisation du corps : elle serait tendance à la désérotisation ou à la désexualisation.

Mais le refus de l'érotisme prend lui-même des significations diverses, et tout d'abord le sens d'une répression, au cas où la tendance h- se manifesterait sur un mode exacerbé (!, ...). Car dans l'acharnement même qu'il met à refuser et à nier la libido, l'individu révèle qu'il ne continue pas moins d'être tenaillé par elle: le besoin érotique est toujours agissant dans son orientation originelle. Plus le h- est tendu, écrit Deri en ce sens (IS, p. 71), et plus il est à interpréter comme une réaction active à son opposé h+. Psychopathologiquement, la tendance h- (! ,...) nourrirait les inhibitions névrotiques de la sexualité.

Mais la tendance h- est susceptible d'une seconde interprétation majeure. A condition de ne pas être accentuée, de se maintenir dans une relative stabilité et de s'allier à certaines tendances précises relevant d'autres facteurs pulsionnels, elle prendrait le sens d'une sublimation: selon une définition traditionnelle, la libido abandonnerait son but sexuel direct, pour se transformer et se réorienter dans une direction sociale, voire spirituelle. Processus que Szondi formule dans les termes d'une transformation de la tendresse, qui se porterait non plus sur la personne, mais sur l'humanité en général : comme tendance sublimée, la tendance h- serait tendance à la tendresse collective, voire même à l'amour de l'humanité. Mais pouvons-nous adhérer à une interprétation toute suspendue à une définition de la tendance h+ que nous avons déjà récusée ? Paradoxalement, la tendresse personnelle ne devrait-elle pas être attribuée au dynamisme de la tendance h- ? Car, selon une vue de

Freud [1], une désexualisation ne conditionne-t-elle pas l'introduction de l'élément personnel dans l'amour? N'est-ce pas sur fond d'une entrave des tendances sexuelles directes que se tissent les relations interhumaines durables, à l'intérieur du couple ou d'une formation collective? Alors que la tendance h+ privilégiait l'activité sexuelle au détriment de la personne, la tendance h- mettrait au centre la (ou les) personne(s) et reléguerait à l'arrière l'activité sexuelle, entravée ou subordonnée au maintien de la stabilité d'un lien.

c) Le facteur s

1. Essence générale

Szondi définit le facteur s, par contraste avec un facteur h dit d'Eros, comme facteur de mort, comme facteur « Thanatos », et cela à nouveau en référence au second dualisme pulsionnel freudien : le facteur s serait responsable de la destruction des liens objectaux. Détermination à laquelle nous ne pouvons donner notre totale adhésion. Car si une destruction est en jeu dans le facteur s, c'est moins la destruction d'un lien objectal, qu'une tendance comme m- connoterait mieux, que parfois, en dernière extrémité, la destruction d'un objet extérieur ou même une destruction tournée vers soi ou autodestruction. On le soupçonne donc, le facteur s n'est pas absolument étranger, ni à une destructivité agressive, ni même à la pulsion de mort freudienne. Cependant, l'affinité qu'il entretient avec l'une comme avec l'autre ne devient intelligible qu'au départ d'une définition moins orientée. Le facteur s, proposerons-nous, est un facteur général d'activité corporelle, se manifestant sous forme de deux tendances antagonistes, s+ et s-.

2. La tendance s+

La tendance s+ indique le mouvement par lequel le corps se rapporte activement au monde et aux objets du monde, prend ces objets, s'empare d'eux, les maîtrise, les manipule.

Mais n'y a-t-il pas comme un passage insensible de la prise active du monde à l'attaque du monde et à son agression? A mesure qu'elle s'accentue et se gonfle quantitativement, la tendance s+, suivant en cela sa pente naturelle, dégénère en une agressivité qui à la limite s'exprimera dans la violence pure, gratuite et dépassionnée et pourra nourrir l'une ou l'autre forme de délinquance, telle l'agression à main armée, accompagnée, dans les cas les plus graves, de meurtre [2].

Mais l'agressivité dont il vient d'être question est-elle identifiable au sadisme — notion à laquelle le facteur s doit son nom?

Tout est ici affaire de définition. Car la mise en forme szondienne des pulsions impose la différenciation d'un facteur d'activité corporelle et d'un

---

[1] Cfr Freud S., Psychologie collective et analyse du moi, dans *Essais de psychanalyse*, Petite Bibliothèque Payot, pp. 169-174.

[2] Les recherches de Waelder (1952) semblent confirmer ce diagnostic. Les personnes condamnées pour délit, chez qui on observe une accentuation de la tendance s+, seraient des voleurs ou des meurtriers caractérisés par une prédisposition à des actes de violence, alors que les individus chez qui apparaît une accentuation de la tendance h+ seraient plutôt des criminels pervers, coupables par exemple d'un attentat aux mœurs (TrD, p. 86).

facteur d'érotisme. En conséquence, le sadisme proprement congénial à la tendance s+ ne sera pas sans plus le sadisme érotique dont la perversion sexuelle du même nom tire son plaisir, mais davantage ce sadisme dont Freud n'avait pas hésité, en de rares moments, à postuler l'existence comme « pulsion d'emprise » (« pulsion non sexuelle, qui ne s'unit que secondairement à la sexualité et dont le but est de dominer l'objet par la force »[1]).

Il n'est donc pas interdit de penser que l'emprise corporelle exercée sur le monde soit le lieu d'une jouissance (« sadique ») non érotique, à laquelle l'approvisionnement virtuel de la tendance h+ pourrait néanmoins ajouter une composante libidinale. Des considérations finales sur quelques formes d'association de l'érotisme et du sadisme d'emprise nous éclaireront sur ce point. Sous une forme simple, l'érotisme et le sadisme contribuent à un acte sexuel qui combine l'obtention du plaisir sexuel à la prise active de l'objet (S++). Mais, lorsque la prise de l'objet sexuel s'accentue pour devenir la source préférentielle du plaisir érotique (S++!), nous entrerions dans un régime proche du sadisme pervers. Enfin, lorsque la composante libidinale s'éclipse et se vide (So+!), surgit le sadisme pur, déconnecté de toute recherche érotique, trouvant son plaisir dans la seule destructivité agressive et risquant de déboucher en son point limite sur le meurtre froid.

3. La tendance s-

La tendance s- est intérieurement beaucoup plus complexe que la tendance s+, et il est difficile d'en ressaisir de manière cohérente tous les aspects.

Au départ, la tendance s- procède d'un refus de l'activité corporelle inhérente au besoin s et à son orientation originelle. Et s'il est vrai que le refus d'agir entraîne une substitution de la passivité à l'activité, nous dirons aussi que la tendance s- est tendance à la passivité. Mais une tendance à la passivité qui se déploie dans deux directions.

Tout d'abord, la passivité est le simple négatif de l'activité. Etre passif, c'est en première instance ne pas agir, se refuser à l'activité. En ce sens, la tendance s- pourrait révéler une inhibition de l'activité, et même, sous forme accentuée, une répression de l'agressivité, susceptible d'induire, chez l'individu de sexe masculin, un trouble d'inhibition de la sexualité, le s- (!, ...) étant comme le signe qu'il craint de pénétrer son partenaire sexuel, en quoi il révèle combien cette pénétration est associée, pour lui, à l'effraction agressive du corps féminin.

Mais ne pas être actif, être passif, c'est aussi s'offrir à la prise du monde, c'est risquer d'avoir à subir, à souffrir les assauts du monde. La tendance s- devient alors tendance, non plus à agir son corps, mais à subir son corps, non plus à agir le monde par son corps, mais à subir le monde dans son corps : elle devient à proprement parler tendance au masochisme.

Mais nous franchissons dès lors un nouveau degré de complexification. Car l'auto-complaisance dans la passivité, le masochisme, s'oriente lui-même dans deux directions, et en premier lieu, en direction d'une sublimation. A la façon dont l'amour sexuel érotique s'était développé, par désexualisation, en amour personnel ou collectif désérotisé, la passivité ou l'offrande du corps se transforme, par désinvestissement du corps, en dévouement pour les autres,

---

[1] J. Laplanche et J.-B. Pontalis, *Vocabulaire de la psychanalyse*, P.U.F., 1967, p. 364.

en don de soi aux autres. A condition de s'accompagner d'autres indices de sublimation, ne serait-ce d'abord que de la tendance h- dans le vecteur S (S--), la tendance s- révèle la disposition d'un individu au don de sa personne. Mais conjoint à l'angoisse de culpabilité, le même dévouement se colorera d'une touche névrotique, en quoi il confinera au masochisme moral : si l'individu s'offre aux autres, c'est alors qu'il se sent coupable d'une faute et tient à se punir pour le mal qu'il leur a fait ou croit leur avoir fait.

Mais n'est-il pas aussi une passivité originaire du corps, elle-même accompagnée d'une possible jouissance ? Le corps pulsionnel humain n'est-il pas le lieu incessant de mouvements subis de tension et de détente ? N'est-ce pas d'ailleurs pour rejoindre cette dimension constitutive de toute pulsion que Freud a posé le concept de pulsion de mort, désignant par là la tendance de la pulsion à retourner à son point zéro de tension ? Et le masochisme, comme masochisme primaire, ne désignerait-il pas le culte d'un mouvement pulsionnel qui aspire à la détente et poussé à son paroxysme s'achève dans le repos éternel de la mort ? Exacerbée, déconnectée d'une sexualité qui vise moins à l'annulation de toute tension (principe de Nirvana) qu'à la stimulation plaisante du corps érogène (principe de plaisir), la tendance s- serait, de l'aveu même de Szondi, tendance élémentaire à l'auto-destruction, qui à la limite désirerait en finir avec un corps toujours tenaillé par le désir et s'accomplirait dans le suicide.

Quant au masochisme sexuel, pas plus que le sadisme sexuel, il n'est pur produit du besoin s, mais résultat d'un fonctionnement combiné des facteurs h et s : la tendance s- n'en est l'indice qu'à condition de s'allier à la tendance h+. Dès ce moment, le sujet cherche un plaisir érotique dans le mouvement même par lequel il offre son corps à la prise active de son partenaire (S+-). Enfin, source préférentielle du plaisir érotique, le masochisme se développe en perversion masochiste (S+-!).

3. La pulsion ou vecteur paroxysmal

a) *Le vecteur du rapport à autrui et à la collectivité*

Trois expressions servent traditionnellement à désigner le vecteur P : on le qualifie tout à la fois de vecteur paroxysmal, de vecteur des affects et de vecteur de l'éthique et de la morale. Mais que vise-t-on sous ces trois dénominations ?

Ainsi qu'entend le signifier la première expression, les manifestations pulsionnelles nourries par le vecteur P ont la propriété d'être paroxysmales, à savoir de procéder par accumulation et décharge brutale d'énergie.

Mais quelle énergie se trouve ainsi accumulée et déchargée ? Une seconde dénomination en précise aussitôt la nature : les manifestations paroxysmales puisent aux sources énergétiques des affects, plus précisément de deux catégories distinctes d'affects selon que les facteurs e ou hy sont concernés. Le facteur e s'alimente à l'énergie d'affects dits brutaux ou grossiers — affects de nature agressive : haine, jalousie, colère, rage, envie,... —, alors que le facteur hy mobilise l'énergie d'affects fins ou doux, de nature érotique.

Enfin, une dernière expression indique que le vecteur P est aussi le lieu d'une défense contre l'accumulation et la décharge d'énergie : défense contre les affects brutaux assurée par l'éthique (facteur e), défense contre les affects doux assurée par la morale (facteur hy).

Toutefois, bien que nous puissions réassumer ces premières désignations, nous ne les jugeons pas encore suffisantes pour cerner le vecteur P dans toute sa spécificité. L'analyse doit donc être poussée plus avant.

On aura remarqué la parenté entre le vecteur S et le vecteur P. Les facteurs e et s ne mobilisent-ils pas tous deux l'agressivité ? Et l'érotisme n'est-il pas engagé dans le facteur hy aussi bien que dans le facteur h ? Mais qu'est-ce donc qui différencie e et s, hy et h ? Nous croyons que les facteurs e et hy, à la différence des facteurs s et h, impliquent une intériorisation de l'agressivité et de l'érotisme, liée à leur expression dans la relation à autrui, en même temps qu'ils prescrivent une défense contre l'agressivité et l'érotisme, liée elle aussi à la relation à autrui, ou plus exactement à la relation aux autres et à la collectivité.

1. Rapport à autrui dans les manifestations paroxysmales non défensives

a) Facteurs s et e

Dans son mode d'expression non défensive, dans le mouvement même par lequel il conduit à une décharge d'affects brutaux, le facteur e implique déjà, par contraste avec le facteur s, une intériorisation de l'agressivité et un rapport constitutif à autrui. Mais en quel sens ? Le facteur s, nous l'avons vu, commande le déploiement d'une activité corporelle en direction du monde extérieur qui s'exprimera éventuellement sous la forme d'une agression physique d'autrui (sans qu'autrui en soit d'ailleurs l'objet nécessaire), alors que le facteur e appelle la haine, la volonté haineuse de nuire à autrui, de lui faire du tort ou du mal. Qui plus est, la haine que nourrit l'énergie des affects brutaux se décharge moins en un acte d'agression directe qu'en un éclatement d'affects, dont le but est de surprendre autrui, comme s'il s'agissait davantage d'exprimer l'agressivité pour autrui que de l'extérioriser sur lui. Qu'il suffise à chacun, pour saisir la différence, de comparer le coup que l'on porte à autrui et la crise de colère brutale qui vient clore un affrontement affectif. Certes, il arrive à l'agression physique d'accompagner la décharge d'affects brutaux. Mais sans doute dans ce cas le facteur s apporte-t-il sa contribution propre, comme d'ailleurs à l'occasion le facteur e colore l'extériorisation agressive prescrite par le facteur s. Ainsi, la conjonction des tendances s+ (!!) et e- (!!) fait craindre l'imminence d'un acte de violence physique, mais d'un acte auquel le facteur e ajoute le caractère d'une passion haineuse. Sans la contribution de la tendance e-, la violence, voire le meurtre restent froids, dépassionnés, non investis d'affects, accompagnés du seul plaisir lié à l'exercice de la pulsion d'emprise.

b) Facteurs h et hy

Nous n'avons pas besoin ici d'un long développement tant sont clairs l'intériorisation et le rapport à autrui. Alors que le facteur h invite à un plaisir érotique éventuellement obtenu à la faveur d'un contact corporel avec autrui, le but du facteur hy dans son orientation non défensive est l'expression de l'érotisme et des affects érotiques pour autrui: non pas tant rechercher la jouissance dans une activité érotique que se montrer à autrui comme être érotique.

2. *Rapport à la collectivité dans les manifestations paroxysmales défensives*

Nous venons de voir que les facteurs e et hy supposent déjà une référence déterminante à autrui là où ils ne régissent encore que la décharge de l'agressivité et de l'érotisme. Mais nous savons que les facteurs paroxysmaux assurent également une fonction de défense contre l'extériorisation affective. Sous cet aspect ils renvoient à titre essentiel moins sans doute à autrui et à la relation intersubjective qu'à une collectivité humaine qui instaure des règles et des lois et organise par là la vie en commun des hommes. Ce qui a d'ailleurs déterminé De Waelhens à désigner le vecteur P comme vecteur du rapport à la loi. Car le facteur e protège aussi contre le mal que nous pouvons faire à autrui : il prescrit une défense contre les affects brutaux et leur expression, que Szondi attribue à l'éthique, aux lois universelles des sociétés humaines, dont le noyau serait l'interdit du meurtre. Quant au facteur hy, il commande aussi la censure contre l'érotisme et son expression visible, que Szondi rapporte à la morale, à savoir aux lois relatives à chaque société qui réglementent les manifestations de la sexualité.

En conclusion, il nous paraît pertinent de définir le vecteur P comme vecteur non pas tant du rapport à la loi, qui n'en désigne que l'un des versants, que du rapport à autrui et à la collectivité des hommes, et cela non pas parce qu'il serait seul à engager un rapport à autrui, mais parce que nos compagnons humains, dans leur être personnel comme dans la communauté qu'ils forment avec nous, y sont constitutivement présents.

b) Le facteur e

1. La tendance e+

La tendance e+ révèle l'affirmation de la censure éthique dirigée contre l'expression des affects brutaux et en particulier contre la poussée au meurtre. L'individu qui assume la tendance e+ se refuse au mal; positivement, il veut le bien de son prochain et de l'humanité en général, il adhère aux grandes valeurs humanistes de justice, tolérance et bonté. Le personnage biblique de Moïse, venu apporter aux hommes la loi de l'interdit du meutre, en est assurément la plus belle figure symbolique.

Bien qu'elle ne soit pas seule concernée, la tendance e+ est sans doute, de toutes les fonctions pulsionnelles, la tendance qui évoque le plus adéquatement le surmoi freudien. Le surmoi, on le sait, se formerait au moment du complexe d'Œdipe, comme son aboutissement et sa résolution même, par intériorisation ou introjection de la loi qui interdit le meurtre du père et la relation incestueuse avec la mère : en termes szondiens, il serait le gardien installé à demeure de la censure éthique. Et la parenté est d'autant plus proche que la tendance e+ a été aussi reconnue comme responsable de ce qui est pour Freud une émanation propre du surmoi, nous voulons parler du sentiment ou de la conscience de culpabilité. Lorsque la tendance e+ s'accentue (!...), elle révèle en effet une forte angoisse de culpabilité : l'individu se sent coupable d'une faute effective ou présumée, qu'il éprouve l'obligation de réparer. Forme de manifestation spécifiquement névrotique et plus encore, selon Szondi, caractéristique de l'hystérie d'angoisse.

2. La tendance e-

A l'inverse, la tendance e- marque le refus de la censure et du contrôle éthique sur la haine, la colère, la rage, bref sur tous les affects brutaux. La figure biblique de Caïn en constitue le symbole le plus parlant.

Exacerbée, la tendance e- (!, ...) révèle une accumulation d'énergie haineuse qui pourrait préluder à une décharge (eo). Nous le savons déjà, même si l'impulsion au meurtre, au mal extrême que nous pouvons commettre à l'endroit d'autrui, lui est inhérente, la tendance e- ne commande pas à proprement parler un acte meurtrier qui serait l'aboutissement limite d'une agression physique d'autrui. Szondi a reconnu dans la crise d'épilepsie le mode d'expression le plus pur de la poussée meurtrière e-. Et c'est là sans doute l'un des mérites les plus importants de Szondi que d'avoir suggéré l'hypothèse d'une articulation entre l'épilepsie et le facteur e et d'avoir ainsi réinséré dans le champ du psychopulsionnel un trouble qui tendait à être accaparé par la seule neurologie. Mais comment rendre compte de la crise épileptique de façon à lire en elle une décharge de la tendance e- ? L'épileptique, répond Szondi, tournerait vers lui-même la poussée meurtrière qui monte en lui : plutôt que de la manifester sur autrui, il la manifesterait sur lui-même dans une sorte de mort et d'anéantissement de soi, et cela comme un aboutissement pur de l'intériorisation affective qui est inhérente au facteur e lui-même. A cet égard, l'approche szondienne de l'épilepsie mériterait d'être enrichie des remarquables analyses que Sartre a consacrées à la crise de colère, cette forme la plus banale de décharge « caïnesque »[1]. Car Sartre voit dans la colère la solution d'un affrontement avec autrui, mais une solution qui, loin de supprimer autrui par une action directe, selon les voies que prescrirait une conscience pragmatique du monde, conduit à une suppression « magique » d'autrui, et cela par une transformation de la conscience ou du rapport au monde opérant via une transformation brutale et explosive du corps. Ne reconnaissons-nous pas dans cette conversion de l'agression en colère ce que nous avons appelé jusqu'ici un mouvement d'intériorisation affective, la tendance e- assurant par elle-même, sans apport adventice, une défense contre le danger d'une agression directe inhérent à la tendance s+ ? Ne reconnaissons-nous pas enfin dans les termes mêmes de l'analyse sartrienne le processus hypothétiquement générateur de la crise épileptique, dès lors terme extrême d'une série d'équivalents « épileptoïdes » dont la crise de colère serait la forme la plus élémentaire ?

c) Le facteur hy

1. La tendance hy+

La tendance hy+ est la tendance à se montrer, à se porter au regard, à se mettre en valeur aux yeux d'autrui, à exprimer ses émotions pour autrui. Elle se manifestera, tantôt sous les traits caractériels d'une démonstrativité émo-

---

[1] Cfr J.-P. Sartre, *Esquisse d'une théorie des émotions* (1939), Nouvelle édition, Hermann, 1960.

tionnelle, tantôt dans le choix socialisé d'une profession qui appelle l'extériorisation affective sous le regard d'autrui (tel le choix de la profession théâtrale), tantôt encore sous le mode d'une conversion hystérique qui utilise le corps et son système moteur aux fins d'une expression symbolique voilée de tendances sexuelles refoulées. Accentuée (!,...), elle pourra préluder à une décharge (hyo), par exemple sous la forme d'un acte d'exhibitionnisme sexuel ou sous la forme d'une crise hystériforme, de ce que Szondi appelle une «tempête de mouvements» hystériforme, par quoi il désigne quelques-uns des symptômes les plus spectaculaires de la grande crise hystérique (cris, tremblements, convulsions,...).

Mais rappelons une dernière fois la distinction entre la tendance hy+ et la tendance h+. Un individu qui assume la tendance hy+ tend à exprimer l'érotisme jusqu'à développer parfois un exhibitionnisme sexuel destiné à surprendre et provoquer autrui. Mais il est loin de toujours joindre l'activité sexuelle proprement dite à l'extériorisation voyante de l'érotisme. Cependant il arrive à la tendance h+ de se combiner avec la tendance hy+ : dans ce cas, l'attitude séductrice, toujours prête à déboucher sur la relation sexuelle, est comme l'amorce d'un contact érotisé; la rencontre érotique se déploie d'abord en préambule séducteur avant de s'achever peut-être dans l'acte sexuel. Au demeurant, l'acte sexuel auquel ne s'associerait pas la dimension d'une expressivité émotionnelle serait un acte extrêmement «frustre» : court-circuitant toute préparation affective, le désir déboucherait quasi directement sur l'acte appelé à lui procurer satisfaction — en quoi se manifeste à nouveau l'intériorisation dont les fonctions de la sexualité sont redevables au vecteur P. Mais il peut tout aussi bien arriver — et le cas n'est sans doute pas moins fréquent — que la tendance h- se trouve conjointe à la tendance hy+ : l'individu qui met en valeur ses appâts et se rend par là attirant et désirable se refuse en même temps à tout contact érotique, telle l'hystérique qui provoque sexuellement autrui mais se dérobe au moment d'en découdre et de passer à l'acte. A la limite la tendance hy+ s'exacerbant ne finirait-elle pas par exclure le contact sexuel lui-même, à la façon dont la tendance e- pouvait exclure, à la limite, l'acte sadique?

2. La tendance hy-

La tendance hy- naît du refus de se montrer ou de se porter au regard : elle est tendance à se cacher et à construire une barrière ou une censure morale à l'encontre de l'expression des émotions, et particulièrement des émotions érotiques.

En d'autres termes, la tendance hy- est tendance à la honte ou à la pudeur, et s'oppose en cela à la tendance e+, responsable du sentiment de culpabilité. Car la honte, à la différence de la culpabilité, n'a rien d'un sentiment qui émane de l'intérieur et s'éveille à l'appel d'une voix de la conscience; elle ne commande pas d'avouer un mal absolu, indépendant du jugement externe d'autrui, mais nous saisit à la vue du regard réprobateur et accusateur qu'autrui pose sur nous; la faute qu'elle nous révèle ne nous étreint qu'à la mesure du soupçon d'autrui, et l'évitement de son regard suffit seul à en apaiser l'angoisse. D'où le fait aussi que la tendance hy- se développe en une forme d'anxiété qui est comme aux antipodes de l'angoisse de culpabilité. On aurait pu l'appeler angoisse de honte si une expression classique du langage psychiatrique n'était apparue comme tout à fait adéquate pour la désigner. Accentuée (!, ...), la tendance hy- peut être révélatrice d'une angoisse sensitive de relation : en ce cas, les individus qui l'assument seront constamment préoccupés de savoir si les autres ne devinent pas les tendances qu'ils portent et cachent en eux ; ils se sentiront et se diront observés, regardés, ils interpréteront les propos d'autrui, croyant y percevoir le signe que leurs tendances honteuses ont été percées à jour, ...

Ajoutons, pour terminer, que la tendance hy- représente sans doute l'une des dimensions les plus courantes de nos relations à autrui. Toute rencontre intersubjective qui confronte les sexes ne mobilise-t-elle pas toujours aussi des motions érotiques que le plus souvent nous nous empressons de dissimuler et retenir en nous et développons dès lors en fantasmes intérieurs ? Car la discrétion, la réserve, la froideur, bref la fermeture d'un corps qui ne doit trahir aucun mouvement affectif, est clairement corrélative d'un renforcement d'une vie imaginaire d'autant plus effervescente et luxuriante que la voie d'une expression directe est barrée. N'est-ce pas là un fait d'expérience courante que chacun est en état de ressaisir par retour sur soi ? N'avons-nous pas tous tendance, alors même que nous cachons nos mouvements érotiques, à nous replier à l'intérieur d'un monde de fantaisie et de rêverie diurne et à y entretenir complaisamment nos émotions réprimées ? C'est pourquoi Szondi a attribué aussi la formation du monde de la fantaisie à l'efficace de la tendance hy- : cette dernière pourrait révéler un repli complaisant dans une vie fantasmatique qui amènerait à la limite à délaisser le monde réel au profit d'un refuge exclusif dans un univers irréel de fantaisie cultivé parfois jusqu'à la mythomanie.

4. La pulsion du moi ou vecteur Sch

a) Le vecteur du rapport à soi et à la réalité

En ce qui concerne le vecteur Sch, nous ne rencontrons guère les problèmes parfois difficiles de dénomination auxquels nous nous sommes heurté jusqu'ici chaque fois qu'il s'agissait de définir l'essence générale d'un vecteur. Tous les interprètes s'accordent en effet à reconnaître que le vecteur Sch est le vecteur du rapport à soi et à la réalité : la personne y est en jeu dans ce qui la constitue comme moi et dans le débat qu'elle engage toujours avec la réalité alors même qu'elle se forme en entrant en rapport à soi. Et si l'on veut bien admettre que le rapport à soi et au réel est sélectivement perturbé dans les schizophrénies, on comprendra que le vecteur du moi ait été appelé aussi vecteur « Sch ».

Mais la relation incessante que le moi institue avec lui-même et la réalité est susceptible de connaître deux grandes orientations contrastées, soit que le moi dépasse ses frontières, s'élargisse ou s'épande pour se trouver ou se perdre dans l'autre, soit qu'il s'enferme dans un espace clos, se restreigne et se replie sur soi pour se poser dès lors face à la réalité comme face à une réalité distincte de lui. D'emblée, Szondi désignera le besoin p comme besoin d'égodiastole (ou besoin d'expansion du moi) et le besoin k comme besoin d'égosystole (ou besoin de rétrécissement du moi), pour les dénommer par la suite à l'aide de deux verbes élémentaires : être et avoir, aptes à ressaisir à leur façon les deux mouvements antagonistes par lesquels le moi entre en relation avec la réalité. Car être l'autre, n'est-ce pas aussi s'épandre en lui, s'élargir à lui ? Et la relation d'avoir n'institue-t-elle pas une distinction entre soi et cela même qu'on a ou possède [1] ?

Mais si Szondi a tenu à intégrer un vecteur du moi dans son schéma quaternaire, c'est assurément aussi pour y faire place à ce que le théorie et la pratique psychanalytique ont articulé sous ce terme. On ne s'étonnera donc pas que Szondi inscrive à l'intérieur du vecteur Sch plusieurs des fonctions reconnues par Freud et la psychanalyse comme mécanismes du moi : projection, identification, introjection, refoulement,... Mais à vrai dire il fait bien davantage que collecter ici ou là quelques concepts déjà construits : à travers sa mise en forme originale des fonctions du moi, il produit un effet de connaissance inédit susceptible de débloquer une impasse de la théorie psychanalytique. A. Zenoni (1974) et J. Schotte (1973-74) d'abord, N. Duruz (1978) ensuite, y ont insisté : à travers la polarité des besoins p et k et leur articulation dans une doctrine cohérente et unifiée du moi, Szondi réconcilie en les intégrant deux versants du moi qui demeurent comme éclatés en l'état actuel du développement de la psychanalyse, à savoir, d'une part, accentué par Lacan, le versant du moi comme instance idéale, imaginaire, narcissique (besoin p), d'autre part, promu par Hartmann et la psychanalyse américaine, le versant d'un moi défensif, représentant des exigences de la réalité (besoin k).

Quant à la promotion d'une pulsion du moi, on devine déjà qu'elle ne restitue en aucune façon le concept infra-psychologique d'un besoin d'autoconservation biologique de soi, que Freud lui-même avait dû abandonner dans un mouvement de rectification conceptuelle. Si le moi est inscrit comme pulsion, c'est pour signifier qu'il ne connaît pas de forme prédéterminée de destin : son devenir est aussi risqué et problématique que tout autre devenir pulsionnel. Mais c'est aussi pour signifier que le moi n'est pas une instance absolument souveraine venant comme s'imposer de l'extérieur à des pulsions dont il ne participerait pas, pour les régler et les contraindre. Et pourtant, la théorisation szondienne du moi emporte bien quelque chose de la problématique d'un moi non-pulsionnel ou extra-pulsionnel, introduite en psychanalyse par Hartmann et son école.

Il est vrai que le moi occupe une place à part dans l'ordre et le système pulsionnel, ce qui nous conduira par la suite à lui consacrer un chapitre propre qui en manifestera l'originalité. Cependant, il est indispensable, pour les besoins de notre exposé actuel, que nous soulignions déjà l'une des particularités du moi, par quoi il bénéficie d'un privilège par rapport aux autres vecteurs et s'élève en quelque façon au-dessus d'eux. Le moi s'explique avec lui-même et la réalité — avec une énergie pulsionnelle propre (la puissance d'être), précisera Szondi, au même titre que les autres pulsions s'expliquent avec une énergie spécifique, telle l'énergie des affects pour le vecteur P. Mais le moi s'explique toujours aussi avec les autres besoins pulsionnels, ou plus exactement il ne se forme lui-même dans un débat toujours périlleux qu'en

---

[1] Dépassant l'intuition encore mal conceptualisée de Szondi, A. Zenoni (1967) a pu fonder la légitimité et démontrer la fécondité d'une définition des fonctions p et k en termes d'être et d'avoir, et cela sur base d'analyses linguistiques aussi bien que phénoménologiques.

s'expliquant avec les besoins pulsionnels constitutifs des trois autres vecteurs. Comme si le moi avait le privilège de reprendre en lui, d'assumer dans son espace, pour les élaborer, tous les autres besoins pulsionnels. C'est pourquoi l'exposé qui vient distinguera toujours à propos de chacune des tendances du moi ce qui relève d'une élaboration d'une énergie propre ou d'une explication du moi avec lui-même et la réalité et ce qui relève d'une élaboration d'un désir, d'un besoin, d'une tendance, qui lui viendrait de l'extérieur, en l'occurence de l'espace des autres vecteurs pulsionnels.

Une dernière remarque avant de nous engager dans l'analyse détaillée des facteurs du moi. On notera immédiatement que notre développement brise la logique qui imposerait de procéder de la tendance positive vers la tendance négative. Nous commençons en effet par présenter la tendance p- pour ne passer qu'ensuite à la tendance p+. Nous suivons en cela l'idée szondienne d'un circuit du moi qui partirait de la tendance p- pour s'achever dans la tendance k- après avoir mobilisé les tendances p+ et k+ (TrP, p. 142).

Les tendances du moi parcoureraient donc un cycle régulier dont la signification serait génétique — c'est dans cette succession qu'elles entreraient en action au cours du développement de l'enfant — et conceptuelle — c'est uniquement dans cet ordre nécessaire que seraient concevables l'enrichissement et la complexification progressifs du rapport à soi et à la réalité.

Après Szondi, l'idée d'un circuit du moi a été reprise par J. Schotte qui a proposé de l'élargir aux autres vecteurs tout en la contredisant sur un point : à son sens le circuit du moi irait de p- vers p+ à travers k+ et k-[1]. Enfin, dans un mémoire récent, J. Servais (1976) en donne une nouvelle formulation (de p- à k- par k+ et p+).

Pour notre part, nous pensons que le débat ainsi engagé est loin d'être encore éclairci. Des arguments divers, relevant en particulier de la psychologie génétique, sont avancés de part et d'autre : les uns empruntent aux stades du développement de l'enfant mis au jour par les psychologues généticiens (à quel circuit du moi correspond le développement de l'enfant?), les autres se réfèrent aux résultats de l'administration du test à des groupes d'enfants (selon quel ordre les fonctions testologiques du moi apparaissent-elles effectivement?). Mais à notre avis, les observations dont nous disposons sur ce plan, sont encore trop maigres et trop équivoques pour que nous puissions trancher dans un sens ou dans un autre, ce que nous préciserons dans une note ultérieure. C'est pourquoi nous nous sommes tenu au déroulement proposé par Szondi, non pas parce que nous le considérons comme le plus valable, mais parce qu'il nous a paru offrir un cadre commode d'exposition. Et cela d'autant plus qu'il ne contredit pas clairement les données de la psychologie génétique auxquelles nous pouvons recourir pour éclairer le développement des fonctions du moi.

b) Le facteur p

1. La tendance p-

a) p- et la puissance d'être

« Je suis l'autre » : telle pourrait être la formule la plus adéquate à définir le rapport à soi et à la réalité instauré par le facteur p. Valable à la fois pour les tendances p+ et p-, elle est toutefois diversement accentuée. Ainsi la tendance p- porte l'accent sur : « l'autre », le « je suis » étant comme entre

---

[1] J. Schotte, 1975-1976, pp. 89-92. Cfr aussi l'excellente mise au point de Jean Melon (TP, pp. 139-144). Notons aussi que notre analyse du vecteur C donne une appréhension de ce que pourrait être un circuit du contact (m+, d-, m-, d+).

parenthèses. En d'autres termes, la puissance d'être, l'énergie interne au facteur p, est retirée au sujet pour être totalement déversée sur l'autre. Au terme du processus, il n'y a donc plus que l'autre : le sujet, sorti de soi, vit désormais au lieu de l'autre.

La tendance p- sera donc définie comme une tendance à la participation originaire, que nous tiendrons avec Szondi pour congéniale à l'existence des « primitifs », si du moins nous osons adhérer encore aux vues, aujourd'hui mises en question, d'un Levy-Bruhl : l'homme « primitif » serait comme diffusé à l'extérieur de lui-même, participant directement de la vie des autres, de la vie de ses dieux, de ses ancêtres, des membres de son clan et de sa famille.

Sur le terrain caractérologique, la tendance p- serait à l'œuvre dans un trait comme l'empathie, manifestée par les individus capables de saisir intuitivement les fines nuances de la vie affective d'autrui.

Au plan génétique, un lien participatif serait repérable dans le premier rapport à autrui, dont Wallon situe l'efflorescence vers 6 mois[1]. A cet âge, on voit s'épanouir, à la faveur d'un stade dit émotif ou affectif, une première forme de sociabilité, marquée par la symbiose affective, par la communication et la contagion des émotions : l'enfant vit émotivement dans l'autre, participe de sa vie affective, sans se ressaisir encore comme soi dans le rapport à l'autre. Peut-être même le premier sourire social de l'enfant véhiculerait-il quelque chose de la participation originaire connotée par la tendance p- : ainsi que l'a établi Spitz, l'enfant y est comme totalement absorbé dans un visage où il reconnaît une forme humaine générale, sans se reconnaître lui-même comme être humain, comme s'il n'identifiait encore l'humanité que dans l'autre, au lieu de l'autre.

Enfin, au niveau psychopathologique, la tendance p- s'exprime dans l'impuissance du moi. Le moi, qui a projeté sa puissance d'être sur le monde, a désormais le sentiment d'être livré sans recours à une toute-puissance extérieure. Dès lors qu'elle est accentuée (!, ...), la tendance p- pourrait être à l'origine des symtômes schizophréniques de l'écho ou du vol de la pensée, comme si nos propres pensées nous venaient du dehors, comme si elles étaient faites ou fabriquées en nous par un autre, comme si nous étaient enlevées.

b) p- et l'élaboration du désir

Si nous traduisons la définition générale de la fonction p- au plan de l'élaboration du désir, nous devons dire que la tendance p- nous entraîne à vivre nos désirs au lieu de l'autre, tout en nous annulant comme sujet de désir. Que serait-ce, par exemple, que vivre un désir haineux sur un mode conforme à la tendance p- ? Assurément, vivre l'autre comme haïssable et ne pas se réfléchir comme haineux ; ou encore, vivre la haine comme si elle était suscitée par l'autre et son caractère détestable, comme si nous n'y avions aucune part.

La tendance p- est donc bien, conformément à sa désignation la plus courante, tendance à la projection des désirs : tendance de l'être humain à

---

[1] Nous nous référons, ici comme dans la suite, à : H. Wallon, *Les origines du caractère chez l'enfant*, P.U.F., 1949.

investir de désirs la réalité, à structurer le monde et ses objets d'après ses désirs, et cela abstraction faite de toute prise de conscience. N'est-ce pas d'ailleurs, ainsi que le remarque Deri (IS, p. 172), sur le principe d'une structuration désirante (le plus souvent: inconsciemment désirante) de la réalité que sont fondées les techniques dites «projectives»?

Mais la vie désirante du monde prend aisément une connotation paranoïde, depuis le moment où elle se développe en une psychologie de l'accusation toujours prête à imputer à autrui («c'est l'autre qui...») jusqu'au point extrême où, à la faveur d'une indistinction de soi et de l'autre, nos propres désirs, inconsciemment chassés dans l'autre, nous reviennent de l'extérieur. Dès cet instant, la tendance p- devient tendance à la projection au sens précis où l'entend la théorie psychanalytique[1]. Car le désir, nié dans l'inconscient, est attribué à l'autre lui-même. Ainsi l'autre n'est plus simplement haïssable, mais il est devenu l'auteur de la haine: c'est lui qui me hait et peut-être même, me haïssant, me persécute. Exacerbée (!, ...), la tendance p- est responsable du délire paranoïde de persécution.

2. *La tendance p+*

a) p+ et la puissance d'être

La tendance p+ lève la parenthèse qui annulait le sujet et le maintenait en suspens aussi longtemps que la projection était seule en état de fonctionnement: le «je suis» est thématiquement accentué. En d'autres termes, le moi parvient à une première reconnaissance de soi, mais, insistons-y, à une reconnaissance qu'il n'obtient encore que par la médiation de l'autre: certes, le moi est, mais il est l'autre, et l'autre, c'est lui. Ou encore, le moi qui avait comme déversé sa puissance d'être dans un monde vécu dès lors comme tout-puissant récupère son énergie un instant aliénée, il se gonfle d'une toute-puissance faite sienne, il s'enfle; ainsi que l'a définie Szondi, reprenant en cela une notion de Jung, la tendance p+ est tendance à l'inflation. S'il n'y avait d'abord que l'autre, à présent il n'y a que moi, mais un moi élargi au monde entier. Le moi est tout et n'est pas sensible aux contradictions internes qui pourraient l'agiter: il est possédé par des ambitendances, à la fois Dieu et diable, homme et femme, homme et animal; identifié à la totalité, il est les deux à la fois.

Au plan génétique, le processus inflatif serait observable dans le rapport à autrui qui se développe entre la première et la troisième année. A cette époque, l'enfant parvient à un repérage thématique de soi: il identifie comme sienne une image, il se reconnaît en elle et en tout ce qui, en dehors de lui, dans le monde interhumain, lui ressemble, y est assimilable. Ainsi, dès cet instant, l'enfant ne participe plus aux émotions d'autrui qu'à condition de percevoir en autrui sa propre image, en quelque sorte de s'y retrouver: il n'y a d'autre que moi, pour ainsi dire, et moi, je suis tout, car tout me renvoie mon image. Structure des rapports intersubjectifs dont Lacan a souligné l'importance dans le procès de formation de la subjectivité et qu'il a promue au rang de

---

[1] Le concept psychanalytique impliquant une expulsion et une localisation dans l'autre de ce qui est méconnu ou refusé en soi (J. Laplanche et J.B. Pontalis, *Vocabulaire de la psychanalyse*, P.U.F., 1967, p. 344).

« stade du miroir », mais que Wallon, bien avant Lacan, avait mise au jour et décrite dans ses formes de manifestations les plus concrètes[1].

Enfin, au niveau psychopathologique, la tendance p+ (!, ...) est à l'œuvre dans le délire paranoïde de grandeur, chez ces personnes qui, au lieu de s'éprouver impuissantes et livrées au monde, se sentent puissantes d'être tel ou tel, Jésus-Christ, Napoléon, la Sainte Vierge,... ou d'être tel et tel à la fois, homme et femme, Dieu et diable, ...

b) p+ et l'élaboration du désir

Ainsi que l'écrit Deri (IS, p. 172), le facteur p n'est pas, au même titre que les autres facteurs, le lieu d'un désir spécifique, mais il ouvre un espace où s'accomplit le redoublement du désir (et des désirs concrets, particuliers, qui s'inscrivent dans les autres vecteurs pulsionnels): il est désir de désir. En d'autres termes, le besoin p est le besoin de vivre ses désirs et de s'exprimer continûment à travers sa vie désirante. Et s'il est vrai que la dialectique de l'affirmation et du refus s'effectue aussi à l'intérieur du facteur p, il en découle que la tendance p+ prolonge un mouvement d'auto-expressivité désirante auquel la tendance p- opposait un démenti. Dès lors qu'il passe de la tendance p- à la tendance p+, le sujet assume en première personne le désir qu'il vivait jusque là projectivement, comme à l'extérieur de lui-même. Pour continuer la signification générale de la tendance p+, nous dirons que le sujet se gonfle de son désir, ou encore qu'il en prend conscience. Car la tendance p+, dira aussi Szondi, est responsable de la fonction proprement humaine de conscience de désir: alors même que l'animal ne dispose que de la seule conscience perceptive, l'homme a la possibilité d'accéder à la conscience de ses désirs qu'il tend d'abord à vivre inconsciemment dans l'autre. Un «je le hais» se substitue ainsi au «il est haïssable», ce qui contribue à atténuer le danger inhérent au désir haineux. Car il n'y a qu'un pas du «il est haïssable» au «il doit être châtié, puni, supprimé», à tel point que la tendance p- est constitutive, avec les tendances m-, e- et s+, de ce que Szondi a appelé le syndrome du meurtrier. Le danger est largement conjuré dès le moment où la haine accède à la conscience de désir: à cet instant, l'objet devient surtout un prétexte à l'entretien de la haine et à l'expression haineuse de soi et n'est plus directement menacé. Plus généralement, quel que soit le désir intéressé, la personne qui s'installe en p+ n'a d'autre souci que de se complaire de manière toute introversive dans un désir dont l'exercice actif et direct est ainsi perpétuellement différé, ce qui la fait apparaître aussi sous les traits d'un être passionnément idéaliste, mais inefficace. Car gagnée et comme possédée par la toute-puissance d'un désir, elle risque de ne pas en apercevoir les bornes ou les limitations. Incapable de mesurer son désir imaginairement grossi aux exigences de la réalité, elle ne débouche que rarement sur une activité transformatrice du réel.

---

[1] L'apparition régulière dans le développement de l'enfant de ces phénomènes concrets relevant sans conteste de la tendance p+ constitue l'une des raisons importantes pour lesquelles nous maintenons la formule proprement szondienne du circuit du moi. C'est ainsi que la reconnaissance de soi dans le miroir intervient régulièrement chez l'enfant entre deux à trois ans (cfr les travaux récents de René Zazzo: La genèse de la conscience de soi, dans *Psychologie de la connaissance de soi*, P.U.F., 1975).

Que la tendance p+ ait bien la signification que nous venons de dire, c'est ce que confirment aussi ses modes d'apparition socialisés. N'est-il pas significatif à cet égard que la tendance p+ soit régulièrement observée chez les personnes qui exercent dans leur activité courante, sous une forme ou sous une autre, une prise de conscience de désir, qu'il s'agisse de psychologues ou encore de certaines catégories d'artistes ? Ainsi, dans une recherche inédite, Deri a pu constater que la tendance p+ était prépondérante chez les écrivains, alors même qu'elle s'atténuait chez les peintres et les sculpteurs, et cela au bénéfice de la tendance p-. Sans doute les uns comme les autres transposent-ils leurs désirs dans la matière même de leur création. Mais les écrivains ne présentent-ils pas la particularité de donner expression verbale à leurs désirs ? Et ne serait-ce pas là d'ailleurs la seule manière d'en opérer en général la prise de conscience ? Pour parler le langage de Freud, une motion pulsionnelle n'accède-t-elle pas au système conscient-préconscient dès lors qu'elle s'inscrit dans le registre des représentations de mots ? Ce qui rejoint à nouveau une observation courante, à savoir que les individus chez qui prédomine la tendance p+ non seulement sont possédés par une vie fantasmatique d'une grande richesse, mais surtout manifestent une vive capacité à transposer en paroles les contenus de leur vie fantasmatique, par quoi ils sont prédisposés à toutes les formes de psychothérapie à base verbale.

c) Le facteur k

1. Les tendances du facteur k et la puissance d'être

a) k+ et la puissance d'être

Nous le savons, le facteur k contracte le moi, le rétrécit, le délimite. A ce titre, il exerce une fonction défensive : il protège le sujet contre le danger d'une expansion démesurée de son moi et de ses désirs dans le monde, et par là assure la santé et l'auto-préservation du moi.

Mais s'il est exact que le facteur k, par la coartation du moi qu'il régit, s'oppose à la dilatation commandée par le facteur p, il n'est pas illégitime de partir, en vue de sa définition, du mouvement par lequel il nie l'orientation du facteur p. Or, qu'est-ce que nier le rapport à soi et au réel instauré par le facteur p, sinon affirmer : « je ne suis pas l'autre » ? Mais que suis-je donc si je ne suis pas l'autre ? Je suis moi-même, pourrait-on dire. La tendance k+, qui assume la direction interne au facteur k, désigne le processus de la formation ou de la cristallisation d'une image de soi qui donne au sujet le sentiment de sa personnalité, de son individualité, de cela même qui le différencie de tout ce qui n'est pas lui. A ce titre, la tendance k+ est proche plus qu'aucune autre du moi psychologique, de cet ensemble d'attributs variés qui constitue une personnalité, qu'il s'agisse d'attributs de caractère ou d'attributs professionnels. La tendance k+, dira Szondi, est responsable de la formation du caractère ou de la constitution de la personnalité professionnelle.

La tendance k+ a donc été reconnue comme une tendance narcissique, mais comme une tendance narcissique très différente de la tendance p+, qui pour sa part n'en usurperait pas la qualité. Car la tendance p+ conduit aussi le sujet à reconnaître une image comme sienne, mais à la reconnaître sur l'autre et dans l'autre : lui-même et l'autre ne s'opposent pas, mais se redoublent indéfiniment. A l'inverse, l'image de soi formée par la tendance k+ oppose le sujet à l'objet, le moi à l'autre. La tendance k+ installe le sujet dans un sentiment d'auto-suffisance qui le coupe émotionnellement de son entourage, en même temps qu'elle le conduit à vivre la réalité comme un univers à organiser, conquérir, contraindre et dominer, comme un champ ouvert à l'action rationnelle et efficace. C'est pourquoi, si l'on a pu définir la tendance k+ comme tendance à l'égocentrisme, on a pu aussi paradoxalement la considérer comme tendance à l'extraversion. Certes, la tendance p+ instaure un constant rapport à l'autre, mais précisément à un autre toujours mélangé des désirs et des fantasmes du sujet. Seule la fonction k+ fonde la possibilité d'un rapport objectif, rationnel, positif — en ce sens extraverti — avec le monde extérieur, notamment à travers la perception. Car, propose aussi Szondi, la tendance k+ est responsable du rapport perceptif avec la réalité.

Au plan génétique, nous pourrions reconnaître l'entrée en jeu de la fonction k+ dans ce que Wallon a appelé la crise de personnalité de trois ans. N'est-ce pas le moment où l'enfant devient vivement conscient de son individualité, où il maîtrise le système des pronoms personnels (je, tu, il), où il s'oppose aux contraintes de son entourage et devient indiscipliné, boudeur, renfermé, comme sont souvent indisciplinés et non conformistes les individus chez qui la fonction k+ est prédominante ?

Enfin, au niveau psychopathologique, la tendance k+ pourra s'exprimer dans l'autisme. Car si le mouvement qu'esquisse la fonction k+ est poussé à la limite (!,...), le moi, se repliant sur soi, risque de couper tout contact avec le monde extérieur. Il y a un sens de la formule « je suis tout » qui est congénial à la fonction k+, non parce que je me prolongerais dans l'univers pour m'identifier à lui, mais bien plutôt parce que l'univers entier serait comme absorbé dans l'espace du moi et disparaîtrait en quelque sorte au bénéfice d'un moi désormais tout-puissant.

b) k- et la puissance d'être

Reprenons la formule de la tendance k+ pour la doubler d'une négation et nous obtenons la signification de la tendance k-. D'un côté, nous avons : « je suis moi-même », à savoir « je suis tel ou tel, je constitue comme miens quelques traits différenciateurs par lesquels je prends consistance face au monde et m'oppose à lui comme à une réalité à modeler ». De l'autre côté, nous obtenons par négation : « je ne suis pas tel ou tel, je renonce à être tel ou tel, j'accepte une limitation de mon être, j'accepte l'épreuve ou le verdict de la réalité ». De sorte que si la tendance k+ marquait la constitution d'une image de soi contre la réalité, la tendance k- marque au contraire la conformation du soi et de l'image de soi à la réalité.

Mais repèrerait-on la fonction k- et son émergence privilégiée à un moment déterminé du développement de l'enfant ? La recherche testologique qu'a conduite Susan Deri a révélé que le facteur k évolue du k+ vers le k± entre la troisième et la cinquième année de l'existence[1]. La tendance k- apparaîtrait

---

[1] Selon Deri (IS, pp. 209-225), les configurations du vecteur Sch se développeraient selon l'ordre suivant : Sch o- (avant trois ans), Sch +- (trois ans), Sch ±- (aux alentours de cinq ans), Sch -- (à partir de six ans). La formule du circuit du moi proposée par Schotte (p -

donc aux alentours de la cinquième année. Et Deri d'ajouter: il doit se produire à cette époque un événement particulièrement « drastique » dans les rapports de l'enfant avec la réalité, un événement qui le contraint au renoncement (IS, p. 222). Or nous savons aussi qu'à la même époque l'enfant traverse la phase œdipienne. Formulons donc l'hypothèse d'une liaison entre l'émergence de la fonction k- et le complexe d'Œdipe qui impose à l'enfant de sexe masculin de reconcer à remplacer son père auprès de sa mère.

Enfin, de même que la fonction k+ peut à la limite passer du « je suis tel ou tel » au « je suis tout », la fonction k- peut évoluer du « je ne suis pas tel ou tel » au « je ne suis rien ». Nous parvenons alors à ce que Szondi appelle la destruction « moïque », à la destruction de tout être soi-même, ou encore à la désimagination, à la destruction de tout idéal ou de toute image de soi, cette forme de destruction alimentant, d'après Szondi, certaines formes de psychose, telles la schizophrénie catatonique ou la manie, ou certaines formes de psychopathie, en particulier les toxicomanies (qui viseraient, par la prise de drogue, l'annulation de toute subjectivité différenciée).

2. Les tendances du facteur k et l'élaboration du désir

Les tendances k+ et k- désignent, outre deux processus formateurs du moi dans son rapport à la réalité, deux modes de la prise de position du sujet par rapport au désir. Il s'agit chaque fois pour le moi de préserver sa cohérence ou son intégrité contre ce qui, du désir, pourrait la menacer. Cependant, dans cette préservation de soi, les fonctions k+ et k- travaillent dans des directions opposées, conformément à leur signification générale: la fonction k+ révèle une prise de position affirmatrice vis-à-vis du désir, elle indique la tendance du moi à affirmer un désir contre la réalité et contre ce qui, dans la réalité, le dément; à l'inverse, la fonction k- révèle une prise de position négatrice par rapport au désir, elle indique la tendance du moi à nier un désir, d'après le verdict de la réalité.

a) La tendance k+ et l'élaboration du désir

En k+, le sujet, plutôt que de renoncer à un désir ou à une représentation de désir que la réalité contredit, préfère se transformer lui-même, exercer un travail sur lui-même, qui lui permette de maintenir envers et contre tout son désir ou sa représentation de désir. Szondi a qualifié ce travail du moi de travail d'introjection et défini dès lors la fonction k+ comme fonction d'introjection.

Repérons d'abord le fonctionnement du processus dans d'autres registres que le registre psychopathologique, dans la socialisation professionnelle et dans la dissolution du complexe d'Œdipe.

Un sujet nourrit un désir qui se heurte à des obstacles en provenance de la

→ k + → k - → p+) serait ainsi confirmée par les résultats testologiques. Il faut toutefois remarquer que seule une reconstruction théorique hypothétique nous permet d'accéder au fonctionnement du moi qui précède trois ans (le test n'étant pas administrable aux enfants avant l'âge de trois ans). Il est donc loisible à chacun, en fonction de ses options théoriques, de postuler avant trois ans un fonctionnement du moi qui inclut ou exclut p+. C'est ainsi qu'on observera que Szondi lui-même intercale entre Scho- et Sch+- deux étapes de fonctionnement du moi qui impliquent p +: Sch o± et Sch +± (et cela, « d'après des considérations théoriques », DP, p. 221).

réalité sociale. Plutôt que de renoncer à son désir, le sujet l'introjecte, l'inscrit dans sa personnalité sous la forme d'un idéal professionnel qui lui ôte son caractère passionnel, le transforme en un intérêt imposant une activité froide et rationnelle sur les objets du monde extérieur, le situe à une place limitée dans son existence et le rend socialement acceptable. Ainsi, plutôt que d'être un sadique destructeur, le sujet deviendra boucher ou chirurgien; plutôt que d'être un délinquant, il deviendra policier.

Le maintien du désir par introjection s'opère aussi à l'occasion de la dissolution du complexe d'Œdipe. Le désir de l'enfant de sexe masculin d'être son père ou de prendre la place de celui-ci auprès de sa mère se heurte à un interdit porté par l'entourage interhumain. L'enfant devra dès lors renoncer à son désir, ou tout au moins il ne pourra le conserver tel quel. Il ne le maintiendra qu'au prix de sa transformation introjective ou de son inscription sous forme d'un idéal: introjectant l'idéal ou la loi du père, il renonce certes à être père dans l'immédiat et à coucher avec sa mère, mais en même temps il est désormais assuré de pouvoir un jour être père à son tour.

Mais la tendance k+ intervient également comme fonction introjective dans le registre psychopathologique, en particulier dans la mélancolie et dans certaines formes de perversion.

Dans la mélancolie, le sujet ne peut abandonner l'investissement désirant d'un objet perdu. Il construit dès lors cet objet en lui-même, l'incorpore ou l'introjecte, selon le mécanisme décrit par Freud dans *Deuil et Mélancolie*. Par là il continue à vivre son désir, mais sous la forme d'un rapport à soi, nourri de la haine (devenue haine de soi) qu'il vouait à l'objet perdu, infidèle.

Par ailleurs, Szondi considère que l'introjection est caractéristique de certaines perversions, essentiellement du fétichisme. Le fétichiste aurait fixé un moment existensiel traumatisant, il en aurait comme photographié certains éléments, qu'il s'efforcerait désormais de retrouver ou de reproduire dans la matérialité du réel. Le processus opère bien dans la direction prescrite par la tendance k+ : une image prélevée sur la scène traumatique s'est cristallisée subjectivement, pour être ensuite reproduite dans le réel le plus positif et le plus cru, par la visualisation, la manipulation ou la possession d'objets qui lui correspondent. Mais pourquoi la formation introjective de l'image d'un geste, d'une posture, d'un vêtement, d'un organe, découpée sur un complexe plus étendu de sensations? Ne serait-ce pas, comme le veut l'hypothèse freudienne, que le sujet s'est trouvé brutalement confronté à une scène qui lui révélait, avec le vide béant du sexe féminin, la différence des sexes et battait en brèche sa représentation d'un seul sexe, le sien? Mais plutôt que de renoncer à cette représentation, et pour ne pas y renoncer, il aurait alors prélevé sur la scène et introjecté un objet ou un geste latéral, anodin, inoffensif, le convainquant, par sa présence intériorisée et sa répétition matérialisée, que rien n'est advenu, qu'il n'y avait là tout au plus qu'un sous-vêtement, un pied, une cuisse.

b) La tendance k- et l'élaboration du désir

La tendance k- agit en sens inverse : au lieu de préserver un désir ou une représentation de désir démentie par la réalité, le sujet accepte le verdict de la réalité et renonce à son désir. Selon la définition de Szondi, la fonction k- révèle la tendance du moi à nier, inhiber, refouler des motions pulsionnelles, des représentations qui menacent l'auto-conservation de la personne. En cela, elle révèle aussi la tendance du moi à s'adapter aux exigences de la morale, de monde environnant, du surmoi.

Comme mécanisme de défense, la tendance k- est proche de ce que la psychanalyse appelle le refoulement: elle est toujours interprétée comme mécanisme névrotique à moins qu'elle ne s'exacerbe, auquel cas elle se développe comme auto-destruction ou désimagination et pointe vers des formes de pathologie psychotique.

B. LA DIALECTIQUE PULSIONNELLE

Jusqu'ici nous avons considéré les constituants du système pulsionnel indépendamment des relations qu'ils instituent entre eux. Or, loin d'être juxtaposés et de se maintenir ainsi dans un état d'indifférence, les constituants pulsionnels élémentaires sont toujours aussi engagés dans un débat mutuel que le terme de dialectique qualifie adéquatement. Car la relation qu'ils nouent à la faveur de ce débat n'est pas une relation de détermination causale univoque, mais bien une relation d'interaction réciproque, placée sous le signe d'un processus d'action-réaction: elle est en ce sens, selon l'usage le plus courant du terme, « dialectique ».

Pour préciser la nature de la relation dialectique qui s'instaure entre les éléments du système pulsionnel, partons, à la manière de Szondi, d'un état pulsionnel (fictif) où seraient données toutes les composantes du système:

$$\pm \ \pm \ \pm \ \pm \ \pm \ \pm \ \pm \ \pm$$

Que se passe-t-il donc dès le moment où les éléments du système pulsionnel se rencontrent en une constellation qui les réunit tous ? De vives tensions se font jour, des forces antagonistes s'affrontent, qu'il s'agisse des tendances à l'intérieur du besoin (ex. h+ ↔ h-), des besoins au sein du vecteur (ex. h ↔ s), des vecteurs eux-mêmes à l'intérieur du système pulsionnel total (en particulier les vecteurs centraux contre les vecteurs périphériques: Sch et P ↔ S et C). Tensions si insupportables qu'elles appellent une élaboration qui contribue à les réduire quelque peu. Car le sujet n'est pas en mesure d'assumer en totalité pareil ensemble de tendances au sein duquel les tensions pulsionnelles jouent à plein. Aussi en écarte-t-il ou en repousse-t-il quelques-unes, pour n'en assumer qu'un nombre limité. Nous dirons qu'il divise ou clive les pulsions, selon une des innombrables formes de répartition momentanée des tendances pulsionnelles entre l'avant-plan et l'arrière-plan. Ainsi, par exemple:

Avant-plan   ± - + o - + - o
Arrière-plan o + - ± + - + ±

Par là, le sujet aura résolu à sa manière les tensions internes au système pulsionnel total. Mais prenons garde de croire qu'il les aurait ainsi supprimées. Le clivage opéré, tout rapport de forces, toute interaction dynamique, n'a pas disparu. Résoudre les tensions par clivage n'équivaut pas à liquider les tensions, mais bien à leur donner une figure spécifique et limitée, qui appelle une analyse dialectique en termes d'interaction dynamique.

Ce sont précisément les diverses formes de clivage des pulsions, qui définissent autant de modalités du fonctionnement dialectique des pulsions, que nous nous proposons d'étudier dans ce chapitre.

Procédant du simple au complexe, nous serons ainsi amenés à considérer successivement cinq formes de la dialectique pulsionnelle :

1. Une première étape nous conduira à analyser les formes de clivage factoriel, aboutissement du débat dialectique des tendances pulsionnelles au sein du facteur pulsionnel.

2. Dans une seconde phase, nous dégagerons les diverses figures auxquelles donne lieu, en conséquence des clivages vectoriels, la dialectique des tendances pulsionnelles au sein du vecteur pulsionnel.

3. Un troisième moment nous amènera à étudier le fonctionnement dialectique des tendances pulsionnelles au sein d'un système couvrant les quatre vecteurs pulsionnels, ou encore les modalités d'interaction des tendances pulsionnelles à l'intérieur de ce que nous appelons une conjoncture pulsionnelle, résultat du clivage instantané du système pulsionnel.

4. Une quatrième étape nous permettra d'aborder une forme de la dialectique pulsionnelle rarement développée pour elle-même encore que très importante et appelant des considérations spécifiques, à savoir la dialectique entre les conjonctures pulsionnelles constitutives d'un profil pulsionnel, par quoi nous soulèverons un problème laissé en friche par Szondi : le problème des déroulements pulsionnels.

5. Dans une cinquième phase, nous achèverons notre parcours par l'examen de l'interaction entre le profil d'avant-plan et les profils d'arrière-plan au sein du profil pulsionnel total.

1. Les clivages factoriels

a) Les formes de clivage factoriel

Le débat dynamique interne au facteur pulsionnel met aux prises deux tendances pulsionnelles antagoniques, positive et négative, celles-là mêmes qui constituent a priori ce dernier. Le clivage qui est appelé à résoudre la tension opère donc ici sur deux tendances : en les assumant et/ou en les repoussant, il donne une forme précise et particulière au débat intrafactoriel.

On le comprend aussitôt, quatre formes de clivage factoriel sont seules possibles, qui correspondent aux réactions pulsionnelles élémentaires : les clivages positif (+) et négatif (-) que nous regroupons sous le titre de clivages factoriels unitendants — l'une ou l'autre des deux tendances est assumée, alors que la tendance antagoniste est repoussée ou écartée —; le clivage nul (o) — aucune des deux tendances n'est assumée, les deux tendances sont écartées —; enfin le clivage ambitendant (±) — les deux tendances sont assumées.

Dans les développements qui suivent, nous adopterons une procédure d'exposition qui nous guidera aussi dans l'analyse des clivages vectoriels : nous énoncerons tout d'abord la signification psychodynamique générale des grandes formes de clivage factoriel, pour en dégager ensuite la signification différenciée, selon le lieu pulsionnel (ici en l'occurence un facteur pulsionnel spécifique) où elles se manifestent. Nous serons aussi amené à indiquer en quelle mesure les clivages sont susceptibles de représenter un danger pulsionnel, et cela d'après leurs caractéristiques psychodynamiques générales d'une part, d'après le contenu spécifique des tendances qu'ils élisent d'autre part.

1. Les clivages unitendants

Dans le clivage factoriel unitendant, l'une des deux tendances d'un facteur est comme déconnectée de sa tendance corrélative: la vie pulsionnelle du facteur bascule dans une direction unilatérale. En quoi le clivage unitendant représente un danger pulsionnel. Car la tendance élue n'est pas contre-balancée par une tendance antagonique qui viendrait l'équilibrer: isolée, elle déploie dès lors ses effets psychodynamiques pleins.

Quant aux significations différenciées des clivages factoriels unitendants, positifs ou négatifs (au nombre de seize: deux par facteur), nous pouvons éviter de les développer ici. Le clivage factoriel unitendant se charge en effet des significations propres à la tendance qu'il assume. Ainsi, pour dégager les significations d'un clivage h- ou d'un clivage e+, il suffit de se reférer aux significations des tendances h- ou e+ telles qu'elles ont été formulées dans notre chapitre précédent. Précisons cependant que le caractère dangereux des clivages unitendants peut varier d'après le contenu spécifique de la tendance assumée, et cela malgré leur signification psychodynamique commune. Ainsi un m- est généralement considéré comme plus dangereux qu'un m+; de même en ce qui concerne e- par rapport à e+. Encore que l'appréciation du danger potentiel interne à un clivage factoriel unitendant doive aussi prendre en compte le clivage factoriel corrélatif, nous l'avons déjà indiqué à propos d'un clivage comme s-, dont la signification est différente selon qu'il est accompagné d'un h+, d'un h- ou d'un ho. De même le danger d'un p- est atténué par la présence corrélative d'un k-, alors qu'il est renforcé par la présence d'un ko.

Enfin, pour terminer, signalons que le clivage factoriel unitendant peut être le lieu d'un danger pulsionnel propre, nous voulons parler du danger pulsionnel par surcharge ou tension quantitative, inscrite sous forme de point(s) d'exclamation. Nous l'avons observé tout au long de notre chapitre précédent, dès le moment où la tendance élue s'accentue (!, !!, !!!), la signification du clivage tend à s'infléchir: ainsi h- devient signe, non plus d'une sublimation de l'Eros, mais d'une répression de la libido. C'est aussi dès ce moment que les clivages unitendants risquent de produire les effets psychopathologiques nourris par les tendances qu'ils élisent, ceux-là mêmes que nous avons relevés dans notre chapitre précédent. L'observation d'un clivage unitendant accentué commande donc d'être attentif à une pathologisation possible, encore que, nous y insistons, l'appréciation ultime de la gravité psychopathologique d'une unitendance factorielle accentuée repose en dernière analyse sur une analyse dialectique globale, mettant en jeu toutes les dimensions de la dialectique pulsionnelle.

2. Le clivage nul

De manière générale, le clivage nul (o) indique qu'un besoin n'est pas dynamiquement actif dans la vie pulsionnelle du sujet. Mais pourquoi n'est-il pas actif ? Deux réponses sont possibles, entre lesquelles Szondi oscille. Le besoin est adynamique, 1. soit parce que son énergie, qui s'était accumulée, a été déchargée, en quoi le clivage nul révélerait une décharge pulsionnelle dans une action pulsionnelle, 2. soit parce que, de manière générale, il ne s'accumule pas et donc ne pousse pas à l'action ou à la décharge pulsionnelle : le clivage nul révélerait l'absence ou la faiblesse relative d'un dynamisme pulsionnel. Ainsi le clivage ho peut indiquer que le sujet vient de décharger son besoin érotique dans un acte érotique (acte sexuel, contact corporel intime, masturbation,...) ou inversement que le besoin érotique est le plus souvent adynamique dans la vie pulsionnelle du sujet et dès lors ne le prédispose pas à l'exercice d'activités érotiques.

En conséquence, le clivage nul peut être le lieu de deux formes de danger pulsionnel tout à fait distinctes. Il représentera un danger, soit au titre d'une décharge d'un besoin s'extériorisant en manifestations comportementales (au cas où serait observé par exemple un clivage eo, danger d'un éclatement d'affects brutaux), soit au titre de l'absence d'un besoin dont la présence serait utile, voire indispensable à la santé pulsionnelle (ainsi du besoin k de prise de position vis-à-vis des désirs, dont le clivage ko révèle l'absence).

Mais examinons à présent les significations différenciées des clivages nuls.

Vecteur S

Nous connaissons déjà les significations du clivage ho. Quant au clivage so, il s'interprétera, soit comme décharge du besoin d'activité, soit comme absence relative du même besoin.

Vecteur P

Le clivage eo révèle, soit une décharge paroxysmale des affects brutaux sous forme d'un accès épileptiforme (crise épileptique ou plus généralement équivalent épileptoïde : migraine, asthme,...), soit l'affaiblissement de la censure éthique.

De la même manière, le clivage hyo pourrait être le signe d'une décharge des affects doux à la faveur d'une crise émotionnelle de type hystériforme (cris, pleurs, «tempête de mouvements»,...) ou renvoyer à la faiblesse de la censure morale.

Vecteur Sch

Les clivages nuls du vecteur Sch ne sont pas interprétés en terme de décharge. Ainsi le clivage ko n'est jamais interprété comme effectuation d'un processus d'introjection. En conséquence, le clivage ko indique l'absence de prise de position affirmatrice ou négatrice vis-à-vis des désirs, de même que le clivage po révèle que les désirs sont comme évacués de la «conscience de désir», ou encore que l'investissement désirant du monde fait défaut.

Vecteur C

Le clivage mo signifie, soit la satisfaction momentanée du besoin d'accrochage (par exemple dans la prise orale d'un objet chez le toxicomane alcoolique qui vient de traverser une crise éthylique), soit la faiblesse du même besoin d'accrochage (peut-être parce que le contact s'établit à un niveau infantile régressif, quasi fusionnel, excluant toute tension dynamique).

Enfin le clivage do révèle, soit la décharge du besoin de recherche (par exemple dans la consommation parfois débridée d'un objet nouveau, qui apaise temporairement l'aspiration à un renouvellement des contacts), soit l'absence ou le défaut de tout besoin de recherche.

Mais si deux possibilités extrêmes s'offrent en général à l'interprétation des clivages nuls, une question se pose : pour quelle interprétation opter dans les cas concrets ? Le choix est souvent délicat et difficile. Tout au moins peut-on l'éclairer en différenciant deux situations extrêmes.

Il arrive parfois au clivage nul d'apparaître dans une succession qui l'associe à un clivage unitendant. Dans ce cas, une interprétation en terme de décharge pourra souvent être retenue. Donnons l'exemple modèle d'une succession régulière du h+!! et du ho : le passage du h+!! au ho (suivi d'une recharge de la tendance érotique) nous permet ici de présumer la décharge du besoin érotique dans un acte érotique. Notons cependant qu'une pareille interprétation ne peut être élargie à tous les déroulements qui mènent du clivage unitendant au clivage nul; si certains déroulements de ce type sont aisément traductibles en terme de décharge (ainsi, parmi d'autres, le passage du e- au eo : décharge de la tendance caïnesque dans un acte paroxysmal de nature épileptoïde, ou le passage du m+ ou mo : décharge de la tendance à l'accrochage par prise d'un objet), d'autres par contre le sont plus difficilement. Oserons-nous parler d'une décharge d'amour sublimé ou collectif là où nous observons le passage d'un h- à un ho ? Oserons-nous parler de la décharge d'une tendance au bien ou d'une angoisse de culpabilité (dans un acte de réparation) là où nous observons le passage d'un e+ à un eo ?

Mais il arrive aussi qu'un clivage nul se maintienne de manière stable à l'intérieur du profil. En pareil cas nous pencherons plutôt pour une interprétation en terme de faiblesse ou d'absence. Ainsi, si un ho apparaît 8, 9, voire même 10 fois, nous songerons à la relative faiblesse du besoin érotique dans la vie pulsionnelle du sujet.

Pour nous résumer : deux possibilités extrêmes d'interprétation des clivages nuls, qu'un critère relatif au déroulement pulsionnel sert parfois à départager. Encore que souvent la situation soit ambiguë et mal définie. L'incertitude dans laquelle nous nous trouvons impose alors de ne pas mettre d'accent particulier sur les clivages nuls.

3. *Le clivage ambitendant*

Trois significations possibles sont attribuées au clivage ambitendant : fonctionnant à un niveau prédialectique, il serait l'indice de ce que Szondi appelle la forme ambitendante originaire d'un besoin pulsionnel non encore différencié en tendances antagoniques; inscrit dans la dialectique pulsionnelle, il serait le signe d'une manière proprement ambivalente de résoudre la tension interne au besoin; enfin, surmontant la dialectique pulsionnelle, il serait l'indice d'une intégration supérieure du besoin et de ses deux tendances, réconciliées au-delà de leur opposition.

Mais précisons aussitôt que les trois interprétations ne sont pas à mettre sur le même pied. En effet, la première comme la dernière ne sont invoquées que dans des cas rares et exceptionnels. On peut même se demander si le diagnostic expérimental des pulsions, méthodologiquement fondé sur le principe du clivage des pulsions (puisque, du fait même de son mode d'administration, il exclut inévitablement certaines tendances), est apte à ressaisir un fonctionnement qui se situerait, soit en deçà, soit au delà du clivage des pulsions. Mais il n'en demeure pas moins que, de l'avis de Szondi, certains clivages ambitendants seraient à interpréter en termes de la première ou de la dernière signification. Examinons ces cas.

La première signification concernerait exclusivement les clivages ambitendants du vecteur sexuel, en particulier lorsqu'ils seraient réunis dans la constellation S±±, révélatrice de la forme ambitendante originaire d'une sexualité hermaphrodite et bisexuelle.

Quant à la troisième signification, elle n'est retenue que pour l'interprétation des clivages ambitendants du vecteur Sch (et dans une moindre mesure, des clivages ambitendants du vecteur P), mais à la condition que les clivages k± et p± apparaissent conjointement, demeurent relativement stables à l'intérieur du profil et soient accompagnés de certains clivages vectoriels correlatifs (en particulier de S--). Sch ±± pourrait alors révéler la forme supérieure d'un moi qui arriverait à concilier en lui-même les tendances contradictoires de Sch: nous aurions là l'image du moi Pontifex oppositorum, qui surmonte tous les dilemmes, toutes les oppositions. Cas si rare qu'il est quasiment exclu de le rencontrer dans la pratique. Szondi lui-même n'en cite qu'un seul exemple, celui du « psychohygiéniste », qui n'est rien d'autre que le sien propre (TrD, p. 183)!

Mais la seconde signification est assurément la plus courante, et c'est elle qui sera envisagée en priorité. Confronté aux deux tendances opposées antagoniques d'un besoin, le sujet décide de les assumer. En quoi le clivage ambitendant évite aussi bien le danger inhérent au clivage nul (puisque le besoin est présent au lieu d'être absent) que le danger inhérent au clivage unitendant (puisque les deux tendances sont présentes et donc s'équilibrent l'une l'autre). Mais assumant deux tendances contradictoires, le sujet est aussi la proie d'une tension péniblement ressentie: si le clivage ambitendant est sans doute le moins dangereux de tous les clivages, il est en même temps le plus inconfortable pour le sujet qui le vit. En bref, inscrit dans la logique d'un fonctionnement dialectique des pulsions, le clivage ambitendant a la signification d'un dilemme, qui s'exprime sous la forme d'une alternative et se particularise aisément selon le besoin.

h± ou le dilemme érotique: « Dois-je satisfaire ma libido sous sa forme originaire ou la sublimer? Chercher le plaisir pour lui-même ou l'inscrire dans le contexte d'une liaison amoureuse stable? »

s± ou le dilemme sado-masochiste: « Dois-je agresser l'autre ou m'offrir à lui? Le dominer ou être dominé par lui? »

e± ou le dilemme éthique: « Dois-je m'adonner au mal ou me vouer au bien? »

hy± ou le dilemme moral: « Dois-je montrer mes tendances érotiques ou les cacher? »

k± ou le dilemme dans l'affirmation: « Dois-je assumer ou refuser un désir? Dois-je m'affirmer ou me nier moi-même? »

p± ou le dilemme dans la prise de conscience: « Dois-je me gonfler d'un désir ou l'évacuer de ma conscience? Dois-je me perdre dans l'autre ou me ressaisir moi-même dans mon investissement de la réalité? »

m± ou le dilemme dans l'accrochage: « Dois-je m'accrocher à l'objet ou me détacher de lui? »

d± ou le dilemme dans la recherche: « Dois-je coller à l'ancien objet ou chercher de nouveaux objets? »

b) *Méthodes quantitatives*

Parmi les toutes premières méthodes d'interprétation mises au point par Szondi dès 1947, nous comptons ces méthodes qu'il a lui-même appelées méthodes quantitatives. Par la suite, Szondi devait les opposer aux méthodes dialectiques qui au fil du temps prenaient de plus en plus de poids.

Pour notre part, nous considérons qu'une pareille opposition entre méthodes quantitatives et méthodes dialectiques est peu justifiée. Certes, les méthodes quantitatives sont basées sur des calculs et conduisent à l'établissement d'indices numériques. Mais que mesurent-elles, sinon des clivages pulsionnels, résultant du fonctionnement dialectique des pulsions? Et sur quoi reposerait l'interprétation des clivages ainsi mesurés, sinon sur leur signification dialectique? C'est pourquoi nous avons décidé de réinsérer les méthodes dites quantitatives dans le seul cadre où elles prennent sens, à savoir dans le cadre de la dialectique pulsionnelle.

Nous exposerons ici les méthodes quantitatives qui s'articulent sur la dialectique intrafactorielle, et cela en référence à un profil concret dont nous donnons d'emblée l'ensemble des indices numériques (Tableau V).

C'est ainsi que nous examinerons successivement le quotient de tension de tendances, le pourcentage de réactions symptomatiques, le degré de tension quantitative et enfin la formule pulsionnelle.

1. Le quotient de tension de tendances

Mode de calcul

Nous calculons d'abord, pour chacun des facteurs pulsionnels, la somme des clivages nuls, que nous inscrivons dans la rangée Σo. Puis, par addition des sommes factorielles, nous établissons le nombre total des clivages nuls du profil pulsionnel. Nous procédons de même pour les clivages ambitendants et obtenons ainsi la somme totale des clivages ambitendants du profil ($\Sigma \pm$). Enfin, nous divisons la somme totale des clivages nuls par la somme totale des clivages ambitendants, ce qui nous donne précisément le quotient de tension de tendances. En l'occurrence ici,

$$\frac{\Sigma o}{\Sigma \pm} = \frac{13}{9} = 1{,}44.$$

Interprétation

L'interprétation du quotient de tension de tendances est basée sur la signification générale des clivages nuls et ambitendants.

Le clivage nul est ici considéré comme signe d'une décharge pulsionnelle : il révélerait l'extériorisation comportementale du besoin. Quant au clivage ambitendant, indice d'un dilemme ambivalenciel ou d'une hésitation entre approbation et désapprobation du besoin, il révélerait à l'inverse une inhibition comportementale.

Trois situations plus précises seraient à différencier :

1. les sujets dont le comportement est exagérément inhibé présenteraient un quotient de tension de tendances inférieur à 1 ($\Sigma \pm$ supérieur à Σo), ce que nous observerions notamment chez les obsessionnels et les schizoïdes;

2. un quotient de tension de tendances situé entre 1 et 3 s'inscrirait dans les limites de la normale;

3. enfin, un quotient de tension de tendances qui s'élèverait au-delà de 3,

LA THEORIE DES PULSIONS 91

Tableau V : Profil d'avant-plan
et méthodes quantitatives

Vordergrundprofile (VGP)

Nr.	S h	S s	P e	P hy	Sch k	Sch p	C d	C m		Existenzform	
1	+!	+!!	0	−	0	−	0	−!		2	7
2	+	+	−	−	−!	+	−	0		13	11
3	+!	+	+!	0	−	+	−	−		7	11
4	+!	+	+!	−	−	+!	0	−		7	12
5	+!	+!	+!	−	−	+	0	−		7	11
6	+	+!	−	−	−	+	−	−!		13	7
7	+!	+!	+!	−	0	+	0	−!		7	11
8	+	+!!	+!	−	−	+	−	−		7	3
9	+!	+!	+!	0	−	+!	−	0		13	7
10	+	+!!	+!	0	1	0	0	3			

	Σ 0										
Tend. Sp. Gr.	Σ ±	0	1	2	3	0	5	2	13	Σ 0 = 1,44	
		0	7	0	0	0	0	0	9	Σ ±	
Quant. Sp. Gr.		0	8	2	3	2	5	2		22 Sy % = 27,5 %	
		5	10	0	1	1	0	3		Σ ! = 19	
Dur		2,5		4		0		13		Dur = 42/17 = 2,5	
Moll		0		6		11		0		Moll	
Σ Soz. +		10		7		7		2		Soz. Index 26/59 = 44 %	
Σ Soz. −		15		3		4		11			

I. Trieblinnäus-Verrechnung :

a) Triebformel :

$$\frac{e^{+}_{8}}{d^{o}_{5}; k^{-}_{3}; hy^{-}_{2}; h^{+}_{2}; m^{-}_{2}} \\ h^{+}_{o}\ ;\ s_{o}^{+!}$$

b) Latenzproportionen : $\dfrac{Phy^{-}}{6} : \dfrac{Cm^{-}}{3} : \dfrac{Schp^{+}}{1} : \dfrac{Shs^{+!}}{0}$

c) Triebklasse : Phy^{-}

jusqu'à 5, voire même jusqu'à 10, révélerait un sujet particulièrement excité, dont les tensions pulsionnelles se déchargent sans frein à travers le comportement; c'est ainsi que le quotient de tension de tendances serait particulièrement élevé chez les hystériques, les épileptiques et les maniaco-dépressifs.

Mais le quotient de tension de tendances n'est pas sans appeler une attitude de réserve critique, dans la mesure surtout où il interprète univoquement le clivage nul comme indice d'une décharge, alors même que le clivage nul, nous l'avons vu, s'offre parfois à une autre interprétation.

2. Le pourcentage de réactions symptomatiques

Mode de calcul

Pour chacun des facteurs, nous effectuons la somme des clivages nuls et des clivages ambitendants ($\Sigma o + \Sigma \pm$), que nous inscrivons dans la rangée Tend. Sp. Gr. (Tendenzspannungsgrad: degré de tension de tendances). Nous additionnons les degrés de tension de tendances des huit facteurs pulsionnels et obtenons ainsi le nombre total des clivages nuls et ambitendants du profil. On voit que ce nombre s'élève ici à 22. Il ne nous reste plus dès lors qu'une opération à effectuer: nous multiplions la somme totale des clivages nuls et ambitendants par 100 et la divisons par 80. Nous obtenons ainsi le pourcentage de réactions symptomatiques, calculé selon la formule générale:

$$Sy\% = (\Sigma o + \Sigma \pm) \times \frac{100}{80}$$

Ici en l'occurrence

$$Sy\% = 22 \times \frac{100}{80} = 27,5\%.$$

Notons que le chiffre qui figure au dénominateur de la formule exprime le nombre total de clivages factoriels du profil. Il n'est égal à 80 qu'au cas où le test a été administré 10 fois. Il doit donc être modifié si le test a été administré 9 fois ($8 \times 9 = 72$), 8 fois ($8 \times 8 = 64$),...

Interprétation

On voit immédiatement que le pourcentage de réactions symptomatiques assimile les clivages nuls et ambitendants sous le titre de «réactions symptomatiques». Quel est donc le fondement de cette assimilation?

Et tout d'abord qu'entend Szondi par «symptomatique»? Il semble bien que Szondi identifie les notions de «symptomatique» et de «cliniquement visible»: les facteurs symptomatiques seraient les facteurs qui se manifestent dans la clinique visible d'un cas, par opposition aux facteurs qui agissent à un niveau inconscient et non directement visible. Szondi dira en ce sens que les facteurs où prédominent les clivages nuls régissent des manifestations visibles ou symptômes de nature objective, le besoin déchargé s'extériorisant dans le comportement, alors que les facteurs où prédomine le clivage ambitendant donne lieu à des manifestations cliniques ou symptômes de nature interne, subjective : le besoin s'exprime, non pas au plan d'un comportement externe, mais au plan d'un vécu subjectif, sous la forme d'une tension intérieure.

Ce point élucidé, nous devrions comprendre aussi pourquoi Szondi prétend mesurer le degré de *tension* de tendances d'un facteur via la sommation des clivages nuls et ambivalents qui y apparaissent. Szondi se réfère très clairement ici à la tension intrafactorielle qui résulte de la présence conjointe de deux tendances antagoniques : « sous le nom de tension de tendances, nous désignons la tension pulsionnelle qui naît entre les tendances, génétiquement antagoniques d'un besoin » (DP, p. 67). Mais dès lors, une question se pose : la tension, définie en ces termes, n'est-elle pas propre au clivage ambitendant ? Pourquoi l'élargir au clivage nul, ce qu'effectue concrètement le calcul du « degré de tension de tendances » ? Sur ce point, Szondi fait appel à l'hypothèse d'un cycle pulsionnel qui conduirait naturellement du ± au o : le o s'inscrirait dans le régime de la tension pulsionnelle au titre de sa décharge.

Nous acceptons provisoirement ces significations, sur lesquelles nous aurons à revenir de manière critique, pour signaler que le pourcentage de réactions symptomatiques, situé normalement entre 20 % et 30 %, doit s'interpréter en conjonction avec le quotient de tension de tendances. Le pourcentage de réactions symptomatiques ne nous donne en effet qu'une information encore très vague, sur l'importance prise par les « symptômes » dans la vie d'un sujet, qui demande à être précisée par le quotient de tension de tendances. Ainsi, l'obsessionnel présente en général un Sy % élevé, supérieur à 30 %. Mais quelle forme prennent les symptômes de l'obsessionnel ? Le quotient de tension de tendances, inférieur à 1, nous répond : les symptômes de l'obsessionnel sont surtout « subjectifs ». Autre exemple : le Sy % du maniaco-dépressif est généralement inférieur à 30 %. Cependant, des formes excessives de manifestations symptomatiques ne sont pas exclues. Car le quotient de tension de tendances est généralement très élevé : les symptômes « objectifs » prédominent, et la rareté des clivages ambitendants explique la relative faiblesse du Sy %.

3. *Les degrés de tension quantitative*

Les degrés de tension quantitative se calculent en effectuant la somme des accentuations qui apparaissent à l'intérieur de chaque série factorielle. Nous inscrirons les nombres obtenus dans la rangée Quant. Sp. Gr. (Quantumspannungsgrad ou degré de tension quantitative). Nous pouvons établir aussi la somme totale des accentuations du profil. Ici, $\Sigma! = 19$.

En fait, nous ne disposons pas de critères précis et numériques d'interprétation des degrés de tension quantitative. A ce jour, aucune norme n'a été établie. L'apparente objectivité du chiffre est donc ici de peu d'utilité. Certes, les degrés de tension quantitative attirent notre attention sur les lieux de surcharge ou de tension pulsionnelle exacerbée (par exemple ici, la tendance s+ et accessoirement les tendances h+ et m-). Mais la seule inspection du regard suffit sans doute à obtenir cette information, dont l'interprétation dialectique, nous le savons, doit faire grand cas.

4. La formule pulsionnelle

Mode de calcul

La formule pulsionnelle complète répartit les huit facteurs pulsionnels en trois groupes : 1. le groupe des *facteurs symptomatiques* est composé des facteurs dont le degré de tension de tendances est égal ou supérieur à 6 ; 2. font partie du groupe des facteurs *submanifestes* ou *sublatents,* les facteurs dont le degré de tension de tendances est situé entre 5 et 2 ; 3. enfin, constituent le groupe des facteurs *racines* ou *pathogènes* les facteurs dont le degré de tension de tendances est égal à 1 ou à o.

Concrètement, la formule pulsionnelle s'inscrira sur la feuille de protocole dans le grand rectangle qui figure en haut sous l'expression « Triebformel » (formule pulsionnelle). Les huit facteurs seront inscrits par ordre décroissant de leur degré de tension de tendances, les facteurs symptomatiques en haut, les facteurs submanifestes au centre, les facteurs racines en bas. A côté de l'initiale de chaque facteur, on ajoutera, en-dessous le degré de tension de tendances, au-dessus le clivage dominant.

Ce qui donne bien pour le cas qui nous intéresse :

$$\frac{e_8^{\pm}}{\dfrac{d_5^{o,-}\ ;\ k_3^{-}\ ;\ hy_2^{-}\ ;\ p_2^{+}\ ;\ m_2^{-}}{h_o^{+}\ ;\ s_o^{+!}}}$$

On calcule aussi une formule pulsionnelle abrégée, qui comporte au numérateur le plus important des facteurs symptomatiques, au dénominateur le plus important des facteurs racines. Soit ici :

$$\frac{e_8^{\pm}}{s_o^{+!}}$$

Interprétation et remarques critiques

L'interprétation de la formule pulsionnelle, comme de la plupart des indices dont il est question dans ce paragraphe, est fondée sur les significations générales attribuées aux divers clivages factoriels.

On aura déjà constaté que les facteurs dits symptomatiques sont dominés par les clivages nuls et/ou ambitendants : conformément au principe qui guide aussi l'interprétation du Sy %, ils s'exprimeraient dans les manifestations visibles de la clinique. Coincés entre les facteurs symptomatiques et les facteurs racines, les facteurs submanifestes ou sublatents, dont les clivages sont les plus diversifiés, n'appellent pas de considérations propres. Quant aux facteurs racines, ce sont des facteurs dominés par le clivage unitendant, à savoir par une tendance univoque, régulièrement présente, et ne parvenant guère ni à se satisfaire dans l'action, ni à accéder (sur un mode problématique) à la conscience « intérieure » du sujet (du fait de la rareté et des clivages nuls et des clivages ambitendants). En conséquence, les facteurs racines seraient révélateurs de tendances insatisfaites, dynamisant, de l'inconscient, la vie pulsionnelle du sujet. Articulant alors en une vue unitaire la dialectique des facteurs symptomatiques et des facteurs racines, Szondi dira que les facteurs symptomatiques révèlent les lieux de manifestation d'une maladie, alors que les facteurs racines en révèlent les fondements inconscients cachés, en quel sens ils méritent aussi d'être appelés « pathogènes ». Ainsi, nous référant à la formule pulsionnelle abrégée de notre exemple, nous serons amenés à affirmer que le dynamisme inconscient d'une tendance agressive hypertendue (s + accentué) se dissimule derrière l'ambivalence éthique (e±) qui domine le tableau clinique visible, et en nourrit la production.

Mais que penser de la formule pulsionnelle? A notre sens, l'appréciation doit être nuancée.

Face à un profil pulsionnel, il est certainement utile et fécond de parcourir verticalement les huit facteurs en vue d'y déceler des clivages caractéristiques, ce qu'effectue précisément la formule pulsionnelle. Mais reste à savoir si les modalités de groupement et d'interprétation que privilégie la formule pulsionnelle sont pertinents.

Remarquons d'abord que la formule pulsionnelle met surtout l'accent sur les facteurs caractérisés par la présence régulière d'un clivage dominant (ce que sont souvent, bien que non nécessairement, les facteurs symptomatiques et les facteurs racines). A l'inverse, les facteurs au sein desquels se succèdent des clivages très variables (les facteurs dits submanifestes) sont négligés, alors même qu'ils appelleraient, selon nous, une considération attentive. Nous y reviendrons lorsqu'il sera question des déroulements pulsionnels.

Mais, cette distinction étant présupposée, la formule pulsionnelle pratique une première opération : elle additionne les clivages nuls et les clivages ambitendants et ainsi les assimile les uns aux autres, et cela sous le titre de clivages « symptomatiques ». Mais y a-t-il une signification commune aux clivages nuls et ambitendants qui justifie une pareille assimilation? Et si oui, cette signification commune est-elle celle que Szondi énonce? C'est ici que nous apparaît un des points les plus contestables de la formule pulsionnelle.

A la lumière des significations que sont susceptibles de revêtir les clivages nuls et ambitendants, comment oser encore les qualifier univoquement de symptomatiques? Comment oser attribuer, par exemple, à une succession factorielle de dix clivages nuls la signification d'une manifestation symptomatique, alors même qu'elle signifierait plutôt une absence de manifestation? Néanmoins, il n'est pas exclu que clivages nuls et clivages ambitendants ne partagent une signification fondamentale que nous désignerions volontiers en terme d'un adynamisme, adynamisme par absence pure et simple du besoin dans le cas du clivage nul, adynamisme par blocage du besoin, résultant de l'auto-équilibration de ses deux tendances dans le cas du clivage ambitendant. En quoi alors clivages nuls et clivages ambitendants viendraient comme s'opposer globalement aux clivages unitendants, additionnés et regroupés par la formule pulsionnelle à la faveur d'une seconde opération. Nous touchons sans doute là un des éléments les moins discutables de la formule pulsionnelle, à savoir que les facteurs dominés par un clivage unitendant et basculant par là dans une direction univoque, sont des lieux de dynamisme pulsionnel important auxquels toute interprétation dialectique doit être particulièrement attentive.

Pour nous résumer sur ce point, nous dirons que l'examen précieux et même nécessaire des successions de clivages factoriels appelle des analyses fines et diversifiées, que les critères, souvent grossiers et parfois contestables dans leur univocité, de la formule pulsionnelle ne rendent pas toujours possibles.

Mais, pour terminer, nous devons marquer une dernière limite de la formule pulsionnelle, commune d'ailleurs à tous les modes d'analyse qui demeurent enfermés dans le facteur pulsionnel. La formule pulsionnelle aboutit à couper le clivage factoriel du clivage qui l'accompagne au sein du vecteur et se trouve toujours appelé à nuancer la signification du premier. Ainsi, dans le cas qui nous occupe, les clivages h+ et m- sont coupés, respectivement du clivage s+ et du clivage do. Bref, la formule pulsionnelle ne prend pas en compte la dialectique interfactorielle ou intravectorielle, à laquelle nous devons dès à présent venir.

2. Les clivages vectoriels

a) *Les formes de clivage vectoriel*

Quatre tendances interagissent au sein du vecteur, et la tension qui résulte de leur débat va ici à nouveau se trouver résolue par clivage. En fait, il existe, en tout et pour tout, seize modes de solution de la tension intravectorielle, qui définissent autant de formes de clivage. On a classiquement réparti les seize clivages vectoriels en cinq groupes, que nous allons tout d'abord passer brièvement en revue.

 1. Les clivages unitendants : +o, -o, o+, o-

Une tendance est assumée, les trois autres sont écartées.

 2. Les clivages bitendants : ++, --, +-, -+, o±, ±o

Deux tendances sont assumées, les deux autres sont écartées.

 3. Les clivages tritendants : +±, -±, ±+, ±-

Trois tendances sont assumées, une tendance est écartée.

 4. Le clivage quadritendant : ±±

Les quatre tendances sont assumées, aucune n'est écartée.

 5. La clivage nul ou double nul : oo

Les quatre tendances sont écartées, aucune n'est assumée.
Mais examinons dans le détail les formes de clivage vectoriel.

1. Les clivages unitendants

Nous pouvons transposer ici ce que nous avons déjà dit à propos des clivages factoriels unitendants. Une tendance se présente à l'état isolé et n'est donc pas équilibrée par l'action d'autres tendances du vecteur. En conséquence, comme aime à le dire Szondi, elle tend à un règne illimité sur la vie pulsionnelle (du vecteur): son effet dynamique propre peut se donner libre cours. En quoi le clivage vectoriel unitendant est le lieu d'un danger pulsionnel, qui demande cependant à être nuancé, tout à la fois d'après la nature de la tendance assumée (ainsi un clivage comme Co+ sera considéré comme moins dangereux que le clivage Co-) et d'après le contenu des clivages vectoriels corrélatifs (en particulier d'après le contenu du clivage corrélatif du moi), susceptibles, soit de le limiter, soit de le renforcer davantage. C'est donc ici aussi que la tendance élue risque de produire des effets pathogènes, surtout si elle est accentuée (toujours sous réserve de ce qui se joue dans les autres vecteurs pulsionnels), et cela bien davantage encore qu'en cas de clivage factoriel unitendant. Car l'unitendance factorielle (+ ou -) n'est pas élaborée par l'action éventuellement protectrice du facteur corrélatif, ici tout à fait vide (o) et donc adynamique.

Dans la mesure où le clivage unitendant se charge de la signification propre à la tendance qu'il a élue, il nous suffit à nouveau, pour formuler les significations différenciées des clivages vectoriels unitendants, de nous référer aux données de notre paragraphe A. Nous résumons ces données dans le tableau VI.

2. *Les clivages bitendants*

Les clivages bitendants sont eux-mêmes répartis en trois groupes. De quelle manière ?

Travaillons sur une constellation composée des quatre tendances qui constituent a priori le vecteur :

$$+ \quad +$$
$$- \quad -$$

Nous pouvons tout d'abord opérer une coupe horizontale :

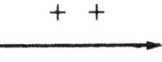

De part et d'autre de la ligne horizontale, nous trouvons : en haut ++, en bas --. Nous avons ainsi les clivages bitendants dits horizontaux.

Mais nous pouvons aussi articuler les tendances, deux par deux, selon une direction diagonale :

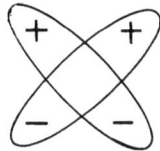

Nous obtenons par là les clivages bitendants appelés diagonaux : +-, -+.

Enfin, nous pouvons décomposer la constellation selon une ligne verticale :

Tableau VI : Significations majeures des clivages vectoriels unitendants.

	S	P	Sch	C
+ o	Dominance de l'érotisme sensuel.	Dominance de la censure éthique.	Introjection totale. Auto-suffisance narcissique. Affirmation introjective des désirs.	Dominance de la recherche d'objets nouveaux.
Avec !	Frustrations libidinales. Tensions sexuelles prégénitales.	Angoisse de culpabilité. Phobie.	Psychopathologie: schizophrénie autistique, perversions, mélancolie.	Recherche toujours relancée et insatisfaite d'un objet perdu.
- o	Dominance de la désérotisation. Sublimation de la sexualité.	Dominance des affects cainesques.	Négation totale ou refoulement. Négation de soi et de ses désirs au bénéfice de la réalité.	Dominance de la conservation d'objets anciens. Caractère anal.
Avec !	Répression de la sexualité.	Danger d'une attaque épileptiforme.	Auto-destruction. Désimagination. Psych.: catatonie.	Rigidité excessive, bloquant toute possibilité de changement objectal.
o +	Dominance de l'activité corporelle.	Dominance des affects doux. Tendance à se montrer.	Inflation totale. Gonflement de soi. Prise de conscience et élaboration imaginaire des désirs jusqu'au délire de grandeurs (Psych.: schizophrénie paranoïde).	Dominance de l'accrochage.
Avec !	Sadisme d'emprise.	Danger d'une crise hystériforme ou d'un acte d'exhibitionnisme sexuel.		Accrochage forcené à un objet perdu (névrose d'acceptation) ou à un objet-ersatz (toxicomanies).
o -	Dominance de la passivité.	Dominance de la censure morale. Tendance à se cacher.	Projection totale. Diffusion participative de soi.	Dominance du détachement. Isolement. Solitude. Contact hypomaniaque.
Avec !	Répression de l'agressivité ou masochisme.	Angoisse sensitive de relations. Penchant à la mythomanie.	Projection des désirs jusqu'au délire de persécution (Psych.: schizophrénie paranoïde).	Détachement de tout objet a priori décevant. Psych.: manie.
	(TrD, p. 100)	(TrD, p. 124)	(TrD, p. 171)	(TrD, p. 200)

Assumées seules, les deux tendances qui figurent, soit à gauche, soit à droite de la ligne verticale, constituent un clivage bitendant dit vertical, dont les deux formes seront: ±o, o±.

Mais discutons à présent la nature et le sens de ces diverses formes de clivage bitendant.

a) Les clivages bitendants horizontaux (alliages)

De tous les clivages bitendants, les clivages horizontaux sont sans doute les moins dangereux. En effet, les deux tendances qu'ils élisent sont généralement de direction opposée, en sorte qu'elles aboutissent à se contrôler l'une l'autre ou à s'auto-équilibrer: le danger pulsionnel représenté par l'une est ainsi rendu inoffensif par la présence et l'action équilibrante de l'autre. Nous observerons cependant que cette règle psychodynamique générale s'applique diversement selon les cas concrets. De plus, si le clivage horizontal est rarement dangereux, il contribue parfois à engendrer une vive tension subjective, qui en rend pénible la prise en charge par l'individu.

Mais examinons dans le détail les clivages horizontaux des quatre vecteurs pulsionnels.

Vecteur S

Image de la *sexualité normale* ou de la sexualité *de l'homme de tous les jours*, qui aspire au contact érotique (h+) et tend à obtenir satisfaction par prise active d'un objet (s+). Grâce à la tendance s+, la tendance h+ ne s'enferme pas dans l'immanence du corps, mais cherche à obtenir la jouissance immanente qu'elle vise par la rencontre et la prise d'un objet extérieur au corps; en sens inverse, grâce à la tendance h+, la dimension agressive de s+ est adoucie.

Des hypertonies quantitatives (S+!+!) pourraient témoigner d'une vive insatisfaction érotique (h+!), ainsi que d'une agressivité réactionnelle à la frustration libidinale (s+!). L'image S++, surchargée d'accentuations, est fréquente dans toutes les formes de la pathologie mentale.

S--

Image de la *sexualité sublimée*, constituée par un alliage de la désexualisation (h-) et du don de soi (s-).

L'absence d'hypertonie quantitative et un haut degré de maturité du moi (cfr les clivages vectoriels du vecteur Sch) renforcent l'interprétation de cette image en terme de sublimation.

Le processus d'auto-équilibration est ici moins évident.

Vecteur P

Le commentaire des clivages horizontaux du vecteur P fait apparaître pour la première fois la possibilité d'une élaboration des tendances de l'un des besoins par les tendances inhérentes au besoin corrélatif. En l'occurence, pour ce qui concerne le vecteur P, les tendances à se montrer (hy+) ou à se cacher (hy-) sont susceptibles d'élaborer les tendances au mal (e-) ou au bien (e+); en direction inverse, la censure éthique (e+) est en état d'élaborer la charge des affects doux (hy+). Mais observons le phénomène sur le cas des deux clivages horizontaux du vecteur P.

P++

La tendance au bien (e+), la bonté, la générosité, sont portées au regard ou exhibées (hy+) : hy+ élabore e+. En direction inverse, le contrôle ou la censure du surmoi (e+) tempère les tendances exhibitionnistes (hy+) : e+ élabore hy+.

Szondi appelle cette image l'image du *flux* ou de la *marée des affects* (Affektflut). Au plan théorique, la dénomination choisie par Szondi n'est pas clairement justifiée, si ce n'est que le clivage P++ inclut la tendance hy+, révélatrice de la dramatisation expressive du désir et des émotions. Mais sans doute, une constatation empirique a-t-elle été déterminante dans le choix de pareille dénomination : selon Szondi, l'image apparaîtrait de manière régulière chez les individus disposés à des « tempêtes de mouvement » hystériformes, et cela surtout lorsqu'elle précède la décharge Poo[1]. A ce titre, elle est partie constitutive du syndrome de l'hystérie, sous-tendant les phénomènes de théâtralisation émotionnelle caractéristiques de cette névrose.

P--

La tendance au mal, l'exigence caïnesque (e-) est cachée ou dissimulée (hy-) : la tendance hy- contrôle et équilibre la tendance e-.

Image, précise encore Szondi, de la *panique* et de l'*oppression intérieure*, voire de la paralysie et de l'immobilisation. Comme si au flux (P++) venait se substituer en P-- le blocage paralysant des affects, la répression oppressante de toute extériorisation émotionnelle, ce que pourrait fonder en partie l'élaboration équilibrante mais inconfortable et pénible de la charge des affects agressifs (e-) par la censure morale (hy-). Mais dénomination justifiée davantage ici à nouveau par une constatation clinique que par une déduction théorique : le clivage P-- se rencontrerait fréquemment chez des sujets souffrant d'une anxiété flottante ou diffuse (non phobiquement cristallisée sur un objet précis et exclusif).

Vecteur Sch

Sch ++

Cette image est appelée image du *narcissisme total*, et cela parce qu'elle conjoint les deux tendances du moi qui connotent le narcissisme. Mais les deux tendances narcissiques élues travaillent aussi dans des directions opposées : la tendance du moi à se gonfler et à s'élargir (p+) vient contrebalancer la tendance du moi à se rétrécir et à s'individualiser (k+) et inversement. La froideur efficace et matérialiste du k+ est réchauffée par la passion désirante du p+ : la capacité de maîtrise rationnelle est ainsi mise au service de la réalisation d'un idéal. Inversement, la passion désirante du p+, qui à elle seule risque de s'entretenir introversivement sans jamais déboucher sur l'action efficace, réussit, grâce à la collaboration du k+, à se traduire en entreprises matérielles et réalistes; ou encore, selon la formule de Deri, la

---

[1] Il faut savoir comme Szondi a opéré originellement pour désigner les clivages vectoriels : il rassemblait en tas les protocoles pulsionnels caractérisés par le même clivage vectoriel et cherchait ensuite, sur la base de l'examen des dossiers cliniques, le point que les sujets testés pouvaient avoir en commun. On comprend dès lors que les dénominations szondiennes doivent être soumises à un réexamen critique.

fusion émotionnelle avec le monde (p+) est corrigée par une constante prise de distance (k+), qui prend régulièrement la forme d'une conceptualisation ou d'une intellectualisation du désir (IS, pp. 248-255).

On comprend dès lors que cette image soit considérée comme l'image d'un moi « développé ». On la rencontre le plus souvent chez les intellectuels adultes. Elle est généralement absente des tableaux psychopathologiques.

| Sch -- |

Nous avons affaire ici au *moi* dit *adapté* ou *discipliné*. D'une part, les désirs sont vécus projectivement, à la manière d'une sollicitation immédiate qui émane du monde, sans aucune forme de prise de conscience (p-). Mais d'autre part, ces mêmes désirs vécus projectivement sont niés (k-), en quoi le moi s'adapte ou se conforme aux exigences de la réalité sociale. Le danger projectif est ainsi équilibré par la fonction négatrice.

Le moi adapté ou discipliné est tout d'abord caractéristique de l'homme de tous les jours, de l'individu terre à terre, vivant dans une réalité plate, non transcendée par un idéal imaginaire ou personnel, tout prêt à s'insérer dans une organisation sociale de masse. Mais en même temps, accompagné d'accentuations, il apparaît dans de nombreuses formes de pathologie non névrotique, là où précisément les désirs pathogènes ne passent pas par le relais de la fonction imaginaire (IS, pp. 229-232). C'est ainsi que nous rencontrons le moi dit adapté dans les troubles psychosomatiques [1] (selon la formule freudienne des névroses actuelles, des tensions désirantes érotiques n'y sont pas prises en charge par l'ordre des représentations psychiques et se déchargent de manière directe dans l'appareil somatique), dans la psychose maniaque (l'agressivité rageuse s'y défoule immédiatement dans une action destructrice exercée sur l'environnement), voire assez paradoxalement dans certaines formes de psychopathie criminelle parmi les plus violentes (les tendances à la violence agressive n'étant pas relayées imaginairement ou symboliquement, dès lors que la censure faiblit momentanément, elles éclatent sous leur forme la plus crue).

Vecteur C

| C++ |

Nous observons à nouveau la conjonction de deux tendances de direction opposée. D'une part, la recherche trouve un aboutissement momentané dans la prise d'un objet, ce qui en tempère le caractère éperdu. D'autre part, l'accrochage à un objet se complète de la recherche d'autres objets. C'est pourquoi aussi on a désigné cette image comme l'image d'un *contact dispersé, double* ou *pluraliste*, ou encore d'un contact bilatéral ou multilatéral : le contact se déploie en investissements dispersés d'une multiplicité d'objets. Cette forme du contact serait fréquente dans les cas de psychopathie et de perversion.

| C-- |

Si deux tendances opposées, au détachement et à la conservation, se

---

[1] Nous renvoyons sur ce point aux remarquables travaux de Jean Melon (1971; 1973; TP, pp. 293-315).

conjuguent bien ici, leur réunion conduit néanmoins à une situation difficile et inconfortable. Car la conservation ou le collage porte sur un objet désinvesti. Ou mieux encore, le détachement par rapport à un objet s'accompagne du refus de partir à la recherche d'un objet nouveau. En quoi se développe une situation de total retrait ou de complet isolement par rapport au monde : le *contact vital* avec la réalité est *rompu* ou *perdu* (Kontaktsperre). Contact malheureux par excellence, estime Szondi.

Notons cependant que cette image ne doit pas être l'objet d'une péjoration unilatérale. Si sa potentialité autistique peut se trouver confirmée dans des configurations d'allure franchement schizomorphe — ainsi dans le syndrome dit du bloc irréel (p- d- m-), qui marquerait l'entrée dans la psychose —, elle peut aussi s'insérer dans un tableau humanisé, et cela lorsqu'elle s'accompagne d'autres signes de sublimation, tels un clivage S-- et un niveau élevé de développement du moi. Dans ce dernier cas, le renoncement à une vie de contact heureuse prend la signification d'un auto-sacrifice au service d'une fin humanitaire.

b) Les clivages bitendants diagonaux

Dans le clivage diagonal, à l'opposé de ce qui se déroule dans le clivage horizontal, les deux tendances élues travaillent dans la même direction, de sorte que, au lieu de se contrarier et par là de s'équilibrer, elles tendent à se confirmer et donc à se renforcer l'une l'autre. Ou encore, autre formulation générale : dans le clivage diagonal, l'une des deux directions internes au vecteur s'isole, écartant une seconde direction opposée, et en conséquence se développe à l'état pur, sans aucun contrepoids. D'où le caractère réputé dangereux des clivages diagonaux. Encore que, nous le verrons, la règle psychodynamique de la confirmation mutuelle des tendances s'applique diversement selon les vecteurs, de même que le caractère dangereux des configurations diagonales varie d'une configuration à l'autre.

Vecteur S

Une division s'instaurerait ici entre une direction féminine (S+-) et une direction masculine (S-+) de la sexualité. A telle enseigne que la présence de ces images pourrait être l'indice de tendances homosexuelles.

| S +- |

Image de l'*érotisme passif*.

L'érotisation du corps se conjoint au refus de l'activité. Le plaisir sensuel tend à s'obtenir dans l'offrande passive du corps.

| S -+ |

Image de la *virilité agressive*.

Le corps sensuel, érotique, est désinvesti, au bénéfice exclusif d'un rapport corporel actif, rude et agressif, avec le monde. Dans certains cas rares d'humanisme militant, l'activité est mise au service d'une cause humanitaire (en quel sens Szondi parle de sado-humanisme ou de sadisme culturel). Ou encore, l'agressivité s'exerce dans un contexte socialisé.

On le voit, les clivages diagonaux du vecteur S opposent un être doux et passif, tendre et soumissif, soucieux de cultiver l'immanence sensuelle de son corps, à un être rude et actif, brusque et agressif, négligeant dans son corps ce qui en ferait un vecteur de sollicitation érotique. Nous reconnaîtrons là assurément ce qui dans notre culture et ses représentations dominantes correspond à la féminité d'une part, à la masculinité d'autre part. En ce sens, l'homme qui assumerait un clivage S+- passera aisément pour efféminé, alors que la femme qui se constituerait sur le modèle du clivage S-+ sera volontiers tenue pour une femme virile. Mais devrait-on en conclure que le premier ou la seconde opère aussi un choix d'objet homosexuel? Nous n'en voyons pas la nécessité. Les clivages diagonaux du vecteur S qualifient deux modes d'être sexuels, l'un à tendance passive, l'autre à orientation active, qui peuvent être vécus aussi bien par l'homme que par la femme, et cela dans des relations hétérosexuelles aussi bien qu'homosexuelles. D'ailleurs, de l'aveu de Szondi lui-même, les indices d'un choix d'objet homosexuel doivent davantage être cherchés du côté du vecteur du moi. Nous y reviendrons.

Vecteur P

Le vecteur se trouve clairement partagé entre deux directions, entre une vie affective étroitement contrôlée par les censures éthique et morale d'une part, entre une vie affective libérée de toute censure d'autre part.

| P +- |

Image du *doux Abel*.

Les deux tendances élues révèlent le contrôle sur la vie affective: contrôle exercé sur les affects brutaux et leur expression par la censure éthique (e+), contrôle exercé sur les affects fins et leur expression par la censure morale (hy-). Il s'agit là en conséquence d'un clivage diagonal peu dangereux, connotant un effort d'humanisation des pulsions. Toutefois, lorsqu'il est accentué, il est l'indice d'un contrôle trop rigide des affects, souvent mis au service d'une défense névrotique contre les tensions pulsionnelles opérant dans les vecteurs S ou C.

| P -+ |

Image du *Caïn pur*.

A l'inverse, les deux tendances élues révèlent l'absence de tout contrôle exercé sur la vie affective. Les affects caïnesques s'accumulent en même temps que les tendances érotiques sont portées au regard. Ou encore, selon le principe d'une interprétation corrélative, les affects caïnesques accumulés tendent à être portés au regard. La malignité et l'impudence se substituent à la bonté et à la discrétion délicate.

Vecteur Sch

Le renforcement mutuel des tendances apparaît ici moins clairement, de même que le clivage de la vie pulsionnelle en deux directions unilatérales, encore que certains aient parlé, pour désigner les deux clivages diagonaux du vecteur Sch, d'un axe psychotique du moi (Sch +-) d'une part, d'un axe névrotique du moi (Sch-+) d'autre part (TP, p. 144).

| Sch +- |

Image de l'*autisme* ou du moi autistique indiscipliné.

Les désirs sont tout à la fois projetés et introjectés (introprojection). Selon une formulation dialectique: le moi introjecte (k+) un objet inconsciemment structuré d'après ses désirs (p-) ou encore: il est lui-même (k+) cet objet dans lequel il transpose projectivement ses désirs (p-), à la manière par exemple dont l'enfant, à l'époque d'efflorescence du jeu symbolique, s'identifie à des personnages qu'il a formés du matériau de ses désirs, est le roi, la reine, l'éléphant, le lion,... (IS, p. 217).

Ce clivage se rencontre essentiellement dans des formes de pathologie psychotique. Citons à titre paradigmatique:

- la psychose mélancolique.

Selon la formule szondienne inspirée de Freud, le mélancolique : 1. vit une relation désirante à un objet, marquée du sceau de l'ambivalence haineuse, et cela en-deçà de toute prise de conscience (p-) (le mélancolique ignore tout, disait Freud, de ce qu'il a perdu et hait) ; 2. introjecte cet objet (k+), en telle sorte qu'il vit sa relation désirante à l'objet comme relation à lui-même (en conséquence, se hait lui-même).

- la psychose paranoïaque.

A la différence du schizophrène paranoïde en phase de délire des grandeurs (Scho+!!), qui se gonfle imaginairement d'un personnage, le paranoïaque quitterait le registre de l'identification fantasmatique coupée du réel (p+), pour produire une identification «réaliste» (k+): plutôt que de se prendre fantasmatiquement pour un personnage, il incarnerait le personnage sur lequel il a projeté inconsciemment ses désirs, et cela dans un rapport effectif au réel (selon les modalités du rapport au monde caractéristique de la fonction k+).

Sch -+

Image de l'*inhibition* ou du moi inhibé.

A un premier niveau, ce clivage du moi apparaît comme conflictuel et nous oblige donc à abandonner notre principe d'une confirmation mutuelle des tendances. Car les deux tendances élues entrent ici en conflit. Le moi nie (k-) un désir dont par ailleurs il se gonfle (p+); ou encore, le moi oppose à sa volonté de tout être l'exigence de réalité. Et dans la mesure où le désir parvient à la conscience (p+), le moi vit le conflit sous la forme d'une tension subjectivement ressentie entre ses ambitions et la réalité. A cet égard, le terme d'inhibition est particulièrement adéquat à qualifier l'état d'un moi qui se sent incapable de réaliser, voire se refuse à réaliser, sous la pression de forces internes, certaines ambitions ou certains désirs que néanmoins il éprouve vivement.

Mais à un autre niveau, les deux fonctions constitutives de cette image se complètent. Combinant la négation (en terme freudien, le refoulement) et l'élaboration imaginaire du désir (la transposition indirecte et voilée du désir dans l'ordre des représentations psychiques), ce clivage dessine le tableau d'un moi foncièrement névrotique.

Vecteur C

Le renforcement mutuel des tendances et la polarisation univoque de la vie pulsionnelle sont ici particulièrement nets.

C-+

Image du *contact fidèle* ou de la fidélité dans le contact. L'accrochage à l'objet est renforcé par la conservation et la rétention durable de l'objet.

Contrairement à notre principe général, cette image est généralement considérée comme peu dangereuse. Encore qu'elle dénote, surtout si elle est accentuée, une trop forte exclusivité du contact, qui risque de compromettre un travail de deuil.

Ajoutons encore que Szondi définit cette image comme image du contact incestueux. Mais à notre sens, cette interprétation doit être évitée dans ce qu'elle pourrait avoir de systématique. Car elle associe trop univoquement un contenu précis (l'objet incestueux, père ou mère) à un mode de fonctionnement formel, qui doit être conçu dans toute sa généralité. A ce propos, Deri écrit très justement: «cette image n'implique pas nécessairement un attachement clair à l'un des deux parents, mais signifie que quelque chose (une personne, une idée ou une chose) est investi avec la même intensité que l'a été le premier objet principal de la libido» (IS, p. 147).

$\boxed{C+-}$

Image du *contact infidèle* ou de l'infidélité dans le contact. La recherche de nouveaux objets vient appuyer le détachement pour connoter une incapacité de s'attacher durablement à quelqu'objet que ce soit. Situation de contact assez dangereuse, mais sans doute moins malheureuse que la situation révélée par le clivage C--. Car la recherche de nouveaux objets, toujours insatisfaite il est vrai, vient ici assurer une perpétuelle diversion à cet isolement dans lequel le clivage C-- risque d'enfermer.

c) Les clivages bitendants verticaux

Le clivage vertical assume un besoin complet avec ses deux tendances et écarte le besoin corrélatif. Il en résulte ce que Szondi appelle l'isolation du besoin: l'un des deux besoins constitutifs du vecteur se trouve isolé de son besoin corrélatif. Autre conséquence du clivage vertical: le vecteur est occupé par un besoin ambitendant. En telle sorte que la formulation spécifique des divers clivages verticaux est simple: chaque fois, le doute ou le dilemme connoté par le clivage factoriel ambitendant élu domine la vie du vecteur. Ainsi:

Vecteur S

La vie sexuelle est dominée, soit par le dilemme érotique (S±o), soit par le dilemme sado-masochiste (So±).

Vecteur P

La vie affective est dominée, soit par le dilemme éthique (P±o), soit par le dilemme moral (Po±).

A propos du clivage Po±, Szondi précise qu'il donne lieu cliniquement à des plaintes ou lamentations hystériformes. Pour notre part, nous tendons à voir dans ce dernier énoncé un résultat de la recherche empirique, dont le fondement théorique n'est pas clair.

Vecteur C

La vie du contact est dominée, soit par le dilemme dans la recherche (C±o), soit par le dilemme dans l'accrochage, lui-même souvent accompagné de tristesse et d'humeur dépressive (Co±).

Mais le clivage vertical est aussi appelé clivage compulsif. Dans cette dénomination, la constatation empirique est sans doute intervenue pour une part importante. En effet, là où apparaît un nombre important de clivages verticaux, il est courant d'observer aussi des phénomènes compulsifs dans la symptomatologie clinique. En particulier, la névrose obsessionnelle, dont le tableau clinique est précisément dominé par la compulsion, se caractérise à l'état pur par une association de quatre clivages verticaux (selon Szondi: ± o ± o ± o o ±). Ici toutefois, le fondement théorique est quasi évident. Car qu'est-ce que la compulsion, sinon, selon la définition la plus classique, une tendance incoercible à poser un acte, à concevoir une pensée, à laquelle s'oppose de manière tout aussi contrainte une volonté contraire ? Bref, n'est-ce point par excellence un phénomène de doute ou de dilemme, la mise en scène d'une ambivalence, qu'elle soit érotique (S±o) ou haineuse (P±o) ? Il reste cependant que de tous les clivages verticaux, un clivage particulier serait à dégager au titre de clivage compulsif par excellence, nous voulons parler du clivage Sch±o. Il nous faut, pour terminer, réserver une place à part aux clivages verticaux du moi.

Sch ±o

Deux dénominations qualifient traditionnellement cette image.

Il s'agirait tout d'abord du *moi compulsif* obsessionnel, dont Szondi a tenté de démontrer l'affinité avec la névrose obsessionnelle en y reconnaissant un processus d'intro-négation (k±). Car, sous des modalités qui peuvent être diverses, l'obsessionnel affirme et nie tout à la fois.

Ainsi, il peut affirmer et nier tout à la fois une même motion pulsionnelle, ce qu'il met en scène dans un acte symptomatique à deux temps, le premier acte donnant libre cours à la pulsion, le second acte venant contredire et annuler le premier (selon le processus défensif de l'annulation rétroactive). Ou encore, confronté à des ambitendances ou à des couples de tendances opposées (par exemple e±), l'obsessionnel peut se défendre, d'une part en niant (k-) l'une des tendances (e- : la haine, la cruauté, ...), d'autre part en introjectant et incorporant dans son caractère l'autre tendance (e+ : la bonté, la pitié, ...), au titre d'une formation réactionnelle (k+).

Mais la même image est aussi définie comme image du *moi masculin* ou viril. A tel point que l'homosexualité féminine se caractériserait par les deux clivages S-+ et Sch±o : l'homosexuelle féminine vraie assumerait, outre une sexualité virile agressive, un idéal du moi masculin, qui la conduirait à élire la femme comme objet sexuel. Pour notre part, nous croyons qu'il est difficile de légitimer cette dernière dénomination, si ce n'est au nom d'une caractérologie culturellement déterminée. Car il est vrai que le facteur k, qui ici domine seul et à l'état complet le tableau, est gros de tous les traits caractériels qui, dans notre culture, sont attribués aux hommes (la positivité, la rationalité, la froideur matérialiste, etc.).

Sch o±

De nouveau, deux dénominations.

D'une part, nous avons affaire à l'image du *moi abandonné*. Nouveau cas, semble-t-il, où la connaissance empirique a précédé de loin la compréhension théorique (IS, p. 182). En effet, on a constaté au départ que les individus traversant une crise dans la relation à leur plus important objet d'amour se caractérisaient souvent par le clivage Scho±. D'où l'on a pu conclure : « la personne qui manifeste le p± se sent abandonnée par l'objet de son amour » (IS, p. 182). Encore fallait-il en un second temps chercher à comprendre la liaison entre le sentiment d'abandon et la fonction pulsionnelle p±. Il semble que la liaison puisse se concevoir en deux sens divergents, mais nullement exclusifs l'un de l'autre. D'une part, la crise dans la relation à l'objet, laissant planer la menace d'un abandon ou d'une perte, pourrait susciter dans le moi la prise de conscience d'un désir (p+) vécu d'abord sur un mode participatif (p-), à l'époque où la relation à l'objet était sans problème. Ainsi que l'écrit Deri : « Il paraît logique qu'en temps de crise, lorsque la fusion dans un objet d'amour rencontre des difficultés dans la réalité, le besoin lui-même soit ressenti de manière plus aiguë » (IS, pp. 182-183). Inversement, tout mouvement de prise de conscience de soi ou de reprise de soi (p+) sur fond d'un état initial de fusion participative (p-) n'est-il pas apte à éveiller le sentiment que l'autre, avec lequel je me confondais jusqu'alors, se retire de moi, me fait défaut, bref m'abandonne ?

Mais la même image est aussi considérée comme l'image du *moi féminin*. Nous devrions répéter ici mot pour mot ce que nous avions déjà dit à propos de l'interprétation du clivage Sch±o comme indice d'un moi masculin. Seule une caractérologie discutable, parce qu'idéologiquement marquée, paraît justifier l'interprétation. Car vivre sur le mode prévalent de la fonction p, c'est bien vivre sur le mode de ce que notre culture tient pour féminin (l'intuition, le sentiment, la passion enflammée, etc.). Mais Szondi veut dire bien davantage. Selon lui, assumer le clivage Scho± équivaut à assumer un idéal du moi féminin, à vouloir être femme. En conséquence, l'homosexualité masculine vraie serait caractérisée par les deux clivages S+- et Scho±.

3. *Les clivages tritendants*

Les clivages tritendants comptent parmi les plus complexes. Aussi s'offrent-ils à de multiples possibilités d'interprétation. En vue de mettre de l'ordre dans ces dernières, nous proposons d'en différencier deux : (a) une interprétation en fonction des tendances présentes ; (b) une interprétation en fonction de la tendance absente.

a) L'interprétation des clivages tritendants en fonction des tendances présentes

Le principe consiste ici à interpréter le clivage tritendant en terme d'une dialectique entre un groupe de deux tendances d'une part et la troisième tendance isolée d'autre part. Mais on devine aussitôt que les deux tendances groupées peuvent être : 1. soit les tendances qui résultent du clivage vertical (±) ; 2. soit les tendances qui résultent du clivage diagonal (+- ou -+) ; 3. soit encore les tendances qui résultent du clivage horizontal (+ + ou --). En sorte que cette première possibilité d'interprétation se décompose elle-même en trois formes particulières, dont nous dresserons ci-après l'éventail exhaustif sur la base de quatre exemples appartenant chacun à l'un des quatre types de clivage tritendant.

		S + ±	P - ±	Sch ± +	C ± -
Formes	1.	h+ ↔ s±	e- ↔ hy±	k±·↔ p+	d± ↔ m-
de	2.	S+- ↔ s+	P-+ ↔ hy-	Sch-+ ↔ k+	C+- ↔ d-
décomposition	3.	S++ ↔ s-	P-- ↔ hy+	Sch++ ↔ k-	C-- ↔ d+

Mais examinons dans le détail la signification psychodynamique générale de ces trois formes d'interprétation, qui, nous le verrons, doit dans bien des cas être nuancée, voire même renversée.

1. ± contre + ou -

Le doute ambivalenciel protège contre le danger représenté par le clivage factoriel unitendant. En d'autres termes, une défense s'exerce du clivage factoriel ambitendant ± sur le clivage factoriel unitendant + ou -. Exemples :

Sch±-   La compulsion (k±) protège contre le danger de la projection (p-).
P-±   Le dilemme moral (hy±) protège contre le danger des tendances caïnesques (e-).

Mais il arrive que la relation doive être renversée. En ce cas, c'est le clivage factoriel unitendant qui élabore l'ambivalence et protège contre elle, en particulier lorsque le clivage factoriel unitendant est l'indice d'un mode d'être défensif. Exemples :

P±-   Le Caïn douteur (±) se cache (hy-), le dilemme éthique (e±) se dissimule (hy-) : le hy- élabore le e±.
Sch-±   Le moi nie (k-) l'abandon (p±) ou se refuse à accepter (k-) la féminité (p±) : le k- élabore le p±.

2. + ou - contre +- ou -+

Le danger du clivage diagonal est adouci par la présence d'une tendance modératrice. Exemple :

P-±   Le Caïn pur (P-+) se dissimule (hy-) ; le danger du Caïn est ainsi modéré par la tendance à se cacher.

Mais à nouveau, la relation peut s'inverser dans certains cas, et c'est alors le clivage diagonal qui protège contre la tendance isolée, elle-même lieu d'un fort danger potentiel. Exemple :

Sch-±   Le moi inhibe (Sch-+) un désir projeté (p-) ; le clivage diagonal protège contre une tendance dangereuse.

3. ++ ou -- contre + ou -

Le clivage horizontal peu dangereux est perturbé par la tendance isolée. Exemple :

S±-   La sexualité sublimée (S--) est perturbée par la tendance érotique (h+) ; la sublimation n'est pas entièrement accomplie.

Mais il arrive aussi que la relation se renverse, précisément dans les cas où les clivages horizontaux sont eux-mêmes dangereux. Exemple :

C-±   La tendance à l'accrochage (m+) modère le danger de la perte totale du contact (C--).

Mais que dire en général, quelles que soient les formes particulières de leur décomposition, du caractère dangereux des modes de clivages tritendants ? A cette question, on peut répondre que les modes de clivages tritendants, interprétés en fonction des tendances présentes, sont relativement peu dangereux, et cela dans la mesure où la force qui tendrait à faire basculer la vie pulsionnelle dans une direction unilatérale est toujours contrecarrée par une force antagoniste. Toutefois, les clivages tritendants sont toujours aussi corrélatifs d'une situation de dilemme aigu et donc difficile à vivre pour le sujet.

b) L'interprétation des clivages tritendants en fonction de la tendance absente

La tritendance est un mode de clivage qui assume toutes les tendances du vecteur à l'exception d'une seule. Il est donc toujours possible de polariser l'interprétation, non sur les tendances présentes, mais sur la tendance qui fait défaut et par là révèle un danger d'autant plus grand qu'elle est elle-même importante pour la préservation de la santé pulsionnelle.

A vrai dire, cette interprétation, Szondi l'a surtout développée à propos du clivage Sch-±, dont la signification majeure de moi de la *dépersonnalisation* ou de l'*aliénation* est précisément fondée sur l'absence de la fonction k+. On sait en effet que la tendance k+ donne au moi le sentiment de sa personnalité par rapport à un monde extérieur perçu comme distinct de lui-même. La personne à qui elle fait défaut perdrait donc les points de repère qui lui permettent de se différencier et du même coup perdrait son rapport à la réalité; elle deviendrait étrangère à elle-même et au monde (s'aliénerait).

Nous venons donc de voir quelles sont les diverses possibilités d'interprétation d'un clivage tritendant. Nous pourrions à présent passer systématiquement en revue les seize tritendances vectorielles (quatre tritendances par vecteur). Mais nous estimons que les indications et les exemples déjà fournis suffisent pour que chacun s'essaye avec succès à en dégager lui-même les multiples significations. Toutefois il nous importe d'apporter encore deux compléments. Tout d'abord de développer plus complètement un exemple qui nous fera percevoir plus concrètement les problèmes soulevés par l'interprétation des tritendances. Ensuite, de dire un mot de trois clivages tritendants dont nous n'avons pas parlé jusqu'ici et qui ont reçu une interprétation tout à fait particulière.

Un exemple développé: le clivage tritendant C-±

Analyse

a) Selon les tendances présentes

a-1. Selon le clivage vertical: d-/m±
 La personne colle à un objet ancien, mais s'interroge: vais-je continuer à m'accrocher à lui ou vais-je m'en détacher?
 (La protection assurée par le m± contre le d- n'est pas claire.)

a-2. Selon le clivage diagonal: C-+/m-
 La personne est accrochée à un objet ancien qu'elle tend à retenir, mais en même temps doute de son accrochage et esquisse un mouvement de détachement.
 (L'exclusivité du contact est modérée par le désaccrochage, ou inversement la fidélité protège contre le détachement.)

a-3. Selon le clivage horizontal: C--/m+
La personne tend à couper tout contact à l'objet et à s'isoler, sans qu'elle ait encore tout à fait renoncé à l'accrochage.
(Le danger de la perte du contact est tempéré par l'accrochage.)

b) *Selon la tendance absente: absence de d+*
La personne ne part pas à la recherche d'un nouvel objet.

Commentaires

L'analyse des multiples significations du clivage C-± nous aide à soulever une question que le lecteur n'a sans doute pas manqué de se poser: pour quelle signification opter dans tel ou tel cas? On voit en réalité à la lumière de notre exemple que les diverses interprétations ne sont pas mutuellement exclusives. Ainsi, les interprétations a-1. et a-2. sont pratiquement identiques. Néanmoins les accentuations peuvent être différentes. Nous contrasterions volontiers ici les interprétations a-1. et a-2. et l'interprétation a-3. Allons-nous être frappé par ce que le clivage contient de contact fidèle, d'attachement durable à un objet, ou bien par ce qu'il charrie d'une perte de contact? En d'autres termes, avons-nous affaire à un sujet qui commence à douter d'un attachement ancien ou à un sujet quasiment enfermé dans une situation d'isolement que seules quelques traces d'accrochage viennent encore tempérer? Là est sans doute la véritable option interprétative. Encore que la divergence ne soit pas absolue. Le risque ne serait-il pas que ce sujet, accomplissant le détachement (m-), se retrouve seul, sans appui (C--), d'autant plus qu'il ne fait pas mine de partir à la recherche (absence de d+)? Mais l'interprétation ne pourra progresser et l'alternative ne pourra être tranchée que si nous insérons le clivage momentané dans une dialectique plus vaste et en particulier à l'intérieur d'un déroulement pulsionnel. Car il est à peu près exclu que le sujet se maintienne de bout en bout dans le seul clivage C-±. En sorte que nous pourrons trouver confirmation de l'une ou l'autre de nos deux directions interprétatives selon que les autres clivages vectoriels du contact accentuent le pôle C-+ ou le pôle C--.

Trois clivages tritendants particuliers

C+±

Image du *contact dépressif* mélancolique.

La confiance basale dans l'objet de tenue est ébranlée (m±). Dans cet état d'insécurité et de doute ambivalenciel, s'engage un mouvement de recherche d'un objet-ersatz substitutif (d+), nécessairement décevant parce que toujours inadéquat à remplacer l'objet primitif.

Sch ±-

Image du *moi fugueur* ou du moi paroxysmal.

L'observation empirique aurait vérifié la corrélation du clivage Sch±- et d'une tendance clinique (souvent déchargée sur un mode explosif ou paroxysmal) à la fugue, au vagabondage, au changement de lieu, de résidence, de travail professionnel...
Resterait cependant à articuler la constatation clinique et la signification théorique du clivage. Pour sa part, Szondi privilégie le découpage vertical: le moi se protègerait contre la projection et la fusion participative (p-) par une activité compulsive (k±). Mais va-t-il de soi que la compulsion doive se manifester ici comme une «compulsion irrésistible à quitter le lieu de résidence, à vagabonder ou à voyager» (TrD, p. 163)? Quant à Deri, elle opte

pour une décomposition diagonale. Des désirs autistiques (Sch+-) se heurteraient aux limitations de la réalité (k-). Pour se délivrer de la tension liée à un tel conflit, le moi se livrerait alors à une activité ininterrompue, jamais relâchée, désordonnée et constamment variée (IS, pp. 222-223).

Mais n'a-t-on pas à nouveau cristallisé un mode de fonctionnement formel général autour d'un contenu trop précis (la fugue) ? Comme il est sans doute vrai aussi du clivage :

| Sch ±+ |

L'obligation est faite au chercheur de dériver un contenu empirique qui résulte de l'observation clinique (la *compulsion au travail*, travail ménager, travail intellectuel, travail professionnel,...) du jeu des trois fonctions théoriques qui constituent le clivage. Plusieurs voies s'offrent. La partition verticale aurait notre préférence : l'idéal inflatif d'être (p+) est élaboré par les deux processus du facteur k— il est partiellement introjecté, transmué en un idéal réaliste qui trouve à s'incarner dans un rapport positif ou fonctionnel à la réalité (k+), mais aussi partiellement nié, limité, réfréné (k-). Au même titre que la configuration Sch++, il s'agirait de l'image d'un moi développé, souvent rencontrée chez des intellectuels productifs (plus efficaces encore que les personnes chez qui prédomine le clivage Sch++, car capables de renoncer à une part de leurs ambitions), dont le travail créateur conserve toutefois une note compulsive d'être exécuté dans l'atmosphère d'un perpétuel dilemme entre l'affirmation et la négation.

4. Le clivage quadritendant

Les significations fondamentales du clivage quadritendant recoupent les trois grands modes d'interprétation du clivage factoriel ambitendant. La quadritendance s'interprétera en effet en termes d'une indifférenciation, ou d'une ambivalence proprement dite, ou encore d'une intégration.

a) L'indifférenciation pourrait qualifier dans certains cas le clivage S±±, image de la bisexualité originaire qui précéderait toute forme de structuration différenciée de la sexualité.

b) Le plus souvent, le clivage quadritendant sera interprété comme l'indice d'une maximisation de tous les dilemmes internes à un vecteur. Ainsi :
- le clivage C±± maximise les dilemmes du contact : le dilemme de la recherche (d±) et de l'accrochage (m±), le dilemme de la fidélité (C-+) et de l'infidélité (C+-), le dilemme de la fermeture du contact (C--) et de son ouverture multilatérale (C++);
- le clivage S±± condense tous les dilemmes de la sexualité : le dilemme de l'immanence sensuelle (h±) et de la transcendance active (s±), de la tendresse et de l'agression (h± contre s±), le dilemme de la masculinité (S-+) et de la féminité (S+-), le dilemme de l'adhésion positive à la sexualité (S++) et de sa négation sublimante (S--);
- le clivage P±± maximise les dilemmes de la vie affective : le dilemme des affects brutaux (e±) et des affects doux (hy±), le dilemme du Caïn (P-+) et de l'Abel (P+-), le dilemme du flux des affects (P++) et de leur blocage (P--).

c) Au cas où seraient présents de manière particulièrement nette et convergente d'autres signes importants de sublimation, les clivages quadritendants du centre pulsionnel (P± ±, Sch± ±) pourraient être interprétés comme signes d'une intégration réconciliatrice, soit des tendances de la vie affective, soit des tendances du moi.

Notons enfin que la constellation Sch± ± pourrait aussi signifier la mobilisation panique de toutes ses défenses par un moi qui pressent une catastrophe ou un danger imminent (dans la phobie, ou dans l'épilepsie à l'approche de la crise) ou s'organise en vue de liquider un choc ou un traumatisme (dans la névrose traumatique en particulier).

5. *Le clivage nul ou double nul*

Comme la signification du clivage factoriel nul, l'interprétation du clivage vectoriel nul ou double nul (oo) oscille entre deux pôles extrêmes :

a) la décharge temporaire d'une pulsion dans une action pulsionnelle. Ainsi,

Soo : décharge de la sexualité dans un acte sexuel (hétérosexuel, homosexuel, masturbatoire,...);
Poo : décharge affective dans une crise paroxysmale épileptiforme ou hystériforme;
Coo : satisfaction infantile et régressive du contact.

b) l'absence durable d'une pulsion généralement adynamique. Ainsi,

Soo : faiblesse de la sexualité;
Poo : absence de toute censure éthico-morale;
Schoo : défaut d'élaboration des besoins et dangers pulsionnels par un moi inconsistant, changeant, fluide, « polyplastique »;
Coo : annulation de la vie de contact.

Pointons cependant l'interprétation d'un clivage double nul qui n'est à proprement parler assimilable à aucun des deux pôles que nous venons de différencier. En effet, le clivage Schoo peut aussi connoter un effacement temporaire du moi, sans qu'il soit légitime de parler vraiment d'une décharge de l'énergie du moi dans une action pulsionnelle. Ainsi, dans l'épilepsie, le moi, à la faveur d'un passage brusque du Sch± ± au Schoo, s'anéantirait provisoirement, en telle sorte que les affects brutaux pourraient alors se manifester et se décharger à l'état brut dans la crise épileptique.

b) *Méthodes quantitatives*

1. *Les classes pulsionnelles*

De toutes les méthodes quantitatives congéniales à la dialectique intravectorielle, la plus célèbre s'organise autour de la classe pulsionnelle. Toutefois, elle comporte aussi, en-deçà : le calcul des proportions de latence, au-delà : le recours au Linné des pulsions.

a) *Les proportions de latence*

Mode de calcul

Nous considérons chaque vecteur en particulier, et soustrayons son degré de tension de tendances le moins élevé de son degré de tension de tendances le plus élevé. Ensuite, nous inscrivons, d'après leurs initiales, les quatre vecteurs les uns à la suite des autres, et cela par ordre décroissant de leur différence de tension intravectorielle. Puis nous traçons, sous l'initiale des vecteurs, une ligne horizontale, en dessous de laquelle nous indiquons le chiffre correspondant à la différence de leurs degrés de tension de tendances. Enfin, à côté de l'initiale du vecteur, nous inscrivons son facteur au degré de tension de tendances le plus bas, et à droite de ce facteur son mode de clivage dominant (à condition qu'il en ait un).

Considérons notre profil de référence (p. 91).

Nous obtenons bien pour ce qui concerne les proportions de latence :

$$\frac{\text{Phy-}}{6} \; ; \; \frac{\text{Cm-}}{3} \; ; \; \frac{\text{Schp+}}{1} \; ; \; \frac{\text{Shs+!}}{0}$$

Mode d'interprétation

On le voit, le calcul des proportions de latence est fondé sur un critère relevant d'une dialectique interfactorielle ou intravectorielle. La méthode des proportions de latence aboutit à distinguer, d'une part les vecteurs à proportion de latence élevée, dans lesquels l'un des facteurs est, selon le langage de la formule pulsionnelle, symptomatique (y prédomine le o ou le ±) alors que le second est un facteur racine (y prédomine le + ou le -), d'autre part les vecteurs à proportion de latence basse, dans lesquels les deux facteurs sont soit symptomatiques (o±, ±o, oo, ±±), soit racines (--, ++, -+, +-). Ce qui conduit Szondi à interpréter la proportion de latence élevée comme révélatrice d'un danger vectoriel. Dans ce cas en effet, un facteur univoquement tendu ou chargé (+ ou -) développe une poussée dynamique qui n'est pas contrebalancée par l'action de son facteur corrélatif, lui-même déchargé (o) ou en tout cas bloqué ou immobilisé (±). En d'autres termes, l'un des besoins se satisfait, alors même que le second reste constamment insatisfait et dès lors agit seul, sans frein, dans les profondeurs du psychisme. Inversement, une proportion de latence basse serait l'indice d'une porte de sortie ou d'une soupape pulsionnelle ainsi que l'appelle Szondi, à l'aide de laquelle le sujet tenterait de se décharger de la tension accumulée dans le vecteur dangereux à proportion de latence élevée, opérant ainsi au titre de « ventilateur » pulsionnel (ou de vecteur ventile).

On remarquera que la dialectique ici postulée entre vecteurs tendus et vecteurs détendus est homologue à la dialectique entre facteurs racines et facteurs symptomatiques de la formule pulsionnelle. Toutefois, les proportions de latence sont appelées à nuancer la formule pulsionnelle. Du fait même de leur sensibilité à une dialectique intravectorielle non prise en compte par la formule pulsionnelle, elles sont en état de faire apparaître des dangers voilés par la formule pulsionnelle et d'en modérer d'autres grossis par cette dernière. Ainsi, pour ce qui concerne notre profil de référence, on voit que le vecteur P y apparaît comme le vecteur le plus dynamique et en particulier son facteur hy, non seulement parce que celui-ci (hy-) tend à être univoquement tendu (dialectique intrafactorielle), mais surtout parce que le facteur corrélatif e (e±) n'exerce sur lui aucun contrôle équilibrant (dialectique intravectorielle). Les proportions de latence attribuent donc au facteur hy et à sa tendance hy- une importance dynamique que ne leur conférait pas la formule pulsionnelle. Mais on observe inversement que le vecteur S se présente comme vecteur ventile. Le danger inhérent aux facteurs h (h+) et s (s+)

considérés à l'état isolé (dialectique intrafactorielle) est nuancé par le contrôle qu'ils exercent l'un sur l'autre dans le clivage horizontal (S++) (dialectique intravectorielle).

Il reste cependant que, malgré leur sensibilité dialectique supérieure, les proportions de latence méritent d'être l'objet d'une sérieuse critique. Outre le fait qu'elles-mêmes négligent des dimensions plus englobantes de la dialectique pulsionnelle, et en première instance la dimension d'une dialectique intervectorielle, on doit leur reprocher de ne différencier que très grossièrement des modes de clivage vectoriel qu'elles se bornent à répartir en deux groupes : d'un côté les clivages unitendants et tritendants considérés comme clivages dangereux, d'un autre côté les clivages bitendants, quadritendant et double nul considérés comme clivages ventiles. On doit rappeler à cet égard que la méthode des proportions de latence est une des premières méthodes d'interprétation que Szondi ait développée. Or, la suite de l'œuvre devait amener Szondi à analyser beaucoup plus finement les divers modes de clivage vectoriel dans leur fonctionnement dynamique propre, ce dont nous avons rendu compte tout au long de notre paragraphe précédent. On peut donc se demander si la méthode des proportions de latence n'est pas aujourd'hui caduque. En tout cas, nous sommes en droit de nous poser de nombreuses questions dont nous ne détacherons que quelques-unes à titre illustratif. Est-il légitime d'assimiler unitendances et tritendances, et encore bien de les assimiler sous l'étiquette de clivages pathogènes dangereux ? Ces deux modes de clivage n'ont-ils pas une signification dynamique spécifique ? La tritendance n'est-elle pas en état d'exercer une protection par le biais de l'ambivalence factorielle, là où précisément l'unitendance livrait la vie pulsionnelle du vecteur à la dominance exclusive d'une seule fonction ? De la même façon, est-il légitime d'assimiler les diverses catégories de bitendances et de les assimiler sous la dénomination de clivages ventiles ? Les bitendances horizontales et diagonales ont-elles une signification identique ? Les bitendances horizontales ne signalent-elles pas des lieux d'équilibration, alors même que les bitendances diagonales font basculer la vie pulsionnelle dans une direction univoque dangereuse ? A notre sens, l'interprétation dialectique non quantitative, informée des apports les plus récents et conduite selon des règles fines et nuancées, permet aujourd'hui de se passer d'une méthode des proportions de latence par trop sommaire, bien plus conduit souvent à l'infirmer. Ainsi, pour en rester à notre exemple, il nous paraît aberrant de considérer ce qui se joue dans le vecteur S comme l'indice d'une ventilation pulsionnelle opérant via la sexualité : le vecteur S, couplant deux tendances positives exacerbées (h+! s+!!), est dans ce profil un vecteur éminemment tendu et dangereux.

b) *Les classes pulsionnelles*
Mode d'établissement

Le calcul des proportions de latence conduit directement à l'établissement de la classe pulsionnelle. La classe pulsionnelle d'un profil est en effet identique au vecteur dans lequel la différence des degrés de tension de tendances est la plus élevée (bref à proportion de latence la plus élevée), complété par son facteur unitendant et par le signe qui symbolise la direction positive ou négative de l'unitendance factorielle. Dans notre exemple, nous inscrirons donc la classe pulsionnelle sous la forme: Phy-.

Ajoutons que l'on distingue des classes pulsionnelles de danger et des classes pulsionnelles ventiles.

Une classe pulsionnelle est dite classe de danger lorsque sa différence de tension intravectorielle est égale ou supérieure à 5. De plus, le danger de la classe pulsionnelle peut, soit apparaître seul, soit s'accompagner d'un ou plusieurs dangers secondaires (à savoir d'un ou plusieurs vecteurs à proportion de latence égale ou supérieure à 5). On parlera, dans le premier cas de l'existence d'un seul danger, dans le second cas de l'existence de deux, trois ou quatre dangers.

Une classe pulsionnelle est dite classe ventile, lorsque sa différence de tension intravectorielle est inférieure à 5. Une classe ventile peut être triventile ou quadriventile. Elle est dite triventile lorsque la différence entre la proportion de latence la plus élevée et la proportion de latence la plus basse est au moins égale à 3. Elle est dite quadriventile lorsque cette différence est inférieure à 3.

Quelques exemples

Exemple 1

$$\frac{Schk+}{8}, \frac{Sh-}{3}, \frac{Pe+}{2}, \frac{Cm-}{1},$$

Classe pulsionnelle: Schk+.
Classe pulsionnelle de danger; 1 danger.

Exemple 2

$$\frac{Cm+}{7}, \frac{Sh+}{6}, \frac{Phy-}{5}, \frac{Sch}{0},$$

Classe pulsionnelle: Cm+.
Classe pulsionnelle de danger; 3 dangers.

Exemple 3

$$\frac{Sh-}{4}, \frac{Phy-}{2}, \frac{Sch}{0}, \frac{C}{0},$$

Classe pulsionnelle: Sh-.
Classe ventile; triventile.

Exemple 4

$$\frac{Cd+}{2}, \frac{Ss+}{1}, \frac{Schp-}{1}, \frac{P}{0}$$

Classe pulsionnelle: Cd+.
Classe ventile; quadriventile.

Mode d'interprétation

L'interprétation des classes pulsionnelles peut se développer dans trois directions.

Tout d'abord, elle peut s'appuyer sur les indications générales qui guident aussi l'interprétation des proportions de latence. Ainsi, la classe pulsionnelle révèle le vecteur, le facteur et la tendance les plus dynamiquement actifs et perturbateurs du profil. Ainsi, une classe pulsionnelle quadriventile indique que le sujet mobilise un maximum de lieux pulsionnels en vue d'une décharge ou d'une ventilation... Les remarques critiques adressées à la méthode des proportions de latence sont ici aussi d'application.

Elle peut ensuite se référer aux descriptions des diverses classes pulsionnelles. On le devine, il existe en tout et pour tout seize classes pulsionnelles, quatre classes pulsionnelles par vecteur (ainsi pour le vecteur S: Sh+, Sh-, Ss+, Ss-). Or Szondi, combinant les considérations théoriques et les constatations cliniques, a eu le souci de dégager, sous la forme de tableaux de personnalité, les grandes caractéristiques des sujets chez qui prédomine telle ou telle classe pulsionnelle. Le lecteur pourra consulter à ce sujet le DP (descriptions abrégées: pp. 86-95; descriptions détaillées: pp. 273-293). Il trouvera également un résumé dans TP (pp. 168-169).

Enfin, la classe pulsionnelle peut conduire à la consultation du «Linné des pulsions», dont nous devons dire à présent un mot particulier.

c) Le Linné des pulsions

La consultation du Linné des pulsions couronne l'édifice des grandes méthodes quantitatives développées par Szondi à l'époque où il commence à mettre en route l'interprétation du test.

Par Linné des pulsions, on désigne un petit volume (Szondi, 1960) qui dresse une sorte de catalogue des espèces pulsionnelles sur le modèle du catalogue des espèces végétales de Linné. Il n'est pas possible ici d'entrer dans le détail de la procédure qui guide la circulation à l'intérieur du Linné des pulsions. Chaque lecteur qui en fera l'acquisition pourra aisément s'y retrouver seul. Nous donnons cependant le principe général de la méthode. Il s'agit en s'appuyant sur la classe pulsionnelle et sur la formule pulsionnelle de parvenir à une ou plusieurs étiquettes psychiatriques, établies sur une base empirique et supposées caractéristiques du sujet. Ainsi, par exemple, le sujet chez qui prédomineraient la classe pulsionnelle Phy+ et la formule pulsionnelle $\frac{ke}{hsdhy}$ serait «alcoolique» et souffrirait d'«homosexualité latente» (p. 38). On le voit, cette méthode pêche par toutes les horreurs de la classification psychiatrique, fixiste et enfermante, contre lesquelles à sa manière Szondi a aussi protesté. Aussi cette méthode tend-elle aujourd'hui à être abandonnée. Elle doit pour le moins être utilisée avec la plus extrême prudence. Au même titre que toutes les autres méthodes quantitatives quelles qu'elles soient, elle ne peut être employée que comme méthode d'appoint, dans le contexte d'une interprétation essentiellement guidée par les règles de la dialectique pulsionnelle et donc aussi corrigée, nuancée (voire même, dans certains cas, récusée) par celles-ci.

2. Les index proportionnels

Szondi a considéré les méthodes proportionnelles comme méthodes spécifiques, distinctes aussi bien des méthodes dialectiques que des méthodes quantitatives. Pour notre part, les méthodes proportionnelles nous paraissent tout à fait assimilables aux méthodes quantitatives, et cela dans la mesure où elles s'appuient sur le calcul et le chiffre. De plus, elles privilégient le niveau de la dialectique vectorielle. C'est pourquoi nous en traiterons ici.

Ces méthodes ou index proportionnels intéressent deux dimensions partielles de l'existence: la dimension de la psychosexualité et la dimension de la sociabilité. Ils supposent que chacune de ces dimensions est susceptible de s'orienter dans deux directions exclusives l'une de l'autre, pour la première dans une direction masculine ou féminine, pour la seconde dans une direction positive ou négative. Aussi se proposent-ils de déterminer les proportions de tendances masculines ou féminines révélées par un sujet (index psychosexuel), ainsi que les proportions de ses tendances sociales positives ou sociales négatives (index psychosocial).

a) L'index psychosexuel ou index Dur-Moll

Mode de calcul

On passe en revue systématiquement, vecteur par vecteur, les réactions vectorielles du profil et l'on compte au fur et à mesure, d'une part les réactions masculines ou réactions Dur, d'autre part les réactions féminines ou réactions Moll[1]. Pour effectuer le décompte, on se réfère à un tableau qui attribue à chacune des 64 réactions vectorielles possibles (16 réactions par vecteur) une note, soit de masculinité (D), soit de féminité (M). Nous donnons ci-après une variante de ce tableau.

Les résultats s'inscrivent sur la feuille de notation, vecteur par vecteur, dans les rangées prévues à cette fin, ainsi que le révèle notre profil de référence (p. 91).

Précisons que tout point d'exclamation donne droit à une note supplémentaire D ou M selon la nature de la réaction vectorielle accentuée. Ainsi S+!+!! donnera lieu à 4 notes Dur. L'index psychosexuel total s'obtient en effectuant successivement la somme des réactions Dur et la somme des réactions Moll des quatre vecteurs et en divisant ensuite la première par la seconde. Notre sujet obtient ici :

$$\frac{\text{Dur}}{\text{Moll}} = \frac{42}{17} = 2,5$$

Quelques normes d'interprétation

Chez l'individu de sexe masculin, l'index s'installe normalement aux alentours de $\frac{2}{1}$, alors que chez les individus de sexe féminin, les réactions Moll tendent normalement à l'emporter sur les réactions Dur.

Une inversion du rapport pourrait révéler une problématique d'homosexualité. Ainsi, les réactions Moll prédominent nettement chez les homosexuels passifs de sexe masculin, dans une proportion qui avoisine 1 sur 3 et s'élève parfois jusqu'à 1 sur 5. Inversement, chez les homosexuels de sexe féminin, nous observons souvent un déplacement de l'index au bénéfice des réactions Dur.

Enfin, certains syndromes psychopathologiques se caractérisent aussi par les particularités de leur index psychosexuel. Chez les paranoïaques de sexe masculin, dont l'homosexualité latente est un trait classiquement reconnu, l'index s'inverse au profit des réactions Moll. Quant aux psychopathes criminels, leur index atteste une particulière accentuation des tendances Dur.

---

[1] Szondi a utilisé métaphoriquement, pour désigner la polarité masculin-féminin, le couple de termes Dur-Moll, qui en allemand appartient exclusivement au vocabulaire musical et connote respectivement les gammes majeure et mineure.

TABLEAU VII

Critères d'attribution des réactions psychosexuelles et psychosociales

		S	M	M	D	M	D	M	D	M	D	M	D	M	D	D	D	M
DUR/	P	M	M	M	M	D	D	M	M	M	M	M	D	M	D	D	D	D
	Sch.	M	M	M	M	D	D	D	M	M	D	D	M	D	M	M	M	D
MOLL	C	M	M	M	D	M	M	M	D	D	D	D	D	D	D	M	M	D
Vektorbild:		oo	o±	o+	o·	±o	±±	±+	+o	±+	++	±·	·o	+·	+±	+·	+·	+·
	S	+	·	·	·	+	·	+	·	·	+	·	·	+	·	+	·	+
SOZ +/	P	·	+	·	·	+	+	+	·	+	+	+	·	+	·	·	·	·
	Sch.	·	·	·	·	+	+	+	·	·	+	·	·	+	+	+	+	+
SOZ –	C	+	·	+	·	+	·	·	·	·	+	·	·	+	+	+	+	·

b) L'index psychosocial

L'index psychosocial se calcule selon les mêmes principes que l'index psychosexuel, à cette différence près que toute accentuation a systématiquement valeur de réaction sociale négative. On consultera donc à nouveau le tableau de la p. 118 qui attribue à toute réaction vectorielle une note de sociabilité positive (soc+) ou négative (soc-) et on aboutira à un index de proportions psychosociales obtenu selon la formule :

$$\frac{(\text{soc}+) \times 100}{(\text{soc}+) + (\text{soc}-)}$$

On observera que notre profil exemplatif donne à cet égard :

$$\frac{26}{26 + 33}\% = 44\%$$

Quelques normes d'interprétation

L'index psychosocial s'établit normalement entre 40 % et 50 %. Néanmoins, dans certains cas, il se déplace, soit vers le haut, soit vers le bas. Ainsi chez les névrotiques, il dépasse souvent les 60 %, ce qui atteste la sévérité des exigences sociales portées par leur surmoi; de même, chez les personnes qui exercent une profession de type social, il tend fréquemment à s'élever au-delà des 50 %. A l'inverse, dans les tableaux psychopathiques ou psychotiques, il tend à descendre en dessous des 40 %.

c) Remarque critique

Le mode de construction des index proportionnels serait assurément à discuter. On pourrait se demander en particulier d'après quels critères les 64 clivages vectoriels ont été répartis entre les catégories « Dur » et « Moll » ou entre les catégories « soc+ » et « soc- ». Est-ce une déduction théorique, elle-même guidée par un concept a priori de la différence des sexes ou de l'adaptation sociale, qui a présidé à la répartition? Ou bien au contraire, la répartition finale a-t-elle été décidée au terme de tâtonnements empiriques, les index proportionnels étant reconnus valides dès l'instant où leurs résultats numériques différenciaient adéquatement des groupes cliniques (un groupe d'hommes « normaux » et un groupe de femmes « normales », un groupe d'individus socialement adaptés et un groupe d'individus socialement inadaptés) ?

Mais quelle que soit la procédure qui ait régi leur construction, il n'en demeure pas moins que les index proportionnels s'appuient nécessairement sur des critères définissant ce qu'est un individu « masculin » ou « féminin », un individu « socialement adapté » ou « socialement inadapté ». Or ces critères ont toute chance de correspondre non aux attributs d'une nature humaine universelle, mais aux normes historiques d'une société particulière. En quoi les index proportionnels, en stigmatisant les déviants, risquent de participer à une entreprise de normalisation sociale, et cela sous le couvert idéologique de propriétés inhérentes à la nature psychologique des individus. Sous cet aspect, leur usage doit être l'objet de la plus extrême méfiance.

3. Les clivages globaux instantanés ou conjonctures pulsionnelles

Franchissant une nouvelle étape dans notre mouvement de complexification dialectique croissante, nous abordons dans ce paragraphe les clivages globaux instantanés : globaux parce qu'ils concernent le système pulsionnel total dans l'ensemble de ses vecteurs, instantanés parce qu'ils s'opèrent à un moment donné du temps.

Pour désigner ces clivages, nous avons proposé un terme inédit, que la communauté szondienne n'a pas encore repris à son compte : le terme de conjoncture pulsionnelle. Ce terme a en effet le mérite de connoter « la rencontre de certains événements en un même point » (Littré), en l'occurence la rencontre de clivages pulsionnels élémentaires venant se conjuguer pour former une unité provisoire; de plus il inclut aussi l'idée d'une rencontre momentanée, circonstancielle, non définitivement arrêtée : la conjonction des clivages pulsionnels qui s'organisent en un ensemble conjoncturel ne nous livre qu'un instantané photographique d'un processus toujours plus ou moins fluctuant ou mouvant.

Acceptons donc le terme et demandons-nous comment opère l'interprétation d'une conjoncture pulsionnelle. Deux voies s'offrent, dont on peut découvrir les traces chez Szondi dès la première édition du TrD. La première voie consiste à travailler sur les significations théoriques attribuées aux clivages factoriels et vectoriels élémentaires de façon à combiner ces dernières selon certaines règles psychodynamiques et à parvenir ainsi à une représentation d'ensemble de la conjoncture pulsionnelle. Nous appellerons cette démarche, principalement basée sur un travail théorique, une démarche de construction théorique. Quant à la seconde voie interprétative, elle consiste à reconnaître dans une conjoncture pulsionnelle et dans les divers clivages qui la composent les signes d'une image clinique ou syndromatique spécifique, qui servira dès lors à qualifier la conjoncture. Nous appellerons cette démarche, plus immédiatement soucieuse d'une liaison à la clinique psychopathologique, une démarche de corrélation clinique.

a) *Une démarche de construction théorique : la méthode centre-périphérie*

Mettons tout d'abord en évidence deux processus psychodynamiques qui travaillent le système pulsionnel dans son ensemble et pourraient en conséquence guider l'interprétation de la conjoncture pulsionnelle.

D'une part, une relation dynamique s'instaure au sein du système pulsionnel total entre les pulsions ou vecteurs de la périphérie (vecteurs S et C) et les pulsions ou vecteurs du centre (vecteurs P et Sch). La distinction entre les vecteurs S et C et les vecteurs P et Sch est en effet davantage qu'une distinction topographique : elle est, selon les termes de Szondi, une distinction dynamique-fonctionnelle, qu'on peut en première approximation situer dans les termes suivants. Les vecteurs périphériques révèlent les mouvements pulsionnels par lesquels le monde et en particulier le monde interhumain se trouve investi de la manière la plus immédiate, alors que les vecteurs centraux indiquent comment les mouvements pulsionnels de la périphérie se trouvent repris et élaborés par le sujet sur un mode plus intériorisé. On devine qu'une pareille interaction dynamique inspire une méthode de lecture de la conjoncture qui articule la périphérie et le centre après avoir procédé successivement à leur analyse séparée.

Mais d'autre part, une seconde relation, mettant aux prises les lieux de danger et les lieux de protection, pourrait dynamiser le système pulsionnel total. Pour sa part, Szondi a tendance à identifier les deux modes de liaison dynamique que nous venons de distinguer. Car il est vrai que le second recoupe largement le premier. La périphérie est par excellence le lieu des dangers pulsionnels, alors que le centre est par excellence le lieu de la défense, de la censure, de la prise de position protectrice contre les dangers pulsionnels de la périphérie. Le recouvrement n'est pas absolu, ne serait-ce que parce que les vecteurs centraux peuvent à l'évidence être eux aussi le lieu de dangers pulsionnels (danger par tension quantitative, danger par clivage unitendant, ...) et de dangers qui, lorsqu'ils affectent le moi, sont parmi les plus graves et fondent les formes les plus sévères de la pathologie mentale (les schizophrénies). C'est pourquoi une seconde méthode de lecture de la conjoncture est concevable, qui relève tout d'abord les lieux de dangers pulsionnels où qu'ils apparaissent (éventuellement dans le centre) et relève ensuite les lieux de protection où qu'ils apparaissent (éventuellement dans la périphérie).

Malgré l'existence des deux approches interprétatives que nous venons de différencier, nous nous bornerons ici à en développer une seule, la méthode centre-périphérie, qui procède en trois étapes:
1. l'interprétation dialectique de la périphérie;
2. l'interprétation dialectique du centre;
3. l'articulation dialectique de la périphérie et du centre.

1. L'interprétation dialectique de la périphérie

Le principe est ici de jeter un regard sur les quatre clivages factoriels qui composent la périphérie en vue d'aboutir à une vue synoptique de celle-ci, qui ne se limite pas à une sommation extrinsèque ou à une juxtaposition mosaïque des significations élémentaires, mais les concatènent et les infléchissent. Mais qu'entendons-nous par là?

Par concaténation de significations nous entendons la mise en liaison de significations élémentaires en telle sorte qu'elles viennent s'intégrer dans une phrase unique, intelligible et cohérente. Pour illustrer cette définition, donnons-nous la périphérie suivante :

$$\begin{array}{cc} S & C \\ +!+ & -+! \end{array}$$

Cette périphérie juxtapose, d'une part un attachement fidèle (C-+) anxieux (m+!) et une sexualité positive dite normale (S++), lieu d'une tension érotique insatisfaite (h+!). Adoptant un présupposé, qui bien souvent aide l'interprétation dialectique, à savoir que l'objet des investissements du contact et de la sexualité est un seul et même objet, vraisemblablement ici une personne, nous pourrions dire, au titre d'une interprétation possible, que le sujet, inquiet (m+!) de son objet d'accrochage fidèle (C-+), cherche activement (s+) un contact érotique (h+!) avec lui. On le voit, une phrase a été formulée, qui enchaîne les divers constituants pulsionnels de la périphérie. Nous pourrions même aller au-delà et au départ des deux clivages les plus frappants (h+!

et m+!) nous demander par exemple si la demande de relation érotique (h+!) n'est pas le canal privilégié par lequel le sujet traduit sa quête anxieuse de sécurité ou d'acceptation (m+!).

Mais tournons-nous à présent vers le second processus dit d'infléchissement de significations. Nous entendons par là qu'un clivage à la signification plurivoque prend une signification plus précise (et donc infléchit sa signification dans une direction davantage univoque) dès l'instant où il doit s'interpréter en conjonction avec les clivages qui l'accompagnent. Soit par exemple le clivage So-, interprété comme signe de passivité ou de masochisme. Mais quel sens prend la passivité ? Comment s'exprime le masochisme ? Le clivage corrélatif du contact nous aidera à répondre. Donnons-nous donc les trois périphéries suivantes et interprétons la passivité qui chaque fois y apparaît :

	S	C
1.	o-	--
2.	o-	oo
3.	o-	-+

1. La passivité prend place dans le contexte d'un contact malheureux (C--). Elle peut prendre la signification d'un laisser aller, d'un abandon au malheur, d'une auto-complaisance dans le malheur (« ayant perdu mon objet, je puis tout endurer, tout peut désormais m'arriver »).

2. La passivité s'inscrit dans le cadre d'un contact infantile régressif (Coo). Elle pourrait être l'indice d'une demande d'être pris sur le mode d'un maternage infantile ou d'une tendance à passer par tous les caprices d'un objet avec qui l'on vit une relation de type quasi fusionnel.

3. La passivité prend place dans le contexte d'un contact fidèle (C-+). La périphérie n'étant pas chargée des accentuations qui lui donneraient une connotation névrotique, la passivité peut s'interpréter dans la direction sublimatoire d'un dévouement à l'objet d'accrochage stable.

2. L'interprétation dialectique du centre

L'analyse dialectique du centre s'efforcera de dégager une vue synoptique en se conformant aux deux principes de la concaténation et de l'infléchissement.

Concaténation

Donnons ici les exemples les plus simples, qui associent le même clivage paroxysmal à diverses formes de clivage du moi :

	P	Sch
1.	-+	+o
2.	-+	o-
3.	-+	--
4.	-+	±±
5.	-+	-+

Dans tous les cas, le Caïn pur (P-+) se trouve élaboré par un mécanisme ou une prise de position spécifique du moi :

1. Le sujet introjecte (k+) le Caïn, sous la forme d'un mode d'existence qui lui permet de vivre le Caïn dans un rapport positif au monde tout en le

limitant et l'inscrivant à sa place dans la personnalité (comme trait de caractère ou comme mode d'existence professionnel socialisé).

2. Le sujet projette (p-) le Caïn : il vit ses tensions caïnesques sous forme de sollicitations qui émanent immédiatement du monde sans passer par le relais de la prise de conscience.

3. Le sujet projette (p-) et nie (k-) tout à la fois le Caïn. Il s'agit en quelque sorte d'un Caïn adapté (Sch--) ou discipliné, dans les deux sens que cette dernière expression peut recouvrir : le sujet est en état de renoncer à ses exigences caïnesques, tout en étant aussi susceptible de les exercer strictement dans des cadres socialement établis (dans une organisation fasciste de masse).

4. Le sujet pressent la catastrophe (Sch$\pm\pm$) et mobilise sur un mode panique toutes ses défenses pour faire face au Caïn.

5. Le sujet se gonfle (p+) du Caïn tout en le niant (k-). Il inhibe (Sch-+) le Caïn : il est possédé par des représentations fantasmatiques qui mettent en scène le désir caïnesque (p+), mais en même temps il les travestit névrotiquement (k-); il se trouve engagé dans une lutte intérieure (Sch-+) contre celles-ci et ce qui en transparaît au niveau conscient.

Infléchissement

Soit deux variantes du centre :

	P	Sch
1.	o-	o-
2.	o-	-o

Nous reconnaissons dans ces deux centres un vecteur paroxysmal dominé par la tendance à se cacher (hy-). Mais la manière même dont pourrait être vécue la tendance hy- s'infléchit d'après le contenu du clivage corrélatif du moi :

1. Ce que le clivage Po- peut comporter de connotation paranoïde est renforcé par le clivage projectif du moi (Scho-). Le sujet projette sur les autres des désirs qui risquent de lui faire retour de l'extérieur (p-). En sorte que le regard d'autrui lui apparaît alors comme le véhicule du désir qu'il a chassé à l'extérieur de lui-même. Ainsi, au cas où il serait par exemple animé d'un désir homosexuel projeté, il pourrait interpréter le regard et plus généralement les expressions et les attitudes d'une personne de son propre sexe comme signes d'une invitation ou d'une sollicitation homosexuelle (hy-).

2. Le sujet nie un désir (k-) et tend en conséquence à éviter les situations susceptibles de l'éveiller. En ce sens, il pourra se sentir mal à l'aise devant autrui, chercher à se protéger de lui et de sa présence par le retrait sur soi, voire par la fuite (hy-), et cela dans la mesure où la rencontre d'autrui lui ferait craindre inconsciemment la sollicitation de son désir refoulé.

3. L'articulation d'ensemble de la périphérie et du centre

L'analyse conduite selon la méthode centre-périphérie se conclut par la prise d'une vue d'ensemble de la conjoncture totale. Il s'agit en quelque sorte d'opérer une concaténation finale qui intègre en une unité intelligible et cohérente les significations découlant de l'interprétation de la périphérie et les significations résultant de l'analyse du centre. Par ailleurs, il n'est pas exclu qu'au cours de cette opération ultime d'articulation, des significations restées relativement plurivoques puissent être nuancées ou infléchies.

Nous connaissons déjà la règle dialectique qui préside à la concaténation terminale. Selon les formulations de Szondi, la périphérie nous renseignerait sur les dangers pulsionnels qui se forment dans le registre des relations interhumaines de la vie sexuelle et de la vie de contact, alors que le centre révèlerait les défenses psychiques à l'aide desquelles le sujet tente de se préserver des dangers périphériques (TrD, p. 211). En bref, deux questions mériteraient chaque fois d'être soulevées: quels dangers pulsionnels habitent la périphérie? En quelle mesure et selon quelles modalités le centre protège-t-il contre ces dangers périphériques?

Pour concrétiser la méthode, référons-nous aux exemples que Szondi lui-même a choisis pour illustrer ses principes interprétatifs (TrD, pp. 214-215).

Soit les conjonctures totales suivantes:

	S	P	Sch	C
1.	+!!-!	+ ! !o	o o	-!-!
2.	+!!-!	- ! !o	o o	-!-!
3.	+!!-!	o +!!	o o	-!-!
4.	+!!-!	o - !!	o o	-!-!
5.	+!!-!	o o	+ ! !o	-!-!
6.	+!!-!	o o	- ! !o	-!-!
7.	+!!-!	o o	o +!!	-!-!
8.	+!!-!	o o	o - !!	-!-!

1. Analyse de la périphérie

Nous avons affaire dans ces huit cas à une périphérie identique:

S   C
+!!-!   -!-!

La périphérie frappe d'abord par l'importance des accentuations qui nous appellent à majorer les dangers révélés par le contenu des tendances élues.

Le vecteur C est occupé par le contact malheureux. Le sujet se détache d'un objet et désespère d'en trouver un autre. C'en est fini pour lui d'un objet décevant et sa déception même le dissuade de jamais en chercher un autre. Le vecteur S nous signale d'abord un corps lieu d'une tension érotique extrêmement vive et insatisfaite. La sexualité se trouve en quelque sorte sans objet (C--) et s'exacerbe à vide. A quoi s'ajoute une passivité masochiste qui prend la connotation d'un abandon et d'un laisser aller, et bien plus fait craindre, du fait même du contexte où elle s'insère, que le sujet ne veuille en finir avec une existence malheureuse et un corps d'où émanent d'énormes tensions, difficilement tolérables parce que sans issue.

En un mot, et c'est là la conclusion à laquelle aboutit Szondi, la périphérie révèle un danger suicidaire. Encore que nous risquons en nous arrêtant à cet énoncé, de donner un contenu empirique trop précis à la dynamique des tendances périphériques. Car il n'est pas exclu que la considération du centre ne conduise à nuancer une conclusion prématurément péremptoire. Que le sujet tende à s'auto-sacrifier, assurément. Qu'il y tende sous les espèces d'un acte suicidaire au sens strict, c'est peut-être moins sûr. Nous l'observerons au moins dans un cas. Mais l'hypothèse est vraisemblable, et dès lors s'ouvre la question: le sujet, animé d'une tendance suicidaire, se suicidera-t-il en fait?

« La réponse à cette question dépend naturellement de la force ou de la faiblesse du centre » (TrD, p. 213).

2. Analyse du centre

Les huit centres distincts qui caractérisent nos conjonctures de référence ont tous un point commun : ils sont quasiment vides (trois clivages factoriels nuls), si ce n'est qu'un facteur est occupé par une tendance (clivage factoriel unitendant) elle-même exacerbée. L'interprétation en est donc très simple et n'appelle pas de concaténation dialectique, puisque domine une seule tendance (la tendance éthique e+, ou la tendance caïnesque e-,...) qui se développe à plein (!!). Situation bien évidemment exceptionnelle, très rarement rencontrée dans la pratique, mais invoquée ici à titre didactique. Car nous pourrons découvrir sur ces exemples comment chaque tendance du centre est en état d'élaborer un danger périphérique.

3. Articulation de la périphérie et du centre

Quelle que soit la tendance spécifique élue par le centre, ce dernier est « faible » puisque quasiment vide. Le danger suicidaire est donc mal protégé. L'acte suicidaire est à craindre dans tous les cas. Le pronostic de destin sera toujours défavorable. Toutefois, certains centres assurent l'ébauche d'une défense protectrice, alors que d'autres renforcent le danger. Il peut même arriver que le contenu de la tendance centrale amène un retour sur la signification présomptivement acquise de la périphérie et oblige à nuancer ou infléchir son interprétation en terme de danger suicidaire. Par ailleurs, la forme du suicide pourrait être différente selon la nature de la tendance qui travaille le danger périphérique.

Commentons donc successivement les huit conjonctures d'après leur variante centrale.

$$1. \quad \begin{array}{cc} P & Sch \\ +!!o & oo \end{array}$$

Si nous considérons le danger suicidaire comme acquis au terme de l'interprétation de la périphérie, nous dirons que le clivage e+!! est susceptible de freiner la tendance suicidaire. Car la tendance suicidaire est culpabilisée : le sujet hésite à lui donner libre cours du fait même des énormes scrupules de conscience qu'elle éveille en lui.

Cependant, dans ce cas, l'importance de la tendance éthique et des idéaux humanitaires qu'elle connote pourrait autoriser une réorientation de la signification du masochisme périphérique : le sujet s'auto-sacrifie (s-!) en s'adonnant jusqu'à totale abnégation à un mouvement humanitaire, social, politique, religieux,... Et si nous tenons à tout prix à inscrire encore le danger suicidaire, nous ajouterons qu'il se voue à un mouvement humanitaire qui peut exiger le sacrifice d'une vie : il sera prêt s'il le faut à mourir pour la cause qu'il défend.

$$2. \quad \begin{array}{cc} P & Sch \\ -!!o & oo \end{array}$$

Le danger suicidaire n'est pas protégé, mais tout au contraire renforcé. Le suicide pourra être exécuté sur un mode paroxystique, à savoir sous la forme d'un accès soudain, brutal et explosif. Ou encore, il pourra prendre les traits du suicide épileptoïde, par saut dans le vide par exemple.

	3.	P	Sch
		o+!!	oo

La tendance suicidaire est mise en scène, en quoi le suicide a tendance à être différé, la démonstration suicidaire prenant plus d'importance que l'acte lui-même. En fait, nous avons affaire au cas typique de la tentative de suicide hystériforme: l'acte suicidaire est annoncé avec fracas, sur un ton menaçant, à des fins de chantage affectif; il est exécuté spectaculairement, de façon à être découvert; bien souvent, il est organisé de manière à en éviter l'issue. Mais les tentatives de suicide se répétant, l'une d'entre elles pourra s'avérer fatale.

	4.	P	Sch
		o-!!	oo

Le sujet a honte de ses tendances suicidaires, il s'efforce de les dissimuler et d'en garder le secret pour lui seul, jusqu'à ce qu'il commette un suicide pudique et discret, loin des regards et de la présence d'autrui.

	5.	P	Sch
		oo	+!!o

Le sujet affirme sa tendance au suicide. Il assume et prend en charge un suicide qui se chargera de tous les traits congéniaux à la fonction k+: la programmation positiviste, le calcul, le soin et la netteté méticuleuse, la froideur, le calme, la dignité sereine.

	6.	P	Sch
		oo	-!!o

Cette sixième conjoncture est celle qui présente, sans doute, la plus grande difficulté d'interprétation. La tendance k- est tendance à la négation. Mais oserions-nous parler ici d'un sujet qui nie ses tendances suicidaires, auquel cas nous rencontrerions le rempart le plus efficace contre le suicide? Car on sait aussi que la tendance k- accentuée s'interprète préférentiellement en termes de destruction de toute image de soi. Or, dès l'instant où nous décidons de retenir cette dernière signification, nous sommes confrontés au délicat problème de la différenciation à établir entre les tendances s-(!) et k-(!) interprétées toutes deux comme tendances à l'auto-destruction. Quelle nuance la tendance k- ajoute-t-elle donc à la tendance s-? Pour répondre à cette question, il est utile de repartir du mouvement par lequel la tendance k- nie la tendance k+. Nous pourrions dire alors que la tendance k- vise à annuler la distinction entre le moi et le non-moi que la tendance k+ institue et qu'à ce titre, elle accentue le danger suicidaire. Il est clair en effet que la mort suicidaire peut contribuer à suspendre l'individualisation du moi par rapport au non-moi, sans être pour autant la seule forme d'expression de pareille tendance. Ainsi, la toxicomanie, fréquemment caractérisée au niveau psychopulsionnel par l'accentuation de la tendance k-, pourrait en constituer une autre modalité d'apparition: elle aussi conduit à la destruction de soi-même, à la suppression du sentiment d'être une personne individuelle, discontinue, clairement différenciée de l'entourage. Bref, le clivage k-!! pourrait ajouter à la tendance suicidaire une nuance de destruction « moïque » dans le sens qui vient d'être défini: la mort suicidaire pourrait survenir dans ce cas comme point d'aboutissement d'une entreprise d'auto-destruction, par exemple après une crise excessive de drogue.

        7.   P   Sch
             oo   o+!!

Le sujet se gonfle de ses tendances suicidaires, avec ce que cela comporte d'ambiguïté : se gonfler d'une tendance suicidaire, c'est abonder dans son sens, mais aussi lui donner accès à un espace de prise de conscience, d'élaboration imaginaire, qui peut en différer la manifestation immédiatement agie.

        8.   P   Sch
             oo   o-!!

Le danger suicidaire est assurément très mal protégé par une tendance qui connote le vécu désirant le plus brut, le moins élaboré. Il reste cependant difficile d'articuler significativement la tendance p- et le désir suicidaire. Que pourrait signifier en effet « vivre son désir suicidaire au lieu de l'autre » ? Peut-être devrait-on songer à un acte suicidaire exécuté dans une atmosphère d'inconscience, comme si le suicide émanait de l'autre (un homme traverse la rue, une voiture le renverse, il est écrasé, mort).

b) *Une démarche de corrélation clinique : la méthode des formes d'existence*

La méthode des formes d'existence est la dernière en date des grandes méthodes d'interprétation du test. Développée d'abord par A. Beeli (1965), reprise et modifiée ensuite par Szondi (TrD, 1972)[1], elle couvre l'entièreté du registre pulsionnel en état de fonctionnement, y compris les deux profils complémentaires d'arrière-plan. Toutefois, nous avons décidé de la présenter dès à présent, et cela tout simplement parce qu'elle s'appuie sur l'analyse des conjonctures pulsionnelles.

Le principe de la méthode des formes d'existence est simple. Il consiste à passer en revue successivement les conjonctures pulsionnelles, y compris les conjonctures des deux plans complémentaires, et d'attribuer à chacune la (ou les) forme(s) d'existence qu'elle révèle. Une fois établies les formes d'existence caractéristiques des trente conjonctures du profil pulsionnel total, il est alors possible de calculer un index dit de danger, point d'aboutissement ultime de la méthode. Mais entrons dans le détail, en suivant la méthode de Szondi.

1. *Le catalogue des formes d'existence*

Reprenant la numérotation de Beeli, mais assimilant les formes d'existence 11 et 15, Szondi construit le catalogue suivant :

A. Formes d'existence dangereuses   N°

    I. Formes d'existence sexuelle extrêmes
       Homosexuelle (masculine ou féminine)   10
       Perverse (sado-masochiste)   9

---

[1] On trouvera également une présentation de la méthode des formes d'existence dans l'*Introduction à l'analyse du destin*, 1972, en particulier dans les pp. 31-42.

II. Formes d'existence paroxysmale extrêmes
    Epileptiforme   13
    Hystériforme   14

III. Formes d'existence du moi extrêmes
    Prépsychotique   1
    Paranoïde projective   2
    Paranoïde inflative   3
    Héboïde   4
    Catatoniforme   5

IV. Formes d'existence d'humeur et de contact extrêmes
    Dépressive-mélancolique   6
    Maniaque   7
    Psychopathique   8

B. Formes d'existence protectrices
    Hypocondriaque   11 (ou 15)
    Obsessionnelle   12
    De l'homme de la rue   16
    Humanisée   17

2. Le diagnostic des formes d'existence

Nous le savons déjà, il s'agit d'attribuer à chaque conjoncture pulsionnelle la (ou les) forme(s) d'existence qui lui correspond(ent). Deux cas sont à différencier. Ou bien la conjoncture représente à l'état pur une seule forme d'existence, qui lui sera dès lors attribuée. Ou bien — cas fréquent — la conjoncture est impure : elle contient les signes caractéristiques de deux ou même de plusieurs formes d'existence. En ce cas, deux formes d'existence (au maximum) lui sont assignées. Les formes d'existence sont inscrites dans le protocole sous forme de leur numéro, et cela à côté de chaque conjoncture dans la colonne « Existenzform » (cfr notre protocole de référence p. 91).

Reste à savoir selon quel procédé les formes d'existence sont assignées aux conjonctures. Pour sa part, Szondi détaille sous forme de tableaux publiés dans la troisième édition du TrD (cfr tableaux VIII, pp. 129-132), les signes pulsionnels qui caractérisent les diverses formes d'existence.

Mission étant conférée à l'interprète de se guider d'après les indications fournies par les tableaux en vue de relever dans chaque conjoncture les symptômes de telle ou telle forme d'existence. A vrai dire, ces tableaux pourraient appeler de très nombreux commentaires. Bornons-nous aux deux principaux. On voit tout d'abord que toute forme d'existence présente entre trois et cinq variantes, différenciées sous forme des lettres a, b, c (d, e). L'attribution d'une forme d'existence est donc légitime si les clivages factoriels ou vectoriels caractéristiques d'une variante se conjuguent dans la conjoncture. Ainsi la conjonction conjoncturelle des clivages so, Poo et Sch± - autorise l'attribution de la forme d'existence épileptiforme 13 (variante b). Enfin, un coup d'œil jeté sur les tableaux permet aussi de découvrir

TABLEAUX VIII Symptômes testologiques pour la détermination des 17 formes d'existence

A. FORMES D'EXISTENCE DE DANGER		Numéro des formes d'existence	Dans le Vecteur Sexuel S =	Dans le Vecteur Paroxysmal P =	Dans le Vecteur du Moi Sch =	Dans le Vecteur du Contact C =
Formes caractérologiques	Formes cliniques-psychiatriques					
I. Formes d'existence sexuelle				♂ ♀	♂	(±+,o+,±±,+o)
hommes féminins femmes masculines	inversion, homosexualité, travestisme	10 a	♂ −+(!!)/o−(!!) ±± ±± / +s ou ±h		±+ ±+ / o+ o− / ±+ ±+	Syndrome classificatoire
		b	♀ −(!)+/o +/ ±+ ±+ / +s		oo / +o / +o / (−!o)(−!+)	++
		c	+!!h, −!!h −s	−hy	(−o)	
caractères sexuels contre-nature	perversion, sadisme, sado-masochisme, etc.	9 a	+!!s (o+,o+!,−+!,±+!)		+!k ±+ ++!/ ++	Syndrome du plaisir p d m +(!) ±(!) et ±o o o variantes
		b	−!!s		(−+, −±, −o, o+)	
		c	±s		+o (oo,++)	−!d
		d	−+!	+!+ (o+,o±−)	+−, ±±,−!±,−!+,−!o +o, o+, oo,+(!)−, o−,−(!)−(!)	−!m, o−/±+, −−
II. Formes d'existence affectives-paroxystiques						
justiciers, colériques, vindicatifs, jaloux, envieux	affects meurtriers, forme d'existence épileptiforme	13 a	(+!s,+!!s,o+,−!+)	−+(!) −+!,−±,±± o−(!) ±±, o±	−+, −!, ±, o+, o±, ++!, ±± ±−	(aussi +m ou om)
		b	−s,−!s,−!!s,os,±s	−+(!),−o,−±,oo,o+,±± ±−	−+, −!, ±, o+, o±, ++!, ±± ±−	(Centre épileptiforme)
		c		−−,−!	−−,−!,−−!	
		d		−!e,+!e −!,+!,−!+	oo, ±±, ±−, −±, −+, +−, o+, +o	−m ±! non valable (meurtrier épileptique)
		e		−ϑ	(−p)	
acteurs, comédiens, se portent au regard, se cachent, menteurs	hystériformes	14 a		+!hy, −!hy (Hyst. de conv.)	−o, −+, −! (−!±, oo, ++)	(+!m, −!m)
		b		−+,oo,−!,±,±±,o+	−o, −+, −(!)±, ±−, o−, oo	(Hystéro-épil.)
		c		+o (phobie) −	±!±, ±+, oo (+±, +−, ±−)	

A. FORMES D'EXISTENCE DE DANGER

Formes caractérologiques	Formes cliniques-psychiatriques	Numéro des formes d'existence		Dans le Vecteur Sexuel S =	Dans le Vecteur Paroxysmal P =	Dans le Vecteur du Moi Sch =		Dans le Vecteur du Contact C =	
						k	p	d	m
III. Formes d'existence du moi									
étrangers au monde, irréels, nient la vie	prépsychotiques ou suicidaires	1	a			(-)	-	-	-
			b			+	-	-	-
			c			o	-	-	-
			d			±	-	-	-	± non valable
égocentriques, méfiants, cherchent un bouc émissaire	paranoïdes projectifs	2	a			-!p, -!!p (même seul!)			
			b			+-, o- (sans!) avec clivages diagonaux (+-) dans 1 ou 2 vecteurs			
			c	(o-)	ò-	ò- (même sans !) +!-			
			d	+-	+-	ò-	(o-)	+-	(centre projectif)
possédés, orgueilleux,	paranoïdes inflatifs	3	a			+!p, +!!p, +!!!p (même seul) ++!, ++!!, ±!			
			b			o+ (sans !), ++ avec clivages diagonaux dans 1-2 vecteurs			
narcissiques			c	+-	+!	-+!	o+	-+, o-	(syndr. class.)
			d		o+	o+ (centre inflatif)			
versatiles, pathétiquement et théâtralement bizarres	héboïdes	4	a		-!hy	-!k		oo, -	ò-
			b	(+!h, +!!h)	-!hy				
			c		+!hy	-!k	(-!p)	oo, -	ò-
			d		o-!(!!)	-!(!) (centre héboïde)			

A. FORMES D'EXISTENCE DE DANGER		Numéro des formes d'existence		Dans le Vecteur Sexuel S =	Dans le Vecteur Paroxysmal P =	Dans le Vecteur du Moi Sch =	Dans le Vecteur du Contact C =
Formes caractérologiques	Formes cliniques-psychiatriques						
nient tout, destructifs, auto-destructeurs	catatoniformes	5	a			-!!o, -!o, -!!±	-!
			b	(-!!s, +!!s)	-o	-!k -!!k (op)	(centre catatonif.)
			c		(-±, o-, o±)	-!!-	-! (suicide)
			d	+!+!!, (o+!)	-!o (o-, --)	-!o (-!±)	-!-, oo (syndr. class.)
IV. Formes d'existence d'humeur et de contact		6	a	-(!)s (±s)	(-+, o+, oo)	+(!)k	+(!)d, ±d (syndr. class.)
	dépressifs, mélancoliques		b	os		+(!)k, (±k)	+(!)d, ±d
	profonds, auto-accusateurs		c				+!!d, +!!!d
			d	+!s, os		-!-, -!+, -!±	+-, oo (U. Moser) (dépression chronique)
exaltés, hyperjoyeux, hyperactifs	hypomaniaques, maniaques	7	a		oo, -+(+-), o-		0-, o-! (!!) --(!)
			b	++!, +o, +!+!!		-!k	o- (même sans !) --
			c	++!!		-!-, -!o	o-, -- (syndr. class.)
particularités socialement anormales	psychopathiques	8	a		(oe) -!hy	ok (op) même sans syndrome de plaisir { +p ±p op } avec	++ ±± -(!)± oo syndrome de plaisir et variantes
			b	+!h, (-!s), (+!s)	ohy	ok	
			c			-!k	
			d		(oo, -+)	-!k +-	+!m («Sucht»)

B. EXISTENCES PROTECTRICES

Formes caractérologiques	Formes cliniques psychiatriques	Numéro des formes d'existence		Dans le Vecteur Sexuel S =	Dans le Vecteur Paroxysmal P =	Dans le Vecteur du Moi Sch =	Dans le Vecteur du Contact C =
hyperscrupuleux, besoin de culpabilité et de punition	hypocondriaques, organo-névrotiques	11 et 15	a		+-, +!-	+!!-, o-, ±-	-(!)o, -+	
			b		+-(!), ±-, o-		-(!)	
			c			-!		névrose d'organe (15)
			d	(-s)	(oo, o+)			+!m, +!!m névrose d'acceptation
impulsions obsessionnelles; hypertatillons, se maîtrisent	actes compulsifs, névrose obsessionnelle	12	a	impulsions obsessionnelles:	2 ou 3 réactions ±	(-±, -+, -!±, -!+, oo)	
			b	actes obsessionnels:	idem	même sans ±k	
			c			±o avec 1-2 réactions ± dans les autres vecteurs	
						+o (chronique)	
s'adaptent, renoncent	hommes de la rue socialisés	16	a	++	+o, +!+, ++!, +-	-+, -o, -!-, -!+, -!o	
			b	±+, ±±, -+, -!+, -+!		idem	
			c	-!		idem	
			d	±+, -±		idem	
			e	++, ±±, +o, ++		±+ (travailleur forcené)	(o+)
êtres humains spirituellement humanisés		17	a	-!	-!-, -!	±±, ±+ ++	
			b	-o, -!o		idem	
			c	±+, -±		idem	

l'importance relative des signes : certains d'entre eux, entre parenthèses, sont accessoires et leur présence n'est pas nécessaire au diagnostic (ainsi, la présence en C des clivages ±+ ou o+ ou +± ou +o n'est pas nécessaire à l'attribution de la forme d'existence 10 dans ses variantes a ou b); à l'autre extrême, d'autres signes, encadrés, sont considérés comme les plus significatifs, bien que la présence des signes qui ne sont ni encadrés ni entre parenthèses puisse être aussi déterminante dans le diagnostic (le clivage P-- est un élément tout aussi déterminant de l'attribution de la forme d'existence 14 dans sa variante c que le clivage P+o).

On le devine, le diagnostic des formes d'existence n'est pas toujours une opération simple. Mais nous aurons l'occasion dans la suite d'examiner quelques exemples qui nous introduiront plus concrètement à la pratique de la méthode.

3. L'index de danger

L'index de danger est identique au rapport entre le total des formes d'existence dangereuses et le total des formes d'existence protectrices des trois profils pulsionnels.

Un index de danger normal devrait s'établir aux alentours de 1 : 1, ce que des recherches effectuées sur des échantillons de sujets normaux (notamment sur un groupe d'ouvriers-mineurs et sur un groupe d'instituteurs) auraient vérifié. Par contre, si l'index atteint ou dépasse la proportion de 2 : 1, le pronostic de destin serait défavorable et une psychothérapie de type analytique contre-indiquée.

4. Le profil pulsionnel

Introduction à la problématique des déroulements pulsionnels

Une conjoncture pulsionnelle isolée n'épuise jamais la problématique d'un sujet : elle doit toujours être insérée dans un ensemble plus vaste, le profil pulsionnel, qui l'englobe et la nuance. Mais comment procéder en face d'un profil pulsionnel ?

Deux procédures extrêmes, deux modes de circulation à l'intérieur du profil, paraissent possibles. La première détache les ensembles horizontaux que constituent les conjonctures pulsionnelles et les examine successivement. Quant à la seconde, elle privilégie une dimension verticale, découpe le profil selon les facteurs et les vecteurs, analyse successivement les séries factorielles et vectorielles pour parvenir enfin à une interprétation d'ensemble du profil. Mais à vrai dire, ces deux procédures ne sont nullement exclusives. Bien au contraire, elles doivent être complétées l'une par l'autre.

Cependant, quoi qu'il en soit d'une telle alternative, il reste que l'interprétation du profil pulsionnel appelle à considérer des clivages qui se succèdent ou se déroulent dans le temps. De là découle, selon nous, le problème interprétatif fondamental soulevé par le profil. C'est pourquoi nous placerons ce paragraphe sous le signe des déroulements pulsionnels. Par souci d'analyse, nous considérerons successivement les déroulements factoriels, les déroulements vectoriels et enfin les déroulements « conjoncturels ».

a) Les déroulements factoriels

Il s'agit ici d'examiner les dix clivages successifs qui caractérisent un facteur. Deux phénomènes méritent d'être observés à cette occasion: la variabilité et la forme du déroulement.

1. L'index de variabilité

Une première question doit être soulevée devant une série factorielle: le même clivage se répète-t-il de manière constante? Ou bien les clivages varient-ils d'une conjoncture à l'autre?

Plusieurs auteurs se sont efforcés d'approcher la question dans une optique quantitative et à cette fin ont mis au point un index numérique de variabilité (IV). Nous ne retiendrons ici que la version simple et maniable de Berta et Silvera (1962), qui consiste à compter un point chaque fois qu'un changement s'opère dans une série factorielle. Un indice de variabilité fluctuant entre zéro et neuf est ainsi attribué à chaque facteur et l'addition des huit indices factoriels donne lieu au calcul d'un indice de variabilité globale (IVG).

Notre profil de référence (p. 91) nous donne les résultats suivants:

```
     h s e hy k p d m
IV   0 0 4 3  5 4 5 3    IVG = 24
```

Au plan interprétatif, l'index de variabilité nous renseigne sur l'importance de la rigidité ou de la déstructuration de la vie pulsionnelle. Un indice trop élevé signale l'anarchie et la perte de contrôle; un indice trop bas témoigne d'une fixité qui compromet le changement et l'adaptation. Une souplesse qui exclut la rigidité sans verser dans le chaos, bref une position moyenne, tel paraît être l'idéal. A ce titre, l'index de variabilité globale se situerait normalement entre dix et trente-cinq, les valeurs qui tombent en dessous de dix ou dépassent trente-cinq apparaissant en général dans des formes de pathologie psychotiques graves, en particulier dans les schizophrénies[1]. Il faut toutefois signaler que malgré son intérêt, l'index de variabilité présente des limites. Un même index quantitatif peut en effet correspondre à des situations qualitativement distinctes. Considérons par exemple les deux séries factorielles suivantes:

```
    +    ±
    +    -
    -    ±
    +    ±
    ±    +
    o    ±
    +    -
    ±    ±
    ±    ±
    -    +
```

---

[1] Sur ce point, on consultera J. Melon (1974a).

Dans les deux cas, l'index de variabilité s'élève à 7. Et cependant, du point de vue de leur déroulement, les deux séries sont très différentes. Dans la première, nous observons toutes les formes de clivage dans une succession incohérente, alors que dans la seconde, nous découvrons une variabilité qui procède très régulièrement du clivage unitendant vers le clivage ambitendant et inversement. Ce qui a la portée de nous indiquer que le calcul de l'index quantitatif doit être nuancé par une analyse qualitative des formes de déroulement.

2. Les formes du déroulement

Susan Deri est sans doute la seule à avoir porté une attention soigneuse aux formes de déroulement factoriel, pour en proposer une sorte de typologie (IS, p. 38 ss.). C'est ainsi qu'elle distingue trois grands modes de succession factorielle :
- Certaines successions mettent en jeu le clivage nul, dans un déroulement qui conduit du clivage nul (o) vers un clivage unitendant positif (+) ou négatif (-), ou inversement. L'interprétation pourra s'effectuer ici en termes de décharge-recharge ou de charge-décharge, avec toutefois les nuances qu'impose l'ambiguïté de la signification des clivages nuls, ce dont nous avons déjà parlé antérieurement.
- D'autres successions impliquent le clivage ambitendant, selon deux variantes principales. Soit le déroulement concerne le clivage ambitendant et un clivage unitendant positif ou négatif. En ce cas, le sujet est confronté avec une ambivalence qu'il cherche à dénouer par l'élection d'une tendance. Soit la succession concerne le clivage ambitendant et le clivage nul, auquel cas Szondi tend à parler d'un passage de la charge (±) à la décharge comportementale (o) du besoin, encore qu'une autre interprétation ne puisse être exclue : en évacuant le besoin, le sujet se débarrasserait provisoirement d'une ambivalence pénible qu'il n'arrive pas à élaborer.
- Enfin, certains déroulements mettent en jeu exclusivement les clivages unitendants positif et négatif (succession du + vers le - ou du - vers le +). En pareille circonstance, deux situations seraient à différencier. D'une part il peut arriver qu'un clivage contraire apparaisse isolément dans une série par ailleurs très uniforme (par exemple un clivage négatif s'insère dans une succession de clivages positifs). Selon Susan Deri, un tel phénomène doit être apprécié favorablement, car il révèle que le sujet n'est pas figé sur des positions exclusives, mais est capable de changer d'attitude lorsque les circonstances l'exigent. Mais d'autre part, il peut arriver aussi que la série factorielle comporte de fréquents renversements du + vers le - et du - vers le +. Toujours selon Deri, pareille caractéristique, observée dans les psychoses et certaines formes de psychopathie instable, serait l'indice qu'un processus psychopathologique est en cours dans le facteur.

Ajoutons que les toutes dernières hypothèses que nous venons de formuler ont été à la base de la construction d'un index quantitatif dit de désorganisation (ID). Pour chaque série factorielle, on calcule une fraction qui porte en dénominateur le nombre total des clivages unitendants (+ et -) et en numérateur le nombre des clivages unitendants minoritaires (+ ou -). Plus la fraction est proche de zéro et plus les clivages unitendants sont uniformes; plus la fraction est élevée et proche de 0,5, plus la série factorielle comporte à la fois des clivages positifs et négatifs. L'addition des numérateurs et dénominateurs des huit fractions factorielles permet enfin d'obtenir un index de désorganisation globale (IDG), dont la valeur doit normalement se situer en dessous de 0,10 [1]. Notre profil illustratif (p. 91) nous donne les chiffres suivants:

$$\frac{h}{10} \quad \frac{s}{10} \quad \frac{e}{2} \quad \frac{hy}{8} \quad \frac{k}{7} \quad \frac{p}{8} \quad \frac{d}{5} \quad \frac{m}{8} \quad \text{IDG} = \frac{1}{58}$$

Nous en terminons là avec l'analyse des déroulements factoriels, si ce n'est que nous devons faire mention d'un phénomène très particulier, qui relève, lui aussi, de la succession factorielle. On a en effet observé que le facteur e était le facteur le plus fluctuant, sans doute parce qu'il est le facteur paroxysmal par excellence, soumis en conséquence à des processus fréquents d'accumulation et de décharge.

b) Les déroulements vectoriels

Il s'agit à présent de repérer les processus qui se développent à l'intérieur de la succession de dix clivages vectoriels. Malheureusement, sur ce point, la littérature et l'expérience de l'Analyse du destin ne nous offrent guère d'outils généraux d'analyse. Aussi nous bornerons-nous à deux remarques.

Nous le savons déjà, il est toujours indispensable de nuancer la signification d'un clivage factoriel par la signification du clivage corrélatif. En conséquence, chaque fois que nous observerons une fluctuation factorielle, il sera important d'en enrichir le sens d'après l'évolution concomitante du facteur corrélatif. Ainsi, si nous relevons dans le facteur m un passage du ± vers le -, nous nous demanderons si le facteur d connaît une transformation parallèle. Dès cet instant, nous serons attentifs au déroulement vectoriel, qui pourrait conduire par exemple d'un C-± à un C+-: le sujet parvient à se détacher (m± → m-) et en même temps s'ouvre à de nouveaux investissements objectaux (d- → d+).

Pour le reste, nous ne relevons dans la littérature qu'une seule notation intéressante et significativement nous la devons à nouveau à Susan Deri, qui a attiré l'attention sur une forme particulière de déroulement vectoriel connue désormais sous le nom de «succession en miroir» (IS, pp. 43-44). On parlera de succession en miroir lorsqu'une série vectorielle comporte deux clivages qui sont comme le reflet exact l'un de l'autre, par exemple les clivages o- et -o. Les successions en miroir de clivages bitendants diagonaux (passage du +- au -+ ou du -+ au +-) seraient tout spécialement révélatrices d'un processus psychopathologique grave, et cela d'autant plus qu'elles se produiraient brusque-

---

[1] Sur ce point, cfr J. Melon et M. Timsit-Berthier (1974b).

ment et sans transition; ainsi, observées dans le vecteur Sch, elles caractériseraient l'entrée dans la schizophrénie.

c) *Les déroulements conjoncturels*

1. *Une multiplicité de formes d'existence*

Le profil pulsionnel est le lieu de plusieurs conjonctures dont la variété même témoigne de la multiplicité des possibilités d'existence d'un sujet. Car, comme aime à le dire le vieux Szondi, l'être humain n'a pas un destin, mais une multiplicité de possibilités de destin. Jamais il ne peut être enfermé dans une étiquette univoque qui prétendrait en résumer les caractéristiques. Toujours le faisceau entier de ses potentialités doit être déployé. En quoi devient intelligible aussi la nécessité de répéter la procédure testologique, dont les résultats fluctuants d'une administration à l'autre ne sont pas l'indice d'un déficit psychométrique, d'une absence de fidélité, mais bien d'une sensibilité à capter un éventail de formes diverses. Au plan interprétatif, il en découle une instruction claire: il importe en présence d'un profil d'établir un inventaire des formes d'existence en vue de saisir les voies multiples qu'elles ouvrent au destin du sujet. Soit par exemple le profil suivant:

Nr.	Soz.-Wert	S		P		Sch		C		Existenzform	
		h	s	e	hy	k	p	d	m		
1		−!	o	+	+	o	+	+	−!	3	
2		−!	o	+	+	+	+	+	−	6	
3		−!!	o	+	±	o	+!!	o	−!	3	
4		−!	o	+	+	o	+!	−	−!	3	
5		−!	o	+	±	o	+!	o	−	3	
6		−	o	+	±	+	+	±	−	17	
7		−	−	+	±	+	+	−	−	17	
8		−	−	+	±	+	+!	−	−	17	3
9		o	o	±	±	o	+!!	−	−	3	
10		o	−	±	±!	+	+	−	−	17	

Un regard vertical fait assurément apparaître des constantes: en particulier, là où se condensent la plupart des tensions quantitatives, le détachement (m-), la désexualisation (h-), l'inflation (p+). Le sujet se retire du monde, refuse l'accrochage à l'objet (m-) et le lien érotique (h-), pour s'absorber dans un monde d'idéaux personnels (p+). Cependant, un regard horizontal permet de diversifier un tableau jusque là univoque. Car les tendances stables se répétant d'une conjoncture à l'autre s'associent de manière variée à d'autres tendances pour former avec elles des ensembles conjoncturels distincts. Ou bien les tendances constantes se combinent en clivages vectoriels unitendants (S-o, Po+, Co-) dans une conjoncture paranoïde inflative dont la troisième administration donne l'aperçu le plus saisissant. Ou bien elles s'organisent sous forme de clivages bitendants horizontaux (S--, Sch++, C--) dans une conjoncture humanisée dont la septième administration offre l'exemplaire le plus net. En effet, s'il est vrai que le sujet est confronté à un danger pulsionnel majeur que connote le couplage périphérique des tendances m- (!) et h- (!), il est en état de l'élaborer selon deux voies divergentes. Son destin est partagé entre deux directions possibles : renchérir sur son isolement (h-!, m-!) pour verser dans un délire paranoïde qui le coupe du monde commun des hommes (Scho+!), ou mettre sa retraite et son renoncement (S--, C--) au service de la construction d'un idéal humanitaire (Sch++) qui le restitue créativement à la communauté interhumaine. On observera d'ailleurs que l'inventaire des formes d'existence manifeste bien le balancement entre la forme d'existence 3 et la forme d'existence 17.

Mais malgré son importance, l'inventaire des possibilités de destin guidé par la méthode des formes d'existence souffre d'un défaut. Il est clair qu'une forme d'existence n'a pas de valeur de position : elle a même valeur quelle que soit la position qu'occupe la conjoncture dans la succession temporelle. Bref, la méthode des formes d'existence n'est pas sensible au déroulement en tant que tel; elle n'a pas ce souci d'analyser le flux qui pourrait emporter les facteurs et vecteurs du registre pulsionnel total dans un mouvement significatif et cohérent. C'est donc à ce dernier point que nous devons venir, en évoquant tout d'abord les hypothèses proposées par Claude Van Reeth.

2. Le déroulement temporel des conjonctures selon Cl. Van Reeth

Dans un petit article suggestif (1971), Van Reeth a proposé quelques hypothèses générales destinées à ressaisir la signification de la succession des conjonctures pulsionnelles. Selon lui, la première conjoncture aurait le sens d'une « carte de visite » : le sujet y offrirait de lui-même une image limitée aux seuls aspects superficiels qu'il souhaite livrer au regard d'autrui. Mais petit à petit, à mesure que l'administration progresse, il abandonnerait les traits de l'apparence pour se révéler davantage en profondeur, jusqu'aux conjonctures centrales 4, 5, 6, auxquelles Van Reeth confère le statut de conjonctures nucléaires, reflétant les réelles possibilités structurales du sujet. Enfin, à mesure que l'administration s'achemine vers sa fin, le sujet se refermerait progressivement, pour réassumer dans la dixième conjoncture l'image qu'avait déjà offerte la première.

On ne peut cacher l'intérêt que présente pareille analyse. Elle a tout d'abord le mérite de restituer l'administration du test et ce qu'elle révèle comme modes d'existence pulsionnelle au contexte d'une relation clinique qui a sa cohérence et sa dynamique temporelle propre. Par ailleurs, les hypothèses de Van Reeth s'appuient sur des constatations empiriques que l'interprète du test a régulièrement l'occasion de vérifier.

Cependant, les principes de Van Reeth nous paraissent dangereux dans ce qu'ils pourraient avoir de systématique et d'exclusif. Est-il exact que les vraies possibilités structurales d'un sujet se révèlent toujours dans les conjonctures 4, 5 et 6, à telle enseigne que l'interprétation devrait chaque fois détacher et privilégier les conjonctures centrales pour y découvrir l'essentiel ? On peut en douter. De plus, les déroulements concrets sont loin de toujours être conformes au modèle circulaire de Van Reeth. Certains profils connaissent une évolution continue, qui jamais ne restitue en fin de parcours l'image de départ. D'autres profils se stabilisent définitivement dès la troisième ou la quatrième conjoncture etc. Bref, si Van Reeth a ouvert à la recherche une problématique importante, il n'a tout au plus mis au jour qu'une forme de déroulement pulsionnel. L'éventail complet de ces formes reste encore aujourd'hui à établir.

Quant à nous, dans l'attention de plus en plus soutenue que nous avons portée aux déroulements conjoncturels globaux, nous avons progressivement choisi de systématiser une méthode que l'on pourrait appeler « méthode des déroulements intervectoriels ».

3. Les déroulements intervectoriels

La mise au jour des déroulements intervectoriels est le point d'aboutissement de l'analyse verticale du profil, en même temps qu'elle restitue les résultats de cette dernière à la conjoncture totale. Elle représente donc ce moment où viennent se conjoindre et s'unifier lecture verticale et lecture horizontale. Mais de quoi s'agit-il ?

Dans une phase antérieure, rappelons-le, nous avons procédé à une inspection séparée des facteurs et des vecteurs et nous avons relevé à cette occasion des déroulements significatifs. Nous avons à présent à nous demander si des mouvements affectant un facteur ou un vecteur ne s'accompagnent pas de mouvements qui affecteraient au même instant un ou plusieurs autres vecteurs. Si la réponse devait être positive, nous aurions ainsi dégagé un déroulement qui emporte sinon le système pulsionnel total, en tout cas les conjonctures dans plusieurs de leurs composantes.

Mais exemplifions cette méthode d'analyse sur un profil concret, composé de six conjonctures :

Nr.	Soz.-Wert	S		P		Sch		C		Existenzform	
		h	s	e	hy	k	p	d	m		
1		−	−	+	+	−	o	+	±	14	
2		±	−	+	o	−	+	o	±	14	
3		±	o	+!!	o	−	±	o	−	14	(12)
4		+	o	+	−	−	+	o	±	11	
5		−	o	+!	o	o	±	±	±	8	(12)
6		−	o	+!	+	o	±	±	−	12	(14)

Jetons d'abord un coup d'œil sur le tableau des formes d'existence.

Nous voyons que prédomine la forme d'existence hystériforme n° 14. La seule inspection du centre permettait d'ailleurs de détecter la problématique hystérique et hystérophobique : dominent dans le vecteur Sch des mécanismes de défense hystériformes (Sch-o, -+, -±) ; dominent dans le vecteur P des processus paroxysmaux hystériformes et hystérophobiques (P++ ; passage du P++ au P+o, corrélatif d'une « tempête de mouvements hystériforme » ; P+!o, caractéristique de l'hystérie d'angoisse ou de la névrose phobique). Par ailleurs, nous relevons aussi une (demi) forme d'existence psychopathique (8) et le recours à des mécanismes de protection obsessionnels (12) et hypocondriaques (11). Ajoutons encore que pour l'essentiel, l'inventaire des formes d'existence recoupe le tableau clinique. Le profil est donné en effet par une jeune femme se plaignant notamment de symptômes d'anxiété dont il n'est pas simple de différencier cliniquement la nature phobique ou obsessionnelle (par exemple : peur de l'étouffement dans un lieu clos, claustrophobie ; mais aussi crainte d'avoir laissé ouvert le robinet de gaz, donnant lieu à de nombreuses vérifications compulsives).

Le diagnostic des formes d'existence reste cependant trop grossier que pour nous aider à pénétrer de manière fine dans la problématique du sujet. Seule l'analyse des déroulements nous permettra de progresser dans cette voie.

Observons tout d'abord les déroulements factoriels et vectoriels qui dans ce profil sont très nombreux : il n'est aucun vecteur qui ne soit d'une manière ou d'une autre en mouvement.

Vecteur S

L'évolution la plus significative affecte ici le facteur h. Le sujet est partagé entre le refus et l'assomption positive de l'érotisme. La succession conduit du refus (h-) à l'assomption (h+) à travers une phase d'ambivalence (h±), puis à un retour sur une position de refus (h-).

Vecteur P

Apparemment, le facteur e est très stable. Cependant, il connaît une évolution quantitative non négligeable : l'angoisse de culpabilité se tend, puis se relâche pour se tendre à nouveau. Quant au facteur hy, sa fluctuation connote bien la problématique hystérique de par la succession alternée de la tendance à la démonstration (hy+) et de la tendance à la dissimulation (hy-), elle-même ponctuée par des moments de décharge (hyo) qui pourraient coïncider avec les crises d'anxiété phobique (P +!o).

Vecteur Sch

Le vecteur Sch connaît une remarquable évolution graduelle qui mène à travers deux formes transitoires (Sch-+, Sch-±), de la négation de soi et du refoulement du désir (Sch-o) au dilemme de la conscience de soi et du désir (Scho±) : Vais-je me ressaisir moi-même ou me perdre dans l'autre ? Vais-je poser un désir comme mien ou être l'objet du désir de l'autre ?

Vecteur C

L'essentiel du débat se résume en une explication avec un objet d'attachement, engagée dans sa phase d'ambivalence (m±) et ponctuée ici ou là d'un mouvement de détachement (m-) rapidement rentré et mis en question (retour au m±). Quant à la recherche d'un nouvel objet embryonnairement articulée (d+), elle est très vite obturée ou immobilisée (do, d±) : un lien de dépendance non dénoué jette une ombre sur la possibilité d'investir un nouvel objet.

Mais il nous importe à présent d'interconnecter les fluctuations intravectorielles que nous venons de dégager. Bien que les possibilités de liaison intervectorielle soient multiples, nous nous contenterons de mettre au jour le déroulement conjoncturel qui nous paraît le plus apte à ressaisir le mouvement existensiel du sujet. Il nous semble en effet légitime de nouer un lien entre les évolutions qui affectent les vecteurs P, Sch et C, en particulier dans leurs facteurs e, p, m.

Considérant l'évolution qui s'opère au moment de la troisième conjoncture, nous découvrons tout d'abord que le mouvement de détachement (m-) s'accompagne d'une exacerbation de l'angoisse de culpabilité (e+!!). Nous parlerons donc selon notre principe de concaténation, d'un détachement culpabilisé. Et effectivement, notre sujet est occupé à se libérer avec hésitation et incertitude (m±) d'un lien de dépendance à sa mère, qu'elle vit comme étouffant. Elle vient de quitter le toit familial pour s'installer dans une petite chambre où elle vit seule (m-). Mais elle n'est pas sans éprouver des remords torturants de conscience (e+!!), alimentés par le chantage affectif de sa mère : en l'abandonnant ne vais-je pas nuire à ma mère, menacer sa santé, voire la détruire ? Dans l'existence concrète du sujet, les velléités de détachement suscitent bien une culpabilité (m-, e+!!) que peut seule apaiser la reprise du contact (conjoncture 4 : e+!! → e+, m- → m±), mais qui renaît à mesure que se prépare et s'effectue un nouveau détachement (conjonctures 5 et 6 : e+ → e+!, m± → m-).

Nous pouvons ensuite compléter l'analyse en y incluant la fluctuation corrélative qui s'opère dans le facteur p. En effet, la première apparition du clivage p± est contemporaine de l'émergence de la tendance au détachement (conjoncture 3). Par la suite, après une éclipse temporaire associée à la reprise de l'accrochage (conjoncture 4), le même clivage p± refait surface, en même temps que se gonfle la censure éthique (conjonctures 5 et 6) et se réeffectue le détachement (conjoncture 6). Le sujet paie donc un sentiment d'abandon (p±, Scho±) pour prix du détachement qu'il cherche à opérer. Ou encore, livré à la solitude du détachement (m-), le sujet pose la question de sa propre identité (p±) : puis-je encore être moi-même sans cet autre que je suis en voie de perdre ? Ne dois-je pas retourner à cet autre qui me fait défaut pour me refondre en lui (apparition du p- dans le passage du p+ au p±) ? Et il est vrai que la prise de distance, l'éloignement du toit familial, éveille en lui le sentiment d'une impuissance à être soi, à exister dans un monde désormais vécu comme menaçant ou dangereux. Il est significatif à cet égard que les symptômes d'anxiété éclatent préférentiellement lorsque notre sujet se retrouve livré à soi et s'éprouve dès lors comme seul responsable de lui-même et de son environnement : tout devient alors prétexte à une inquiétude qui se cristallise par déplacement sur telle ou telle situation (l'étroitesse d'un lieu clos et étouffant, la menace d'un réchaud à gaz dont le robinet n'aurait pas été fermé...).

Par ce bref exemple, nous croyons avoir fait ressortir la nature et l'intérêt d'une enquête centrée sur les déroulements intervectoriels. Ajoutons encore, pour terminer, que la recherche pourrait s'orienter dans l'avenir vers la mise au jour de déroulements intervectoriels typiques. Ainsi nous avons déjà évoqué ce que pourrait être un déroulement épileptoïde emportant les vecteurs P et Sch, dans une évolution qui conduirait de e-!! Sch±± à eoSchoo. Dans le même ordre d'idées, J. Schotte (1972) a commencé d'élaborer la théorie d'un déroulement dépressivo-maniaque, affectant en concomitance les facteurs s, k, d et m, dans le passage du s- au s+, du k+ au k-, du d+ au do, du m± au m-. Mais, comme le suggère Schotte, il pourrait être intéressant de poursuivre plus avant cette direction de recherche, en vue de dégager un éventail complet des mouvements existentiels, qui viendraient opportunément compléter les tableaux par trop statiques et figés des formes d'existence.

Conclusions

Est-il possible au terme de ce paragraphe de dégager une stratégie d'interprétation du profil pulsionnel ? Nous l'avons dit d'emblée, deux voies d'analyse divergentes, horizontale et verticale, s'offrent à l'interprète. A notre sens toutes deux méritent d'être empruntées. Mais au départ, elles ne pourront l'être que séparément, l'une à la suite de l'autre, car chacune a ses exigences propres et appelle des manipulations spécifiques. Elles devront cependant finir par confluer dans une analyse qui les rassemble, ce pour quoi notre méthode des déroulements intervectoriels nous paraît l'intermédiaire idéal. Mais expliquons-nous plus précisément.

Au point de départ, nous devons décider de commencer par l'une des deux directions interprétatives. Optons par exemple pour la direction horizontale. Nous sommes donc amenés tout d'abord à examiner successivement les diverses conjonctures du profil. Nous analysons leur dynamique selon le principe dialectique centre-périphérie. Nous leur attribuons une ou deux formes d'existence. A la fin, nous jetons un premier coup d'œil d'ensemble sur le profil, en prenant soin de relever ses orientations dominantes, mais aussi sa diversité, la multiplicité de ses formes d'existence, voire déjà quelques-unes des fluctuations marquantes qui le caractérisent. Puis, parvenu en ce point, nous inversons la direction de notre regard et adoptons le principe de la lecture verticale. Nous calculons les index de variabilité et de désorganisation, analysons les huit séries factorielles et les quatre séries vectorielles, pour en dégager chaque fois aussi bien les directions dominantes que les changements significatifs. Enfin, nous nous efforçons d'interconnecter les évolutions vectorielles, par quoi nous opérons un retour sur la dimension horizontale, dont l'analyse se trouve enrichie de l'apport fin et nuancé de la méthode des déroulements intervectoriels.

5. Le profil pulsionnel total

Introduction à la méthode avant-plan — arrière-plan

Jusqu'à présent, notre analyse ne s'est intéressée qu'au profil dit d'avant-plan. Mais elle ne sera considérée comme complète et achevée qu'après avoir pris en considération les données des profils d'arrière-plan. A quel propos se pose la question: quelles significations respectives attribuer aux trois profils pulsionnels?

En fait, personne n'est en état aujourd'hui de donner une réponse sûre et définitive à la question. Plusieurs hypothèses circulent, que nous nous efforcerons de formuler et dont nous dégagerons les conséquences pour l'interprétation. Nous nous attarderons ensuite quelque peu sur l'arrière-plan empirique, pour développer enfin une stratégie d'interprétation du profil pulsionnel total, que nous illustrerons par l'analyse d'un cas concret.

a) De la signification des trois profils pulsionnels

Il arrive à Szondi de formuler et de mettre en œuvre concrètement dans l'interprétation une hypothèse que nous pourrions énoncer dans les termes suivants: la vie pulsionnelle totale d'un sujet serait régie par le fonctionnement et le jeu complémentaire de l'avant-plan et de l'arrière-plan théorique. Quant à la signification respective des deux plans, elle découle de la transposition à leur interrelation d'un schème dialectique que nous avons déjà maintes fois rencontré: l'avant-plan ferait office d'une façade qui correspondrait aux symptômes les plus manifestes d'un sujet, alors même que l'arrière-plan théorique révélerait les racines profondes, les fondements dynamiques cachés des symptômes visibles inscrits à l'avant-plan.

Il est clair que si nous devions adopter cette hypothèse, la moins généralement retenue, l'interprétation du profil total serait profondément affectée. Car l'accent majeur devrait être mis alors sur le profil d'arrière-plan théorique : c'est ce dernier qu'il importerait d'analyser avec le plus de minutie, puisque c'est lui qui nous introduirait aux dynamismes les plus cruciaux de la vie pulsionnelle d'un sujet. Quant à l'arrière-plan empirique, on voit mal la place qui lui serait accordée.

Une seconde hypothèse s'articule elle aussi sur la relation entre l'avant-plan et l'arrière-plan théorique, mais ouvre déjà la voie à une interprétation de l'arrière-plan empirique. Elle postule entre les deux plans un rapport de forces qui tourne à l'avantage de l'avant-plan. Certaines tendances, plus fortes, plus puissantes, seraient arrivées à dominer d'autres tendances et occuperaient dès lors le devant de la scène, reléguant à l'arrière les secondes.

On le voit, les dynamismes les plus décisifs sont révélés ici par l'avant-plan. Il n'empêche toutefois que l'arrière-plan est réel : les tendances qu'il abrite font partie de l'éventail des possibilités du sujet et trouvent à s'exercer dans sa vie pulsionnelle. Mais de quelle façon s'y exercent-elles ? De manière variable selon leur force. En effet, s'il est vrai que les tendances d'arrière-plan sont dominées par les tendances d'avant-plan, elles peuvent l'être aussi en intensité variable. A cet égard, deux possibilités méritent d'être différenciées.

Soit les tendances d'arrière-plan ont une force quasi égale à la force des tendances d'avant-plan. Le débat dynamique est très instable et toujours incertain. Les tendances d'arrière-plan sont en état à chaque instant de renverser la vapeur et de s'imposer à leur tour. En pareil cas, tendances d'avant-plan et tendances d'arrière-plan se manifestent « quasi côte à côte » (IchA, p. 281) : les grands choix d'une existence seraient guidés tout autant par les unes que par les autres.

Soit les tendances d'arrière-plan sont très largement dominées par les tendances d'avant-plan. Auquel cas elles ne se manifesteront que très faiblement, sous forme d'une légère coloration, ou très indirectement, par des voies très détournées, par exemple dans certains rêves.

Reste à savoir comment départager ces deux possibilités extrêmes. Comment évaluer l'intensité quantitative du rapport de forces qui se développe entre l'avant-plan et l'arrière-plan ? C'est précisément ici que Szondi a l'idée de faire appel à l'arrière-plan empirique, interprété selon la méthode classique d'une analyse des concordances. Il s'agit en fait de procéder à une confrontation systématique, facteur par facteur, vecteur par vecteur, des tendances de l'arrière-plan empirique avec les tendances concomitantes de l'avant-plan et de l'arrière-plan théorique. Selon que les tendances de l'arrière-plan empirique confirment l'avant-plan ou l'arrière-plan théorique, nous conclurons, soit à la domination quasi exclusive de l'avant-plan dans ce secteur de la vie pulsionnelle, auquel cas l'arrière-plan théorique ne mérite pas d'être pris en considération, soit à la force de certaines tendances de l'arrière-plan théorique sur lesquelles il importe de compter.

Notre deuxième hypothèse commande donc une procédure très claire d'interprétation du profil total qui se déroule en trois phases : 1. interprétation de l'avant-plan; 2. analyse des concordances; 3. interprétation d'ensemble du profil fondée sur l'avant-plan et les tendances de l'arrière-plan théorique confirmées par l'arrière-plan empirique.

Mais nous devons formuler une troisième hypothèse, qui correspond sans doute à la pratique actuelle de la plupart des interprètes du test.

Nous venons de le voir, la deuxième hypothèse accordait déjà une place à l'arrière-plan empirique, mais dans un sens très limitatif. Aucune valeur propre ne lui était reconnue. Pur produit fictif d'une manipulation technique, il n'était pas doté d'une réalité autonome, que seul était en droit de revendiquer l'arrière-plan théorique.

Or, la communauté des interprètes du test a été progressivement gagnée par un sentiment de méfiance vis-à-vis du ThKP, en même temps que se renforçait l'intérêt et la confiance dans l'EKP, au point même que la situation soit aujourd'hui renversée du tout au tout : l'arrière-plan théorique est pure fiction, seul l'arrière-plan empirique abrite des orientations effectives de la vie pulsionnelle du sujet.

Mais sur quoi repose ce que nous devons bien appeler en l'état actuel un sentiment, en l'absence jusqu'ici de toute argumentation rationnelle et de toute recherche empirico-clinique décisive ? Sur deux faits, semble-t-il. Tout d'abord, la prise en compte de l'arrière-plan théorique comme arrière-plan réel autorise des formes d'interprétation souvent arbitraires : puisque ce qui fait défaut au VGP est (par principe de construction) présent au ThKP, il sera toujours possible à l'interprète de déceler au ThKP ce dont l'absence au VGP le gênait. A quel moment il verse dans une procédure qui risque de dérober le test à toute épreuve de falsification, et dont Szondi nous a malheureusement trop souvent donné l'exemple. Mais plus fondamentalement l'arrière-plan empirique repose sur des choix de photos effectivement posés. Nous avons donc toute raison de penser que ces choix effectifs révèlent des tendances tout aussi réelles que les choix posés à l'occasion de la première phase de l'administration du test.

Pour notre part, nous avons choisi d'adopter provisoirement cette dernière hypothèse. Jusqu'au jour où des travaux plus poussés nous obligeront à une éventuelle révision. C'est donc aussi dans la perspective que dessine cette hypothèse que nous réfléchirons un moment sur la signification possible de l'arrière-plan empirique, avant de dégager une stratégie d'interprétation du profil pulsionnel total.

b) *De la signification de l'arrière-plan empirique*

Pour appuyer nos quelques réflexions sur la signification de l'EKP, rien ne vaut de repartir de l'épreuve testologique et de la manière dont se trouve pratiquement établi l'arrière-plan empirique.

Au cours du premier choix, un sujet, confronté à six visages d'homosexuels, choisit négativement trois d'entre eux et laisse les trois autres par rapport auxquels il ne se prononce pas. A la suite du premier choix, nous le créditons donc d'un clivage h- : par la répulsion significative qu'il a manifestée vis-à-vis des photos d'homosexuels, il a désapprouvé le besoin « sensuel » que ces photos véhiculent et révélé ainsi la tendance négative du besoin h. Mais au cours du second choix, les trois visages d'homosexuels qu'il avait écartés lui sont à nouveau présentés. Supposons qu'il les choisisse tous trois positivement. Nous sommes conduits cette fois à le créditer d'un clivage h+ : par son attrait, notre sujet a approuvé le besoin et manifesté sa tendance positive. Correspondant à une prise de position effective vis-à-vis de photos porteuses d'un dynamisme pulsionnel, cette tendance h+ a le statut d'une tendance réelle. Encore faudrait-il comprendre la signification qu'elle revêt, et en particulier ce qui pourrait la différencier de la tendance h- manifestée à la faveur du premier choix.

Il semble que deux significations extrêmes puissent être attribuées à l'arrière-plan empirique, bien qu'elles ne soient peut-être pas aussi exclusives qu'il peut paraître en un premier temps. Pour les introduire, nous utiliserons au départ une métaphore empruntée au langage de la topique freudienne, qu'il nous faudra cependant aussitôt mettre en question.

Tout d'abord nous rencontrons chez les interprètes du test une tendance à interpréter l'arrière-plan empirique en terme d'inconscience. Une tendance révélée par l'arrière-plan empirique serait une tendance exclue, barrée, refoulée. Derrière une tendance consciente à la désérotisation et à la sublimation (h-) se dissimulerait l'orientation originelle du besoin érotique, que le sujet s'efforcerait certes de censurer, mais qui de l'inconscient presserait et exercerait un effet dynamique. La sublimation réussie aurait appelé à l'EKP une confirmation de la tendance h- manifestée au moment du premier choix. Dans une autre formulation quelque peu différente, faisant appel à des catégories temporelles, on dira couramment que les tendances de l'EKP correspondent moins à des tendances actuellement exercées ou mobilisées (celles-là mêmes que révélerait l'avant-plan) qu'à des tendances anciennes, sortes de reliquats du passé, témoignages d'époques déjà révolues, ou à des tendances potentielles, provisoirement sous le boisseau, mais que l'avenir pourra peut-être un jour actualiser.

C'est en quelque sorte la relation la plus souvent postulée par Szondi entre VGP et ThKP qui se trouve ici transposée au rapport entre VGP et EKP. Mais on voit aussitôt l'objection à laquelle se prête pareille hypothèse. Car si vraiment la tendance h+ était une tendance refoulée au sens fort, pourquoi le sujet l'aurait-il manifestée à l'occasion du second choix ?

Nous voici alors conduit à formuler une seconde hypothèse. Les tendances de l'arrière-plan empirique relèveraient du préconscient. L'arrière-plan empirique n'aurait pas le statut d'un inconscient, mais serait plutôt un second avant-plan ou un avant-plan complémentaire, situé du point de vue topique au même niveau que l'avant-plan. Car, répétons-le, si le sujet libère la tendance h+ au moment du second choix, n'est-ce pas qu'elle est pour lui actuellement disponible et peut circuler librement, pénétrer sans peine jusqu'à sa conscience ? En quoi la conjonction des tendances h- (VGP) et h+ (EKP) serait l'indice d'une véritable ambivalence érotique, subjectivement donnée à la conscience du sujet.

Cependant, malgré l'appui de base que nous sommes désormais tenté d'apporter à la seconde hypothèse, nous estimons qu'elle doit être nuancée par la première. Pour les raisons que nous venons de dire, l'arrière-plan empirique ne peut être considéré comme l'équivalent rigoureux de l'inconscient freudien, séparé de l'avant-plan par la barre du refoulement. Mais il est vrai aussi que l'on ne peut pas purement et simplement niveler l'avant-plan et l'arrière-plan empirique. La référence à l'épreuve testologique est à nouveau éclairante. Notre sujet a d'abord choisi la tendance h-, qui se présentait comme la plus urgente, la plus disponible, et ce n'est que dans un second temps qu'il a livré la tendance h+. Il n'est donc pas faux de dire que la première recouvrait ou dissimulait la seconde ou encore que la seconde a été un moment activement mise à l'écart. C'est dire que la topique freudienne n'est pas adéquatement applicable à la relation entre avant-plan et arrière-plan empirique. Au sens strict, l'arrière-plan empirique n'est pas inconscient, mais il n'est pas non plus préconscient; ou plus exactement, dans une formulation très insatisfaisante, il est préconscient, mais moins que l'avant-plan! Avant-plan et arrière-plan empirique sont aussi engagés dans un rapport de forces dynamique dont l'avant-plan est le temporaire vainqueur. Mais répétons-le encore, nous en sommes réduit en l'état actuel de la recherche à des énoncés provisoires et nécessairement insuffisants.

Remarquons, pour terminer, qu'il serait possible d'opérer une revalorisation de l'arrière-plan théorique comme seul lieu des tendances exclues, comme seul « arrière-plan véritable ». Car la thèse de Szondi selon laquelle les tendances pulsionnelles dans leur entièreté sont offertes à tout sujet au titre de possibilités ne doit pas être trop légèrement négligée. En tout cas, si nous l'adoptions, nous serions amenés à considérer comme tendances barrées les tendances du ThKP qui ne sont pas confirmées par l'EKP. Ainsi, si un sujet donnait la tendance h- à la fois au VGP et à l'EKP, nous devrions considérer la tendance h+ présente au ThKP comme une tendance qu'il écarte. Resterait à savoir — c'est en ce point que se cristallise le débat — si pareille tendance est refoulée et exerce dans le psychisme le dynamisme que la topique freudienne prête à l'inconscient refoulé ou si elle est (provisoirement: car rien ne peut absolument exclure que le sujet ne l'assume un jour) inactive, écartée du jeu dynamique des pulsions, dont le débat total serait justement ressaisi par la seule dialectique de l'avant-plan et de l'arrière-plan empirique. Pour notre part, nous avons accompli ce dernier pari. C'est pourquoi, dans la stratégie d'interprétation du profil pulsionnel total que nous développons immédiatement, nous ne proposons pas de prendre en considération l'arrière-plan théorique, suivant en cela la majorité des interprètes qui travaillent aujourd'hui avec le test de Szondi.

c) *Une stratégie d'interprétation du profil pulsionnel total*

L'interprétation du profil pulsionnel total commence par l'analyse détaillée du profil d'avant-plan, selon les méthodes que nous avons déjà précisées. Nous n'y revenons pas. Il ne reste plus alors à l'interprète que d'examiner l'arrière-plan empirique. Comment donc analyser celui-ci?

Une première possibilité consisterait à analyser l'arrière-plan en tant que tel, comme un plan autonome, et cela selon la procédure déjà utilisée pour l'avant-plan, puis à clôturer l'interprétation par une confrontation ultime entre avant-plan et arrière-plan empirique.

Pour notre part, nous ne voudrions point absolument exclure cette première possibilité. Tout au moins doit-on savoir qu'elle se heurte à une difficulté, qui appelle en tout cas sa rectification et peut même conduire à privilégier une autre stratégie d'interprétation. Mais quelle est donc cette difficulté?

Cette difficulté résulte des contraintes qui pèsent sur le second choix. Nous voulons dire par là que les choix opérés à l'occasion de la première phase de l'administration du test limitent les possibilités de choix au cours de la seconde phase. Le fait nous est déjà connu, puisqu'il s'inscrit explicitement dans ce que nous avons appelé le zéro contraint ou forcé (noté $\varnothing$). Mais en réalité, le même phénomène opère dans tous les cas, à des intensités et selon des formes variables. N'en citons que deux exemples auxquels nous sommes particulièrement sensible. Supposons qu'un sujet donne un clivage nul à l'occasion du premier choix. Nous comprenons aussitôt que toutes les possibilités ne lui sont plus ouvertes au moment du second choix. Il a d'abord choisi un maximum de deux photos d'une catégorie psychiatrique; les photos qu'il n'a pas choisies (quatre au minimum) lui sont ensuite présentées à nouveau, et cette fois il est contraint de prendre position par rapport à elles: il pourra donner un clivage positif, un clivage négatif ou un clivage ambitendant, mais il ne pourra en aucun cas répéter son clivage nul. De la même manière, si un sujet a donné à l'occasion du premier choix un clivage ambitendant selon une distribution de choix bruts $\frac{2}{2}$, il pourra donner au moment du second choix un clivage positif ($\frac{2}{0}$), un clivage négatif ($\frac{0}{2}$) ou un clivage nul ($\frac{1}{1}$), mais il ne pourra pas comme tel répéter son clivage ambitendant. Mais observons le clivage nul $\frac{1}{1}$ du second choix. Ne peut-on supposer que si le sujet est réellement ambivalent vis-à-vis des photos du facteur et du besoin qu'elles véhiculent, il n'a trouvé d'autre moyen d'exprimer son ambivalence au second choix qu'à travers un clivage nul qui répartit les deux photos restantes en sympathique et antipathique. Assez paradoxalement, le clivage nul non contraint du second choix pourrait avoir la signification d'un clivage ambitendant. Ce qui indique bien que les clivages de l'arrière-plan empirique ne peuvent pas tout à fait s'interpréter à la manière des clivages de l'avant-plan, ainsi que l'effectue illégitimement une interprétation de l'EKP comme plan autonome.

Avant de tirer les conséquences de ceci au plan de la stratégie globale d'interprétation, donnons l'exemple de deux conjonctures concomitantes d'avant-plan et d'arrière-plan empirique:

	S	P	Sch	C
VGP	+o	o±	o±	o-
EKP	o+!!	±o	±o	-!+

Face à cette double conjoncture, nous pourrions adopter une première stratégie d'interprétation: tout d'abord considérer les deux conjonctures comme conjonctures autonomes, les interpréter séparément, pour ensuite les confronter globalement. Dans cette perspective, nous serions vraisemblablement amenés à établir un net contraste entre les deux conjonctures. Ainsi, nous soulignerions ce que la première peut signifier d'une problématique «féminine» d'abandon hystériforme: convaincu d'être abandonné (Scho±) par un objet qui me fait défaut, dont je suis détaché (Co-), je m'exhibe devant lui, sur un mode ambivalent (Po±), dans mes tendances érotiques (S+o). A l'inverse, nous relèverions dans la seconde les traces d'un mode d'existence «viril», tout occupé à élaborer à la manière obsessionnelle (P±o, Sch±o) des tendances agressives, voire sadiques (So+!!), dirigées sur un objet d'accrochage fidèle (C-!+). En conclusion, nous poserions l'hypothèse d'un balancement de l'existence du sujet entre deux formes d'existence divergentes, dont l'une pourrait éventuellement servir de couverture à l'autre.

Mais une seconde stratégie d'interprétation qui confronte d'emblée les clivages de l'EKP aux clivages du VGP et prend en compte les contraintes de choix, conduit à une vision quelque peu différente. Certes, il est bien vrai qu'à première vue les deux conjonctures sont très divergentes, y compris dans le détail des clivages: aucun des clivages de l'avant-plan ne se trouve reconduit à l'arrière-plan. Cependant, une analyse plus fine, guidée par la conscience des contraintes de choix, oblige à apprécier diversement la différence observable entre les deux périphéries et la divergence (apparente) entre les deux centres. La périphérie de l'avant-plan fonctionne en effet comme une véritable couverture dissimulatrice de l'arrière-plan. Il n'en va pas de même pour le centre.

Considérons d'abord la périphérie pour y observer deux clivages nuls qui sont franchement dissimulateurs. En effet, au moment du premier choix, le sujet n'a pas choisi (ou quasiment pas choisi) de photos de sadiques ni de dépressifs; mais cependant, à l'occasion du second choix, il les a choisies dans une direction univoque, en positif pour les unes (s+!!), en négatif pour les autres (d-!). Le sujet a donc révélé par là une puissante tendance sadique et un puissant collage à l'objet, que nous tenons pour des composantes réelles de son dynamisme pulsionnel actuel. Mais ces tendances réelles, il a aussi préféré ne pas les livrer à l'occasion du premier choix : il s'efforce de les cacher, d'y échapper, de les écarter, de n'y point prêter attention. Nous croyons donc être justifié d'interpréter la périphérie dans son ensemble en terme de dissimulation. Nous avons affaire à un sujet qui se donne en façade comme un être érotique, doux et tendre (h+), comme un être détaché (m-). Et sous cette apparence qu'il adopte pour autrui, se dissimulent, dans un état de plus ou moins grande conscience ou inconscience, des tendances inverses : une forme d'agressivité sadique (s+!!) et un attachement collant, adhésif, persévérant à un objet (d-!), nous dirons selon notre principe de concaténation : une agressivité sadique dirigée sur un objet d'attachement collant.

Par contre, le centre ne justifie pas pareille interprétation. Notre conscience des contraintes de choix nous appelle à voir dans le centre de l'arrière-plan une confirmation de l'avant-plan plutôt que l'émergence d'une orientation inverse divergente (par exemple la substitution d'un moi masculin à un moi féminin). Comme nous l'avons établi, les deux clivages nuls de l'arrière-plan (hyo et ko) sont des quasi-ambivalences : ils continuent en quelque sorte les ambivalences de l'avant-plan. Quant aux clivages ambivalents (e± et k±), ils poursuivent à leur façon les clivages nuls de l'avant-plan, en ce que ces derniers peuvent signifier d'une absence de prise de position, d'un blocage ou d'une immobilisation du dynamisme factoriel. C'est donc d'un centre globalement ambitendant que nous devons parler. Dès lors, nous pouvons dire en conclusion que dans la conjoncture existensielle où nous l'avons saisi, le sujet se montre ambivalent vis-à-vis d'une tendance sadique dirigée sur un objet d'attachement collant, qu'il dissimule sous une apparence de tendresse sensuelle et d'indifférence détachée.

Mais essayons à présent de développer dans plus de détails notre stratégie d'interprétation, non sans répéter encore que si nous ne voulons pas condamner absolument tout examen indépendant de l'arrière-plan, nous tenons à souligner la nécessité de rapporter en dernière instance toutes les données de l'EKP quelles qu'elles soient (conjoncture, clivage vectoriel ou clivage factoriel) aux données correspondantes qui les accompagnent au VGP et d'en nuancer dans cette mesure même le sens.

Ainsi, l'on pourra commencer l'analyse de l'arrière-plan empirique par un examen successif de ses conjonctures, auxquelles seront attribuées une ou deux formes d'existence. Cependant, l'on devra aussitôt confronter les formes d'existence de l'arrière-plan aux formes d'existence qui leur sont contemporaines à l'avant-plan. Il n'est pas indifférent par exemple qu'une forme d'existence obsessionnelle présente à l'EKP soit concomitante d'une forme d'existence paranoïde ou d'une forme d'existence homosexuelle au VGP. De plus, l'attribution des formes d'existence et plus généralement l'analyse dialectique des conjonctures de l'EKP devra veiller à s'appuyer sur des clivages dont le sens n'est pas biaisé par le phénomène des contraintes de choix. Ainsi un clivage nul non contraint (non barré) sera toujours suspecté.

Mais, au même titre que l'interprétation du profil simple, l'interprétation du profil pulsionnel total doit être complétée par une lecture verticale, par un examen des séries factorielles et vectorielles de l'arrière-plan et plus encore par une confrontation des clivages factoriels et vectoriels de l'arrière-plan avec les clivages correspondants de l'avant-plan. C'est ici que la méthode dite des concordances trouve sa juste place. A propos de chaque facteur, nous nous poserons la question: les clivages de l'arrière-plan confirment-ils les clivages de l'avant-plan ou bien révèlent-ils une orientation nouvelle par rapport à l'avant-plan? Dans le premier cas, nous devons considérer que les tendances de l'avant-plan sont très solidement installées, dans le second cas poser que des tendances réelles non apparentes à l'avant-plan et dissimulées par celui-ci animent la vie pulsionnelle du sujet. Précisons que dans la méthode des concordances que nous pratiquons, nous tenons compte des contraintes de choix, en telle sorte que les situations les plus significatives nous paraissent être les suivantes:

Clivages factoriels

VGP		+	-	o	±
EKP	confirmation	+	-	±	o
	orientation nouvelle	-	+	+ ou -	+ ou -

Sur cette base il est possible d'établir un tableau où figurent pour chaque facteur, d'une part les clivages dominants du VGP, d'autre part les clivages dominants de l'EKP, eux-mêmes différenciés selon qu'ils dénotent une confirmation ou une orientation nouvelle. Bien entendu, dans la mesure où il ne retient que les clivages dominants, ce tableau est trop sommaire: il doit être complété par une analyse plus fine qui confronte chaque clivage particulier de l'arrière-plan à son clivage concomitant de l'avant-plan, particulièrement pour les séries factorielles qui donnent lieu à une forte variabilité.

Enfin nous pouvons clôturer notre interprétation par une analyse axée sur les déroulements intervectoriels. Si des évolutions significatives affectent les conjonctures de l'avant-plan, quelles transformations leur correspondent à l'arrière-plan?

On voit ainsi que nous proposons de calquer l'interprétation du profil pulsionnel total sur la démarche qui préside à l'analyse du profil pulsionnel simple. Mais terminons par l'analyse d'un cas concret qui nous permettra d'illustrer nos principes.

d) L'analyse d'un cas concret

Vordergrundprofile (VGP)

Nr.	Soz.-Wert	S		P		Sch		C		Existenzform	
		h	s	e	hy	k	p	d	m		
1		o	±	±	–	±	o	o	+	12	
2		+!	o	–	–	–	–!	+	±	11	(13)
3		+	o	o	–	–!	–	+	+	11	
4		+!	o	+	–	–	–!	–	+	11	
5		+!	o	+	–	–	–	±	+	11	
6		+	o	o	–	–	–!	+	+	11	
7		+	o	+	–	–	–	+	±	11	
8		+!	o	+	–	–	–	±	–	11	
9		+	o	+	–	±	–!	–	o	2	
10		+	o	+	–	–	–!	–	+	11	

L'analyse de l'avant-plan nous aura permis de reconnaître le caractère tout à fait particulier de la première conjoncture, en conformité avec l'hypothèse de Van Reeth, que l'ensemble du déroulement ne confirme toutefois pas (en particulier, les dernières conjonctures ne marquent pas un retour sur les positions de la première). Arrêtons-nous donc un instant sur cette conjoncture exceptionnelle et ce qui y correspond à l'arrière-plan, pour vérifier une nouvelle fois des idées que nous avons émises.

La première conjoncture d'avant-plan est assurément une conjoncture obsessionnelle caractérisée. Cependant, nous aurions tort d'en tirer une conclusion prématurée. Car elle ne révèle nullement la problématique clinique de fond du sujet, qui ne va se libérer que dans la suite. L'accumulation des clivages nuls et ambitendants signe davantage une hésitation à prendre position et à se livrer face à un matériel nouveau, à l'occasion de l'instauration d'un premier contact avec un psychologue. Mais examinons la conjoncture concomitante d'arrière-plan qui confirme notre diagnostic provisoire. Ne prêtons pas trop d'attention à la forme d'existence paranoïde qui s'y révèlerait (du fait du seul clivage p-! : variante a) pour relever plutôt, de manière systématique, les clivages factoriels de l'EKP qui correspondent aux clivages nuls et ambitendants du VGP :

		h	s	e	k	p	d
VGP		o	±	±	±	o	o
EKP	confirmation		o	o			±
	orientation nouvelle	+!				–!	
	donnée ininterprétable				∅		

Nr.	Soz.-Wert	S		P		Sch		C		Existenzform	
		h	s	e	hy	k	p	d	m		
1		+!	0	0	0	∅	−!	±	+	2	
2		0	+!	−	±	−	0	−	∅	14	(13)
3		+	+!	−	−	∅	−	−	0	11	
4		−	±	−	−	+	0	+	+	9	
5		0	±!	±	+	+	−	−	−	13	
6		+	+!	−!	−	0	0	−	+	13	
7		+	±	−	0	+	−	0	+	13	
8		0	±!	−	−	+	−	−	+	13	
9		−	±	−	+	∅	∅	−	+	3	
10		+	±!	−	−	0	0	+	+	13	8

Nous voyons ainsi que dans trois cas, en l'occurrence dans les facteurs s, e et d, l'EKP confirme l'hésitation, l'absence de prise de position du VGP. Par contre, dans les deux autres cas, à savoir dans les facteurs h et p, l'indécision du VGP se trouve infirmée par l'EKP, au profit d'une tendance précise, quantitativement chargée. En d'autres termes, le sujet fait barrage ou silence sur trois dimensions pulsionnelles, par rapport auxquelles il refuse absolument de prendre position et par là de se livrer, alors qu'il s'exprime déjà en termes clairs, malgré une légère réticence, à propos de deux autres besoins pulsionnels. En fait, les tendances h+! et p-! sont des tendances d'emblée disponibles, même si elles sont momentanément recouvertes par une timidité de surface : si l'on tient à la métaphore topique, on pourrait dire qu'elles sont préconscientes et prêtes à migrer vers la conscience, et à cet égard il est hautement significatif que dès la deuxième conjoncture, elles apparaissent à l'avant-plan pour ne plus le quitter. Par contre, les besoins s, e et d sont des lieux pulsionnels à l'intérieur desquels s'exerce une censure beaucoup plus stricte : il n'est pas étonnant que ce soient eux qui abritent les orientations nouvelles les plus significatives de l'EKP. Mais c'est là ce que nous devons vérifier à présent.

Efforçons-nous donc d'examiner les autres conjonctures pulsionnelles en nous concentrant sur l'arrière-plan empirique.

Un premier coup d'œil d'ensemble jeté sur l'EKP considéré à titre de plan autonome fait apparaître la présence importante de formes d'existence épileptiformes, dominantes depuis la cinquième jusqu'à la dernière conjoncture. Celles-ci nous paraissent valablement diagnostiquées (essentiellement selon les variantes a et c), encore qu'elles ne soient pas toujours présentes à l'état pur. C'est pourquoi l'analyse dialectique devra révéler ce que l'étiquette recouvre précisément. Par ailleurs, l'objection que soulève le phénomène des contraintes de choix ne pourrait concerner que les conjonctures 6 et 10, qui comportent chacune un Schoo. Mais en fait, quand bien même ce dernier clivage devrait être converti en Sch ±±, il ne compromettrait point le diagnostic d'une forme d'existence 13 (cfr la variante d: Schoo *ou* Sch±±, e-!, P--).

Mais au-delà de l'inventaire statique et grossier des formes d'existence, une analyse plus fine nous indiquerait que le sujet est aux prises avec une forte agressivité (s+!) dirigée sur un objet qu'il retient du passé (d-): la charge de la tendance s+ coïncide toujours avec la tendance d-, alors que l'agressivité se détend pour s'associer à la passivité (s±) dès l'instant où le sujet esquisse un mouvement de recherche (d+), ce qui pourrait être signe d'une tendance à la perversion sado-masochiste, qui s'inscrit comme telle dans la conjoncture 4 (forme d'existence perverse, combinant le s±, le Sch+o et le C++). Mais comment le centre élabore-t-il le danger périphérique? Tout d'abord il réassume la tension agressive «incestueuse» sur un mode caïnesque (constance du e-): la tendance à exercer une prise active, voire à développer une agressivité physique à l'égard de l'objet ancien, se nourrit d'affects haineux. Quant au moi, s'il commence par se protéger de l'agressivité haineuse par un mécanisme névrotique (conjoncture 2: k-), il en vient rapidement, à partir de la cinquième conjoncture, à abonder dans son sens, l'incorporant autistiquement (Sch+-), pour parfois (conjoncture 6 en particulier), non tellement s'absenter devant elle (Schoo), mais plutôt se mobiliser sur un mode panique pour y faire face (Sch±±).

Mais abandonnons l'examen de l'arrière-plan comme plan autonome et pratiquons notre analyse de concordance, qui ne fera rien d'autre que confirmer notre première impression. Constituons donc le tableau qui confronte les clivages factoriels, pour n'y inscrire, il est vrai, que les données significatives qu'il est en état d'enregistrer:

	s	e	k	p
VGP	o	+	-	-
EKP { confirmation				-
orientation nouvelle	+(!)	-	+	
Tendance absente				+

Notre tentative concrète de construire le tableau des concordances factorielles entre VGP et EKP manifeste clairement les limites de pareil tableau: il ne dégage de données significatives que dans les facteurs dominés par des orientations précises, et cela aussi bien au VGP qu'à l'EKP. Ainsi, dans le cas qui nous occupe, les tendances univoques qui dominent le facteur h (h+) et hy (hy-) au VGP laissent place à l'EKP à des orientations très indécises balançant entre le h+ et le h-, entre le hy- et le hy+. Quant au vecteur C et à ses deux besoins, il est extrêmement mobile: ses quatre tendances sont présentes au VGP comme à l'EKP. Bien entendu, ce dernier fait mérite une attention soigneuse, d'autant plus que le profil d'avant-plan est dans l'ensemble très rigide et que la variabilité du vecteur C marque donc un contraste notoire; mais il ne peut être pris en compte par notre tableau des concordances. Il reste cependant que ce dernier, tout partiel qu'il soit, révèle des faits massifs que nous pouvons résumer comme suit: 1. Derrière une façade très défensive (e+, k-) qui évacue toute problématique d'agressivité (so), le sujet masque l'affirmation (k+) d'une agressivité (s+) caïnesque (e-); 2. De toutes les fonctions pulsionnelles, la fonction p+ de l'élaboration fantasmatique des désirs est la seule vraiment absente, exclue du jeu pulsionnel : nous ne pouvons en aucune manière compter sur elle.

Avant de conclure, il nous faut encore interroger les déroulements. Mais, nous venons de le dire, le profil d'avant-plan est très rigide. La seule évolution notable s'opère dans le passage de la première conjoncture à la deuxième conjoncture, dont nous connaissons déjà le sens : le sujet abandonne son blocage initial pour laisser apparaître, au VGP comme à l'EKP, des tendances qui vont désormais dominer les profils, ainsi les tendances h+, p- et k- (VGP), les tendances s+ et e- (EKP). Pour le reste, il n'est pas possible d'y relever des mouvements conjoncturels significatifs : dès la deuxième conjoncture, le sujet s'installe sur des positions protectrices de nature hypocondriaque-psychosomatique (forme d'existence 11 - 15) qu'il ne quittera plus. De sorte que les changements conjoncturels observables à l'arrière-plan ne peuvent être corrélés à des changements correspondants de l'avant-plan : telle forme d'existence précise de l'EKP n'est pas associée à une forme d'existence spécifique du VGP. Seuls des phénomènes partiels sont constatables. Retenons-en deux. Tout d'abord, l'examen conjoint des conjonctures 6 du VGP et de l'EKP permet de reconnaître une montée particulièrement intense des affects caïnesques, à laquelle le moi répond par une mobilisation défensive. La censure éthique s'efface (eo au VGP), en même temps que l'agressivité haineuse se charge (s+! et e-! à l'EKP); parallèlement le moi renforce sa pente projective (p- accentué au VGP) et se prépare à recourir à tous les mécanismes défensifs du moi (Schoo ayant valeur de Sch$\pm\pm$ à l'EKP). Mais plus intéressant assurément serait d'analyser les mouvements du vecteur C. L'instabilité de l'avant-plan signe le désarroi ambivalenciel d'un sujet qui tente de se divertir (d+) d'un rapport à un objet ancien (C-+) dont il n'arrive pas vraiment à se libérer, malgré ses esquisses de détachement (m-). Comparativement, l'arrière-plan accentue davantage le pôle de la fidélité et de la rétention collante : les formes d- et C-+ y sont plus prégnantes. Ce qui révèle sans doute ce que nous avons déjà dit, à savoir que l'agressivité caïnesque porte sur un objet d'attachement ancien. Mais une confrontation systématique des clivages de l'EKP avec les clivages concomitants du VGP renforce l'impression d'une ambivalence du contact : les mouvements de recherche (d+) du VGP sont souvent corrigés par une tendance à coller à l'objet (d-) à l'EKP (conjonctures 2, 3 et 6) et inversement (conjonctures 4 et 10); à l'infidélité la plus marquée du VGP (C+$\pm$, C$\pm$-) correspondent, dans les conjonctures 2 et 8, le collage et la fidélité (d-, C-+) de l'EKP et à la fidélité du VGP (C-+) correspond, dans les conjonctures 4 et 10, la dispersion multilatérale de l'EKP (C++).

En conclusion, que dire en quelques mots de la problématique d'ensemble du sujet telle qu'elle ressort de l'examen dialectique des deux profils d'avant-plan et d'arrière-plan ? Le sujet s'est construit une armature défensive très solide et très rigide. Les investissements désirants sont exclus de la conscience, refoulés et peut-être liés somatiquement. Mais de quoi le sujet se défend-il ? Quelle énergie pulsionnelle lie-t-il somatiquement ? L'arrière-plan nous répond : le sujet se protège d'une agressivité caïnesque, qui s'inscrit dans le contexte d'une relation de dépendance à un objet de contact. Les données cliniques dont nous disposons confirment notre analyse.

Le sujet se présente sous les allures d'un play-boy, sans aucune conscience de la moindre problématique psychologique : envoyé par son médecin de famille, il attend que le psychologue lui dise ce qui ne va pas et ce qu'il faut faire. Il apparaît écrasé, étouffé par une mère surprotectrice, dont il n'arrive pas à se libérer, si ce n'est sous la forme de liaisons amoureuses sporadiques et sans lendemain. Cliniquement, il souffre de symptômes psychosomatiques, céphalées, vertiges, syncopes. Il est fréquemment pris par des états de tension nerveuse extrêmes, qui ne parviennent pas à se décharger. Il est régulièrement responsable d'accidents de la circulation.

L'analyse du protocole pulsionnel nous aide à ramener la symptomatologie clinique à ses sources dynamiques : l'énergie du facteur e, écartée ou refusée par la censure défensive, se trouve liée sous forme de symptômes psychosomatiques dont Szondi avait reconnu dès l'origine la nature d'équivalents épileptoïdes.

Chapitre II
Considérations sur la psychopathologie pulsionnelle

Comme toute théorie au sens fort, la théorie pulsionnelle de Szondi pose l'existence de processus (en l'occurence de pulsions en état de fonctionnement) non directement accessibles à l'observation sensible. Cependant, pour avoir droit au titre de théorie scientifique, elle doit aussi pouvoir être mise en relation avec des phénomènes empiriques. Nous rencontrons le problème de la liaison entre le système pulsionnel et ses manifestations empiriques, dont les maladies mentales sont sans doute les plus significatives, en tout cas les plus étudiées. Certes, nous n'avons pu éviter de nous référer déjà à maintes reprises, tout au long de notre chapitre précédent, à la pathologie mentale et à ses diverses formes. Toutefois, en raison même de la place qu'elles occupent dans la doctrine psychopulsionnelle de Szondi, il nous importe à présent de leur consacrer un développement propre.

A. Classes nosographiques et catégories psychopulsionnelles

Commençons par nous interroger dans les termes les plus généraux sur la place que la démarche de Szondi confère à la maladie mentale, pour relever un double mouvement: d'une part un saut des classes aux catégories, d'autre part un retour ou une redescente des catégories vers les classes.

1. Le saut des classes aux catégories

Selon Schotte (1963), Szondi aurait opéré un saut des classes vers les catégories, nous précisons: un saut des classes nosographiques de la psychiatrie vers les catégories psychopulsionnelles. Mais de quoi s'agit-il?
Nous le savons, Szondi dénomme ses besoins pulsionnels à l'aide de termes empruntés à la nosographie psychiatrique: homosexualité, épilepsie, manie ... Mais, explique Schotte, dès l'instant où ces termes s'inscrivent dans le

schéma pulsionnel szondien, leur sens est comme transmué. Ils ne désignent plus des classes mutuellement exclusives d'individus malades mentaux, mais des catégories, nous dirons plus simplement : des processus généraux qui concernent non seulement tous les malades mentaux, mais encore tous les êtres humains quels qu'ils soient. Le système des concepts qui s'articulent dans le tableau pulsionnel n'est pas un système de concepts nosographiques, qui aiderait à cataloguer le malade mental (déjà au préalable classé comme malade mental, exclu de la classe des individus sains d'esprit), à l'insérer dans une classe ou une espèce qui le définirait en propre (comme homosexuel, ou comme épileptique, ou comme maniaque,...), mais un système de concepts qui déploie l'éventail complet des dimensions existentielles auxquelles participent tous les êtres humains. En quoi Szondi répéterait le mouvement déjà accompli par Freud, nous inviterait à lever la barrière étanche que nous avons toujours tendance à dresser entre le malade mental et l'homme « normal ». Car le choix de termes nosographiques n'est pas indifférent : il témoigne que le malade mental révèle à chacun de nous une figure irréductible de son humanité, ou, selon le célèbre principe du cristal, manifeste au grand jour, en ses points de rupture, ce qui anime toujours aussi la normalité, mais se trouve en elle plus dissimulée.

Mais avons-nous avec cette formule de Schotte épuisé le débat ? Szondi se contenterait-il de dépasser la frontière classificatoire du normal et du pathologique en direction de la mise au jour de principes humains généraux qui constitueraient autant de composantes de son système pulsionnel ? Nous ne le croyons pas. Szondi n'annule pas purement et simplement la distinction entre la maladie mentale et la normalité psychique. Il ne la suspend que temporairement pour mieux la retrouver en un second temps : il opère aussi un retour ou une redescente des catégories vers les classes.

2. *Le retour des catégories vers les classes*

Certes, les catégories psychopulsionnelles, les facteurs et les tendances pulsionnels (l'accrochage, la sensualité, la projection, ...), sont en tant que telles psychopathologiquement neutres : elles ne qualifient directement ni un état de morbidité mentale, ni de normalité psychique. Cependant, il n'est nullement exclu de redescendre des facteurs et tendances pulsionnels vers la clinique psychopathologique. Car certaines formes spécifiques de combinaison et de fonctionnement des facteurs et tendances pulsionnels ne seraient-elles pas caractéristiques des diverses entités nosographiques que la psychiatrie a répertoriées ? C'est bien là la question que soulève Szondi et à laquelle il répond positivement, soutenant que le diagnostic expérimental des pulsions, qui met précisément en état de fonctionnement les facteurs et tendances pulsionnels, n'est pas « seulement une méthode de recherche de la psychologie des profondeurs, mais aussi un procédé clinique utilisable en vue du psychodiagnostic », ajoutant encore : « on peut même diagnostiquer à l'aveugle les syndromes psychopathologiques cliniques » (TrP, p. 240).

On voit donc que le projet de Szondi n'est pas tant celui d'une suspension pure et simple de la distinction du normal et du pathologique et des distinctions cliniques opérées à l'intérieur du registre psychopathologique que celui d'une fondation ou d'une dérivation explicative de ces distinctions descriptives et classificatoires par le détour d'un corps de concepts théoriques généraux.

Reste une question : comment opérer cette redescente des catégories vers les classes ? Une démarche de déduction a priori se présentait assurément comme la plus congéniale à l'ambition d'une explication théorique. A cet égard, le tableau de Mendeleïev, par lequel Szondi aurait été obsédé, offrait le plus beau des modèles. Car Mendeleïev n'a-t-il pas réussi à dériver tous les corps chimiques concrets, connus et même inconnus, à partir d'une combinatoire de quelques propriétés essentielles ? De la même façon, n'aurait-il pas été possible d'engendrer les syndromes psychopathologiques fondamentaux (nous dirions même : un nombre limité et exhaustif de syndromes psychopathologiques) à partir des possibilités combinatoires des tendances pulsionnelles, qui, toutes innombrables voire infinies qu'elles soient, présentent toutefois quelques constellations que leurs propriétés formelles signalent comme constellations pures.

On peut dire que dans l'ensemble Szondi n'a guère été guidé par cette démarche de déduction théorique a priori, même si, comme nous le verrons, des considérations inspirées de sa théorie pulsionnelle guident parfois ses découpages et ses analyses psychopathologiques. Szondi a préféré suivre la voie de facilité que lui offrait son test. Plutôt que de procéder du système pulsionnel et de ses combinatoires a priori vers la clinique psychopathologique, il est parti de la clinique psychopathologique et des découpages classificatoires qu'elle opère, désignant tel sujet comme mélancolique, tel autre comme épileptique, tel autre encore comme homosexuel. Plus précisément, il a fait fonctionner son instrument sur des groupes de sujets homogènes du point de vue de l'étiquetage psychiatrique (sur un groupe de mélancoliques, par exemple), et puisque le test diagnostique par hypothèse les processus pulsionnels fondateurs, il a pu mettre au jour ainsi des constellations pulsionnelles explicatives des syndromes cliniques (de la mélancolie et des autres classes nosographiques).

Démarche dont Szondi nous présente les résultats majeurs dans la Triebpathologie, une œuvre organisée dans sa partie « syndromatique » par une classification des troubles mentaux, dont les caractéristiques pulsionnelles sont successivement passées en revue. C'est à cette œuvre que nous allons à présent emprunter l'essentiel de nos considérations, en vue tout d'abord d'analyser la classification des troubles mentaux qu'elle promeut, ensuite d'exposer quelques éléments très généraux de la syndromatique pulsionnelle des maladies mentales.

B. La classification szondienne des troubles mentaux

Nous donnons en p. 158 un tableau qui résume la classification szondienne des troubles mentaux telle qu'elle se dégage de la TrP. C'est ce tableau que nous allons commenter tout au long de ce paragraphe.

Il s'agit là au fond d'une classification qu'on pourrait dire classique, inspirée des apports aujourd'hui les mieux établis de la psychopathologie, aussi bien des apports de la psychiatrie kraepelinienne que des apports de la psychanalyse freudienne. Nous y observerons cependant quelques accents personnels, dont il nous importera d'interroger le sens.

Tableau IX : La classification szondienne des maladies mentales (d'après TrP)

LES PSYCHOSES	1. Les schizophrénies	a) paranoïde b) catatonique c) hébéphrénique	projective inflative
	2. La psychose maniaco-dépressive	a) la mélancolie b) la manie	
	3. L'hypocondrie et la dépersonnalisation		
LES PSYCHOPATHIES	1. Les psychopathies sexuelles	a) les perversions	introjectives (fétichisme et masochisme) destructives (sadisme et exhibitionnisme)
		b) l'homosexualité	masculine féminine
	2. Les psychopathies de contact	a) la « Sucht » b) le manque de tenue sexuelle (Sexuelle Haltlosigkeit)	
	3. Les psychopathies criminelles		
LES NEVROSES	1. La névrose du moi (névrose obsessionnelle)	a) l'hystérie de conversion	
	2. Les névroses paroxysmales	b) l'hystérie d'angoisse, la phobie c) l'hystéro-épilepsie, l'épilepsie d'affects, l'épilepsie génuine	

On remarque tout d'abord que le champ de la maladie mentale est divisé en trois groupes majeurs : le groupe des psychoses, le groupe des psychopathies et le groupe des névroses. Considérons successivement chacun de ces groupes.

Le groupe des *psychoses* appelle sans doute le moins de commentaires. Szondi fait essentiellement place en effet aux deux grandes entités qui depuis Kraepelin articule le registre des psychoses endogènes : la schizophrénie dont Kraepelin avait déjà établi les trois formes principales (paranoïde, catatonique et hébéphrénique) et la psychose circulaire ou maniaco-dépressive, oscillant cycliquement entre la mélancolie et la manie. Seules deux particularités sont à observer. On remarque tout d'abord que Szondi inclut parmi les psychoses les deux syndromes de l'hypocondrie et de la dépersonnalisation. Toutefois nous n'avons affaire là en quelque sorte qu'à deux syndromes annexes qui n'ont pas l'importance des deux grandes psychoses endogènes. De plus, leur inscription univoque dans le groupe des psychoses est plus que discutable. Ainsi, on peut penser que l'hypocondrie traverse tout le champ de la psychopathologie, ce que Szondi lui-même a implicitement admis, puisque si la TrP n'en reconnaît que la forme psychotique, l'inventaire des formes d'existence l'installe en position tout aussi univoque d'une formation «protectrice». Il vaut sans doute mieux, à l'instar de Melon (TP, pp. 287-293), ranger les deux syndromes de l'hypocondrie et de la dépersonnalisation parmi les états limites entre la névrose et la psychose. Enfin, nous pouvons noter, au titre d'une seconde particularité, que Szondi différencie une forme projective et une forme inflative de la schizophrénie paranoïde : la première, à dominante persécutive, repose sur le dynamisme de la tendance projective p-, alors que la seconde, dont le délire est caractérisé par une thématique prévalente de grandeur, est fondée par une exaspération de la tendance inflative p+. Pour la première fois, nous remarquons ainsi l'incidence de la théorie des pulsions, présente ici à travers la polarité des tendances p+ et p-, sur la classification psychopathologique. Mais nous l'observerons encore davantage dans l'analyse des deux autres groupes cliniques.

Szondi inclut dans la nébuleuse *« psychopathique »* ce qui s'y trouve couramment rangé, en gros les perversions sexuelles, les toxicomanies et les délinquances criminelles, encore que Szondi opère ici quelques infléchissements qui ne sont pas étrangers à ses perspectives théoriques générales. Mais avant de relever ces derniers, remarquons que la TrP ne consacre aucun développement propre au troisième groupe des psychopathies dites criminelles, pour lesquelles Szondi renvoie au travail de Waelder: *Triebstruktur und Kriminalität* (1952). Attachons-nous donc plus spécialement aux deux premiers groupes, pour y souligner d'emblée ce que nous annoncions : ils sont introduits dans les termes mêmes de la théorie des pulsions. Car si Szondi parle de psychopathies sexuelles, c'est moins pour désigner des troubles qui se manifestent empiriquement au plan de l'activité sexuelle que pour pointer des perturbations qui relèvent du dynamisme de la pulsion ou du vecteur sexuel. De même que s'il individualise des psychopathies de contact, c'est clairement pour indiquer cela même qui les fonde pulsionnellement, à savoir un fonctionnement spécifique de la pulsion ou du vecteur du contact. Mais bien sûr, Szondi vise aussi sous ces termes des formes pathologiques classiquement délimitées.

Les *psychopathies sexuelles* recouvrent ce qui est plus couramment désigné comme perversions sexuelles, même si Szondi utilise le terme de perversion de manière plus limitative qu'il n'est de tradition. Il dégage en effet l'homosexualité dans ses deux variantes masculine et féminine du groupe des perversions qu'il différencie à nouveau d'après un critère congénial à sa théorie des pulsions. Il fait apparaître une affinité, d'une part entre le fétichisme et le masochisme, caractérisés par une prévalence de la fonction introjective k+, d'autre part entre le sadisme et l'exhibitionnisme, dominés par le dynamisme de la fonction négatrice k- s'emballant sur un mode autodestructeur (k-!).

Quant aux *psychopathies de contact*, elles incorporent les toxicomanies. Toutefois, Szondi procède ici à un élargissement conceptuel, qui constitue sans doute l'un des apports les plus remarquables de sa classification des troubles mentaux. Sous le terme de « Sucht », Szondi désigne l'état de « rage » « démangeaison », « fureur » (autant de termes qui ne traduisent que bien inadéquatement le « Sucht » allemand), qui caractérise le rapport au monde de certains individus, poussés impulsivement, sous l'emprise d'un besoin incoercible, à poser un acte électif ou à se procurer un objet tout aussi électif. On reconnaît assurément là l'état du toxicomane, de l'alcoolique ou du drogué. Mais, estime Szondi, la « Sucht » déborde largement la toxicomanie au sens étroit. A la limite, toute activité quelle qu'elle soit (boire, fumer, mais aussi collectionner, jouer, voler,...) est susceptible de dégénérer en Sucht. Toute activité, y compris par exemple l'activité sexuelle. D'où la mise au jour par Szondi d'un syndrome dit de la « Sexuelle Haltlosigkeit » (ou « manque de tenue sexuelle »), dans lequel il faut voir moins un syndrome faisant contrepoint à la « Sucht » qu'une sorte de variante sexuelle de la « Sucht ». Car le « manque de tenue sexuelle » désigne l'état des individus qui se livrent, de manière effrénée, avec « démangeaison », « rage » et « fureur », à l'activité sexuelle. Si au plan clinique ou empirique ce trouble se manifeste bien comme trouble sexuel, il n'est pas à proprement parler un trouble sexuel. Car, comme les toxicomanies et les autres formes de « Sucht », il relève du dynamisme de la pulsion du contact: il résulte d'un échec à assumer la perte de l'objet, la rupture de l'union duelle et témoigne d'une tentative furieuse de reconstituer l'union duelle rompue par le truchement d'un objet ou d'une activité substitutive.

Ainsi donc, si Szondi reprend à son compte une classification psychiatrique traditionnelle, il n'hésite pas cependant à innover sur certains points, à introduire un syndrome original (le « manque de tenue sexuelle »), mais bien davantage à opérer une restructuration par élargissement, qui le conduit à poser un syndrome de la « Sucht » dont les toxicomanies ne seraient qu'une forme particulière, et cela moins pour des raisons strictement cliniques que pour des raisons théoriques liées à la doctrine pulsionnelle et à sa promotion d'une pulsion du contact. Mais observons immédiatement un phénomène analogue au plan de l'organisation du champ des névroses.

Si nous jetons un coup d'œil sur la structuration du *registre névrotique*, nous découvrons en effet que Szondi tout à la fois réassume la distinction sans doute la plus éprouvée entre la névrose obsessionnelle et l'hystérie et procède à une restructuration par élargissement, elle-même corrélative de la mise au jour d'un syndrome nouveau, du moins comme syndrome relevant de la psychopathologie. La différenciation la plus fondamentale se formule à nouveau dans les termes de la théorie pulsionnelle. La névrose obsessionnelle définie comme névrose du moi, à savoir comme névrose fondée sur le dynamisme de la pulsion du moi, s'oppose à des névroses dites paroxysmales elles-mêmes régies par le fonctionnement du vecteur P. Mais à vrai dire c'est dans la délimitation de ce dernier groupe qu'émerge l'originalité la plus marquante. Szondi élargit en individualisant un groupe dont l'hystérie dans ses deux variantes devenues classiques depuis la psychanalyse (hystérie de conversion et hystérie d'angoisse ou phobie) ne constitue qu'une forme particulière, et au même moment fait apparaître un syndrome dont la présence signe une des autres caractéristiques remarquables de la classification szondienne, nous voulons parler de l'épilepsie, désignée comme hystéro-épilepsie, épilepsie d'affects ou épilepsie « génuine ».

Au demeurant, l'apparition de l'épilepsie dans la classification szondienne des troubles mentaux répondait à une nécessité prescrite a priori. Car, bien avant que la TrP ne construise une nosographie psychopathologique, Szondi avait levé le monopole neurologique jeté sur l'épilepsie et réintégré cette dernière dans le registre de la pathologie mentale. D'entrée en jeu, Szondi avait élu l'épilepsie comme une maladie mentale susceptible de véhiculer et de révéler un besoin pulsionnel fondamental, une dimension existentielle universellement humaine. Il était dès lors nécessaire que la redescente des catégories vers les classes conduise à retrouver l'épilepsie, bien plus à la retrouver au voisinage de l'hystérie. Mais cette remarque ne nous permet-elle pas de toucher un point des plus problématiques ? Szondi n'a-t-il pas dès l'origine, avant même son saut vers les catégories, postulé une classification des maladies mentales, celle qui précisément a servi de tremplin à son bond vers les catégories pulsionnelles et se trouve inscrite à même la grille du test ? Ne serait-ce pas là la seule classification véritablement congéniale à la doctrine psychopulsionnelle ? N'est-ce pas elle en fin de compte que la théorie pulsionnelle aurait à fonder ?

Il faut l'avouer, nous sommes loin d'avoir réussi pareille fondation, qu'impose pourtant une exigence de cohérence logique. Dans la TrP la classification des troubles mentaux qui sert de fil conducteur à l'exposé de la syndromatique demeure très largement extérieure à la classification qui sous-tend le système des besoins pulsionnels, même si d'une certaine façon elle l'englobe, faisant figurer côte à côte les schizophrénies paranoïde (p) et catatonique (k), la dépression mélancolique (d) et la manie (m), les perversions, parmi lesquelles le sadisme (s) et l'homosexualité (h), l'hystérie (hy) et l'épilepsie (e). Et pourtant Szondi lui-même a perçu la nécessité d'une sorte de rencontre voire de fusion des deux classifications, puisque le second grand exposé syndromatique de son œuvre, contenu dans la partie « clinique » de la SchaTh (1963) adopte comme cadre organisateur les catégories du schéma pulsionnel et distingue : les troubles de la sexualité (homosexualité et perversion sado-masochiste) les troubles des affects (hystérie et épilepsie), les troubles du moi (essentiellement les schizophrénies, mais aussi la névrose obsessionnelle) et enfin les troubles du contact (parmi lesquels, à côté de la névrose d'acceptation et de la « Sucht », la psychose maniaco-dépressive). Cependant, pareil catalogue nosographique, qui épouse les découpes du système pulsionnel, son organisation en vecteurs et privilégie les troubles inhérents à la classification originaire, garde l'allure d'un pur inventaire empirique. Ainsi, pour ne citer qu'un exemple, Szondi ne nous explique pas à propos de l'homosexualité et du sado-masochisme pourquoi ces deux troubles, et eux seuls, méritent d'être reconnus comme les troubles sexuels les plus fondamentaux et en quelque sorte les plus purs. En conséquence, l'exclusion d'autres formes de perversion ne peut apparaître qu'arbitraire. Il reste donc à montrer que les règles du fonctionnement combinatoire et dialectique des tendances et des facteurs pulsionnels appellent l'engendrement d'un nombre limité de troubles fondamentaux, identiques aux formes pathologiques de la nosographie originelle. Mais, nous l'avons déjà dit, Szondi n'a pas emprunté de manière un tant soit peu systématique la voie de la déduction théorique, en sorte que la classification psychopathologique de l'Analyse du destin demeure jusqu'à nouvel ordre dans un état d'émiettement empirique, et cela malgré les efforts prometteurs mais toujours embryonnaires d'un Schotte, occupé à jeter les bases d'une nosographie renouvelée à la lumière de catégories pulsionnelles elles-mêmes repensées (cfr pp. 54-55).

C'est en vue de contribuer, non tellement à résoudre ce problème qu'à l'éclaircir davantage, que nous développerons à présent quelques considérations sur la syndromatique pulsionnelle des maladies mentales.

C. La syndromatique pulsionnelle des maladies mentales

Dans le paragraphe que nous venons d'achever, nous avons examiné la classification szondienne des maladies mentales, en nous efforçant d'y relever quelques signes qui laissaient transparaître l'influence de la théorie pulsionnelle. Nous allons maintenant tenter d'émettre quelques remarques à propos de la syndromatique pulsionnelle des maladies mentales, à savoir à propos des constellations pulsionnelles typiques, formulées en termes de clivages, qui caractériseraient les diverses formes de la pathologie mentale.

Nous avons toute raison de penser, rappelons-le, que ces constellations ont été établies par Szondi à la faveur d'une démarche empirique opérant via le test, dont nous avons déjà défini les principes généraux.

Toutefois, nous devons avouer que Szondi ne nous donne guère d'indications sur les démarches précises qu'il a accomplies. Jamais il ne nous révèle combien de sujets appartenant à un groupe pathologique ont été testés, selon quelles méthodes il a dégagé de leurs protocoles des caractéristiques pulsionnelles de groupe,... Ici comme ailleurs, le souci méthodologique de Szondi est quasiment nul, ce qui lui a valu des critiques justifiées. En telle sorte que les constellations syndromatiques de la TrP n'ont d'autre statut que celui d'hypothèses de travail et appellent en conséquence des recherches nouvelles conduites selon des procédures méthodologiques rigoureuses, en vue de les confirmer ou de les infirmer, ou encore de les affiner et de les compléter. Pareilles recherches sont en cours et on ne peut dire qu'elles confirment toujours les hypothèses szondiennes.

Cela dit, il ne peut être question pour nous d'entrer ici dans un examen détaillé de la syndromatique des maladies mentales. Sur ce point, nous renvoyons, soit directement à la TrP de Szondi, soit à l'exposé fouillé de Jean Melon (TP, Partie « Syndromatique », pp. 182 ss.), qui s'appuie d'ailleurs étroitement sur la TrP, tout en l'agrémentant çà et là de quelques compléments. Au demeurant, nous avons déjà émaillé notre chapitre précédent de notations relatives à l'apparition des fonctions et clivages pulsionnels dans diverses formes de maladies mentales. Aussi nous limiterons-nous à une seule observation, qui s'insère dans le contexte des préoccupations que nous venons il y a peu d'avouer.

A l'examen attentif de la syndromatique pulsionnelle des maladies mentales, nous avons été frappé par un fait. Même si Szondi s'est laissé emporter par l'observation empirique, il est vrai aussi que sa mise au jour des constellations syndromatiques caractéristiques est constamment guidée par un point de vue théorique relevant de la dialectique pulsionnelle. On découvre en effet que si les troubles pulsionnels affectent toujours un vecteur privilégié parmi les quatre vecteurs pulsionnels, ils affectent aussi dans tous les cas le vecteur du moi. Nous pourrions en vérifier le principe sur toutes les formes de la pathologie pulsionnelle.

En d'autres termes plus précis encore, toute constellation pulsionnelle caractéristique d'un syndrome psychopathologique est dominée à la fois par un danger pulsionnel majeur localisé dans l'un ou l'autre des quatre vecteurs pulsionnels et par un mécanisme du moi. De plus, dans la plupart des cas, hormis dans le cas des psychopathies de contact, il est possible d'assigner aux formes de la pathologie mentale leur danger pulsionnel principal et leur mécanisme du moi caractéristique. A telle enseigne que nous avons pu dresser les tableaux des pp. 164-166.

Pour terminer, nous formulerons trois remarques que nous inspirent ces tableaux.

1. Il peut arriver que le danger pulsionnel majeur et le mécanisme du moi coïncident, précisément dans les cas où le danger pulsionnel majeur est localisé dans le vecteur du moi (le moi étant aussi une pulsion susceptible d'être un lieu de danger pulsionnel): c'est le cas en particulier dans les schizophrénies paranoïde et catatonique, ainsi que dans la névrose obsessionnelle.

2. Dans la perspective d'une fondation psychopulsionnelle de la classification szondienne des maladies mentales que nous avons appelée originelle, nous pouvons remarquer que les huit troubles mentaux qui ont servi de point d'appui au saut catégoriel et à la mise au jour des besoins pulsionnels sont tous dominés par un danger pulsionnel qui a son siège dans les vecteurs et même bien souvent dans les facteurs correspondants.

Mais il ne s'agissait là que d'un juste retour des choses. Car si la manie, par exemple, avait été apte à révéler un besoin d'accrochage, il était logique que la redescente du besoin d'accrochage vers la manie manifeste en elle une exaspération dynamique du besoin d'accrochage. Et de même pour les sept autres formes pathologiques originelles.

3. Malheureusement, la fondation théorique de la classification originelle rencontre aussi des limites évidentes. Il ne nous est pas possible de redescendre en toute rigueur de dangers pulsionnels concevables a priori vers les classes nosographiques. Ainsi, pour ne citer qu'un seul exemple, nous ne pouvons établir une relation stricte entre les dangers pulsionnels qui affectent le moi et le groupe des schizophrénies. S'il est vrai, comme nous l'avons déjà noté, que les schizophrénies paranoïde et catatonique sont bien dominées par

Tableaux X
Caractéristiques pulsionnelles dominantes des troubles mentaux

	SCHIZOPHRÉNIES			PSYCHOSES		PSYCHOSE MANIACO-DEPRESSIVE	
	PARANOÏDE		CATATONIE	HEBEPHRENIE	MELANCOLIE	MANIE
	a) projective	b) inflative					
Siège du danger principal	Sch	Sch	Sch	P	C	C
Modalité du danger principal	p o-!	p o+!	k -!o	hy o-!	d +±	m o-
Mécanisme de défense du moi	,,	,,	,,	-!-!	k +!-	k -!-!

CONSIDÉRATIONS SUR LA PSYCHOPATHOLOGIE PULSIONNELLE

	PSYCHOPATHIES								
	SEXUELLES							DE CONTACT	
	Perversions				Homosexualité				
	Introjectives		Destructives		Masculine	Féminine	« Sucht »	Manque de tenue sexuelle	
	Fétichisme	Masochisme	Sadisme	Exhibition-nisme					
Siège du danger principal	S	S	S	P	S	S	C	C
Modalité du danger principal	o-!	o-!	o+!	o-!	+-	-+	o+!?	o+?
Mécanisme de défense du moi	k +!o	k +!o	-+	-+	o±	±o	oo?	?

	Névrose obsessionnelle	NEVROSES		
		Hystérie de conversion	Névroses paroxysmales	
			Phobie Hystérie d'angoisse	Epilepsie Hystéro-épilepsie Epilepsie d'affects
	Sch	P	P	P
Siège du danger principal				
Modalité du danger principal	± o	+ → + o o	+ o	e - - - o -
Mécanisme de défense du moi	,,	± -	± ±	o o

un danger pulsionnel dont le lieu est le vecteur du moi, il n'est pas vrai que tout danger pulsionnel du moi donne lieu à une schizophrénie (cfr l'exception de la névrose obsessionnelle) pas plus que toute schizophrénie n'est dominée par un danger pulsionnel du moi (cfr l'exception de l'hébéphrénie).

Mais quoi qu'il en soit, malgré les limitations inévitables d'une démarche axée sur l'accueil foisonnant de l'empirique, le principe d'une combinatoire entre un danger pulsionnel principal et un mécanisme du moi pourrait dans l'avenir se révéler heuristique. Notre prochain chapitre nous permettra de reconnaître en lui l'une des lois de fonctionnement de toute totalité structurale.

Chapitre III
Le moi et l'ordre pulsionnel

Pour achever notre troisième partie, il nous reste à développer le troisième point que nous nous étions promis de traiter, à savoir à élucider quelque peu la position du moi à l'intérieur de l'ordre pulsionnel. A vrai dire, nous n'avons pu éviter de fournir déjà quelques indications à cet égard. Ainsi, nous avons souligné que la pulsion du moi avait cette propriété spécifique de toujours s'expliquer aussi avec les autres pulsions (pp. 75-76) et pointé au passage la fonction intégratrice que Szondi attribue au moi, le désignant comme « Pontifex oppositorum » (p. 89). Ce sont ces quelques indications embryonnaires que nous devons à présent systématiser davantage.

Pour ce faire, nous allons emprunter un détour. Il y a bien longtemps déjà (1969), nous avons souligné combien le concept de totalité structurale promu par Louis Althusser était susceptible de jeter une lumière particulière sur le système pulsionnel de Szondi. Aussi rappellerons-nous en termes brefs les composantes essentielles du modèle althussérien, développé en vue de rendre intelligible la conception marxiste de la totalité sociale, pour nous demander ensuite en quel sens il éclaire l'ordre pulsionnel et son fonctionnement, et plus particulièrement la place dévolue au moi.

A. Le concept althussérien de totalité structurale

La totalité sociale articule ce qu'Althusser appelle des instances, à savoir plus précisément, selon les vues classiques du marxisme, les trois instances économique, juridico-politique et idéologique. Ces instances sont elles-mêmes structurées, à savoir composées de divers éléments mis en rapport — ainsi, l'instance économique combine divers éléments : force de travail, objet de production, instrument de production... De plus, elles sont autonomes, et en tant que telles susceptibles d'être l'objet d'un examen propre, qui en construirait, par exemple, l'histoire spécifique. Néanmoins, les instances ne sont autonomes que relativement: elles entretiennent un rapport régi par une loi qui leur assigne un rôle particulier à l'intérieur du tout. Mais à quels principes obéit l'articulation des instances? La réponse introduit deux concepts décisifs.

« Le tout complexe possède l'unité d'une structure articulée à dominante » écrit Althusser[1]. L'une des instances du tout joue, dans une conjoncture donnée, le rôle directeur. L'évolution de la conjoncture transfèrera la dominante d'une instance à l'autre. De plus, toute instance est susceptible d'assumer, à l'un ou l'autre des moments de l'histoire du tout, la fonction de dominante: « Tout type est pensable: conjoncture à dominante politique (crise dans l'Etat), idéologique (combat anti-religieux, comme au XIIIe siècle), économique (grande grève), scientifique (coupure décisive, comme la création de la physique galiléenne) »[2].

Mais qu'est-ce qui détermine l'organisation spécifique du tout complexe articulé à dominante? Qu'est-ce qui règle en dernier ressort le déplacement de la dominante? Une instance déterminante, répond Althusser, et en l'occurence, dans le cas de la totalité sociale, l'instance économique. L'instance économique est certes, en tant qu'instance ou structure régionale, inscrite elle-même en un lieu défini de la structure globale, et donc soumise à la règle de cette structure globale, à savoir la règle de dominance: elle pourra être soumise, dans une conjoncture particulière, à l'efficace d'une autre instance; elle n'est donc pas toujours, comme le veut l'économisme, l'instance dominante du tout social. Mais l'instance économique est aussi une instance décalée par rapport aux autres instances, à la fois dans et hors de la totalité, visible et invisible. En tant qu'excentrée, elle fixe la dominante conjoncturelle et règle la permutation de cette dominante. En ce sens, l'instance économique détermine elle-même la propre position, de dominante ou non, qu'elle occupe, comme instance, dans l'espace du tout articulé.

B. Le système pulsionnel comme totalité articulée à dominante et déterminante

Le système pulsionnel de Szondi est-il susceptible d'être éclairé à la lumière du concept de totalité structurale promu par Althusser?

Tout d'abord, il est assez clair que le système pulsionnel de Szondi est diversifié en régions structurées et relativement autonomes. On aura deviné que nous visons sous le terme de « régions » les quatre vecteurs pulsionnels: 1. complexifiés en éléments plus simples, eux-mêmes en dialectique réciproque (les facteurs et tendances pulsionnels); 2. susceptibles, selon les termes mêmes de Szondi, d'une « intuition d'essence », qui leur assigne une signification propre, indépendante de l'ensemble dont ils participent (TrD, p. 207), tout en étant toujours aussi engagés dans une interaction mutuelle. En conséquence, nous ne nous attarderons guère à cet aspect du problème, pour nous poser une question qui elle nous retiendra plus longuement: le

---

[1] L. Althusser, *Pour Marx*, Maspero, 1966, p. 208.

[2] A. Badiou, Le (re)commencement du matérialisme historique, dans *Critique*, 240, mai 1967, pp. 455-456.

système szondien en état de fonctionnement comprend-il l'équivalent de ce qu'Althusser appelle respectivement une instance dominante et une instance déterminante ? C'est en répondant à cette question que nous ferons apparaître la position privilégiée du moi à l'intérieur de l'ordre pulsionnel, ou mieux encore : ses deux positions privilégiées.

1. Le système pulsionnel comme totalité à dominante : le premier privilège du moi

Il est frappant de constater combien Szondi, analysant une conjoncture, a toujours le souci d'y repérer un danger pulsionnel prévalent. Nous l'avons suffisamment remarqué dans notre chapitre précédent à propos des formes de la pathologie mentale : toute conjoncture psychopathologique typique est dominée par un danger pulsionnel qui a son siège dans l'un des quatre vecteurs pulsionnels. Il ne nous paraît donc nullement forcé d'énoncer comme principe général que le système pulsionnel (la totalité pulsionnelle) est dominé, à tout moment de son fonctionnement (en toute conjoncture), par l'un de ses quatre vecteurs (par l'une des quatre instances du tout), à savoir par ce vecteur qui est le lieu du danger pulsionnel principal.

Mais nous savons déjà aussi que cette règle de dominance doit être complétée. Toute conjoncture est dominée certes par un danger pulsionnel, mais aussi par un mécanisme du moi. D'où un premier privilège du moi, celui-là même que nous avons déjà relevé et qui résulte de la définition de la pulsion du moi comme pulsion qui, outre son énergie pulsionnelle propre, élabore les autres pulsions, les accueille dans son espace pour les soumettre à ses processus prévalents (projection et/ou inflation et/ou introjection et/ou négation) et ainsi les transformer.

Toutefois, là n'est peut-être pas le seul privilège du moi. Le moi ne serait pas seulement une composante toujours décisive d'un fonctionnement pulsionnel dominé par un danger qu'il combat, nuance ou infléchit, mais il aurait aussi le statut d'instance déterminante de la totalité pulsionnelle régissant en quelque sorte le jeu d'ensemble de la dialectique pulsionnelle, y compris la propre fonction défensive qu'il remplit face à un danger pulsionnel dominant.

Mais pour dégager ce second privilège du moi, le texte szondien doit être soumis à une opération créatrice, nous voulons dire par là que si Szondi a d'une certaine façon produit le concept du moi comme instance déterminante, il ne l'a que bien peu affirmé en termes explicites. Il nous faut donc accomplir l'effort de l'extraire thématiquement des textes qui le présupposent.

2. Le système pulsionnel comme totalité à déterminante : le second privilège du moi

Nous nous proposons de circuler à travers quelques textes de Szondi en vue de dégager une conception du moi comme « instance déterminante invisible ». Nous montrerons d'abord comment Szondi pose l'existence d'une instance psychique « plus haute » (« déterminante ») responsable du clivage des pulsions. Interrogeant ensuite les mécanismes qui divisent ou clivent les pulsions, nous observerons qu'il s'agit de mécanismes du moi, à quel moment nous pourrons conclure que cette instance plus haute responsable du clivage des pulsions n'est autre que le moi lui-même. Il ne nous restera plus qu'à établir que ce moi « déterminant » est un moi « invisible » et nous serons alors en état d'esquisser, à titre d'hypothèse, une théorie cohérente d'ensemble.

a) Une instance psychique plus haute

Il arrive à Szondi, dans la SchaTh en particulier, de s'interroger sur la relation qui lierait danger pulsionnel dominant et mécanisme de défense du moi. Lequel cause l'autre?

Le mécanisme du moi produit-il le danger pulsionnel? Szondi le laisse parfois entendre. Ainsi il écrit: « la préphase de l'introjection (Sch = $+\pm$), l'intégration (Sch = $\pm\pm$), la compulsion (Sch = $\pm$ o) et la fuite (Sch = $\pm$ -) peuvent, dans certaines circonstances, paralyser totalement la sexualité, et plus précisément sous forme d'asexualité, d'abstinence, de frigidité (S = oo)» (IchA, p. 358).

Mais à d'autres moments, Szondi renverse la relation de causalité. Ce serait plutôt le danger pulsionnel qui imposerait un mécanisme de défense du moi. Les modifications du moi, se demande Szondi au cours de la discussion des troubles des affects (hystérie et épilepsie), sont-elles primairement conditionnées par les paroxysmes affectifs (vecteur P) ou inversement (SchaTh, p. 357)? Et il répond: « dans ces maladies, les paroxysmes affectifs jouent le rôle principal. Ce sont ces paroxysmes qui produisent dans le moi un mode spécial de division ... la modification du moi s'installe secondairement, comme défense contre les exigences des affects...» (SchaTh, p. 359).

Szondi hésite donc quant à la direction de la causalité: procède-t-elle du mécanisme du moi au danger pulsionnel ou inversement? Mais sommes-nous contraints de nous enfermer dans l'alternative? Le mécanisme du moi et le danger pulsionnel ne sont-ils pas les éléments d'une dialectique dirigée d'ailleurs? Référons-nous à un texte capital. Szondi y évoque la dialectique d'une image sexuelle et d'une image du moi, en l'occurence la dialectique qui se joue, dans la conjoncture de l'homme de tous les jours, entre l'alliage de la sexualité (S++) et l'alliage du moi (Sch--). Szondi écrit alors: « on pourrait supposer que l'alliage du moi veille à l'alliage de la sexualité. Ou inversement: que l'alliage de la sexualité conditionne l'alliage du moi. Une troisième hypothèse serait qu'il existe dans la vie psychique de l'être humain une instance plus haute qui veille aussi bien à l'alliage dans la sexualité qu'à l'alliage dans le moi» (SchaTh, pp. 317-318).

On voit donc comment Szondi produit dans ce tout dernier texte le concept d'une instance « plus haute », qui équivaut à l'instance « déterminante » du modèle althussérien. Car cette instance régit bien les formes prises par les deux composantes « dominantes » de la conjoncture dite de « l'homme de tous les jours », à savoir par le vecteur dominant S (S++) et par le vecteur Sch, siège du mécanisme du moi (Sch--). Or, dans la théorie pulsionnelle de Szondi, cette instance déterminante ne peut être que l'instance responsable du clivage des pulsions, puisque toutes les formes de la dialectique pulsionnelle (ici en l'occurrence les formes S++ et Sch--) sont identiques à des modalités du clivage des tendances pulsionnelles réparties entre l'avant-plan et l'arrière-plan théorique. Tournons-nous donc, pour relancer notre propos, vers quelques textes qui analysent les mécanismes formateurs des deux plans clivés de la vie pulsionnelle.

b) Le moi comme instance déterminante

Szondi évoque le plus souvent une différence de force de pénétration entre les tendances d'avant-plan et les tendances d'arrière-plan. Il écrit : « par suite de la force différente des tendances élémentaires, certaines tendances, précisément celles qui sont ... plus fortes, poussent (drängen) à l'avant-plan de la vie pulsionnelle; par contre, les tendances plus faibles sont poussées (gedrängt) à l'arrière par les plus fortes » (TrD, p. 99). L'avant-plan pousse donc l'arrière-plan.

Mais les besoins évacués de l'avant (o) et accumulés à l'arrière avec leurs deux tendances élémentaires (±), seront parfois interprétés comme besoins refoulés. Commentant les clivages do et hyo de l'avant-plan, Szondi écrit : « l'homme refoule (verdrängt) ses gros besoins anaux (do) ..., et les tendances exhibitionnistes (hyo) » (TrP, p. 479).

Enfin, il n'est pas rare que Szondi souligne la possibilité d'une relation de négation entre l'avant-plan et l'arrière-plan : « Ainsi, l'avant-moi de l'homme inhibé (Sch = -+) nie énergiquement son contre-pied dans l'inconscient, à savoir l'arrière-moi autistique-indiscipliné (Sch = +-) » (IchA, pp. 221-222).

Des termes de la série « poussée », « refoulement », « négation », sont donc fréquemment invoqués par Szondi pour situer la relation entre les tendances d'avant-plan et les tendances d'arrière-plan. Mais ils ne sont pas les seuls.

Dans les pp. 141-142 de la TrP, Szondi retrace une genèse quasi mythique du clivage de la vie pulsionnelle. Par l'entrée en jeu du mécanisme d'inflation, quelques tendances pulsionnelles seraient arrachées aux couches les plus profondes de l'inconscient, et parviendraient aux limites de la conscience. Ou encore, certaines tendances, plus fortes et plus rapides, réussiraient à gagner l'avant-plan de l'inconscient, représenté par l'espace d'inflation (p+), abandonnant derrière elles d'autres tendances, plus faibles et moins vivaces, condamnées à demeurer à l'arrière de l'inconscient que représente l'espace de projection (p-).

Les quelques notes éparses que nous venons de rassembler ont pour portée d'indiquer que des mécanismes s'exercent sur l'ensemble des tendances d'avant-plan ou d'arrière-plan. L'arrière-plan est poussé, refoulé, nié, par l'avant-plan, avions-nous d'abord remarqué. Mais nous avons appris aussi que les tendances d'avant-plan étaient soumises à un processus d'inflation, et que les tendances de l'arrière-plan occupaient l'espace de la projection. Et, ajouterons-nous dès à présent, nous citerons bientôt un texte dans lequel il est question d'une introjection des tendances d'avant-plan. Or, nous le savons, les mécanismes d'introjection et de négation, d'inflation et de projection sont des mécanismes du moi. Que conclure, sinon que l'instance plus haute, déterminante, qui agit sur l'avant-plan et l'arrière-plan et opère par là leur clivage, est assimilable à un moi? Mais quel est donc ce moi?

c) Le moi déterminant invisible

Avant de suggérer une réponse, précisons dans quel sens nous entendons ici les termes « visible » et « invisible ». Nous qualifions de visibles les clivages qui s'inscrivent explicitement dans le protocole pulsionnel. Ainsi le clivage Sch±+, inscrit dans le protocole comme composante d'une conjoncture pulsionnelle, révèle le mécanisme visible du moi. Par contraste, nous qualifions le moi déterminant d'invisible, parce que précisément il n'apparaît pas comme tel dans la constellation des instances telle que la rend intégralement thématique le protocole pulsionnel.

Mais reprenons notre question: quel est le moi qui opère le clivage des pulsions selon les processus qui lui sont congéniaux: l'introjection et la négation, l'inflation et la projection? La réponse de Szondi est: le moi visible d'avant-plan. Le moi d'avant-plan agirait donc à la fois sur l'ensemble des tendances de l'avant-plan et sur l'ensemble des tendances de l'arrière-plan.

Mais d'une part, est-il légitime d'affirmer que le moi visible d'avant-plan agit sur l'ensemble des tendances de l'avant-plan? N'agit-il pas plutôt, selon la règle que prescrit la dialectique pulsionnelle, sur les tendances de la périphérie? Citons un cas particulier exemplaire: le moi, dit Szondi, introjecte (k+) une figure dépressive (k+, d+, s-) (Icha, p. 390). En d'autres termes, l'avant-moi introjectif (Sch = +o) contribue à déterminer, comme mécanisme de défense du moi, et conjointement aux clivages s- (le masochisme) et d+ (la tendance à partir à la recherche), une conjoncture pulsionnelle dépressive, mais en même temps élabore sur le mode de l'introjection l'ensemble de la conjoncture pulsionnelle, à laquelle il participe aussi à titre de constituant. Est-il plausible que le mécanisme visible du moi s'exerce à la fois sur la périphérie et sur l'ensemble des tendances visibles, y compris sur les tendances du moi lui-même?

D'autre part, est-il légitime d'affirmer que le moi visible d'avant-plan agit sur la conjoncture pulsionnelle de l'arrière-plan? C'est en tout cas ce que Szondi soutient à plusieurs reprises. Les mécanismes de défense de l'avant-plan sont dirigés, non seulement contre les tendances de la périphérie, mais aussi contre les tendances de l'arrière-plan. Ainsi, « les objets du processus de refoulement qui apparaît à l'avant-plan doivent toujours être cherchés à l'arrière-plan réel» (TrD, p. 242). Autre exemple: en conclusion d'une analyse de cas, Szondi écrit: «l'avant-plan tente par différents mécanismes de défense de se défendre contre le même arrière-plan» (TrP, p. 233). Mais les mécanismes qui assurent la dialectique Avant-plan-Arrière-plan sont-ils visibles? En d'autres termes, si un moi est responsable de l'articulation Avant-plan-Arrière-plan, n'est-ce pas un moi déterminant invisible plutôt que l'avant-moi visible?

Pour situer le problème dans toute son acuïté, reprenons l'analyse de l'exemple que nous avons déjà évoqué. Un moi introjecte une conjoncture dépressive, que Szondi attribue par ailleurs à un ancêtre (selon les anciennes options génétiques qui continuent d'infiltrer la doctrine psychopulsionnelle). Les clivages d'avant-plan d+, s-, k+ révèlent l'ancêtre dépressif; de plus le moi introjectif (k+) indique l'assomption personnelle de cet ancêtre. Or, si l'on accepte le principe selon lequel l'avant-plan entretient avec l'arrière-plan une relation définie par la défense du moi de l'avant-plan, le même moi qui introjecte l'avant-plan devrait aussi introjecter l'arrière-plan. Précisons que l'arrière-plan est occupé par le père et l'oncle maternel caïnesques. Or, que soutient Szondi? Que le moi repousse à l'arrière-plan ces ancêtres caïnesques: «Il ne veut pas accepter ces ancêtres. Il ne peut pas s'identifier à ces ancêtres paroxysmaux-sadiques» (IchA, p. 396).

Nous butons donc sur une contradiction indiscutable: l'introjection, l'assomption personnelle de l'avant-plan dans son ensemble, est indiquée par le mécanisme du moi visible à l'avant-plan; mais l'arrière-plan quant à lui est interprété comme ce qui se trouve nié par le moi en dépit même du mécanisme de l'avant-plan.

Nous nous trouvons donc devant la nécessité d'une clarification théorique qui mette un terme à la contradiction que nous venons de relever. C'est pourquoi nous oserons, pour conclure, quelques hypothèses, qui ne nous paraissent nullement forcées, mais serrent et prolongent d'aussi près que possible de multiples suggestions théoriques de Szondi.

Le système pulsionnel en état de fonctionnement — ou mieux : la dialectique pulsionnelle dont les formes sont déposées à l'état visible dans le protocole pulsionnel — est régi par une instance déterminante. Cette instance n'est autre que le moi, à savoir une instance de la totalité pulsionnelle, mais qui a cette particularité d'être à la fois présente et absente, visible et invisible[1]. Comme instance présente ou visible, le moi intervient toujours comme une composante décisive de la dialectique, sous forme d'un mécanisme de défense qui élabore les dangers pulsionnels. Comme instance absente ou invisible (ou, pour reprendre les termes de Szondi, comme « moi Pontifex oppositorum »), il opère le clivage des pulsions, dont les modalités sont précisément identiques aux constellations de la dialectique visible. Et pour cette opération, il ne dispose que des quatre fonctions selon lesquelles agit tout moi, qu'il soit visible ou invisible : la projection (p-), l'inflation (p+), l'introjection (k+), la négation (k-). Plus précisément encore — et c'est en ce point surtout que nous tranchons pour lever les contradictions dans lesquelles Szondi s'est empêtré —, le moi déterminant invisible agit selon des mécanismes permanents par lesquels il constitue l'avant-plan et l'arrière-plan dans leur division, quel que soit par ailleurs le mécanisme visible du moi : se gonflant de certaines tendances (p+) et les introjectant (k+), il constitue l'avant-plan; niant-projetant (k-, p-) certaines autres tendances, il constitue l'arrière-plan. En d'autres termes, l'avant-plan serait soumis en permanence, de la part du moi déterminant, aux processus d'inflation et d'introjection, et l'arrière-plan soumis, de la part du même moi, aux processus de négation et de projection.

Que ces propositions soient grosses d'implications, qu'elles relancent à leur manière certaines problématiques que nous avons cru provisoirement closes, nous en sommes parfaitement conscient. Mais nous n'en avons pas encore fini avec elles : nous en développerons plus avant certaines potentialités dans notre dernière partie, qui nous conduit à un retour explicite sur le test en vue d'en interroger la validité.

---

[1] Szondi a parfaitement reconnu, en termes métaphoriques, cette double position du moi, lorsqu'il compare le moi à un capitaine de bâteau, qui, du haut de sa tour de guet, surveille et dirige les opérations; mais le capitaine n'est pas toujours sérieux, ajoute-t-il, et descend parfois de son poste d'observation privilégié pour occuper en bas une place particulière (IchA, p. 160).

Quatrième partie
Questions à propos de la validité du test de Szondi

Toute notre troisième partie s'est développée dans une sorte de mise entre parenthèses du test de Szondi. Non pas qu'elle lui était absolument étrangère. Bien au contraire, dans son premier chapitre en particulier, elle exposait les concepts et les principes théoriques qui président à l'interprétation des résultats du test. Mais en même temps elle faisait comme s'il allait de soi que le test diagnostique des pulsions organisées selon la théorie qu'elle formulait. Bref, elle présupposait sa validité. Notre ouvrage serait donc assurément incomplet s'il n'opérait un ultime retour sur le test lui-même, pour en questionner la validité. Tel est le sens de notre quatrième et dernière partie.

Il nous a paru progressivement pertinent de distinguer trois dimensions de la validité du test de Szondi, que nous appelons respectivement : validité théorique, validité de construction, validité empirico-clinique. Nous nous efforcerons donc, tout d'abord de définir ces trois aspects de la validité, pour ensuite consacrer à chacun d'entre eux un exposé propre, dont l'ambition ne sera pas de clore le débat, mais plus modestement de l'ouvrir.

A. Les trois dimensions de la validité du test de Szondi

Pour définir les trois dimensions de la validité, nous ferons appel au « génotest », à savoir au test de Szondi tel qu'il pourrait fonctionner dans le contexte de la doctrine génétique des pulsions. Certes, ce n'est point là ce qui nous intéresse directement, puisque, comme tous les praticiens, nous utilisons le test comme « diagnostic expérimental des pulsions ». Cependant le « génotest » nous offre un modèle simple, qui nous permet d'illustrer aisément les trois aspects de la validité que nous différencions. C'est exclusivement à ce titre que nous nous y référons.

Le thème d'une *validité théorique* n'est guère familier au psychométricien. Nous avons cependant cru devoir l'introduire dès 1971 pour pointer une question que soulève inévitablement toute tentative de fondation scientifique du test de Szondi. Ce dernier prétend en effet effectuer un saut qui conduit de réactions comportementales visibles (les choix de photos de malades mentaux) vers des entités ou des processus hypothétiques invisibles (les gènes latents ou les tendances pulsionnelles). Dès lors, le test ne sera valide que s'il s'appuie sur une théorie explicite du choix qui fonde ce saut.

A cet égard, nous avons déjà montré que la doctrine génétique des pulsions inclut une hypothèse théorique fondatrice du choix testologique, à savoir l'hypothèse du génotropisme qui articule les actes de choix « génotropes » de l'individu (y compris l'acte de choix guidé par l'attirance amoureuse) et le bagage génétique latent.

Quant à la *validité de construction*, elle ne doit pas être confondue avec ce que les psychométriciens anglo-saxons appellent couramment « construct validity ». Nous avons expliqué ailleurs pourquoi il nous paraît erroné et source de confusions de traduire « construct validity » par « validité de construction » (1971, p. 534). La « construct validity » est plus justement validité de « construct » ou, selon notre propre expression, validité d'« attribut », qui relève à proprement parler de ce que nous appelons ici une validité empirico-clinique. Cependant, nous avons cru bon de dégager sous le titre de validité de construction une dimension spécifique de la validité du test de Szondi, et cela parce qu'elle se rapporte à la manière dont le test est construit. Car le test, dans le détail de son matériel et de ses procédures, est-il construit de façon à permettre l'appréhension des entités ou processus hypothétiques qu'il prétend diagnostiquer ? Telle est la question que soulève le thème de la validité de construction.

Nous avons montré aussi comment le test, dans son matériel, ses instructions et ses résultats, était articulé sur la doctrine génétique des pulsions, en particulier sur l'hypothèse du génotropisme. Cependant, un examen plus attentif nous amène à relever l'un ou l'autre décalage entre l'hypothèse théorique fondatrice (nécessaire au titre de l'exigence d'une validité théorique) et le détail du procédé testologique. Par exemple, l'hypothèse du génotropisme postule l'attraction réciproque des conducteurs (ou des individus hétérozygotes). Or, le test est composé de visages de malades mentaux, à savoir d'homozygotes. En toute rigueur, l'articulation correcte du test sur la doctrine du choix n'appelait-elle pas la construction d'un matériel composé d'individus hétérozygotes ?

Enfin l'exigence d'une *validité empirico-clinique*, sans doute la plus proche des préoccupations traditionnelles de la psychométrie, soulève la question suivante : est-il possible de dégager à partir des résultats du test des conclusions précises et cohérentes, formulées en termes empiriques ou observationnels, qui puissent elles-mêmes être confirmées par des observations empiriques indépendantes ?

Szondi lui-même nous a donné plusieurs exemples d'une pareille démarche de validation empirique[1]. Citons seulement celui qu'il expose dans les pages 123 à 124 de la Scha. Ayant administré son « géno-test » à un prêtre catholique de 40 ans, Szondi croit pouvoir affirmer sur la base des résultats que cet individu est conducteur (porteur du gène latent) de l'épilepsie, de la paranoïa et du sadisme (affirmation théorique fondée sur la doctrine du génotropisme appliquée au procédé testologique). Il en

---

[1] Cfr Scha, pp. 123-129; TrD, pp. 390-391; IchA, p. 82.

dégage comme conclusions empiriques que : 1. les gènes récessifs responsables de l'e, la p, et le s, se transmettent dans la famille du sujet de génération en génération et donc apparaissent régulièrement, soit sous forme de maladie mentale manifeste, soit sous forme de choix génotropique (choix en amour et amitié, choix professionnel); 2. le sujet lui-même est guidé dans ses choix génotropiques (empiriquement observables) par la latence des gènes e, p et s. Szondi vérifie enfin ses conclusions hypothétiquement déduites de la doctrine génétique par des observations empiriques recueillies par l'enquête généalogique d'une part, par la méthode biographique d'autre part.

B. La validité théorique

Nous abandonnons dès à présent toute référence au test de Szondi comme géno-test pour ne plus le considérer que comme « diagnostic expérimental des pulsions », et lui adressons d'abord à ce titre la question que soulève l'exigence de validité théorique.

A vrai dire, nous avons déjà suggéré que sur ce point le texte explicite de Szondi nous laisse tout à fait dépourvu. Jamais Szondi ne formule une doctrine psychopulsionnelle du choix qui fonderait en termes explicites le saut opéré des choix testologiques vers les tendances pulsionnelles (par exemple : le saut d'un choix de cinq photos de maniaques vers l'exacerbation de la tendance à l'accrochage). Nous en sommes donc réduit ici à engager une recherche exploratoire, dont la prétention est moins de résoudre le problème que d'aider à le poser et à l'ouvrir par là aux travaux de nos successeurs.

Nous procéderons en deux étapes. Tout d'abord, nous esquisserons les éléments de ce qui nous apparaît dans l'œuvre du dernier Szondi comme une doctrine révisée du choix (en général). Puis nous interrogerons le choix testologique proprement dit, formulerons quelques hypothèses destinées à rendre compte de son fonctionnement, dont aucune, nous le verrons, ne nous semblera satisfaisante.

1. Une doctrine révisée du choix

Nous connaissons la doctrine originelle du choix que formule Szondi : les grandes figures du destin et du choix destinal y sont attribuées aux effets d'un bagage génétique pulsionnel. Or, à mesure que le champ d'investigation de Szondi se déplaçait d'un terrain génétique sur un terrain proprement psychopulsionnel, la conception du choix devait elle-même se modifier à l'appel des transformations générales de la doctrine. Un énoncé résume à lui seul cette modification : le choix est désormais une œuvre du moi, et non plus un effet de gènes pulsionnels. Mais reste à savoir en quel sens le moi choisit et par son choix donne visage ou figure à son destin. C'est ce que nous allons préciser en projetant sur la dernière doctrine du choix le concept de ce que nous avons appelé un moi déterminant invisible.

Que nous dit le dernier Szondi, sinon que le moi (identique pour nous au moi déterminant) est confronté à une gerbe d'orientations ou de tendances pulsionnelles qu'il ne constitue pas mais qui lui sont offertes et par rapport auxquelles il doit prendre position, modelant par là même son destin. Car il n'est pas dans l'œuvre du dernier Szondi de définition plus constante et plus répétitive du destin que celle qui l'assimile à la conséquence d'une prise de position libre du moi, exercée sur une somme finie de possibilités d'existence pulsionnelles données a priori.

Mais comment le moi choisit-il ? Nous le savons, il choisit en clivant les tendances, en les écartelant selon deux opérations divergentes mais simultanées, qui orientent de manière spécifique le destin : l'assomption d'une part, le rejet d'autre part. Cela même que le moi aura assumé à l'avant-plan d'après un mécanisme d'introjection-inflation constituera ce que Szondi a appelé dans un sens large son caractère, défini comme « cette partie du destin gravée dans le moi par introjection » (IchA, p. 370). Une partie du destin elle-même plus ou moins maladive ou plus ou moins socialisée selon le contenu des tendances ainsi introjectées (analysées d'après les méthodes dialectiques qui confrontent la périphérie et le centre, le danger pulsionnel et le mécanisme du moi). Car quel est le mécanisme responsable du choix des symptômes morbides et du choix de la profession ? L'introjection, répond le dernier Szondi[1]. A quoi nous ajoutons : l'introjection opérée par le moi déterminant qui assume une part des tendances pulsionnelles et les inscrit à l'avant-plan. Mais qu'advient-il des tendances niées, rejetées, occupant la scène de l'arrière-plan ? Demeurent-elles inactives, comme en état de léthargie ? Ou interviennent-elles de quelque manière pour régir une facette du destin ? Les tendances écartées, niées (dont le contenu devra lui aussi être analysé selon les mêmes méthodes dialectiques), répond Szondi, sont aussi des tendances projetées, qui dès lors, conformément à la pente propre au processus de projection, reviennent au sujet de l'extérieur sous forme d'une sollicitation ou d'une interpellation : le sujet s'intéresse en quelque sorte aux personnes sur lesquelles il appréhende ses propres tendances niées et projetées. En termes plus précis encore, un mécanisme de projection, opéré sur l'arrière-plan par le moi déterminant, serait responsable du choix en amour et amitié[2].

Nous croyons avoir ainsi esquissé les perspectives que dessine l'œuvre du dernier Szondi : les grandes figures du choix destinal (choix en amour et en amitié, choix de la profession, choix de la maladie), qui étaient autrefois rapportées à l'hérédité, sont à présent reconnues comme l'œuvre du moi déterminant.

C'est peut-être ici que nous percevons le mieux en quoi la conception d'un moi déterminant est grosse d'implications. Car elle aboutit à reconnaître l'arrière-plan théorique comme lieu de possibilités d'existence niées, mais néanmoins réelles et actives, responsables en particulier de certains actes de choix de l'individu, à savoir de ses choix en amour et amitié. En l'état actuel, il existe donc bien une contradiction entre les conclusions auxquelles conduisent les développements théoriques de l'œuvre szondienne et la pratique spontanée de l'interprétation du test qui tend à négliger l'arrière-plan théorique.

Seules des recherches empiriques, interrogeant la manière dont l'arrière-plan se manifeste effectivement dans le destin concret des individus, seraient à notre sens susceptibles de faire progresser la problématique.

Mais reste une question : dans quelle mesure la doctrine révisée du choix éclaire-t-elle le processus du choix qui s'opère au moment de l'administration du test ? La dynamique du choix testologique doit être à présent examinée.

---

[1] Sur l'introjection comme facteur de choix, cfr IchA, pp. 214-217.

[2] Sur la projection comme facteur de choix, cfr IchA, pp. 172-176.

2. *Le processus du choix testologique*

C'est sans doute Susan Deri qui s'est affrontée de la manière la plus explicite à la problématique du choix testologique, et cela dans un article intitulé : « Genotropism in the framework of a unified theory of choice » (1963). Considérons donc un moment les idées essentielles que développe cet article, concernant à la fois la signification du matériel et la signification de l'acte de choix. Car, dans la mesure où le choix testologique s'exerce sur un matériel précis, il ne sera lui-même élucidé que si le contenu du matériel est au préalable déterminé. Que nous dit Deri à ce sujet ? D'après elle, les sujets photographiés se caractériseraient par un déséquilibre qui affecterait de manière privilégiée l'un des huit besoins pulsionnels. Ainsi, les sadiques seraient caractérisés en propre par une exacerbation déséquilibrante du besoin s. De plus, l'excès de tension pulsionnelle affleurerait ou transparaîtrait à même la physionomie des malades représentés, selon un principe nécessairement imposé par le fonctionnement du test, à savoir que « la forme de la face reflète les qualités psychologiques internes de la personne » (p. 42).

Mais que se passe-t-il alors du côté du sujet qui se trouve confronté aux photos ? Selon Deri, ce dernier réagira face aux photos en fonction des tensions qui déséquilibrent sa propre structuration pulsionnelle. Plus précisément, le besoin qui se trouve dans l'état relativement le plus élevé de déséquilibre déterminera le choix de photos spécifiques. Par exemple, l'individu dont le besoin homosexuel est dans un état actuel de déséquilibre, sera attiré par les visages d'homosexuels, sur lesquels transparaît précisément un besoin excessif de tendresse sensuelle.

Ce corps d'hypothèses a l'insigne mérite d'exister et par là d'engager un débat sur une problématique à notre sens cruciale. De plus, il accorde une juste attention à la nature du matériel, dont nous n'aborderons la discussion que dans notre prochain paragraphe. Néanmoins, quant à l'analyse du processus de choix proprement dit, il présente deux lacunes graves. D'une part, il ne rend pas compte de la différence entre choix de sympathie et choix d'antipathie. En somme, Deri considère un choix défini comme activité dirigée et donc n'explique tout au plus que l'intérêt porté par un sujet à telle ou telle photo, mais non le choix positif ou négatif. D'autre part, l'explication de l'intérêt ou de l'attrait (au sens non qualifié le plus large d'être concerné par ou d'être poussé vers) laisse elle-même à désirer. Pourquoi un sujet dont le besoin h est déséquilibré sera-t-il attiré par les photos qui laissent transparaître le même déséquilibre ? Deri recourt ici aux principes de la psychologie de la forme. La déséquilibration appelle une rééquilibration obtenue par la constitution d'une forme qui réunit les semblables. Sur ce point, nous adressons à Deri le reproche d'avoir cru trouver dans une doctrine extrinsèque ce qu'elle aurait pu chercher à l'intérieur même de l'Analyse du destin. Or, s'il est une exigence que pose la doctrine psychopulsionnelle de Szondi, c'est bien de faire place dans le choix au moi et à ses mécanismes, ici tout à fait absents. Le choix, y compris le choix testologique, est l'œuvre d'un moi (déterminant) prenant position par rapport aux dynamismes pulsionnels que lui offrent à l'état exacerbé les photos du test. Essayons donc de compléter dans cette ligne les hypothèses de Deri.

Soit un sujet dont les huit besoins pulsionnels sont en état relatif de charge ou de décharge, de déséquilibre ou d'équilibre. Nous posons nous aussi qu'il sera interpellé par les visages qui révèlent un déséquilibre analogue au sien, à ceci près que nous faisons intervenir à présent un mécanisme du moi pour fonder cette interpellation. Le sujet (ou identiquement : le moi déterminant) projette sur le monde ses besoins pulsionnels chargés, qui lui reviennent du dehors comme sollicitation : le sujet est intéressé par les visages sur lesquels il appréhende les besoins qu'il a chassés, par projection, à l'extérieur de lui-même. Mais nous n'en sommes toujours là qu'à une phase d'interpellation non différenciée. Car le sujet doit encore choisir positivement ou négativement les photos qui l'interpellent. C'est ici qu'entrerait en action la fonction k, pour déterminer la prise de position. Il est très significatif à cet égard que Deri elle-même, dans son *Introduction to the Szondi test*, ait fait appel à des mécanismes relevant du facteur k pour expliquer les choix positif et négatif. Soit, dit-elle, le sujet s'identifie au processus motivationnel (au besoin) offert par la photo qui l'interpelle, auquel cas il choisit positivement; soit il se contre-identifie au même processus motivationnel, auquel cas il choisit négativement (p. 34). Or Szondi a rapporté explicitement l'identification et la contre-identification respectivement à l'introjection k+ et la négation k- (IchA, p. 217). Nous osons donc affirmer que le choix positif, adressant un « oui » au besoin, est l'œuvre de la fonction k+, alors que le choix négatif, lui adressant un « non », repose sur le dynamisme de la fonction k-. Car : « l'introjection dit oui ..., la négation dit non », a aussi écrit Szondi (IchA, p. 218).

Nous croyons avoir ainsi répondu aux objections que nous avions adressées au corps d'hypothèses de Deri : le moi et ses mécanismes interviennent dans le choix testologique; la différenciation entre choix positif et choix négatif est fondée. Cependant, nos dernières hypothèses, qui nous apparaissent dans l'état actuel comme les plus satisfaisantes, appellent une remarque importante. Le lecteur qui a présents à l'esprit les développements de notre deuxième partie aura déjà observé que nos hypothèses sont en parfaite harmonie avec ce que nous avons reconnu comme un état intermédiaire de la doctrine szondienne, révélé par la 1re édition du TrD (1947). La quantité de choix révèle l'état de charge ou de décharge du besoin (nous ajouterons à présent : via un mécanisme de projection). Quant à la qualité du choix, elle résulte d'une prise de position approbatrice ou désapprobatrice du moi par rapport à la direction originaire du besoin. Par contre, nos hypothèses sont clairement incompatibles avec l'état final d'une doctrine szondienne qui reconnaît la réalité aprioristique des tendances pulsionnelles et fonde la construction corrélative d'un arrière-plan (théorique) réel. Car elles présupposent par exemple que la tendance négative est constituée par la prise de position négatrice du moi, ou encore que le besoin non chargé (o), sur lequel ne fonctionne pas la projection, n'exerce aucun dynamisme dans la vie pulsionnelle du sujet. En face de cette situation, deux attitudes sont possibles : ou bien nous récusons nos hypothèses au nom d'une doctrine à laquelle nous faisons crédit, ou bien inversement nos hypothèses, en ce qu'elles nous paraissent aujourd'hui les seules à fonder le choix et la pratique testologique, nous conduisent à opérer un retour destructeur sur la dernière doctrine de Szondi, en particulier à contester la thèse d'un arrière-plan théorique réel. Car bien entendu la situation serait beaucoup plus simple si la dernière doctrine de Szondi était en état d'expliquer le choix testologique. Malheureusement il n'en est rien. C'est ce qu'il nous reste à suggérer.

Nous l'avons vu, Szondi aboutit à formuler une théorie (révisée) du choix en amour et en amitié, qui s'inscrit de manière tout à fait cohérente dans l'ensemble de ses dernières options doctrinales. Qu'affirme cette théorie? Que la direction du choix en amour et amitié est déterminée par la composition de l'arrière-plan théorique : le moi nie-projette un arrière-plan, qui lui revient du dehors comme attraction[1]. Ainsi, un sujet sera attiré par un sadique, parce qu'il porte en lui, dans son arrière-plan, une figure existensielle sadique[2]. Or, si nous appliquons ce principe à la lettre, nous nous heurtons à une contradiction de prime abord insurmontable. C'est ce qu'il nous suffira de remarquer pour être en droit d'écarter cette hypothèse comme une hypothèse incompatible avec la pratique testologique et donc impuissante à la fonder.

Soit un sujet dont l'arrière-plan est occupé par une figure sadique, qui donc présente entre autres, à l'arrière-plan, la tendance s+ (!!). Ce sujet projette le sadisme et se trouve attiré par des individus sadiques. En toute logique, le même sujet manifestera la même attirance au moment de l'administration du test et produira le clivage s+(!!). En conséquence, la tendance s-(!!) apparaîtra dans son arrière-plan (tel qu'il est hypothétiquement reconstitué par l'épreuve du test). Nous sommes donc conduits à affirmer que le même individu présente à l'arrière-plan tout à la fois la tendance s+ (selon notre hypothèse initiale) et la tendance s- (selon une déduction fondée tout à la fois sur la doctrine du choix en amour et en amitié et la pratique testologique courante de construction de l'arrière-plan théorique).

C. La validité de construction

Le travail de validation théorique s'efforce de formuler les principes les plus généraux qui président au fonctionnement du test. Mais, ces principes généraux explicités, ils appellent aussitôt un prolongement concret. Car le test, dans son matériel, dans sa procédure, obéit-il effectivement aux exigences que prescrivent les hypothèses théoriques de fonctionnement? Dès l'instant où nous soulevons cette question, nous sommes transportés sur le terrain de la validité de construction.

Pour notre part, nous avons pris connaissance de la majorité des travaux qui dans les trente dernières années ont été consacrés à des questions relevant de la validité de construction. A la réflexion, il nous a paru possible de les ordonner autour de trois exigences postulées par le fonctionnement du test, que nous formulerons comme suit :

1. les photos du test représentent des sujets qui manifestent une affinité particulière avec l'un des huit besoins pulsionnels;
2. les photos sont en état de solliciter, chez le sujet qui les regarde, le besoin pulsionnel qui leur est congénial;
3. les réactions de choix d'un sujet vis-à-vis des photos révèlent sa situation ou sa position par rapport au besoin que les photos sollicitent.

---

[1] On trouvera l'affirmation la plus explicite de cet énoncé à la p. 176 de la IchA.

[2] C'est là un cas que Szondi évoque explicitement dans les pp. 238-246 du TrD : « Le choix de son époux pervers, sadique, est dirigé par le déplacement de cette figure existensielle sadique cachée dans son propre arrière-plan psychique. Elle a choisi ce sadique parce qu'elle porte en elle une figure existensielle sadique, meurtrière ». (TrD, p. 243).

Il est exclu que nous discutions dans le détail et de manière exhaustive les trois propositions énoncées ci-dessus, à la lumière des nombreux travaux qui ont prétendu les vérifier. Aussi nous contenterons-nous de les passer en revue, pour souligner chaque fois quelques-uns des principaux problèmes qu'elles soulèvent.

1. Sujets photographiés et besoins pulsionnels

Il est vraisemblablement crucial pour le fonctionnement du test que les malades mentaux représentés sur les photos manifestent une affinité particulière avec le besoin pulsionnel dont ils sont supposés être les représentants extrêmes.

Mais comment vérifier ce principe, sinon par une connaissance fouillée des malades, de leur histoire et de leur problématique clinique ? Or, que savons-nous à cet égard ? A la vérité, trop peu de chose. Nous savons comment ont été obtenues les photographies : trente-huit photos sont tirées de manuels de psychiatrie, six photos de criminels (étiquetées s) ont été transmises à Szondi par un psychiatre suédois, enfin quatre photos ont été obtenues par Szondi lui-même de patients qu'il devait connaître personnellement (TrD, p. 357). Quant aux renseignements dont nous disposons sur les personnes photographiées, ils sont variables selon les cas, parfois très maigres, parfois un peu plus abondants. De toute manière, ils sont en général trop lacunaires pour que nous puissions adopter une attitude claire quant au lien privilégié que les malades auraient entretenu avec un besoin pulsionnel. A la lumière des données les plus extensives recueillies par Domingues da Silva (1977), il apparaît que neuf malades manifestent une affinité exclusive avec le besoin qu'ils sont censés représenter; quant aux trente-neuf autres, ils manifesteraient tous une affinité partielle avec le besoin, soit dominante (pour vingt-quatre d'entre eux), soit partagée avec un autre besoin (treize), soit secondaire (deux). Mais, répétons-le, ces conclusions, les mieux fondées à l'heure actuelle et dans l'ensemble favorables au test, reposent sur un matériel insuffisant. Il semble exclu que nous puissions dans l'avenir en savoir davantage.

2. Les photos et leur caractère évocateur

Nous effectuons à présent un saut. Car une chose est que les malades représentés s'expliquent de manière privilégiée avec un besoin en état d'exacerbation déséquilibrante, autre chose est que leur visage photographié soit susceptible d'évoquer ou de solliciter le même besoin chez d'autres sujets qui le regarderaient.

Il importe avant tout de soulever une question qui chevauche en quelque sorte nos paragraphes 1 et 2. Car à supposer que nos malades aient avec un besoin pulsionnel l'affinité que nous avons exigée, ne doit-on pas postuler, pour que le test fonctionne, que ce besoin s'exprime à travers leur physionomie ? En d'autres termes, le besoin pulsionnel, exacerbé, déséquilibré, ne viendrait-il pas se matérialiser dans la physionomie et produire par ce truchement son effet évocateur[1]? Il est difficile d'échapper à cette conclusion et à sa conséquence nécessaire, à savoir que les huit malades qui sont supposés révéler le même besoin devraient présenter des caractéristiques physionomiques communes. Malheureusement, la recherche à ce propos n'est guère avancée. A notre connaissance, seul Bellingroth (1962) s'est aventuré sur ce terrain et est parvenu à dégager deux «portraits-robots» caractéristiques respectivement des homosexuels et des sadiques. Quasiment tout reste à entreprendre.

De toute manière, le caractère évocateur des photos peut être approché sans que son médium physionomique soit pris en considération. De nombreuses recherches ont été conduites, qui s'organisent autour d'un principe commun. Des sujets sont priés d'«associer» à propos des photos du test auxquelles ils se trouvent confrontés. L'analyse de leurs associations permet de vérifier s'ils ont reconnu les qualités spécifiques hypothétiquement évoquées par les photos. Mais sur ce fond commun de nettes divergences apparaissent entre deux démarches: l'une plus clinique, misant sur des associations verbales libres et s'inscrivant dans le contexte d'une relation individuelle; l'autre plus expérimentale, procédant au départ d'une liste de qualités déjà codifiées et recueillant le matériel à la faveur d'un examen collectif standardisé. Plutôt que d'exposer chacune des recherches en particulier, nous leur adresserons globalement trois questions: quels sujets choisir? Quel mode de reconnaissance considérer comme adéquat? De quelles qualités s'assurer la reconnaissance?

Quels sujets? Tout sujet est-il susceptible de reconnaître à tout moment les qualités spécifiques de chacune des photos? Ainsi, n'avons-nous pas de sérieuses raisons de penser qu'un sujet dont le besoin est adynamique n'est pas sollicité par les photos évoquant ce besoin? Dès lors ne vaudrait-il pas mieux ne pas lui soumettre les photos pour lesquelles il ne manifeste que de l'indifférence et l'appeler à associer préférentiellement sur les photos qui l'interpellent le plus? C'est bien ainsi que procède Szondi dans la méthode clinique d'association factorielle qu'il nous présente dans son Diagnostic des pulsions (DP, pp. 34-43; TrD, pp. 354-372); il choisit pour base de l'association factorielle les quatre photos qui se sont révélées les plus sympathiques ou antipathiques pour le sujet (TrD, p. 354). Malheureusement, cette restriction, inspirée par une connaissance intérieure de l'Analyse du destin, n'est pas prise en considération par les chercheurs qui se sont réclamés d'une méthodologie expérimentale.

Quel mode de reconnaissance? La reconnaissance des qualités spécifiques des photos qui s'opère par hypothèse au moment de l'administration du test est une reconnaissance infra-verbale, qui se déroule dans le registre de la rencontre visuelle intersubjective. Or, pour vérifier la reconnaissance, tous les chercheurs, y compris les tenants de l'Analyse du destin, ont été contraints de recourir à un matériel d'associations verbales. D'où une question inévitable: à quelles conditions les associations verbales sont-elles sus-

---

[1] Il est significatif d'observer à cet égard que le même malade maniaco-dépressif se trouve représenté à deux reprises dans le jeu des quarante-huit photos, une première fois en phase maniaque (IIIm), une seconde fois en phase dépressive (IVd). Sa mimique exprime deux états psychopulsionnels à ce point distincts que l'identité est à peine reconnaissable.

ceptibles de dévoiler les mouvements perceptivo-affectifs qui sont éveillés dans la rencontre visuelle des visages photographiés ? Le contexte d'une relation clinique individuelle, ouverte à l'émergence des affects les plus intimes, paraît en tout cas plus propice que les conditions standardisées d'une procédure expérimentale qui ne laisse quasiment rien venir à la parole, sinon une réaction verbale enfermée dans le champ étroitement clos d'une codification préétablie.

Quelles qualités ? Par hypothèse, les photos sollicitent un besoin pulsionnel. En d'autres termes, les qualités reconnues sur un mode non verbal par le sujet qui choisit une photo seraient des qualités inhérentes au besoin pulsionnel congénial à la photo. Nous avouons certes que la notion de qualités « pulsionnelles », exclusivement dévoilées par des associations psychopulsionnelles profondes, reste une notion floue. En particulier, il n'est pas toujours simple de différencier lesdites qualités pulsionnelles de qualités formulables en termes de descriptions caractérologiques de personnalité. Toujours est-il que nous sommes autorisés à rejeter comme non pertinentes certaines qualités qui s'écartent par trop visiblement d'un registre pulsionnel profond, telles ces qualités que Szondi réfèrent à des « associations objectives superficielles » : qualités esthétiques (beau, laid, ...), intellectuelles (idiot, intelligent,...), psycho-diagnostiques (schizophrène, maniaque,...). Du même coup, plusieurs recherches expérimentales se trouvent invalidées.

Ainsi, nous ne voyons pas très bien en quelle mesure la reconnaissance de l'appartenance psychiatrique des photos par des personnes supposées compétentes (psychiatre, psychologue clinicien, infirmier psychiatrique) apportent une quelconque contribution au problème que nous soulevons ici [1]. Car le fonctionnement du test ne présuppose nullement la reconnaissance d'une photo m comme photo de maniaque, la reconnaissance d'une photo p comme photo de schizophrène paranoïde, ... Par contre une telle recherche pourrait vérifier qu'une configuration faciale commune est significativement associée aux malades des huit groupes représentés dans le test, de telle sorte que des professionnels entraînés seraient capables de poser un diagnostic correct sur la seule base de l'examen physionomique d'un patient.

Quant aux recherches qui se sont efforcées de vérifier l'attribution aux photos de descriptions de personnalité conformes aux catégories szondiennes [2], elles sont un peu moins discutables, dans la mesure où certaines qualités caractérielles formulées dans les termes non techniques du langage courant pourraient traduire ce qui se trouve éveillé à la vue des photos. Elles sont néanmoins sujettes aux critiques déjà énoncées : l'atmosphère d'une recherche collective standardisée n'est guère favorable à l'expression des émois psychopulsionnels.

Nous concluerons donc avec Szondi que le contrôle du caractère évocateur des photos devrait exclure comme inutilisables les associations superficielles, au bénéfice des seules associations psychopulsionnelles profondes, propres à libérer un matériel inconscient, ce qui n'a malheureusement guère été respecté (TrD, p. 356). Est-ce dire que le caractère évocateur des photos est démontré ? Nullement. Nous ne voulons point voiler les insuffisances crian-

---

[1] Parmi les recherches soucieuses de vérifier l'attribution aux photos de leur qualité psychodiagnostique, citons : Rabin (1950 a et b), Best et Szollosi (1953), Steinberg (1953) et Silverstein (1957).

[2] Parmi ces recherches, citons : Klopfer et Borstelmann (1950), Wallen (1951), Dudek et Patterson (1952) et Davis et Raimy (1952).

tes des recherches conduites jusqu'ici par les tenants de l'Analyse du destin. Car Szondi aussi bien que Deri se contente d'affirmations triomphalistes, ne donnant par ailleurs que quelques exemples choisis d'associations verbales (TrD, pp. 356-361; IS, pp. 17-20), que nous pouvons difficilement tenir pour des corroborations empiriques sérieuses. On voit donc que pour nous des travaux décisifs restent à nouveau à entreprendre. Au demeurant, nous croyons qu'ils devraient conjuguer les méthodes expérimentale et clinique, beaucoup moins incompatibles que nous ne l'avons laissé entendre jusqu'ici. Car ils devraient, conformément aux prescriptions de la méthode expérimentale, être guidés par des hypothèses clairement formulées (falsifiables), que viendrait corroborer ou infirmer un matériel empirique rigoureusement et méthodiquement recueilli et analysé. Mais ils devraient aussi s'appuyer sur un matériel d'associations verbales (profondes) recueillies en situation d'entretien clinique.

Domingues da Silva a récemment engagé une recherche exploratoire qui s'efforce de respecter au mieux ces deux conditions. Les conclusions provisoires auxquelles il a abouti sont plus que nuancées: plus de la moitié des photos évoquent le besoin pulsionnel supposé; par contre, plusieurs d'entre elles ne l'évoquent pas ou l'évoquent insuffisamment. Le matériel du test serait donc partiellement invalidé et appellerait d'importants aménagements (1977, Vol. I, pp. 117-124 et 141-152).

3. Réactions de choix et état du besoin pulsionnel

Mais supposons établi que les photos du test sollicitent le besoin qui leur est congénial. Une dernière question se pose: les réactions de choix vis-à-vis des photos relevant d'un même facteur sont-elles révélatrices de l'état d'un besoin pulsionnel?

Une première voie d'approche du problème repose sur une hypothèse qui n'est pas conforme à la pratique du test. Certains raisonnent comme suit: si un besoin spécifique (par ex. un besoin d'accrochage) régit les réactions de choix vis-à-vis des photos d'une même série factorielle (vis-à-vis des photos de maniaques), à telle enseigne que ces réactions puissent être tenues comme révélatrices du besoin, alors un même sujet devrait tendre à réagir de manière identique vis-à-vis des photos de la série factorielle. Le besoin pulsionnel est en quelque sorte assimilé à un « construct » psychologique qui se manifeste sous la forme d'un comportement constant. L'hypothèse commandera alors, soit une démarche qui opère via le calcul des corrélations[1], soit une démarche plus fine encore, qui recourt à l'analyse factorielle[2]. Que les résultats de ces recherches aient été unanimement négatifs n'a pas de quoi nous étonner. Car elles s'appuient sur un présupposé qui se trouve explicitement contredit par le fonctionnement concret du test. Un besoin ne détermine nullement dans tous les cas une réaction constante, soit de sympathie, soit d'antipathie. Il

---

[1] On procédera à la fois à des corrélations intrafactorielles (par ex. hl-h3 ou s2-s5) et à des corrélations interfactorielles (par ex. hl-s6 ou e1-p5). Au contraire des secondes, les premières devraient être significativement positives. Parmi les recherches qui ont utilisé cette méthode, citons: Lubin et Malloy (1951), Cohen et Feigenbaum (1954) et Gordon et Lambert (1954).

[2] Parmi les recherches qui ont procédé à une analyse factorielle des photos, citons: Guertin (1951b) et Gordon (1953).

arrive que le sujet se situe de manière ambivalente vis-à-vis du besoin et dès lors réagisse à la fois sous forme de sympathie et d'antipathie.

Nous écarterons donc comme inadéquates des recherches viciées par une mécompréhension notoire du test.

Mais une seconde voie d'approche est beaucoup plus pertinente. Nous nous y attacherons davantage.

Esquissons d'abord la problématique avant de l'examiner dans le détail. Même si les besoins pulsionnels interviennent dans le choix des photos, il est loin d'être exclu que d'autres facteurs extrapulsionnels (par ex. la beauté des visages) puissent aussi influencer le choix. A supposer que ce soit le cas, deux possibilités se présentent : ou bien les facteurs extrapulsionnels ont été tenus constants, ou bien ils ne l'ont pas été. Dans cette dernière éventualité, le test n'est-il pas mis en question comme révélateur de processus pulsionnels ? Mais précisons.

Plusieurs chercheurs ont mis en évidence l'incidence de facteurs extrapulsionnels sur le choix des photos.

Ainsi, Szollosi, Lamphiear et Best (1951) montrent que certaines photos sont systématiquement plus choisies que d'autres photos relevant du même facteur (ainsi la photo Vh est significativement plus choisie que d'autres photos d'homosexuels). De son côté, Guertin (1950) montre qu'un même sujet tend à privilégier une photo particulière au détriment d'autres photos de la même série factorielle. Or ces faits ne peuvent être expliqués par l'influence des déterminants pulsionnels.

Quelques auteurs ont été ainsi conduits à établir un classement des photos selon ce qu'ils appellent leur degré de popularité[1]. Car certaines photos seraient en général plus attirantes, d'autres photos en général plus repoussantes, quelles que soient par ailleurs les caractéristiques pulsionnelles individuelles des sujets. Quant aux raisons de la popularité différentielle des photos, elles ne sont guère élucidées. On peut penser que la qualité esthétique des visages joue un rôle. Mais au fond peu importe : la seule existence de cette popularité différentielle suffirait à mettre en question le test.

En effet, le test donne le même poids pulsionnel à des choix de photos dont le degré de popularité est très différent. Or l'opération est illégitime. Car une signification nettement moindre devrait être accordée au choix d'une photo dont le degré de popularité est très élevé. Le test est donc vicié à la base.

Mais qu'ont à rétorquer les partisans de l'Analyse du destin ? Nous exposerons les arguments développés par deux auteurs et d'abord par Szondi lui-même.

Dans le chapitre XXVII du TrD, intitulé « A propos du fonctionnement du test », Szondi nous informe qu'il a pris en compte la problématique de la popularité différentielle des photos ou de ce qu'il appelle pour sa part la tonalité générale de sympathie ou d'antipathie des photos, mais bien plus qu'il a veillé à une répartition inégale de la tonalité de sympathie à l'intérieur de chaque série factorielle : trois photos seraient plutôt sympathiques ou attirantes, trois photos seraient par contre plutôt antipathiques ou repoussantes. Ce dont il rattache la nécessité à une exigence a priori qui devait présider à la construction du test :

---

[1] Citons Szollosi, Lamphiear et Best (1951), Guertin (1951a) Borstelmann et Klopfer (1951).

L'homme de la rue devait fournir au test un profil de tous les jours plus ou moins «général», qui corresponde effectivement à la psychologie de l'homme moyen, à savoir:

$$+ \; + \; - \; - \; - \; - \; o \; +$$

Car si les six photos représentent des êtres humains extrêmement beaux, attirant tous en général l'homme de la rue, alors le profil de l'homme de tous les jours manifestera des réactions positives correctes, alors que les fonctions négatives (par ex. les fonctions de l'angoisse, de l'adaptation, etc.) seront par contre diagnostiquement incertaines, dans la mesure où le sujet aura dû choisir sous la contrainte douze photos antipathiques parmi des photos qui ne lui sont pas véritablement antipathiques (p. 377).

Szondi nous semble confondre ici, d'une part le fait qu'une photo puisse être en général ou en moyenne (si l'on veut: pour un homme «moyen») attirante ou repoussante, d'autre part le fait que pour des raisons intrinsèques à sa structure pulsionnelle, l'homme de tous les jours doive ressentir comme attirantes les photos de certaines séries factorielles et comme repoussantes les photos d'autres séries factorielles. Or, si l'on opère une distinction claire entre la tonalité générale de sympathie et la structure pulsionnelle intrinsèque, la répartition inégale de la tonalité de sympathie n'apparaît plus justifiée, du moins au nom de l'argument invoqué par Szondi. Car, à supposer même que toutes les photos soient également attirantes en général, les composantes du dynamisme pulsionnel contribueront à les départager en plus sympathiques et en plus antipathiques.

La confusion entretenue par Szondi se traduit d'ailleurs en énoncés apparemment contradictoires. Ainsi, tout juste après avoir affirmé que des six photos d'un facteur une moitié devait être attirante et une autre moitié repoussante pour l'homme de la rue (p. 377), il écrit: «Dans la sélection des photos des catégories k et p trois photos au moins devaient être repoussantes et pas plus d'une photo attirante pour l'homme de la rue» (p. 378). Seule une claire différenciation (gommée par Szondi) entre la popularité «moyenne» des photos et l'attrait suscité par la structure pulsionnelle de l'homme de tous les jours permet de lever la contradiction.

Que conclure en ce point sinon que l'argumentation de Szondi n'est pas convaincante? Mais tournons-nous à présent vers Schubert (1954), un autre représentant de l'Analyse du destin, qui formule une remarque intéressante.

Selon lui, la présence dans chaque série factorielle de photos plutôt attirantes et de photos plutôt repoussantes n'empêche nullement l'individu humain de réagir selon l'état de ses besoins pulsionnels. Ainsi, si un individu, du fait de sa structure pulsionnelle, tend à ressentir comme antipathiques les homosexuels, il rejettera comme antipathiques les deux ou trois homosexuels en général repoussants et ignorera les homosexuels attirants; et si, toujours du fait de sa structure pulsionnelle, il tend à ressentir comme violemment antipathiques les homosexuels, alors sa tendance négative pourra même aller à l'encontre du caractère généralement attirant de l'une ou l'autre photo d'homosexuel. Donc, conclut l'auteur, une répartition inégale des tonalités de sympathie ne compromet pas le fonctionnement du test.

Toutefois, malgré son intérêt, cette dernière observation demeure insuffisante. Car il est étrange qu'à aucun moment n'ait été pris en considération un caractère essentiel du matériel testologique, à savoir son organisation en six séries de huit photos. Or ce fait bouleverse les données de la problématique, au point d'avoir conduit les plus intelliggents des contradicteurs de l'Analyse du destin (Guertin d'une part, Borstelman et Klopfer d'autre part) à nuancer leur position critique initiale. Au fond, ont-ils fait remarquer, si l'on veut égaliser les déterminants extrapulsionnels du choix, l'essentiel n'est pas de contrôler l'égalité de la tonalité de sympathie à l'intérieur des groupes factoriels, mais de la contrôler à l'intérieur des six séries de huit photos. Et chacun de proposer alors une version modifiée du test, qui obéirait davantage à cette exigence.

Nous tenons, pour terminer, à apporter une contribution personnelle à la problématique, basée sur la prise en compte de l'organisation du test en six séries.

Supposons un homme de la rue dont nous connaissons a priori la structure pulsionnelle. Supposons de plus que cet homme de la rue, confronté successivement à chacune des six séries du test, choisisse d'après sa structure pulsionnelle postulée, mais aussi d'après les tonalités relatives de sympathie et d'antipathie constitutives de chaque série. Et demandons-nous comment devrait être organisé le matériel du test pour que cet homme de la rue nous livre, en conséquence de ses réactions testologiques, un profil pulsionnel identique à son profil a priori. Nous sommes arrivé à la conclusion qu'une répartition inégale des tonalités de sympathie au sein de chaque série, non seulement n'est pas préjudiciable au fonctionnement du test, mais bien plus lui est nécessaire, et cela pour les raisons qui justifiaient, aux yeux de Szondi, une répartition inégale au sein des séries factorielles: si la répartition était égale, certains choix seraient diagnostiquement incertains (Szondi). Supposons en effet un homme de la rue qui présente dans son centre pulsionnel quatre tendances négatives et supposons qu'il soit chaque fois confronté à des séries de photos égalisées du point de vue de la tonalité de sympathie. Dans ces conditions, il trouvera antipathiques les photos e, hy, k et p. Or il ne peut en choisir que deux comme antipathiques. Lesquelles choisira-t-il? Il devra s'en remettre au hasard ou à quelques associations personnelles. En conséquence, au terme des six séries, il n'est pas du tout sûr qu'il livre les clivages factoriels e-, hy-, k- et p-. Par contre, si la répartition des tonalités de sympathie est inégale au sein d'une même série, il choisira comme négatives les photos plutôt repoussantes et ignorera les photos plutôt attirantes (par ex. il choisira négativement dans la série I les photos k et hy qui sont plutôt repoussantes, et ignorera les photos e et p qui sont plutôt attirantes). Mais on voit aussitôt que la répartition inégale des tonalités de sympathie au sein de chacune des six séries n'est pas suffisante. Il importe aussi que la nature des photos plutôt attirantes et plutôt repoussantes varie d'une série à l'autre. On comprend par exemple que les huit photos d'épileptiques ne doivent pas se situer en position systématique de photos attirantes, car s'il en était ainsi, notre homme de la rue ne les choisirait jamais négativement et donc ne livrerait pas le clivage e- conforme à sa structure pulsionnelle a priori. Il semble donc qu'une condition d'inégalité à l'intérieur de chacune des huit séries factorielles doive se conjoindre à la condition d'inégalité à l'intérieur de chacune des six séries. Pour que le test fonctionne, un équilibre subtil devrait être réalisé quant à la répartition des tonalités de sympathie à l'intérieur des huit groupes factoriels comme des six séries constitutives du test. Cet équilibre est-il effectivement réalisé? C'est là une question que nous laisserons ouverte à la recherche ultérieure.

D. La validité empirico-clinique

Rappelons d'abord la signification de la démarche de validation empirique ou empirico-clinique, dans laquelle on reconnaîtra aisément ce que les psychométriciens anglo-saxons appellent « construct validity ». Le but poursuivi est de vérifier si le test de Szondi saisit effectivement ce qu'il prétend saisir. A cette fin, on procédera à une comparaison des données recueillies par le test avec des données empiriques indépendantes. Ainsi, le test de Szondi prétend atteindre certaines fonctions psychologiques : on comparera ses résultats avec des données empiriques qui appréhendent les mêmes fonctions. Ou encore, le test de Szondi prétend être la base d'un diagnostic psychopathologique : on comparera ses résultats avec ce que la clinique permet d'observer.

C'est dans ce dernier registre que se sont développées les tentatives de validation empirico-clinique les plus significatives. C'est pourquoi nous nous y référerons de manière privilégiée. Mais nous voudrions au préalable établir une distinction qui nous paraît très éclairante.

1. Validation forte et validation faible

Les travaux qui ont un rapport à notre problématique peuvent revendiquer, soit une validation forte, soit une validation faible. Qu'entendons-nous par là ?

Par démarche de validation forte, nous désignons une démarche qui obéit au critère poppérien de falsifiabilité. Une hypothèse est formulée qui, au vu des résultats empiriques recueillis, pourra être, soit corroborée, soit falsifiée. Une embûche est tendue au test, dont ce dernier sortira ou vainqueur ou vaincu.

Citons comme exemple la recherche récente d'Alfred Vannesse (1977).

Vannesse analyse le discours sur Dieu de 100 sujets selon les catégories du système psycho-pulsionnel de Szondi. Ainsi, certains énoncés lui paraissent relever de la fonction h+, d'autres de la fonction m-, d'autres encore de la fonction k+. Il procède ensuite à une comparaison avec les résultats du Szondi : les sujets qui ont tendance à parler de Dieu selon la dimension p+ devraient présenter au Szondi une tendance p+ significativement élevée, et de même pour les quinze autres tendances pulsionnelles. La confrontation conduite à l'aide du test X^2 donne dans chaque cas des résultats hautement significatifs. Le test de Szondi sort ainsi (provisoirement) corroboré de l'épreuve.

Par démarche de validation faible, nous entendons une démarche qui n'obéit pas au critère de falsifiabilité. On procède bien dans ce cas à une confrontation entre les données du Szondi et des données empiriques indépendantes. Mais les données empiriques et leur corrélation sont interprétées après coup. Donnons un exemple. Supposons que nous souhaitions confronter les données du Szondi avec les données du Rorschach dans un but de validation. Première possibilité : nous procédons au départ d'une hypothèse falsifiable. Eu égard à la signification théorique (provisoirement acquise) des données du Szondi et des données du Rorschach, nous postulons par exemple que les sujets qui donnent au Szondi un important pourcentage de tendances p+ doivent donner au Rorschach un pourcentage significativement élevé de grandes kinesthésies. Nous opérons ensuite le contrôle empirique de l'hypothèse. Seconde possibilité : nous observons d'abord et constatons par exemple une corrélation significative entre la tendance p+ et le nombre de grandes kinesthésies. Puis nous interprétons : eu égard à la théorie de Szondi et à la théorie de Rorschach, le résultat est hautement significatif[1]. Mais on

---

[1] C'est là la méthode qu'a adoptée Jean Melon (1975-1976, cfr en particulier pp. 64-123).

voit aussitôt que cette seconde possibilité est très dangereuse, car elle se prête à toutes les manipulations. Il est toujours possible de manipuler la théorie de manière à fonder n'importe quelle corrélation empirique, et cela d'autant plus que la théorie est elle-même souple et parfois confuse. Nous ne croyons pas cependant que ce type de démarche soit toujours illégitime. Dans certains cas, l'interprétation après coup de corrélations empiriques paraît rigoureuse et probante. Malheureusement, dans d'autres cas trop nombreux, l'interprétation est arbitraire et donne l'impression que la théorie du test de Szondi est compatible avec n'importe quelle observation et est donc de ce fait même non falsifiable.

Mais observons le fonctionnement de la distinction que nous venons d'opérer sur le terrain du diagnostic psychopathologique.

2. La validité du test de Szondi comme outil de diagnostic psychopathologique

Deux méthodes ont été utilisées en vue d'éprouver la validité du test de Szondi comme outil de diagnostic psychopathologique. Une première méthode met l'accent sur l'analyse individuelle; une seconde méthode privilégie l'analyse de groupe.

a) L'analyse centrée sur l'individu : la méthode du diagnostic aveugle

Le principe de la méthode est simple. Un diagnostic émis à l'aveugle par un interprète du test est confronté avec le diagnostic établi par un psychiatre ou un psychologue sur base de l'examen clinique.

Plusieurs expériences ont été tentées dans cette direction. Nous nous limiterons ici aux deux expériences les plus connues : l'expérience de Delay-Pruschy et l'expérience de Moser[1].

L'expérience conduite par Delay et son équipe (1953), à laquelle collabora une spécialiste du Szondi, Mme R. Pruschy-Bejarano, utilisa la méthode de l'appariement. Elle porta sur dix sujets dont étaient connus : 1. le diagnostic clinique émis par le psychiatre, 2. le diagnostic établi à l'aveugle par Pruschy. Il s'agissait pour les participants à l'expérience (le psychiatre, Mme Pruschy et sept autres juges) d'établir une correspondance entre le diagnostic psychiatrique et le diagnostic szondien. L'expérience se solda par un échec quasi total.

A propos de cet échec, Mme Pruschy (1953) s'est longuement expliquée. Il est intéressant de l'écouter, car, si sa réponse est pertinente, elle peut aussi apparaître comme une forme de dérobade à toute expérience falsificatrice de validité. Nous ne nous attarderons pas sur le fait que les conditions que Pruschy avait exigées au préalable pour une épreuve d'appariement adéquate n'avaient pas été réalisées (des cas francs et typiques, non organiques et non soumis à une thérapeutique biologique). Car, avoue Pruschy, même si ces conditions avaient été remplies, il n'est pas dit que la méthode d'appariement aurait été davantage appropriée au test de Szondi. La méthode d'appariement repose en effet sur la mise en correspondance de deux diagnostics aussi précis et univoques que possible. Or le test de Szondi n'a pas pour signification

---

[1] Parmi les autres expériences intéressantes, on pourrait aussi citer H. Mignot et J. Gabel, 1952.

d'aboutir à un diagnostic univoque. Il a plutôt pour visée de restituer la complexité de la vie pulsionnelle d'un sujet et d'esquisser l'éventail pluridimensionnel de ses possibilités d'existence. En conséquence, s'il doit être éprouvé, c'est moins dans sa capacité à enfermer le sujet dans une étiquette unique que dans sa capacité à ressaisir les fines nuances de l'existence et de l'histoire personnelle d'un sujet. D'où la méthode de validation congéniale au test de Szondi que propose Pruschy : une analyse comparative précise et très poussée de chacun des diagnostics szondiens considéré dans toutes ses nuances avec les plus menus détails de chaque histoire de malade. Lorsque la confrontation est conduite de cette manière, il ressort que : « beaucoup de divergences sont plus apparentes que réelles » (p. 478) et que la valeur diagnostique du test peut être constatée, car il est alors possible de « retrouver, à travers le test de Szondi, en expérience aveugle, la phénoménologie et la pathogénie des cas étudiés » (p. 499).

Moser (1955) partage les mêmes options. Moser a procédé à une expérience sur quarante cas selon une méthodologie moins sévère (à potentialité moins rigoureusement falsificatrice) que la méthode d'appariement. Les diagnostics étaient comparés et leur correspondance était appréciée à la fois par l'interprète du test et par le psychiatre responsable du diagnostic clinique. Dans trente-quatre cas, la correspondance fut parfaite. Dans trois cas, l'échec fut total. Enfin dans cinq cas, les diagnostics à l'aveugle se révélèrent partiellement erronés. Cependant dans la plupart des cas d'erreur, un examen plus fouillé permit de constater que l'échec n'était qu'apparent, soit que les données du diagnostic clinique se manifestèrent dans le test à la faveur d'une relecture plus fine du protocole pulsionnel (ex. cas 26), soit inversement que le diagnostic szondien se trouva confirmé par une analyse plus nuancée de la clinique (ex. cas 3).

On aperçoit le problème que soulève pareil échange d'arguments. A leur manière, les objections de Pruschy et Moser à l'égard d'une épreuve de validation fondée sur l'idéal d'une univocité diagnostique sont parfaitement légitimes. Il est vrai que le test de Szondi n'a pas pour vocation d'étiqueter et de classer un sujet dans une et une seule catégorie nosographique, mais d'établir la complexité d'une dynamique pulsionnelle inconsciente. Cependant, si l'on assume jusqu'au bout une telle option, on devrait aussi avoir le courage de reconnaître la quasi impossibilité d'une validation stricte du Szondi. Car la méthode de validation qui nous est offerte comme voie alternative autorise toutes les manipulations. Si l'on prend en compte les mille détails d'une histoire personnelle ou d'un tableau clinique, on parviendra toujours à y découvrir ce qu'on désire trouver au titre d'un indice confirmatoire des résultats du test. Bref, cette méthode échappe au critère de falsifiabilité.

b) L'analyse centrée sur le groupe

On ne se préoccupe pas ici de comparer un protocole individuel avec un diagnostic ou un tableau clinique individuel, mais bien de confronter les caractéristiques communes de protocoles pulsionnels avec les caractéristiques cliniques communes des sujets, formulées le plus souvent en termes de critères nosographiques. Plus précisément encore, on s'efforce de vérifier si des signes testologiques précis permettent de différencier les groupes psychopathologiques.

Nous savons déjà à cet égard que Szondi a formulé dans la TrP des hypothèses quant aux signes psychopulsionnels qui spécifient les diverses entités psychiatriques. D'où le souci de certains chercheurs de contrôler les hypothèses szondiennes à la faveur d'une démarche obéissant à un critère de validation forte.

Citons deux recherches parmi les plus célèbres, qui ont chacune abouti à un résultat négatif.

Rauhala (1958) analyse les protocoles de cent schizophrènes et découvre que les signes considérés par Szondi comme caractéristiques de la schizophrénie ne permettent de différencier son groupe de schizophrènes ni d'un groupe contrôle, ni d'un groupe d'élèves infirmières.

David et Rabinowitz (1952) travaillent sur deux groupes de sujets: un groupe de cent épileptiques et un groupe de cent homosexuels. De manière générale, les protocoles szondiens des deux groupes ne se différencient pas significativement si l'on considère les signes supposés spécifiques de l'épileptique d'une part, de l'homosexuel d'autre part.

Mais quelles pourraient être les réponses des partisans de l'Analyse du destin en face de résultats aussi apparemment dévastateurs?

Un disciple de Szondi, A. Beeli (1952), a répondu à Rauhala. Tout d'abord, il problématise l'analyse statistique de groupe. D'une part, l'analyse statistique tend à briser l'unité dialectique d'une conjoncture ou d'un profil pulsionnel: elle isole le clivage factoriel ou le clivage vectoriel des clivages corrélatifs. Or l'interprétation d'un Szondi et de ce qu'il peut révéler d'une problématique psychopathologique doit reposer sur une forme de raisonnement dialectique, qui n'a d'occasion de se développer qu'à la faveur d'une analyse individualisée d'un protocole. D'autre part, la méthode statistique privilégie les réactions les plus fréquentes au détriment des réactions isolées. Or une réaction isolée, que seule à nouveau l'analyse individuelle est en état de prendre en considération, peut être tout aussi significative d'une problématique psychopathologique qu'un ensemble de réactions majoritaires et dominantes. Ainsi, écrit Beeli, il suffit d'une seule réaction Scho-! à l'intérieur d'une série de dix conjonctures pulsionnelles pour que notre attention soit attirée sur la possibilité d'une forme d'existence paranoïde. Ces deux insuffisances de la méthode statistique expliquent pourquoi David et Rabinowitz ont abouti à des résultats nettement plus positifs lorsqu'ils ont substitué à l'analyse statistique de groupe une analyse fondée sur l'appréciation individualisée de chaque protocole.

Dans un travail ultérieur (1953), David et Rabinowitz ont soumis les mêmes protocoles de cent épileptiques et de cent homosexuels à des spécialistes du Szondi. Ceux-ci ont alors réparti les deux cents protocoles en deux groupes sur la base d'une analyse individuelle à l'aveugle, à savoir en un groupe d'épileptiques d'une part et un groupe d'homosexuels d'autre part. Les résultats obtenus furent cette fois franchement encourageants, même si les interprètes commirent encore plusieurs erreurs.

Bref on peut se demander jusqu'à quel point la méthode statistique est une méthode adéquate de validation des techniques psychodiagnostiques et dans quelle mesure d'autres méthodes ne sont pas plus appropriées, à savoir l'analyse syndromatique individuelle et le diagnostic aveugle. Nous sommes ainsi renvoyés à l'analyse centrée sur l'individu, dont nous avons déjà souligné le caractère problématique. La validité empirico-clinique du test de Szondi comme outil diagnostique demeure entière.

Mais Beeli adresse un autre reproche à la recherche de Rauhala, que Moser a formulé en termes plus généraux. Les caractéristiques cliniques des sujets dont les protocoles szondiens sont considérés dans les analyses de groupe sont souvent trop grossières. Ainsi il est trop grossier de parler d'épileptique ou d'homosexuel en général. Car il existe de multiples formes d'épilepsie ou d'homosexualité. De même en ce qui concerne la schizophrénie. La schizophrénie évolue dans le temps : la forme aiguë qu'elle revêt au moment de son éclosion doit être différenciée de sa forme chronique. Or le syndrome expérimental établi par Szondi n'intéresse que la forme aiguë initiale de la schizophrénie, alors que Rauhala a travaillé sur des schizophrènes en phase terminale.

A nouveau, nous devons dire que la réponse de Beeli est pertinente, mais en même temps qu'elle vient très mal à propos. Car, comme nous l'avons relevé déjà, Szondi lui-même ne nous indique jamais avec précision quelles sont les caractéristiques cliniques des malades sur lesquels il a établi ses syndromes expérimentaux. On ne peut raisonnablement exiger des critiques ce qu'on n'exige pas du maître. Par les défauts méthodologiques qui marquent ses œuvres, Szondi est le premier responsable des lacunes que l'on impute à tort à ses successeurs.

Pour terminer, nous aimerions faire état d'un courant de recherche qui s'est développé depuis une dizaine d'années et qui, s'il ne tranche pas de manière décisive la question de la validité du test comme instrument diagnostique, atteste tout au moins sa fécondité possible dans le registre d'une exploration de la structure différentielle des maladies mentales. Au plan méthodologique, ces recherches commencent par sélectionner des protocoles pulsionnels de sujets qui présentent une caractéristique psychopathologique commune. Ensuite elles examinent les protocoles selon les règles d'une méthodologie statistique. Ainsi, elles aboutissent à établir un profil de groupe. Or ces travaux mettent régulièrement au jour des structures pulsionnelles qui confirment sinon Szondi[1], du moins ce que la psychopathologie tient pour caractéristique des syndromes concernés. Nous ne citerons ici comme exemplative que la recherche récente de Bruno Paisana (1977), consacrée à la névrose d'angoisse et l'hystérie d'angoisse[2]. Le profil type de la névrose d'angoisse se présente comme suit :

h	s	e	hy	k	p	d	m
+!	+(!)	+	-(!)	-(!)	-(!)	-	+!
	-(!)						

Interprété dans le langage de la doctrine szondienne, ce profil confirme l'analyse psychodynamique de la névrose d'angoisse produite par Freud. On peut notamment y reconnaître la stase libidinale (h+!) et le refus d'une prise

---

[1] Bien au contraire, ils ont souvent infirmé des syndromes établis par Szondi dans la TrP. Ainsi à la lumière des recherches récents, le clivage vectoriel P+ o ne peut être retenu comme caractéristique de la phobie pas plus que le clivage P++ ne peut être considéré comme prototypique de l'hystérie de conversion.

[2] Cfr aussi M. Legrand et B. Paisana, 1977.

en charge psychique des tensions pulsionnelles (Sch-!-!). Par ailleurs, le profil type de l'hystérie d'angoisse (ou de la phobie) présente des différences significatives par rapport au profil type de la névrose d'angoisse, en quoi le test de Szondi manifeste sa capacité à discriminer les structures psychopathologiques. Bien plus, la différence concerne en particulier la dimension qui, aux yeux de Freud, démarque le plus décisivement l'hystérie d'angoisse de la névrose d'angoisse : dans la substitution du p+ au p-, l'hystérie d'angoisse révèle cela même qui fait défaut à la névrose d'angoisse, à savoir l'accession des tensions pulsionnelles au registre des représentations psychiques.

Mais nous savons que pareilles recherches ne relèvent que d'une démarche de validation faible. Selon la sévérité de nos critères de scientificité, nous rejetterons le test de Szondi, que nous considérerons comme un instrument falsifié (ou sinon falsifié, infalsifiable), ou nous le retiendrons présomptivement comme outil fécond de recherche psychopathologique.

Conclusions générales

Comment conclure, sinon en rappelant notre objectif: pénétrer de l'intérieur l'univers de Léopold Szondi, nous insinuer dans le mouvement même de l'œuvre et de la pratique, y repérer chemin faisant les tensions, les contradictions, les lacunes, elles-mêmes promesses d'évolution. C'est pourquoi nous avons formulé peu de critiques extrinsèques. Non pas que celles-ci nous paraissent impertinentes. Tout au contraire, l'œuvre de Szondi devrait être interrogée épistémologiquement quant à ce qu'elle pourrait inclure d'un mentalisme constitutif: est-il pertinent de chercher l'explication des choix concrets qui scandent un destin humain dans des entités inobservables ? Ne devrait-on pas privilégier l'ordre des conditions concrètes d'existence et d'environnement [1] ? Elle devrait aussi être interrogée socio-politiquement: par le sens affiné qu'elle conserve au clivage du normal et du pathologique, n'est-elle pas en état de participer aux nouvelles formes de contrôle social qui s'installent avec le triomphe progressif d'une psychiatrie rénovée, diffusée capillairement dans les pores du tissu social [2] ? Au demeurant, les critiques épistémologique et socio-politique ne devraient-elles pas converger ? Le détour illusoire par l'ordre des entités psychopulsionnelles internes n'empêche-t-il pas la confrontation avec les conditions de production concrètes, y compris sociales, de ce qui se donne comme « maladies mentales » ? Nous l'avouons: ces critiques sont pour nous pertinentes et nous les développerons dans d'autres publications [3]. Mais elles nous ont paru prématurées. Car, comme l'écrit Richelle à propos de Skinner: encore faut-il connaître avant de critiquer. Tel est notre vœu au terme de cet ouvrage: avoir en quelque mesure introduit le public francophone à une connaissance théorique et pratique de Szondi et par là avoir ouvert l'espace d'une critique.

---

[1] La critique skinnérienne, remarquablement illustrée par le dernier ouvrage de Marc Richelle, *B.F. Skinner ou le péril behavioriste* (Mardaga, 1978), aurait ici sa place.

[2] Cfr les perspectives ouvertes par Robert Castel dans *Le psychanalysme*, Maspero, 1973.

[3] Nous avons nous-même déjà, avec Sami Arbache, engagé la critique du test de Szondi comme « outil disciplinaire » de savoir-pouvoir (S. Arbache et M. Legrand, 1977).

Bibliographie

La bibliographie est limitée aux travaux qui concernent de manière directe le domaine de l'Analyse du destin. On trouvera la bibliographie la plus complète dans : Dino LARESE, *Léopold Szondi* (1976).

a) Œuvres de SZONDI

Œuvres originales

Contributions to Fate Analysis I. *Analysis of Marriages*, An attempt at a theory of choice in love, dans Acta Psychologica, 1937, 3, Martinus Nijhof, La Haye.

Schicksalsanalyse, Wahl in Liebe, Freundschaft, Beruf, Krankheit und Tod, Schwabe, Bâle, 1944 (3e édition refondue et élargie : 1965).

Lehrbuch der experimentellen Triebdiagnostik, Hans Huber, Berne, 1947 (2e édition totalement refondue : 1960; 3e édition élargie : 1972).

Triebpathologie, Elemente der exakten Triebpsychologie und Triebpsychiatrie, Hans Huber, Berne, 1952.

Ich-Analyse, Die Grundlage zur Vereinigung der Tiefenpsychologie, Hans Huber, Berne, 1956.

Trieblinnäus-Band, Hans Huber, Berne, 1960.

Schicksalsanalytische Therapie, Ein Lehrbuch der passiven und aktiven analytischen Psychotherapie, Hans Huber, Berne, 1963.

Freiheit und Zwang im Schicksal des Einzelnen, Hans Huber, Berne, 1968.

Kain, Gestalten des Bösen, Hans Huber, Berne, 1969.

Moses, Antwort auf Kain, Hans Huber, Berne, 1973.

En Français

Diagnostic expérimental des pulsions, (Traduction du « Lehrbuch der experimentellen Triebdiagnostik », 1re édition, 1947, par Ruth Pruschy-Bejarano), Bibliothèque de Psychiatrie, P.U.F., 1952, (2e édition : 1973).

Introduction à l'Analyse du destin, Tome I, Psychologie générale du destin, (Traduction de conférences prononcées par Szondi à l'Université de Zurich en 1962-1963, inédites en allemand, par Cl. Van Reeth), Pathei Mathos, Nauwelaerts, Louvain, 1972.

Liberté et contrainte dans le destin des individus, (Traduction de « Freiheit und Zwang im Schicksal des Einzelnen », par Cl. Van Reeth), Textes et études anthropologiques, Desclée de Brouwer, 1975.

b) Travaux de l'Ecole de Louvain

Beaucoup de travaux de l'Ecole de Louvain sont déposés dans des cours, thèses, mémoires ou documents inédits. Tout lecteur désireux d'obtenir l'un de ces travaux inédits sous forme de photocopies est prié de s'adresser au Centre de psychologie différentielle et clinique, Faculté de psychologie et des sciences de l'éducation, voie du roman pays, 20, B-1348 Louvain-la-Neuve.

S. ARBACHE & M. LEGRAND, *Le diagnostic expérimental des pulsions : un dispositif disciplinaire de savoir-pouvoir ?* Communication inédite au Colloque Szondi de Cerisy-la-Salle, août 1977.

R. BUCHER, L'angoisse dans le test de Szondi, dans *Revue de psychologie et des sciences de l'éducation,* 1971, 6, n° 4, pp. 510-527.

R. BUCHER, *Depression und Melancholie,* Eine historische und klinisch-triebpsychologische Untersuchung zur Klassifizierung und Struktur der Depressionsformen, I et II, Thèse doctorale, Louvain, 1975. Publiée chez Hans Huber, Berne.

R. BUCHER, La classification des états dépressifs et le test de Szondi, dans *Annales médico-psychologiques,* Masson, Paris, T. 1, 133e année, n° 3, pp. 317-345.

J. CORNET, Introduction à la doctrine szondienne des clivages du moi, dans *Revue de psychologie et des sciences de l'éducation*, 1971, 6, n° 4, pp. 456-464.

L. DE ANDRADE, *L'épilepsie et les épilepsies*, Esquisse d'une confrontation entre neuropsychiatrie et Schicksalsanalyse, Thèse inédite, Louvain, 1975.

A. DE WAELHENS, Sujet et système dans la pensée de Szondi, dans *Contributions à l'Analyse du destin*, Szondiana VIII, Nauwelaerts, Louvain, 1971, pp. 301-313.

N. DURUZ, *Narcissisme et Analyse du Moi*, Confrontation et reprise des apports freudiens et szondiens, Thèse inédite, Louvain, 1978.

A. LEBAS & J. MELON, Les vieux schizophrènes asiliaires, dans *Beiträge zur Anwendung des Szonditestes*, Szondiana X, 1974, Hans Huber, Berne, pp. 39-54.

M. LEGRAND, Après le cinquième Colloque de Schicksalsanalyse, dans *Revue philosophique de Louvain*, nov. 1969, 67, pp. 613-628.

M. LEGRAND, Théorie génétique et validation du test de Szondi, dans *Revue de psychologie et des sciences de l'éducation*, 1971, 6, n° 4, pp. 528-540.

M. LEGRAND, Essai d'analyse épistémologique de l'œuvre de Szondi, dans *Psychanalyse, Schicksalsanalyse et Epistémologie*, Deuxième partie, pp. 390-685, Thèse inédite, Louvain, 1972.

M. LEGRAND, *Théorie pulsionnelle et diagnostic expérimental*, Communication inédite au 6ᵉ Colloque de l'Association internationale de recherche en psychologie du destin, Zurich, août 1972.

M. LEGRAND & B. PAISANA, *Angoisse et hystérie*, Contributions à la psychopathologie des névroses, Communication inédite au Colloque Szondi de Cerisy-la-Salle, août 1977.

M. LEGRAND, *La dialectique de l'avant-plan et de l'arrière-plan*, Remarques à propos du statut des plans complémentaires, Communication inédite au VIIIᵉ Colloque de l'Association internationale de recherche en Analyse du destin, Pamplona, août 1978.

J. MELON, Le profil psychosomatique au test de Szondi, dans *Annales médico-psychologiques*, 1971, 129, pp. 273-281.

J. MELON, L'intérêt du test de Szondi en recherche psychosomatique, dans *Les Feuillets psychiatriques de Liège*, 1971, 4, n° 2, pp. 187-195.

J. MELON & S. BOURDOUXHE, Test de Szondi et psychosomatique, dans *Les Feuillets psychiatriques de Liège*, 1973, 6, n° 1, pp. 5-25.

J. MELON, De la signification de l'indice de variabilité dans le test de Szondi, dans *Beiträge zur Anwendung des Szonditestes*, Szondiana X, 1974a, Hans Huber, Berne, pp. 83-85.

J. MELON & M. TIMSIT-BERTHIER, De quelques corrélations significatives entre les données du test de Szondi, l'étude des activités corticales lentes et la clinique psychiatrique, dans *Beiträge zur Anwendung des Szonditestes*, Szondiana X, 1974b, Hans Huber, Berne, pp. 86-109.

J. MELON, *Théorie et pratique du Szondi*, Presses Universitaires de Liège, 1975.

J. MELON, *Figures du Moi*, Szondi, Rorschach et Freud, Thèse inédite, Liège, 1975-76.

J. MELON, *Les circuits pulsionnels*, Cycles et structure, Communication inédite au Colloque Szondi de Cerisy-la-Salle, août 1977.

Th. NEFF, *Représentation de Dieu et structure de la personnalité*, Thèse inédite, Louvain, 1976.

B. PAISANA, *La névrose d'angoisse et l'hystérie d'angoisse dans l'œuvre de Freud et dans le test de Szondi*, Mémoire inédit, Louvain, 1977.

J. SCHOTTE, Notice pour introduire le problème structural de la Schicksalsanalyse, dans *Festschrift Léopold Szondi*, Szondiana V, 1963, Hans Huber, Berne, pp. 144-201.

J. SCHOTTE, *La Schicksalsanalyse*, Cours inédit, Louvain, 1967-68.

J. SCHOTTE, *Les formes de clivages du moi*, Cours inédit, Louvain, 1970-71.

J. SCHOTTE, Psychanalyse et Schicksalsanalyse, dans *Contributions à l'Analyse du destin*, Szondiana VIII, Nauwelaerts, Louvain, 1971, pp. 334-341.

J. SCHOTTE, Présentation du Docteur Léopold Szondi, dans *Revue de psychologie et des sciences de l'éducation*, 1971, 6, n° 4, pp. 419-427.

J. SCHOTTE, *L'œuvre de Szondi : Une théorie des moments ou dimensions constitutifs de l'acte d'exister*, Cours inédit, Louvain, 1971-72.

J. SCHOTTE, *Perspectives thérapeutiques de la Schicksalsanalyse*, Cours inédit, Louvain, 1972.
J. SCHOTTE, *L'Analyse du moi*, Cours inédit, Louvain, 1973-74.
J. SCHOTTE, Notes pour rouvrir un dialogue sur la psychanalyse, pratique et science humaine clinique, dans *Dialogues en Sciences humaines*, Publications des Facultés Universitaires Saint-Louis, Bruxelles, 1975, pp. 96-126.
J. SCHOTTE, *Recherches Nouvelles sur les fondements de l'Analyse du destin*, Cours inédit, Louvain, 1975-1976.
J. SCHOTTE, *(Dé)négation et négativité*, Freud, Lacan, le langage et Szondi, Cours inédit, Louvain, 1976-77.
J. SCHOTTE, *La nosographie psychiatrique comme patho-analyse de notre condition*, Cours inédit, Louvain, 1977-78.
J. SERVAIS, Le système du moi, Mémoire inédit, Louvain, 1976.
A. VANNESSE, *Relations entre langage religieux et structures pulsionnelles*, Recherche expérimentale à l'aide du test-Szondi, Thèse inédite, Louvain, 1977.
Cl. VAN REETH, Le déroulement temporel des profils comme méthode d'interprétation du test de Szondi, dans *Contributions à l'Analyse du destin, Szondiana VIII*, Nauwelaerts, Louvain, 1971, pp. 259-265.
Cl. VAN REETH, Du compte au mythe, Introduction à la pensée de Szondi (suivi d'une discussion avec J. Laplanche, J. Schotte, P. Fedida, J. Gagey) dans *Psychanalyse à l'Université*, Tome 3, n° 10, Mars 1978, pp. 297-340.
A. VERGOTE, Complexe d'Œdipe et Complexe de Caïn, Ethique, psychanalyse et analyse du destin, dans *Revue de psychologie et des sciences de l'éducation*, 1971, 6, n° 4, pp. 446-455.
A. ZENONI, *La dialectique de l'être et de l'avoir dans le système de Szondi*, Mémoire inédit, Louvain, 1967.
A. ZENONI, Catégories szondiennes du vecteur Sch et aspects du langage, dans *Contributions à l'Analyse du destin, Szondiana VIII*, Nauwelaerts, Louvain, 1971, pp. 283-297.
A. ZENONI, *Analyse du Moi et langage*, Essai d'articulation des théories analytiques du moi, Thèse inédite, Louvain, 1974.

c) **Travaux concernant la validité du test de Szondi**

A. BEELI, Bemerkungen zur Arbeit von L. Rauhala « Über die Validität von Szondis Syndromatik der Schizophrenie », dans *Schweizerische Zeitschrift für Psychologie*, 1958, 17, pp. 198-208.
F. BELLINGROTH, Faktorielle Gesichtsschemata im Szondi-test als Reizschemata für faktorielle Antriebsgestimmtheit, dans *Beiträge zur Diagnostik, Prognostik und Therapie des Schicksals, Szondiana III*, 1962, Hans Huber, Berne, pp. 133-136.
H.L. BEST & E. SZOLLOSI, Recognition as a criterion in the Szondi test, dans *Journal of clinical psychology*, 1953, 9, pp. 75-76.
L.J. BORSTELMANN & W.G. KLOPFER, Does the Szondi test reflect individuality? The affective valences of the Szondi pictures, dans *Journal of personnality*, 1951, 19, pp. 421-439.
J. COHEN & L. FEIGENBAUM, The assumption of additivity on the Szondi test, dans *Journal of projective techniques*, 1954, 18, pp. 11-16.
H.P. DAVID & W. RABINOWITZ, Szondi patterns in epileptic and homosexual males, dans *Journal of consulting psychology*, 1952, 16, pp. 247-250.
H.P. DAVID, M. ORNE & W. RABINOWITZ, Qualitative and quantitative Szondi diagnosis, dans *Journal of projective techniques*, 1953, 17, pp. 75-78.
N.E. DAVIS & V.C. RAIMY, Stimulus functions of the Szondi cards, dans *Journal of clinical psychology*, 1952, 8, pp. 155-160.
J. DELAY, P. PICHOT, J. PERSE & P. DENIKER, La validité des tests de personnalité en psychiatrie V, Etude sur la validité du test de Szondi, dans *Annales médico-psychologiques*, nov. 1953, tome II, n° 4, pp. 449-467.
S. DERI, Genotropism in the framework of a unified theory of choice, dans *Festschrift Léopold Szondi, Szondiana V*, 1963, Hans Huber, Berne, pp. 39-74.

A. DOMINGUES DA SILVA, *Portraits et personnalité*, Etude des 48 portraits du test de Szondi et de leur utilisation en psychologie clinique, Mémoire inédit, Louvain, 1977.
F.J. DUDEK & H.O. PATTERSON, Relationships among the Szondi test items, dans *Journal of consulting psychology*, 1952, 16, pp. 389-394.
L.V. GORDON, A factor analysis of the 48 Szondi pictures, dans *Journal of psychology*, 1953, 36, pp. 387-392.
L.V. GORDON & E.J. LAMBERT, The internal consistency of the Szondi «factors», dans *Journal of social psychology*, 1954, 40, pp. 67-71.
W.H. GUERTIN, A test of a basic assumption of the Szondi, dans *Journal of consulting psychology*, 1950, 14, pp. 404-407.
W.H. GUERTIN, A comparison of the stimulus value of Szondi's pictures with those of normal americans, dans *Journal of clinical psychology*, 1951a, 7, pp. 163-166.
W.H. GUERTIN, A factor analysis of some Szondi pictures, dans *Journal of clinical psychology*, 1951b, 7, pp. 232-235.
W.G. KLOPFER & L.J. BORSTELMANN, The associative valences of the Szondi pictures, dans *Journal of personnality*, 1950, 19, pp. 172-188.
A. LUBIN & M. MALLOY, An empirical test of some assumptions underlying the Szondi test, dans *Journal of abnormal and social psychology*, 1951, 46, pp. 480-484.
H. MIGNOT & J. GABEL, Contribution à la question de la validité du test de Szondi (Quatre «analyses aveugles»), dans *Revue de psychologie appliquée*, 1952, 2, pp. 39-48.
U. MOSER, Validierung, Blinddiagnosen und die Problematik der Krankheitsbegriffes im Szondi-Test, dans *Szondiana II*, Hans Huber, Berne, 1955, pp. 36-64. Trad. fr. sous le titre «A propos du test de Szondi», *Annales médico-psychologiques*, 1954, Tome I, n° 5.
R. PRUSCHY-BEJARANO, De la validité du test de Szondi, dans *Annales médico-psychologiques*, nov. 1953, Tome II, n° 4, pp. 468-499.
A.I. RABIN, Szondi's pictures: Identification of diagnoses, dans *Journal of abnormal and social psychology*, 1950a, 45, pp. 392-395.
A.I. RABIN, Szondi's pictures: Effects of formal training on ability to identify diagnoses, dans *Journal of consulting psychology*, 1950b, 14, pp. 400-403.
L. RAUHALA, Uber die Validität von Szondis Syndromatik der Schizophrenie, dans *Schweizerische Zeitschrift für Psychologie*, 1958, 17, pp. 174-197.
J. SCHUBERT, The stimulus value of the Szondi pictures: A theoretical and empirical study, dans *Journal of projective techniques*, 1954, 18, pp. 95-106.
A.B. SILVERSTEIN, «Diagnosing» Szondi's pictures, dans *Journal of projective techniques*, 1957, 21, pp. 396-398.
A. STEINBERG, Szondi's pictures: discrimination of diagnoses as a function of psychiatric experience and of internal consistency, dans *Journal of projective techniques*, 1953, 17, pp. 340-348.
E. SZOLLOSI, D.E. LAMPHIEAR & H.L. BEST, The stimulus values of the Szondi pictures, dans *Journal of consulting psychology*, 1951, 15, pp. 419-424.
R. WALLEN, Factors affecting the choice of certain Szondi test pictures, dans *Journal of consulting psychology*, 1951, 15, pp. 210-215.

d) Travaux divers

A. BEELI, *Psychotherapie-Prognose mit Hilfe der «Experimentellen Triebdiagnostik»*, Hans Huber, Berne, 1965.
M. BERTA & H. SILVERA, Indice de variabilité dans le test de Szondi, dans *Beiträge zur Diagnostik, Prognostik und Therapie der Schicksals, Szondiana III*, 1962, Hans Huber, Berne, pp. 142-146.
S. DERI, *Introduction to the Szondi test*, Theory and Practice, Grune et Stratton, New York, 1949.
W. HUTH, *Wahl und Schicksal*, Hans Huber, Berne, 1978.
D. LARESE, *Leopold Szondi*, Eine Lebensskizze, Amriswiler Bücherei, 1976.
R. PRUSCHY & R. STORA, *Socialiser les pulsions*, Fleurus, Paris, 1975.

J. RUDRAUF, *C'est toi qui le diras...*, Fleurus, Paris, 1975.
E. STUMPER, *Triebstruktur und Geisteskrankheiten*, Hans Huber, Berne, 1956.
H. WAELDER, *Triebstruktur und Kriminalität*, Hans Huber, Berne, 1952.

Table des matières

PREFACE par Jean OURY ... 5
AVANT-PROPOS ... 11
INTRODUCTION : Léopold Szondi et l'Analyse du destin ... 13

Première partie
ANALYSE DU DESTIN ET DOCTRINE GENETIQUE DES PULSIONS ... 17
A. Destin et figures du destin ... 17
B. La détermination génético-biologique des figures du destin ou choix destinaux ... 18
   1. La détermination génético-biologique des figures morbides du destin (maladies mentales et morts suicidaires) ... 18
   2. La détermination génético-biologique des figures socialisées du destin (choix amoureux, choix professionnel) : le génotropisme ... 19
C. La doctrine génétique des pulsions ... 22
Conclusions ... 26
Annexe : Quelques notions de génétique ... 28

Deuxième partie
LE DIAGNOSTIC EXPERIMENTAL DES PULSIONS ET LE MOUVEMENT DE LA PRATIQUE SZONDIENNE ... 29
A. Première présentation du test de Szondi ... 30
   1. Le matériel du test ... 30
   2. L'administration du test ... 31
   3. L'inscription des résultats bruts ... 31
   4. La transformation des résultats bruts en réactions pulsionnelles et la constitution des profils pulsionnels ... 33
B. Le test et le mouvement de la pratique szondienne ... 37
   1. Le test dans la doctrine génétique ... 37
   2. L'excès du test sur la doctrine génétique ... 38
   3. Le test dans la doctrine des pulsions ... 39
      a) Premier moment :
         l'Analyse du destin (1944) ... 39
      b) Deuxième moment :
         le Diagnostic des pulsions (1947) ... 40
      c) Troisième moment :
         la pathologie pulsionnelle (1952) ... 43
Conclusions ... 47

Troisième partie
LA DOCTRINE PSYCHOPULSIONNELLE 49
CHAPITRE I : La théorie des pulsions 51
  A. Le système pulsionnel et ses constituants élémentaires 51
    1. La pulsion ou vecteur du contact 56
      a) Le vecteur du rapport à l'objet 56
      b) Les mouvements objectaux du contact 57
      c) Normalité et maladivité du contact 60
    2. La pulsion ou vecteur sexuel 63
      a) Le vecteur du rapport au corps 63
      b) Le facteur h 64
      c) Le facteur s 67
    3. La pulsion ou vecteur paroxysmal 69
      a) Le vecteur du rapport à autrui et à la collectivité 69
      b) Le facteur e 71
      c) Le facteur hy 72
    4. La pulsion du moi ou vecteur Sch 74
      a) Le vecteur du rapport à soi et à la réalité 74
      b) Le facteur p 76
      c) Le facteur k 80
  B. La dialectique pulsionnelle 84
    1. Les clivages factoriels 85
      a) Les formes de clivage factoriel 85
        1. Les clivages unitendants 86
        2. Le clivage nul 86
        3. Le clivage ambitendant 88
      b) Méthodes quantitatives 89
        1. Le quotient de tension de tendances 90
        2. Le pourcentage de réactions symptomatiques 92
        3. Les degrés de tension quantitative 93
        4. La formule pulsionnelle 94
    2. Les clivages vectoriels 96
      a) Les formes de clivage vectoriel 96
        1. Les clivages unitendants 96
        2. Les clivages bitendants 97
        3. Les clivages tritendants 107
        4. Le clivage quadritendant 111
        5. Le clivage nul ou double nul 112
      b) Méthodes quantitatives 112
        1. Les classes pulsionnelles 112
        2. Les index proportionnels 116
    3. Les clivages globaux instantanés ou conjonctures pulsionnelles ... 120
      a) Une démarche de construction théorique : la méthode centre-périphérie ... 120
      b) Une démarche de corrélation clinique : la méthode des formes d'existence ... 127
    4. Le profil pulsionnel : Introduction à la problématique des déroulements pulsionnels ... 133
      a) Les déroulements factoriels 134
      b) Les déroulements vectoriels 136
      c) Les déroulements conjoncturels 137
    5. Le profil pulsionnel total : Introduction à la méthode avant-plan — arrière-plan. ... 142
      a) De la signification des trois profils pulsionnels 142
      b) De la signification de l'arrière-plan empirique 144
      c) Une stratégie d'interprétation du profil pulsionnel total ... 146
      d) L'analyse d'un cas concret 150
CHAPITRE II : Considérations sur la psychopathologie pulsionnelle ... 155
  A. Classes nosographiques et catégories psychopulsionnelles 155
  B. La classification szondienne des troubles mentaux 157
  C. La syndromatique pulsionnelle des maladies mentales 162

CHAPITRE III : Le moi et l'ordre pulsionnel	169
A. Le concept althussérien de totalité structurale	169
B. Le système pulsionnel comme totalité articulée à dominante et déterminante	170

Quatrième partie

QUESTIONS A PROPOS DE LA VALIDITE DU TEST DE SZONDI	177
A. Les trois dimensions de la validité du test de Szondi	177
B. La validité théorique	179
C. La validité de construction	183
D. La validité empirico-clinique	190
CONCLUSIONS GENERALES	197
BIBLIOGRAPHIE	198

PSYCHOLOGIE ET SCIENCES HUMAINES
collection publiée sous la direction de MARC RICHELLE

1. Dr Paul Chauchard
   LA MAITRISE DE SOI, *8ᵉ éd.*
5. François Duyckaerts
   LA FORMATION DU LIEN SEXUEL, *9ᵉ éd.*
7. Paul-A. Osterrieth
   FAIRE DES ADULTES, *14ᵉ éd.*
9. Daniel Widlöcher
   L'INTERPRETATION DES DESSINS D'ENFANTS, *9ᵉ éd.*
11. Berthe Reymond-Rivier
    LE DEVELOPPEMENT SOCIAL DE L'ENFANT ET DE L'ADOLESCENT, *8ᵉ éd.*
12. Maurice Dongier
    NEVROSES ET TROUBLES PSYCHOSOMATIQUES, *7ᵉ éd.*
15. Roger Mucchielli
    INTRODUCTION A LA PSYCHOLOGIE STRUCTURALE, *3ᵉ éd.*
16. Claude Köhler
    JEUNES DEFICIENTS MENTAUX, *4ᵉ éd.*
21. Dr P. Geissmann et Dr R. Durand
    LES METHODES DE RELAXATION, *3ᵉ éd.*
22. H. T. Klinkhamer-Steketée
    PSYCHOTHERAPIE PAR LE JEU, *3ᵉ éd.*
23. Louis Corman
    L'EXAMEN PSYCHOLOGIQUE D'UN ENFANT, *3ᵉ éd.*
24. Marc Richelle
    POURQUOI LES PSYCHOLOGUES?, *6ᵉ éd.*
25. Lucien Israel
    LE MEDECIN FACE AU MALADE, *4ᵉ éd.*
26. Francine Robaye-Geelen
    L'ENFANT AU CERVEAU BLESSE, *2ᵉ éd.*
27. B. F. Skinner
    LA REVOLUTION SCIENTIFIQUE DE L'ENSEIGNEMENT, *3ᵉ éd.*
28. Colette Durieu
    LA REEDUCATION DES APHASIQUES
29. J.C. Ruwet
    ETHOLOGIE: BIOLOGIE DU COMPORTEMENT, *3ᵉ éd.*
30. Eugénie De Keyser
    ART ET MESURE DE L'ESPACE
32. Ernest Natalis
    CARREFOURS PSYCHOPEDAGOGIQUES
33. E. Hartmann
    BIOLOGIE DU REVE
34. Georges Bastin
    DICTIONNAIRE DE LA PSYCHOLOGIE SEXUELLE
35. Louis Corman
    PSYCHO-PATHOLOGIE DE LA RIVALITE FRATERNELLE
36. Dr G. Varenne
    L'ABUS DES DROGUES
37. Christian Debuyst, Julienne Joos
    L'ENFANT ET L'ADOLESCENT VOLEURS
38. B.-F. Skinner
    L'ANALYSE EXPERIMENTALE DU COMPORTEMENT, *2ᵉ éd.*
39. D.J. West
    HOMOSEXUALITE
40. R. Droz et M. Rahmy
    LIRE PIAGET, *3ᵉ éd.*
41. José M.R. Delgado
    LE CONDITIONNEMENT DU CERVEAU ET LA LIBERTE DE L'ESPRIT
42. Denis Szabo, Denis Gagné, Alice Parizeau
    L'ADOLESCENT ET LA SOCIETE, *2ᵉ éd.*
43. Pierre Oléron
    LANGAGE ET DEVELOPPEMENT MENTAL, *2ᵉ éd.*
44. Roger Mucchielli
    ANALYSE EXISTENTIELLE ET PSYCHOTHERAPIE PHENOMENO-STRUCTURALE
45. Gertrud L. Wyatt
    LA RELATION MERE-ENFANT ET L'ACQUISITION DU LANGAGE, *2ᵉ éd.*
46. Dr. Etienne De Greeff
    AMOUR ET CRIMES D'AMOUR
47. Louis Corman
    L'EDUCATION ECLAIREE PAR LA PSYCHANALYSE
48. Jean-Claude Benoit et Mario Berta
    L'ACTIVATION PSYCHOTHERAPIQUE
49. T. Ayllon et N. Azrin
    TRAITEMENT COMPORTEMENTAL EN INSTITUTION PSYCHIATRIQUE

50 G. Rucquoy
LA CONSULTATION CONJUGALE
51 R. Titone
LE BILINGUISME PRECOCE
52 G. Kellens
BANQUEROUTE ET BANQUEROUTIERS
53 François Duyckaerts
CONSCIENCE ET PRISE DE CONSCIENCE
54 Jacques Launay, Jacques Levine et Gilbert Maurey
LE REVE EVEILLE-DIRIGE ET L'INCONSCIENT
55 Alain Lieury
LA MEMOIRE
56 Louis Corman
NARCISSISME ET FRUSTRATION D'AMOUR
57 E. Hartmann
LES FONCTIONS DU SOMMEIL
58 Jean-Marie Paisse
L'UNIVERS SYMBOLIQUE DE L'ENFANT ARRIERE MENTAL
59 Jacques Van Rillaer
L'AGRESSIVITE HUMAINE
60 Georges Mounin
LINGUISTIQUE ET TRADUCTION
61 Jérôme Kagan
COMPRENDRE L'ENFANT
62 Michael S. Gazzaniga
LE CERVEAU DEDOUBLE
63 Paul Cazayus
L'APHASIE
64 X. Seron, J.L. Lambert, M. Van der Linden
LA MODIFICATION DU COMPORTEMENT
65 W. Huber
INTRODUCTION A LA PSYCHOLOGIE DE LA PERSONNALITE
66 Emile Meurice
PSYCHIATRIE ET VIE SOCIALE
67 J. Château, H. Gratiot-Alphandéry, R. Doron et P. Cazayus
LES GRANDES PSYCHOLOGIES MODERNES
68 P. Sifnéos
PSYCHOTHERAPIE BREVE ET CRISE EMOTIONNELLE
69 Marc Richelle
B.F. SKINNER OU LE PERIL BEHAVIORISTE
70 J.P. Bronckart
THEORIES DU LANGAGE
71 Anika Lemaire
JACQUES LACAN, 2e éd. revue et augmentée
72 J.L. Lambert
INTRODUCTION A L'ARRIERATION MENTALE
73 T.G.R. Bower
DEVELOPPEMENT PSYCHOLOGIQUE DE LA PREMIERE ENFANCE
74 J. Rondal
LANGAGE ET EDUCATION
75 Sheila Kitzinger
PREPARER A L'ACCOUCHEMENT
76 Ovide Fontaine
INTRODUCTION AUX THERAPIES COMPORTEMENTALES
77 Jacques-Philippe Leyens
PSYCHOLOGIE SOCIALE
78 Jean Rondal
VOTRE ENFANT APPREND A PARLER
79 Michel Legrand
LE TEST DE SZONDI

Cet ouvrage a été publié en collaboration
avec les PRESSES UNIVERSITAIRES DE NAMUR,
Rempart de la Vierge, 8 - 5000 NAMUR (Belgique)

LEOPOLD SZONDI
SON TEST, SA DOCTRINE